Financial Management
and
Management Accounting

Financial Management and Management Accounting

CA. C Rama Gopal
F.C.A., F.C.S., CAIIB., A.I.B. (London-Part I)
Professor and Head of Finance Department
V.N.S. Institute of Management, Bhopal
Member, Board of Studies (Management)
Barkatullah University, Bhopal

PUBLISHING FOR ONE WORLD

NEW AGE INTERNATIONAL (P) LIMITED, PUBLISHERS
New Delhi • Bangalore • Chennai • Cochin • Guwahati • Hyderabad
Jalandhar • Kolkata • Lucknow • Mumbai • Ranchi
Visit us at **www.newagepublishers.com**

Published by New Age International (P) Ltd., Publishers
First Edition: 2011
Reprint: 2012

BRANCHES

- **Bangalore** 37/10, 8th Cross (Near Hanuman Temple), Azad Nagar, Chamarajpet, Bangalore-560 018
  Tel.: (080) 26756823, Telefax: 26756820, E-mail: bangalore@newagepublishers.com
- **Chennai** 26, Damodaran Street, T. Nagar, Chennai-600 017
  Tel.: (044) 24353401, Telefax: 24351463, E-mail: chennai@newagepublishers.com
- **Cochin** CC-39/1016, Carrier Station Road, Ernakulam South, Cochin-682 016
  Tel.: (0484) 2377004, Telefax: 4051303, E-mail: cochin@newagepublishers.com
- **Guwahati** Hemsen Complex, Mohd. Shah Road, Paltan Bazar, Near Starline Hotel, Guwahati-781 008
  Tel.: (0361) 2513881, Telefax: 2543669, E-mail: guwahati@newagepublishers.com
- **Hyderabad** 105, 1st Floor, Madhiray Kaveri Tower, 3-2-19, Azam Jahi Road, Nimboliadda, Hyderabad-500 027
  Tel.: (040) 24652456, Telefax: 24652457, E-mail: hyderabad@newagepublishers.com
- **Kolkata** RDB Chambers (Formerly Lotus Cinema) 106A, 1st Floor, S.N. Banerjee Road, Kolkata-700 014
  Tel.: (033) 22273773, Telefax: 22275247, E-mail: kolkata@newagepublishers.com
- **Lucknow** 16-A, Jopling Road, Lucknow-226 001
  Tel.: (0522) 2209578, 4045297, Telefax: 2204098, E-mail: lucknow@newagepublishers.com
- **Mumbai** 142C, Victor House, Ground Floor, N.M. Joshi Marg, Lower Parel, Mumbai-400 013
  Tel.: (022) 24927869, Telefax: 24915415, E-mail: mumbai@newagepublishers.com
- **New Delhi** 22, Golden House, Daryaganj, New Delhi-110 002
  Tel.: (011) 23262368, 23262370, Telefax: 43551305, E-mail: sales@newagepublishers.com

ISBN : 978-81-224-3038-7

₹ 395.00

C-12-06-6380

Printed in India at Mohanlal Printers, Delhi.
Typeset at In-house, Delhi.

PUBLISHING FOR ONE WORLD

NEW AGE INTERNATIONAL (P) LIMITED, PUBLISHERS
7/30 A, Darya Ganj, New Delhi-110002
Visit us at **www.newagepublishers.com**

DEDICATED

TO

LORD VENKATESWARA

BALANCE SHEET OF LIFE

Our Creative Ideas are our Assets

Knowledge is our Capital

Friends are our General Reserves

Our Prejudiced Views are our Liabilities

Heart is our Current Asset

Soul is our Fixed Asset

Brain is our Fixed Deposit

Thinking is our Current Account

Character & Morals, our Stock-in-Trade

Values & Behavior are our Goodwill

Our Birth is our Opening Balance!

Our Death is our Closing Balance!

Patience is our Interest Earned

Achievement is our Dividend

Children are our Bonus Issues

Education is Brands/Patents

Buying this Book is your Investment

Something to Share

This is my fifth book. I give a pat on my back for this achievement. You may wonder, is it self bragging? I often tell my students when you feel that you have finished a big job reasonably well, a matter of self assessment, just give a pat on your back. No one else has time in this world to do this for you. That gives happiness and the needed drive to you for doing the next big job with greater zeal and self-generated motivation. Do you agree with me that I deserve a small pat? Next time you do, look to the positive change you would notice in yourself to face the next challenge-you wish to welcome. The small happiness works as a stimulus for striding towards bigger aims.

My students are the real and great motivators for writing books. They wonder that I write the books directly on the computer and design as well as solve the problems, without any intermediary script. I take pride that I have developed this ability and tell them 'Nothing is impossible to achieve at any age, make a sincere beginning and your genuineness takes you to the desired end'.

To explain difficult concepts, I always ask, is it essential to use complex language? Do not blame students, if they do not understand as the creator (author) has created the barrier, complex language, I believe. Why to punish students on two fronts - a new subject and equally with a difficult language to understand, easily? My continuing quest is how to improve myself with simple language, explaining the concepts directly that is understood by non-English medium and non-Commerce students. The above lot of students does not have enough books. **This book is for those who want simple language, straight communication and understanding the subject on first reading.** I enjoy when I see their smiles that convey their unsaid appreciation, without conveying at times. My beaming students are the greatest inspiration for writing as they often ask me 'Sir, what next'?

My great family admirers are my brother, Dr. C. Srinivasulu, who is a practicing physician who tells me that an author is born in the family that has not happened earlier, son-in-law Mr. L.V.J. Kishore (U.S.A) who takes keen interest in my work despite his busy schedule and cousin Mr. V.V.N Gupta who loves to find time to read my books though fully busy in his blooming business.

My wife, often, is worried how I would spend my time, once I retire from the hectic corporate life. After more than three decades of corporate service, when I have chosen teaching line, I have never dreamt that I would develop this hobby of writing books. Now, my wife—Sandhya is no longer worried as she knows several titles are standing up in queue, waiting impatiently for their turn to go through my computer hands. I tell the projects not to rush me - one at a time which my grandson Theer says from his childhood. Message is very clear. **Destination is very important but the process of reaching the destination must also be made enjoyable, which is rather more important. Once we change our life style in this direction along with 'winning attitude', we can learn the art of living happily and can make others around us too happy.** Plan your journey in such a way that when you are reaching top, people around you, in particular your family members should also enjoy as they give their life time to you.

CA. C. Rama Gopal

Acknowledgement

I acknowledge the support and encouragement of my well-wishers in writing this book.

Miryala Kalyana Chakravarthi,
Stamford, U.S.A

Lingamallu Kishore,
Newjersey, U.S.A.

Mrs. C. Radhika,
Stamford, U.S.A.

Mrs. Lingamallu Dheera,
Newjersey, U.S.A.

Dr. C. Srinivasulu,
Vijayapuri North–508203
Andhra Pradesh

CA. T. Gangadhar,
California, U.S.A.

Dr. Sudhir Sharma,
Chairman, V.N.S. Group, Bhopal

Sh. J.K. Singh,
Secretary, V.N.S. Group, Bhopal

Dr. P.K. Chopra,
Director,
V.N.S. Institute of Management,
Bhopal

Dr. D.P. Sharma,
Ex-Vice Chancellor, Barkatulla University, Bhopal

Dr. Sameer Sharma,
Director, People's Group, Bhopal

Colonel V.G. Kondalkar,
Professor, People's Group, Bhopal

Dr. Vikas Shrotriya
Reader, Department of Management Studies,
Swami Keshvanand Institute of Technology,
Management & Gramothan, Jaipur (Rajasthan)

Prof. S.K. Bagchi
Banking & Finance, NMIMS University, Mumbai.

Dr. Salman Nusrat Zaidi
Professor, Oman Government College,
Muscat, Oman

Dr. Bijay Bhujabal
Member of the Faculty, ICFAI Business School,
ICFAI University, Dehradun.

Dr. Ramakanta Patra
Principal, NSHM Business School,
Durgapur, West Bengal.

Contents

CHAPTER 1

Financial Management An Overview

1.1 INTRODUCTION

Financial Management is concerned with planning, directing, monitoring, organizing and controlling monetary resources of an organization. Financial Management simply deals with management of money matters. Management of funds is a critical aspect of financial management. The process of financial management takes place: at the individual as well as organization levels. Our area of dealing is from the view- point of organization.

'Financial Management' is a combination of two words, 'Finance' and 'Management'. Finance is the lifeblood of any business enterprise. No business activity can be imagined, without finance. It has been rightly said that business needs money to make more money. However, money begets money, when it is properly managed. Efficient management of business is closely linked with efficient management of its finances. Financial Management is that specialized function of general management, which is related to the procurement of finance and its effective utilization for the achievement of common goal of the organization.

1.2 MEANING OF FINANCE

Finance is defined as the provision of money at the time, it is required. Finance is the art and science of managing money. There is no human being, without blood. Similarly, there is no organization that does not require finance, irrespective of the activity, it is engaged in. The way blood is needed for a person to live, so is the requirement of finance to any firm for its survival and growth. Without adequate finance, no organization can possibly achieve its objectives.

Ray G. Jones and Dean Dudley observe that the word 'finance' comes directly from the Latin word *'finis'*. As a management function, finance has special meaning. Finance function may be defined as the procurement of funds and their effective utilization.

Howard and Uption (1952) defined finance as "the administrative area or set of administrative function in an organization which have to do with the management of flow of cash so that the organization will have the means to carry out its objectives as satisfactory as possible and, at the same time, meet its obligations as they become due."

Distinction between Money and Finance: Money is expressed in currency. Money can be any country's currency, which is in the hands of any person or organization. Finance is also money, any country's currency, which is owned by any person or organization, but lent to others, used to buy an asset or make investment opportunities. The distinction between money and finance can be explained in another way.

> **If you hold currency, it is money, while you lend it over to others for buying or investing in investment opportunities, it becomes finance.**

It is curious to find that the same currency changes its role from 'Money' to 'Finance', with the change of hands. Let us illustrate. Money raised by a bank, in the form of deposits from public, becomes finance when it is lent to borrowers. If it is granted to buy/ construct a home, it becomes a home loan. It is a vehicle loan, when the amount is lent for buying a car. The amount becomes 'Project Finance', if lent to entrepreneur to start or expand a project.

> **If you hold money, it does not give any return. You part money in the form of finance, either by way of loan or investment, it starts getting return. Is it not interesting?**

1.3 FUNCTIONS AND IMPORTANCE OF FINANCE

In general, the term "Finance" is understood as the provision of funds, as and when needed. Finance is the essential requirement—*sine qua non*—of every organization.

Required Everywhere: All activities, be it production, marketing, human resources development, purchases and even research and development, depend on the adequate and timely availability of finance both for commencement and their smooth continuation to completion. Blood is needed for every human being. Similarly, there is no organization that does not require finance, irrespective of its activities. The way blood is required for a person to live, so be the finance to any firm for its survival and growth. Finance is regarded as the life-blood of every business enterprise.

Efficient Utilization—More Important: Finance function is the most important function of all business activities. The efficient management of business enterprise is, closely, linked with the efficient management of its finances. The need of finance starts with the setting up of business. Its growth and expansion require more funds. Funds have to be raised from various sources. Such sources have to be selected keeping in view their relation to the implications, in particular, its risks attached. Receiving money, alone, is not important. Terms and conditions, while receiving money are more important. Cost of funds is an important element. Its utilization is rather more important. If funds are utilised properly, repayment would be possible and easier, too. Care has to be exercised to match the inflow and outflow of funds. Needless to say, profitability of any firm is dependent on its cost as well as its efficient utilization.

1.4 FINANCE AND RELATED DISCIPLINES

Financial Management is not an independent area, but an integral part of overall management. As a subject too, Financial Management had been a branch of Economics till 1890. Later, it has evolved into a separate discipline. It draws heavily on Economics to explain its theoretical concepts, even today. The subject is of immense interest to academicians and practicing managers. Academicians take interest as there are several controversies and no unanimous opinion is, still, found. Again, the subject is a matter of great challenge to practicing managers as business affords a lot of scope to expand, with ever-growing competition. Every decision-making process involves finance, demanding new innovative products and techniques to use them to the utmost advantage of the firm. Finance managers often do feel in real life why this subsequent thinking did not come to them earlier, to solve their problems. Threat to survive sharpens the thinking process.

1.4.1 Finance and Economics

Economics has two broad areas, viz. Macroeconomics and Microeconomics.

Macroeconomics is concerned with overall institutional and international environment in which the firm must operate. In other words, macroeconomics is the environment in which an industry operates, which is not controllable by any individual firm. They are the external factors, which are beyond the control of the company. They relate primarily to

- State of the economy
- Government policy

When we analyse our problems from the viewpoint of the whole economy, it is a macro economics. Institutional environment encompasses banking system, capital markets, financial intermediaries, credit policies of The Reserve Bank of India, structure and growth of financial system, monetary and economic policies of the government, which vary periodically. Their awareness and adoption to change for the firm is vital. Business firms operate in the macroeconomic environment. Unless the finance managers understand the implications of the policy and assess the impact they make to the business, and change accordingly, business firms cannot survive, let alone grow. Finance managers have to understand the broad economic environment in which their firms work. To be successful, they cannot afford to function in isolation. They should recognize the impact of each decision, be it monetary or credit policy, in terms of their relative cost and availability of funds. For example, when the economy faces slump, it is not advisable to go for expansion activities. Similarly, when the economy experiences an uptrend, firm can opt for trading on equity for financing as larger profits are assured to most of the firms. That policy helps the firm to increase earnings per share. Finance managers have to update their knowledge and make detailed analysis in respect of matters affecting the company to apprise the management for the timely changes to be introduced.

Microeconomics is firm's specific environment and also controllable. Microeconomic factors deal with the internal conditions of the firm. A few important factors are as under:

1. **Nature and Size of Enterprise:** Firms differ in activities and their size. Their capital structure and methods of financing also depend on their size. A manufacturing firm or public utility organization would require more fixed assets, so their capital structure is large. Small firms can obtain their fixed assets even on lease. But, large firms would construct their own building and assemble their own plants. Unlike big firms, small firms do not enjoy goodwill in the capital market and are largely dependent on internal finances.
2. **Level of Risk and Stability in Earnings:** Risk influences the financial decisions of the firm. Greater the risk, firm has to retain more profits, rather than adopting a liberal dividend policy. Firms that enjoy stable earnings prefer fixed-cost capital, such as preference shares and debentures as they can pay the fixed amount of interest, without difficulty, from their earnings. Where stable earnings do not exist, financing is done through equity as there is no commitment to pay fixed and regular dividend.
3. **Liquidity Position:** Dividend, normally, is paid out of cash. Firms with a sound liquidity position can adopt liberal dividend policy. If there is illiquidity in the firm, it affects nature of financing and dividend decisions.
4. **Pattern of Ownership:** In a closely-held company, ownership lies in a few hands. It is easier to convince them that a conservative dividend policy is good to them, if the policy is in the interests of the company. Where there are many shareholders, their wishes matter the most in decision-making. Their preferences cannot be ignored, while designing dividend policy.
5. **Attitude of Management:** Though listed last, importance of attitude of management is not the least. If the firm is conservative, greater importance is given to liquidity, rather than the profitability. More investment is made in current assets. The finance manager tries to tread a beaten path, preferring to avoid fixed obligations for raising additional capital, even if debt capital is advantageous. On the other hand, finance manager in an aggressive firm stresses profitability, sacrificing importance of liquidity. Additional capital is raised by debt, accepting the risk of debt to take advantage of the debt. Alternatively, preference may be given to conduct the business with lesser current assets.

An experienced finance manager, with prudence, can manoeuvre and absorb the impact of internal and external factors to some extent.

> **A prudent finance manager would prefer a compromise between risk and return, equally between profitability and liquidity.**

Supply and demand relationship, profit maximization, pricing strategies, risk and return determination and marginal analysis are the few examples of relevant microeconomic theories used in financial management. The rationale of depreciating assets is rooted in microeconomic theory. Product pricing strategies is one of the common issues that are, often faced. The primary principle of financial management, **Marginal Analysis or Cost Benefit Analysis,** is one of the important areas that is frequently applied. Comparison of cost with the corresponding benefit is essential for decision-making, as benefit in excess of cost only increases profit. Knowledge of basic microeconomics is essential for all finance managers.

Let us illustrate. A proposal has come for consideration to replace an existing manual stone crusher by a mechanized stone crusher. Existing stone crusher can be sold at ₹ 10,000, while the new mechanized stone crusher involves a cash outlay of ₹ 75,000. The total benefits from the new mechanized stone crusher and manual crusher are ₹ 1,20,000 and ₹ 22,000 respectively. Applying Marginal Analysis, we get:

		₹
Benefits from new crusher	1,20,000	
Less: Benefits from old crusher	22,000	
Marginal Benefit (A) **(Incremental Benefit)**		98,000
Cost of new crusher	75,000	
Less: Proceeds from the sale of old crusher	10,000	
Marginal Cost (B) **(Additional Cost)**		65,000
Net Benefits (A–B)	33,000	

As the decision results into a net benefit, cost benefit analysis recommends acceptance of the proposal to the firm.

> **Stated simply, economics is closely intertwined with finance, the subject of finance has since long been known as 'Economics of Finance'.**

1.4.2 Finance and Accounting

Much of the modern business is not possible without accounting information. It is an accepted fact that business is finance oriented. It is the process of using money to make money. Accounting generates information/data related to activities/operations of a firm, dealing in goods or services. Necessary input is provided by accounting for finance function. Accounting is a source of most information, which management uses for decision-making. Management is heavily dependant on accounting for operating facts.

Finance is closely related to accounting. Accounting is the data collection process, dealing with accurate reporting, while finance is a managerial or decision-making process. Accounting provides the input for finance. Finance is wide, while accounting is its part. Finance is referred to with greater respect than accounting. In many organizations, finance is entrusted only to those who enjoy the trust of the top management.

End products of accounting—profit and loss account, balance sheet, sources and application of funds statement and cash flow statement—assist finance managers in assessing the past performance and understanding the future directions of the firm.

There are two key differences between accounting and finance. One relates to treatment of funds and the other relates to decision-making.

Treatment of Funds: Accrual system of accounting is the backbone of accounting, which forms the basis for determination of operating results. Revenue is recognized at the point of sale, irrespective of its realization of sale proceeds. In other words, collection of cash has no significance. Similarly, expenses are recognized when they are incurred, not at the time of payment. Payment of expense is not relevant at all. A firm may be quite profitable in the accounting sense, but, still, struggling, even, to make small cash payments due to liquidity problems. In fact, such a book profit firm cannot survive very long. Solvency is always a challenge, if it is not the focus of the firm.

For treatment of funds, finance is based on cash flows. Funds mean inflow and outflow of cash. Sales, when actually realized, are inflows and expenses when paid are outflows. Here, the importance is on solvency, i.e. ability to maintain cash obligations as and when they fall due for payment. Insolvency situation is avoided. The goal of the firm is to maintain the necessary cash flows, to meet its obligations and finance the assets needed for the firm.

Let us illustrate with a small example the difference in treatment between accounting and finance for transactions in a year:

		₹
Sales	:	20,00,000
Cost of sales or purchases	:	14,00,000
Opening & Closing stock	:	Nil
Collections from sales	:	4,00,000
Payments to suppliers	:	12,00,000

Accounting View (Profit and Loss Account)		**Financial View (Cash Flow Statement)**	
Sales	₹ 20,00,000	Cash inflows	₹ 4,00,000
Less: Costs	14, 00,000	*Less*: Cash outflow	12,00,000
Net Profit	6,00,000	*Net Cash outflow	(8,00,000)

*** Net Cash outflow is the resultant of current year operations. This is negative, indicating that opening cash balance has gone towards reduction of cash flow, resulting in reduced closing cash balance at the end of the year.**

The picture clearly shows that the firm is highly profitable in the accounting sense. However, if this type of performance continues, there would be heavy shortage of cash, resulting in liquidity crunch. Very soon, the firm would not survive, due to inadequate cash flows to meet its obligations. Financial collapse is imminent. In financial terms, firm is heading for insolvency. In other words, a highly profitable firm, in accounting sense, is heading towards insolvency.

Financial view exposes what accounting treatment eclipses.

Decision-making: Accounting and finance differ in their purpose. The purpose of accounting is collection and presentation of data. The data so made available is used by the finance manager for decision-making. It does not mean that accountants never make decisions and finance managers never collect data. Their focus is different. Accountants collect accurate data and finance managers plan, control and make decisions. In a way, finance begins where accounting ends.

1.4.3 Finance and Other Related Disciplines

Finance also draws support from other related disciplines, such as production, marketing and quantitative methods. Finance is a service function to meet the needs of production and marketing. If the firm decides to produce and sell more, capital expenditure projects may be needed, for which finance manager has to arrange funds. Such a decision also would have impact on the projected cash flows. In those areas, production and finance managers need to work closely for optimum investment in plant and machinery. Finance is becoming a complex area and so tools of analysis developed in the quantitative methods area are helpful in analyzing the complex financial management problems.

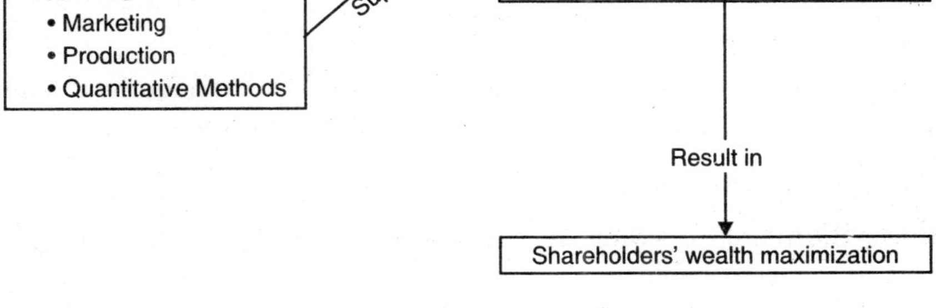

Fig. 1.1: Impact of important disciplines on financial management

1.5 MEANING AND DEFINITION—FINANCIAL MANAGEMENT

The general meaning of finance refers to the provision of funds, as and when needed. However, as management function, the term 'Financial Management' has a distinct meaning. **Financial management deals with the study of procuring funds and its effective and judicious utilization, in terms of the overall objectives of the firm, and expectations of the providers of funds.** The basic objective is to maximize the value of the firm. **The purpose is to achieve maximization of share value to the owners, i.e. equity shareholders.**

The objective of every company is to create value for its shareholders. Market price of equity share is the barometer for showing the real 'Value'. The basic objective of financial management is to maximize the shareholders' wealth, represented by the market value of equity shares.

Financial Management is concerned with three activities:

- **Anticipating financial needs, which means estimating requirements of the firm in terms of long-term and short-term needs or investment in fixed and current assets.**
- **Acquiring financial resources from different sources to meet the financial needs.**
- **Allocating funds to maximize shareholders' wealth.**

The term financial management has been defined differently by various authors. Some of the authoritative definitions are given below:

1. "Financial Management is concerned with the efficient use of an important economic resource, namely, Capital Funds." – **Solomon**
2. "Financial Management is concerned with the managerial decisions that result in the acquisition and financing of short-term and long-term credits for the firm." – **Phillioppatus**
3. "Financial Management is concerned with the acquisition, financing and management of assets with some overall goal in mind."– **James C. Van Horne**
4. "Financial Management deals with procurement of funds and their effective utilization in the business." – **S.C. Kuchhal**

From the above definitions, two basic aspects of financial management emerge.

A. Procurement of funds.

B. Effective and judicious utilization of funds.

Financial management has become so important that it has given birth to Financial Management as a separate subject.

1.6 NATURE OF FINANCIAL MANAGEMENT

Financial management refers to that part of management activity, which is concerned with the planning and controlling of firm's financial resources. Financial management is a part of overall management. All business decisions involve finance. Where finance is needed, role of finance manager is inevitable. **Financial management deals with raising of funds from various sources, dependent on the availability and existing capital structure of the organization.** The sources must be suitable and economical to the organization. Emphasis of financial management is more on its efficient utilization, rather than raising of funds alone.

The scope and complexity of financial management has been widening with the growth of business in different diverse directions. As business competition increases, with a greater pace, more support of financial management is needed, in a more innovative way to make the business grow, ahead of others.

1.7 IMPORTANCE—FINANCIAL MANAGEMENT

The main importance of financial management can be listed as under:

1. It is necessary for the smooth running of the organization.
2. It facilitates to evaluate the profitability of operational activities of the organization.
3. From the view point of profitability, decision-making is geared at all functional levels.

1.8 NEED OF FINANCIAL MANAGEMENT

Financial management is concerned with optimum utilization of resources. Resources are limited, particularly in developing countries like India. So, the focus, everywhere, is to take maximum benefit, in the form of output, from the limited inputs.

Financial management is needed in every type of organization, be it public or private sector. Its importance exists equally in both profit oriented and non-profit organizations. In fact, need of financial management is more in loss-making organizations to turn them to profitable enterprises. Study reveals many organizations have sustained losses, due to absence of professional financial management.

1.9 SCOPE—FINANCIAL MANAGEMENT

Over the years notable changes have occurred in financial management both in its scope and areas of coverage. **Study of changes that have taken place, over the years, is known as "Scope of Financial Management".**

For easy understanding of changes, it is necessary to divide the scope of financial management into two approaches. Broadly, the two approaches and their emphasis are:

Traditional Approach—Procurement of Funds
Modern Approach—Effective Utilization of Funds

Traditional Approach

The scope of finance function was treated in the narrow sense as procurement or arrangement of funds. A finance manager was treated as just provider of funds, when organization felt its need. **The utilization or administering resources was considered outside the purview of the finance function. It was felt that the finance manager had no role to play in the decision-making for its utilization.** Others used to take decisions regarding its application in the organization, without the involvement of finance personnel. Finance manager had been treated, in fact, as an outsider with a very specific and limited function, supplier of funds, to perform when the need of funds was felt by the organization.

As per this approach, the following aspects only were included in the scope of financial management:

(i) Estimation of requirements of finance.

(ii) Arrangement of funds from financial institutions.

(iii) Arrangement of funds through diverse financial instruments such as shares, debentures, bonds and loans.

(iv) Looking after the accounting and legal work connected with the raising of funds, and

(v) Preparation of financial statements and managing cash levels needed to pay day-to-day maturing obligations.

Limitations

The traditional approach was evolved during the 1920s and 1930s period and continued till 1950. The approach had been discarded due to the following limitations:

(i) **No Involvement in Application of Funds:** The finance manager had not been involved in decision-making of the allocation of funds. He had been ignored in internal decision-making process and treated as an outsider.

(ii) **No Involvement in Day-to-day Management:** The focus was on providing long-term funds from a combination of sources. This process was more of one time happening. The finance manager was not involved in day-to-day administration of working capital management. Smooth functioning of the firm depends on working capital management, where the finance manager was not involved and allowed to play any role.

(iii) **Not Associated in Decision-making–Allocation of Funds:** The issue of allocation of funds was kept outside his functioning. He had not been involved in decision-making for its judicious utilization.

(iv) **Outsider-looking-in Approach:** The subject of finance has moved around the suppliers of funds (investors, financial institutions, banks, etc.) who are outsiders. The approach has been outsider-looking-in approach, since finance manager has never been involved in internal decision-making process.

Raising finance was an infrequent event. Its natural implication was that the issues involved in working capital management were not in the purview of the finance function. In nutshell, during the traditional phase, the finance manager was called upon, in particular, when his speciality was required to locate new sources of funds, as and when the requirement of funds was felt.

The following issues, as pointed by Solomon, were ignored in the scope of financial management, under this approach:

(A) Should an enterprise commit capital funds to a certain purpose?

(B) Do the expected returns meet financial standards of performance?

(C) How should these standards be set and what is the cost of capital funds to the enterprise?

(D) How does the cost vary with the mixture of financing methods used?

The traditional approach has failed to provide answers to the above questions due to narrow scope. Traditional approach has outlived its utility in the changed business situation. The scope of finance function has undergone a sea change, with the emergence of different capital instruments.

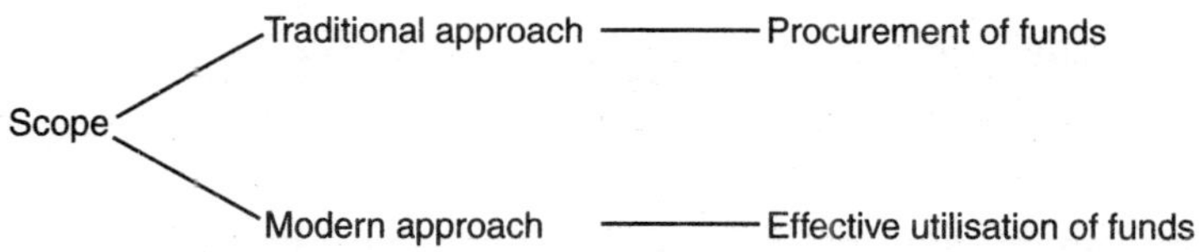

Fig. 1.2: Scope of financial management

Modern Approach

Modern approach has started during mid 1950s. The approach and utility of financial management has started changing in a revolutionary manner. Modern approach provides answers to those questions which traditional approach has failed to provide.

Financial management is considered as vital and an integral part of overall management. Its scope is wider, as it covers both procurement of funds and its efficient allocation. Allocation is not a just haphazard process. Its effective utilization and allocation among various investments helps to maximize shareholders' wealth.

The emphasis of Financial Management has been shifted from raising funds to the effective and judicious utilization of funds. The modern approach is analytical way of looking into the financial problems of the firm.

The main contents of this new approach are:

(A) What is the total volume of funds an enterprise should commit?

(B) What specific assets an enterprise should acquire?

(C) How should the funds required be financed?

Advice of finance manager is required at every moment, whenever any decision with involvement of funds is taken. There is hardly any activity that does not involve funds.

In the words of Solomon, **"The central issue of financial policy is the use of funds. It is helpful in achieving the broad financial goals which an enterprise sets for itself".**

Now-a-days, the finance manager is required to look into the financial implications of every decision to be taken by the firm. He is involved before taking any decision, during its review and, finally, when the final outcome is judged. In other words, his association has been continuous in every decision-making process from inception till its end.

Check Your Understanding

(A) State whether the following statements are True or False

1. Government monetary policy influences the firm's financial decisions.
2. Corporate financial decisions are based on microeconomic factors only.
3. The objective of wealth maximization serves the interests of different groups directly or indirectly related to the firm.
4. Macroeconomics deals with the internal factors affecting the firm.
5. An efficient finance manager closely follows both macro and microeconomic factors that influence the activities of the firm.
6. Financial management does not have any relationship with other disciplines.
7. Irrespective of slump or uptrend of economy, expansion activities are to be undertaken.
8. Credit policy of the government influences the nature of a firm's financial decisions.
9. Analysis of external environment by finance manager helps in identifying opportunities and threats to the firm.
10. Basic knowledge of economics is not necessary for a finance manager.
11. Efficient management of business is closely linked with efficient management of finances.
12. Finance holds key to all economic activities.

(B) Objective Questions (Identify what is most appropriate)

1. Profit maximization is made when

   (i) marginal revenue is < marginal cost

   (ii) marginal revenue is > marginal cost

   (iii) marginal revenue = marginal cost

2. Corporate financial decisions are influenced by
   (i) macroeconomic factors only
   (ii) microeconomic factors only
   (iii) both macroeconomic and microeconomic factors
3. Traditionally, the role of finance manager was restricted to
   (i) efficient utilization of funds
   (ii) acquisition of funds
   (iii) acquisition and efficient utilization of funds
4. Financial management is mainly concerned with
   (i) efficient management of business
   (ii) providing funds
   (iii) acquisition and efficient utilization of financial resources

Answers

1. (iii) 2. (iii) 3. (ii) 4. (iii)

Descriptive Questions

1. Explain the meaning and importance of finance. **(1.1 to 1.3)**
2. Draw a distinction between 'Finance' and 'Money' with suitable examples. **(1.1 & 1.2)**
3. In what ways do macro and microeconomic factors influence corporate financial decisions? **(1.4 & 1.4.1)**
4. How finance is related to macro-economic and micro-economic problems? **(1.4 & 1.4.1)**
5. Describe the close relationship between 'finance' and 'economics' and explain the need for a finance manager to possess basic knowledge of economics. **(1.4 & 1.4.1)**
6. "The subject of finance has since long been known as 'economics of finance"—Discuss. **(1.4 & 1.4.1)**
7. What are the major differences between accounting and finance in respect of cash flows? **(1.4.2)**
8. Describe the relationship between finance and other related disciplines. **(1.4 & 1.4.1, 1.4.2 and 1.4.3)**
9. Define 'Financial management' and explain its nature, need and importance. **(1.5 to 1.8)**
10. Explain the scope of financial management. **(1.5 and 1.9)**
11. "The horizons of Financial Management have changed substantially in scope and complexity over the years"—Justify the statement. **(1.9)**
12. Write short notes on the following:
    (A) Money and Finance **(1.2)**
    (B) Financial Management **(1.5)**
13. Market price of equity share is the barometer for showing the real 'value' of the company.

14. The basic objective of financial management is to maximize the shareholders' wealth, represented by the market value of equity shares.
15. It is not the function of the finance manager to look into the financial implications of marketing decisions.

Answers

1. True	2. False	3. True	4. False	5. True	6. False	7. False	8. True
9. True	10. False	11. True	12. True	13. True	14. True	15. False	

Interview Questions

Q.1. Is there any difference between 'Money' and 'Finance'? If so, illustrate your views?

Ans. 'Money' and 'Finance' are different. Any form of currency held is money. Money changes its role to finance when it is used as an investment or lent to others. Let us take an example to explain their difference. Money raised by a bank in the form of deposits becomes finance when the amount is lent. It becomes vehicle finance when the loan is sanctioned for the purchase of a vehicle and the same amount, when lent for buying a home, becomes home loan.

Q.2. What is the basic objective of 'Financial Management'?

Ans. The basic objective of 'Financial Management' is to maximize the shareholders' wealth. Maximization of shareholders' wealth occurs when the price of the equity share is at its peak.

CHAPTER 2

Functions of Financial Management

2.1 INTRODUCTION

Finance holds key to all economic activities. Every other function in business organization needs finance. It is appropriately said that the finance needs an overall knowledge of the environment in which it is needed. It is in this sense that finance is, often, described as part of the nervous system in business.

A good measure of specialization coupled with sensitivity to general trends and, in particular, appreciation of the requirements of other departments, in the right perspective, makes an ideal combination for the success of finance function.

Many times finance function fails because finance personnel lack understanding of the overall environment of the business in which the finance function must operate.

2.2 RELATIONSHIP OF FINANCE WITH OTHER MANAGEMENT FUNCTIONS

There exists an inseparable relationship between finance on one hand and other management functions, such as purchase, production, marketing, personnel and other functions on the other hand. Most of these functions in a business are undertaken on the availability of funds. For example, recruitment and promotion of employees in the production department is clearly a responsibility of the production department. However, it requires payment of wages, salaries and other benefits, involving finance. To increase production, an existing machine may need replacement or a new machine is additionally required, which needs finance, affecting the outflows in a significant manner. Formulation of sales promotion policies fall within the purview of marketing function, but advertising and other sales promotion activities need cash outlays. So, financial resources are affected.

To work efficiently, finance function has to generate finance, and for this purpose it depends on the coordination of different business functions or departments.

Financial policies of the firm are to be devised in such a manner that the requirements of the other functional areas are adequately met. Financial management provides oxygen to the life of a firm by providing timely, adequate and uninterrupted availability of funds throughout the firm to achieve its ultimate objectives.

Finance functions are closely connected with production, marketing and other functions and it is difficult to separate them.

A brief, hereunder, is presented about the relationship between finance and other business functions:

Financial Management and Materials Management

Materials department in a manufacturing firm covers procurement, storage, maintenance and supply of materials and stores. Materials are sufficiently kept so that production schedule continues smoothly and, at the same time, they remain in good condition. Materials, generally, constitute a substantial part of the cost of production. Cost of production can be substantially controlled and reduced by a strict vigil on the material movement. If materials are procured on economic terms and used in effective manner, firm can achieve maximum productivity. The finance manager and the material manager may discuss together in determining economic order quantity, determination of stock level, safety level and perpetual inventory system, etc. The finance manager can effectively arrange availability of cash for making payment of bills, when they fall due, when he is closely associated in the above function.

Financial Management and Production Management

The job of the production department in a firm is to provide production facilities, keep production cycle running, arrange skilled and unskilled labour, provide storage of finished goods and ensure maximum capacity utilisation, etc. Cost of production assumes a substantial part in the total cost. Finance manager interacts with the production manager to control cost of production. Production department wants to increase availability of machinery, installation of materials monitoring devices, safety devices and better production facilities. All these decisions involve financial requirements. So, finance has a significant role to play.

Financial Management and Personnel Management

Success or failure of every business depends on the efficiency or otherwise of persons who are entrusted to handle the respective functions. The personnel department is concerned with recruitment, training and placement of staff in right places for the firm. A sound personnel policy includes proper wage structure, incentives, promotion opportunity and human resource development. Again, all these matters affect finance. Personnel Department plays an important role in increasing the productivity of employees which, in turn, improves the profitability. The expenditure incurred on the personnel department and return it generates, as reflected in the increased productivity of the employees, should be considered in framing a sound personnel policy.

The personnel department has to work closely with the finance department while evaluating the incentive schemes, revision of pay scales, employees' welfare measures, lay offs, etc. Therefore, the relationship between both the departments has to be intimate.

Financial Management and Marketing Management

The Marketing department is concerned with the selling activity of goods and services to customers. This department is entrusted with the responsibility of developing, marketing, selling, advertisement and other related policies to achieve the sales target. It has to create the brand image for the firm's products. All these decisions involve financial implications. While choosing different distribution channels, media of advertisement and sales promotion devices, cost benefit analysis should be the guiding factor. Any change in distribution function affects cash flows significantly. The marketing manager has to interact with the finance manager in the process of finalizing these decisions.

For example, the marketing manager should not arbitrarily relax credit terms, just to achieve sales targets. If a greater credit period is extended, more funds get tied up in receivables, involving increased cost. Greater period of credit has to be justified with increased sales and/or greater contribution that improve profits of the firm. The financial implications of the proposed credit policy, price wars and advertisement policy have to be evaluated jointly to reach a mutual consensus in the interest of the firm.

Financial Management and Research and Development Management

Normally, research and development activities do not yield immediate and fast results. They take more time to give results, involve activities requiring huge funds. There should be a constant endeavour for improvement and sophistication to the existing product. Unless newer varieties are introduced, present products of the firm are likely to go out of existence. If the expenditure on R & D is disproportionate to the financial capacity of the firm, it cripples the enterprise. On the other hand, if there is a heavy cut down of expenditure on this front, scope of diversification and improvement would be affected. So, it is necessary to bring a balance between the necessary R & D activity and availability of funds. This exercise is possible only through the joint efforts of the finance manager and the person at the helm of affairs of R & D department.

All this indicates that a closer interaction between finance and all other functional departments on a continuous basis is essential and only joint effort can achieve the goals of the enterprise.

An interesting question is where is the separation between the other functional managements and the finance function, entrusted with the task of providing funds, to meet the cost of production and marketing operations? There are no clear cut answers.

A company that has a tight financial position gives more weight to financial considerations and devises the strategies for other departments in the light of the financial constraints. On the other hand, a company, which has a comfortable and regular supply of funds, will be more flexible in formulating strategies for production and marketing departments. The general feeling in most of the organizations is that the finance department has more important place to play than others. In real life, it is not so. Only the concerted and combined efforts of all the departments only help in achieving the objectives of the management.

2.3 AIMS OF FINANCE FUNCTION

The primary function of finance is to make availability of funds, as and when needed and at the same time ensure their judicious utilisation. The following are the aims of finance function:

1. **Acquiring Sufficient and Suitable Funds:** The primary aim of finance function is to assess the needs of the enterprise properly and procure funds in time. Time is also an important element in meeting the needs of the organization. If the funds are not available at the time of need, the firm may become sick or at least, the profitability of the firm would be definitely adversely affected.

   It is necessary that the funds should be reasonably adequate to the demands of the firm. The funds should be raised from different sources, commensurate to the nature of business and risk profile of the organization. When the nature of business is such that the production does not commence immediately and requires long gestation period, it is necessary to have the long-term sources like share capital, debentures and long-term loan, etc. A concern with longer gestation period does not have profits for some years. So, the firm should rely more on permanent capital like share capital to avoid interest burden on the borrowing component during the gestation period.
2. **Proper Utilization of Funds:** Raising funds is important. More important is their proper utilisation. If proper utilisation of funds were not made, there would be no revenue generation. Benefits should always exceed cost of funds so that the organization can be profitable. Beneficial projects only are to be undertaken. So, it is all the more necessary that careful planning and cost-benefit analysis should be made before the actual commencement of projects.
3. **Increasing Profitability:** Profitability is necessary for every organization. The planning and control functions of finance aim at increasing profitability of the firm. To achieve profitability, the cost of funds should be low. Idle funds do not yield any return, but incur cost. So, the organization should avoid idle funds. Finance function also requires matching of cost and returns of funds. If funds are used efficiently, profitability gets a boost. To improve profits, products yielding lower profits may be replaced with those giving higher benefits. For this, a continuous review and look out for better products within the existing infrastructure is needed.

4. **Maximising Firm's Value:** The ultimate aim of finance function is maximising the value of the firm, which is reflected in wealth maximization of shareholders. The market value of the equity shares is an indicator of the wealth maximization.

2.4 FUNCTIONS OF FINANCE

Finance function is the most important function of a business. Finance is closely connected with production, marketing and other activities. If finance is not adequate, progress of all these activities retards significantly. In the absence of finance, all these activities come to a halt. In fact, only with finance, a business activity can be commenced, sustained and expanded. Finance is required everywhere, be it for production, marketing, human resource development or undertaking research activity. **Understanding the universality and importance of finance, finance manager is associated, in modern business, in all activities as no activity can exist without funds.**

When a decision involves finance, it is viewed as a financial decision in a business firm. In all the following financial areas of decision-making, the role of finance manager is vital. We can classify the finance functions or financial decisions into four major groups:

(A) Investment decision or long-term asset mix decision

(B) Financing decision or capital mix decision

(C) Liquidity decision or short-term asset mix decision

(D) Dividend decision or profit allocation decision

Finance functions do not necessarily occur in sequence. But, decisions have to be taken with the objective of maximizing shareholders' wealth. The finance manager has to manage funds for their optimum utilisation. While procuring funds, he has to ensure risk; cost and control considerations are properly balanced under a given situation.

Finance functions are explained below in a greater detail.

(A) Investment Decision

Investment decisions relate to selection of assets in which funds are to be invested by the firm. Investment alternatives are numerous. Resources are scarce and limited. They have to be rationed and discretely used. Investment decisions allocate and ration the resources among the competing investment alternatives or opportunities. The effort is to find out the projects, which are acceptable.

Investment decisions relate to the total amount of assets to be held and their composition in the form of fixed and current assets. Both the factors, total as well as composition, influence the risk the organization is exposed to. The more important aspect is how the investors perceive the risk.

The investment decisions result in purchase of assets. Assets can be classified under two broad categories:

(i) Long-term investment decisions: Long-term assets

(ii) Short-term investment decisions: Short-term assets

Long-term investment decisions: Purchase of fixed assets, like plant and machinery, land and building etc. are long-term investment decisions.

Investment in long-term assets is popularly known as "capital budgeting'.

Capital Budgeting decisions relate to acquisition of fixed assets. The fixed assets are long-term, in nature. Basically, fixed assets create earnings for the firm. They give benefit in future period. It is difficult to measure benefits derived from them, with total accuracy, as future is uncertain.

The investment decision is important not only for setting up new units but also for expansion of the existing units. Such decisions generally are irreversible. Often, reversal of decisions results in substantial loss. When a brand new car is sold, even after a day of its purchase, still, the next buyer treats the vehicle as a second-hand car. The transaction, invariably, results in heavy loss, even, for a short period of owning. So, the finance manager has to evaluate profitability of every investment proposal carefully, before funds are committed to them.

Short-term Investment Decisions: Acquiring current assets (raw materials, work-in-progress, finished goods, debtors, etc.) is a short-term investment decision. Short-term assets are to be converted into cash within the financial year without diminution (reduction) in value.

The short-term investment decisions are popularly termed as working capital management.

It relates to management of current assets. The finance manager has to allocate among cash and cash equivalents, receivables and inventories. Though these current assets do not directly contribute to the earnings, their existence is necessary for proper, efficient and optimum utilisation of fixed assets.

For a movie to progress, both hero and heroine are needed. In the same way, if fixed assets are heroes, current assets are heroines to the financial success story of an organization.

Acquisition of Assets alone, not Sufficient: Apart from acquisition of new assets, the flip side of investment – disinvestment-must not be ignored. Assets that can no longer be, economically justified for retention need to be reduced, eliminated or replaced, at the earliest, before they lose their value significantly. In other words, acquisition and disinvestment are to be treated as an ongoing exercise investment function.

(B) Financing Decision

Once investment decision is made, the next step is how to raise finance for the concerned investment.

Financing decision is concerned with the mix or composition of the sources of raising the funds, required by the firm. In other words, it is related to the pattern of financing.

Here, the finance manager is concerned with the make up of the left hand side of the balance sheet. In financing decision, the finance manager is required to determine the proportion of equity and debt, which is known as capital structure. There are two main sources of funds, shareholders' funds (variable in the form of dividend) and borrowed funds (fixed interest-bearing). These sources have their own peculiar characteristics. The key distinction lies in the fixed commitment. Interest has to be paid on borrowed funds, irrespective of the profitability of the firm. Interest has to be paid, even if the firm incurs loss and this permanent obligation is not there with the funds raised from the shareholders. **The borrowed funds are relatively cheaper compared to shareholders' funds; however they carry risk.** This risk is known as financial risk, i.e. risk of insolvency due to non-payment of interest or non-repayment of borrowed capital.

Financing decision relates to determination of proportion of debt and capital.

On the other hand, the shareholders' funds constitute a permanent source to the firm. The shareholders' funds could be from equity shareholders or preference shareholders. Equity share capital is not repayable and does not have fixed commitment in the form of dividend. However, preference share capital has a fixed commitment in the form of dividend and is redeemable, if they are redeemable preference shares.

Barring a few exceptions, every firm tries to employ both borrowed funds and shareholders' funds to finance its activities. The employment of these funds, in combination, is known as financial leverage. Financial leverage provides profitability, but carries risk. Without risk, there is no return. This is the case in every walk of life!

When the return on capital employed (equity and borrowed funds) is greater than the rate of interest paid on the debt, shareholders' return gets magnified or increased. In a period of inflation, this would be advantageous, while it is a disadvantage or great curse in times of recession.

Example:

Total Investment:	₹	1,00,000
Return		15%
Composition of Investment:		
Equity	₹	60,000
Debt @ 7% interest	₹	40,000
Return on investment @15%	₹	15,000
Interest on Debt 7% on ₹ 40,000	₹	2,800
Earnings Available to Equity Shareholders	₹	12,200

Return on equity (ignoring tax) is 20%, which is at the expense of debt as they get 7% interest only.

In the normal course, equity would get a return of 15%. But, they enjoy 20% due to financing by a combination of debt and equity.

This area would be discussed in detail in the later chapter while dealing with leverages.

The finance manager follows that combination of raising funds which is optimal mix of debt and equity. The optimal mix minimizes the risk and maximizes the wealth of shareholders.

(C) Liquidity Decision

Liquidity decision is concerned with the management of current assets.

> **Liquidity means having enough cash to pay bills and meet obligations, as and when they fall due for payment.**

Basically, liquidity management is Working Capital Management. Working Capital Management is concerned with the management of current assets. It is concerned with short-term survival. Short term-survival is a prerequisite for long-term survival.

When more funds are tied up in current assets, the firm would enjoy greater liquidity. In consequence, the firm would not experience any difficulty in making payment of debts, as and when they fall due. With excess liquidity, there would be no default in payments. So, there would be no threat of insolvency for failure of payments. However, funds have economic cost. Idle current assets do not earn anything. Higher liquidity is at the cost of profitability. Profitability would suffer with more idle funds. Investment in current assets, in general, affects the overall profitability, liquidity and risk of a firm. **A proper balance must be maintained between liquidity and profitability of the firm. This is the key area, where finance manager has to play a significant role. The strategy is in ensuring a trade-off between liquidity and profitability.** This is, indeed, a balancing act and continuous process. It is a continuous process as the conditions and requirements of business change from time to time. In accordance with the requirements of the firm, the liquidity has to vary and in consequence, profitability changes. This is the major dimension of liquidity decision-working capital management. Working capital management is day-to-day problem to the finance manager. His skills of financial management are put to test almost daily.

(D) Dividend Decision

Dividend: The term 'dividend' relates to the portion of profit, which is distributed to shareholders of the company. It is a reward or compensation to them for their investment made in the firm. The dividend can be declared from the current profits or accumulated profits.

Dividend decision is concerned with the amount of profits to be distributed and retained in the firm.

Which course should be followed—dividend distribution or retention of profits? Normally, companies distribute certain amount in the form of dividend, in a stable manner, to meet the expectations of shareholders and balance is retained within the organization for expansion. If dividend is not distributed, shareholders would be greatly dissatisfied. Non-declaration of dividend affects the market price of equity shares severely. One significant element in the dividend decision is, therefore, the dividend payout ratio, i.e. what proportion of dividend is to be paid to the shareholders.

The dividend decision depends mainly on the preference of the equity shareholders and investment opportunities, available within the firm.

A higher rate of dividend, beyond the market expectations, immediately increases the market price of shares. However, it leaves a small amount in the form of retained earnings for expansion. The business that reinvests less will tend to grow slow. The other alternative is to raise funds in the market for expansion. Equally, it is not a desirable decision to retain all the profits for expansion, without distributing any amount in the form of dividend.

There is no ready-made answer to how much is to be distributed and what portion is to be retained. Retention of profit is related to

- Reinvestment opportunities available to the firm.
- Alternative rate of return available to equity shareholders, if they invest themselves.

2.5 INTER-RELATIONSHIP OF FINANCE FUNCTIONS OR DECISIONS

All the finance functions or decisions relating to investment function, financing function, liquidity function and dividend function—are inter-related and inter-connected. They are inter-related because the goal of all functions is one and the same. Their ultimate objective is only one—achievement of maximization of shareholders' wealth or maximising the market value of shares.

All financial decisions are not independent; they are interrelated to each other. An optimal combination of decisions relating to investment, financing and dividends will maximize the value of the firm to its shareholders.

Let us illustrate both these aspects, with an example.

Interrelationship between "Investment and Financing Decisions": If a firm wants to undertake a project requiring funds, this investment decision cannot be taken, in isolation, without considering the availability of finances, which is a financing decision. Both the decisions are inter-connected.

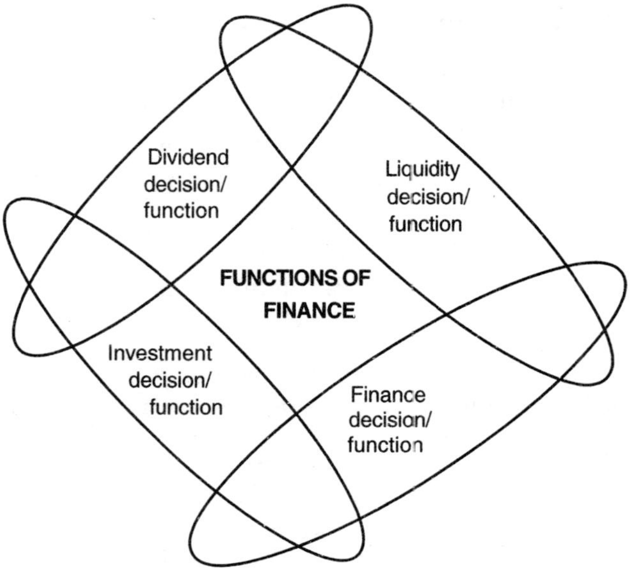

Fig. 2.1: Inter-relationship of finance functions

Example: Firm plans to make an investment of ₹ 12 crores involving fixed assets ₹ 10 crores and ₹ 2 crores in current assets. So, investment decision is ₹ 12 crores. The total funds required to finance total assets are ₹ 12 crores, which is also the financing decision. Financing decision means knowing the total amount required for raising and finalizing the various instruments for finance.

Interrelationship Between "Financing Decision and Dividend Decision": The firm has two options to finance the project, either from internal resources or raising funds, externally, from the market. If the firm decides to meet the total project cost only from internal resources, the profits, otherwise available for distribution in the form of dividend, have to be retained to meet the project cost. Here, the financing decision has influenced the dividend decision. Continuing the example, the firm has decided to raise external resources of ₹ 11 crores and balance ₹ 1 crore from internal resources. So, profits available for dividend have been reduced by ₹ 1 crore. Financing decision to meet a part of the project cost from internal resources has influenced the dividend rate of the company. In other words, financing decision has affected dividend decision.

Interrelationship Between "Dividend Decision and Liquidity Decision": Dividend payment results in the outgo of cash. If the firm does not make adequate planning for payment of cash to pay dividend, despite adequate profits, the firm would experience liquidity problem.

Interrelationship Between "Investment Decision and Liquidity Decision": If the firm allocates more funds for fixed assets, lesser amount would be available for current assets. In the above example, if there is a cost escalation in acquiring fixed assets by ₹ 50 lakhs, only ₹ 1.50 crores would be available for current assets, in case the firm does not want to increase the project cost. So, liquidity problem has started, from the very beginning of the project. Here, investment decision has affected liquidity decision.

So, an efficient financial management takes the optimal decision by considering the implications or impact of all the decisions, together, on the market value of the company's equity shares. The decision has to be taken considering all the aspects, simultaneously.

No Function is Superior: All the functions are important. Importance of the function depends on the situation of the firm. If a firm has adequate investment opportunities, but experiences difficulty to raise funds, the financing function is superior to the firm at that juncture. It does not mean that investment decision is always less important as compared to financing decision.

The essence is that no financial function or decision is superior to others.

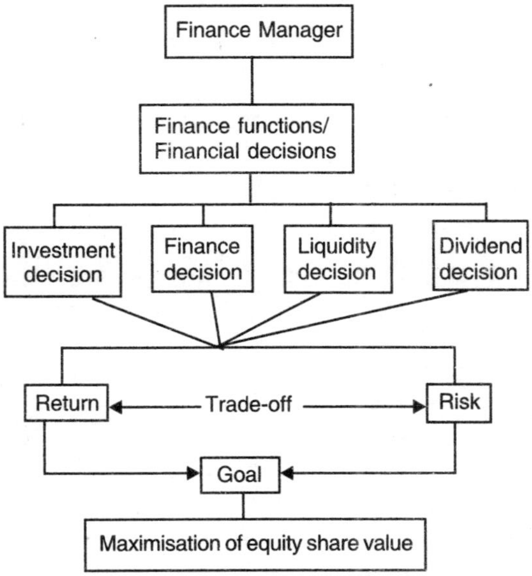

Fig. 2.2: Goal of financial management

2.6 LIQUIDITY VS. PROFITABILITY (RISK–RETURN TRADE OFF)

In course of performance of duties, a finance manager has to take from time to time various types of financial decisions related to investment, financing, liquidity and dividend, as detailed above. In every area of financial management, the finance manager is always faced with the dilemma of liquidity vs. profitability. He has to strike a balance between the two.

Liquidity means that the firm has:

(A) Adequate cash to pay bills/obligations as and when they fall due, and

(B) Sufficient cash reserves to meet emergencies and unforeseen demands, at all time.

Profitability goal, on the other hand, requires that funds of the firm are to be used in such a way to yield the highest return.

Liquidity and Profitability are Conflicting Decisions. When one increases, the other decreases. More liquidity results in less profitability and vice versa. In financial decisions, both liquidity and profitability cannot increase and decrease simultaneously at the same time.

The finance manager has to face the conflict between liquidity and profitability, as all the financial decisions involve both.

Example: A firm may borrow more, beyond the risk-free limit, to take the advantage of cheap interest rate. This decision increases the liquidity to meet the requirements of the firm. However, the firm has to pay committed fixed interest rate, at fixed time, irrespective of the return the liquidity (funds) gives. Profitability suffers in this process of decision, if the expected return does not materialise. This is the risk the organization faces by this financial decision.

Example: If the firm maintains a higher level of raw materials in anticipation of increase in price, efforts are made to approach profitability. However, liquidity suffers. Same case, a liberal credit policy is likely to increase sales and, in turn profitability may also improve, but liquidity would be endangered.

If profitability increases, liquidity decreases and vice versa. Both cannot be achieved, at the same time, at the highest level.

Risk: Risk is defined as the variability of the expected return from the investment.

Risk is the chance when actual outcomes may differ from those expected.

Risk is associated with uncertainty. When an investment is made, we are not sure of the return we get, unless the instrument guarantees a fixed return, at the time of investment. Guaranteed instruments do not carry a higher return. We may plan for 25% return, at the time of investment. But, the investment may yield only 20% return or it may give 30%, more than the planned return.

Return: Return is measured as a gain or profit expected to be made, over a period, at the time of making the investment.

Example: If an investor makes a deposit in a nationalised bank carrying an interest of 7% p.a., the investment is virtually risk free for repayment both principal and interest. However, if a similar amount is invested in the equity shares, there is no certainty for the amount of dividend or even for getting back initial investment as market price may fall subsequently at the time of sale. The expected dividend may or may not materialise. In other words, the dividend amount may vary or the company may not declare dividend at all. A bank deposit is a safe investment, while equity shares are not so. So, **risk is associated with the quality of investment.**

The relationship between risk and return can be expressed as follows:

Return = Risk free rate + Risk premium

Risk free rate is a compensation or reward for time and risk premium for risk. Risk and return go hand in hand. Higher the risk, higher the required return expected. It is only an expectation at the time of investment. There is no guarantee that the return would be definitely higher. If one wants to make an investment, without risk, the return is always lower. For this reason only, deposit in a bank and post office carry lower returns, compared to equity shares.

Every financial decision involves liquidity and profitability implications, which carries risk as well as return. However, the quantum of risk differs from one decision to another. Equally, the return from all the decisions is not uniform and also varies, even from time to time.

Relationship Between Liquidity, Profitability and Risk Return

Let us take an example to explain the above concept.

If higher inventories in the form of raw materials are built, in anticipation of an increase in price, more funds are locked in inventories. So, organization may experience problems in making other payments, in time. If the expected price increase materialises, firm enjoys a boost in profits due to the wind fall return the decision yields. The expected increase in price is a contingent event. In other words, the increase in price may or may not happen. But, the firm immediately suffers liquidity problems. This is the price firm has to pay, which, otherwise, is the risk the firm carries.

Risk and return always go together, hand in hand. More the risk, chances of a higher return may exist. It has to be remembered that there is no guarantee of higher returns with higher risk. The classical example is lottery. There is a great risk, if one invests in a lottery. However, there is no guarantee that one would win the lottery. There is a direct relationship between higher risk and higher return, however, with no certainty. In the above example, building higher inventories, more than required, is a higher risk decision. This higher risk has created liquidity problem. But, the benefit of higher return is also available. Higher risk, on the one hand, endangers liquidity and higher returns, on the other hand, increases profitability.

Liquidity and profitability are conflicting, while risk and return go together. The pictorial presentation explains the relationship, better:

For a finance manager, if profitability is the left hand, liquidity is the right hand. Both the hands are essential. No one is less important in discharging the functions of finance. To discharge the functions of finance, efficiently and effectively, both liquidity and profitability are equally essential. The real challenge to a finance manager is in bringing a balanced approach between the two, looking to the priorities of the organization.

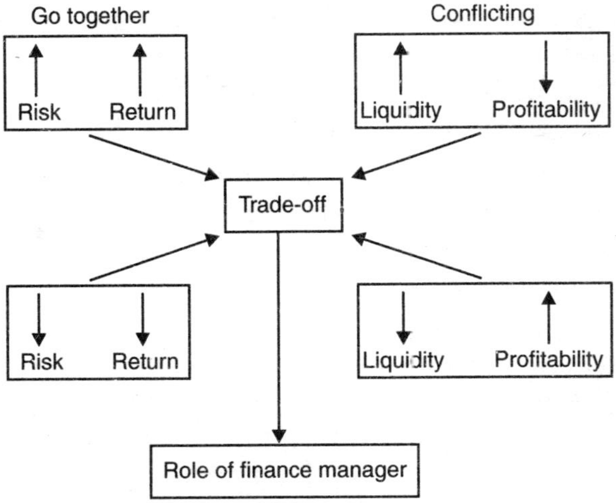

Fig. 2.3: Role of finance manager
Relationship between Risk-Return vs Liquidity-Profitability

Balanced Approach: A finance manager cannot avoid the risk altogether while taking decisions. At the same time, he should not take decisions, considering the returns aspect only. At the time of taking any financial decision, the finance manager has to weigh both the risks and returns in the proposed decision and optimise the risk and returns, at the same time. A proper balance between risk and return should be maintained by the finance manager to maximize the market value of shares.

An efficient finance manager fixes that level of operations where both risk and return are optimized. That particular combination, where both risk and return are optimised is known as Risk–Return Trade off.

Basic Objective of Finance Manager: An efficient finance manager fixes that level of operations, where he can achieve maximization of shareholders' wealth. Such a level is termed as risk-return trade off. **Every finance manager attempts to achieve that trade-off in every finance decision.** At this level, the market value of the company's shares would be maximum. To achieve maximum return, funds flowing in and out of the firm are to be constantly monitored to ensure their safety and proper utilisation.

2.7 ROLE OF FINANCE MANAGER

The finance manager handles finance. The role of finance manager is pivotal. He can change the fortunes of the organization with proper planning, monitoring and timely guidance. If the manager is not competent, even a profitable organization may dwindle or even sink. The finance manager is now responsible in shaping the fortunes of the enterprise.

The role of finance manager in a modern business is pervasive in all the activities of any business firm, including its production and marketing.

It has been rightly said, money begets money. Business needs money to make more money. However, business can make money, when it is properly managed. The financial history is replete with stories how even the profitable organizations were wound up, when the management of finance had turned bad, due to mismanagement of financial affairs.

It is misunderstood, in some corners, that the role of finance manager is important only in private organizations. It is not so. His role is important both in private and public sectors. He has a positive role to play in every type of organization. Even in non-profit making organizations, his role exists as long as there is involvement of funds.

Influences Fortunes of Firm: The history of failures of organizations is worth studying. **Many firms have failed, not because of inefficiency of production, inability in marketing or non-availability of funds but due to the absence of competent finance manager.** In many public sector undertakings, in particular, state government undertakings, importance is given to the appointment of peons, more than adequately, but not to the appointment of competent professional manager in finance, even after the lapse of several years. That is the real secret of numerous loss-making organizations in public sector! Over the years, the picture has been changing, but only after the real damage has already occurred in those public sector undertakings, due to the non-appointment of professional finance managers, at the time of formation of those undertakings. In several public sector undertakings, the presence of competent finance manager is often found inconvenient. A finance manager cannot play any significant role in the public sector, unless he is given the necessary freedom.

> **Modern financial management is concerned with anticipation, acquiring and allocation of funds effectively.**

Exists Everywhere: Well said, the role of finance manager, in modern times is universal and pervasive. We find rarely any activity, which does not involve finance. Even entertainment in a firm requires financial management due to financial implications. In modern business, no decision is taken without the consultation of finance. Even in recruitment, the presence of finance representative has been a normal feature. Only the level of finance representative changes, dependent upon the status of position for which recruitment is held. At times, people working in other departments feel that the finance manager has been interfering in all matters even when they are unconnected to him. It is due to inadequate understanding of the role of finance manager and expectations expected of him in modern business. The finance manager can definitely contribute to the overall development of the organization, provided he is competent and allowed to perform his functions independently.

In his new role, in the words of Solomon, the finance manager must find answers for the following three questions:

- How large should an enterprise be, and how fast should it grow?
- How should the funds be raised?
- In what form, should the firm hold its assets?

To sum up, finance functions or decisions include the following important areas, where the finance manager has to contribute:

- Investment decision or long term asset-mix decision
- Finance decision or capital-mix decision
- Liquidity decision or short-term asset mix decision
- Dividend decision or profit allocation decision

The main objective of all the above decisions is to increase the value of shares, held by the equity shareholders. **The finance manager has to strive for shareholders' wealth maximization.**

Focus on the Functions of Finance Manager: While discharging his functions, the finance manager has to focus his attention on the following aspects to maximize the shareholders' wealth:

1. Procuring funds, at the lowest cost, as and when necessary.
2. Investing funds in those assets, which are more profitable, and
3. Distributing dividends to shareholders to meet their expectations and facilitate expansion to achieve the long-term goals of organization.

Role of Finance Manager, Post Liberalization: The role of finance manager, post liberalization, has become more important, complex and demanding. He has to function in the changed economic and financial environment, in particular, in the following areas:

- Abolition of Monopolies and Restrictive Trade Practices Act and its replacement by the Competition Act, with effect from 1st September, 2009.
- Enactment of a liberalized Foreign Exchange Management Act (FEMA), repealing Foreign Exchange Regulation Act.
- Abolition of Capital Issues (Control) Act and setting up of Securities and Exchange Board of India (SEBI) for the regulation and development of securities and protection of the interests of investors.
- Enactment of the Insurance Regulatory and Development Authority (IRDA), breaking the monopoly of LIC and GIC as well as its subsidiaries.
- Convertibility of rupee.
- Credit rating.
- Access to Euro-issues, American Depository Receipts (ADRS) and opportunities to raise finances, internationally, at cheaper interest rates, compared to local interest rates.
- Emergence of highly innovative financial instruments.
- Opportunities of liberalised foreign investments in India.
- Sophisticated money market.

Social Responsibility

Social responsibility is not clearly defined. However, no firm can afford to ignore social responsibility as it has to function, in society, as an integral part. Maximizing shareholders' wealth does not mean neglecting social responsibility. It is the function of every management to protect the interests of consumers, pay fair wages to employees, and involve itself in environmental issues, such as clean air and water, along with maintaining fair trading practices to all parties concerned.

Social responsibility means taking financial decisions, beyond the economic activity.

It is well recognized that the very existence of the firm largely depends on being socially responsive and responsible.

Check Your Understanding

(A) State whether the following statements are True or False

1. Finance holds key to all economic activities.
2. Investment in long-term assets is popularly known as "capital budgeting'.
3. Investment decision relates to determination of proportion of debt and capital.
4. An efficient finance manager fixes that level of operations, where both risk and return are optimized.
5. Dividend decision depends mainly on the investment opportunities, available within the firm, ignoring preferences and expectations of the equity shareholders.
6. All finance functions are independent.
7. All the functions of finance are important and importance of the relative function depends on the situation of the firm.
8. Key function of a finance manager is to maintain a proper balance between liquidity and profitability of the firm.
9. Dividend relates to the portion of profit, which is retained, without distributing to shareholders of the company.
10. Liquidity and profitability go together.
11. In current times, function of finance is limited to supply of funds to the requirements of the organization.
12. Dividend can be declared from the current as well as cumulative profits of an organization.
13. The finance decisions can be classified into four basic kinds: investment decisions, financing decisions, liquidity decisions and dividend decisions.
14. Liquidity means having enough cash to meet the bills and obligations, as and when they fall due for payment.
15. Modern financial management is concerned with anticipation, acquiring and allocation of funds, effectively.
16. A finance manager's concern must be to maintain profitability rather than liquidity.
17. Financing decision relates to determination of proportion of debt and capital.

18. In financial decisions, both liquidity and profitability can increase as well as decrease simultaneously.
19. Risk and return go hand in hand.
20. The role of finance manager, in a modern business, is pervasive in all the activities of business firm, including production and marketing.
21. Financing function is not a function of finance.

Answers:

1. True	2. True	3. False	4. True	5. False	6. False	7. True	8. True
9. False	10. False	11. False	12. True	13. True.	14. True	15. True	16. False
17. True	18. False	19. True	20. True	21. False			

(B) Objective Questions (Identify what is most appropriate)

1. Financial management is mainly concerned with
   (i) The efficient management of every activity of business;
   (ii) Arrangement of funds required to the firm;
   (iii) Obtaining required funds in the appropriate mix and utilising them efficiently.
2. Finance decisions involve
   (i) Investment, sales and dividend decisions;
   (ii) Financing, investment and dividend decisions;
   (iii) Finance, investment and cash decisions.
3. Financial management helps in
   (i) Short-term planning of company's activities;
   (ii) Estimating the total funds' requirement and their proper utilisation in fixed assets and working capital;
   (iii) Profit planning of the firm.

Answers

1. iii 2. ii 3. ii

(C) Fill in the blanks

1. One who takes financial risks is called the ______________.
2. The finance function provides the ______________ required by the business enterprises.
3. Ownership is divorced from the ______________ in a limited company.

Answers

1. Entrepreneur 2. Funds 3. Management

Descriptive Questions

1. Explain the relationship of finance with other management functions. **(2.1 and 2.2)**
2. In addition to the raising of funds, financial management is directly concerned with production, marketing and all other functions within an organization. Explain with suitable examples the interrelationship with other functions. **(2.1 and 2.2)**
3. Finance functions are closely connected with production, marketing and other functions and it is difficult to separate finance function from these functions. Discuss. **(2.1 and 2.2)**
4. Explain the aims of finance function. **(2.3)**
5. Explain the basic finance functions. **(2.4)**
6. Describe the prominent areas of financial decision-making. **(2.4)**
7. Examine and illustrate with examples the interrelationship among the investment, financing and dividend decisions with an example and analyze the superiority amongst the different decisions. **(2.5)**
8. "An optimal combination of decisions relating to investment, financing and dividends will maximize the value of the firm to its shareholders". Examine. **(2.5)**
9. For a finance manager, if profitability is the left hand, liquidity is the right hand. Both the hands are essential. No one is less important in discharging the functions of finance.' Justify the statement. **(2.6)**
10. "Liquidity and profitability are competing goals of the finance manager". Comment. **(2.6 and 2.6.1)**
11. In financial decisions, both liquidity and profitability cannot increase and decrease simultaneously. Discuss. **(2.6)**
12. Describe the role of finance manager in a modern business. **(2.7)**
13. What role should the finance manager play in the modern enterprise? **(2.7)**
14. The financial manager plays a pivotal role in the multifarious facets of a business enterprise. Do you advocate his role as interference or contribution? **(2.7)**
15. Write short notes on the following:
    (A) Liquidity decision **(2.4)**
    (B) Risk-Return trade off **(2.6)**

Interview Questions

Q.1. What is meant by Risk' in financial management?

Ans. Risk is the chance that actual outcome may differ from those expected. The actual outcome can be better or worse than what is expected. In a financial decision, element of assessing 'risk' is important and significant.

Q.2. What is the relationship between risk and return?

Ans. Risk and return always go hand in hand. When there is more risk, return would also be more. Investment in a speculative project gives more returns. Here, risk is great and, equally, returns. Investment in equity shares gives more returns, but, at the same time, they are risky too. Investment in a safe mode like a bank deposit gives less return as there is, virtually, no risk with such investment.

Risk and return are like two sides of a coin. When you have a coin, both of them are with you. You can not avoid one to have another.

Q.3. What is the basic function of a finance manager and what care he is expected to take while performing?

Ans. The basic function of a finance manager is to maximize the shareholders' wealth. At the time of discharging finance functions or taking decisions, he has to weigh both the risk and return, involved in each decision. He has to maintain a proper balance between risk and return and try to bring a trade off between risk and return to maximize the shareholders' wealth.

No function is free from risk, but wisdom lies in bringing a balance between risk and return.

Q.4. What is meant by liquidity?

Ans. Liquidity means arranging adequate cash and cash equivalent resources to meet the financial obligations, as and when they fall due for payment. The basic intention is to find adequate cash at all times to make payments, in time, while retaining no idle cash.

He should have enough reserves to meet the unforeseen emergencies.

Q.5. What would happen if the firm does not have adequate liquidity?

Ans. When the firm does not have sufficient liquidity, it would experience difficulty in making timely payments. There would be repeated defaults. If the crunch (shortage) of funds continues, suppliers would not be willing to sell goods on credit. When the message spreads in the market that the firm is not having sufficient funds to make payments and delaying payment on due dates, suppliers and service providers would like to make them available only on cash payments. Finally, liquidity crisis may even force the firm to be wound up.

Q.6. Explain the relationship between liquidity and profitability?

Ans. Liquidity and profitability conflict with each other. If the firm has more than required liquidity, there would be no defaults in payments. Problem of not finding adequate cash to meet the financial obligations, as and when they fall due, does not arise. However, funds carry cost. Idle or excessive funds erode profits. In consequence, if more funds are tied up in liquid form, the immediate casualty would be profitability. When firms maintain less liquid funds to improve profitability, profitability would be higher. But, firms experience problem often in honouring the financial commitments in time.

Liquidity and profitability have an inverse relationship. Both liquidity and profitability cannot be achieved, simultaneously, in excessive proportions. Role of finance manager is to bring a balanced compromise between liquidity and profitability to maximize the shareholders' wealth, which is the basic function of finance manager.

❍❍

CHAPTER

3

Objectives of Financial Management

3.1 INTRODUCTION

The objective of a company is to create value to its shareholders. The modern day finance manager is instrumental to achieve value creation to the company. To be successful, the finance manager has to be a team player, actively and constructively associated in operations, marketing and company's overall strategy.

Every firm should have a goal or objective to achieve. In the context of that objective, the finance manager evaluates the decisions to be taken. A goal of the firm may be defined as 'a target against which its performance can be measured'. Several goals of financial management have been cited. The goals are maximization of sales revenue, net profit, return on investment, size of the firm, percentage of market share, etc. The problem is to identify one of these several goals.

It is generally agreed that the financial goal of the firm should be the maximization of owners' economic welfare. Owners' economic welfare can be maximized with the Shareholders' Wealth Maximization (SWM), as reflected in the market value of the equity shares.

3.2 CHARACTERISTICS OF A GOOD OPERATIONAL DECISION CRITERION

The objective of financial management can be achieved by following the widely accepted approaches:

(A) Profit maximization

(B) Wealth maximization

Frequently, profit maximization is regarded as the proper and final objective of the firm. But, this is not an inclusive goal. In other words, goal is beyond 'Profit Maximization'. Value creation is the final objective of financial management, which can happen through wealth maximization alone.

An appropriate operational (financial) decision criterion should

a. Be precise and exact,
b. Recognize the time value of money,
c. Be based on 'Bigger the Better' principle, and
d. Consider both 'quantity' and 'quality' dimensions.

3.3 OBJECTIVES OF FINANCIAL MANAGEMENT

Now, let us examine which approach, profit maximization or wealth maximization would comply with all the characteristics of a good operational decision criterion.

3.3.1 Profit Maximization

Profit earning is the primary motivating factor for any economic activity. Business is also an economic activity. So, every business seeks profit. Profit earning is the real barometer to measure the efficiency of business firm. If an enterprise fails to make profit, capital invested is eroded and this situation prolongs the enterprise, ultimately ceases to exist.

According to this approach, actions that increase total profits/EPS should be undertaken and those that decrease total profits/EPS are to be avoided.

The term 'profit' refers to the amount of income, which is due to the owners of business, whether distributed in the form of dividend or not. Profitability is an operational concept. In other words, profitability refers to a situation where output exceeds input, i.e. the value created by the use of resources is more than the total of input resources. Profitability refers to Earnings Before Interest and Taxes (EBIT).

Arguments in Support

1. **Aim of Business:** According to this approach, actions that increase profit should be undertaken and those that decrease profit are to be avoided. The approach is, indeed, simple. It implies that all the financial management decisions—the investment, financing and dividend decisions–should be oriented towards maximization of profits.
2. **Barometer for Measuring Efficiency:** Real test for measuring comparative performance of firms is profit. So, this is the ground of rationality.
3. **Economic Conditions Change:** Business may undergo recession, depression and severe competition as economic conditions do not remain the same always. When conditions are favourable, firm has to make more profits to withstand the unfavourable situations later. Firm can rely on the past earnings, if it sustains loss.

So, every firm has to concentrate to make more money, when the going is good.

4. **Facilitates Growth:** Firm can accumulate profits, which could be a supporting or main source of finance for expansion and growth.
5. **Social Goals:** Personal objectives are primary to everyone. If profits are high, a business firm can meet its personal objectives and can also help the society for socio-economic welfare. If profits are small, who allocates funds for social benefits? So, profitability is essential for fulfilling social goals.

   In view of the above, it is argued that every firm should be guided by the aim of profit maximization.

Criticism: The arguments against profit maximization and main technical flaws of this criterion are as follows:

(A) Ambiguity-Vague: The term 'profit' is vague and has different interpretations. It means different things to different people. It can be pre-tax or post-tax profit. It is not clear whether it is short-term profit or long-term profit. Does it mean operating profit or profit available for shareholders? The other equivalent term, often used, is 'Return'. Return can be on total capital employed or total assets or shareholders equity and so on.

Further, it is also possible that the net profits may increase, but earning per share may decline. To illustrate, a firm has issued 1,000 equity shares and has made a net profit of ₹ 10,000. So, the earnings per share (EPS) are ₹ 10 per share. Later, the firm has increased the number of equity shares, further by 2,000, making the total number of equity shares 3,000. After increase of share capital, the net profit of the firm has been ₹ 15,000. The net profit has increased by 50% from ₹ 10,000 to ₹ 15,000, but EPS has declined from ₹ 10 to ₹ 5. In such a situation, the market value of the share does not increase, despite more profits. In fact, there would be a fall in market price of equity share, due to reduction in EPS.

Year	Equity Shares	Net Profit	Earning Per Share (EPS)
2008	1,000	10,000	₹ 10
2009	3,000	15,000	₹ 5

The above situation explains that maximization of profits does not increase the economic welfare of the owners.

> **Profit maximization concept is neither precise nor exact. A loose expression like profit cannot form the basis for operational criterion for financial management.**

(B) Timing and Value of Money-Ignored: The concept of profit maximization does not help in making a choice between projects giving different benefits, spread over a period of time. It ignores the difference in time in respect of benefits arising from the similar amount of investment. **The fact that a rupee received today is more valuable than the rupee receivable in future, is ignored in this concept.** It gives equal importance to all earnings though receivable in different periods. Hence, it ignores time value of money.

The following illustration explains how time value of money is ignored.

Time Pattern of Benefits (Profits)

(₹ In lakhs)

	Alternative A	**Alternative B**
First year	5	Nil
Second year	10	10
Third year	5	10
Total	**20**	**20**

If profit maximization were the decision criterion, both the alternatives would be ranked equally, as the amount of profit is the same in both the alternatives.

'A' provides higher returns in earlier years. In case of 'B', the returns are more in later years. The returns, arising in the earlier years, can always be reinvested to earn extra returns. **The basic dictum in financial planning is "Earlier, the Better".** This is referred to as time value of money. Profit maximization criterion does not differentiate the returns received at different periods. Costs and benefits, received over a period, are treated alike, irrespective of their timings. This is not a true and real picture. Benefits received in the earlier years are more valuable than the equivalent benefits received in the later years. The assumption of equal value is inconsistent with the real world situation.

(C) Quality (Certainty) of Benefits: This is the most important technical objection or limitation. The term 'Quality' refers to degree of certainty, with which benefit can be expected to materialize. If certainty of benefit is more, higher quality of benefit can be expected. Profit maximization gives weight to the size of returns, but not to the certainty of returns. Basically, investors are risk averse, i.e. they want to avoid or at least minimize risk. So, the investors give preference to those returns, which are certain, even with small variations over the years.

Two firms may have the same expected earnings to shareholders, but if the earnings of one firm stream vacillate considerably, when compared to the other firm, it will be more risky.

This concept can be understood from the following example:

Uncertainty about Expected Benefits (Profits)

(₹ In lakhs)

State of Economy	**Alternative A**	**Alternative B**
Recession (Period I)	90	Nil
Normal (Period II)	100	100
Boom (Period III)	110	200
Total	**300**	**300**

Returns in both the cases are identical in the normal situation. However, returns vary widely during recession and boom, in both the alternatives, and fluctuate depending on the state of economy. But, range of variation is very wide in case of alternative B, while it is narrow in the alternative A.

To put it differently, earnings associated with alternative 'B' are more uncertain and risky, with no returns during the recession period and highest returns in the boom period. In recession period, it is difficult to survive, let alone make money and it is easy for all firms to make profits during the boom.

Obviously, alternative 'A' is better from the point of risk and certainty.

Profit maximization considers size only and gives no weight to quality. So, profit maximization criterion is inappropriate and unsustainable as operational objective in the financial management decisions of different kinds—investment, financing and dividend decisions of a firm. It ignores two important dimensions, namely, (i) risk, and (ii) time value of money.

So, the last characteristic of a good operational decision criterion—'quantity and quality' is also ignored by profit maximization theory.

> **In boom times, almost every firm makes good profits. However, during recession period, only a few firms, with foresight, prudence and financial wisdom, can only survive.**
>
> **When many U.S. banks have collapsed, during the recession period, none of the banks in India have failed, rather tottered. U.S. industry is admiring the Indian wisdom for its financial management. True test of financial management is not in boom times, but in time of recession.**

(D) Change in Organization Structure: Principle of profit maximization was earlier accepted when the structure of the business was sole proprietorship. The sole proprietor managed the business individually and was the recipient of total profits. As total profit belonged to him, his wealth maximized. This was the picture in 19th century, when the business was totally self-managed.

Over a period, the sole proprietorship concept has changed to Joint Stock Company. In this changed structure, there is divorce between ownership and management. Shareholders own the company, while professional managers manage the business. There are several stakeholders in the joint stock company—shareholders, customers, employees, government and society. Due to varied stakeholders, their interests are diverse and the finance manager has to reconcile their divergent and conflicting interests. To achieve the objective of profit maximization, it is not possible to ignore the interests of other stake holders such as customers, employees and society, just to promote the narrow interests of shareholders.

In the changed scenario, the concept of 'profit maximization' is unrealistic and inappropriate.

(E) Social Welfare may be Ignored: Due to profit maximization objective, business may produce goods and services, which may not be necessary and beneficial to the society. So, it is indeed doubtful how far the profit maximization objective serves or promotes the social welfare, let alone optimizes social welfare.

(F) Ignores Financing and Dividend Aspects: The profit maximization concept concentrates on profitability aspect alone, and impact of financing and dividend decisions on the market value of shares are totally ignored.

Let us explain the point further. A firm may borrow, beyond its capacity, to finance the projects on hand. The firm's main concern is to maximize the profit alone, ignoring the financial risk—risk of insolvency due to non-payment of interest and repayment of principal. Totally ignoring risks associated with the huge borrowing is not in the interests of the organization. So, it cannot be said that such type of borrowing is to promote economic welfare of shareholders as risk aspect has been altogether ignored. More so, this heavy risk is likely to dampen the market price of shares.

Normally, dividend decision influences market price of equity shares. Even if the firm declares a higher dividend rate than the preceding year, still, market price of the equity share may decline, if the market expectations are not fulfilled. In such a situation, even if the firm makes more profit and ignores the expectations of shareholders in respect of dividend, it is unlikely that the market value of shares would improve. The logic is simple. The real owners–equity shareholders may not appreciate this type of working.

Profit maximization is not an inclusive goal for maximization of shareholders' wealth.

Through profit maximization, shareholders' wealth maximization can be achieved. However, profit maximization is not an inclusive goal. The term 'inclusive goal' means that the objective should not serve the interests of one section, i.e. shareholders' alone, it should satisfy the diverse interests of all stakeholders, such as creditors, consumers, government and all those parties who have a link with the company. This is not happening with the objective of profit maximization. So, profit maximization is not a proper objective of financial management.

Let us examine whether wealth maximization is a better objective of financial management compared to profit maximization.

3.3.2 Wealth Maximization

Wealth maximization of the firm is the most appropriate objective of the enterprise. The principle of wealth maximization implies that the fundamental objective of the firm is to maximize the value of its equity shares. The wealth created by a company is reflected in the market value of the company's equity shares. This situation indicates efficiency of management.

When this objective is achieved, the net worth of the firm would be high. When net worth is high, earnings per share (EPS) would be at its peak. When EPS is high, market price of share would also be high. The shareholders' wealth would be maximum as wealth of the shareholder is a product of number of shares held and its market price.

> **Shareholders' current wealth in a firm = Number of equity shares owned X current market price.**

Characteristics of a Good Operational Decision Criterion:

The wealth maximization criterion is based on the concept of cash flows. Cash flows refer to the firm's future cash flows. In case of profit maximization criterion, the accounting profit is the basis of the measurement of benefits.

Cash flow is a better concept: The concept of cash flows is better than the accounting profit on account of the following reasons:

1. **Precision Concept:** Cash flow is a precise concept, with a definite connotation. Cash flow means inflow and outflow of cash, connected to operational aspects of a business. Cash flow may not be actual profits. An organization may be in profits, but still may experience cash flow problems.
2. **Quality Dimension:** The more certain the cash flows are, better is the quality of benefits and higher would be the value. Conversely, the less certain the flows are, the lower the quality and, therefore, value of benefits is also lower. So, quality dimension is complied with.
3. **Time Concept:** Cash flows are discounted (taking the opportunity cost of capital) to arrive at the present value, which reflects the recognition of time value of money.
4. **Quantity Dimension:** Bigger cash flows, after discounting, would result in increased value. So, quantity aspect is also complied with. All financial decisions should be based on cost-benefit analysis. Financial action has to be undertaken only when benefit exceeds cost. Conversely, if cost is more than benefit, the decision will not serve the purpose of maximizing the wealth. So, those actions should be rejected. 'The bigger, the better' principle is recognized.

> **Wealth maximization complies with all the characteristics of a good operational decision criterion.**

Maximization of Market Price: Here, price refers to market price, in the long run. The long run means a period long enough so that a normalized price can be worked out. Market price, over a long-term, serves as a performance index of the company's progress.

At times, in some firms, management may make decisions to get the short-term advantage, at the expense of the long run. For instance, a company may cut its research and development expenses significantly, in order to increase current earnings. This action increases the current earnings immediately. This may result in the increase of current market price. However, the firm is likely to suffer, without significant research and development and the result will be a sharp drop in the market price, in the long run.

The market price of a share is linked to three functions of finance:

Investment Decision: Once expansion news appears, market price flares, anticipating faster development.

Financing Decision: Once the news appears about a big loan is raised, at a cheap interest rate in the international market, the market price goes up.

Dividend Decision: If a company declares a dividend below the expectations of market, the market price takes a dip. Market price is also dependent on other factors like market sentiments about the proposed investment, economic and political issues.

Maximizing Economic Welfare of Shareholders: The objective of maximization of wealth is the primary goal of financial decision-making. Any financial action which creates wealth or which has a net present worth above zero is desirable and should be undertaken. If two desirable courses of action are mutually exclusive (only one of the two projects can be undertaken, which is the most suitable or economical), the decision should be to do that action which shows the highest amount of net present value.

> **Finance Manager should concentrate on maximizing earnings per equity share.**

The value of the equity share largely depends on earnings per share. Earnings per share (EPS) depend on the net worth of the firm. This objective is also consistent with the objective of maximizing the economic welfare of the shareholders.

Formula for Shareholders' Wealth Maximization: Net present value concept can be used to measure the shareholders' wealth maximization. The net present value or worth can be defined, explicitly in the following way:

$$W = \frac{A_1}{(1+k)} + \frac{A_2}{(1+k)^2} + \ldots\ldots \frac{A_n}{(1+k)^\eta} - C_0$$

$$= \Sigma \frac{A_t}{(1+k)^t} - C_0$$

Σ = Sigma (sum)

A = Stream of benefits expected to occur to the firm

K = Appropriate discount rate (cost of capital)

W = Wealth

t assumes values from 1 to η

C_0 = Cost of action

Assumption: The underlying assumption is that the shares are traded in an efficient capital market. In practice, the share price is subject to the influence of several extra forces/factors. The overall economic and political scenario in the country influences the market price of a share. More often, the market price of a share may fluctuate on account of speculative activities. All the factors are assumed to be given and constant in this objective.

> **Profit maximization can be considered as a part of the wealth maximization strategy' it should never be permitted to overshadow the latter.**

3.3.3 Criticism of Wealth Maximization

Wealth maximization is criticized by certain financial theorists on the following grounds:

1. **Socially not desirable:** The objective of wealth maximization is not necessarily socially desirable.
2. **Benefits others too:** There is some controversy whether the objective of maximization of wealth is of the firm or stockholders. If wealth of firm were maximized, it would be benefiting the interests of debenture holders and preference shareholders too.
3. **Conflict of interest:** In corporate sector, ownership and management are separate, unlike in a sole proprietorship. Management acts as the agents of real owners, i.e. shareholders. However, there is always a possibility of conflict of interest between the shareholders' interests and managerial interests. The managers may act to maximize their managerial utility, but not the wealth of stockholders of the firm. A particular decision may be taken to exhibit their managerial utility and that decision may not be in the exclusive interests of the firm. Many a time, individuals place their personal preferences and selfish interests above the institutional interests.

3.3.4 Superiority of Wealth Maximization Compared to Profit Maximization

The objective of Shareholders' Wealth Maximization (SWM) is an appropriate and operationally feasible criterion to select among the alternative financial actions.

Wealth Maximization is superior to Profit Maximization for the following reasons:

1. **All Factors Considered:** Profit maximization is dependent on total profits of the firm alone. This objective does not consider the effect of earnings per share, dividend paid per share or any other return to the shareholders. More so, this objective does not consider the risk factor the firm may undertake in maximizing the profits.

   Wealth maximization considers all factors, such as cash flows, earnings per share, return to shareholders, dividend declared per share and also impact of risk involved in different decisions. In fact, the discount rate reflects the associated degree of risk of the project and mix of financing the project. Where the debt equity ratio of the relevant project is more, discount rate would be more as the project carries more risk.
2. **Cash Flows, not Accounting Profit:** Measuring benefits in terms of cash flows avoids the ambiguity, associated with accounting profits.

   Total profits is the basis for calculation of profit maximization. Profits may not be, totally, realized. For calculating wealth maximization, cash flows are the basis. Cash flows are more realistic as they relate to actual inflows and outflows of cash. As the basis for calculation is more realistic, the result is also more realistic in respect of wealth maximization.
3. **Dividend Declaration:** Firm that wishes to maximize profits would refrain from declaring dividends. Firm would like to retain all profits to reinvest in business for expansion. Shareholders do not appreciate this approach.

The objective of wealth maximization would permit the firm to declare regular dividends to the shareholders. Shareholders certainly prefer declaration of dividend.

> **Profit maximization can be considered as a part of wealth maximization strategy. In other words, wealth maximization is an extension of profit maximization. Profit maximization cannot be allowed to overshadow wealth maximization.**

3.3.5 Relationship between Profit Maximization and Wealth Maximization

When the finance manager manages the available financial resources efficiently, and everything goes according to plan, due to his effective control, the result is higher profits. How are the profits utilized? A part of the profits are distributed to shareholders to satisfy their expectations and ensure their loyalty towards the company, retaining the balance in business for expansion. The process continues over a period of time and, in consequence, value of the firm increases. Increase in value of the firm is reflected in the form of increased earnings per share (EPS) of the firm. As a result, market price of the shares goes up, in consequence. Finally, market price of a share is the growth index of the company concerned.

Value maximization or wealth maximization is almost universally accepted as an appropriate objective of financial management.

> **It can be said that wealth maximization is considered to be the main objective of financial management, in comparison to profit maximization.**

3.4 OTHER OBJECTIVES OF FINANCIAL MANAGEMENT

Besides the above basic objectives, the following are the other goals of financial management:

1. Ensuring a fair return to shareholders.
2. Ensuring maximum operational efficiency by efficient and effective utilization of finances.
3. Coordination among the various departments of business concern to ensure smooth functioning of the operations.
4. Building up of reserves for expansion and growth.
5. Ensuring financial discipline in the organization.

3.5 MEASURING SHAREHOLDERS' VALUE CREATION

Maximizing the shareholder value is considered as one of the fundamental goals of all businesses. Everywhere, top management is expected to maximize shareholders' value.

Maximizing shareholders' value everywhere is becoming the new corporate standard. Shareholders' wealth is measured in terms of the returns they receive on their investment.

The returns can either be in the form of dividends or in the form of capital appreciation or both. Capital appreciation, in turn, depends on the subsequent changes in the market value of shares. This market value of shares is influenced by a number of factors, which can be company specific, industry specific and macro-economic in nature.

Investors provide funds to the company and expect a certain minimum return. This minimum return is known as 'opportunity cost' to the investors or the minimum return that shareholders can earn, elsewhere. If the company provides more return than the return expected by the shareholders, the company is creating additional value.

> **New concepts, such as Economic Value Added (EVA) and Market Value Added (MVA), are used with traditional measures, such as ROI, ROE, EPS, ROCE and DPS, etc.**

For measuring the corporate financial performance, there are accounting profitability measures and shareholders' value based measures. Accounting profitability measures include ROI, ROE, EPS, ROCE and DPS, etc. Shareholders value based measures include EVA and MVA.

3.6 METHODS OF MEASURING SHAREHOLDERS' VALUE CREATION

There are basically two methods to measure shareholders value creation. They are:

(A) Economic Value Added

(B) Market Value Added

> **The concept 'Economic Value Added' is based on the principle of 'Profit Maximization', while the concept 'Market Value Added' is based on 'Wealth Maximization.**

3.6.1 Economic Value Added

'Economic Value Added' is a method to calculate true economic profit of a corporation. This provides formula and answer for determining whether a company is creating wealth or not.

The concept of Economic Value Added was introduced by a New York based consulting firm, Stern Stewart & Co., in early eighties.

The corporate sector in India is gradually recognizing the importance of EVA. As a result of this, some Indian companies, viz., Infosys Technologies Ltd., Hindustan Lever Ltd., Ranbaxy Laboratories Ltd., Samtel India Ltd. etc., have started calculating EVA. Infosys Technologies Ltd. is the first Indian company to report its EVA in the annual report.

> **EVA is return earned by the company in excess of the minimum expected return of the shareholders.**

EVA is an excess profit of a firm, after charging cost on capital invested. EVA essentially seeks to measure company's actual rate of return as against the required rate of return.

To put it simply, EVA is the difference between Net Operating Profit After Tax (NOPAT) and the capital charge for both debt and equity. Debt and equity are the normal sources of finance and providers of these sources expect a certain minimum return. The return expected by both of them (shareholders and lenders) is the aggregate of cost of capital. If NOPAT exceeds the aggregate cost of capital, EVA is positive and if it is less than aggregate cost of capital, EVA is negative.

EVA = Net Operating Profit, After Tax – (Weighted Average Cost of Capital x Invested Capital)

Shareholders of the company will receive a positive value added, when the return from the capital employed in the business operations is greater than the aggregate cost of capital.

Computation of EVA: While computing EVA, capital employed represents capital invested at the beginning of the year. The logic behind taking beginning capital for computing EVA is that a company would take, at least, one-year to earn the return on investment. Calculation of EVA involves some tricky issues. Each element of EVA, therefore, has been discussed, individually. EVA requires three different inputs for its computation. They are given below:

(A) Net Operating Profit, After Tax (NOPAT)

(B) Invested Capital

(C) Weighted Average Cost of Capital (WACC)

Net Operating Profit, After Tax (NOPAT): Operating profit is that income which is derived from business operations. Any income, not connected to business is excluded. Stewart has defined NOPAT as the "Profits derived from company's operations, after taxes, but before financing costs and non-cash book keeping entries". Examples of non-cash book keeping entries are preliminary expenses written off, amortization of expenses, goodwill written off. They do not involve any cash outgo. However, such non-cash book keeping entries do not include depreciation since depreciation is considered as a true economic expense. In other words, NOPAT is equal to the income available to shareholders plus interest expenses (after tax).

NOPAT = Net profit, after tax + Interest expenses + Non-cash expenses (Amortisation exp + Preliminary exp + Goodwill written off etc.)

Invested Capital/Capital Employed: Capital employed is the aggregate of net worth and interest bearing borrowings, secured as well as unsecured.

Invested capital or capital employed refers to total assets net of current liabilities (non-interest bearing liabilities). From an operating perspective, invested capital can be defined as Net Fixed Assets plus Investments plus Net current assets. Net current assets denote current assets net of non-interest bearing current liabilities.

From a financing perspective, it can be defined as Net Worth plus total borrowings. Total borrowings denote all interest bearing debts.

Capital Employed = Net worth + Interest bearing debts

Weighted Average Cost of Capital (WACC): For calculating WACC, cost of each source of capital is calculated, separately, and then weights are assigned to each source on the basis of proportion of a particular source in the total capital employed. Weights can be assigned on market value basis or book value basis.

WACC = E/CE × Ke + LTB/CE × Kd

Where E = Equity Capital, CE = Capital Employed, LTB = Long-term Borrowings,
Ke = Cost of Equity Capital, Kd = Cost of Debt Capital

WACC includes two specific costs, viz. (i) cost of equity (Ke), (ii) cost of debt (Kd)

Increase of EVA: EVA increases in the following circumstances:

(A) **No additional capital:** Operating profit increases, without employing additional capital, i.e. through greater efficiency. In other words, the existing resources are put to effective use.

(B) **Introduction of additional capital:** Additional capital is invested in such projects that give higher returns than the cost of producing new capital. Surplus goes towards increasing EVA.

(C) **Liquidation of unproductive capital:** Unproductive capital is liquidated. In other words, projects that are not giving required returns are closed or liquidated. For this, a constant review is needed.

Illustration No. 1

From the following condensed financial information, calculate Economic Value Added and offer comments on wealth maximization.

Profit and Loss Account of Rajesh Ltd. for the year ended March, 2009

(₹)

To operating expenses	40,000	By Gross Profit	5,60,000
Interest on debentures	30,000	Dividend on Investments	20,000
Preliminary expenses written of	5,000		
Selling expenses	20,000		
Administrative expenses	10,000		
Depreciation	25,000		
Income tax	50,000		
Net profit	4,00,000		
	5,80,000		**5,80,000**

Balance Sheet of Rajesh Ltd. as on 31st March, 2009

(₹)

Liabilities		Assets	
Equity share capital (F.V. ₹ 10)	9,00,000	Fixed assets (Net)	8,50,000
Preference share capital	3,00,000	Cash	10,000
Profit and loss account	1,00,000	Bank	90,000
General reserves	2,00,000	Sundry debtors	4,00,000
Revaluation reserve	3,00,000	Stock	2,50,000
12% debentures	2,50,000	Investments	4,00,000
Sundry creditors	1,50,000	Goodwill	2,30,000
Outstanding expenses	1,00,000	Preliminary expenses (not yet written off)	70,000
	23,00,000		**23,00,000**

Cost of equity capital is 20% and cost of debt capital is 12%.

Solution

First, net operating profit is to be calculated. While calculating net operating profit, dividend on investments is to be deducted as it is not operating income. Preliminary expenses written off are to be added as it is not an operating expense. Depreciation is considered as a true economic expense, hence needs no adjustment. Interest on debentures is to be added as debentures are treated as part of capital employed.

Net Operating Profit, After Tax (NOPAT) = 4,00,000 – 20,000 + 5,000 + 30,000 = 4,15,000

Now, capital employed is to be calculated.

Capital employed does not include revaluation reserve.

Capital Employed = Equity Share Capital + Preference Share Capital + Profit and Loss Account + General Reserves + Debentures

= 9,00,000 + 3,00,000 + 1,00,000 + 2,00,000 + 2,50,000

= 17,50,000

Weighted Average Cost of Capital is to be calculated.

$$WACC = E/CE \times Ke + LTB/CE \times Kd$$

Where E = Equity Capital, CE = Capital Employed, LTB = Long-term Borrowings, Ke = Cost of Equity Capital, Kd = Cost of Debt Capital

$$\text{WACC} = \frac{9,00,000}{17,50,000} \times 20 + \frac{2,50,000}{17,50,000} \times 12$$

$$= 10.28 + 1.71 = 11.99\,\%$$

Cost of capital = Capital employed × WACC

= 17,50,000 × 11.99%

= 2,09,825

EVA = Net Operating Profit, After Tax – (Weighted Average Cost of Capital × Invested Capital)

= 4,15,000 – 2,09,825 = ₹ 2,05,175

Comments on Wealth Maximization: EVA represents the value added to shareholders by generating profit in excess of the cost of capital employed in the business. Here, ₹ 2,05,175 is the value addition to the company, above the cost of capital employed. So, EVA is positive.

3.6.2 Market Value Added (MVA)

With a view to measure shareholders' value, Stewart used the term Market Value Added (MVA). Market Value Added (MVA) is defined as "the difference between market value of invested capital and book value of invested capital of a company at a given period of time". Market value of invested capital refers to the market value of equity capital and debt capital. But, the market value of debt is not easily available, as debts are not, generally traded. Thus, the definition of MVA can be stated as market capitalization less net worth. Market capitalization is the product of closing share price and number of outstanding shares as on that date, i.e., date of balance sheet, whereas net worth is the sum of equity capital, reserves and surplus, net of revaluation reserve less accumulated losses and miscellaneous expenditure.

MVA = Market Capitalization – Net Worth

Market Capitalization = (Closing Share Price × Number of Outstanding Shares) + Debentures

MVA is considered as a measure of shareholders' wealth. MVA denotes the extent to which the market has added value to the net worth of a company. An increase in MVA infers maximization of shareholders' wealth. This is because shareholders want to see appreciation in stock price. MVA can improve, if market capitalization increases for the same level of net worth or decreased net worth of a company.

'Market Value Added' concept facilitates measurement of shareholders' wealth, based on 'Wealth Maximization' in a firm.

MVA provides the stock market's assessment of how efficiently a company is using capital. A positive MVA indicates that a company is building value for its shareholders and a negative MVA indicates that a company is destroying shareholders' value.

Note: Revaluation reserve is not a part of capital employed, while it is a part of net worth.

Illustration No. 2

Based on the information contained in Illustration No. 1, calculate Market Value Added. Market value of equity share (FV ₹ 10) is ₹ 25 as on the date of balance sheet.

Solution

MVA can be stated as market capitalization less net worth. Market capitalization is the product of closing share price and number of outstanding shares as on balance sheet date. While calculating market capitalization, debentures are ignored as they are not, normally quoted.

MVA = Market Capitalization – Net Worth

Market Capitalization = Closing Share Price × Number of Outstanding Shares

= (25 × 90,000)

= 22,50,000

Net worth is the sum of equity capital, reserves and surplus, net of revaluation reserve less accumulated losses and miscellaneous expenditure.

Net Worth = Equity Share Capital + Preference Share Capital + Profit and Loss Account + General Reserves + Revaluation Reserves – Preliminary Expenses

= 9,00,000 + 3,00,000 + 1,00,000 + 2,00,000 + 3,00,000 – 70,000

= 17,30,000

MVA = Market Capitalization – Net Worth

= 22,50,000 – 17,30,000

= 5,20,000

So, MVA is positive by ₹ 5,20,000.

3.7 CONFLICT OF GOALS

Conflict Between Departmental Goal and Firm Goal: There are several departments in a firm, such as sales department, purchase department, production department and marketing department, etc. There may be conflicts among the goals of these departments. Moreover, the internal operative goal of the department may conflict with the goal of the firm. At times, the departmental head may fail to visualize the ultimate corporate goal, which is more important to achieve. It is necessary to resolve these conflicts to achieve the goal of the firm.

Diverse Interests of Stakeholders: Company is a complex organization. There are various stakeholders in a company, other than the shareholders. They are creditors, debenture holders, employees, customers and society who have their own interest in the organization.

The interests of stakeholders are different. Every group wants to evaluate the performance of management from its own objective view point. Each group recognizes the efficiency of management only when their interests are satisfied. So, management has to satisfy all the groups. By achieving wealth maximization, management can satisfy all stakeholders. Shareholders are benefited with the maximization of their equity share prices in the market. Market is defined as the place where the shares are quoted, e.g. Bombay Stock Exchange or National Stock Exchange. Creditors feel more secured about the refund of their principal as well as interest amount. Employees get better salaries and can have better career, with improved working conditions.

The real focus of wealth maximization is on the satisfaction of customers through production of goods and services, with better quality. Unless the customers are satisfied, there would be no survival for the organization. Even the Government can secure higher revenue through higher tax collection, due to increase in profits. Society also gets the benefit, when the firm shares a part of its wealth to the common benefit of the members of the society. Society, in general, gets the gain in the long-run.

Social Responsibility: Maximizing shareholder's wealth does not imply that management should ignore social responsibility. Protecting the interests of consumers, paying fair wages to employees, maintaining fair hiring practices, higher concern for safety issues and becoming involved in environmental issues such as clean air and water are some of the issues of social responsibility. The very existence of corporate now depends on their being socially responsible. Laws can make the companies legally responsible to a large extent but their own ethical values can make them really socially responsible in spirit and actual practice. Public image is built with social responsibility of the firm which indirectly goes to the maximization of the shareholders' wealth.

Concentration on Easily Attainable Goals: In case of corporate firms, the ownership is held by the shareholders, while the management is in the hands of Board of Directors and senior management who work as functional directors or heads. The owners set the goals for management to achieve. Certain goals are easy, while others may be difficult to achieve. In a company, the decision-making authority lies in the hands of management. The management may concentrate on easily attainable goals like achievement of production and ignore the effect of the other variables on the market price of the share.

Differing Viewpoints: Usually, the shareholders are scattered and ill organized to control the Board of Directors. Board of Directors may tend to develop their own goals on account of their functional autonomy. More so, now, the professionals hold the senior management positions. This may result in differing viewpoints between the shareholders and management. The professional management may alienate from the viewpoint of the shareholders. This situation did not prevail there, earlier, when sole proprietorship firms largely conducted the business.

Survival of Management: The survival of management will be threatened, if any objective of the stakeholders remains unfulfilled.

Every management wants to survive, satisfying the interests of all stakeholders, over a long run. So, the management cannot pursue its own personal goals too long because of the continuous supervision by the company's owners, employees, creditors, customers and Government.

The responsibility of the management is to maintain a balance between the goals of various groups. The objective of wealth maximization may be in general harmony with the interests of the various groups, such as owners, employees, creditors and society.

Long-term goal of shareholders' wealth maximization can be achieved by maintaining positive relationship with the stakeholders, which would avoid stakeholders' turnover, conflict and litigation. In brief, a firm can achieve its objective better with cooperation, rather than with conflict with all stakeholders.

3.8 ORGANIZATION OF FINANCE FUNCTION IN A MULTI-DIVISIONAL INDIAN COMPANY

Structure not Standardized: The finance function is very vital for every business firm. A firm should give proper attention to the structure and organization of its finance department. However, the structure of the finance department is not standardised.

There is no tailor made structure of finance function.

The structure depends upon several factors' the such as nature of business transactions, size of the business, type of financing operations, capabilities of finance executives and, in particular, requirements and expectations of top management. When the sole proprietor conducts his business, he performs even the finance function. With the increase in size of business, joint stock companies have been formed. As there is a divorce in ownership and management, professionals handle this important function.

Changing Nature of Corporate Financial Work: In some firms, the walls between finance and line management are being torn down. Financial control is becoming a shared responsibility for all members of the management team. This shared responsibility is creating a new ethic of financial communication and information sharing. Line managers are now required to be more be financially literate, while financial managers are required to share information, communicate, and become more business literate. Furthermore, financial executives are being asked to accept more responsibility for the achievement of "non-financial" aspects of business performance, such as product quality and customer service.

Freedom with Accountability: Due to development of corporate functioning, the finance function is centralized due to its importance. Organization of the finance function differs from company to company, dependent upon their respective needs and financial philosophy. More so, the role of finance has been increasing as the realization has been

Source: Patrick J. Keating and Stephen F. Jablonsky, *Changing Roles of Financial Management: Getting Close to Business* (Morristown, NJ: Financial Executives Research Foundation, (1990), p 5.

gaining ground gradually, that the survival and growth of business are more dependent on the finance function. The finance function is delegated to a top management executive who is designated as General Manager (Finance), Executive Director (Finance), Chief Financial Officer (CFO) or even Vice-President (Finance). The finance chief is a member of the top management and is closely associated with the formulation of policies as well as decision-making. Below the top head, various functions are described and responsibilities assigned to avoid overlapping and, at the same time, they are given freedom of functioning, with the necessary accountability.

Structure Chart: Basically, there are two most important functions—the accounting and finance functions. **The accounting and control functions are performed by Controller, while the Treasurer performs the financing activities of the firm.** Both these functionaries work under the close supervision of Vice-President (Finance).

An illustrative organization chart of finance function of management in a large, multi-divisional Indian company is shown, diagrammatically, below:

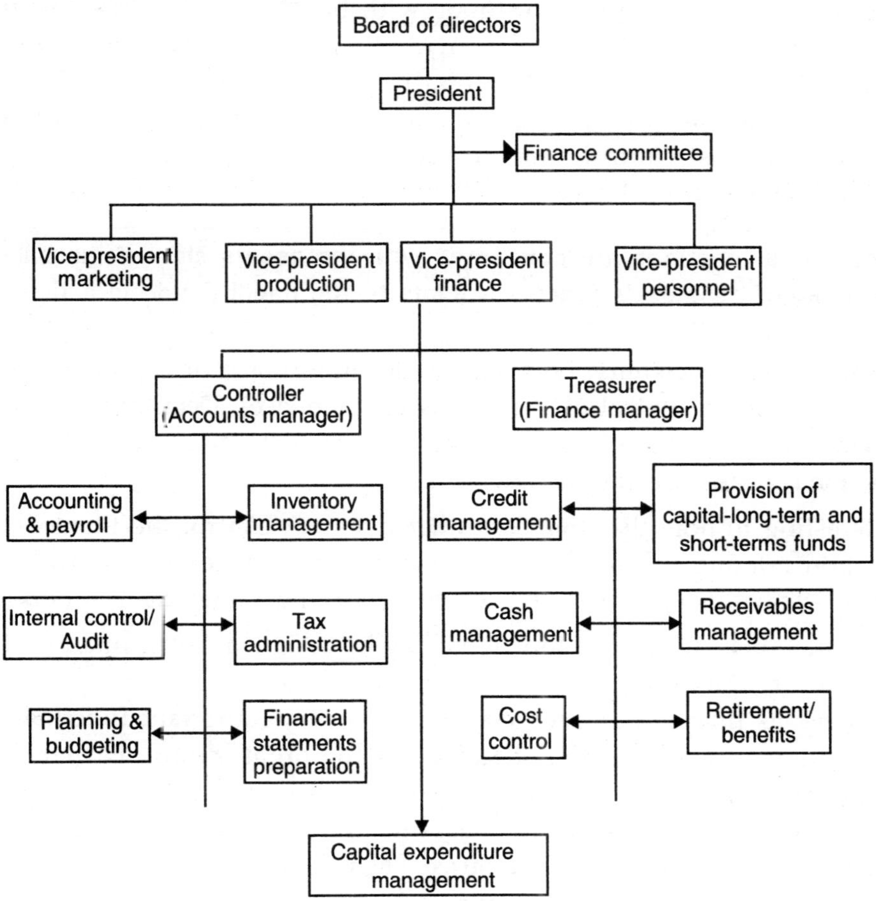

Fig. 3.1: Organization of Finance Function in a Multi-division Indian Company

The organization chart shows that the Vice-President (Finance) is supported by two deputies, known as:

1. Controller or Comptroller (Accounts Manager)
2. Treasurer (Finance Manager)

Controller's Functions: The functions of controller are related mainly to accounting and control. Controller's functions, basically, include financial accounting, preparation of financial and annual reports, inventory management, planning and budgeting, payroll, all types of tax administration, statutory and internal audit, economic appraisal and reporting and internal control. In some organizations, he is designated as 'Accounts Manager'.

Treasurer's Functions: The functions of Treasurer are related mainly with the financing activities of the firm. The major duties of Treasurer include forecasting of financial needs, present and future, both long-term and short-term and arranging required funds, at economic cost, in time. He is to coordinate with banks and financial institutions. The main function of Treasurer is to plan, provide the needed capital and working capital funds and their management. Additionally, he assumes responsibility for cash management and for administering the flow of cash, management of receivables, retirement benefits, cost control and protecting funds and securities. The treasurer is also designated as Finance Manager.

Controller's functions are concerned with the assets side of the balance sheet, while treasurer's functions relate to the liability side in a firm.

Capital Expenditure Decisions: Looking to the importance of capital expenditure, the function is under direct control of Vice-President (Finance). Decisions relating to capital expenditure are taken through Finance Committee, presided over by the President, where all the functional heads are the members.

It is interesting to note that the Controller does not control the finances. He utilises the information relating to finance for planning and management control. The routine functions are always delegated to the officers, working under their supervision.

Additional Functions: Additional functions may be assigned to the finance division. But, the culture, of late, has been to allow the finance chief to concentrate on the finance functions, alone, as finance has been considered a very important function, demanding full time attention to maintain the efficiency of the organization. Earlier, Government reporting and insurance functions used to be handled by the finance. Now, they are handled by the Company Secretary to enable the Vice-President (Finance) to concentrate on the management of the financial resources. His duties are not compounded with the other duties, generally, in large companies.

Treasurer	Controller
1. Provision of capital (Both long-term and short-term funds)	1. Accounting function
2. Maintaining relationship with banks and financial institutions	2. Preparation of financial statements and annual report
3. Credit management	3. Planning and budgetary control
4. Cash management	4. Statutory audit and Internal audit
5. Receivables management	5. Tax administration
6. Protection of funds and securities	6. Internal control
7. Cost control	7. Economic appraisal

Controller vs. Treasurer: Both the terms 'Controller' and 'Treasurer' are used in the United States of America, where the total finance functions are divided between them. Many a time, their functions overlap with each other. Both these designations have not become popular in India and these functions are performed by the Manager (Accounts) and Manager (Finance). However, in private sector, with modern management, there is always the trend now to designate people with some new nomenclature.

As already stated, the functions of finance largely depend on the various factors and, above all, the competence and professional background of the person who handles the functions.

Check Your Understanding

(A) State whether the following statements are True or False

1. Maximizing market price of equity share is the final objective of financial management.
2. According to the approach of profit maximization, actions that decrease profit should be undertaken and those that increase profit are to be avoided.
3. The objective of every company is to maximize value of the equity shares held by its shareholders.
4. The term 'Profit' is vague and ambiguous for advocating profit maximization concept.
5. Profit maximization concept recognizes the principle of 'Time Value of Money'.
6. In the context of growing joint stock company practice, it is possible to ignore the interests of customers, employees and society to promote the interests of shareholders of the company, alone.
7. All companies can make good profits in recession times.
8. Profit maximization fails to take social consideration into account.
9. Management's prime goal is shareholders' wealth maximization, which, in turn, serves the benefit of all stakeholders.
10. The wealth maximization criterion is based on the concept of cash flows, while accounting profit is the basis in profit maximization concept.
11. Value of an equity share largely depends on earnings per share.

12. Profit maximization can be considered as a part of wealth maximization strategy.
13. Market price of a share is not the growth index of the company.
14. Stakeholders of a company include employees, customers, suppliers, creditors, owners and society who have a direct link to the firm.
15. All financial decisions carry a certain element of 'Risk'.
16. The concept 'Economic Value Added' is based on the principle of 'Profit Maximization', while the concept 'Market Value Added' is based on 'Wealth Maximization.
17. It is not possible to increase the operating profit, without employing additional capital, even with greater efficiency.
18. Shareholders' wealth maximization cannot be measured though 'Market Value Added' concept.
19. The finance chief is a member of top management and is closely associated with the formulation of policies as well as decision-making.
20. The functions of controller are related mainly to accounting and control.

Answers

1. True	2. False	3. True	4. True	5. False	6. False	7. False	8. True
9. True	10. True	11. True	12. True	13. False	14. True	15. True	16. True
17. False	18. False	19. True	20. True.				

(B) Objective Questions (Identify what is most appropriate)

1. The appropriate objective of an enterprise is
   (i) Maximization of owner's wealth
   (ii) Maximization of net profits
   (iii) Maximization of sales
2. Basic objective of financial management is
   (i) Maximization of profits
   (ii) Maximization of shareholders' wealth
   (iii) Ensuring financial discipline in the firm
3. If all companies had the objective of maximizing shareholder wealth, would people overall tend to be
   (i) better off (ii) worse off (iii) neutral

Answers

1. i 2. ii 3. iii

(C) Fill in the blanks:

1. The ____________________ side of the balance sheet is managed by the Comptroller.
2. Amongst the functions of ____________________, raising finance is a primary function.

Answers

1. Assets 2. Treasurer

Descriptive Questions

1. 'Profit maximization is not an inclusive goal for maximization of shareholders' wealth as it suffers from several limitations. Discuss. **(3.1, 3.2 and 3.3.1)**
2. Describe the good characteristics of a financial decision criterion and critically examine whether 'Profit Maximization' fulfils the selection criteria. **(3.2 and 3.3.1)**
3. "The Profit Maximization is not an operationally feasible criterion". Illustrate your views with suitable examples. **(3.2 and 3.3.1)**
4. "The goal of profit maximization does not provide an operationally useful criterion for measuring the success of business operation". Comment. **(3.2 and 3.3.1)**
5. Of the two objectives of financial management, viz. profit maximization and wealth maximization, which one do you think is a better operational guide for a finance manager and justify it with reasons? **(3.2, 3.3.1 and 3.3.2)**
6. In what ways is the wealth maximization objective superior to the profit maximization objective. Explain? **(3.2, 3.3.1 and 3.3.2)**
7. "Goal of wealth maximization is a better operational criterion than profit maximization"– Illustrate. **(3.2, 3.3.1 and 3.3.2)**
8. Why should a company concentrate primarily on wealth maximization instead of profit maximization? **(3.2, 3.3.1 and 3.3.2)**
9. 'Wealth maximization is a better approach to achieve value creation for shareholders' – Discuss along with criticism leveled against. **(3.3.2, 3.3.3 and 3.3.4)**
10. Describe the objectives of Financial Management. **(3.3, 3.3.1, 3.3.2, 3.3.4 and 3.4)**
11. Describe different methods of measuring Shareholders' Value Creation. **(3.5, 3.6, 3.6.1 and 3.6.2)**
12. How 'Economic Value Added' and 'Market Value Added' concepts are used in measuring shareholders value creation? **(3.5, 3.6, 3.6.1 and 3.6.2)**
13. When can there be conflicts between owners and management's goals? How wealth maximization can take care of this? **(3.7)**
14. Draw an illustrative chart of a multi-divisional Indian Company showing the finance functions? What functions do the financial officers perform? **(3.8)**
15. How should the finance function of a large enterprise be organized? What functions are performed by the finance division? Do you advocate additional functions to them? **(3.8)**
16. Write short notes on
    (A) Market Value Added **(3.6.2)**
    (B) Functions of Controller and Treasurer **(3.8)**
    (C) Economic Value Added **(3.6.1)**

Interview Questions

Q.1. If a person does not want to become a finance manager, what is the need to understand financial management?

Ans. Every person aspires for growth. More and more business organizations are reducing various layers in corporate pyramid to reduce costs and boost productivity. As a result, responsibilities of the remaining management positions are broadened. To become a successful manager, one has necessarily to be, a team player, who has the knowledge and ability to move not just vertically within the organization, but horizontally as well. So, mastery of basic financial management skills is a key ingredient, essential to move ahead of others.

Q.2. Does profit maximization always result in wealth maximization of shareholders?

Ans. Profit maximization may not always result in wealth maximization of shareholders. Profits may increase, but earnings per share may fall. As a result, market price of share falls. In such an event, shareholders' wealth maximization does not occur.

Q.3. If profits increase, is it necessary to increase earnings per share?

Ans. Increase in profits may or may not result in increased earnings per share. Increase in profits may happen, still earnings per share falls, if increase in profits is not proportionate to the increase in the number of equity shares.

The following picture would explain the situation, clearly.

Year	Equity Shares	Net Profit	Earning Per Share (EPS)
2008	1,000	10,000	₹ 10
2009	3,000	15,000	₹ 5

Net profit has increased, but earnings per share have decreased, due to increase in equity shares more than the increase in profit.

Q.4. What is the meaning of 'Risk'?

Ans. The term 'Risk' refers to the chance that actual outcome may differ from the original expectation.

Q.5. What is meant by value creation in a company? How it is measured?

Ans. Investors, both equity providers and lenders, invest in a company in anticipation of certain amount of return. If the operating profits of a company, after tax, are in excess of the cost of capital invested, there is value addition. If the net operating profit, after tax (NOPAT) is positive, there is value addition. In case, NOPAT is negative, there is decrease in value to the company.

Value creation is measured either on the basis of 'Economic Value Added' and/or 'Market Value Added' concepts.

❍ ❍

CHAPTER 4

Analysis of Financial Statements

4.1 INTRODUCTION

The basic limitation of the traditional financial statements, balance sheet and profit and loss account, is they do not give all the relevant and required information for knowing the strength and weakness of a firm. However, they provide extremely useful information about the summarized view of the financial position and operations of a firm. The balance sheet mirrors the financial position on a particular date, in terms of structure of assets, liabilities and owner's equity, like a snap shot. The profit and loss account shows the operational results during a particular period, in terms of revenue generated and costs incurred for achieving them. As the financial information is in absolute amounts, they are not readily understandable. The answer is 'Analysis of Financial Statements'.

> **Analysis of financial statements refers to the application of different tools to know the behaviour of the accounting information.**

Much can be learnt by analyzing the financial statements.

4.2 PURPOSE OF FINANCIAL ANALYSIS

Every management is interested to know the strength and weakness of the firm it runs, in terms of finance. Absolute figures in the financial statements—Profit and Loss Account and Balance Sheet—are always big and difficult to understand easily. Analysis of financial statements helps the management in understanding the figures better for quicker and meaningful decisions along with corrective actions in time.

The term 'Financial Analysis' is also known as analysis and interpretation of financial statements. The purpose of financial analysis is to diagnose the information content in financial statements so as to judge the profitability, financial soundness of the firm and chalk out ways to improve the existing performance.

4.3 MAIN OBJECTIVE OF FINANCIAL ANALYSIS

Different parties are interested in the financial statements for different purposes and look to them from their own angle. The objective of the different parties is not the same. Their requirements are not uniform. So, every one is interested to use them for his own requirement. A lender is interested for repayment of the money lent and interest assured at the time of lending. Shareholder is concerned for earnings and appreciation of the investment he has made. Their objectives are not common so their approach and the information they look for is different.

4.4 USERS OF FINANCIAL ANALYSIS

The management of the firm as well as interested parties, outside the firm, can undertake financial analysis. Outsiders of the firm are owners (shareholders), creditors, intending investors and others, particularly the potential lenders.

Nature of Analysis: The nature of the analysis depends upon their purpose or requirement. They make the necessary analysis and take the decision, based on their assessment of the results obtained.

Trade Creditors are those who have supplied goods and services to the firm. They are interested in their timely repayment. So, before they supply or render service, they want to be sure that the firm would be in a position to pay their dues, in a short period, as assured to them. They analyze the firm's short-term liquidity position. The term 'liquidity' refers to the ability of the firm to pay, as and when the obligations and debts fall due for payment.

Firm would be in a position to meet the current obligations, if the cash receipts match payments in terms of time.

Suppliers of Long-term Debt are those who provide loans for a long period. They are concerned with the firm's long-term solvency and survival, which depends on profitability and cash generation. Before they lend, they want to assure themselves that the organization would be able to generate adequate liquid funds to pay the loan installment and interest. They are more concerned with the future outlook, rather than the past, based on the projections of the firm. They analyze the historical data, based on the financial statements, to determine the basis and reasonableness of the projections to decide the future financial standing of the firm.

Shareholders and investors invest their money in the firm's shares to earn dividend and appreciation of share value. They are concerned with the firm's **present and future profitability**. The ability of the company to pay dividend depends on the future prospects and earning capacity of the organization. They would have more confidence in those firms, which show steady growth in earnings. They are also interested in the firm's financial structure to the extent it influences the firm's earning ability.

Employees and Management: The importance of trust and harmonious relationship between the employees and management requires no more emphasis for accelerated growth of the firm. If the employees feel confident of assured employment, more salaries, retirement benefits and fast track career growth, in future, their loyalty would be assured. Employees look for stability and profitability in financial statements.

Management of the firm would be interested in every aspect of financial analysis. Management is concerned with the effective and efficient utilization of resources, analyzing the financial statements and other information available to them.

Government regulates the functioning of all organizations for the benefit of public. It has to generate adequate revenue for this purpose. Collection of taxes and information for deciding future policies are based on the financial statements of the firms.

It is clear that the different users need the financial statements for different purposes.

Requirements of users of financial statements are different, not uniform. The aim of the financial statements is to provide the information required for their divergent needs.

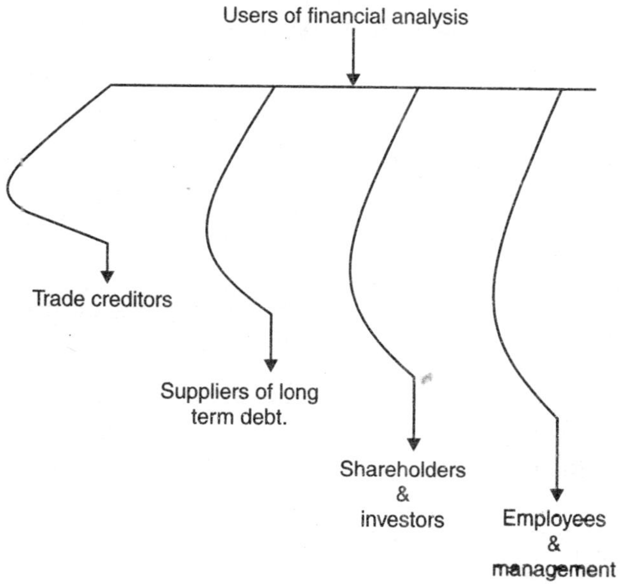

Fig. 4.1: Users of financial analysis

4.5 DIFFERENT TERMS OF FINANCIAL STATEMENTS USED IN RATIO ANALYSIS

To have understanding of ratios, it is necessary to know how the required information can be calculated:

Statement of cost of goods sold

Raw materials	xxx
Direct labour	xxx
Depreciation	xxx
Other manufacturing expenses	xxx
	xxx
Add: Opening stock in process	xxx
	xxx
Less: Closing stock in process	xxx
Cost of Production	**xxx**
Add: Opening stock of finished goods	xxx
	xxx
Less: Closing stock of finished goods	xxx
Cost of Sales/Cost of Goods Sold	xxx

Break up of Profit and Loss Account for the year ending ......

A.	Net Sales	xxx
B.	Cost of sales (cost of Goods sold)	xxx
C.	Gross Profit (A–B)	xxx
D.	*Less:* Selling, General & Administrative expenses	xxx
E.	Operating income (C–D)	xxx
F.	*Add:* Other income	xxx
G.	Earning before interest and tax (EBIT) (E+F)	xxx
H.	*Less:* Interest	xxx
I.	Profit before tax (PBT) (G–H)	xxx
J.	Provision for tax	xxx
K.	Profit after tax (PAT) (I–J)	xxx
L.	Dividend distributed	xxx
M.	Retained earnings (K–L)	xxx

Break up of Balance Sheet as on...

A. Net Worth

Equity share capital	xxx	
Preference share capital	xxx	
Reserves	xxx	
Net worth		xxx

B. Long-term Borrowings			
Debentures	xxx		
Others	xxx		
Long-term debt	xxx		
Long-term borrowings			xxx
C. Capital Employed (A+B)	**xxx**		
D. Fixed Assets			
Gross block	xxx		
Less: depreciation	xxx		
Net block		xxx	
Other non-current assets (Trade Investments etc.)		xxx	
Net fixed assets			xxx
E. Current Assets			
Inventories:			
Raw material	xxx		
Stock in process	xxx		
Finished goods	xxx		
Inventories		xxx	
Debtors		xxx	
Cash and bank balance		xxx	
Others		xxx	
Current assets			xxx
F. *Less*: Current Liabilities			
Trade creditors	xxx		
Bank overdraft / Cash credit	xxx		
Provisions and others	xxx		
Current liabilities		xxx	
G. Net Current Assets (E–F)		**xxx**	
H. Net Assets (D+G)		**xxx**	

The above statement shows

Net Assets (H) = Capital Employed (C)

4.6 TYPES OF FINANCIAL ANALYSIS

Financial analysis can be classified into two categories depending upon

(i) Material used, and

(ii) Method of Analysis

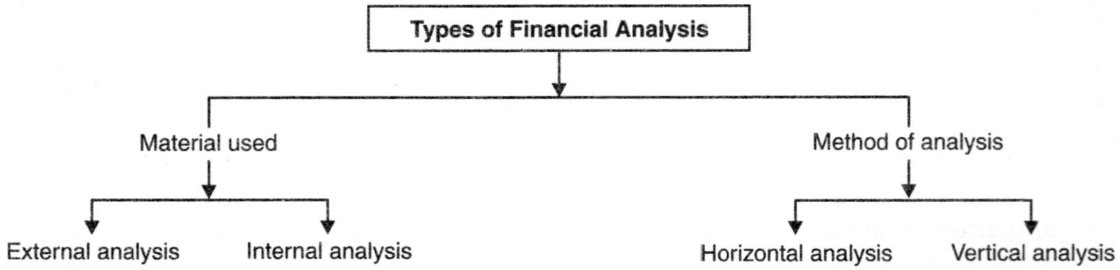

Types of Financial Analysis

(i) On the Basis of Material Used: According to this category, financial analysis can be of two types. They are:

(A) External Analysis: Those people who do not have access to the internal records of the firm do this analysis. Basically, they are creditors, present and potential investors, credit agencies and the general public. Normally, except select employees in the firm, all others do not have access to the internal records. More so, there is always a time lag for the publication of accounts, after their preparation. So, updated or recent information is not available for analysis. Due to this inherent limitation, this type of analysis serves a limited purpose as the analysis is based on the published final accounts, audited or not audited. However, of late, the position has significantly improved due to government regulations to make the published accounts more frequent, transparent and detailed.

(B) Internal Analysis: Those persons, who have an access to the books of accounts, financial and other records of the firm, do this analysis. Basically, the employees and executives of the firm, who have access to the records, can do this analysis. Even, the government agencies can also do when they have the statutory powers to access the records. This analysis would be more meaningful and useful as the analysis is made on the basis of full records and with a specific objective. The management of the firm would, invariably, adopt internal analysis for managerial purposes.

(ii) Method of Analysis: Based on the method, financial analysis can be of two types. They are Horizontal Analysis and Vertical Analysis.

Horizontal Analysis: Horizontal Analysis refers to the comparison of financial data of a company for several years. Horizontal analysis helps to observe changes in the financial variables over the years. For this analysis, base or standard year is first chosen as a starting point. Any year may be taken as the base year, but, generally, the starting or initial year is taken as the base year. Base year has to be a normal or representative year. All the financial figures are presented in a horizontal manner. Keeping the data of base year in the beginning, the data of the different years are kept in separate columns.

> **Horizontal Analysis measures the change of position of business over a number of years. Horizontal analysis is also known as 'Dynamic Analysis' as it is based on the data from year to year rather than the data of any one year.**

With horizontal analysis, it is possible for the firm to focus on those items, which have changed significantly. As comparison for several years is made with a base year, a trend is likely to emerge. Trend can be improvement, deterioration, stagnancy or fluctuating trend. Based on the trends observed, management can make a rationale judgment about the past and chalk out suitable plans for the future.

> **Comparative statements and trend analysis are the two tools that use horizontal analysis. Attention of the management would be focussed on those items, which have changed significantly. Based on the prevailing trend, it is possible for the firm to make a rational forecast about the future progress.**

The purpose of the analysis is to identify strengths and weaknesses of the firm. Comparison of the item, over several years, shows the development/deterioration trend. The management would be able to get insight of the strength or problem for necessary action in time.

Vertical Analysis: Vertical analysis refers to the study of relationship of the various items contained in the financial statement of one accounting period. For example, the ratios of different items of cost for a particular period are calculated with the sales for that period. So, sales are taken as 100 and each expense is taken as a percentage of sales, i.e. 100. Such analysis is useful in comparing the performance of several companies in the same group or industry, or divisions or departments in the same company. **Vertical analysis is also known as 'Static Analysis'. This has got its name as the analysis is confined to one year's figures.** As vertical analysis is limited for one year, this is not considered as conducive analysis.

> **Common-size financial statements and ratio analysis are the two tools employed in vertical analysis.**

Combined use of Horizontal and Vertical Analysis: Both the analysis can be used simultaneously. Vertical analysis can be used along with horizontal analysis to make it more effective and meaningful.

> **Horizontal analysis is used for comparing data of several years of one firm, while vertical analysis is used for comparing the relative performance of different firms, in the same industry, for one particular period or a year.**

Illustration No. 1

From the following statement of cost of goods manufactured of Monica Private Ltd., present the data in a suitable form for analysis:

	2009	2008
Raw materials:		
Opening stock	40,000	30,000
Purchases	1,20,000	1,10,000
	1,60,000	1,40,000
Closing stock	10,000	40,000
Materials consumed	1,50,000	1,00,000
Direct labour	32,000	25,000
Manufacturing expenses	18,000	15,000
Depreciation	10,000	12,000
	2,10,000	1,52,000
Variation of goods – stock in process		
Opening stock	12,000	9,000
Closing stock	8,000	12,000
Increase/decrease	4,000	(3,000)
Cost of production	2,14,000	1,49,000

Solution

₹

Monica Private Limited
Comparative statement of cost of production (cost of goods manufactured)

	Amount		Percentage of cost of production		Increase/Decrease	
	2009	2008	2009	2008	Amount	Percentage
Raw materials used	1,50,000	1,00,000	70.09	67.11	+ 50,000	+ 50.00
Direct labour	32,000	25,000	14.95	16.78	+ 7,000	+ 28.00
Manufacturing expenses	18,000	15,000	8.41	10.06	+ 3,000	+ 20.00
Depreciation	10,000	12,000	4.67	8.05	– 2,000	– 16.67
	2,10,000	1,52,000	98.12	102.00	+ 58,000	+ 38.16
Less: Adjustment for increase / decrease in stock-in-process*	4,000	3,000	1.88	2.00	+ 7,000	
Cost of production (cost of goods manufactured)	2,14,000	1,49,000	100.00	100.00	+ 65,000	+ 43.62

Note: * **Stock-in-process:** To arrive at the cost of production, opening stock-in-process is added, while closing stock-in-process is deducted.

Illustration No. 2

The following figures relate to the trading activities of Chandu Ltd. for the year ending on 31st March, 2004:

	₹		₹
Sales	5,20,000	Opening stock	76,250
Purchases	3,22,250	Closing stock	98,500
Selling and distribution expenses:		Sales return	20,000
		Administrative expenses:	
Salaries	15,300		
Advertisement	4,700	Salaries	27,000
Travelling	2,000	Rent	2,700
Non-operating income:		Stationery, postage	2,500
		Depreciation	9,300
Dividend on shares	9,000	Other charges	16,500
Profit on sale of assets	3,000	Provision for taxation	40,000
Non-operating expenses			
Loss on sale of shares	4,000		

Rearrange the above figures in a form suitable for analysis.

(B.U., M.B.A., 2004)

Solution

Income from Operations			
Sales after returns (5,20,000 – 20,000)		5,00,000	
Less: Cost of goods sold:			
Opening stock	76,250		
Add: Purchases	3,22,250		
	3,98,500		
Less: Closing stock	98,500		
Cost of goods sold		3,00,000	
		2,00,000	
Less: Depreciation		9,300	
Gross Profit			**1,90,700**
***Less:* Operating Expenses:**			
Selling & Distribution Expenses			
Salaries	15,300		
Advertisement	4,700		
Travelling	2,000		
		22,000	

Contd...

Administrative Expenses			
Salaries 27,000			
Rent 2,700			
Stationery, Postage 2,500			
Other charges 16,500			
		48,700	70,700
Operating Profit			**1,20,000**
Add: **Non-operating Income**			
Dividend on shares	9,000		
Profit on Sale of assets	3,000	12,000	
Less: **Non-operating Expenses**			
Loss on sale of Shares	4,000	4,000	
Add: **Net Non-operating Income**			**8,000**
Profit Before Tax			1,28,000
Less: Provision for taxation			40,000
Profit After Tax			88,000

4.7 MAJOR TOOLS OF FINANCIAL ANALYSIS

Various tools or techniques are used in the financial analysis. The main objective of any analytical method is simple presentation of data in a relevant manner, even for a complex problem for quick understanding. Its basic purpose is to drow the attention of management on the problem area for solution.

The most important tools for financial analysis are:

(a) Comparative Financial Statements,
(b) Trend Analysis or Trend Ratios,
(c) Common Size Statements,
(d) Ratio Analysis,
(e) Fund Flow Analysis, and
(f) Cash Flow Analysis.

4.8 COMPARATIVE FINANCIAL STATEMENTS

Generally, two financial statements (balance sheet and profit and loss account) are prepared in comparative form for financial analysis.

Comparative financial statements indicate the direction of movement with respect to financial position and operating results of the firm.

These statements can be equally useful for inter-firm comparison.

Method of Preparation: Information in the financial statements, both profit and loss account and balance sheet, has to be grouped and placed, side-by-side, for two or more years. The next column has to show the amount of change in absolute amount and the last column is for percentage of increase or decrease. From this, it is possible to draw reasonable conclusions about the direction, progress or deterioration of operational efficiency and financial position of the business and the factors that have contributed.

The importance of comparative financial statements can be understood from the requirement of the Companies Act, 1956 which makes it obligatory for all companies to prepare the final accounts of companies by presenting current as well as the previous years figures.

It is obligatory under Companies Act, 1956 for all companies to prepare the final accounts of companies by presenting current as well as previous years figures. For comparison, figures have to be regrouped, if necessary.

4.8.1 Guideline for Interpreting Financial Statements

While interpreting comparative balance sheet and profit and loss account, the following aspects are to be studied. Students have to comment on these matters, while presenting their answer on analysis of financial statements.

(A) Short-term financial position and liquidity: For studying current financial position or short-term financial position, working capital position is to be studied for both the years. Working capital is the excess of current assets over current liabilities. Increase in working capital indicates improvement in the current financial position of the business. If there is an increase in current assets, with a similar increase in current liabilities, there would be no increase in working capital. Decrease of working capital is anxiety causing, if the existing working capital position is not excessive. Reasons for decrease in working capital are to be examined further, as this would create payment problems to the firm.

Liquidity position of the firm is also to be studied. Liquidity is a key factor for the smooth functioning of the firm. Current assets minus inventory, when compared with current liabilities, liquidity position would be known. If inventory increases, working capital increases, but liquidity does not increase. Increase of inventory alone is not a satisfactory position.

(B) Long-term financial position: It is always desirable that the increase in fixed assets are to be financed by increase in long-term sources such as equity share capital, debentures, long-term loans and profits etc. Reason is fixed assets are permanent in business. So, permanent funds only are to finance them, not temporary funds like working capital. So long as permanent funds (sources) meet permanent needs (uses), there is no problem to the firm. So, a comparison of increase in fixed assets is to be made with an increase in long-term sources. If increase in long-term sources exceeds the increase in fixed assets, it shows that the firm has used part of its long-term sources for working capital needs, in addition to fixed assets. This is a sound policy. On the other hand, if increase in fixed assets is more than the increase in long-term sources, it is an indication that working capital is diverted for purchase of fixed assets, which is not a wise policy. So a comparison of change in long-term sources is to be made with the change in fixed assets to understand and comment on long-term financial position of the company.

(C) Profitability: Profitability of the firm is an important issue. Whether the firm has made profits or not, it is important to ascertain. A comparison of profit of the current year, shown in profit and loss account with previous year shows the direction of profitability. A comparison of increase in balance in profit and loss account and reserves gives the idea that the firm has retained part of profits for further growth, even after distribution of dividend. A comparison of dividend payment gives the idea whether the firm is satisfying the expectations of the shareholders or not. At times, firm may skip dividend payment to show an increase in financial position, which would not be a satisfactory situation.

(D) Operating profits: An increase in sales need not necessarily result in increase in operating profits. If costs are more than revenue, profits decrease. If increase in cost of sales is more than the increase in sales, operating profits decrease due to increase in selling and distribution costs and administrative costs. Expenses, which have gone up, have to be identified for control. An increase in profit comes from increase in sales and control on costs. Profits can increase, due to increase in sales or control of expenses alone, due to managerial efficiency.

Illustration No. 3

From the condensed financial statements of Smitha Jain & Co. Ltd., engaged in retail business of women speciality items, prepare comparative financial statements in vertical form. Comment on them.

Trading & Profit and Loss Account of Smitha Jain & Co. Ltd. (₹)

Particulars	2008	2009	Particulars	2008	2009
To opening stock	40,000	35,000	By sales	50,000	62,000
Purchases	30,000	40,500	Closing stock	35,000	32,000
Gross profit	15,000	18,500			
	85,000	94,000		85,000	94,000
Salaries	2,000	1,000	By gross profit	15,000	18,500
Rent	500	500			
Other operating expenses	5,000	12,500			
Net profit	7,500	4,500			
	15,000	18,500		15,000	18,500

Summarized Balance Sheet of Smitha Jain & Co. Ltd.

(₹)

Liabilities	2008	2009	Assets	2008	2009
Equity share capital	72,500	1,02,500	Fixed assets	50,500	2,08,500
			Investments	10,000	2,000
Reserves	23,000	20,000	Stock	20,000	10,000
Secured loan	10,000	1,13,000	Debtors	25,000	15,000
Bank cash credit account	5,000	3,000	Cash & Bank balance	10,000	5,000
Sundry creditors	5,000	2,000			
	1,15,500	2,40,500		1,15,500	2,40,500

Inquiries reveal that the firm has been experiencing difficulty in making payments and not getting adequate supply of stock.

Solution

Comparative Income Statement of Smitha Jain & Co. Ltd.

Particulars	2008	2009	Absolute change	Percentage of change
Sales	50,000	62,000	+12,000	+24.00 %
Less: Cost of sales (Opening stock + purchases – Closing stock)	35,000	43,500	+ 8,500	+ 24.28 %
Gross profit	15,000	18,500	+ 3,500	+ 23.33 %
Less: Total expenses	7,500	14,000	+6,500	+ 86.67 %
Net profit	7,500	4,500	–3,000	– 40%

Comparative Summarized Balance Sheet of Smitha Jain & Co. Ltd.

Liabilities	2008	2009	Absolute change	Percentage of change
Long Term Sources				
Equity share capital	72,500	1,02,500	30,000	+ 41.38 %
Reserves	23,000	20,000	– 3,000	–13.04 %
Secured loan	10,000	1,13,000	1,03,000	+ 10.30 %
	1,05,500	2,35,500	1,30,000	123.22 %
Applications				
Fixed assets (A)	50,500	2,08,500	1,58,000	312.87 %
Investments (B)	10,000	2,000	– 8,000	– 80.00 %
Current assets	55,000	30,000	– 25,000	– 45.45 %
Current liabilities	10,000	5,000	– 5,000	
Net working capital (C)	45,000	25,000	– 20,000	– 50 %
Total (A+B+C)	1,05,500	2,35,500	1,30,000	– 44.44 %
				123.22 %

Interpretation

1. **Increase in Sales and Gross Margin:** Sales have increased by 24%, with almost similar increase in Gross Profit by 23.33%. This indicates that the spread (difference) between the selling price and purchase price for both the years is almost the same.
2. **Reduction in Net Profit:** There has been a significant reduction of net profit by 40%, despite increase in sales by 24%. The culprit is the other operating expense that has increased by ₹ 6,500 (increase of 86.67%), while sales have just increased by 24% only. Control is essential on these expenses for improving profitability.
3. **Long-term Sources:** There has been an increase of long-term sources by ₹ 1,30,000, comprising mainly of equity share capital ₹ 30,000 and secured loan for ₹ 1,03,000. There has been a reduction in reserves by ₹ 3,000.
4. **Diversion of Short-term Sources to Long-term Uses:** Fixed assets have increased by ₹ 1,58,000, which are financed by the long-term sources of ₹ 1,30,000, disposal of investments by ₹ 8,000 and the balance amount of ₹ 20,000 out of the working capital diversion. Diversion of working capital for the purchase of fixed assets is not a wise policy, more so when the firm is already experiencing difficulty in making payments to suppliers.
5. **Decrease in Reserves:** Reserves have decreased by ₹ 3,000 in the year 2009. This indicates that the withdrawal of profits is more than the amount of profit earned in the year 2009. In other words, earlier years' profits have been used for declaring dividend.
6. **Final Comments:**

   (A) Short-term Sources Used for Long-term Uses: Diversion of working capital for the purchase of fixed assets is a wrong policy. Normally, a part of working capital is to be financed by long-term sources. Here, it is a reverse situation. There has been diversion of working capital for long-term use, purchase of fixed assets. This is, indeed, a wrong policy.

(B) Not Healthy Function: Normally, a portion of profits is to be retained in the organization. Here, withdrawal of profits is more than the earning made by the organization. This approach does not speak very well of the organization's functioning.

(C) Lack of Effective Control on Expenses: Control on other operating expenses is essential as there has been a significant increase by 86.67%.

(D) Improvement of Profits: A proper strategy is to be drawn up to improve profits, which have reduced.

Illustration No. 4

From the following balance sheet of Shyam Ltd., prepare comparative balance sheet for the year 2007 and 2008.

Draw tentative conclusions after preparing 'CBS'.

[₹ in lakhs]

Assets	31.12.07	31.12.08
Fixed assets:		
Premises [less dep.]	1,200	1,140
Plant & Machinery [less dep.]	800	1,000
Furniture [less dep.]	200	170
Total fixed assets	**2,200**	**2,310**
Investments	400	300
Current assets:		
Stock	600	600
Debtors	400	300
Cash & Bank	140	156
Total current assets	**1,140**	**1,056**
Total Assets	**3,740**	**3,666**
Liabilities	**31.12.07**	**31.12.08**
Equity share capital	1,000	1,000
8% Preference share capital	400	600
Reserves & Surplus	400	500
Total proprietors' funds	**1,800**	**2,100**
Secured loans:		
10% Debentures	700	400
Current liabilities:		
Sundry creditors	600	700
Bills payable	400	350
Taxes payable	240	116
Total current liabilities	**1,240**	**1,166**
Total liabilities	1,940	1,566
Total Capital & Liabilities	**3,740**	**3,666**

Solution

[₹ in lakhs]

Assets	₹ 31.12.07	₹ 31.12.08	Amount of increase or decrease in 2008	Percentage of increase or decrease in 2008
Fixed assets:				
Premises [less dep.]	1,200	1,140	– 60	– 5.00 %
Plant & machinery [less dep.]	800	1,000	200	25.00 %
Furniture [less dep.]	200	170	– 30	– 15.00 %
Total fixed assets (A)	**2,200**	**2,310**	**110**	**5.00 %**
Investments (B)	400	300	–100	– 25.00 %
Current assets:				
Stock	600	600	—	—
Debtors	400	300	– 100	– 25.00 %
Cash & bank	140	156	16	11.43 %
Total current assets (C)	**1,140**	**1,056**	**– 84**	**– 7.37 %**
Total assets (A+B+C)	3,740	3,666	– 74	– 1.98 %
8% Preference share capital	400	600	+ 200	+ 50.00 %
Equity share capital	1,000	1,000	—	—
Reserves & surplus	400	500	+ 100	+ 25.00 %
Total proprietors' funds	**1,800**	**2,100**	**+ 300**	**+ 16.67 %**
Secured loans:				
10% Debentures	700	400	– 300	– 42.86 %
Current liabilities:				
Sundry creditors	600	700	+ 100	+ 16.67 %
Bills payable	400	350	– 50	– 12.50 %
Taxes payable	240	116	– 124	– 51.68 %
Total current liabilities (D)	**1,240**	**1,166**	**– 74**	**– 5.97 %**
Total liabilities	1,940	1,566	– 374	– 19.28 %
Total capital & liabilities	3,740	3,666	– 74	– 1.98 %
Net working capital (C –D)	– 100	– 110	–10	– 10 %

Tentative Conclusions

Policy for Financing Fixed Assets: Fixed assets are to be financed from long-term sources. This company does not follow this universal policy. Total fixed assets added during the year 2008 ₹ 110 lakhs [i.e., about 5%] compared to 2007, for which long-term investments worth ₹ 100 lakhs have been realized. Even after using the proceeds of investments for the purchase of fixed assets, there is still a shortfall of ₹ 10 lakhs.

Total Proprietors' funds have gone up by ₹ 300 lakhs. Total long-term sources in the form of preference share capital has been raised by ₹ 200 lakhs and reserves have gone up by ₹ 100 lakhs with retained profits. However, these funds are used for redemption of debentures. As a result, there has been no help for fixed assets from this increase.

The level of net working capital has gone down by ₹ 10 lakhs. It implies that there has been an addition to fixed assets with a decrease in net working capital, which reflects a poor financial policy.

Current Assets are to Increase with Fixed Assets: Fixed assets are meant for production. Job of current assets is to facilitate production. Fixed assets are to be supported by current assets for improvement in business.

In fact, there has been a diversion of current assets to acquire fixed assets. In the earlier year itself, the current ratio is below the normal level of 2:1. Earlier current ratio (0.92) has gone down further (0.90) in the current year. When there is an increase of fixed assets, current assets have to increase during the current year. On the other hand, there is a diversion of current assets for acquisition of fixed assets, which is a wrong approach again.

Unsatisfactory Short-term (Working Capital) Position: The relationship between the total current assets and total current liabilities is also not satisfactory as the current ratio is around 1 in both the years. Net working capital in the year 2007 has been negative (100 lakhs), which has further gone drawn to 110 lakhs, indicating highly inadequate working capital situation of the firm.

Redemption of Debentures: Increase in the preference share capital of ₹ 200 lakhs might have been made for the purpose of redemption of debentures. Reserves have gone up by 100 lakhs, which shows the improving trend in profits. The redemption of debentures has been made from the proceeds of the fresh issue of Preference Share Capital and increase in profits. One long-term source is used for redeeming another long-term use, which is a reasonable approach.

Increase in Profits: Increase of reserves is an indication of profitability. There has been an increase in reserves by ₹ 100 lakhs, which indicates the operational activities of the firm are profitable.

Overall Recommendation: Firm has to initiate immediate steps for improving working capital position. Firm has to consider the need of raising long-term funds for rectifying the current situation.

4.9 TREND ANALYSIS OR TREND RATIOS

Trend analysis is a statistical device applied in the analysis of financial statements to reveal the trend of items with the passage of time.

Absolute figures are difficult to understand, in particular when they are big amounts. One can understand better and immediately if the statement says that there has been an increase of 50% in sales over a period of five years, rather than mentioning the absolute amount of sales for the different years.

Trend analysis involves calculation of percentage of changes in financial statement items for a number of successive years.

> **In trend analysis, financial data, containing absolute amounts of large numbers, are substituted by percentages to show brevity and ready readability for management to present trend for suitable action, where necessary.**

Purpose: Trend analysis provides an opportunity to understand the direction of changes over a long period. Annual reports of many companies publish the summary of operating results and selected financial indicators of five or more years. It provides an opportunity to perform trend analysis from the published reports.

Method of Calculation and Presentation: Data for several years is placed in a horizontal manner. This type of presentation of data for a series of years gives meaningful information in respect of growth and deterioration for each item. Base year period is selected to present the data from that year onwards. **Base year figures are taken as 100 and each year's figures are expressed as a percentage of the base year. In other words, each year figure is divided by base year and its percentage is arrived.** Most important point about the base year is the basis for calculation of different items of various years. **Base year does not change.** For example, if sales figures for the years 2005 to 2009 are to be studied, sales of 2005 will be taken as 100 and the percentage of sales for all other years will be calculated in relation to the base year. Base year need not always be the initial year. Carefulness is needed in selection of the base year. Base year has to be normal and representative in all respects, so that distorted results/analysis does not emerge.

If a figure in other year is less than the figure in the base year, the percentage will be less than 100 and it will be more than 100 if the figure of the other year is more than the base year figure.

Precautions: The following precautions must be exercised in preparing trend analysis:

1. **Base Year:** Base year or period should be selected carefully. Base year should be a normal or representative period, neither big or nor small. For any reason, if base year is not properly chosen, it may not give correct idea about the financial data. Generally, the initial year is taken as the base year. Any intervening or middle year can be taken as the base year, if the initial year is not found to be the normal year. If the figure of base year is very small, the percentages calculated based on base year do not give a true picture of the financial data.

2. **No Significant Change in Accounting Policies:** There should not be any material or significant changes in the accounting policies over the years covered for analysis. Consistency is necessary for the entire period to ensure comparability.

3. **Adjustment to be made for Price Variations:** The figures are also to be adjusted for the price variations during that period. If sales have grown by 90% during the period of three years, say from 2006 to 2009, the entire growth may not be due to increase in volumes alone, some growth could be due to increase in selling price. Actual growth can be understood, if suitable price increase adjustment is made.

Illustration No. 5

From the following data of Sathyavathi & Co., present trend analysis, taking the year 2006 as the base, draw conclusion.

Particulars	Year 2006	Year 2007	Year 2008	Year 2009
Net sales	50,000	30,000	1,00,000	1,50,000
Cost of goods sold	30,000	25,000	50,000	80,000
Expenses	6,000	4,000	9,000	11,000

Solution

Particulars	Year 2006	Year 2007	Year 2008	Year 2009	Trend percentage (Base year 2006)			
					2006	2007	2008	2009
Net sales	50,000	30,000	1,00,000	1,50,000	100	60	200	300
Cost of goods sold	30,000	25,000	50,000	80,000	100	83	167	267
Gross profit	20,000	5,000	50,000	70,000	100	25	250	350
Less: Expenses	6,000	4,000	9,000	11,000	100	67	150	183
Net profit	14,000	1,000	41,000	59,000	100	7	293	421

Method of Calculation: Using 2006 as the base year, the sales value in 2007 is shown below:

$$\text{Index in 2007} = \frac{\text{2007 sales}}{\text{2006 sales}} \times 100$$

$$= \frac{30{,}000}{50{,}000} \times 100$$

$$= 60$$

Interpretation: The year 2007 has been a very bad year. However, progress during the years 2008 and 2009 has been spectacular. Not only decline has been arrested, but significant growth has been made in those two years. During the year 2007, sales have gone down by 40%. However, production expenses and other expenses have gone down by 17% and 33% respectively. In other words, both these expenses have not similarly fallen, in line with sales. This means that a substantial portion of production and other expenses are fixed in nature. In consequence, the net profit has fallen significantly. This has resulted in decrease in net profit by 93%, though sales have fallen by 40%.

However, a substantial recovery has been made in the years 2008 and 2009. During the years 2008 and 2009, sales have gone up by 100% and 200 % respectively, but net profit has increased by 193 % and 321 %. It means the increase in net profit has excelled the increase in sales.

Conclusion: Behaviour of net profit during the years 2008 and 2009 confirms that substantial portion of expenses in production and other expenses are fixed in character.

This has contributed to an increase in net profit in percentage, compared to that of increase in sales.

Illustration No. 6

Make a trend analysis from the following figures of Ayusha Khan & Co., engaged in making ready garments for children. Take 2004 year as the base year and interpret.

Year	Sales	Stock	Profit before tax (PBT)
2004	1830	720	315
2005	2320	790	390
2006	2756	830	465
2007	3120	956	530
2008	3900	1169	687

Solution

Statement Showing Trend Analysis (Base Year 2004)

Year	Sales		Stock		Profit before tax (PBT)	
	Amount	Trend percentage	Amount	Trend percentage	Amount	Trend percentage
2004	1830	100	720	100	315	100
2005	2320	127	790	110	390	124
2006	2756	151	830	115	465	148
2007	3120	170	956	133	530	168
2008	3900	213	1169	162	687	218

Interpretation

1. Sales have continuously increased over the years up to 2008. The percentage is 213 in the year 2008, compared to 100 in 2004. In other words, sales have doubled over a period of four years. Progress over a period of four years is quite satisfactory.
2. Stock figures have increased steadily over the period indicating that the manufacturing activity—garments making—is in good progress.
3. Profit before tax has substantially increased. In the four-year period, it has more than doubled. The comparative increase of profit is a bit low in the year 2007, while it has been higher in the year 2008.
4. Out of all the years, performance in the year 2008 has been more impressive as profit before tax is 218%, while the sales are 213%. In other words, improvement in PBT has exceeded the increase in sales.

4.10 COMMON-SIZE STATEMENTS (CSS)

The common size financial statements are valuable in making comparisons between the firms in the same industry.

One of the simplest ways to understand financial statements is to examine the relationship of the various components to the total, comprising all such components. It is always difficult to understand when the amounts are in absolute amounts. When we compare the financial statements of two companies, say Theer & Co. and Tarkh & Co., and want to know which company enjoys lower cost of sales, absolute amounts create difficulty to understand. If sales of Theer Co. are ₹ 12 lakhs and cost of goods sold is ₹ 7 lakhs, while the respective figures for Tarkh & Co. are ₹ 22 lakhs and ₹ 17 lakhs respectively, it is difficult to say which company's cost of goods sold is less. When they are expressed that the cost of goods sold of Theer & Co. is 58% of sales, while it is 77% for Tarkh & Co., one finds the presentation understandable. Immediately, we understand that Theer & Co. enjoys a better gross margin, compared to Tarkh & Co. Since the magnitude of absolute numbers is removed, it is, comparatively, easy to understand.

The common-size statements, balance sheet and income statement are shown in analytical percentages. The CSS represents the relationship of different items, contained in the financial statement, with some common item by expressing each item as a percentage of the common item.

Preparation: The common-size statements may be prepared in the following ways:

(1) The totals of assets and liabilities in the balance sheet are taken as 100.

(2) The individual assets are expressed as a percentage of total assets, i.e. 100. Different liabilities are calculated as a percentage in relation to total liabilities. For example, if total assets are ₹ 10 lakhs and debtors' value is ₹ 1,00,000, debtors will be 10% of the total assets.

$$\frac{1,00,000}{10,00,000} \times 100$$

(3) Similarly, in Common Size Income Statement, each item is stated as percentage of the net sales. The percentages for different items are computed by dividing the absolute amount of that item by the common base (i.e. net sales) and then multiplying it by 100. The percentages, so calculated, can be easily compared with the corresponding percentages, in some other period.

Purpose: Impact of increase or decrease is immediately known as each item is compared to a common standard base of a fixed value, i.e. 100. Bulky figures are reduced to percentages for an early and immediate understanding.

To draw conclusion, items in the profit and loss account are to be compared with volume of sales. Significant relationship is to be established between the relevant items. For example, once a relationship is established between selling expenses and sales, a reduction in sales should at once result in reduction of selling expenses. If selling expenses do not, proportionately, decrease with the fall in sales, percentage of selling expenses increases. Similarly, increase in sales may increase selling expenses, but not administrative and financial expenses. In other words, percentage of fixed expenses should decrease with increase in volume of sales and vice versa, while percentage of variable expenses has to remain the same.

The common size statements are most useful in making comparisons between the firms in the same industry and for the same firm for a series of years, as each individual item is compared as a percentage to the total, which is always taken as 100.

Inter-firm comparison: Inter-firm comparison can be made to decide which firm has performed, more efficiently, during the same period and reasons can also be explained through analysis of common size statements of both the firms in the same industry.

Approach of comparative financial statements and common size statements: In comparative financial statements, comparison of financial statements of different years for the same firm is made, while comparison between different firms for the same year is made in common size statements.

Illustration No. 7

From the following balance sheets, prepare Common Size Balance Sheet.

Balance Sheet of Dotty Ltd.

[₹ in thousands]

	31.12.01	**31.12.02**
Share capital	250	250
Reserves	100	172
Debentures	180	150
Term loan	30	50
Creditors	70	36
Total	**630**	**658**
Fixed assets	500	500
Less: accumulated dep.	80	115
Net fixed assets	420	385
Cash	55	85
Debtors	65	75
Inventories	90	113
Total	**630**	**658**

(B.U., M.B.A., 2003)

Solution

Common Size Balance Sheet (₹ in thousands)

	31.12.01 ₹	%	31.12.02 ₹	%
Assets				
Fixed Assets (Net) (A)	**420**	**66.67**	**385**	**58.51**
Current Assets:				
Cash	55	8.74	85	12.92
Debtors	65	10.31	75	11.40
Inventories	90	14.28	113	17.17
Total Current Assets (B)	**210**	**33.33**	**273**	**41.49**
Total Assets (A + B)	**630**	**100.00**	**658**	**100.00**
Liabilities:				
Capital and Reserves:				
Share capital	250	39.68	250	37.99
Reserves	100	15.87	172	26.14
Total Capital and Reserves (A)	**350**	**55.55**	**422**	**64.13**
Long-term Debts				
Debentures	180	28.57	150	22.80
Term loan	30	4.76	50	7.60
Total Long-term Debts (B)	**210**	**33.33**	**200**	**30.40**
Current Liabilities				
Creditors	70	11.12	36	5.47
Total Current Liabilities (C)	**70**	**11.12**	**36**	**5.47**
Total Debt (B+C)	**280**	**44.45**	**236**	**35.87**
Total Liabilities (A+B+C)	**630**	**100.00**	**658**	**100.00**

Illustration No. 8

Following are the Income Statement and Balance Sheet of Theer & Co. for the year 2005 and 2006. Prepare the CIS and CBS for these two years.

Draw tentative conclusions.

Income Statements for the year 2005 – 2006

[₹]

	2005	2006		2005	2006
To cost of goods sold	5,00,000	3,75,000	By net sales	6,00,000	5,00,000
To General expenses	10,000	10,000			
To Selling expenses	15,000	20,000			
To Net profit	75,000	95,000			
	6,00,000	5,00,000		6,00,000	5,00,000

Balance Sheet as on 31st December, 2005 and 2006

[₹]

Liabilities	2005	2006	Assets	2005	2006
Capital	3,00,000	4,00,000	Land	50,000	50,000
Reserves	1,50,000	72,500	Building	1,50,000	1,35,000
Secured loans	50,000	75,000	Plant	1,50,000	1,35,000
Creditors	1,00,000	1,37,500	Furniture	50,000	70,000
Outstanding expenses	50,000	75,000	Cash	80,000	90,000
			Debtors	70,000	1,30,000
			Finished stock	1,00,000	1,50,000
	6,50,000	7,60,000		6,50,000	7,60,000

Solution

Common Size Income Statement

	Amount (₹)		Percentages	
	2005	2006	2005	2006
Net sales	6,00,000	5,00,000	100.00	100.00
Less: Cost of goods sold	5,00,000	3,75,000	83.33	75.00
Gross: Profit (1)	1,00,000	1,25,000	16.67	25.00
Less: General expenses	10,000	10,000	1.67	2.00
Selling expenses	15,000	20,000	2.50	4.00
Total operating expenses (2)	25,000	30,000	4.17	6.00
Net Profit (1 – 2)	75,000	95,000	12.50	19.00

Common Size Balance Sheet

	Amount (₹)		Percentages	
	2005	2006	2005	2006
Land	50,000	50,000	7.70	6.58
Building	1,50,000	1,35,000	23.07	17.76
Plant	1,50,000	1,35,000	23.07	17.76
Furniture	50,000	70,000	7.70	9.21
Total fixed assets (1)	4,00,000	3,90,000	61.54	51.31
Cash	80,000	90,000	12.31	11.84
Debtors	70,000	1,30,000	10.76	17.10
Finished stock	1,00,000	1,50,000	15.39	19.75
Total current assets (2)	2,50,000	3,70,000	38.46	48.69
Total assets (1+2)	**6,50,000**	**7,60,000**	**100**	**100**

Contd...

Capital	3,00,000	4,00,000	46.15	52.63
Reserves	1,50,000	72,500	23.08	9.54
Net worth (3)	4,50,000	4,72,500	69.23	62.17
Secured loans	50,000	75,000	7.70	9.87
Creditors	1,00,000	1,37,500	15.37	18.09
Outstanding expenses	50,000	75,000	7.70	9.87
Total liabilities (4)	2,00,000	2,87,500	30.77	37.83
Net worth + Total Liabilities (3+4)	6,50,000	7,60,000	100	100

Tentative Conclusions:

1. **Profitability:** Sales have gone down by ₹ 1,00,000. However, net profit has increased by 6.5% [12.5% (2005) to 19% (2006)]. The net increase is due to a combination of the reduction of cost of goods sold by 8.33% [83.33% (2005) to 75% (2006)] and increase of total operating expenses by 1.83%. There is reduction in sales, along with increase in profits. This indicates that the firm has concentrated on the improvement of profitability, even sacrificing total quantum in sales.
2. **Cost of Production:** There has been a significant improvement in reduction of the cost of production in 2006, compared to 2005 as cost of sales has gone down from 83.33% (2005) to 75% (2006).
3. **Control on Operating Expenses:** Operating expenses have gone up by 1.83%. With the reduction in sales, selling expenses might not have reduced. Once we have break up of expenses, area where control is needed can be identified. For further improvement of profitability, control on operating expenses is required. Inventory control would improve the profitability further.
4. **Accumulation of Stocks:** The percentage of finished stock has gone up from 15.39% to 19.75%, despite fall in sales. This indicates that the firm is experiencing accumulation of stocks.

Illustration No. 9

From the following data of X Ltd., compared with industry and its immediate competitor, shown in horizontal and vertical analysis, draw meaningful conclusion and recommend action proposed:

Horizontal Analysis for X Ltd.

Item	2005 (Base year)	2006	2007	2008
Sales	100 %	120 %	140 %	190 %
Cost of sales	100 %	89 %	83 %	81 %
Selling & administrative expenses	100 %	97 %	94 %	90 %
Financial expenses	100 %	124 %	155 %	210 %
Profit	100 %	101 %	100 %	101 %

Vertical Analysis for X Ltd. Compared with Industry and its Immediate Competitor (Year 2008)

Item	X Ltd.	Industry average	Immediate competitor (Z Ltd).
Sales	100	100	100
Cost of sales	63	72	71
Selling & administrative expenses	6	7	7
Financial expenses	21	13	12
Profit	10	8	10

Solution

Horizontal Analysis: When we look at the performance of X Ltd. from the year 2005 to 2008, horizontal analysis reveals that in percentage sales has been progressively inproving in a steady and healthy manner. Cost of sales as well as selling and administrative expenses have been falling year after year. This shows their control and resultant improvement in their respective areas, in terms of reduction in costs, year after year. Financial expenses of X Ltd. have been increasing year after year. To a certain extent, increase is reasonable as more funds are needed to support increasing trend in sales. However, percentage of increase in financial expenses is more than that in sales, which does not appear justifiable. This reflects the deteriorating control on financial expenses. While production, selling and administrative departments have been better controlling costs, this type of performance is not seen with finance department. Severity of the increase in financial expenses is so significant, and in consequence, trend of net profit in X Ltd. is stagnant.

Vertical Analysis: The above trend, shown in horizontal analysis, is confirmed from the vertical analysis. The percentage of financial expenses in X Ltd. for the year 2008 is more than the industry as well as its immediate competitor. On other hand, share of expenses of production and purchase departments is less, when compared with industry as well as immediate competitor. Control of expenses in those departments is reflected in the cost of sales. Even share of selling and administrative expenses is also less.

Both horizontal and vertical analysis confirms that purchase, production and selling and administrative departments have been improving their performance year after year, with lesser percentage of increase, compared to percentage of increase in sales.

Conclusion: The efficiency of purchase, production, and selling and administrative departments is neutralized by the inefficiency of finance division in X Ltd. This situation requires further investigation to improve its profitability. Even, in the absence of efficiency of finance division, it is interesting to note, profitability of X Ltd. is still higher than the industry and equal to its immediate competitor. Profits have been stagnant during the years 2005-08. If finance division's performance is improved, X Ltd. can improve its profitability further.

A combined horizontal and vertical analysis indicates the areas where focus of action and improvement is immediately essential to show better results.

Check Your Understanding

(A) State whether the following statements are True or False

1. Comparative financial statements indicate the direction of the movement of the firm.
2. It is not obligatory under Companies Act, 1956 for all companies to prepare the final accounts of companies by presenting current year, along with comparative figures of previous year.
3. External analysis is better than the internal analysis.
4. In horizontal analysis, balance sheets of different years of the same firm are kept side by side for comparison.
5. Ratio analysis is one of the major tools of financial analysis.
6. The traditional financial statements provide all the relevant and required information to show the strength and weakness of the company.
7. The purpose of financial analysis is to diagnose the information content in financial statements so as to judge the profitability, the financial soundness of the firm and chalk out the way to improve the existing performance.
8. 'Liquidity' refers to the ability of the firm to pay, as and when the obligations and debts fall due for payment.
9. Different parties need the financial statements for the same purpose.
10. Horizontal analysis is used for comparing data of several years of one firm, while vertical analysis is used for comparing the relative performance of different firms in the same industry for the same period.
11. Net worth plus long-term borrowings is equal to capital employed.
12. Net worth includes long-term and short-term borrowings.
13. In trend analysis, base year is taken as 100 for each component and other years' figures are compared to calculate the relevant percentage of that year to understand the direction of change.
14. In trend analysis, even if the figure of base year is very small, the percentages of other years, calculated based on base year, give a true picture of the financial data.
15. In Common-size Statements (CSS), each asset is reduced to percentage of the total assets for comparing with the preceding year's figures to draw meaningful conclusion.
16. In comparative financial statements, comparison of financial statements of different years for the same firm is made, while comparison between different firms for the same year is made in common size statements.

Answers

1. True 2. False 3. False 4. True 5. True 6. False 7. True 8. True
9. False 10. True 11. True 12. False 13. True 14. False 15. True 16. True.

(B) Objective Questions (Identify what is most appropriate)

1. Financial analysis is meant for
   (i) Identifying strength of a firm.
   (ii) Identifying weakness of a firm.
   (iii) Identifying strengths and weaknesses of a firm.

2. Financial analysis can be made from
   (i) Profit and Loss Account.
   (ii) Balance Sheet.
   (iii) Items in Profit and Loss Account and Balance Sheet, by establishing relationship.

3. Financial analysis is meant for the following category.
   (i) Trade creditors.
   (ii) Trade creditors and suppliers of long-term debt.
   (iii) Investors.
   (iv) Management.
   (v) All above categories specified in (i), (ii), (iii) and (iv).

Answers

1. (iii) 2. (iii) 3. (v)

Descriptive Questions

1. What is the need of analysis of financial statements? **(4.1 and 4.2)**
2. What is meant by 'Financial Analysis'? Discuss the purpose and objective of the analysis of financial statements for management and others interested in the business. **(4.2 to 4.4)**
3. What are the objectives of analysis of financial statements? Who are the users of financial analysis? **(4.3 and 4.4)**
4. Show the break up of a balance sheet in a vertical form and establish Net Assets = Capital employed. **(4.5)**
5. Write a brief note on the computation of net worth and capital employed. **(4.5)**
6. Explain the different types of financial analysis. **(4.6)**
7. What are the major tools of financial analysis and explain any three of them? **(4.7 to 4.10)**
8. Explain the purpose of comparative financial statements. Explain the technique for their preparation. **(4.8)**
9. Discuss the different aspects to be examined while interpreting comparative financial statements. **(4.8)**
10. Discuss the method of preparing Common Size Statement and explain whether inter-firm comparison and analysis is possible. **(4.10)**

Interview Questions

Q.1. Loss is reduced from capital account while presenting a balance sheet in a partnership firm. However, loss amount is shown as an asset separately in the balance sheet of a limited company. Why?

Ans. A partnership firm is a personal business belonging to a few individuals. Investment in a limited company is made by different shareholders, unlike a partnership firm. When loss appears, separately, on the assets side of the balance sheet, it is easily known to every one, who reads the balance sheet. Presentation in this manner alerts the investors, who read the financial statements, before they invest. The Companies Act also prescribes the standard format of balance sheet. From the view-point of transparency and to meet the requirements of schedule VI of Companies Act, loss is to be separately shown on the assets side in the balance sheet.

Q.2. What is the basic purpose of analysis of financial statements?

Ans. Management is interested to know the strength and weakness of the firm, in terms of finance. Absolute figures in the financial statements—Profit and Loss Account and Balance Sheet—are always big and difficult to understand, easily. Analysis of financial statements helps the management to understand the figures better for quicker and meaningful decisions.

Q.3. Name some of the tools available for analysis of financial statements.

Ans. The most important tools for financial analysis are:

(a) Comparative Financial Statements
(b) Trend Analysis or Trend Ratios
(c) Common Size Statements
(d) Ratio Analysis
(e) Fund Flow Analysis
(f) Cash Flow Analysis

Q.4. What do you understand by Trend Analysis?

Ans. Trend analysis helps in understanding the direction of movement of the firm, in terms of its operational results and financial position.

Q.5. What is meant by retained earnings and state its purpose?

Ans. Retained earnings are a part of profits which is retained in the business after payment of dividend. In other words, the left out amount of profits in the firm is called retained earnings. The purpose of retained earnings is for expansion and meeting the unforeseen situation of loss, the firm may face. When the firm sustains loss in a particular year, retained profits can be used for payment of dividend to satisfy the expectations of the shareholders.

Q.6. What is meant by operating profit?

Ans. Operating profit is the profit earned by the firm from its main or core activity, before deducting interest and tax.

Q.7. What is EBIT and state its purpose?

Ans. EBIT stands for earnings before interest and tax. EBIT is an aggregate of operating profits of the firm and its non-operating profits, before deducting interest and tax. In the absence of non-operating profits, operating profit of the firm becomes EBIT. EBIT shows whether the firm is profitable or not, even ignoring the incidence of financial charges and tax burden.

Q.8. Give an example to explain that you understand the difference between operating income and non-operating income?

Ans. Hotel President owns its own premises and is running its boarding and lodging business in the first and second floor of its premises, renting out its ground floor to State Bank of India. Boarding and lodging business is its main activity and income from this source is called operating income. Rent from the State Bank of India is its secondary source of income, which is called non-operating income, as this rental income is not connected to its main source of income.

❍❍

CHAPTER

5

Ratio Analysis

5.1 RATIO ANALYSIS AND ITS NEED

The traditional financial statements–Profit and Loss Account and Balance Sheet—do not give all the information related to the financial operations of a firm. Profit and Loss Account shows the results of operations, while Balance Sheet mirrors the financial position on a particular date in respect of assets, liabilities and owner's equity. No doubt, the information they provide is extremely useful. Much can be learnt from them, but not from the shape the information is in.

> **Ratio analysis is the process of determination and interpretation of numerical relationship based on financial statements.**

Accounting ratios are derived from Profit and Loss Account and Balance Sheet. Analysis of financial statements is an important aid to financial analysis. For proper analysis, three requirements are essential.

- Selection of appropriate information from financial statements, relevant to the decision,
- Arrange the information to highlight its significant relationship, and
- Draw inferences and conclusions.

The focus of financial analysis is on identification of key figures and highlighting the significant relationship that exists between them.

Ratio analysis is an important and powerful technique or method, generally used for analysis of financial statements. Ratios are used as yardstick for evaluating the financial condition and performance of a firm. Analysis and interpretation of various accounting ratios gives a better understanding of financial condition and performance of the firm in a better manner than the perusal of financial statements.

5.2 MEANING OF FINANCIAL RATIO

Ratio is derived by dividing one number by another number. Simply, it is a quotient of two arithmetical numbers. Wixon, Kell and Bedford in their book, *'Accountant's Handbook'* have defined ratio as "an expression of the quantitative relationship between two numbers. "A financial ratio or ratio is a relationship between two accounting figures, expressed mathematically. Ratio analysis helps us to ascertain the financial condition of the firm. In financial analysis, a ratio is compared against a benchmark for evaluating the financial position and performance of a firm. Financial ratios help us to summarize large quantities of financial data to make qualitative judgment about the firm's financial performance.

5.3 SCOPE OF ACCOUNTING RATIOS OR RATIO ANALYSIS

A single figure, by itself, has no meaning. For instance, it is stated that the net profits of a company is, say, ₹ 5 lakhs. It throws no light on the adequacy or otherwise. The figure of net profit has to be studied in relation to other variables. How does it stand in relation to sales, total assets and capital employed? If a comparison is made with other firms in the industry or its immediate competitor, meaningful conclusions can be drawn. Accounting ratios are indicators. They serve as pointers for further investigation. With a single financial ratio, no conclusion is to be arrived at. The ratios are to be studied in relation to each other, in comparison of the past ratios of the firm as well as ratios of the industry, better with its immediate competitors to understand their relative significance and impact.

Accounting ratios are the symptoms of health of an organization like blood pressure, pulse or temperature of an individual. A physician never comes to any conclusion, based on one symptom. In a similar manner, accounting ratios are the indicators for further investigation.

After calculating one ratio, no conclusion is to be arrived at. Ratios are to be studied together, not in isolation. Quite often, ratios are looked upon as ends in themselves rather than as means to an end. Ratios alone are not sufficient for taking final decisions. They cannot be taken as final to decide about good or bad financial position of the business. Ratio analysis throws the weak or strong areas of the firm. Though they are indicators, too much reliance should not be put on them.

Each ratio tells a story, individually. They are to be heard, but, no decision is to be taken on its individual story alone. After hearing stories of all ratios, collectively, final conclusion can be arrived at for the proposed action to be taken.

5.3.1 Advantages of Ratio Analysis

The following are the advantages of Ratio Analysis

1. **Simplifies Understanding of Financial Statements:** It facilitates accounting information in a summarized and simplified form to understand the financial statements in a quick and better manner.
2. **Facilitates Inter-firm Comparison:** Ratio analysis provides data for inter-firm comparison. They also reveal strong firms and weak firms, overvalued and undervalued firms.
3. **Makes Intra-firm Comparison Possible:** It makes comparison of performance of various divisions or departments in a firm. This facilitates the management to reward as well pull for better performance.
4. **Helps in Performing Management Functions:** It helps the management to discharge, effectively, the functions of management, such as planning, organizing, controlling, directing and forecasting.
5. **Prompt Decisions:** It provides information to management in taking prompt decisions and corrective actions in time.
6. **Profitable and Unprofitable Activities:** It helps in identifying profitable and unprofitable activities to help the management in improving their efficiency and achieving higher profits.
7. **Fixation of Responsibilities:** It provides assistance in fixing responsibilities for taking correcting action by the concerned in time.
8. **Improved Performance of Business:** It helps to improve the performance in respect of liquidity, solvency and profitability position of the business.

"Ratios can assist the management in its basic functions of forecasting, planning, coordination, control and communication."

– Batty J., Management Accounting

5.4 DIFFERENCES BETWEEN ANALYSIS AND INTERPRETATION OF FINANCIAL STATEMENTS

The terms analysis and interpretation are used term synonymously. However, they differ in the following respects:

1. The term 'analysis' is narrow, while the term 'interpretation' is broader, which includes 'analysis' too.
2. Analysis is the first step and interpretation follows.
3. Analysis implies classification of data in a logical order. Interpretation is concerned with the explanation of reasons for the results.

Analysis means methodical classification of data and presentation in a simplified form for easy understanding. Interpretation means assigning reasons for the behaviour in respect of the data, presented in the simplified form.

Once analysis is made, interpretation should follow. Only analysis does not serve any purpose, without interpretation. Interpretation is not possible without making the analysis. Both careful analysis and meaningful interpretation are important. Analysis and interpretation are complementary to each other. Both are essential. They are not independent, they go hand in hand.

Both the terms 'analysis' and interpretation can be explained with a simple example. An MBA class at VNS IT Institute (Bhopal) has intake strength of 60 students. Admission of students is 50 in the first round of counselling and its actual composition is not known. Once we classify the students, it is found that 35 are male and 15 are female. This classification of data is known as 'analysis'. So, the conclusion is 70% admissions are of male and 30% are female students in the current year. If admissions were 80% male students and 20% were female students during the last year, the current year trend is for female students' preference for MBA at his institute. The interpretation; there is a change in the trend of admissions. Reason for preference by female students may need further investigation. Female preference or bias, interpretation, would not have been possible without analysis of the actual data. Simple analysis of this data would not have served any purpose, if conclusion by interpretation is not derived.

Analysis of ratios, without interpretation, is meaningless and interpretation, without analysis, is impossible.

To have meaningful utilization of analysis, it is necessary to be clear to whom the analysis is made and their purpose or requirement for analysis. **Once the purpose is clear, the required ratios can be identified**. There are different formulae available for different ratios. For example, for calculation of debt-equity ratio, some authors take total liabilities, while others take only long-term liabilities for computation. Different reasoning is given for the treatment adopted. Similarly, while calculating current ratio, current liabilities are calculated, differently. Some authors include short-term bank borrowing in current liabilities, while some do not include, again, for different interpretations.

What is important and necessary is consistent approach. The same formulae and similar treatment have to be used for all the years of comparison. The approach should be equally uniform for all the firms for which comparison is made. Otherwise, distorted results would emerge and the interpretation based on the results would be meaningless.

Once the results are calculated, interpretation is necessary to understand and come to some prima facie signals. The results are not the end, they are the beginning for further investigation.

5.5 STANDARDS OF COMPARISON

A single ratio is not meaningful. For proper interpretation and understanding, ratios are to be compared. Comparison can be with

- **Past ratios,** i.e. ratios from previous years' financial statements of the same firm.
- **Competitors' ratios,** i.e. similar ratios of the nearest successful competitors.
- **Industry ratios,** i.e. ratios of the industry to which the firm belongs to.
- **Projected ratios,** i.e. ratios developed by the firm which were prepared earlier, and projected to achieve.

5.6 TYPES OF RATIOS

Several ratios can be grouped into various classes, according to the activity or function they perform. We have already discussed in the previous chapter that there are several groups of persons—creditors, investors, lenders, management and public—interested in interpretation of the financial statements. Each group identifies those ratios, relevant to its requirements. They wish to interpret ratios for those purposes they are interested in to take appropriate decisions to serve their own individual interests. In view of the diverse requirements of the various users of ratios, the ratios can be classified into four categories:

A. **Liquidity Ratios:** They measure the firm's ability to meet current obligations.

B. **Leverage Ratios:** These ratios show the proportion of debt and equity in financing the firm's assets.

C. **Activity Ratios:** They reflect the firm's efficiency in utilizing the assets.

D. **Profitability Ratios:** These ratios measure overall performance and effectiveness of the firm.

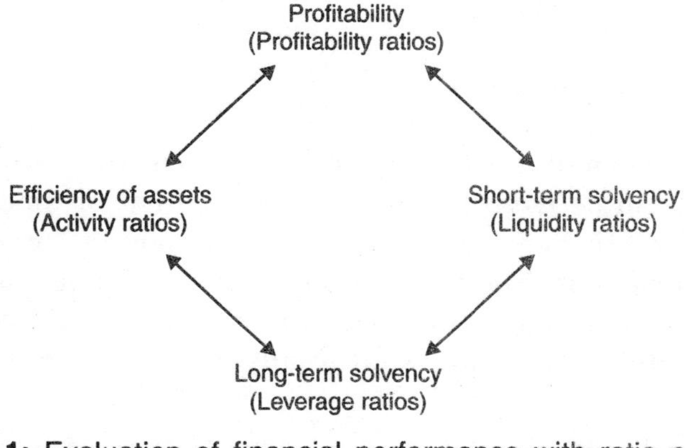

Fig. 5.1: Evaluation of financial performance with ratio analysis

5.7 LIQUIDITY RATIOS

Liquidity ratios are used to test the short-term solvency or liquidity position of the company. Liquidity ratios are highly useful to creditors and commercial banks that provide short-term credit. Short-term refers to a period not exceeding one year. Liquidity ratios measure the firm's ability to meet the current obligations, as and when they fall due. These ratios provide an answer whether short-term liabilities can be paid out of short-term assets or not.

A firm should ensure that it does not suffer from lack of liquidity, equally excess liquidity.

In the absence of adequate liquidity, the firm would not be able to pay creditors, who have supplied goods and services on the promised due date. Firm's goodwill suffers, in case of default in payment. In fact, dissatisfied suppliers, normally, refuse to supply, further. Who can finance, indefinitely? Loss of creditworthiness may even result in legal problems, finally culminating in the closure of business of a company. If the firm maintains more liquidity, it will not experience any difficulty in making payments. However, a higher degree of liquidity is bad, as idle assets earn nothing, while there is cost for the funds. The firm's funds will be, unnecessarily, tied up in liquid assets. In consequence, profitability suffers.

Both inadequate and excess liquidity are not desirable. It is necessary for the firm to strike a proper balance between high liquidity and lack of liquidity.

The important ratios, which fall in this category, are as follows:

5.7.1 Current Ratio

Current ratio is defined as the relationship between current assets and current liabilities. It is also known as working capital ratio. This is calculated by dividing total current assets by total current liabilities.

$$\text{Current ratio} = \frac{\text{Current assets}}{\text{Current liabilities}}$$

The two basic components of the ratio are current assets and current liabilities. Current assets are those that can be realized within a short period of time, generally, one year. Similarly, current liabilities are those that are to be paid, as originally contemplated, within a period of one year. The components of current assets and current liabilities are shown hereunder. It is significant to note that even prepaid expenses are included in current assets as they have been paid, in advance, and are not needed to be paid again.

Similarly, **current liabilities include bank overdraft or cash credit account as they are, normally, sanctioned by the bank for a period of one year.** Technically, they are sanctioned for one year, but banks renew them, unless there are significant adverse reasons or firm does not seek renewal. **Reason for inclusion of bank overdraft in current liability category is the availability of official written sanction of bank for one year, only.**

Treatment of Bank Overdraft/Cash Credit: There is a difference of opinion about the treatment of bank overdraft/cash credit. Some authors treat them as current liabilities, while others treat as part of long-term liabilities. Bank sanctions overdraft/cash credit limit for a period of one year only. In the normal course, after the expiry of one year, the firm has to repay the borrowing. Firm does not, normally, repay as the bank renews the limit, at its request. However, the written sanction of the borrowing is invariably for one year only. **Unless bank renews the limit, technically, firm cannot avail the limit, further. We have treated Bank overdraft/cash credit as current liability, throughout the book.** Some authors treat them as long-term borrowings. The reason is firm continues to enjoy the borrowing, indefinitely, as bank renews the sanction, without much difficulty. Normally, bank gives renewal sanction, at the request of the firm, after submission of the required data, unless there are adverse features in the conduct of the account. **Students are advised to give specific mention of their treatment and give reasoning for the treatment given, either as current liabilities or long-term liabilities.** Whatever approach is adopted, the treatment is to be consistently followed.

COMPONENTS OF CURRENT RATIO

Current Assets	Current Liabilities
1. Cash in hand	1. Sundry creditors
2. Cash at bank	2. Bills payable
3. Marketable securities (short-term)	3. Bank overdraft/Cash credit
4. Short-term investments	4. Short-term advances
5. Sundry debtors, net of provision for bad and doubtful debts	5. Outstanding expenses
6. Bills receivable	6. Provision for income-tax
7. Inventory—Raw materials	7. Proposed dividend
8. —Work in process	8. Unclaimed dividend.
9. —Finished goods	9. Income Received in advance
10. Prepaid expenses	
11. Advance tax paid	
12. Accrued income	

Rationale of Current Ratio: As a conventional rule, a current ratio of 2:1 is considered satisfactory. The rule is based on the logic that in the worst situation, even if the value of current assets becomes half, the firm still will be able to meet its obligations fully. A 'two to one ratio' is referred to as 'Rule of thumb' or arbitrary standard of the liquidity of the firm. This current ratio represents a margin of safety for creditors. The need for safety margin is unevenness in flow of funds. If flows are smooth and uniform, margin can be small. All the current liabilities are to be paid in full. However, current assets available to liquidate them are subject to shrinkage for various reasons. While recovering sundry debtors, there can be bad debts. Inventories may become obsolete and become unsaleable. Unexpected losses may arise in marketable securities. A satisfactory current ratio can only meet these situations and satisfy its obligations, even when the value of the current assets declines.

Current Ratio of 2:1 should not be blindly and mechanically followed in an arbitrary manner. Firms with less than 2:1 ratio may be meeting the liabilities, without difficulty, though firms with a ratio of more than 2:1 may be struggling to meet their obligations to pay.

A current ratio of 1.33: 1 is considered as the minimum acceptable level by banks for providing working capital finance. Looking at the mere ratio in figures, no conclusion is to be arrived at.

Interpretation of Current Ratio: Current ratio is a measure of short-term solvency. If the current ratio is 1.5:1, the safety margin is 50%. A slight decline in the value of current assets may adversely affect the ability of the firm to meet its obligations. In case, if current assets fall by 50%, a rupee of sundry creditor can get only 75 paisa. In case, the current ratio is 3:1, the cushion is 200%. Even, if the value of current assets falls by a similar 50%, still there would be a cushion of 50% to current liabilities. From the view point of creditors, a high current ratio is always welcome. However, a very high current ratio may indicate slackness of management practices as the firm may have high level of inventories and a large amount of receivables, due to inadequate efforts on the front of collections. If the borrowing capacity of the firm is not adequately utilized, it is also an indication that the firm is not fully availing its opportunities. Therefore, a firm should have a reasonable current ratio. What is a satisfactory ratio depends on the nature of industry, conditions in capital market, ability of the firm to raise short-term funds and availability of short-term finances, in case of urgent need. For example, wholesale firms which buy goods on cash basis and extend credit to retailers require a high current ratio. On the other hand, retailers normally enjoy credit from wholesalers at the time of purchase and sell mostly on cash basis. Such firms need to have lower current ratio.

Current ratio is a test of quantity, not test of quality. It is essential to verify the composition and quality of assets before finally taking a decision about the adequacy of the ratio.

Composition of Current Assets More Important Than Current Ratio: Composition and quality of current assets are more important to comment on adequacy of current ratio Decision is not to be based on crude figures of current ratio alone.

Two companies may have the same amount of working capital, still, one firm's debt paying ability may be much weaker than the other. By collecting debtors more speedily, and managing the inventory efficiently, a firm may be able to meet the current obligations, even though its current ratio is lower than the standard ratio. On the other hand, a firm, with a higher current ratio, may be struggling to pay the creditors, even though its ratio is more than the standard ratio. Unless the composition of current assets and other ratios are anlayzed, one should not conclude, merely based on one ratio.

The current ratio is a crude-and-quick measure of the firm's liquidity. It is not a conclusive index of real liquidity of the firm. Current ratio is quantitative rather than a qualitative index of liquidity. It is quantitative as it refers to total current assets, without making a distinction of the proportion of current assets. Current ratio does not distinguish between highly liquid cash and highly illiquid inventory. This ratio treats both the situations alike. In real life, it is not so. Cash is immediately available for payments, while inventory is to be sold, more often, on credit and later to be collected. A qualitative measure takes into account the proportion of various types of current assets.

Causes for Favourable and Unfavourable Current Ratio: A high current ratio, due to the following causes, may not be favourable for the following reasons:

1. Slow-moving or dead stock/s, piled up due to poor sales.
2. Figure of debtors may be high as debtors are not capable of paying or debt collection system of the firm is not satisfactory.
3. Cash or bank balances may be high, due to idle funds.

On the other hand, a low current ratio may be due to the following reasons:

1. Insufficiency of funds to pay creditors.
2. Firm may be trading beyond resources and the resources are inadequate to the high volume of trade.

5.7.2 Problem of Window Dressing

Current assets and current liabilities are manipulated to show the current ratio is an artificially better way which is known as window dressing. In other words, current ratio presented is more favourable than the actual one. When such a manipulation is made, the current ratio loses its significance.

When current assets and current liabilities are manipulated to show a better picture than what is real, it is known as Window Dressing.

Let's assume that current assets are ₹ 90,000 and current liabilities are ₹ 60,000 in the normal times. Here, the current ratio is 1.5, which is not satisfactory. Firm makes special efforts, just before the end of the year, to realize ₹ 30,000 from debtors and pay off the creditors to that extent. In consequence, current assets become 60,000 and current liabilities 30,000. Now, the current ratio is 2. This ratio is considered, now, satisfactory. The position of current assets and current liabilities is not the true picture, as they do not appear, always, in the normal times. With efforts, the firm has managed to realize the debtors and paid the creditors, deliberately, to show a rosy picture, only at the end of the year.

Liabilities			Assets		
	Normal (except year end)	Year end only		Normal (except year end)	Year end only
			Cash	1,000	1,000
Creditors	40,000	10,000	Debtors	59,000	29,000
Bills payable	20,000	20,000	Stock	30,000	30,000
Total current liabilities *	60,000	30,000	Total current assets *	90,000	60,000
			Current ratio = Current Assets / Current liabilities	90,000 / 60,000 = 1.5	60,000 / 30,000 = 2

* Total current assets and total current liabilities are extracted from balance sheet, hence they are not equal.

Window dressing can be created in the following ways:

(i) Over valuation of closing stock.

(ii) Treating a short-term liability as long-term liability.

(iii) Omission of a liability.

(iv) Including obsolete inventory in the closing stock, instead of writing off.

(v) Inadequate provision for bad and doubtful debts. Not treating debtors as bad even though not recoverable and continuing to exhibit as if they are still recoverable.

(vi) Clearing creditors at the end of the year, bringing pressure on debtors for collection, only at the end of the year, to show a better picture.

The purpose of window dressing is to show a rosy picture of the firm, which is not a normal reality. The inference drawn on such a ratio will be faulty and deceptive.

Limitations of Current Ratio: Though current ratio is one of the important ratios for measuring liquidity, it suffers from the following limitations:

1. It is a crude measurement of liquidity. It measures only the quantity, not quality of current assets. All current assets are treated alike.
2. Ratio is calculated from the figures of the balance sheet, at the end of the year. This can be manipulated to show a better position, than what is actually at the end of the year.
3. Even if the ratio is favourable, the firm, still, may be in financial trouble as the current assets may consist more of non-moving stocks and unrealizable debtors. Current ratio is not a conclusive index of liquidity.
4. Current ratio differs from industry to industry and line of business.
5. If credit received from creditors is different from credit extended to debtors, the ratio would be different from the desirable ratio.

5.7.3 Liquid/Quick/Acid Test Ratio/Near Money Ratio

Liquid ratio establishes the relationship between liquid assets and current liabilities. Liquid assets are those that can be converted into cash, quickly, without loss of value. Cash and balance in current account with bank are the most liquid assets. Other assets that are considered, relatively, liquid are debtors, bills receivable and marketable securities (temporary, quoted investments purchased, instead of holding idle cash). Inventories and prepaid expenses are excluded from this category. Normally, most of the sales are on credit basis, in the normal course of business. So, the first stage in a sale is credit sale and the second stage is its realization. Inventory is excluded from liquid assets, as even the first stage of sale is not over. Inventories are considered less liquid as they require time for realising into cash and have a tendency to fluctuate, in value, at the time of realization. Prepaid expenses cannot be recovered in cash, normally; hence they are excluded.

$$\text{Quick ratio} = \frac{\text{Liquid assets}^*}{\text{Current liabilities}}$$

***inventories and prepaid expenses are excluded**

Interpretation of Liquid Ratio: Liquid ratio of 1:1 is, normally, considered satisfactory. However, firms with the ratio of more than 1:1 need not be liquid and those having less than the standard need not, necessarily, be illiquid. It depends more on the composition of liquid assets. Debtors, normally, constitute a major part in liquid assets. If the debtors are slow paying, doubtful and long outstanding, they may not be totally liquid. So, firms even with high liquid ratio, containing such type of debtors, may experience the problem in meeting the current obligations, as and when they fall due. On the other hand, inventories may not be, totally, non-liquid. To a certain extent, they may be available to meet the current obligations. So, all firms not having the liquid ratio of 1:1 may not experience difficulty in meeting the current obligations, depending on the efficient realization of inventories. On the other hand, firms with a better ratio (more than 1:1) may still struggle, if their debtors are not realized as per the schedule.

Quick ratio is a more stringent test of liquidity than the current ratio.

5.7.4 Cash Ratio or Absolute Liquid Ratio

Cash is the most liquid asset. Although receivables (debtors) and bills receivable are, generally, better realizable than inventories, there are doubts regarding their realization, more so in time. So, they are not considered immediately available for making payments and so are excluded for the calculation of cash ratio.

$$\text{Cash ratio} = \frac{\text{Cash \& Bank + Short-term Securities}}{\text{Current liabilities}}$$

Cash ratio of 1:2 is considered acceptable. It means ₹ 1 liquid assets are considered adequate to pay ₹ 2 of current liabilities, as all the creditors are not expected to demand cash, at the same time. More so, cash may be realized, at least something, from debtors and inventories too. Besides, sanctioned working capital limits of the bank are not always fully utilized and the unutilized drawing power is always available to the firm for immediate withdrawal of cash.

Illustration No. 1

From the following balance sheets of Richa Dixit & Co., calculate relevant liquidity ratios and interpret the company's liquid position.

Balance Sheet of Richa Dixit & Co.

(in lakhs)

	31.12.08	31.12.09
Share capital	250	250
Reserve	100	172
Debentures	120	120
Long-term loan	60	30
Creditors	50	22
Cash credit account from Bank	20	14
Provision for tax	30	50
Total	**630**	**658**

Fixed assets	500	500
Less: Accumulated dep.	80	115
Net fixed assets	420	385
Cash	55	85
Debtors	65	75
Inventories	70	83
Marketable securities	20	30
Total	**630**	**658**

Solution

Note: Cash credit is treated as current liability as bank sanctions the facility for a period of one year only. Some authors treat it as long-term liability as the funds remain with the firm almost in a permanent manner, as banks generally renew the sanction, if the conduct of the account is satisfactory.

Students are advised to specify the assumption with reasoning, clearly.

$$\text{Current ratio} = \frac{\text{Current assets}}{\text{Current liabilities}}$$

$$: \frac{\text{Cash + Inventories + Debtors + Market securities}}{\text{Creditors + Bank cash credit + Provision for tax}}$$

$$\text{Year 2008} \quad : \frac{55+65+70+20}{50+20+30}$$

$$: \frac{210}{100} : 2.1$$

Year 2009 : $\frac{85+75+83+30}{22+14+50}$

$= \frac{273}{86} = 3.17$

Liquid ratio : $\frac{\text{Liquid assets}}{\text{Current liabilities}}$

: $\frac{\text{Cash + Debtors + Marketable securities}}{\text{Creditors + Bank cash credit + Provision for tax}}$

Year 2008 : $\frac{55+65+20}{50+20+30}$

: $\frac{140}{100}$: 1.4

Year 2009 : $\frac{85+75+30}{22+14+50}$

$= \frac{190}{86} = 2.21$

Cash ratio or Absolute liquid ratio = $\frac{\text{Cash + Marketable securities}}{\text{Creditors + Bank cash credit account + Provision for tax}}$

Year 2008 : $\frac{55+20}{50+20+30}$

: $\frac{75}{100}$: 0.75

Year 2009 : $\frac{85+30}{22+14+50}$

$= \frac{115}{86} = 1.34$

Interpretation

Current Ratio: Normal current ratio, accepted as a thumb rule, is 2:1. In this case, the current ratio of Richa Dixit & Co. is 2.1 for the year 2008, which has improved to 3.17 for the next year 2009. So, current ratio is satisfactory. But, the current ratio shows that there are excessive idle funds, which is evident from the increased cash balance from 55 lakhs to 85 lakhs. Idle funds do not yield any return. In case, the increased cash holding has become a long-term feature, the firm can park the excessive idle funds in some marketable securities to get some additional return. In case, these excess funds are held for a short period only, it is ok.

Liquidity Ratio: Liquidity ratio of the firm for the year is 1.4 and has improved to 2.21. Normal liquidity ratio is 1:1 and so the liquidity ratio is satisfactory. Presence of idle cash funds, again, is confirmed.

Cash Ratio or Absolute Liquid Ratio: Cash ratio or Absolute liquid ratio is 0.75, which has, again, improved to 1.34. Normal ratio is 1:2. The cash ratio or absolute liquid ratio is also equally satisfactory. Presence of idle cash funds again is confirmed.

Conclusion about excessive idle funds is confirmed from the above three ratios.

Conclusion: Liquidity ratios of the firm are satisfactory and can meet its current obligations in time. However, attention of the firm is needed about the excessive idle funds.

Illustration No. 2

The following figures are extracted from the balance sheets of Sonal Ltd. as on 31st December.

[₹ in lakhs]

	2008	**2009**
Assets		
Fixed assets	140	200
Cash	1	2
Cash at bank	2	1
Debtors	90	60
Bills receivable	12	10
Stock	15	12
Prepaid expenses	6	2
Advance income tax	3	1
Total	269	288
Liabilities		
Equity share capital	120	120
General reserves	80	63
Share premium	14	14
Bank overdraft	22	35
Creditors	22	45
Bills payable	3	5
Provision for income tax	8	6
Total	269	288

Calculate any two liquidity ratios and comment on financial prudence of the company.

Solution

$$\text{Current ratio} = \frac{\text{Current assets}}{\text{Current liabilities}}$$

$$= \text{Cash + Cash at bank + Debtors + Bills receivable + Stock + Prepaid expenses + Advance income tax/Bank overdraft + Creditors + Bills payable + Provision for income tax}$$

Year 2008 $= \dfrac{1+2+90+12+15+6+3}{22+22+3+8}$

$= \dfrac{129}{55} = 2.34$

Year 2009 $= \dfrac{2+1+60+10+12+2+1}{35+45+5+6}$

$= \dfrac{88}{91} = 0.97$

Liquid Ratio $= \dfrac{\text{Liquid assets}}{\text{Current liabilities}}$

= Cash + Cash at Bank + Debtors +Bills receivable/Bank overdraft + Creditors + Bills Payable + Provision for income tax

Year 2008 $= \dfrac{1+2+90+12}{22+22+3+8}$

$= \dfrac{105}{55} = 1.91$

Year 2009 $= \dfrac{2+1+60+10}{35+45+5+6}$

$= \dfrac{73}{91} = 0.80$

Current Ratio: Acceptable normal current ratio is 2:1. In this case, the current ratio is 2.34 for the year 2008, which was satisfactory for that year. But, the ratio has reduced, drastically to 0.97 for the next year 2009.

So, current ratio is not satisfactory.

Liquidity Ratio: Liquidity ratio of the firm for the year 2008 is 1.91. Rule of thumb is 1:1. So, for the year 2008, the ratio is satisfactory. However, the ratio has slipped to 0.80. So, liquidity ratio for the year 2009 too is not satisfactory.

Conclusion: Regarding financial prudence of the company concerned, the firm has diverted its short-term sources for long-term uses. Current liabilities are short-term sources, while current assets are short-term uses. Current liabilities are to be used for the purchase of current assets only. In fact, a part of long-term sources are also to be used for short-term uses, such as current assets. In this case, a reverse situation has happened. Firm's fixed assets have gone up by ₹ 60 lakhs during the year 2009. This increase in fixed assets has come from short-term sources in the absence of increase in long-term sources—share capital, share premium and general reserves. For this reason only, both current and liquid ratios fell down drastically much below the acceptable levels in the year 2009, though they were satisfactory in the year 2008.

Even the general reserves have gone down from ₹ 80 lakhs to ₹ 63 lakhs. Reduction of ₹ 17 lakhs in general reserves may be due to loss or payment of dividend from general reserves, in the absence of profits, in the year 2009.

On account of these adverse features, firm's financial management is poor.

Illustration No. 3

A credit manager of Axis Bank Ltd. has received two applications from different firms, seeking working capital facility in the form of cash credit account. Quota fixed for the branch is almost over and only one of the applications can be sanctioned. Based on the following data, examine the relevant liquidity ratios and recommend only one application, with the reasons for recommendation.

Particulars	Company X Ltd. Amount (₹)	Company Z Ltd. Amount (₹)
Assets		
Cash balance	10,000	2,000
Bank balance	2,000	1,000
Debtors	40,000	90,000
Inventories:		
Raw materials	12,000	75,000
Finished goods	85,000	5,000
Fixed assets	30,000	1,00,000
Total	**1,79,000**	**2,73,000**
Liabilities		
Equity share capital	25,000	1,36,000
Preference share capital	5,000	12,000
Retained earnings	2,000	10,000
Long-term loans	15,000	30,000
Creditors	80,000	84,000
Bills payable	25,000	1,000
Outstanding expenses	12,000	—
Income received in advance	15,000	—
Total	**1,79,000**	**2,73,000**

Solution

Bank would examine liquidity ratios of both the firms to decide about which application is to be considered for sanction of working capital limit.

The relevant liquidity ratios to the bank are as under:

(1) Current Ratio,

(2) Liquid Ratio, and

(3) Cash Ratio

$$\text{Current Ratio} = \frac{\text{Current assets}}{\text{Current liabilities}}$$

$$\text{X Ltd.} = \frac{\text{Cash + Bank + Debtors + Inventories}}{\text{Bills payable + Outstanding expenses + Income received in advance}}$$

$$= \frac{10{,}000 + 2{,}000 + 40{,}000 + 12{,}000 + 85{,}000}{80{,}000 + 25{,}000 + 12{,}000 + 15{,}000}$$

$$= \frac{149}{132} = 1.13$$

$$\text{Z Ltd.} = \frac{2{,}000 + 1{,}000 + 90{,}000 + 75{,}000 + 5{,}000}{84{,}000 + 1{,}000}$$

$$= \frac{173}{85} = 2.03$$

$$\text{Liquid ratio} = \frac{\text{Liquid assets}}{\text{Current liabilities}}$$

$$\frac{\text{Cash + Bank + Debtors}}{\text{Creditors + Bills payable + Outstanding expenses + Income received in advance}}$$

$$\text{X Ltd.} = \frac{10{,}000 + 2{,}000 + 40{,}000}{80{,}000 + 25{,}000 + 12{,}000 + 15{,}000}$$

$$= \frac{52}{132} = 0.39$$

$$\text{Z Ltd.} = \frac{2{,}000 + 1{,}000 + 90{,}000}{84{,}000 + 1{,}000}$$

$$= \frac{93}{85} = 1.09$$

Cash ratio or Absolute liquid ratio =

$$\frac{\text{Cash+Bank}}{\text{Creditors + Bills payable + Outstanding expenses+Income received in advance}}$$

$$\text{X Ltd.} = \frac{10{,}000 + 2{,}000}{80{,}000 + 25{,}000 + 12{,}000 + 15{,}000}$$

$$= \frac{12}{132} = 0.09$$

$$\text{Z Ltd.} = \frac{2{,}000 + 1{,}000}{84{,}000 + 1{,}000}$$

$$= \frac{3}{85} = 0.03$$

Once, we tabulate the results of both the companies, the consolidated position, against the standard ratios, is as under:

Name of Liquidity Ratio	Standard Ratio	X Ltd.	Z Ltd.
Current ratio	2 : 1	1.13 : 1	2.03 : 1
Liquidity ratio	1 : 1	0.39 : 1	1.09 : 1
Cash ratio	1 : 2 or 0.50	0.09 : 1	0.03 : 1

Final Recommendation: Z Ltd. enjoys better current ratio and liquid ratio, compared to X Ltd. These ratios of Z Ltd. also comply with the standard norms that are acceptable. However, cash ratio of both the firms, X Ltd. and Z Ltd. is less than the standard ratio.

In view of the foregoing, application of Z Ltd. would be considered by the bank for sanction of working capital limit.

Illustration No. 4

Assuming that the current ratio is 2:1, what is the effect of each of the following transactions, individually, on the current ratio? State whether the ratio will improve, or decline, or have no change, taking any imaginary figures.

(A) Payment of current liabilities

(B) Sale of fixed assets for cash

(C) Cash collected from debtors

(D) Bills receivable dishonoured

(E) Issue of debentures

(F) Redemption of redeemable preference shares

(G) Cash purchases of stock

(H) Purchase of fixed assets on credit basis

Solution

Let us suppose that the current assets (CA) are ₹ 4 lakhs and current liabilities (CL) are ₹ 2 lakhs. In such a case, current ratio (CA: CL) is 2:1.

Effect of each transaction, in the absence of other transactions, on current ratio would be as under:

(A) Payment of Current Liabilities: Assume that current liability of ₹ 1 lakh is paid. Cash balance reduces by ₹ 1 lakh and current liabilities, say creditors, also reduce by ₹1 lakh. Now, current assets are ₹ 3 lakhs and current liabilities are ₹1 lakh. Current ratio becomes 3:1. So, current ratio gets improved.

(B) Sale of Fixed Assets for Cash: Consider that fixed assets are sold for ₹ 1 lakh. So, current assets become ₹ 5 lakhs (Cash balance increases), with no change in current liabilities. So, current ratio is 2.5:1. Current ratio has improved.

(C) Cash Collected from Debtors: Say, debtors for ₹ 1 lakh are collected. Debtors decrease by ₹ 1 lakh and to the same extent, cash increases by ₹ 1 lakh. There is no change in total current assets and current liabilities as a result of this transaction. One form of current asset is changed to another form of current asset. There is no effect on current ratio.

(D) Bills Receivable Dishonoured: Debtor, who has accepted the bill of exchange, has dishonoured it on the due date. Presume that bill receivable for ₹ 1 lakh is dishonoured. So, bills receivable is reduced by ₹ 1 lakh and debtors increase by ₹ 1 lakh. Both debtors and bills receivable are part of current assets. One of the current assets increases, while another decrease for the same amount. So there is no change in the total amount of current assets. There is no change in the current liabilities. Current ratio remains the same.

(E) Issue of Debentures: Let us presume that debentures are issued for ₹ 1 lakh. So, current assets become ₹ 5 lakhs, with no change in current liabilities. Now, ratio becomes 2.5 : 1. In this way, current ratio increases.

(F) Redemption of Redeemable Preference Shares: When preference shares, say ₹ 1 lakh, are redeemed, cash balance decreases by that amount and so current assets become ₹ 3 lakhs, with no change in current liabilities. So, current ratio is now 1.5 : 1. Current ratio declines.

(G) Cash Purchases of Stock: Cash purchases, say ₹ 1 lakh, are made then stock increases by ₹ 1 lakh and cash balance decreases by the same amount. In other words, there is no change in the current assets. There is no change in current liabilities too. Current ratio remains the same.

(H) Purchase of Fixed Assets on Credit Basis: When fixed assets are purchased, say by ₹ 1 lakh, their value increases by ₹ 1 lakh. There is no change in the current assets. Current assets are still ₹ 4 lakhs. However, current liabilities increase to ₹ 3 lakhs. from ₹ 2 lakhs. So, current ratio is now 1.33 : 1. Current ratio declines.

Tutorial note: Take the same amount for each transaction. Think about each transaction independently without considering other transactions.

Illustration No. 5

Current ratio = 2.8
Acid-test ratio = 1.5
Working capital = ₹ 1,62,000

Find out

(A) Current assets
(B) Current liabilities
(C) Liquid assets **(B.U., MBA, June, 2004)**

Solution

Current ratio = 2.8

It means, if current assets are 280, current liabilities are 100.

$$\text{Current ratio} = \frac{\text{Current assets}}{\text{Current liabilities}}$$

$$= \frac{280}{100}$$

$$= 2.8$$

Working capital = Current assets – Current liabilities

= 2.8 – 1

= 1.8

Working capital = 1,62,000

In such a case, if 1.8 is ₹ 1,62,000 current assets (2.8) would be ₹ 2,52,000 and current liabilities (1) would be ₹ 90,000.

The correctness can be checked with the current ratio.

$$\text{Current ratio} = \frac{2,52,000}{90,000}$$

$$= 2.8$$

$$\text{Acid test ratio or liquid ratio} = \frac{\text{Liquid assets}}{\text{Current liabilities}}$$

Liquid assets = Current assets – Stock

Liquid ratio is 1.5. It means, if current liabilities are 1, liquid assets are 1.5.

Current liabilities are ₹ 90,000, so liquid assets are ₹ 1,35,000.

$$\text{Acid test ratio or liquid ratio} = \frac{1,35,000}{90,000}$$

$$= 1.5$$

(A) Current assets = ₹ 2,52,000

(B) Current liabilities = ₹ 90,000

(C) Liquid assets = ₹ 1,35,000

5.8 LEVERAGE RATIOS

Solvency ratios are of two types, short-term solvency and long-term solvency. The financial position of a firm can be analyzed from these two perspectives or angles.

Liquidity ratios speak about short-term solvency. They are discussed above. Long-term solvency is understood through leverage ratios.

Leverage ratios indicate the long-term solvency of the firm.

> **Leverage ratios indicate the mix of debt and owners' equity in financing the assets of the firm.**

These ratios measure the extent of debt financing in a firm.

To whom these ratios are important? Short-term creditors like suppliers of raw materials and banks that provide working capital are concerned with short-term solvency of the firm. On the other hand, long-term creditors like debenture holders, financial institutions that provide long-term capital are concerned with long-term solvency. In fact, it is necessary for the firm to have short-term as well as long-term solvency for financial strength. Long-term solvency relate to the firm's ability to meet

(i) Interest on the debt, and

(ii) Instalment on the principal amount on the due date.

5.8.1 Debt-Equity Ratio

Debt-equity ratio is also known as external-internal equity ratio. **This ratio is calculated to measure the relative claims of outsiders and owners against the firm's assets.** The ratio shows the relationship between the external equities (outsiders' funds) and internal equities (shareholders' funds).

This ratio can be calculated in two ways. The numerator can only be long-term debt, such as debentures, mortgages or long-term loans. Alternatively, it can be total debt that includes both long-term and short-term liabilities. **We are of the opinion that current liabilities (short-term liabilities) should also be included in the total debt for calculating debt equity ratio.**

$$\text{Debt-equity ratio} = \frac{\text{Total debt}}{\text{Net worth}^*}$$

Or

$$\frac{\text{Long-term debt}}{\text{Net worth}^*}$$

***Net worth = Equity share capital + Preference share capital + Reserves and surplus**

The accumulated losses and deferred expenses, if any, should be deducted to arrive at net worth.

Treatment of Preference Share Capital: There is a difference of opinion on the inclusion of preference share capital in outsiders' funds (numerator) or shareholders' funds (denominator). The reason for including in numerator (total debt) is that the funds bear a fixed commitment in the form of dividend to the firm, similar to interest on debentures. If preference share capital is treated as borrowing, it is to be included in the numerator. It may be noted though the preference share capital bears the obligation of fixed dividend, yet, it is not in the nature of debt, a basic aspect to be remembered.

The preference share capital does not bring any financial risk to the firm, in the absence of profit and non-payment of dividend, which is the basic character of debt.

We are of the opinion to treat the preference share capital as shareholders' funds and be included in the net worth (denominator). Students are advised to give specific mention of the treatment and substantiate with reasoning.

Interpretation of Debt-Equity Ratio: As a general rule, there should be a mix of debt and equity. The owners want to conduct business with maximum outsiders' funds to take less risk for their investment. At the same time, they want to maximize their earnings at the cost and risk of outsiders' funds. Outsiders (lenders and creditors) want the owners' share on a higher side in the business so that their risk would be lower, with more safety to their funds.

Debt-equity ratio indicates the extent to which debt financing has been used in business. This ratio shows the level of dependence on the outsiders.

Total debt to net worth of 1:1 is considered satisfactory as a thumb rule. In some businesses, a high ratio of 2:1 or, even more, may be considered satisfactory, say, for example in the case of contractor's business. It all depends upon the financial policy of the firm, risk bearing profile, nature of business and industry average. Generally speaking, the long-term creditors welcome a low ratio as owners' funds provide the necessary cushion to them in the event of liquidation. It is a better approach to compare the DE ratio of the firm with that of the industry to which it belongs to for proper evaluation of the risk character of the firm. Every industry has its own peculiar characteristics relating to capital requirements. For example, in case of basic and heavy industries, the DE ratio is always higher compared to manufacturing concerns.

Impact of High Ratio: A high debt-equity ratio may be unfavourable as the firm may not be able to raise further borrowing, without paying higher interest, and accepting stringent conditions. This situation creates undue pressures and unfavourable conditions to the firm from the creditors.

Debt-trap: During the period of low profits, a high debt financed firm experiences difficulty to meet the fixed interest obligations on term-loan and debentures. Even to meet the working capital needs, the firm finds difficulty in getting credit. Creditors who agree to finance put stringent conditions, such as higher interest rate or more collateral security (secondary security) to cover their risk. In other words, it has to borrow on highly unfavourable terms. Thus, the firm gets entangled in debt-trap.

5.8.2 Proprietary Ratio

It is a different form of debt-equity ratio. This ratio establishes relationship between the proprietor's funds and the total tangible assets. The ratio is calculated as under:

$$\text{Proprietary ratio} = \frac{\text{Total shareholders' funds}}{\text{Total tangible assets}}$$

Tangible assets are calculated by eliminating value of goodwill and preliminary expenses, etc. from the value of total assets.

Significance

This ratio is of particular importance to the creditors and other lenders to the firm. They can find out the proportion of shareholders' funds in the total assets of the business. A higher proprietary ratio indicates a lower level of risk to the creditors.

> **Higher the proprietary ratio, the better it is. Higher ratio provides relatively less risk and more comfort to the creditors in the event of winding up of the company.**

In the event of liquidation, owners normally lose their money. With lower proprietary ratio greater risk would occur to the creditors as a part of their money may be also lost in the event of liquidation of the company.

> **Proprietary ratio measures conservatism of capital structure and shows the extent of threat to the outside creditors and lenders in the event of forceful liquidation of the company.**

5.8.3 Total Debt Ratio (TD Ratio)

Total debt ratio compares the total debts (long-term as well as short-term) with total assets.

$$\text{Total debt ratio} = \frac{\text{Total debt}}{\text{Total assets}}$$

$$= \frac{\text{Long term debts} + \text{Current liabilities}}{\text{Total assets}}$$

Interpretation of Total Debt Ratio: This ratio depicts the proportion of total assets financed by total liabilities. Impliedly, the shareholders finance the remaining assets.

> **A higher DE ratio or TD ratio shows the firm is trading on equity.**

In case, the rate of return of the firm is more than the cost of debt, it implies higher return to the shareholders. On the other hand, a lower ratio implies low risk to lenders and creditors of the firm and non-existence of trading on equity. So, neither higher nor lower ratio is desirable from the point of view of the shareholders.

> **A higher ratio is a threat to the solvency of the firm. A lower ratio is an indication that the firm may be missing the available opportunities to improve profitability.**

What we require is a balanced proportion of debt and equity so as to take care of the interests of the lenders, shareholders and firm, as a whole.

5.8.4 Coverage Ratios

Debt ratios are static and fail to indicate the ability of the firm to meet interest obligations.

The interest coverage ratio is used to test the firm's debt-servicing capacity.

The interest coverage ratio shows the number of times the interest charges are covered by funds that are ordinarily available to pay interest charges.

As taxes are computed on earnings after deducting interest, earnings before taxes are taken. Depreciation is a non-cash item. Therefore, funds equal to depreciation are also available for payment of interest charges. So, the interest coverage ratio is computed by dividing the earnings before depreciation, interest and taxes (EBDIT) by interest charges.

$$\text{Interest coverage} = \frac{\text{EBDIT}}{\text{Interest}}$$

Interpretation of Coverage Ratio: This ratio indicates the extent to which earnings can fall, without causing any embarrassment to the firm, regarding the payment of interest charges. The higher the IC ratio, better it is both for the firm and lenders. For the firm, the probability of default in payment of interest is reduced and for the lenders, the firm is considered to be less risky. However, too high a ratio indicates that the firm is very conservative in not using the debt to its best advantage of the shareholders. On the other hand, a lower coverage ratio indicates the excessive use of debt. When the coverage ratio is low, compared to the industry, it should improve its operational efficiency or retire the debt early, preferably expensive debt to have a coverage ratio comparable to the industry. It is well said, a single soldier cannot afford to be tipsy while the whole army is sober!

Limitations

1. IC ratio is based on the accrual concept of accounting. In practice, the interest is to be paid in cash. Therefore, it is better to compare the interest liability with the cash profits (based on cash inflows and outflows, both for incomes and expenses) of the firm.
2. This ratio also ignores the liability related to repayment of instalment of the firm.

Illustration No. 6

From the following balance sheets, calculate the relevant ratios and interpret the company's financial position.

Balance Sheet of Sirish Verma Ltd.

[₹ in lakhs]

	31.12.08	31.12.09
Share capital	250	250
Reserve	100	172
Debentures	180	150
Term loan	30	50
Bills payable	10	12
Creditors	60	24
	630	**658**
Fixed assets	500	500
Less: Accumulated dep.	80	115
Net fixed assets	420	385
Cash	55	85
Debtors	50	65
Bills receivable	15	10
Inventories	85	100
Prepaid expenses	5	13
	630	**658**

Solution

From the above Balance Sheet of Sirish Verma Ltd., the following ratios have been calculated for both the years.

(i) Current ratio $= \dfrac{\text{Current assets}}{\text{Current liabilities}}$

$= \dfrac{\text{Cash + Debtors + Bills receivable + Inventories + Prepaid expenses}}{\text{Bills payable + Creditors}}$

Year 2008 $= \dfrac{55+50+15+85+5}{10+60} = \dfrac{210}{70} = 3$

Year 2009 $= \dfrac{85+65+10+100+13}{12+24} = \dfrac{273}{36} = 7.58$

(ii) Liquid ratio $= \dfrac{\text{Liquid assets}}{\text{Current liabilities}}$

$= \dfrac{\text{Cash + debtors + bills receivable}}{\text{Bills payable + Creditors}}$

Year 2008 $= \dfrac{55+50+15}{10+60} = \dfrac{120}{70} = 1.71$

Year 2009 $= \dfrac{85+65+10}{12+24} = \dfrac{160}{36} = 4.44$

Solvency Ratio: Solvency ratios are of two types—short-term solvency and long-term solvency.

Short-term solvency ratios are current ratio and liquidity ratio. They are already solved above. In long-term solvency ratios, the most important ratio is debt-equity ratio.

$$\text{Debt-equity ratio} = \frac{\text{Total debt}}{\text{Shareholders' funds}}$$

Total debt represents both the long-term debt as well as short-term debt.

$$\text{Year 2008} = \frac{180 + 30 + 10 + 60}{250 + 100} = \frac{280}{350} = 0.8$$

$$\text{Year 2009} = \frac{150 + 50 + 12 + 24}{250 + 172} = \frac{236}{422} = 0.56$$

Some authors treat debt means only long-term debt. We have treated debt means both long-term and short-term debt as debt is a debt, whatever it may be.

Interpretation: Current ratio and liquidity ratios normally show short-term solvency of the firm it should be 2:1. For the year 2008, it has been 3 which has improved further to 7.58 for the year 2009. Main reason is idle cash balance. From 55 lakhs, it has gone up to 85, indicating that idle funds remain unutilized. This is confirmed by the liquidity ratio which has gone up from 1.71 to 4.44. This reflects the bad financial management of the firm as cash carries costs. These idle funds would have affected the profitability of the firm adversely.

Debt-equity ratio has been 0.8 for the year 2008 that has decreased further to 0.56. Normally, this ratio can be 2:1, depending on the industry the firm belongs to. This ratio shows the unutilized borrowing ability of the firm.

Finally, the financial management of the firm, overall, does not appear to be satisfactory.

Illustration No. 7

Calculate debt-equity ratio from the following balance sheet. Interpret the ratio. Remya Ltd. wants to raise a long-term loan of ₹ 4 lakhs from the market. Discuss its possibility to secure the loan at a competitive interest rate.

Balance Sheet of Ramya Ltd. as on 31st March, 2009

Liabilities	₹	Assets	₹
40,000 Equity shares of ₹ 10 each	4,00,000	Fixed assets	19,00,000
1,000 9% Preference shares of ₹ 100 each	1,00,000	Current assets	5,00,000
		Preliminary expenses	1,00,000
		Profit and loss account	60,000
General reserve	2,00,000		
Capital reserve	50,000		
Reserve for contingencies	10,000		
8% Debentures of ₹ 100 each	10,00,000		
Current liabilities	8,00,000		
	25,60,000		25,60,000

Solution

$$\text{Debt-equity ratio} = \frac{\text{Total outsiders debts}}{\text{Net worth*}}$$

= Long-term debts (debentures) + Current liabilities/Equity share capital + Preference share capital + All reserves – Profit and Loss account (debit balance) – Preliminary expenses (deferred expenses)

= 10,00,000 + 8,00,000/4,00,000 + 1,00,000 + 2,00,000 + 50,000 + 10,000 – 1,00,000 – 60,000

$$= \frac{18{,}00{,}000}{6{,}00{,}000} = 3$$

* While calculating net worth, accumulated loss in profit and loss account and deferred expenses, if any, are to be excluded.

Interpretation of Debt-equity Ratio: The debt-equity ratio is calculated to measure long-term solvency of the firm. This ratio also speaks about the financing policy adopted by the company. Generally speaking, a low ratio is favourable from the view point of long-term creditors, as it provides a greater safety margin to them.

Generally, a ratio of 1 : 1 is considered satisfactory. In some business, even a ratio of 2 : 1 is acceptable. What is an acceptable ratio depends on the nature of business and average ratio prevailing in the industry. However, in the current case, the debt-equity ratio is 3 : 1, which is rather very high. When the debt-equity ratio is high, borrowing company experiences difficulty to raise further long-term loans. Even if the firm is able to secure loans, it is highly difficult to secure at competitive interest rate. Firm should be ready to give higher interest rate and provide more collateral (secondary) security to give comfort to the loan provider. Lenders stipulate tougher conditions, even when they are willing to lend at higher interest rates to secure themselves.

5.9 ACTIVITY RATIOS

Firm invests funds of outsiders (lenders and creditors) and shareholders in various assets in business to make sales and profits. The better the management of assets, more would be sales and higher would be the profit.

Activity ratios reflect the management of assets and their effective utilization. If assets were converted into sales, with speed, profits would be more. Activity ratios bring out the relationship between the assets and sales.

These ratios are called Turnover Ratios. For example, funds invested in inventories are converted or turned over into sales. Activity ratios are employed to evaluate the efficiency with which the firm manages and utilizes the assets, in particular, debtors and stock.

Importance of Activity Ratios: Both current ratio and acid test ratio may give misleading results. If current assets include high volume of debtors, due to slow credit collections, current assets would be high, resulting in a high current and acid test ratio. These ratios fail to show the movement of debtors, as they do not exhibit the quality of debtors. Similarly, if inventories were non-moving or obsolete and not written off, current ratio would be high. It is important to calculate the turnover of these assets to ascertain their quality and how efficiently these assets are used in the business.

5.9.1 Inventory Turnover Ratio/Inventory Velocity

Inventory turnover ratio is also known as stock turnover ratio. This ratio shows the speed with which stock is turned over. It shows the number of times, stock is rolled over in a year. This is calculated by dividing cost of goods sold by average inventory.

$$\textbf{Inventory Turnover Ratio} = \frac{\textbf{Cost of goods sold}}{\textbf{Average inventory at cost}}$$

$$\text{Average inventory} = \frac{\text{Opening stock} + \text{Closing stock}}{2}$$

$$\begin{aligned}\text{Cost of goods sold} &= \text{Opening stock} + \text{Purchases} - \text{Closing stock}\\ &= \text{Net sales} - \text{Gross profit}\end{aligned}$$

Interpretation

It is better to compare the turnover ratio with the industry or its immediate competitor.

> **Inventory turnover ratio shows the velocity of stocks. A higher ratio is an indication that the firm is moving the stocks better; so, profitability in such a situation would be more. However, a very high ratio may show that the firm has been maintaining only fast moving stocks. The firm may not be maintaining the total range, with a low level of inventory, and so may be missing business opportunities, which may otherwise be available.**

Points for Consideration: Two points are worth noting in the formula, which are as follows:

(a) Instead of sales, cost of goods sold is to be taken, as inventory is valued at cost so that both numerator and denominator are on the same basis. If there is no possibility to calculate cost of sales, sales may be taken for calculating the ratio.

(b) It is the normal practice to liquidate the stocks at the end of the year. So, it is often advocated to take the average of opening stock and closing stock for a better picture. The situation does not, really, improve. Reason is simple. Closing stock of last year becomes the opening stock of the current year. At the end of last year too, liquidation of stocks would have occurred to bring out a better picture. So, averaging opening stock and closing stock at the end of the year, alone, may not show a real picture, if the firm has the tendency of liquidating the stocks, at the end of the year, to improve the ratio. Better ratio and picture would be available if the opening and closing inventory of each month are taken and average is arrived at.

However, in a situation where the stock figures at the end of every month are not available, average of opening and closing inventory at the end of the year is to be taken. In case, cost of goods sold is not available, sales are to be taken in their place. But, the ratio, in such a case, may not give totally satisfactory findings.

Days of Inventory Holdings: If we want to know the holding of inventory in the form of number of days, the following formula helps us.

$$\text{No. of Days of Inventory Holding} = \frac{360}{\text{Inventory turnover ratio}}$$

Ideal Standard: There is no standard ratio.

The ratio depends upon the nature of business. The ratio has to be compared with the ratio of the industry, other firms or past ratio of the same firm.

> **Every firm has to maintain certain level of inventory, be it raw materials or finished goods to carry on the business smoothly without interruption of production and loss of business opportunities. Inventory Turnover Ratio is a test of inventory management.**

This level of inventory should be neither too high nor too low. If the ratio is too high, it is an indication of the following:

(i) Blocking unnecessary funds that can be utilized somewhere else, more profitably.
(ii) Unnecessary payment for extra godown space for piled stocks.
(iii) Greater chances of obsolescence and pilferage.
(iv) Likely deterioration in quality.
(v) Above all, slow movement of stocks means slow recovery of cash, tied in stocks.

On the other hand, if the ratio is too low:

(i) Stoppage of production, in the absence of continuous availability of raw materials, and
(ii) Loss of business opportunities as full range of finished goods is not available, at all times.

To avoid the situation, the firm should know the position, periodically, whether it is carrying excessive or inadequate stocks for necessary corrective action in time.

In the ratio analysis, readers would have observed, by now, that it is difficult to lay down specific standards. It is always better to compare the ratios of the firm with the ratios of industry and other firms, in competition, for proper evaluation of the performance of the firm.

5.9.2 Debtors' (Receivables) Turnover Ratio/Debtors' Velocity

Firms sell goods on cash and credit. As and when goods are sold on credit, debtors (receivables) appear in accounts. Debtors are expected to be converted into cash over a short period, and they are included in current assets. To judge the quality or liquidity of debtors, financial analysts apply three ratios, which are:

(a) Debtors' turnover ratio
(b) Collection period
(c) Aging schedule of debtors

Debtors' Turnover Ratio/Debtors Velocity: Debtors turnover is found out by dividing credit sales by average debtors.

$$\text{Debtors' turnover ratio} = \frac{\text{Credit sales}}{\text{Average debtors}}$$

Debtors' turnover ratio indicates the number of times debtors are turned over each year. The higher the debtors' turnover, more efficient is the management of credit. If Bills Receivable is outstanding, they are to be added to the debtors as bills receivable have come into balance sheet, in place of debtors, which are, still, outstanding.

Debtors' turnover ratio is also known as debtors' velocity. However, if debtors' velocity is expressed in months, are to be converted into number as debtors' turnover ratio is always expressed in numbers. If debtors' velocity is stated as 3 months, in terms of numbers it is 4 (12/3).

Collection Period: The collection period is calculated in the following way:

$$\text{Collection period} = \frac{360^*}{\text{Debtors' turnover ratio}}$$

* 360 days are taken in place of 365 for convenience in calculation only.

Signals of Collection Period: Debtors' turnover ratio indicates the speed of their collection. The shorter the period of collection, the better is the quality of debtors. A short collection period indicates the efficiency of credit management. The average collection period should be compared with the credit terms and policy of the firm to judge the quality of collection efficiency.

Suppose the firm's credit policy is to extend 45 days credit and on calculation, the actual collection period is 60 days. This shows the laxity in collection. An excessively long collection period implies an inefficient credit and collection policy. On the other hand, too low a collection period is also not a favourable signal. The firm may be extending credit only to those customers, whose creditworthiness is beyond doubt so that there would be total certainty of payment, with no bad debts. The firm may succeed with no bad debts. But, in the process of rigid credit standards to have no bad debts, the firm may be missing the existing sales opportunities and, equally, possible improved profitability. If credit period is relaxed more, the firm may gain more sales and improved profitability, even after providing for the losses towards bad debts. The best way is to compare the collection period of the firm with the industry's average collection period and decide whether the firm has to make any change in the credit policy.

Aging Schedule: The average collection period measures the quality of debtors in the aggregate way. The aging schedule gives the detailed break up of debtors, according to the length of time, they have been outstanding. The aging schedule gives more information than the collection period as it spots the slow-paying debtors. Through this process, the firm can focus on those debtors, where attention is required to improve the collection efforts.

The different debtors, classified according to the age, are as under:

Aging Schedule of Debtors, as on...

Outstanding Period (Days)	**Debtors** (₹)	**% of Total**
0–30	2,00,000	20
31–35	1,80,000	18
36–40	1,20,000	12
41–50	1,00,000	10
51 and above	4,00,000	40
Total	10,00,000	100

Assume, the firm has a policy of allowing credit for 35 days. Out of the above total debtors, 62% are overdue. In other words, almost two thirds—a very big proportion—of the debtors have not been paying, in time. It is a serious situation. This requires an immediate and thorough review of the credit administration and in particular, selection of customers to whom goods are to be sold on credit in future. Otherwise, shortly, the firm would face a grave problem with major debtors remaining unpaid, affecting liquidity as well as profitability seriously. So, it may be necessary to initiate legal action, if necessary, in respect of 40% of the debtors, the last category in the above schedule, as they are likely to cause serious damage to the business. The chunk is high and age wise anxiety causing. As the period is above 51 days, a further detailed analysis is essential about the age of the debtors on a case-to-case basis.

5.9.3 Total Assets Turnover Ratio

Assets are used to generate sales. If the firm manages the assets more efficiently, sales would be more and profits would be equally up. This ratio is calculated by dividing sales by total assets.

$$\text{Total Assets Turnover Ratio} = \frac{\text{Sales}}{\text{Total assets}}$$

Importance: A firm's ability to make sales indicates its operating performance.

Caution: This ratio should be interpreted carefully. Between the two firms, a firm having old assets, with lower depreciated book value of fixed assets, may generate a higher ratio, compared a firm with new fixed assets purchased, recently. The firm, with old assets, may generate a misleading impression of higher turnover, without any actual improvement in sales.

5.9.4 Working Capital Turnover Ratio

The WCT ratio indicates the velocity of utilization of working capital of the firm during the year. The working capital refers to net working capital, which is equal to total current assets less current liabilities. The ratio is calculated as follows:

$$\text{Working Capital Ratio} = \frac{\text{Cost of sales or sales}}{\text{Average working capital}}$$

Working capital average can be calculated by averaging working capital at the beginning and end of the year.

Importance: This ratio measures the efficiency of working capital management. A higher ratio indicates efficient utilization of working capital and a low ratio shows otherwise. A high working capital ratio indicates a lower investment in working capital which has generated more volume of sales. Higher ratio improves the profitability of the firm. But, a very high ratio is also not desirable for any firm. This may also imply overtrading, as there may be inadequacy of working capital to support the increasing volume of sales. This may be a risky proposition to the firm. The ratio is to be compared with the trend of the other firms in the industry for different periods to understand the working capital ratio in its correct perspective, as far as possible.

5.9.5 Creditors/Payable Turnover Ratio

In course of business operations of the firm, a firm has to make credit purchases and incur short-term liabilities. Before the supply of goods, suppliers can check up the ratio to understand the normal payment period taken by the firm, for goods supplied by its creditors. The ratio calculated is similar to debtors' turnover ratio. In place of debtors, creditors are to be substituted and credit purchases in place of credit sales. The ratio can be calculated as under:

$$\text{Creditors' Turnover Ratio} = \frac{\text{Credit purchases}}{\text{Average trade creditors + Average bills payable}}$$

Creditors' Turnover Ratio is also known as Creditors' Velocity. However, if creditors' velocity is expressed in numbers, numbers is to be converted into months to ascertain the period of holding of creditors. If creditors' velocity is stated as 2, in terms of months it is 6 (12/2).

Similarly, to understand the number of days if the creditors are outstanding, the ratio is

$$\text{Payment Period} = \frac{360}{\text{Creditors' Turnover Ratio}}$$

Interpretation of Payment Period

If the period is more, it indicates that the firm defaults its payments and enjoys longer period of credit from the suppliers. Creditors can understand that they may be getting false promises, unless the picture has changed after the preparation of the financial statements they are going through in short run this position may improve, the profitability of the firm. But, the firm may be missing discounts and paying more prices for the goods purchased. To make proper interpretation, a comparative comparison of the period of credit with the other firms is needed.

Creditors' turnover ratio indicates the number of days the creditors are outstanding for payment. If the number of days is lower than the assured period of payment, it indicates liquidity of the firm. This would be good news to the suppliers as they can expect the payment within the assured period.

The following illustration explains the composition of and quality of current assets is more important to comment on adequacy of current ratio, not merely basing on crude figures of current ratio.

Illustration No. 8

Balance Sheet as on 31st March, 2006

[₹ in thousands]

	X	Z		X	Z
Liabilities			**Assets**		
Share capital	400	600	Fixed assets	100	100
Sundry creditors	600	400	Cash	50	10
			Stock	150	700
			Debtors	700	190
	1,000	1,000		1,000	1,000

Further inquires reveal the following information in respect of X and Z:

	Standard (Industry)	X	Z
Stock holding	3 months' turnover	2 months	6 months
Debtors' collection Period	30 days	20 days	100 days
Creditors' payment Period	30 days	30 days	90 days

(i) Calculate the current ratio of X and Z Ltd.

(ii) Why it is not desirable to draw conclusion after calculating the current ratio alone, without considering the composition of current assets and current liabilities?

(iii) Can the current ratio show the quality of assets? Comment on the composition of quality of current assets of both X and Z, based on the above information.

(iv) Any further comments you would like to make.

(v) What is the final conclusion?

Solution

$$\text{Current Ratio} = \frac{\text{Current Assets}}{\text{Current Liablities}}$$

$$= \frac{\text{Cash+Stock+Debtors}}{\text{Creditors}}$$

$$\text{Current Ratio of X} = \frac{50+150+700}{600}$$

$$= 1.5$$

$$\text{Current Ratio of Z} = \frac{10+700+190}{400}$$

$$= 2.25$$

(i) **Current Ratio of X and Z:** The current ratio of Z is 2.25, which appears better as it exceeds the standard ratio of 2, while the ratio of X is 1.5, low compared to the standard. The current ratio of Z is better than X. This is the picture, without considering other relevant factors.

(ii) **Stock Holding Ratio of X and Z:** When we look at the stock-holding, it is 2 months for X, while stock holding of the industry is 3 months' turnover. It indicates that X is holding less quantity of stocks, when compared with the norm of the industry. Similarly, debtors' collection period is 20 days against the average of industry 30 days. It shows that X is extending lesser period of credit on its credit sales. Alternatively, firm is choosing only those selective customers, whose integrity is beyond doubt and do not pose any problem for realizations. For these reasons, X may not be experiencing any liquidity problem, even with a lesser current ratio of 1.5.

Against this picture, Z is holding debtors for a longer period (100 days), against the industry average of 30 days. It means that Z is not receiving the collections in time. Collection efforts are slack. Z is also delaying creditors and is taking 90 days credit, against the industry's norm of 30 days. Its stock holding is also 6 months, against the industry's average of 3 months. For these reasons, current ratio of Z is better. But, this is not a healthy trend for Z. No credit comes without costs. Profits of Z may be under pressure. Further analysis gives answers.

Conclusion: Based on the current ratio alone, ratio of Z (2.25) is better, compared to X (1.5). However, further analysis has revealed that Z holds higher stocks and debtors, in terms of days, compared to industry, which is the reason for a higher current ratio. Z is taking more time too for payment of its creditors. On the other hand, X, even with a lower current ratio, is able to manage its stock and debtors, at a lower level, and is also more prompt in payments to creditors.

No conclusion is to be drawn based on current ratio alone. No ratio is to be studied in isolation. Ratios are to be studied together. Conclusion is to be drawn only after careful analysis of all the ratios.

(iii) **Quality of Assets: Current ratio does not show the quality of assets.** Current ratio shows the picture in quantity, but not in terms of quality.

(iv) **Further Comments:** It is desirable further to seek confirmation that X has not been missing business opportunities due to limited holding of stocks and quick realization of debtors. The above analysis indicates that X has been collecting its debtors, more speedily, and managing the inventory efficiently. For these reasons, X is able to meet the current obligations, even though its current ratio is lower than the standard ratio.

Final Conclusion: Unless the composition and quality of current assets and other ratios are analyzed, one should not conclude merely on the basis of one ratio alone.

Illustration No. 9

(A) The only current assets possessed by a firm are: cash ₹ 1,05,000, inventories ₹ 5,60,000 and debtors ₹ 4,20,000. If the current ratio for the firm is 2:1, determine its current liabilities.

(B) At the close of the year, a company has an inventory of ₹ 1,50,000 and cost of goods sold ₹ 9,75,000. If the company's turnover ratio is 5, determine the opening balance of inventory.

(B.U., MBA, 2004)

Solution

	₹
(A) Current assets	
Cash	1,05,000
Inventories	5,60,000
Debtors	4,20,000
Total current assets	10, 85,000

Current ratio of the firm is 2:1. If current assets are 2, current liabilities are 1.

$$\text{Current ratio} = \frac{\text{Current assets}}{\text{Current liabilities}} = 2$$

$$\frac{10{,}85{,}000}{\text{Current liabilities}} = 2$$

$$\text{Current liabilities} = \frac{10{,}85{,}000}{2}$$

$$= 5{,}42{,}500$$

(B) $$\text{Stock turnover ratio} = \frac{\text{Cost of goods sold}}{(\text{Opening stock} + \text{Closing stock})/2}$$

$$\frac{9{,}75{,}000}{(\text{Opening stock} + 1{,}50{,}000)/2} = 5$$

$$\frac{19{,}50{,}000}{(\text{Opening stock} + 1{,}50{,}000)} = 5$$

$$5\,(\text{Opening stock} + 1{,}50{,}000) = 19{,}50{,}000$$

$$5 \times \text{Opening stock} + 7{,}50{,}000 = 19{,}50{,}000$$

$$\text{Opening stock} = \frac{19{,}50{,}000 - 7{,}50{,}000}{5}$$

$$= \frac{12,00,000}{5}$$

$$= 2,40,000$$

The correctness can be checked with the calculation of an average stock, (2,40,000 + 1,50,000)/2 which works out to 1,95,000.

$$\frac{9,75,000}{1,95,000} = 5$$

So, opening stock = 2,40,000

Tutorial Note: In examinations, students are advised to check the correctness of their answer with the formulae, once the required information is found out.

Illustration No. 10

Complete the following Balance Sheet, assuming that only the Equity Share Capital and Retained Earning figures are given.

Liabilities	₹	Assets	₹
Equity share Capital	1,20,000	Fixed assets	?
		Stock	?
Retained earnings	1,20,000	Debtors	?
Creditors	?	Cash	?
Total (₹)	?	Total (₹)	?

Total debt is two-third of net worth. Turnover of total assets is 1.8;

30 days sales are in the form of debtors; turnover of inventory is 5; cost of goods sold in the year is ₹ 3,60,000; and the acid test is 1:1.

(B.U., MBA, 2003)

Solution

Total debt is two-third of net worth.

Net worth = Equity share capital + Retained earnings

= 1,20,000 + 1,20,000

= 2,40,000

Therefore, total debts, Creditors $= 2,40,000 \times \frac{2}{3} = 1,60,000$

Total liabilities = Equity capital + Retained earnings + Creditors

= 1,20,000 + 1,20,000 + 1,60,000

= 4,00,000

$$\text{Total liabilities} = \text{Total assets} = 4,00,000$$

$$\text{Inventory turnover ratio} = 5$$

$$\frac{\text{Cost of goods sold}}{\text{Stock}} = 5$$

$$\frac{3,60,000}{\text{Stock}} = 5$$

$$\text{Stock} = \frac{3,60,000}{5} = 72,000$$

Turnover of Total Assets is 1.8

Total assets have turned over 1.8 times. It implies that the firm has generated a sale of ₹ 1.8 for every rupee invested in total assets.

$$\text{Assets turnover ratio} = \frac{\text{Sales}}{\text{Total assets}} = 1.8$$

$$\text{Sales} = \text{Total assets} \times 1.8$$

$$= 4,00,000 \times 1.8$$

$$= 7,20,000$$

30 days sales are in the form of debtors. In other words, debtors have turned over 12 times in a year.

$$\text{Debtors turnover} = \frac{\text{Sales}}{\text{Debtors}} = 12$$

$$\text{Debtors} = \frac{\text{Sales}}{12}$$

$$= \frac{7,20,000}{12} = 60,000$$

Alternative way is

$$\text{Sales collection period} = \frac{\text{Debtors}}{\text{Sales}} \times 360 = 30$$

$$= \frac{\text{Debtors}}{7,20,000} \times 360 = 30$$

$$\text{Debtors} = \frac{7,20,000 \times 30}{360}$$

$$= 60,000$$

Acid test ratio 1:1

$$\text{Acid test ratio} = \frac{\text{Current assets} - \text{Inventory}}{\text{Current liabilities}}$$

In this ratio, there are only cash and debtors other than stock in current assets.

So, total cash and debtors are equal to current liabilities (creditors), i.e. ₹ 1,60,000.

Cash + Debtors = ₹ 1,60,000

Cash = ₹ 1,60,000 – Debtors

= ₹ 1,60,000 – 60,000

= ₹ 1,00,000

Now, let us fill the figures in the balance sheet.

Balance Sheet as on ....

Liabilities	₹	Assets	₹
Equity Capital	1,20,000	Fixed Assets *	1,68,000
Retained Earnings	1,20,000	Stock	72,000
Creditors	1,60,000	Debtors	60,000
		Cash	1,00,000
	4,00,000		4,00,000

* Balancing figure

5.10 PROFITABILITY RATIOS

The last group of financial ratios, more often used, is profitability ratios. Profit is the difference between revenue and expenses over a period, usually, one year. Revenue is sales plus other incomes.

Profitability ratios are to measure the operating efficiency of the company. Besides management, lenders and owners of the company are interested in the analysis of the profitability of the firm.

If profits are adequate, there would be no difficulty, normally, for lenders to get interest payment and repayment of principal. Owners want to get required rate of return on investment. The finance manager should evaluate the efficiency of the company in terms of profits. So, profit is important to every one associated with the firm.

Generally, two major types of profitability ratios are calculated:

- Profitability ratios based on sales, and
- Profitability ratios based on investment

5.10.1 Profitability Ratios Based on Sales

Profit is a factor of sales. Profit is earned after meeting all expenses, as and when sales are made. These ratios can be further divided into

- Gross Profit Ratio
- Expenses Ratios
- Net Profit Margin Ratio

(A) Gross Profit Ratio: The first ratio in relation to sales is gross profit ratio or gross margin ratio. The ratio can be calculated by

$$\text{Gross profit ratio} = \frac{\text{Sales} - \text{Cost of goods sold}}{\text{Sales}} \times 100$$

$$= \frac{\text{Gross profit}}{\text{Sales}} \times 100$$

Importance: The ratio reflects the efficiency with which a firm produces/sells its different products.

> **Gross profit ratio indicates the spread between the cost of goods sold and sales. An analysis gives the clues to the management how to improve the depressed profit margins. The ratio indicates the extent to which the selling price can decline, without resulting in losses on operations of a firm.**

Reasons for High Gross Profit ratio: High gross profit ratio is a sign of good management. Reasons could be:

- High selling price, cost of goods remaining constant,
- Lower cost of goods sold, sales price remaining constant,
- A combination of factors in selling price and costs of different products, widening the margin,
- An increase in proportion of volume of sales of those products that carry a higher margin, and
- Overvaluation of closing stock due to misleading factors.

Reasons for fall in gross profit ratio: Reasons may be:

- Purchase of raw materials at unfavourable rates,
- Over investment and/or inefficient utilization of plant and machinery, resulting in higher cost of production,
- Excessive competition, compelling to sell at reduced prices.

The finance manager has to analyze the reasons for the fall and initiate the necessary action, to improve the situation.

(B) Net Profit Ratio: Net profit is obtained after deducting operating expenses, interest and taxes from gross profit. The net profit ratio is calculated by

$$\text{Net profit ratio} = \frac{\text{Profit after tax}}{\text{Sales}} \times 100$$

Net profit includes non-operating income. So the later may be deducted to arrive at profitability arising from operations.

Interpretation

Net profit ratio indicates the overall efficiency of the management in manufacturing, administering and selling the products. Net profit has a direct relationship with the return on investment. If net profit is high, with no change in investment, return on investment would be high. If there is fall in profits, return on investment would also go down.

For a meaningful understanding, both the ratios—gross profit and net profit ratios—have to be interpreted together. If gross margin increases but net margin declines, this indicates that operating expenses have gone up. Further analysis has to be made which operating expense has contributed to the declining position for control. Reverse situation is also possible with gross margin declining and net margin going up. This could be due to increase of cost of production, without any change in selling price, and operating expenses reducing more to compensate the change.

The crux is that both the gross profit ratio and net profit ratio are to be analyzed, together, to find out the causes of increase/decline of profit for control and corrective action.

(C) Operating Expenses Ratios: To identify the cause of fall or rise in net profit, each operating expense ratio is to be calculated. This can be calculated by

$$\text{Operating expenses ratio} = \frac{\text{Operating expense}}{\text{Sales}} \times 100$$

The behaviour of specific expenditure is to be seen in comparison to the earlier years in the same firm. This throws light on the managerial policies and actions. For example, advertisement expenditure may go up, from year to year, with no significant increase in sales. This may be due to ineffective sales promotional expenditure in not bringing increased sales, despite more expenditure on advertisement. A general rise in advertisement expenses throughout the industry or inefficiency of marketing/advertisement department of the firm, alone, may be the contributing factor. The real reason can be better understood once the comparative ratios of the same expenditure in the other firms of the same industry are known for suitable action.

5.10.2 Profitability Ratios Based on Investment

Equity shareholders are the owners of the company. Profits belong to the owners of the firm who have invested their funds, in anticipation of return. If preference shares exist, profits after tax and dividend due to preference shareholders are to be considered for calculation of the return to equity shareholders. It is not important, whether the profits are distributed to the equity shareholders or left in the firm as retained earnings. The profitability of a firm can be analyzed from the point of view of owners in different perspectives, as follows:

(A) Return on Investment: The term investment may refer to total assets or net assets.

Return on investment is the primary ratio that is most popularly used to measure the overall profitability and efficiency of business.

(i) **Return on Total Assets:** 'Total assets' is the total amount appearing on the assets side of the balance sheet. However, in calculating total assets, fictitious assets like preliminary expenses, accumulated losses and discount on issue of shares are to be excluded. However, intangible assets like goodwill, patents and trademarks are to be included. Reason is that these intangible assets contribute for the development of sales and business, while the fictitious assets do not add anything for the growth in business.

When return on investment is calculated on total assets, it is called ROTA.

Total assets are related to operating profit. Operating profit is EBIT, in the absence of other income. EBIT is arrived at by adding financial charges (interest etc.) and tax to net operating profit. By this, we are separating financing effect from the operating effect.

When the profit and loss account includes non-operating income, non-operating income is excluded from the net profits while calculating EBIT. In a similar manner, non –operating assets are to be excluded from total assets. For example, if income from investments is excluded to arrive at EBIT, investments (non-operating assets) too are to be deducted from total assets. In other words, both numerator and denominator are to stand on similar footing for comparison.

The formula is

$$\text{ROI} = \text{ROTA} = \frac{\text{EBIT}}{\text{Total Assets}}$$

The above formula for ROTA ratio is commonly followed. The above formula is advocated on the ground that taxes are not controllable by the management. More so, firm's opportunities for availing tax incentives also differ, depending on the location, which is one of the many factors. So, it may be more prudent to use profits, before-tax, to calculate ROI.

Another alternative way to calculate ROTA is:

$$\text{ROI} = \text{ROTA} = \frac{\text{EBIT}(1-\text{T})}{\text{Total Assets}}$$

All said and done, what is left to the shareholders is the final amount of profit, after tax. Tax Management is also necessary, which is a significant part of management. So, some firms advocate the alternative formula. When we have different formulae, it is necessary to use the right formula, understanding the requirement of the situation.

Any one of the formulae can be used for comparison. The same formula is to be used for all the years for consistency.

(ii) **Return on Capital Employed:** Another way to calculate return on investment is through capital employed or net assets. Net assets are equal to net fixed assets plus current assets minus current liabilities. **Net assets are equal to capital employed. So, net assets and capital employed convey the same meaning, though called differently.**

Capital employed can be calculated in two ways:

Capital employed = Net worth + Long-term borrowings

OR

= Net fixed assets + Current assets – Current liabilities

Net worth includes preference share capital too, as already stated.

> **Return on net assets is called RONA. As net assets are equal to capital employed, the terms RONA and ROCE indicate the same. This ratio indicates the overall efficiency of business, before tax.**

The formula for calculation is

$$\text{ROI} = \begin{matrix}\text{RONA}\\ \text{OR}\\ \text{ROCE}\end{matrix} = \frac{\text{EBIT}}{\text{Capital employed}}$$

Adjustments: Firm may be having some investments, not connected to the business. Such investments and their income are not related to the business. So, both require adjustment. Investments are to be excluded from capital employed and income from investments is to be deducted from EBIT. This treatment is necessary for proper matching.

Another interesting point is interest. Interest on long-term loans only is to be added to arrive at EBIT, but not interest on the short-term loans as short-term loans are not included in the capital employed.

Both the numerator and denominator should always match with each other, otherwise distorted results appear.

Another alternative way is

$$\text{ROI} = \begin{matrix}\text{RONA}\\ \text{OR}\\ \text{ROCE}\end{matrix} = \frac{\text{EBIT}(1-\text{T})}{\text{Capital employed}}$$

The above ratio indicates the overall efficiency of business after tax.

Interpretation

1. ROI (ROTA and RONA) measure the overall efficiency of business.
2. The owners are interested in knowing the profitability of the firm in relation to the total assets and amount invested in the firm. A higher percentage of return on capital employed satisfies the owners that their funds are profitably utilized.
3. It indicates the efficiency of the management of various departments as funds are kept at its disposal for making investment in assets.

4. If the firm increases its size, but is unable to increase its profits proportionately, ROI (both ROTA and RONA) decreases. In such a case, increasing the size of the firm does not advance the welfare of the owners.
5. Inter-firm comparison is useful. Both the ratios of a particular firm should be compared with the industry average or its immediate competitor to understand the efficiency of the management in managing the assets profitably. So, a higher rate of return on capital employed, without comparison, does not imply that the firm is managed efficiently. Once a comparison is made with other firms, having similar characteristics, in the same industry, a fair conclusion is possible.
6. Ratios help in formulating the borrowing policy of the firm. The rate of interest on the borrowings should always be lower than the return on capital employed. Funds are to be borrowed only then.
7. With both the ratios, the outsiders like bankers, financial institutions and creditors know the viability of the firm so that they can lend funds comfortably.

Tutorial Note: There are several types of formulae for calculation of ROI, followed by different authors. Students are advised to give their assumption regarding computation.

(B) Return on Equity: In the real sense, equity shareholders are the real owners of the company. They assume the risk in the firm. Preference shareholders enjoy fixed rate of dividend and preference for payment of dividend, before dividend is distributed to equity shareholders. Similarly, in the event of the liquidation of the company, preference share capital has to be repaid first, before refunding to equity shareholders. Net profits after tax, after payment of dividend to preference shareholders, entirely belong to the equity shareholders. Equity shareholders would be interested to know what their real return is on the funds that belong to them.

This ratio for return on equity is calculated as under:

$$\text{Return on equity} = \frac{\text{Profit after tax} - \text{Preference dividend}}{\text{Equity shareholders' funds}}$$

Equity shareholders' funds are equity share capital, accumulated reserves (both general reserves and capital reserves), share premium and balance in profit and loss account less accumulated losses, if any. **Preference shareholders are not to be included as the dividend due to them has already been deducted from profits after tax.**

Interpretation

1. ROE indicates how well the firm has used the resources of owners.
2. Earning a satisfactory return is the most desirable objective of a business. This ratio is of great interest to the management as it is their responsibility to maximize the owners' welfare.

3. This ratio is more meaningful to equity shareholders as they are interested to know their return. Interpretation of this ratio is similar to return on investments. Higher the ratio, better it is to equity shareholders.

(C) Earnings Per Share: The profitability of the equity shareholders can be measured in other ways. One such measure is to calculate the earnings per equity share. The earnings per equity share is calculated by

$$\text{Earnings per equity share} = \frac{\text{Net profit after tax} - \text{Preference dividend}}{\text{Number of equity shares outstanding}}$$

Interpretation

1. EPS simply shows the profitability of the firm per equity share basis.
2. EPS calculation, over the years, indicates how the firm's earning power, per share basis, has changed over the years.
3. EPS of the firm is to be compared with the industry and its immediate competing firm to understand the relative performance of the firm.
4. As a profitability index, it is a widely used ratio.

Bonus Issue Adjustment: Adjustments for bonus issue should be made, while comparing EPS, over a period of time. Bonus shares are additional free shares issued to the existing equity shareholders, out of the profits of the company. Reserves and surplus profit is utilized for issue of bonus shares by transferring the amount to the equity share capital account. In the process of issue of bonus shares, there is no inflow or outflow of cash to the firm. If bonus shares 1:3 are issued, an existing shareholder, holding 3 shares, gets extra 1 share freely. Suppose, the market price of the share, before bonus issue, is ₹ 100, his total wealth was ₹ 300. Immediate to the issue of bonus shares, there is no increase in the wealth of the shareholders, even though additional shares are received. The reason is share price falls, normally, after bonus issue. The share price gets diluted to ₹ 75 (around), after issue, and so his total wealth remains the same i.e. ₹ 300 (75 × 4). The total wealth of a shareholder, before and after bonus issue immediately remains the same. EPS when calculated, after the issue of bonus shares, requires adjustment for proper comparison. For example, if a bonus issue in the proportion of 1:3 is made, then the adjustment factor 4/3 should be applied to adjust EPS of the year in which the bonus is made as well as the subsequent years. After the issue of bonus shares, if EPS is 9 for the subsequent year, and then adjusted EPS would be 12 (9 × 4/3) for comparison to the EPS of previous year. In other words, EPS 12 (after issue of bonus shares) is equal to EPS 9 (before issue of bonus shares), which is a right comparison.

EPS has to be adjusted to reflect the correct earning position, in view of the increased number of equity shares.

(D) Dividends Per Share (DPS): After payment of dividend to preference shareholders, balance net profit belongs to equity shareholders, whether distributed in the form of dividend or retained in business. However, equity shareholders are interested in the amount of dividend, distributed to them. Dividend per share is calculated as under:

$$\text{DPS} = \frac{\text{Total dividend distributed to equity shareholders}}{\text{Number of equity shares outstanding}}$$

Investors, both existing and potential, are interested in DPS rather than EPS.

(E) Dividend Pay-out Ratio or Pay-out Ratio: Dividend pay-out ratio is calculated to find out the proportion of dividend distributed out of earnings per share. For example, if the firm has an EPS and DPS of ₹ 5 and ₹ 3 respectively, DP ratio is 3/5, i.e. 60%. So, the firm has distributed 60% of PAT (profits after tax) as dividend among its shareholders. The ratio is calculated by

$$\text{Pay-out ratio} = \frac{\text{Dividend per equity share}}{\text{Earnings per equity share}}$$

Earnings not distributed are impliedly retained in the business for the purpose of expansion and growth of the firm. The proportion of retained earnings is equal to 1 – DP ratio. Hence, in the above case, the retained earnings ratio is 40%.

(F) Dividend Yield Ratio: Shareholders are the true owners, interested in the earnings distributed and paid to them as dividend. Therefore, dividend yield ratio is calculated to evaluate the relationship between the dividends paid per share and the market value of the share.

$$\text{Dividend yield ratio} = \frac{\text{Dividend per equity share}}{\text{Market value per equity share}}$$

(G) Price Earnings Ratio: This is the ratio that establishes the relationship between the market price of a share and its EPS. This ratio indicates the number of times the market price is covered by the earnings per share.

The ratio is calculated as per the following formula:

$$\text{Price earnings ratio} = \frac{\text{Market price per equity share}}{\text{Earnings per equity share}}$$

The price earnings ratio indicates investors' judgement or expectations about the firm's future performance. It signifies the number of years, in which the earnings can be equal to market price of share. This ratio is widely used by the security analysts and investors to decide whether to buy or sell the shares of a particular company at that price.

Generally, higher the price-earnings ratio, better it is for the management of that firm. If the P/E ratio falls, it is a cause of anxiety to the management of the firm as the investor's perception about the future performance of the company is not expected to be good. So, the management has to look into the causes for the fall of the ratio.

'Good Buy Decision'

> **For those who want to buy equity shares in a firm, if the P/E ratio of that company is low, compared to its competing firms, the equity shares of that company is a 'good buy', provided they anticipate the future performance of the company would also be brighter.**

For example, if the market price of X Ltd. is ₹ 80 and its EPS is 4, its P/E ratio is 20. Equally good performing company Z Ltd., its competitor in the industry, is quoted at ₹ 200 with EPS 8. So, its P/E ratio is 25. By calculating the P/E ratio, investor can decide whether the share of X Ltd. is undervalued and worth buying or not.

Significance

> **Price-earning ratio helps the investor in deciding whether to buy the shares of a company, at a particular market price, or book profit by selling at that rate.**

The decision also depends on the investor's perception about the future market.

(H) Capital Gearing Ratio: Capital gearing ratio refers to the proportion between fixed interest/dividend bearing funds to non-fixed interest/dividend bearing funds. The fixed interest/dividend-bearing funds include funds provided by the debenture holders and preference shareholders. Funds provided by equity shareholders do not bear fixed commitment, unlike preference shareholders and debenture holders.

In case the total amount of preference share capital, other fixed interest bearing loans and debentures exceed the equity shareholders' funds, the firm is said to be "high geared". In other words, if the capital-gearing ratio is more than one, it is said to be high geared. On the other hand, if preference share capital and other fixed interest bearing loans are less than equity shareholders' funds, capital gearing ratio is less than one, the firm is said to be "low geared". In case both are equal, the capital structure is said to be "even geared".

For computation of capital gearing ratio, funds that belong to equity shareholders, such as equity share capital, share premium and other reserves are to be considered. The capital-gearing ratio can be ascertained as under:

> **Capital gearing ratio = (Preference share capital + Debentures + Long-term Loan)/(Equity share capital + Reserves and surplus)**

Interpretation: If the capital gearing ratio is high, the profits available to equity shareholders would be subject to wider fluctuations, compared to a company that has a low gearing ratio.

Impact of Recession on Highly Geared Firms: During the recession period, all firms, generally, experience a steep fall in sales and profits of firms are always under great pressure. Profits start showing down, southward. In a high geared firm, proportion of fixed interest bearing long-term debts and debentures is always more than the non-fixed interest/dividend bearing funds. In other words, capital gearing is more than one. Firms have to pay fixed commitment of interest, whether there are profits or not. Firms cannot avoid payment of interest as the contractual obligations are of a long-term nature. In consequence, recession is a great curse to highly geared firms as profits available to equity shareholders are subject to wide fluctuations.

Recession is a big curse to highly geared firms.

Share prices of a high-geared firm are more speculative in nature than a low-geared firm. It is highly desirable to find out the capital-gearing ratio of the firms, before making investments, in particular, during recession times. Firms having higher capital gearing would fare more badly, compared to firms with lower gearing. It is desirable to avoid investment in high geared firms during the recession times.

These four financial ratios allow a good financial analyst to quickly and efficiently address the following questions or concerns:

Liquidity Ratios

- Can the company continue to pay its liabilities and debts, in time, as promised?

Leverage Ratios

- Is the company more burdened in the form of debt/borrowing, compared to the industry to which it belongs?

Activity Ratios

- Whether the assets are utilized efficiently?

Profitability Ratios

- What return the company is making on its capital investment? Is it competitive, compared to the industry return?

Illustration No. 11

Balance Sheet of Ram Ltd.

(₹)

Liabilities		Assets	
Equity share capital	80,000	Intangible assets	48,000
Reserves & surplus	40,000	Fixed assets	1,12,000
Mortgage	64,000	Investments	8,000
Bank overdraft	8,000	Stock	24,000
Creditors	32,000	Debtors	24,000
Provision for tax	16,000	Bank balance	24,000
	2,40,000		2,40,000

Calculate the following ratios:

(i) Current Ratio,

(ii) Liquid Ratio,

(iii) Solvency Ratio,

(iv) Proprietary Ratio, and

(v) Gearing Ratio.

(B.U., MBA, 2009)

Solution

Note: While calculating ratios, it is presumed, investments shown in the problem are short-term assets and money has been parked for a short-term duration. Hence, they are treated as current assets. Bank overdraft is treated as a current liability. Investments are also liquid assets as idle funds are parked for short-term duration. **It is better to make the assumptions made, at the beginning, while solving the problem, where more than one interpretation is possible.**

From the Balance Sheet of Ram Ltd., the following ratios have been calculated.

$$\text{(i) Current ratio} = \frac{\text{Current assets}}{\text{Current liabilities}}$$

$$= \frac{\text{Investment + Stock + Debtors + Bank balance}}{\text{Bank overdraft + Creditors + Provision for tax}}$$

$$= \frac{8{,}000 + 24{,}000 + 24{,}000 + 24{,}000}{8{,}000 + 32{,}000 + 16{,}000}$$

$$= \frac{80{,}000}{56{,}000} = 1.43$$

$$\text{(ii) Liquid ratio} = \frac{\text{Liquid assets}}{\text{Current liabilities}}$$

$$= \frac{\text{Bank balance + Debtors + Investments}}{\text{Bank overdraft + Creditors + Provision for tax}}$$

$$= \frac{24{,}000 + 24{,}000 + 8{,}000}{56{,}000}$$

$$= 1.00$$

Solvency Ratio: Solvency ratios are of two types—short-term solvency and long-term solvency.

Short-term solvency ratios are current ratio and liquidity ratio. They are solved above. In long-term solvency ratios, the most important ratio is debt-equity ratio.

$$\text{Debt-equity ratio} = \frac{\text{Total debt}}{\text{Shareholders' funds}}$$

Total debt represents both long-term debt as well as short-term debt.

$$= \frac{64{,}000 + 8{,}000 + 32{,}000 + 16{,}000}{80{,}000 + 40{,}000}$$

$$= 1{:}1$$

Some authors treat the debt as long-term debt only. We have treated debt as both long-term and short-term debt, as debt is a debt, whatever it may be.

(iv) $$\text{Proprietary ratio} = \frac{\text{Total shareholders' funds}}{\text{Total tangible assets}}$$

$$= \frac{80{,}000 + 40{,}000}{1{,}92{,}000}$$

$$= 0.625$$

(Tangible assets does not include goodwill)

(v) $$\text{Gearing ratio} = \frac{\text{Long-term loan (Mortgage)}}{\text{Equity share capital + Reserves and surplus}}$$

$$= \frac{64{,}000}{1{,}20{,}000}$$

$$= 0.53$$

Gearing ratio and capital gearing ratio are one and the same. Bank overdraft is not to be included in the numerator as it can be repaid and does not have fixed commitment.

Illustration No. 12

From the following available details, prepare balance sheet of Dimpy & Co. as on 31st March, 2006 and compute proprietary funds.

(a) Net Worth Turnover Ratio (on cost of sales) = 2

(b) Fixed Assets Turnover Ratio (on cost of sales) = 4

(c) Gross Profits Turnover Ratio = 20%

(d) Creditors Velocity = 73 days

(e) Debtors Velocity = 2 months

(f) Stock Velocity = 6

Reserves and surplus amount to ₹ 10,000. Closing stock was ₹ 5,000 in excess of opening stock. Gross profit was ₹ 60,000.

You can make the necessary assumption, where required.

Solution

Total Sales:

Gross profit was ₹ 60,000 and Gross profits turnover ratio = 20%

$$\text{Gross profit ratio} = \frac{\text{Gross profit}}{\text{Total sales}}$$

$$20\% = \frac{60{,}000}{\text{Total sales}}$$

$$\text{Total sales} = \frac{60{,}000}{20\%}$$

$$\text{Total sales} = 60{,}000 \times \frac{100}{20}$$

$$= 3{,}00{,}000$$

Debtors

Debtors velocity = 2 months. Debtors are turning over 6 times in a year.

$$\frac{\text{Sales}}{\text{Debtors}} = 6$$

$$\text{Debtors} = \frac{\text{Sales}}{6}$$

$$= \frac{3{,}00{,}000}{6}$$

$$= 50{,}000$$

Cost of Sales

$$\text{Cost of sales} = \text{Sales} - \text{Gross profit}$$

$$= 3{,}00{,}000 - 60{,}000$$

$$= 2{,}40{,}000$$

Net Worth

Net worth turnover ratio (on cost of sales) = 2

$$\frac{\text{Cost of sales}}{\text{Net worth}} = 2$$

$$\text{Net worth} = \frac{\text{Cost of sales}}{2}$$

$$= \frac{2{,}40{,}000}{2}$$

$$= 1{,}20{,}000$$

$$\text{Net worth} = \text{Capital} + \text{Reserves}$$

Capital = Net worth – Reserves

= 1,20,000 – 10,000

= 1,10,000

Fixed Assets

Fixed assets turnover ratio (on cost of sales) = 4

$$\frac{\text{Cost of sales}}{\text{Fixed assets}} = 4$$

$$\text{Fixed assets} = \frac{\text{Cost of sales}}{4}$$

$$= \frac{2{,}40{,}000}{4} = 60{,}000$$

Stock

Stock velocity = 6

$$\frac{\text{Cost of sales}}{\text{Average stock}} = 6$$

$$\text{Average stock} = \frac{\text{Cost of sales}}{6}$$

$$\frac{2{,}40{,}000}{6} = 40{,}000$$

$$\text{Average stock} = \frac{\text{Opening stock + Closing stock}}{2}$$

Closing stock was excess by ₹ 5,000, compared to opening stock. In other words, opening stock was lower than closing stock by ₹ 5,000.

Closing stock = 40,000 + 5,000/2

= 42,500

Opening stock = 42,500 – 5,000

= 37,500

The correctness can be checked:

$$\text{Average stock} = \frac{37{,}500 + 42{,}500}{2}$$

= 40,000

Purchases

To arrive at purchases, let us prepare Trading Account to get the balancing figure.

Trading Account

	₹		₹
To opening stock	37,500	By sales	3,00,000
Purchases*	2,45,000	Closing stock	42,500
Gross profit	60,000		
Total	**3,42,500**	**Total**	**3,42,500**

* Balancing figure–Purchases

Alternative way

Cost of sales	=	2,40,000
Increase in closing stock		5,000
Purchases		2,45,000

Creditors

Creditors velocity = 73 days. In other words, creditors have turned over 5 times in a year.

$$\text{Creditors turnover ratio} = \frac{\text{Purchases}}{\text{Creditors}}$$

$$\frac{\text{Purchases}}{\text{Creditors}} = 5$$

$$\text{Creditors} = \frac{\text{Purchases}}{5}$$

$$= \frac{2{,}45{,}000}{5}$$

$$= 49{,}000$$

Balance Sheet of Dimpy & Co. as on 31st March, 2006

Liabilities	₹	Assets	₹
Capital	1,10,000	Fixed assets	60,000
Reserves & surplus	10,000	Cash *	16,500
		Debtors	50,000
Creditors	49,000	Stock	42,500
	1,69,000		1,69,000

* Balancing figure.

Proprietary funds

Capital	=	1,10,000
Reserves and Surplus		10,000
Total		1,20,000

Tutorial Note: Both the terms, Debtors Turnover Ratio and Debtors Velocity, convey the same meaning. However, the problem has stated the velocity in months, so months are converted into number.

Illustration No. 13

There are two companies, X and Y, which have assets and liabilities of similar value. However, there is a difference in their capital gearing. The share capital of the two companies is:

X Ltd.:	**₹**
10,000 7% Preference shares of ₹ 10 each	1,00,000
500 Equity shares of ₹ 10 each	5,000
Total share capital	1,05,000

Y Ltd.:	
1,000 7% Preference shares of ₹ 10 each	10,000
9,500 Equity shares of ₹ 10 each	95,000
Total share capital	1,05,000

Assume that profits of both X Ltd. and Y Ltd. for different years are as under:

2008	₹ 20,000
2009	8,000

1. Calculate the capital-gearing ratio of companies X Ltd. and Y Ltd. Find out which company is highly geared and which is low geared.
2. Establish that the profits and dividend available to the equity shareholders would depend on the capital gearing of the companies, though total share capital and profits of both companies are one and the same.
3. Which company's shares are more speculative?

Solution

1. Capital gearing ratio $= \dfrac{\text{Fixed dividend/interest bearing funds}}{\text{Non-fixed dividend/interest bearing funds}}$

$$= \frac{\text{Preference share capital + Debentures + Long-term loan}}{\text{Equity share capital + Reserves and surplus}}$$

$$\text{X Ltd.} = \frac{1{,}00{,}000}{5{,}000} = 20$$

$$\text{Y Ltd.} = \frac{10{,}000}{95{,}000} = 0.11$$

The company that has gearing more than 1 is highly geared and company whose gearing is less than 1 is low geared. So, gearing of X Ltd. is abnormally high as its capital gearing is 20, while gearing of Y Ltd. is very low geared as its gearing is 0.11.

2. Now, let us prove that dividend available to equity shareholders depend on the capital gearing of the respective companies, though total capital, profits, amount of assets and other liabilities are one and the same.

	Year 2008 Dividend available to equity share capital	Year 2009 Dividend available to equity share capital
X Ltd.:		
Profits	20,000	8,000
Less: Pref. dividend	7,000	7,000
Profit available to equity shareholders	13,000 = 260 %	1,000 = 20 %
Equity share capital	5,000	5,000
Y Ltd.:		
Profits	20,000	8,000
Less: Pref. dividend	700	700
Balance available to Equity shareholders	19,300 = 20.3 %	7,300 = 7.7 %
Equity share capital	95,000	95,000

Conclusion: Profits of both the companies X Ltd. and Y Ltd., are one and the same. Total capital of both the companies is also that same ₹ 1,05,000. Assets and other liabilities of both the companies are also the same. However, Capital gearing of X Ltd. is very high (20), while capital gearing of Y Ltd. is very low (0.11). When the profits are high, highly geared firm X Ltd. enjoys high profits on equity share capital (260%), against equity share capital of low-geared firm Y Ltd. (20%). A steep increase in profits has benefited equity shareholders of a highly geared firm.

With fall in profits from ₹ 20,000 to ₹ 8,000, profits of X Ltd., available to equity shareholders, has fallen from 260% to 20.3%. Fall is 92.2%. However, share of profits, available to equity shareholders of Y Ltd., has fallen from 20 % to 7.7%. Fall is only 61.5%. Equally, a steep fall in profits has adversely affected equity shareholders of a highly geared firm.

3. There is wide fluctuation in profits from ₹ 20,000 to ₹ 8,000. As a consequence, dividend to equity shareholders of a high-geared firm is subject to wide fluctuations (260% to 20.3%), compared to a low-geared firm (20 % to 7.7 %). Fall in share of profits available to equity shareholders is very steep in a high-geared firm, compared to a low-geared firm. Market value of equity share of a company depends on profits as well as dividend declared. So, share prices of a high-geared firm is more speculative than a low-geared firm.

Conclusion: X Ltd. equity shares are more speculative as the company is highly-geared as compared to Y Ltd.

5.11 TRADING ON EQUITY

Normally, assets of the firm are financed by debt and equity. Suppliers of the debt would look to the equity as margin of safety. The use of debt in financing the assets has a number of implications:

Implications of Debt: Firstly, debt is more risky to the firm, compared to equity. Whether the firm makes profit or not, interest on debt has to be paid. If interest and instalment are not paid, there may even be a threat of insolvency.

Secondly, debt is advantageous to the equity shareholders. The equity shareholders can retain control with a limited stake. They can find a way to magnify their earnings. When the firm is able to earn on borrowed funds higher than the interest rate paid, the return to owners would be magnified.

Thirdly, if the firm is burdened with more debt, it experiences greater difficulty in raising funds at the normal interest rate. If the firm's equity is thin, the financial risk to the creditors is high. Then, lenders demand a higher interest rate as compensation for assuming higher risk and also impose stringent conditions, even though they lend.

To illustrate, when the return on investment of a firm, say, is 20% and firm is able to borrow at 12%, the firm is able to make a saving of 8% by utilizing the borrowed funds. In the absence of borrowing, the equity shareholders would get a return of 20%, ignoring taxes. Due to borrowing, a saving of 8% is occurring. This saving of 8% increases the return of equity shareholders, resulting in more than 20%.

The process of magnifying the earnings of equity shareholders through the use of debt is called "Financial Leverage" or "Financial Gearing" or "Trading on Equity".

It is important to note that if the interest rate is higher than the rate of return on the project, it is not desirable to borrow, as the return on equity would get reduced.

A small illustration would better explain the picture.

Illustration No. 14

A company has equity share capital of ₹ 10,000 (F.V. ₹ 100) and 10% Debentures (F.V. ₹ 100) ₹ 40,000. Company's Profits are ₹ 50,000. Calculate the return to debenture holders and equity shareholder and interpret the reason for difference in return between debenture holders and equity shareholders, even though their face value is one and the same. Explain the reason for the difference.

Ignore income-tax.

Solution

Company's profits = 50,000

Interest on debentures = 4,000

Balance amount of profit available to equity shareholders = 46,000

$$\text{Earnings per equity share} = \frac{\text{Net Profit availbale to equity shareholders}}{\text{Number of equity shares outstanding}}$$

$$= \frac{46{,}000}{100}$$

= ₹ 460

Reason for difference in return: Each debenture holder, carrying a face value of ₹ 100, gets an interest of ₹ 10, while each equity shareholder, carrying a similar face value of ₹ 100, a return of ₹ 460. This is due to trading on equity. Equity shareholders get the gets advantage, at the expense of debenture holders.

Relationship between ROCE and Cost of Debt and Impact on ROE: When the return on capital employed is greater than the cost of debt, it is advantageous to borrow as the return on equity goes up. At the expense of debt, the beneficiaries are the equity shareholders. The risk the firm would experience on long-term borrowings is in the form of cost of debt as interest burden is permanent. Additionally, when the earnings fall, the ROCE also falls. But, in the process, the equity shareholders are the real sufferers! With the fall of ROCE, the return on equity goes down.

Debt can prove to be either beneficial or detrimental to the interests of equity shareholders. This may be an advantage and also a disadvantage to the equity shareholders. This is called trading on equity, which is a double-edged sword. The key is the relationship between the ROCE and cost of debt.

The concept of 'Trading on Equity' can be explained with the following example.

Illustration No. 15

Calculate the capital gearing from the following information:

	₹
Equity Share Capital	3,00,000
Reserves	2,00,000
5% Debentures	4,00,000
6% Preference Share Capital	3,00,000
10% Long-term Loan	1,00,000
	13,00,000

The firm earns a profit of ₹ 4,00,000, before interest and tax. Calculate the capital-gearing ratio and test it for 'Trading on Equity'. Tax rate may be taken at 50%.

Solution

The capital-gearing ratio has been calculated as follows:

Capital Gearing Ratio = (Preference share capital + Debentures + Long-term loan/(Equity share capital + Reserves and surplus)

(3,00,000 + 4,00,000 + 1,00,000)/(3,00,000 + 2,00,000) = 8,00,000/5,00,000 = 1.6

Since the capital-gearing ratio is more than one, the firm is said to be highly geared.

As the firm is highly geared, there should be 'Trading on Equity'. This can be verified as follows:

	₹
Profit, as given	4,00,000
Less Interest (20,000 + 10,000)	30,000
	3,70,000
Less Tax (at 50%)	1,85,000
Profit after tax	1,85,000
Less 6% Preference Dividend	18,000
Profit available to equity shareholders	1, 67,000

$$\text{Return on equity to shareholders} = \frac{\text{Profit after tax} - \text{Preference dividend}}{\text{Equity shareholders' funds}}$$

$$= \frac{\text{Profit available to equity shareholders}}{\text{Equity shareholders' funds}}$$

$$= \frac{1,67,000}{5,00,000} \times 100$$

$$= 33.4\%$$

Equity shareholders' funds comprise of both equity share capital and reserves.

$$\text{Return on capital employed} = \frac{\text{EBIT}}{\text{Capital employed}}$$

Capital employed = Net worth + Long-term borrowings

= (3,00,000 + 3,00,000 + 2,00,000) + (4,00,000 + 1,00,000)

$$= \frac{4,00,000}{13,00,000} \times 100$$

$$= 30.76\%$$

The return on capital employed is only 30.76%, while the return on equity shareholders' funds is 33.4%. The equity shareholders have been benefited, at the expense of fixed charge bearing funds. So, there is 'Trading on Equity'.

Tutorial Note: Equity Shareholders' funds do not include Preference share capital, while net worth includes Preference share capital.

5.12 IMPACT OF CAPITAL GEARING RATIO

If the rate of return on total capital employed is more than the average cost of fixed charge bearing funds, the residue goes to the benefit of equity shareholders. The surplus earned on the fixed charge bearing funds can be utilized for paying dividend to the equity shareholders, at a rate higher than the return on the total capital employed in the company. As a result, the return on equity would be more than the return on total capital employed. The process of magnifying the earnings, through the use of debt, is beneficial to equity shareholders.

However, the leverage can also work in the opposite direction too. When the return on capital employed falls below the cost of debt, the fall in return on equity would be higher. The equity shareholders suffer more. **So, a higher gearing ratio can prove to its advantage as well as disadvantage.**

> **The capital-gearing ratio influences the return to equity shareholders. Higher the capital gearing ratio, the impact, benefit as well as loss on equity shareholders would be greater.**

A change in EBIT results in a corresponding similar change; either increase or fall in return on capital employed. However, the corresponding change in ROE would be greater. When the capital-gearing ratio is high, an increase of EBIT would result in a higher increase of ROE. If the EBIT increases, say, by 25%, the increase of ROCE would be 25%. But, ROE would increase more than 25%. Similarly, if EBIT falls by 25%, the fall in ROCE would be 25%. But, the decrease in ROE would be more than 25%. A proper balance between the two funds (fixed charge and non-fixed charge bearing funds) is necessary in order to keep the cost of capital and risk at the minimum.

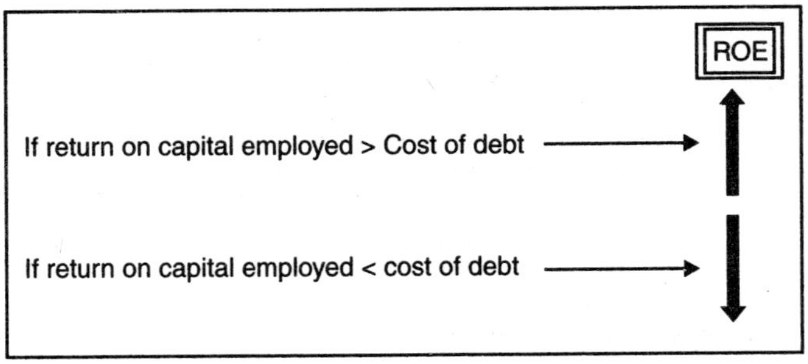

Fig. 5.2: Relationship between ROCE and cost of Debt and Impact of ROE

Illustration No. 16

The capital employed in a business has been financed as under:

	₹
Equity Share Capital	6,00,000
7% Preference Share Capital	4,00,000
6% Debentures	8,00,000
Reserves and Surplus	2,00,000
	20,00,000

The company earns a profit of ₹ 4,00,000 before interest. Tax rate may be taken 50%.

You are required to:

(A) Explain the principles of "Trading on Equity" and test the data for the principle.

(B) Elaborate the impact of changes in EBIT, both increase and decrease, on Return on capital employed (ROCE) and return on equity (ROE) with suitable examples, making the required valid assumption.

(B.U., MBA, 2003)

Solution

(A) The process of using the debt in capital employed to magnify the return of equity shareholders is called "Trading on Equity".

The extent of benefit of debt depends on capital gearing ratio. If capital gearing of the company is more than one, with the increase of EBIT, there would be a similar corresponding increase in ROCE. Similarly, ROE also increases. But, the important point is the % increase of ROE would be more than % increase of EBIT. The reverse is also true. To explain further, if EBIT increases by 10%, ROCE increases by 10%. But, ROE increases more than by 10%. If EBIT falls by 10%, the ROCE also falls similarly by 10%. But, ROE falls more than 10%. **For this reason, "Trading on Equity" is said to be a double-edged sword.**

The capital-gearing ratio can be ascertained as under:

Capital gearing ratio = (Preference share capital + Debentures)/(Equity share capital + Reserves and surplus)

$$= \frac{4,00,000 + 8,00,000}{6,00,000 + 2,00,000}$$

$$= \frac{12,00,000}{8,00,000} = 1.5$$

As the capital-gearing ratio of the company is more than one, the company is said to be 'highly geared'.

(B) Impact of Change in EBIT on ROCE and ROE

Capital employed = Equity share capital + Reserves + Preference share capital + Debentures + Long-term loan

= 6,00,000 + 2,00,000 + 4,00,000 + 8,00,000

= 20,00,000

$$\text{Return on capital employed} = \frac{\text{EBIT}}{\text{Capital employed}}$$

$$\text{Return on capital employed} = \frac{4,00,000}{20,00,000} \times 100$$

= 20%

$$\text{Return on equity} = \frac{\text{Profit after tax} - \text{Preference dividend}}{\text{Equity shareholders' funds}}$$

Profits available to equity shareholders:

EBIT	4,00,000
Less: Interest on debentures	
6% on ₹ 8,00,000	48,000
	3,52,000
Tax @ 50%	1,76,000

Profit after tax	1,76,000
7% Preference dividend on ₹ 4,00,000	28,000
Profits available to equity shareholders	1,48,000

$$\text{Return on equity} = \frac{\text{Profit after tax} - \text{Preference dividend}}{\text{Equity shareholders' funds}}$$

$$= \frac{1,48,000}{8,00,000} \times 100 = 18.5\%$$

Let us presume that there is a change of EBIT by 50%.

If EBIT increases by 50%:

EBIT becomes ₹ 6,00,000

$$\text{Return on capital employed} = \frac{6,00,000}{20,00,000} \times 100$$

$$= 30\%$$

Profits available to Equity shareholders:

EBIT	6,00,000
Less: Interest on debentures 6% on ₹ 8,00,000	48,000
	5,52,000
Tax @ 50%	2,76,000
Profit after tax	2,76,000
7% Preference Dividend on ₹ 4,00,000	28,000
Profits available to equity shareholders	2,48,000

$$\text{Return on equity to shareholders} = \frac{\text{Profit after tax} - \text{Preference dividend}}{\text{Equity shareholders' funds}}$$

$$= \frac{2,48,000}{8,00,000} \times 100 = 31\%$$

So, if EBIT increases by 50%, ROCE also increases by similar 50% (from 20% to 30%).

But ROE has increased by 67.57% (increased from 18.5% to 31% i.e. $\frac{12.5}{18.5} \times 100$)

If EBIT falls by 50%:

EBIT becomes ₹ 2,00,000

$$\text{Return on capital employed} = \frac{2,00,000}{20,00,000} \times 100$$
$$= 10\%$$

Profits available to equity shareholders:

EBIT	2,00,000
Less: Interest on debentures	
6% on ₹ 8,00,000	48,000
	1,52,000
Tax @ 50%	76,000
Profit after tax	76,000
7% Preference Dividend	
on ₹ 4,00,000	28,000
Profits available to equity shareholders	48,000

$$\text{Return on equity} = \frac{\text{Profit after tax – Preference dividend}}{\text{Equity shareholders' funds}}$$

$$= \frac{48,000}{8,00,000} \times 100 = 6\%$$

So, if EBIT falls by 50%, ROCE has also fallen by similar 50% (from 20% to 10%). But ROE has fallen by 67.57% (fell from 18.5% to 6% i.e. $\frac{12.5}{18.5} \times 100$)

This impact can be presented in pictorial presentation for quick understanding:

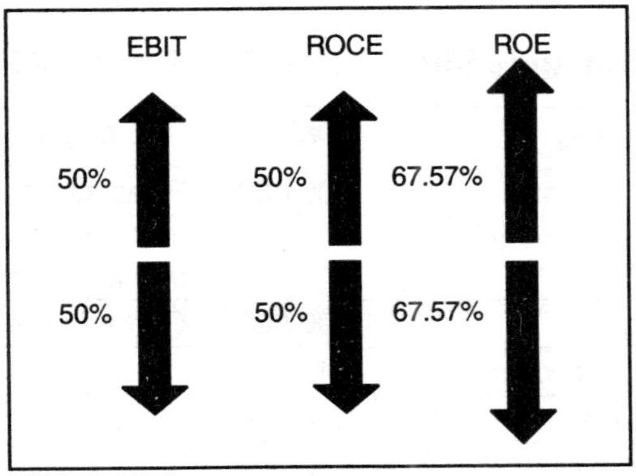

Fig. 5.3: Impact of EBIT on ROCE & ROE in a highly geared firm

Illustration No. 17

From the following information of Cherry & Cherry Company Ltd., prepare the balance sheet and compute the return on capital employed (ROCE), return on total assets (ROTA) and return on equity (ROE):

	₹
Current assets	1,00,000
Investments in treasury bonds	1,00,000
Fixed assets	5,00,000
Sales	5,00,000
Cost of goods sold	3,00,000
10% debentures	1,00,000
Income from treasury bonds	10,000
Interest on debentures	10,000
10% Preference share capital	1,00,000
Equity share capital	2,00,000
Capital reserve	1,00,000
Provision for tax at 30% of net profits	

Solution

Cherry & Cherry Company Ltd.
Profit and Loss Account for the year ended 31st March, 2005

	₹		₹
To cost of goods sold	3,00,000	By sales	5,00,000
To interest on debentures	10,000	By income from	
To provision for taxation	60,000	Treasury bonds	10,000
To net profit after tax	1,40,000		
	5,10,000		5,10,000

Balance Sheet as on 31st March, 2005

Liabilities	₹	Assets	₹
Equity share capital	2,00,000	Fixed assets	5,00,000
10% Pref. share capital	1,00,000	Investments in treasury bonds	1,00,000
Capital reserve	1,00,000	Current assets	1,00,000
Profit and loss account	1,40,000		
10% Debentures	1,00,000		
Provision for taxation*	60,000		
	7,00,000		7,00,000

Return on Capital Employed (ROCE) $= \dfrac{\text{EBIT**}}{\text{Capital employed}}$

EBIT = Net profits + Interest + Tax – Non-operating income
= 1,40,000 + 10,000 + 60,000 – 10,000
= 2,00,000

Capital employed = Net fixed assets + Current assets – Current liabilities (provision for taxation)
= 5,00,000 + 1,00,000 – 60,000
= 5,40,000

Alternatively

Capital employed = Net worth + Long-term loans/borrowings – (Non-current assets)
= (2,00,000 + 1,00,000 + 1,00,000 + 1,40,000) + 1,00,000 – 1,00,000
= 5,40,000

$$\text{Return on capital employed} = \frac{\text{EBIT}}{\text{Capital employed}}$$

$$\text{ROCE} = \frac{2,00,000}{5,40,000} \times 100 = 37.03$$

As operating income (EBIT) does not include non-operating income (income from investments in Treasury Bonds), capital employed also should not include investments in Treasury Bonds.

$$\text{ROTA} = \frac{\text{EBIT}}{\text{Total assets}}$$

$$= \frac{2,00,000}{6,00,000} \times 100 = 33.33$$

$$\text{Return on equity} = \frac{\text{Net profit after tax} - \text{Preference dividend}}{\text{Equity shareholders' funds}}$$

$$= \frac{1,40,000 - 10,000}{2,00,000 + 1,00,000 + 1,40,000}$$

$$= \frac{1,30,000}{4,40,000} \times 100 = 29.55\%$$

*** Provision for Tax is Calculated as under:**

Profits before tax = 5,00,000 + 10,000 – (3,00,000 + 10,000)
= 2,00,000

Tax @ 30% = 60,000

** **EBIT does not include income from Treasury Bonds as it is a non-operating income. So, total assets also should not include the relevant assets – Treasury Bonds. When income is excluded, relevant assets of that income are also to be excluded for proper matching.**

Illustration No. 18

Balance Sheet of Richa Dixit Ltd. as on 31st March, 2009

(₹)

Liabilities		Assets	
Equity share capital	4,00,000	Land	1,00,000
(40,000 Equity shares of ₹ 10 each)		Building	2,00,000
		Plant and machinery stock	50,000
General reserves	50,000		
Profit and loss account	25,000	Debtors	80,000
8 % Debentures	50,000	Bills receivable	1,80,000
Long-term loan	50,000	Bank balance	20,000
Sundry creditors	70,000		45,000
Bills payable	30,000		
	6,75,000		6,75,000

The following information is provided:

Opening Stock:	₹ 40,000
Cash Purchases:	₹ 20,000
Credit Purchases:	₹ 8,00,000
Cash Sales:	₹ .30,000
Credit Sales:	₹ 12,00,000
Profit, after Tax:	₹ 40,000

Profit includes ₹ 10,000, which relates to income from sale of shares, which does not relate to the main activity of the firm.

Tax rate: 50%

Interest: ₹ 20,000

From the above Balance Sheet of Richa Dixit Ltd., calculate the following ratios:

(A) Gross Profit Ratio

(B) Net Profit Ratio

(C) Operating Ratio

(D) Debtors Collection Period

(E) Creditors Velocity

(F) Return on Capital Employed

(G) Return on Equity

Solution

(A) Gross Profit Ratio

Gross profit = (Total sales + Closing stock) – (Opening stock + Total purchases)

= (12,30,000 + 80,000) – (40,000 + 8,20,000)

= 4,50,000

$$\text{Gross profit ratio} = \frac{\text{Gross profit}}{\text{Sales}} \times 100$$

$$= \frac{4{,}50{,}000}{12{,}30{,}000} \times 100$$

= 36.58%

$$\textbf{(B) Net Profit Ratio} = \frac{\text{Profit after tax}}{\text{Sales}} \times 100$$

$$= \frac{40{,}000}{12{,}30{,}000} \times 100$$

= 3.25%

$$\textbf{(C) Operating Ratio} = \frac{\text{Operating profit}}{\text{Sales}} \times 100$$

Profit after tax = 40,000

Profit, before tax (tax rate 50%) = 80,000

Interest = 20,000

EBIT = 1,00,000

EBIT includes operating profit and non-operating profit. EBIT includes ₹ 10,000 from the sale of investments, not related to the main activity of the firm. So, this amount is to be excluded to arrive at operating profit. So, operating profit is ₹ 90,000.

$$\text{Operating ratio} = \frac{90{,}000}{12{,}30{,}000} \times 100$$

= 7.32 %

$$\textbf{(D) Debtors Collection Period} = \frac{\text{Debtors + Bills receivable}}{\text{Credit sales}} \times 365$$

$$= \frac{1{,}80{,}000 + 20{,}000}{12{,}00{,}000} \times 365$$

= 61 days

(E) Creditors Velocity* $= \dfrac{\text{Credit purchases}}{\text{Creditors + Bills payable}}$

$$= \frac{8,00,000}{70,000 + 30,000}$$

$$= 8$$

***Velocity means speed. Creditors' velocity ratio means number of times, the credit purchases have turned over. Creditors 'velocity is expressed in numbers while creditors' turnover ratio is shown in months.**

(F) Return on Capital Employed $= \dfrac{\text{EBIT}}{\text{Capital employed}}$

Capital employed = Equity share capital + Reserves + Debentures + Long-term loans

$$\text{Return on capital employed} = \frac{1,00,000}{5,75,000} \times 100$$

$$= 17.39\%$$

$$\text{Return on equity} = \frac{\text{Net profit after tax}}{\text{Equity shareholders' funds}} \times 100$$

Equity shareholders' funds = Equity share capital + Reserves + Profit and loss account

= 4,00,000 + 50,000 + 25,000

$$\text{Return on equity} = \frac{40,000}{4,75,000} \times 100$$

$$= 8.42\%$$

Illustration No. 19

Prepare balance sheet as on 31 March, 2009 from the following information:

Current ratio	= 1.50	Fixed assets to proprietary funds	= 0.75
Working capital	= ₹ 75,000	Net worth	= ₹ 4,00,000
Trade investments	= ₹ 30,000	Reserves and surplus	= ₹ 1,00,000
Total sales	= ₹ 12,00,000	Long-term loan	= ₹ 50,000
Cash sales	= ₹ 2,00,000	Total purchases	= ₹ 9,00,000
Gross profit ratio	= 25%	Cash purchases	= ₹ 3,00,000
Stock turnover ratio	= 9	Creditors turnover ratio	= 60
Debtors turnover ratio	= 20	Marketable investments	= ₹ 30,000

Treat the balancing item as goodwill/capital reserve.

Solution

$$\text{Current ratio} = \frac{\text{Current assets}}{\text{Current liabilities}} = 1.5$$

Current assets = 1.5

Current liabilities = 1

Working capital = 75,000

= Current assets – Current liabilities

= 1.5 – 1 = 0.5 = 75,000

So, current assets: 2,25,000

Current liabilities : 1,50,000

Total sales – Cash sales = Credit sales

Credit sales = 12,00,000 – 2,00,000 = 10,00,000

$$\text{Debtors turnover ratio} = \frac{\text{Credit sales}}{\text{Debtors}} = 20$$

$$\text{Debtors} = \frac{\text{Credit sales}}{20}$$

$$= \frac{10{,}00{,}000}{20}$$

$$= 50{,}000$$

Total sales = 12,00,000

$$\frac{\text{Gross profit 25\%}}{\text{Cost of sales}} = \frac{3{,}00{,}000}{9{,}00{,}00}$$

$$\text{Stock turnover ratio} = \frac{\text{Cost of sales}}{\text{Stock}} = 9$$

$$\text{Stock} = \frac{9{,}00{,}000}{9} = 1{,}00{,}000$$

$$\text{Fixed assets to Proprietary funds} = \frac{\text{Fixed assets}}{\text{Net worth}} = 0.75$$

Fixed assets = Net worth × 0.75

4,00,000 × 0.75 = 3,00,000

Net worth = Share capital + Reserves

Reserves and surplus = ₹ 1,00,000

$$\text{Share capital} = \text{Net worth} - \text{Reserves and surplus}$$
$$= 4{,}00{,}000 - 1{,}00{,}000 = 3{,}00{,}000$$

$$\text{Creditors turnover ratio} = \frac{\text{Credit purchases}}{\text{Creditors}} = 60$$

$$\text{Creditors} = \frac{6{,}00{,}000}{60} = 10{,}000$$

$$\text{Current assets} = \text{Cash/bank} + \text{Marketable investments} + \text{Debtors} + \text{Stock}$$

$$\text{Cash/bank} = \text{Current assets} - (\text{Marketable investments} + \text{Debtors} + \text{Stock})$$
$$= 2{,}25{,}000 - (30{,}000 + 50{,}000 + 1{,}00{,}000)$$
$$= 45{,}000$$

Balance Sheet as on 31st March, 2009

Liabilities		Assets	
Share capital	3,00,000	Fixed assets	3,00,000
Reserves and surplus	1,00,000	Stock	1,00,000
Long-term loan	50,000	Debtors	50,000
Creditors	10,000	Marketable investments*	30,000
Other current liabilities	1,40,000	Cash/bank	45,000
		Goodwill**	75,000
	6,00,000		6,00,000

*** Marketable investments are a part of current assets, which are held by the firm to park their excess funds, for a short period.**

**** Goodwill is the balancing figure on assets side. In case, the balancing figure appears on the liability side, it would be capital reserve.**

Illustration No. 20

From the following information presented by a firm for the year ended 31-3-2009. Prepare the Balance Sheet.

Sales to Net worth	5 times.
Current liabilities to Net worth	50%
Total Debt to Net worth	60%
Fixed Assets to Net worth	60%
Current Ratio	2
Sales to Stock	10 times
Debtors velocity	9 times
Annual velocity	₹ 15 Lakhs
Cash sales	40%

(MBA, B.U., 2010)

Solution

Annual velocity is annual sales.

Annual sales = 15,00,000

Sales to stock = 10 times

Stock has turned over 10 times in a year.

$$\text{Stock} = \frac{15,00,000}{10} = 1,50,000$$

Sales to net worth = 5 times

$$\text{Net worth} = \frac{15,00,000}{5} = 3,00,000$$

Current liabilities to net worth = 50 %

Current liabilities = 1,50,000

Total debt is 60 % of net worth

Total debt = 1,80,000

Total debt comprises long – term debt and short – term debt (current liabilities).

Long – term debt (long term loan/debentures) = Total debt – current liabilities

= 1,80,000 – 1,50,000 = 30,000

Fixed assets is 60 % of net worth

Fixed assets = 1,80,000

Cash sales is = 40 % of total sales

40 % of 15,00,000 = 6,00,000

Credit sales = Total sales – Cash sales

= 15,00,000 – 6,00,000 = 9,00,000

Debtors velocity = 9 times

It means debtors have turned over 9 times in a year to form total credit sales.

Debtors = 1,00,000

Current ratio = 2

If current liabilities are 1, current assets are 2.

Current assets = 1,50,000 × 2 = 3,00,000

*Cash and bank is presumed as the balance item in current assets.

Cash & bank = Current assets – (Stock + Debtors)

= 3,00,000 – (1,50,000 + 1,00,000) = 50,000

Balance sheet as on 31st Marth, 2009.

Liabilities		Assets	
Capital and reserves (Net worth)	3,00,000	Fixed assets	1,80,000
		Debtors	1,00,000
Long-term debt	30,000	Stock	1,50,000
Current liabilities	1,50,000	Cash and bank*	50,000
Total	4,80,000	Total	4,80,000

Tip to students: In problems of this nature, students often experience difficulty with 'Where to start'. Start with those areas where amount information is available. In the above problem, 'sales' is the key area with which we started.

5.13 RELEVANCE OF RATIO ANALYSIS FOR PREDICTING FUTURE

The basis to calculate ratio analysis is historical financial statements. Historical financial statements indicate what has happened in the past. The financial analyst is interested to know what would happen in future. Management of the company has the information about the company's future plans and policies. Using the historical data and equipped with the knowledge of future plans and constraints to achieve, management is in a better position to predict future happening to a certain reasonable extent. But, outside analyst has his own limitation and the analysis based on past ratios may not, necessarily, reflect the financial position and performance in the future.

5.14 RATIOS MAY BECOME MEANINGLESS, IF DETACHED FROM DERIVED DETAILS

Ratios are only indicators, not end in themselves: They identify the trends, shift in trends or other factors. They are not to be accepted on their face value. They are helpful in identifying the problem areas of a firm. They show the way for further investigation and meaningful conclusion. They are only the means to achieve a particular end. By themselves, they do not give final results.

Ratios are meaningless, if detached from the details from which they are derived. Ratio is based on the data of the concerned company. So, ratios are relevant to that particular company only, which are based on the circumstances and policies of that company. If those ratios are compared to any other company, where the circumstances and policies adopted are totally different, conclusions drawn based on the divergent data would be meaningless. It may, therefore, be concluded that the ratio analysis, if done mechanically, is not only misleading but, equally, dangerous.

A culprit is located by a detective from the clues he leaves. In ratio analysis, financial analyst does the job of a detective, while analyzing the clues derived from ratio analysis to diagnose the reasons of ill health of a corporate.

The analyst must have practical knowledge as well as experience for calculating the ratios and interpreting the results carefully. Unless the analyst is able to correlate the ratios, he would not be able to arrive at meaningful clues. Remember, ratios are only indicators or signals for the direction to investigate further and conclude with specific conclusions. Conclusions can be drawn only after a careful analysis of all the relevant ratios and gathering detailed information, the inquiries may further require.

Ratios, like statistics, have a set of principles and finality about them, at times, may be misleading. It has been said that "a man who has his head in the oven and his feet in the ice-box is on the average, comfortable"! To say a final word on ratio analysis, conclusions on the study of single ratios, in isolation, are dangerous.

Conclusions can be drawn, only after careful analysis of all the relevant ratios and gathering detailed information, further, necessitated by ratio analysis for clarification/ understanding.

5.15 LIMITATIONS OF RATIO ANALYSIS

Ratio analysis is one of the most powerful tools of financial management. They are simple and easy to understand.

Ratio analysis provides useful clues to investigate further. They must always be compared with:

- Previous ratios in order to assess the trends
- Ratios achieved in other comparable companies

Ratios by themselves mean nothing as they have serious limitations. While using the ratios, caution has to be exercised in respect of the following. The following are some of the limitations:

1. **Absence of Identical Situations:** It is difficult to obtain identical situations for different firms. Circumstances do not remain the same, even, for the same firm between two different periods. Ratios are useful in judging the efficiency of business, only when they are compared with the past results of the firm, with identical circumstances, or with the results of similar businesses. Comparison becomes difficult due to lack of uniformity of situation between the two companies.
2. **Change in Accounting Policies:** Management has a choice about the accounting policies. The management of different companies may adopt different accounting policies regarding valuation of inventories, depreciation, research and development expenditure and treatment of deferred revenue expenditure, etc. Comparison would be meaningful and valuable, if their base is similar. All companies may not be following the same method. For example, one may calculate depreciation on straight-line method, while the other may be following written down value method. Different companies may be following different methods of valuation of closing stock, e.g. FIFO or LIFO.

The differences between the accounting policies, followed by different companies, make the interpretation of ratios difficult.

3. **Based on Historical Data:** The ratios are calculated from past financial statements and so they are no indicators of future. Such ratios may provide information about the past. But, for forecasting the future, there are many factors that may change in future. Market conditions and management policies may not remain the same, as they were earlier.

4. **Qualitative Factors are Ignored:** Ratios are expressed in quantitative form only. Qualitative factors are ignored. A high current ratio may not guarantee liquidity as current assets may be high due to inclusion of obsolete inventory and non-paying debtors.

5. **Ratios are only Indicators and not Final:** Ratios are indicators of financial analysis. They are not end in themselves. At best, they give the clues. They are to be investigated, further, to confirm the direction. They cannot be taken as final regarding good or bad financial position of the business.

Ratio analysis can be used as trigger points for further investigation.

6. **Over use could be dangerous:** Over use of ratios as controls on managers could be dangerous. If too much reliance is placed on ratios, management may concentrate in improving the ratios, rather than dealing with significant issues. For example, reducing assets rather than increasing profits can improve the return on capital employed.

7. **Window Dressing:** The term 'window dressing' means manipulation of accounts in a way so as to conceal the actual facts and present the financial statements in such a way to show better position than what actually it is. For example, a high current ratio is considered as an indicator of satisfactory liquidity position. To show an impressive current ratio, firm may postpone credit purchases. A company may have current assets of ₹ 4,000 and current liabilities of ₹ 2,000. So, its current ratio is 2:1, that is normally considered satisfactory. On inquiry, it has been found that the firm has postponed credit purchases, though needed, just to maintain the ratio in a satisfactory manner. Had the firm made credit purchases ₹ 2,000 for meeting its normal requirements, current assets would have increased to ₹ 6,000 and current liabilities to ₹ 4,000. Then, its current ratio would have declined to 1.5. The firm has concealed the true picture, just by postponing credit purchases, at the end of the year, though they were much needed for its requirements. Similarly, firms may make payments at the end of the year to improve the depressed ratio. In the above situation, if the firm pays ₹ 1,000 to creditors, its current ratio becomes 3.

8. **Problems of Price Level Changes:** Financial analysis, based on accounting ratios, will give misleading results, if effects of change in price level are not taken into account. For example, two companies that have set up plant and machinery in two different periods, with a long gap, may give misleading results. Firm that has purchased the

plant and machinery, quite earlier, would have lower amount towards depreciation, when compared with the firm that has set up the machinery quite later. So, the operating results of both the firms vary substantially. The financial statements of the two firms cannot be compared without making suitable changes to the price level changes.

9. **No Fixed Standards:** No fixed standards can be laid down for ratios. Though current ratio 2:1 is normally required, firms enjoying adequate arrangements with banks to provide additional credit, as and when needed, may be able to manage with lesser current ratio. It is, therefore, necessary to avoid any rules of thumb.

> **Ratios are only a post-mortem of what has happened between the two balance sheet dates. The interim position is not revealed by the ratio analysis.**

5.16 SUMMARY OF RATIOS AND THEIR PURPOSE

(1)	(2) Ratio	(3) Computation Formula	(4) Purpose
1.	**Current ratio**	$\frac{\text{Current assets}}{\text{Current liabilities}}$	Measures short-term debt paying ability.
2.	**Quick (Acid test) ratio**	$\frac{\text{Quick assets}}{\text{Current liabilities}}$	A refined measure of the short-term debt-paying ability of the firm. Measures short-term solvency.
3.	**Gross profit ratio**	$\frac{\text{Gross profit}}{\text{Net sales}} \times 100$	Measures efficiency of company's operations, production and trading activities.
4.	**Net profit ratio**	$\frac{\text{Net profit}}{\text{Net sales}} \times 100$	Shows net margin on sales. One of the important indicators of management's efficiency.

Contd...

5.	**Operating expenses ratio**	$\frac{\text{Operating expense}}{\text{Net sales}} \times 100$	Identifies the exact expense that has contributed efficiency or deterioration in performance and requires attention of management to control, where needed.
6.	**Earning per equity share**	$\frac{\text{Profits available for equity shareholders}}{\text{No. of equity shares}} \times 100$	Shows the amount of earnings available for each equity share.
7.	**Dividend yield**	$\frac{\text{Dividend per equity share}}{\text{Market price share}} \times 100$	Shows the rate of return to equity shareholders, in the form of dividends, based on the market price of the share.
8.	**Price earning ratio**	$\frac{\text{Market price of equity share}}{\text{Earning per equity share}} \times 100$	A guide to investor to buy/sell the equity share at that price.
9.	**Interest coverage**	$\frac{\text{EBDIT}}{\text{Interest}}$	A test for firm's debt servicing capacity. Useful to long-term lenders.
10.	**Debt equity ratio**	$\frac{\text{Total debt}}{\text{Net worth}}$	Depicts extent of total debt financing in business.
11.	**Total debt ratio**	$\frac{\text{Total debt}}{\text{Total assets}}$	Shows the proportion of total assets financed by total liabilities.
12.	**Inventory turnover ratio**	$\frac{\text{Cost of goods sold}}{\text{Average inventory, at cost}}$	Shows efficiency of sales and adequacy of control on inventory holding.
13.	**No. of days inventory holding**	$\frac{360}{\text{Debtors' turnover ratio}}$	Shows the inventory holding, in days, and control on inventory management.

Contd...

14.	**Accounts receivable (Debtors) turnover**	$\frac{\text{Credit sales}}{\text{Average debtors}}$	Measures liquidity of debtors and effectiveness of the credit policy.
15.	**Debtors collection period**	$\frac{360}{\text{Debtors' turnover ratio}}$	Shows period of holding of debtors and indicates effectiveness of collection department.
16.	**Working capital ratio**	$\frac{\text{Cost of sales or sales}}{\text{Average working capital}}$	Shows velocity utilization of working capital.
17.	**Return on Investment, before tax** **(i) ROCE** **(ii) ROTA**	(i) $\frac{\text{EBIT}}{\text{Capital employed}}$ (ii) $\frac{\text{EBIT}}{\text{Total assets}}$	Measures the overall efficiency of business, before tax.
18.	**Return on investment, after tax (ROCE, ROTA)**	$\frac{\text{EBIT}(1-\text{T})}{\text{Capital employed or total assets}}$	Shows overall efficiency of business, after tax.
19.	**Return on equity**	$\frac{\text{Net profit after tax} - \text{Preference dividend}}{\text{Equity shareholders' funds}}$	Measures earning power of equity share holders funds. Management's main responsibility is to take care of the interests of the owners. They try to maximize ROE. This ratio is the index of performance of management.
20.	**Pay-out ratio**	$\frac{\text{Dividend per equity share}}{\text{Earnings per equity share}}$	Shows proportion of payment of dividend out of earnings and stability of dividend policy.
21.	**Capital gearing ratio**	$\frac{\text{Preference share capital} + \text{Debentures} + \text{Long-term Loan}}{\text{Equity share capital} + \text{Reserves and Surplus}}$	Refers to the proportion between fixed commitment funds to non-fixed commitment funds in the total capital employed that influences the variability of profits.

Check Your Understanding

(A) State whether the following statements are True or False

1. Ratio analysis is the process of determination and interpretation of numerical relationship based on financial statements.
2. Ratio is an expression of the qualitative relationship between two numbers.
3. Liquidity ratios are used to test the short-term solvency or liquidity position of the company.
4. Current ratio measures long-term solvency, that is ability to meet long-term obligations.
5. Quick ratio is a more stringent test of liquidity than the current ratio.
6. When current assets and current liabilities are manipulated to show a better picture than what is real, it is known as window dressing.
7. Leverage ratios indicate the mix of debt and owners' equity in financing the liabilities of the firm.
8. Debt trap is a situation when the firm is not able to pay fixed interest obligations, due to low profits, and borrows funds on unfavourable terms to meet the working capital needs.
9. Activity ratios are different from turnover ratios.
10. Leverage ratios indicate the short-term solvency of the firm.
11. The term investment may refer to total assets or net assets.
12. Bonus shares are not free shares, issued to the existing equity shareholders of the company.
13. A highly geared firm is a big curse during the period of recession.
14. Ratios are independent and do not have any relation with the details from which they are derived.
15. A decreased stock turnover ratio usually indicates the expanding business.
16. Rate of return on capital employed is a turnover ratio.
17. 'Acid Test' denotes liquidity.
18. Liabilities are not subject to fall, as they have to be paid.
19. Low gearing is preferable to high gearing from the viewpoint of creditors.
20. Profit is not a factor of sales.

Answers

1. True, 2. False, 3. True, 4. False, 5. True, 6. True, 7. False, 8. True, 9. False, 10. False

11. True, 12. False, 13. True, 14. False, 15. False, 16. False, 17. True, 18. True, 19. True, 20. False

(B) Objective Questions (Identify what is most appropriate)

1. Debt Equity Ratio is a

   (i) Liquidity Ratio (ii) Solvency Ratio (iii) Profitability Ratio (iv) Activity Ratio

2. Calculate the inventory holding in terms of days:

   Opening stock: 10,000;

   Closing stock: 20,000;

   Sales: 40,000; Gross Profit: 10%

   (i) 150 (ii) 30 (iii) 60 (iv) 120

3. For calculating inventory ratio, the following information is more appropriate.
   (i) Opening Stocks (ii) Closing Stock (iii) Sales (iv) Gross Profit (v) Average Stock

4. Which statement is wrong?
   (i) Liquidity ratio–measures firm's ability to meet the current obligations.
   (ii) Activity ratio–reflects efficiency in utilizing assets of the firm.
   (iii) Management is not interested in evaluating every aspect of firm's performance.
   (iv) Accounting data is taken from financial statements.

5. Calculate the current ratio from the following data:
   Bank OD: 20,000; Cash: 15,000; Outstanding expenses: 10,000
   Accrued income: 5,000; Stock: 5,000; Prepaid expenses: 5,000
   (i) 2 : 1 (ii) 1 : 1 (iii) 1.5 : 1 (iv) 1 : 1.5

6. Find out the missing figure if current ratio is 2 : 1.

Work in progress	:	20,000
Bank cash credit	:	5,000
Raw materials	:	10,000
Creditors	:	4,000
Bills payable	:	?

   (i) 10,000 (ii) 9,000 (iii) 12,000 (iv) 6,000.

7. Calculate Quick Ratio from the following.

Debentures	:	10,000
Long-term loan	:	20,000
Cash	:	15,000
Raw materials	:	6,000
Debtors	:	5,000
Creditors	:	5,000
Prepaid expenses	:	5,000

   (i) 3 : 1 (ii) 4 : 1 (iii) 2 : 1 (iv) 1 : 1

8. This ratio is a 'Test of Quantity but not Quality'.
   (i) Quick Ratio (ii) Debt-Equity Ratio (iii) Current Ratio (iv) Dividend Payout Ratio

9. A company can meet its financial obligations, as and when they fall due if
   (i) Current Ratio is 2 : 1.
   (ii) Current Ratio is less than 2 : 1
   (iii) More depends on composition of current assets rather than currant ratio alone.
   (iv) Current assets just cover the current liabilities.

10 Calculate the Net Working Capital

Cash: 5,000; Finished goods: 12,000

Debtors: 20,000; Prepaid expenses: 3,000

Debentures: 4,000; Long-term loan: 5,000

Bank cash credit: 6,000;

Creditors = 10,000

(i) 24,000 (ii) 26,000 (iii) 21,000 (iv) 15,000 (v) 20,000

11. Capital employed means

(i) Net worth (ii) Net worth + Long-term loans

(iii) Current Assets + Current Liabilities (iv) Net Current Assets

12. Cost of goods sold includes

(i) Depreciation (ii) Gross Profit (iii) Administrative expenses (iv) Interest (v) None

Answers

1. (ii), 2. (i), (Take average stock) 3. (v), 4. (iii), 5. (ii),
6. (iv), 7. (ii), 8. (iii), 9. (iii), 10. (i), 11. (ii), 12. (i).

(C) Check your ability in fast calculations

1. Calculate Return on Equity with the following information:

EBIT: 50,000; 6% Debentures: 5,00,000

Tax rate: 50%; Equity share capital: 1,00,000 (Face value ₹10) General reserves: 3,00,000

(i) 10% (ii) 2.5% (iii) 20% (iv) 15% (v) 30%

Ans. (ii)

$$\frac{\text{Profit after tax}}{\text{Equity shareholders' fund}}$$

$$\frac{50{,}000-30{,}000-50\%(50{,}000-30{,}000)}{1{,}00{,}000+3{,}00{,}000}$$

2. Share price, before bonus issue is ₹100. Bonus issue 1 : 4 is made.

What can be the ex-bonus price of a share, if other factors were constant?

(i) 60 (ii) 70 (iii) 80 (iv) 100 (v) 20

Ans. (iii) (For every 4 shares held, one bonus share is issued) $100 \times \frac{4}{5}$.

3. Earnings per share are ₹ 80. Bonus shares are issued in the ratio of 1 : 4 during the year. What is the adjusted earning per share of the year in which bonus is made?

(i) 60 (ii) 70 (iii) 80 (iv) 100 (v) 20

Ans. (iv) $80 \times \frac{5}{4}$.

4. Retained earnings of the firm at the end of the year is ₹ 1,20,000. Dividend paid has been ₹ 30,000. Profits earned is ₹ 50,000. What is the balance of retained earnings at the beginning of the year?

   (i) 1,00,000 (ii) 1,40,000 (iii) 80,000 (iv) 70,000

Ans. (i) Out of the current year's profit of ₹ 50,000, dividend of ₹ 30,000 has been paid, leaving a balance of ₹ 20,000 out of the current year's profits. As the closing balance of the retained profits is ₹ 1,20,000, the opening balance should have been ₹ 1,00,000.

(D) Find out impact of decisions taken

The current ratio of Kishore & Co. is 2 : 1. Which of the following decisions would improve the ratio, which would reduce it and which one would not change it?

1. To pay substantial amount of creditors from the available cash balance.
2. To sell a vehicle, used for carrying staff from their residences to office, for cash at a slight loss.
3. To borrow money for a short period, with a nominal interest rate, executing a promissory note.
4. To purchase marketable investments for cash.
5. To give an interest bearing promissory note to a creditor to whom money was owed on current account.
6. Purchase of a fixed asset.
7. Bills receivable dishonoured.
8. Issue of preference shares.

Answers

1. Improves the ratio 2. Improves the ratio 3. Reduces the ratio 4. No change in the ratio 5. No change in the ratio 6. Reduces the ratio 7. No change 8. Improves the ratio

Tip to students: Take a small example and understand the impact of each transaction.

(E) Analyze and interpret the following situations

Q.1. The age of accounts receivables is 60 days, while credit terms require customers to settle dues in 45 days. What conclusion prima facie can be drawn? Any suggestion for the situation? Which ratio is helpful in determining the age of accounts receivable?

Ans: The age of accounts receivables is 60 days, against the stipulated credit terms of 45 days. The situation shows the slackness of the firm in its efforts of collections from debtors. In consequence, firm may be experiencing liquidity problems. It may be worthwhile to explore the possibility of introducing cash discount for securing early payments to overcome the liquidity problem, if experienced by the firm.

Debtors' turnover ratio gives information about the age of accounts receivables.

Q.2. A provision stores donates rice and wheat for flood relief. Accountant of the firm is of the opinion that donation has not been given in cash, so donation need not be reflected in books of accounts. His reasoning is that transactions that are not expressed in terms of money need not be recorded in books of accounts. As closing stock would be reduced to that extent, profits are reduced, automatically, he reasons. React.

Ans. Accountant's reasoning is wrong. Though the donation is not in terms of money, they can be valued in money value. At cost price, they are to be valued and accounted. If no accounting is made, the donation expense is not recorded in books of accounts. So, accounts do not show a true and fair picture of the state of affairs of the firm.

Only those matters that cannot be valued in terms of money, such as loyalty of employees cannot be recorded in books of accounts.

Match the following

Type of Ratios	Purpose
1. Liquidity ratios	(A) Is return on investment in the firm competitive?
2. Leverage ratios	(B) Whether assets are utilized efficiently in the firm?
3. Activity ratios	(C) Is proportion of debt/borrowing in the company reasonable, compared to the industry to which it belongs?
4. Profitability ratios	(D) Is the firm having ability to pay obligations in time?

Ans:

1. (D) 2. (C) 3. (B) 4. (A).

Descriptive Questions

1. What is a financial ratio? Explain the need of ratio analysis. **(5.2 and 5.1)**
2. Explain the scope of ratio analysis. State the difference between analysis and interpretation of financial statements. **(5.2, 5.3 and 5.4)**
3. What is a financial ratio? In what manner, financial ratios can be compared? **(5.2 and 5.5)**
4. Explain 'analysis without interpretation is meaningless and interpretation without analysis is impossible'. **(5.2, 5.3 and 5.4)**
5. "Ratios are the symptoms of health of an organization like blood pressure, the pulse or temperature of an individual". Explain and state their uses. **(5.3 and 5.3.1)**
6. State the different types of ratios and explain their purpose, briefly. **(5.6)**
7. Describe different types of ratios and standards of comparison for evaluating the performance of the firm. **(5.5 and 5.6)**
8. What is the importance of 'liquidity ratios' and explain any one of them, in detail, with its rationale and interpretation? **(5.7, 5.7.1)**
9. "The higher the current ratio, the larger is the amount of rupees available per rupee of current liability and greater is the safety of funds to short-term creditors". Is it desirable for the firm to maintain high current ratio to ensure protection of their interests? **(5.7)**
10. Is it possible for a firm to have a high current ratio and still experience difficulties in paying its current debt? What are the consequences of a high and low current ratio ? **(5.7.1)**
11. "Composition and quality of current assets is more important than mere adequacy of current ratio"–explain. **(5.7.1)**

12. 'Two companies have the same amount of working capital. One company's debt paying ability is much weaker than the other'–Explain how this could occur. **(5.7.1)**
13. What is a current ratio? State its use and limitations. **(5.7.1)**
14. Describe the different types of ratios. Explain any two ratios in each category with their significance. **(5.2, 5.6, 5.7, 5.7.1, 5.8, 5.8.1 and 5.8.2)**
15. What are the important profitability ratios? How they are calculated? Explain their significance. **(5.10, 5.10.1 and 5.10.2)**
16. Describe the concept, 'Trading on Equity'. Explain the relationship between the return on capital employed and return on equity, with a suitable illustration. **(5.11)**
17. What does capital gearing mean? Elaborate the consequences of significant changes in EBIT, when the firm is highly geared. **(5.10.2.H, 5.12)**
18. Explain the limitations of the ratio analysis. **(5.15)**
19. "Ratios are meaningless if detached from the details from which they are derived." Comment and bring out the limitations of ratio analysis. **(5.13, 5.14 and 5.15)**
20. Write short notes on:
    (A) Window dressing **(5.7.2)**
    (B) Liquid ratio **(5.7.3)**
    (C) Proprietary ratio **(5.8.2)**
    (D) Trading on equity **(5.11)**
    (E) Relevance of ratio analysis for predicting future **(5.13)**

Short Questions/Answers

Q.1. Name the different sources of raising funds for a long-term commitment.

Ans. Equity share capital, preference share capital, debentures and long-term loans provide funds for a long-term commitment. Reserves and share premium amount available in the firm would provide the means for the same purpose.

Q.2. When borrowing is favourable to the equity shareholders?

Ans. Borrowing is favourable to the equity shareholders so long as return on investment is greater than the cost of borrowing. The excess return on investment, after meeting the cost of borrowing, increases the return to equity shareholders.

Q.3. What is meant by "Trading on Equity"?

Ans. The process of magnifying the earnings of equity shareholders through the use of debt is called "Trading on Equity" or "Financial Leverage" or "Financial Gearing".

Normally, assets are financed by capital and debt. Debt financing is advantageous to the equity shareholders. The equity shareholders can retain control with a limited stake. They can find a way to magnify their earnings. When the firm is able to earn on borrowed funds higher than the interest rate paid, the return to owners would be magnified. To illustrate, when the return on investment of a firm, say, is 20% and firm is able to borrow at 12%, borrowing results in a saving of 8% on the funds borrowed, ignoring tax. In consequence, the firm is able to increase the return to equity shareholders with borrowed funds. Interest is an admissible expenditure/deduction for tax calculation. On account of admissibility of interest, tax burden would be low and, in consequence, net profits would be more. In the absence of borrowing, the equity share capital would get a return of 20% only.

If the interest rate is higher than the rate of return on the project, it is not desirable to borrow, as the return on equity would get reduced.

Q.4. Why "Trading on Equity' is called a 'Double edged sword'?

Ans. When the return on capital employed is greater than the cost of debt, it is advantageous to borrow as the return on equity goes up. At the expense of debt, the beneficiaries are the equity shareholders. The risk that firm would experience on long-term borrowings is permanent interest burden. Additionally, when earnings fall, the ROCE also falls. But, in the process, the equity shareholders are the real sufferers. With the fall of ROCE, the return on equity goes down. In other words, debt can prove to be either beneficial or detrimental to the interests of equity shareholders. In other words, borrowing may turn to be an advantage or disadvantage to the equity shareholders. This is called trading on equity, which is a double-edged sword. The key is the relationship between the ROCE and cost of debt.

Q.5. How ratio analysis helps in forecasting or predicting the future performance of a firm?

Ans. Financial statements are historical in their nature as they relate to the past performance of the firm. When ratio analysis is applied to the past financial statements, strength and weakness of the firm could be analyzed and identified. Changes are inevitable as future is not a replica of the past. Only management is aware of the expected changes in policies, in future. So, ratio analysis can be applied by the management to anticipate the future performance/results, after considering the impact of changes in policies to the past financial statements.

An outsider is not aware of the likely changes in policies. So, only management, not public, is in a better position to use ratio analysis to forecast or predict the future performance of a firm.

Q.6. Which assets, fixed assets or current assets, are important to a firm?

Ans. Funds are limited to every firm. Equally, funds have a cost. If more funds were tied up in the current assets, lesser funds would be available for fixed assets. Fixed assets generate production, while current assets support them for generating profits.

In a movie, both hero and heroine are important for the story to move. For every hero, there should be a heroine. If fixed assets are heroes, current assets are heroines. So, both are essential to the firm.

Q.7. What is the importance of liquidity?

Ans. Liquidity means having sufficiency of funds in the firm in right quantum, at the right time. In the absence of liquidity, firm would not be able to make payments on the due date. There would be delay for suppliers of goods and services. Creditors would be unhappy with the repayment behaviour of the firm and may suspend or delay supplies that would affect smooth production. The deficiency of liquidity may lead to short-term insolvency.

Excess liquidity erodes the profitability. It is important for every firm to maintain optimum liquidity which should be neither excessive nor inadequate.

Q.8. Between the two objectives, liquidity and profitability, which objective is important and why?

Ans. Both the two objectives, liquidity and profitability are equally important. Liquidity ensures adequate availability of funds in the firm, in right quantum, at the needed hour. Excess liquidity erodes profitability. Inadequate liquidity does not enable the firm to meet the short-term obligations, promptly and properly. On the other hand, profitability is vital for every organization. Existing and potential investors look towards profitability of the firm. With the fall in profitability, market price of share would crash. Liquidity and profitability are two sides of a coin. When we see one side of the coin, other side is not visible. In a similar manner, firm can enjoy only one of them.

Liquidity and profitability are conflicting objectives. It is essential for every firm to maintain both the objectives in a balanced manner.

Q.9. What is Capital Gearing Ratio and why this is important?

Ans. Capital Gearing Ratio deals with the proportion of fixed cost bearing funds to non-fixed cost bearing funds. Fixed cost bearing funds are such as debentures, long-term loans and preference share capital. Non - fixed cost bearing funds are those funds that belong to equity shareholders.

Capital Gearing Ratio is a double-edged sword. In times of higher profits, equity shareholders would be the beneficiaries. When profits fall, significantly, they are the worst losers.

Q.10. During recession period, who would be the worst sufferers in a highly capital geared firm'?

Ans. Equity share holders of the high capital geared firms are the worst sufferers during the period of recession. Higher the capital gearing ratio, the impact on equity shareholders would be greater.

Reason is during recession times, profits are under constant pressure and in consequence, return on capital employed would fall significantly. Firms that have higher capital gearing ratio would leave lower profits for equity shareholders. In other words, return on equity would go down.

Application of Knowledge

Q.1. Rishi and Anchit have been working as marketing executives, heading their respective product divisions. Both of them enjoy the freedom to fix the inventory level of their products to achieve their marketing targets. Both have achieved their respective targets in a similar manner. Marketing manager of their organization intends to promote only one of them as the vacancy in the ladder is one. Advise their marketing manager about any relevant ratio to evaluate their performance? Explain the reason for the ratio chosen?

Ans. Both the marketing executives have achieved their respective targets in a similar manner. So, marketing manager can consider the inventory holding period of each product to evaluate the individual performance, in terms of cost control, while achieving the respective targets. Inventory holding period shows the period each product is held in godown on an average basis. This ratio is important as larger the inventory, more is the cost incurred by the organization to maintain the level of inventory. The executive, out of Rishi and Anchit, who has maintained lower level of stocks to achieve the target sales, can be rewarded with promotion.

Every organization is cost conscious. Generation of more profit is possible with lesser costs. So, the executive who has achieved the sales target, with lesser level of inventory, is more competent. So, the decision of the marketing manager on the above parameter would be more appropriate.

Q.2. Ayusha has taken the charge of a new organization as CEO. During the first year of her working, it is noticed that the gross margin of the firm has improved, while its net profits have gone down. She is more worried. When gross margin has gone up, do you think her worries are justified? Advise her to reduce her worries.

Ans. Ayusha, CEO, is justified in her worries. Reduction of net profit, despite increase in gross margin, definitely requires serious consideration. This indicates that cost of production has gone down, while the other expenses have increased more than the reduction in cost of production. In consequence, net profit has gone down. Reason for lower net profit is due to increase in expenses. It is necessary to check the individual expense ratio—administration, selling and distribution and financial expenses. Each expense ratio is to be calculated by dividing the amount of expenses by total sales. This ratio analysis provides information which expense has increased, in comparison to the previous year. Reasons for such an increase have to be analyzed minutely. The concerned expenses have to be controlled to achieve higher level of profits.

Q.3. Mohammed, working as marketing executive, believes in extending more credit period (45 days) to achieve higher sales than the present credit period of 30 days. Advise the implication of his thinking. Which ratio helps him in knowing the actual credit period enjoyed by his customers, against the actual credit period extended?

Ans. Credit sale results in debtors. A higher credit period would result in more debtors. Firm's funds are involved in extending credit. Funds involve cost. So, before enlarging the period of credit, it is necessary to ascertain whether extra profit on additional credit sales would cover the additional costs involved in extending larger credit period.

Debtors' collection period ratio helps him in knowing the actual period of credit enjoyed by the customers, which can be compared with the actual period of credit allowed.

Q.4. Santhosh is working as marketing manager. He wants to know how he can monitor recoveries from the customers and whether the follow up in recoveries is adequate or not?

Ans. Debtors' holding period shows the period of credit enjoyed by customers. The actual credit period is to be compared with the credit period allowed to understand the control he has been exercising on his collections. If the actual credit period is in excess of the credit allowed, it is an indication that the control is not adequate.

Indicate whether the following statements are True or False

		True	False
1.	**Generally, the first concern of a financial analyst is a firm's liquidity.**	X	
2.	**The working capital ratio is regarded as fundamental measurement of a company's liquidity.**	X	
3.	**Normally, an analyst would believe that a manufacturing company with a current ratio of 3 to 1 was in serious liquidity trouble.**		X
4.	**The acid test ratio is regarded primarily as a measure of a company's long-term liquidity situation.**		X
5.	**Usually, quick ratio of 1.5 or 1 would be considered satisfactory.**	X	
6.	**The accounts receivable turnover is both a measure of liquidity and a measure of activity.**	X	
7.	**Average receivables may be expressed in terms of the number of days' sales in receivables.**	X	
8.	**The receivable position and the approximate collection time may be evaluated by computing the accounts receivable turnover.**	X	
9.	**The inventory turnover is computed by dividing cost of goods sold by average inventory.**	X	

10.	**Long-term solvency ratios measure the business' short-term ability to meet all financial obligations.**		X
11.	**Normally, a relatively low inventory turn-over is desirable.**		X
12.	**The ratio of the net sales to total assets is often called the profitability ratio.**		X
13.	**Profit margin on sales is a measure of the profit percentage per rupee of sales.**	X	
14.	**Return on investment (ROI) is a measure of overall asset productivity.**	X	
15.	**The price earnings ratio is a measure of the relative attractiveness of equity stock as an investment.**	X	
16.	**The use of borrowed funds to magnify the earnings of equity is known as trading on the equity.**	X	
17.	**The internal users of financial statement are public, all employees and creditors.**		X
18.	**Debt to asset ratio measures the extent to which borrowed funds have been used to finance the acquisition of assets.**	X	
19.	**Horizontal analysis is a technique to compare company's financial condition over a period of time.**	X	

20.	**Vertical analysis is a technique to evaluate each item in a financial statement as a per cent of a base amount or item.**	X	
21.	**The four classification of ratio analysis are liquidity ratios, leverage ratios, profitability ratios and efficiency ratios.**		X
22.	**Liquidity ratio measures the ability of a business to meet the long-term obligations.**		X
23.	**Total asset turnover measures the amount of sales generated by each rupee of asset**	X	

Interview Questions

Q.1. What is 'Net Worth' and explain its significance?

Ans. 'Net Worth' represents the amount that belongs to the owners of the firm. In true sense, equity shareholders are the real owners of the firm. Paid up share capital, general reserves, capital reserves, share premium and balance lying in Profit and Loss Account, totally, constitute net worth. Preference share capital amount is also included in the net worth, as the amount is also permanent in nature to the firm for a long period and there is no threat from their end for repayment.

In fact, net worth is a cushion available to the outside creditors of the firm. A higher net worth ratio provides greater safety to the creditors in the event of any unforeseen circumstances and liquidation.

Q.2. What is 'Window Dressing' and illustrate with a suitable example?

Ans. Presenting a rosy picture, ignoring the real situation is called 'Window Dressing'. Some firms try to present a higher current ratio than the actual situation to create better liquidity impression of the organization. The situation is created intentionally.

This situation is manipulated in the financial statements at the end of the year. A firm normally, may have a current ratio of 1.5 with an average of current assets of ₹ 90,000 and current liabilities of ₹ 60,000. Before the year-end, the firm brings pressure on the debtors and collects ₹ 30,000 to pay its current liabilities. This action reduces the current assets to stand at ₹ 60,000 with current liabilities at ₹ 30,000. This makes a current ratio of 2:1 at the end of the year in financial statements. Outsiders get a rosy impression about the liquidity of the firm by this deceitful method. During the rest of the year, this ratio is not maintained. Ratio is maintained at the end of the year to give false comfort to creditors.

Q.3. What is indicated by Debt-Equity Ratio?

Ans. Debt-Equity Ratio indicates the extent of outsiders' share to the owners' share in the firm's total assets. This ratio reflects the extent of financing by short-term as well as long- term creditors in the ownership of total assets.

This ratio is calculated by dividing the total debt by the net worth. It shows the vulnerability of the firm's dependence on the outsiders for its survival.

Q.4. What is the importance of Ratio Analysis to the management of a firm?

Ans. Ratio analysis helps the management to identify the strength and weakness of their firm, compared with the industry to which their firm belongs.

Q.5. Name any four ratios that the management of every firm is interested in, along with their significance.

Ans. Every management is interested to maintain sufficient liquidity and utmost profitability of the firm they manage. Current ratio shows the liquidity strength of the firm. Net profit ratio gives the net profit margin of the firm that can be compared with the industry about its competitiveness. Net profit ratio is one of the important indicators of management's efficiency.

Return on investment is the primary ratio that is most popularly used to measure the overall profitability and efficiency of business.

Return on equity conveys the return available to their equity shareholders. Equity shareholders are the real owners of the firm. Every management wants to satisfy the real owners. This ratio is an index of the overall efficiency of the firm.

Earnings per share, finally, indicate the rate of earnings the equity shareholders enjoy on the investment made.

Q.6. Gross profit ratio has gone up, but net profit ratio has gone down. What is the possible explanation?

Ans. The possible explanation is that operating expenses have gone up. This normally happens with the fall of net profit ratio, despite the increase in gross profit ratio. Each expense ratio has to be compared with the previous year's ratio to identify where action and control is needed.

Q.7. Why preference shareholders are not called as the real owners of the company?

Ans. Preference shareholders enjoy fixed rate of dividend and preference for payment of dividend, before dividend is distributed to equity shareholders. Similarly, in the event of the liquidation of the company, preference share capital has to be repaid first before refunding to equity shareholders. Preference shareholders enjoy a different status as they do not assume the risk similar to equity shareholders. So, preference shareholders are not called as the real owners of the company.

Q.8. What is meant by Bonus shares? Whether their issue results in the outflow of cash? Justify your statement.

Ans. Bonus shares are additional free shares issued to the existing equity shareholders out of the profits of the company. Bonus issue does not result into outflow of cash.

Reserves and surplus profit is utilized for issue of bonus shares by transferring the amount to the equity share capital account. If bonus shares 1:3 are issued, an existing shareholder, holding 3 shares, gets one extra share freely.

If there is a balance in the share premium account, that amount is first utilized for issue of bonus shares.

Q.9. What is meant by 'EPS'? How EPS is calculated?

Ans. 'EPS' stands for earning per share. EPS is calculated by dividing the net profit, after tax, by the total number of equity shares outstanding.

Q.10. Whether net profit totally belongs to the equity shareholders?

Ans. No, net profit totally does not belong to the equity shareholders. First, dividend due to the preference shareholders is to be paid from the net profit. The rest of net profit belongs to the equity shareholders.

Q.11. What is the relationship between net profits, dividend and retained profits?

Ans. Dividend is a portion of net profit paid to the equity shareholders. Balance amount of profit retained in the firm, after payment of dividend, is called retained profits. After payment of dividend to preference shareholders, the total net profit belongs to the equity shareholders, distributed by way of dividend or retained profits in the firm.

Q.12. Name an important indicator for purchase/sale of a share in respect of market price? Explain the reasoning for the indicator chosen?

Ans. PE ratio is an important indicator for the purchase or sale of a share, depending on its market price. This ratio is calculated by dividing the market price of an equity share by EPS. The PE ratio of the concerned firm is to be compared with the PE ratio of the industry or its competing firms. If PE ratio of the firm is low, in comparison to the industry or its competing firms, the share of that company is worth buying. If the ratio is high in comparison, the share of that company is worth selling. A comparative analysis of PE ratio gives important information for deciding to buy or sell the share of that company at that particular price.

CHAPTER 6

Sources and Application of Funds

6.1 INTRODUCTION

The traditional basic financial statements are profit and loss account and balance sheet. A serious limitation of these financial statements is that they do not show the changes of financial position during a particular period. They fail to provide answers to the following vital questions:

- What factors are responsible for the changes in owner's equity, assets and liabilities?
- Are the long-term sources adequate to finance purchase of fixed assets?
- Is the working capital adequate for the firm?
- Why the firm has not paid dividend in spite of profits?
- How much funds have been generated from operating activities?
- Has the liquidity of the firm improved or deteriorated?

The Statement of Changes in Financial Position overcomes the limitations of the basic financial statements. The most commonly used forms of the Statement of Changes in Financial Position are Sources and Application of Funds (Funds Flow Statement) and Cash Flow Statement.

6.1.1 Need of Funds Flow Statement

Profit and Loss Account and Balance Sheet are the two basic financial statements, as stated above, which are of immense importance to owners, management and investors. When Profit and Loss Account and Balance Sheet are prepared, what is the need of preparing this separate Funds Flow Statement again? Let us discuss, in detail. Balance

Sheet shows the summary of assets and liabilities of a firm. The assets side of the balance sheet shows the deployment of funds, while the liabilities side shows how the resources have been raised. In other words, balance sheet shows sources and uses of finance too. It indicates the financial position of a firm on a particular date.

> **Balance Sheet is a static statement and does not show the causes for the changes in assets and liabilities or movement of finances between two periods. To meet this requirement, funds flow statement is needed.**

Balance Sheet does not show the changes that take place during the period. If loan has been raised and repaid during the same period, balance sheet, at the end of the period, does not show both the transactions. Similarly, Profit and Loss Account shows the expenses and revenues for an accounting period. Profit and Loss Account also reflects the operational results of a business for a particular period, which causes changes in owners' equity partially. Capital raised and funds withdrawn, resulting in change in owner's equity, do not appear either in Profit and Loss Account or Balance Sheet. In other words, Profit and Loss Account explains only partial story in respect of owner's equity. Profit and Loss Account and Balance Sheet provide the basic essential information about the business activities of the firm. **However, both these two statements do not explain the causes for changes in assets, liabilities and owner's equity.** Moreover, usefulness of both balance sheet and profit and loss account is limited and fail to serve the purposes of financial analysis and planning.

In the balance sheet of a proprietary concern/partnership firm, capital introduced and withdrawn (drawings) appear. However, these details do not appear separately, in the balance sheet of a limited company. In consequence, to a reader of financial statements of a limited company, these details are not available.

It is clear, from the above, that Profit and Loss Account and Balance Sheet do not provide, sufficiently, wide range of information to make assessment of the organization by the end user for the purpose of analysis and planning. **So, there is a need to prepare a separate statement that explains the changes in assets and liabilities, from one period of time to the end of another period. The statement is called "Funds Flow Statement".**

One should remember that funds flow statement serves to provide additional details which are not furnished in the traditional financial statements. However, funds flow statement is not a substitute to profit and loss account and balance sheet.

Purposes: Both Profit and Loss Account and Balance Sheet do not explain the changes in assets, liabilities and owners' equity between two dates. So, an additional statement is needed to serve this purpose. Funds Flow Statement serves this purpose. Funds Flow Statement serves the following broad purposes. The Funds Flow Statement shows:

(i) Changes in assets and liabilities, including working capital, between two periods, and

(ii) Utilization of financial resources during the period, such as acquisition of assets, payment of debts and distribution of dividends to shareholders, **etc.**

6.2 CONCEPT OF FUNDS

The term 'Funds' has been defined in a number of ways. They are:

(A) In the Narrow Sense: Here, the term 'funds' refer to cash only. Transactions that involve cash only are taken. **Cash Flow Statement is prepared in this approach, where only cash receipts and disbursements are included. It is a summary of cash transactions.**

(B) In the Popular Sense: 'Funds' refer to working capital, the excess of current assets over current liabilities. Total resources of a business are invested in fixed assets and working capital; the later is partly in the liquid form. **The most popular form of 'Statement of Changes in Financial Position' is "Sources and Application of Funds".**

> **Any increase or decrease in the working capital, on account of a transaction, is known as "Flow of Funds".**

(C) In the Broader Sense: The term 'Funds' refer to financial resources, in whatever form, they may exist. **Statement of Total Financial Resources is prepared as per this approach.** This is a comprehensive statement involving cash and non-cash transactions. Transactions involving money, materials, machinery and others are included. When machinery or building is purchased, in exchange of shares, it is not reported both in cash flow statement and Sources and Application of Funds. Reason is there is no outgo of cash, so does not appear in cash flow statement. There is no change of working capital even. So, it does not appear in the funds flow statement. However, this type of transaction involves financial resources and so finds place in the statement of total financial resources. All types of transactions involving financial resources are included in this statement.

The working capital concept of funds is the most popular one, as already stated, amongst the different ways of defining the term 'Funds'. **In this chapter, when we discuss Sources and Application of Funds, the term 'funds' refer to working capital only.**

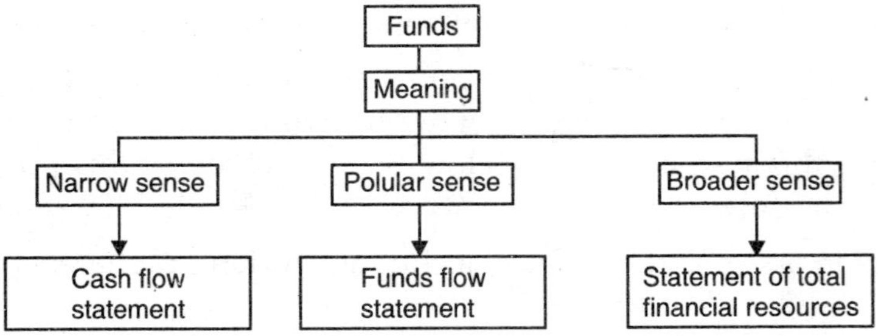

Fig. 6.1: Meaning of 'Funds'

In the context of 'Source and Application of Funds Statement', the term 'Funds' mean 'Working Capital'.

This statement shows the increase or decrease of working capital during a specified period. Further, this statement provides information for the causes or reasons for increase/decrease of working capital. From which sources, working capital is raised or to what purposes there has been diversion of working capital is known from this statement.

In other words, the story behind the change in the financial position between the beginning and end of a period is known.

Funds Flow Statement is called by various names, such as:

(i) Statement of Sources and Uses of Funds,

(ii) Where Got, Where Gone Statement,

(iii) Statement of Inflow and Outflow of Funds,

(iv) Funds Received and Funds Disbursed Statement, and

(v) Statement of Sources and Applications of Funds.

As observed rightly, the key word is 'Funds'.

6.3 MEANING OF FLOW OF FUNDS

The term 'flow' refers to movement of funds. The movement can be in the form of increase or decrease of funds, i.e. working capital. If a transaction creates a change in the quantum of working capital, 'flow' of funds has taken place. The transaction may increase or decrease the existing amount of working capital. Every transaction has two sides. Let us take some examples to explain the concept of flow of funds. Issue of shares for cash results in increase of working capital, it is a transaction of 'Source'. The transaction has resulted in 'inflow' of funds. Purchase of furniture on credit reduces the amount of working capital; it is 'application' of funds. There is outflow of funds with the transaction.

There would be change in working capital, if one of the items is related to current assets or current liabilities. Ask the transaction whether it would result in change—increase or decrease of working capital. If the answer is 'yes', the transaction finds a place in "Working Capital Statement", which is a part of funds flow statement.

If the transaction does not change the amount of working capital, it is said to be non-fund transaction and does not appear in the Funds Flow Statement. In a non-fund transaction, both the items are current or non-current items. The reference is to current assets and current liabilities. If cash is realized from debtors, there is no increase in working capital, as both the items are current items. When machinery has been purchased and in consideration debentures are issued, the transaction has not changed the working capital as both the items are non-current. It is a non-fund transaction. These types of transactions do not appear in the sources and application of funds statement.

***Simple Rule*: The simple rule is to "Ask the transaction, whether it changes working capital, if it is 'YES', the transaction finds a place in Sources and Application of Funds. If the answer is 'NO', no place for the transaction in the Statement.**

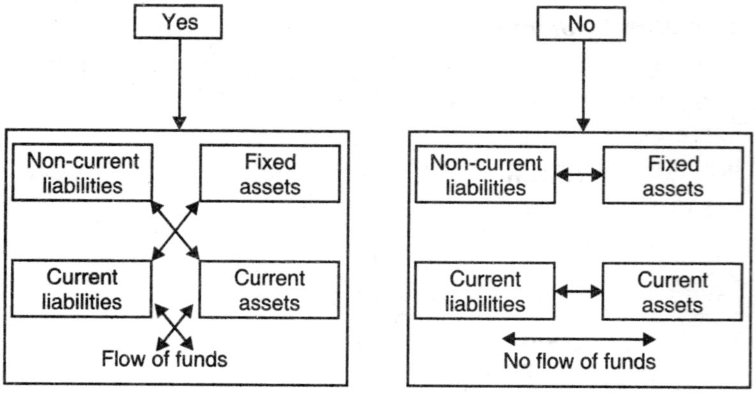

Fig. 6.2: Flow of funds

Flow of Funds is Compared with Natural Love: Funds flow is like natural love. There is always natural attraction between a boy and girl. This is natural love among the opposite genders. If the relationship is between one current asset and another current liability, there is flow of funds. Now-a-days, there is love between the same sex, be it gay or lesbian. If there is a relationship between one current asset with another current asset (gay) and one current liability with another current liability (lesbian), in such cases, there is no flow of fund.

6.4 MEANING AND OBJECTIVES OF FUNDS FLOW STATEMENT

Meaning and Definition: Funds Flow Statement is a device that indicates the various means through which funds have been obtained, during a specified period and the ways they have been used. Simply, it shows the different sources of procuring funds and their varied applications during that period. It shows the inflow and outflow of funds.

> **The term 'funds' refer to working capital. Funds Flow Statement shows the change in financial position of a firm between beginning and ending financial statement dates.**

Foulke defines this statement as: "A statement of sources and application of funds is a device designed to analyze the changes in financial condition of a business enterprise between two dates."

The statement has two sides: the left side shows the sources and the right side presents their uses.

The statement is an important tool for financial analysis for the management, bankers and investors who are interested in knowing the changes in the financial position of the firm. It is a supplement to the financial statements. Banks insist on this statement as and when loan application is submitted for financial assistance.

Now, Funds Flow Statement is a mandatory requirement of reporting in India for limited companies.

Importance and Objectives of Funds Flow Statement: This statement is widely used by the financial institutions, banks, credit rating agencies and management. By preparing the statement, the management can know well, in advance, about the adequacy or otherwise of working capital position for proper planning.

1. **Analysis of Financial Position and Profits:** Balance sheet is a static statement about the financial position, on a particular date. It shows the net effect of various transactions on the operational and financial position of a concern. It does not explain the causes for the change in assets and liabilities between two different dates.

> **The fund's flow statement explains effect on the liquidity position of the organization. At times, even after the firm is profitable, still, it experiences difficulty in meeting normal payments. Firm does not understand reasons for such a situation. Sources and Application of Funds gives the answers for these questions.**

2. **Throws Light on Perplex Questions:** Questions of general interest but answers not available elsewhere are found from this statement, such as:
   - **(i)** Why firm is not able to declare higher dividend, despite increase in profits?
   - **(ii)** Where the proceeds of shares and debentures have gone?
   - **(iii)** In what manner, the sale proceeds of fixed assets have been used?
   - **(iv)** What are the sources of repayment of long-term debts?
   - **(v)** How the increase in working capital requirement is financed and how further requirements would be met?

3. **Information of Profit from Operations and Non-operations:** Profit and Loss Account shows the summary or net effect of operating and non-operating expenses in the form of net profit. In other words, operating and non-operating profit is not calculated and shown separately.

> **Firm may be in net profit, due to non-operation profit, even after offsetting the operating losses. This alarming picture is not known from the profit and loss account for timely action. Funds Flow Statement shows the operating and non-operating profit, separately, that helps timely managerial action.**

4. **Management of Working Capital:** Statement of changes in working capital reveals to management the ways in which working capital was obtained and used in the past. Projections are always prepared by the management to achieve future plans.

A projected statement of working capital may reveal the need of large amount of working capital. In case, the firm is not able to meet the future working capital needs from internal resources, it can plan, in advance, to meet its needs.

5. **Helps in Borrowing Decision:** Now-a-days, banks and other financial institutions insist on the submission of Funds Flow Statement, along with loan application. This helps the bank to assess the working capital needs of the firm.

   Based on this statement, banks consider whether to sanction working capital limits or not and if so, to what extent the limit is to be sanctioned. This statement also facilitates the long-term institutions to appreciate the means of the firm for repaying the installment on a long-term debt. This is a necessary statement both for commercial banks and long-term institutions, while assessing the borrowing needs of the firm.

6. **Knowledge of Sources and Uses:** Sources in the Funds Flow Statement provide knowledge in respect of the various ways funds have been raised. In a similar manner, information in respect of applications or uses gives knowledge about the different ways in which the funds of the firm have been used. Firms may be able to plan future course of action with the information.
7. **Other Information:** Funds Flow Statement provides information which is not precisely available in the financial statements. If the firm purchases building and sells the same in the same accounting year for loss, the transaction does not appear in the Balance Sheet and hence it would not be known. For this reason, Funds Flow Statement is always needed as a supplementary statement.

6.5 UTILITY OF FUNDS FLOW STATEMENT

The versatile utility of Funds Flow Statement to different parties can be summarised as follows:

1. **Management:** The historical Funds Flow Statement (statements of the earlier years) provides the information how the funds were made available and their use in the past. They provide the means to understand why the plans of the earlier years were not achieved. That would be useful information to avoid recurrence in future. Funds Flow Statements can be prepared for future too. Planning can be more effective with their help.

   Funds Flow Statements provide the necessary hints to the management, whether it is necessary for them to review and recast their plans, in a more realistic way, in case the future inflows are not adequate to meet the anticipated outflows.

2. **Financial Institutions:** Commercial banks assess the working capital needs of the firm. Term-lending institutions want to satisfy the repayment capacity of the firm.

Funds Flow Statement provides the information how the firm used the funds earlier. Instances of diversion of sanctioned working capital for acquisition of fixed assets, contrary to the terms of sanction, would be known. The lenders would know firm's style of functioning.

> **Instances are abundant, where working capital limits, sanctioned by banks, are used for purchase of luxurious cars and personal use. Funds Flow Statements show these types of diversion of funds.**

Borrowings may be secured by assets but the financial institutions want to satisfy with the financial integrity of the borrower too. **Financial institutions would know the ways the funds were used, earlier, and future ways of use to judge their repaying ability.**

3. **Debenture Holders:** Debenture holders are long-term creditors of the firm. Their stake is similar to financial institutions, who provide long-term finance. They would get back their money after several years, dependant on the maturity period of the debentures. **Funds Flow Statement shows the position of availability of funds, when debentures fall due for repayment.** To continue to hold the debentures till such time or not, Funds Flow Statement is useful for them to take a suitable decision.
4. **Trade Creditors:** They are the suppliers of goods and services and look for short-term liquidity for payment. Liquidity of the firm and operating profits assure the repayment schedule. **Statement of working capital position indicates how far the firm is liquid to meet the promised payment schedule to review their credit policy.**
5. **Shareholders:** Shareholders are, basically, interested about the financial position of the firm and their future investment plans that generate operating profits. This holds well to the existing as well as potential shareholders. **Future investment plans and the operating profits that are likely to generate would be known from the Funds Flow Statement.**

6.6 SOURCES OF FUNDS

The following are the sources, through which funds come into the business of the firm.

1. **Funds from Operations:** Profits from business is the main source of funds. Profit does not mean the amount that is shown in the profit and loss account. When profit and loss account is prepared, several operating and non-operating expenses are debited. Similarly, operating and non-operating incomes are also credited.

> **Non-operating item is one, which is not connected with the conduct of the business. Examples are loss on sale of assets, preliminary expenses written off and rent received from building, not connected to the business.**

Adjustment is necessary to arrive at the correct profit from business operations. To arrive at operating income, non-operating expenses are to be added and non-operating income is to be deducted from the amount of profit shown in profit and loss account.

Profit from operations is the source as funds are received into the business.

2. **Sale of Fixed Assets:** If any fixed asset, such as land, building, plant and machinery is sold, the total sale proceeds become a source. Sale of fixed assets increases the working capital. However, if one non-current asset (fixed asset) is exchanged for another non-current asset, it does not result in inflow/outflow of funds, as there is no change in the working capital.
3. **Issue of Shares and Debentures:** When shares and debentures are issued to public for cash, cash received is a source. The important point is, if cash is received then only it is a source. In the following instances, it is not to be treated as source:
   (A) Issue of shares and debentures for consideration, other than current assets.
   (B) Conversion of debentures and loans into shares.
   (C) Issue of bonus shares or making partly paid shares as fully paid shares out of the accumulated profits.

The reason is simple. Such above instances do not increase the working capital.

4. **Increase in Long-term Loans:** Long-term loans from financial institutions and banks are a source as they increase the availability of funds.
5. **Decrease in Working Capital:** If the working capital at the end of the period is decreased, compared to the amount at the beginning of the period, it is a source. This can happen due to reduction of current assets or increase of current liabilities. If stock ₹ 60,000 is reduced to ₹ 40,000, working capital is decreased by ₹ 20,000 and the decrease is a source. Similarly, creditors may increase from ₹ 10,000 to ₹ 15,000 and the effect is reduction of working capital by ₹ 5,000. Decrease of working capital is a source of funds.
6. **Non-trading Receipts:** Non-trading receipts like dividend, interest earnings, damages received in legal action and rent etc. are credited to profit and loss account. These items are to be deducted from the net profit to arrive at profit from business operations. So, these items are to be shown separately in the Funds Flow Statement, as they are also sources of funds, not included in the funds from operations.

6.7 IS DEPRECIATION A SOURCE OF FUNDS?

Depreciation means decrease in the value of an asset due to wear and tear, passage of time, obsolescence, exhaustion and accident. It is a part of capital cost of fixed asset, spread over the life of the asset. Depreciation is taken as an operating expense, while arriving at true profits of a business. Depreciation is simply a book entry to arrive at **book** profits. Depreciation is a non-cash item.

It is a myth depreciation is a source. People misunderstand depreciation as a source as it is added to net profits to calculate funds from operations. Funds (Working Capital or Cash) are provided by revenues, but not by depreciation. Depreciation does not affect current assets or current liabilities. Preliminary expenses and goodwill written off are also added to net profits as these transactions do not result in any outflow of cash with them. The same treatment is extended to depreciation, while adding back to net profits to arrive at funds from operations.

Depreciation is neither a direct source nor application of funds. **To qualify it to be a source, depreciation should increase quantum of working capital.** This is not happening. As depreciation does not decrease the working capital, it is also not an application of funds.

Depreciation does not generate funds; it saves funds. For example, if the firm takes the assets on hire, it has to pay rent for them. Payment of rent is avoided by owning assets, which would have resulted in the outflow of funds. So, ownership of assets has only saved funds, but not generated any new funds.

Depreciation is not a direct source of funds. Is it an indirect source of funds? The answer is both YES and NO. When it is an indirect source? If so, to what extent? These are the questions to be answered. Depreciation can be taken as an indirect source of funds in a limited sense. It depends upon circumstances. If the firm is in profits, depreciation acts as a tax shield in helping the firm for reducing tax liability. Income Tax Act permits depreciation as an admissible expenditure to the extent it is provided as per its rules. As a result, taxable profits are reduced and tax liability, in consequence, is reduced. So, to that extent, depreciation is a source.

Depreciation is a source to the extent tax liability is reduced. Due to depreciation, profits available for distribution of dividend gets reduced. But, more funds would be available to the business for expansion. In these circumstances, depreciation is a source. But, when the firm is in loss, question of tax payment does not arise. In those circumstances, depreciation is not a source.

It can be said, with certainty, that depreciation is not a source of funds, directly. So, depreciation is only an indirect source to a limited extent, under certain circumstances.

Depreciation is an expense to be taken into account to arrive at accounting profit, but this has no relevance for calculation of funds from operations. For this reason, depreciation is added back to net profit to calculate funds from operations.

The above point can be understood with a simple example:

	Case I (₹)	Case II (₹)
Income before depreciation	80,000	80,000
Depreciation provided (A)	----	20,000
Taxable income	80,000	60,000
Income tax rate, say 50%	40,000	30,000
Net income after tax (B)	40,000	30,000
Net flow of funds after tax (A+B)	40,000	50,000

In case of II, funds from operations are ₹ 50,000, while they are only ₹ 40,000 in case of I. In case of II, depreciation is a source to the extent of ₹ 10,000 and these funds are, additionally, available to the firm for future expansion.

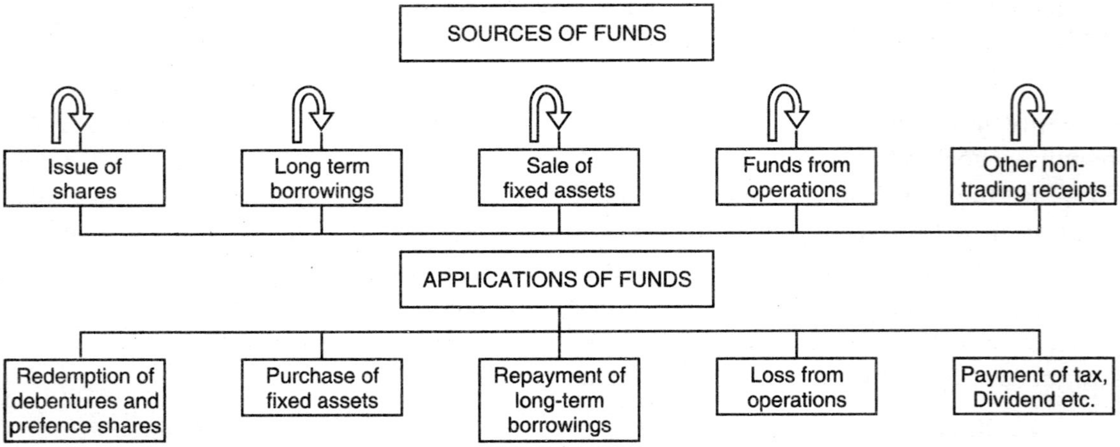

Fig. 6.3: Sources and applications of funds

6.8 APPLICATION OR USES OF FUNDS

1. **Loss from Operations:** Result from trading operations may be loss in a year. Such loss of funds in trading amounts to an application or outflow of funds. Working capital would be the first casualty if the firm sustains loss.
2. **Redemption of Preference Share Capital:** If preference shares are redeemed during the year, redemption decreases the funds and so it is an application. Where redemption happens at premium or discount, the net amount (including premium or after deducting discount) is the use. However, if preference shares are redeemed in exchange of some types of shares or debentures, it does not constitute outflow of funds, as no fund is involved in the transaction.

3. **Repayment of Loans or Redemption of Debentures:** Similar to redemption of preference shares, repayment of loan and redemption of debentures are also uses.
4. **Purchase of Fixed or Non-current Asset:** Purchase of fixed assets such as machinery or building results in application of funds. However, purchase of fixed assets in consideration of issue of shares, debentures or loans is not a use as no funds are involved.
5. **Payment of Dividend and Tax:** Payment of dividend (including interim dividend) and tax are applications. The important point is their actual payment, and then only they become uses. Mere declaration of dividend and provision of tax are not uses.
6. **Any Other Non-trading Payments:** Any other non-trading payments are also uses as they involve outgo of funds. Examples are loss of cash or theft in business.

6.9 PROCEDURE FOR KNOWING WHETHER A TRANSACTION FINDS A PLACE IN FUNDS FLOW STATEMENT

1. Make out the journal entry and find out the accounts involved.
2. Decide whether the accounts concerned are current (concerned with current assets and current liabilities) or non-current (concerned with non-current assets and non-current liabilities).
3. If both the accounts involved are current, i.e. either current assets or current liabilities, it does not result in the flow of funds.
4. If both the accounts are non-current, i.e. either permanent assets or permanent liabilities, the transaction still does not result in the flow of funds.
5. If one of the accounts is concerned with current and the other is non-current, the transaction results in flow of funds.

For the transaction to appear in Funds Flow Statement, it is necessary only if one of the accounts in a transaction should be concerned with current assets or current liabilities. If both the accounts are current or non-current assets/liabilities, the transaction does not appear in Funds Flow Statement.

There is attraction between a male and female. In the normal course, there is no attraction between the species of the same sex. In a similar manner, in a transaction, if both the accounts belong to the same category—current assets or liabilities—there is no funds flow. To appear in a Funds Flow Statement, one of the accounts should only belong to current assets/current liabilities.

Examples

Transaction	Journal Entry	Category of Debit Account	Category of Credit Account	Result—Flow of Funds or not—Reason
1. Cash collected from debtors	Cash A/c ...Dr. To sundry debtors	Current	Current	NO. Both the accounts are current assets. Cash increases with similar decrease in debtors.
2. Goods purchased for cash or credit	Purchases ...Dr. To cash/Creditors A/c	Current	Current	NO. Both the accounts are current assets. Working capital remains the same.
3. Purchase of machinery in exchange of land	Machinery A/c ...Dr. To land A/c	Non-current	Non-current	NO. Both the accounts are non- current assets. Does not affect working capital.
4. Transfer to general reserves	Profit & Loss A/c ...Dr. To general reserves	Non-current	Non-current	NO. Does not affect working capital.
5. Issue of debentures for cash	Cash A/c ... Dr. To debentures	Current	Non-current	YES. One is current asset and another is non-current liability. Cash inflow increases the working capital.
6. Redemption of debentures	Debentures A/c ...Dr. To Cash	Non-current	Current	YES. One is non-current liability and another is current asset. Cash outflow decreases the working capital.
7. Purchase of trade investment	Trade Investment A/c ...Dr To cash	Non-current	Current	Yes. One is non-current asset and another is current asset. Cash outflow decreases the working capital.
8. Writing off fictitious assets, say goodwill	Profit and loss account...Dr. To goodwill account	Non-current	Non-current	No. Both are non-current. Does not change working the capital.

Illustration No. 1

State with reasons whether there is fund flow from the following transactions:

(a) Purchase of machinery for cash ₹ 20,000.

(b) Sale of building ₹ 32,000. The original cost was ₹ 40,000 and accumulated depreciation was ₹ 24,000.

(c) 1,000 shares of ₹ 10 each issued at 11 per share.

(d) Goodwill written off out of profit ₹ 5,000.

(e) ₹ 6,000 declared as divided on equity shares and paid.

(B.U., M.B.A., 2007)

Solution:

Transaction	Journal Entry	Category of Debit Account	Category of Credit Account	Result—Flow of Funds or not—Reason
(a) Purchase of machinery for cash	Machinery A/c ...Dr 20,000 To cash 20,000	Non-current	Current	Yes. One is non-current asset and the other is current asset. Decreases working capital by ₹ 20,000.
(b) Sale proceeds of building, at profit	Cash ....Dr. 32,000 To building 32,000	Current	Non- current	Yes. One is current asset and the other is non-current asset. Increases working capital by ₹ 32,000.
(c) Issue of shares, at premium	Cash ....Dr. 11,000 To share capital 10,000 Share premium 1,000	Current	Non-current Non-current	Yes. One is current and the other accounts are non-current. Increases working capital by ₹ 11,000
(d) Goodwill written off from profit	Profit and loss A/c ...Dr 5,000 To goodwill 5,000	Non-current	Non-current	No. Both the accounts are non-current. Does not change the working capital.
(e) Dividend declared from profits on equity share capital	Profit and loss A/c ...Dr 6,000 To cash 6,000	Non-current	Current	Yes. One account is non-current and the other is current. Decreases working capital by ₹ 6,000.

Impact of Opening Stock/Closing Stock on Funds: Opening stock appears on the debit side of the Profit and Loss Account. Opening stock reduces profit, so it is an application. Closing stock appears on the credit side of the profit and loss account. Due to closing stock, profit increases. Profit is a source. So, closing stock is a source.

Difference between Funds from Operations and Non-operations: The term 'operations' refers to business. At times, the business of the firm may be in loss and still the profit and loss account of the firm may be in profit, due to other incomes, not connected to the business. Let us explain with an example. Hotel President is carrying on the business of boarding and lodging and the hotel is in loss by ₹ 10 lakhs. However, ground floor of the building is let out to State Bank of India, which has been paying an annual rent of ₹ 25 lakhs.

What is the net profit shown in Profit and Loss Account? The profit and loss account shows a profit ₹ 15 lakhs combining operating loss (₹ 10 lakhs) and non-operating income (rental income) ₹ 25 lakhs.

6.10 PREPARATION OF FUNDS FLOW STATEMENT

To prepare Funds Flow Statement, two statements are required to be prepared. They are Statement of Changes in Working Capital and Statement of Funds from Operations. All the information may not always be readily available. Hidden information has to be found out. The entire process of preparation of Funds Flow Statement can be summarised, as under:

(A) Statement of Changes in working capital,

(B) Calculation of funds from operations

(C) Finding out hidden information, if required, and

(D) Preparation of Funds Flow Statement

(A) Statement of Changes in Working Capital

Working capital is the excess of current assets over current liabilities. Every current asset at the end of the year is to be compared with the amount at the beginning of the year to calculate the increase or decrease of working capital. Increase or decrease of working capital is to be recorded in the relevant column. The same procedure is to be repeated in respect of all current liabilities.

All other information is not relevant for preparation of statement of changes in working capital.

Working capital = Current assets − Current liabilities

Increase in current asset	→	Increase in working capital
Decrease in current asset	→	Decrease in working capital
Increase in current liability	→	Decrease in working capital
Decrease in current liability	→	Increase in working capital

Fig. 6.4: Effect on working capital

Illustration No. 2

Prepare a Statement of Changes in working capital from the following Balance Sheets of THEER & Co. Bhopal.

	31st March, 2006	31st March, 2005
Assets		
Goodwill	20,000	15,000
Bank	70,000	60,000
Debtors	40,000	45,000
Bills receivable	10,000	8,000
Closing Stock	20,000	22,000
Long-term investments	5,000	3,000
Building	25,000	15,000
Preliminary expenses	4,000	6,000
	1,94,000	**1,74,000**
Liabilities		
Trade creditors	55,000	60,000
Bills payable	30,000	25,000
Loans (Payable during 2007- ₹ 25,000)	40,000	—
Equity share capital	50,000	80,000
Profit & loss account	19,000	9,000
	1,94,000	**1,74,000**

Solution

Statement of Changes in Working Capital

Particulars	2005	2006	Effect on Working Capital Increase ₹	Decrease ₹
Current Assets:				
Bank	60,000	70,000	10,000	
Debtors	45,000	40,000		5,000
Bills receivable	8,000	10,000	2,000	
Closing stock	22,000	20,000		2,000
	1,35,000	**1,40,000**		
Current Liabilities:				
Trade creditors	60,000	55,000	5,000	
Bills payable	25,000	30,000		5,000
*Loans (Payable during 2007)	------	25,000		25,000
	85,000	**1,10,000**		
Working capital (CA-CL)	50,000	30,000		
Decrease in working capital		20,000	20,000	
	50,000	50,000	37,000	37,000

* **Note:** Out of the total Loan amount ₹ 40,000, only ₹ 25,000 is repayable during the year 2007. Only ₹ 25,000 is current liability, as it becomes payable within one year and so working capital is affected to that extent only.

(B) Calculation of Funds from Operations

The net profit appearing in the Profit and Loss Account need not necessarily be the funds from operations. Certain adjustments are to be made to get funds from operations. Follow the steps as under:

1. Take the net profit figure in Profit and Loss Account as the **BASE**.
2. **Depreciation:** Add back depreciation to the net profit, debited in the Profit and Loss Account, as it does not involve outflow of funds. Depreciation is an expense to be taken into account to arrive at the accounting profit, but this has no relevance for calculation of funds from operations.
3. **Intangible Assets Written Off:** Add back expenses like preliminary expenses, discount on issue of shares and debentures and goodwill written off. These are intangible assets written off to arrive at profit but does not involve outflow of funds.
4. **Incomes not related to Operations or Business:** These are the incomes that are not related to operations but included in Profit and Loss Account to arrive at net profit. These incomes—profit on sale of assets, income from investments and rent from buildings, not connected to business—are to be deducted from net profits.
5. **Non-operating Expenses:** Similarly, non-operating expenses like loss on sale of assets, loss due to theft debited to Profit and Loss Account are to be added back to net profit to arrive at funds from operations.

The intention of the exercise is to find out funds from operations. Instead of net profit, net loss may appear in Profit and Loss Account. Simply, follow a reverse procedure to arrive at funds from operations, in case loss is in Profit and Loss Account. This easy procedure is suggested for students who experience difficulty in appreciating the implication.

Income Statement or Profit and Loss Account is not given: If Income Statement or Profit and Loss Account is not given, information on net profit or loss may be, indirectly, given. Increase in General Reserve and Profit and Loss Accounts, balances appearing between opening and closing balance sheets has to be taken as net profit for the period. Suitable adjustments are to be made for the dividend paid and issue of bonus shares, capitalising profits. Funds from operations can be calculated by preparing Profit and Loss Adjustment Account.

Funds Flow Statement can be prepared in two ways:

1. Report Form
2. T Form or Account Form or Self-Balancing type.

Illustration No. 3

From the following information extracted from the Balance Sheets of Theer & Tarkh Ltd., calculate funds from operations:

	As on 31st March, 2005 (₹)	As on 31st March, 2006 (₹)
Share capital	80,000	1,00,000
General reserve	30,000	35,000
Profit and loss account	40,000	1,00,000
Depreciation fund	15,000	18,000
Goodwill	15,000	10,000
Preliminary expenses	3,000	2,000
Patents	10,000	8,000

Bonus shares have been issued for ₹ 20,000 during 2005-06, capitalising profits from Profit and Loss Account. It is observed in the Profit and Loss Account that an income ₹ 6,000 from sale of machinery has been received.

Solution

	₹
Profit and Loss Account (as on 31st March, 2006)— closing balance	1,00,000
+ Increase in Share Capital (Bonus issue) transferring from Profit and Loss A/c	20,000
+ Transfer to General Reserve	5,000
+ Provision for Depreciation	3,000
+ Goodwill Written Off	5,000
+ Preliminary Expenses Written Off	1,000
+ Patents Written Off	2,000
– Income from Sale of Machinery	6,000
	1,30,000
– Balance in Profit and Loss Account—opening balance (As on 31st March, 2005)	40,000
Funds from Operations	90,000

The funds from operations can be found out in an alternative way by preparing Profit and Loss Adjustment Account.

Dr. **Adjusted Profit and Loss Account** Cr.

Particulars	Amount	Particulars	Amount
To transfer to capital account (Bonus issue)	20,000	By balance b/d	40,000
To transfer to general reserve	5,000	By income from sale of machinery	6,000
To depreciation fund (Provision for depreciation)	3,000	By funds from operations	90,000
To goodwill written off	5,000		
To preliminary expenses written off	1,000		
To patents written off	2,000		
To balance c/d	1,00,000		
	1,36,000		1,36,000

Illustration No. 4

From the following Balance Sheet of a company for the year ending 31st December 1999 and 31st December, 2000, prepare statement showing sources and applications of funds:

Liabilities	31st Dec., 1999	31st Dec., 2000	Assets	31st Dec., 1999	31st Dec., 2000
Share capital	3,00,000	4,00,000	Plant and machinery	50,000	60,000
			Furniture and fixtures	10,000	15,000
P & L A/c	15,000	30,000	Stock in trade	85,000	1,05,000
Sundry creditors	1,00,000	70,000	Debtors	1,60,000	1,50,000
			Cash	1,10,000	1,70,000
	4,15,000	5,00,000		4,15,000	5,00,000

Depreciation has been provided for ₹ 10,000 on plant and machinery. There has been a sale of furniture and fixtures for ₹ 2,000 which was its depreciated cost.

(M.C.A., 2001)

Solution
Statement of Changes in Working Capital

Current Assets	31st Dec., 1999	31st Dec., 2000	Increase	Decrease
Current Assets				
Stock in trade	85,000	1,05,000	20,000	
Debtors	1,60,000	1,50,000		10,000
Cash	1,10,000	1,70,000	60,000	
Total current assets	3,55,000	4,25,000		
Current Liabilities				
Sundry creditors	1,00,000	70,000	30,000	
Total Current Liabilities	1,00,000	70,000		
Working capital	2,55,000	3,55,000		
Increase in working capital	1,00,000			1,00,000
	3,55,000	3,55,000	1,10,000	1,10,000

Dr. Plant and Machinery Account Cr.

To opening balance b/d	50,000	By depreciation	10,000
Bank (purchase of plant and machinery)	20,000	By closing balance c/d	60,000
	70,000		70,000

Dr. Furniture and Fixtures Account Cr.

To opening balance b/d	10,000	By sale of furniture	2,000
Bank (purchase of furniture and fixtures)*	7,000	By closing balance c/d	15,000
	17,000		17,000

Calculation of Profit

Difference in profit and loss account (30,000 –15,000)	15,000	
Depreciation of plant and machinery	10,000	
		25,000

Statement of Sources and Application of Funds

Sources		
Increase in share capital	1,00,000	
Profit	25,000	1,27,000
Sale of furniture and fixtures	2,000	
Application		
Purchase: Plant and machinery	20,000	
Purchase: Furniture and fixtures	7,000	1,27,000
Increase in working capital	1,00,000	

Note: Sale of furniture has been made at depreciated cost ₹ 20,000. So, there is no profit / loss. There is no depreciation on furniture and fixtures.

Illustration No. 5

The Balance Sheet of Moon Ltd. at the end of December, 2000 & 2001 are as follows:

	2000	₹ 2001
Liabilities		
Preference share capital	70,000	75,000
Equity share capital	1,30,000	1,75,000
Creditors	1,00,000	70,000
P. & L. A/C	20,000	30,000
	3,20,000	**3,50,000**
Assets		
Plant & machinery	50,000	60,000
Furniture & fixtures	20,000	75,000
Stock	80,000	50,000
Debtors	70,000	85,000
Cash	1,00,000	80,000
	3,20,000	**3,50,000**

You are required to prepare a Statement of Working Capital Changes and a statement of fund flow from the above data.

Comment on the policy adopted by the company.

(B.U., M.B.A., 2002)

Solution

Statement of Working Capital Changes (₹)

Particulars	2000	2001	Effect of Working	Capital Changes
Current Assets			Increase	Decrease
Stock	80,000	50,000		30,000
Debtors	70,000	85,000	15,000	
Cash	1,00,000	80,000		20,000
	2,50,000	2,15,000		
Current Liabilities				
Creditors	1,00,000	70,000	30,000	
	1,00,000	70,000		
Working Capital	1,50,000	1,45,000		
Decrease in		5,000	5,000	
Working Capital	1,50,000	1,50,000		
			50,000	50,000

Funds Flow Statement for the year ended December, 2001

Sources	₹	Applications	₹
Decrease in working capital	5,000	Purchase of plant and machinery	10,000
Issue of preference shares	5,000	Purchase of furniture and fixtures	55,000
Issue of equity share capital	45,000		
Funds from operations	10,000		65,000
	65,000		

Comments

Long-term Funds: Long-term Funds are ₹ 60,000, comprising of issue of preference shares, equity shares and profit earned by the company during the year 2001.

Long-term Uses: ₹ 65,000 are long-term uses, purchase of machinery, furniture and fixtures.

Profits: Company has made a profit of ₹ 10,000 used for acquisition of fixed assets.

Diversion of working capital: There has been a reduction of working capital by ₹ 5,000, which has been used for long-term uses—fixed assets.

Policy: Usage of long-term sources for long-term uses is proper. But, diversion of short-term sources (working capital) for long-term uses is improper.

However, use of excessive working capital, for purchase of fixed assets is ok.

Illustration No. 6

Following items have been drawn from the Balance Sheet. Compute funds from operations:

	As on 31-3-2007	As on 31-3-2008
Profit and loss account (credit balance)	40,000	60,000
General reserve	15,000	25,000
Goodwill	10,000	5,000
Preliminary expenses accumulated	6,000	3,000
Depreciation on fixed assets	25,000	30,000

(M.C.A., 2001)

Solution

Calculation of Funds from Operations

Profit made in 2007-08		
Difference in Profit and Loss Account	20,000	
Difference in General Reserve	10,000	
		30,000
Goodwill Written Off		5,000
Preliminary Expenses written off		3,000
Depreciation on Fixed Assets		5,000
Funds from Operations		43,000

(C) Finding Out the Hidden Information

While preparing the Funds Flow Statement, one has to analyze the given Balance Sheets. At the end of balance sheets, certain information may be given as notes that give clues for the hidden information. The hidden information may relate to provision and payment of tax, purchase/sale of assets and issue/redemption of shares and debentures.

1. **Provision for Taxation:** There are two ways of dealing with provision for taxation.
   (i) As a current liability
   (ii) As an appropriation of profits

(i) As a Current Liability: Provision for tax may be treated as a current liability, as tax generally is an immediate obligation of the firm to pay to the Government.

> **It is preferable to treat 'Provision of Tax' as current liability, as such a treatment is simple as nothing further is to be done. This approach is recommended for students, if the problem does not stipulate any specific treatment.**

When it is treated as current liability, provision for taxation will appear in the Schedule of Changes in working capital, like other current liabilities. No further treatment is needed in respect of payment of tax and provision of tax made during the year. There is no need to prepare provision for taxation account. The simple rules are as under:

(i) In this case, payment of tax shall not be shown as an application of funds.

(ii) Provision for tax made during the year is not to be added back to the profits to arrive at funds from operations.

The simple rule is to treat provision for tax as current liability and forget further treatment about this matter.

(ii) As an Appropriation of Profit: When provision for tax is treated as an appropriation of profit, follow the treatment as under:

(A) Do not treat 'Provision for Tax' as current liability for the calculation of working capital. In other words, do not include it in the 'Schedule of Changes in Working Capital'.

(B) Show the payment of tax as application in 'Funds Flow Statement'.

(C) Add back 'Provision for Tax' in the current year to the current year's profit to get the operating profit.

So, information for tax payment and provision made for tax in the current year is necessary.

Illustration No. 7

The opening balance in the Provision for Taxation Account, as on 1st January 2005, was ₹ 40,000 and the closing balance, as on 31st December 2005 was ₹ 50,000. The taxes paid during the year amounted to ₹ 35,000. Show the treatment of the item in the Funds Flow Statement:

(i) As Current Liability

(ii) As Appropriation of Profit

Solution

(i) When provision for taxation is treated as current liability

Provision for taxation is treated as current liability and is shown in the schedule of changes in working capital. There is no further treatment in the Funds Flow Statement:

Schedule of Changes in Working Capital

	1-1-2005 ₹	31-12-2005 ₹	Increase in Working Capital ₹	Decrease in Working Capital ₹
Current Liabilities				
Provision for taxation	40,000	50,000		10,000

(ii) As Appropriation of Profit

1. This item will not be shown in the Schedule of Changes in the working capital.
2. Taxes paid during the year, ₹ 35,000, is an Application of Funds and will appear on the application side of Funds Flow Statement.

Funds Flow Statement for the year ended 31-12-2005

Sources	₹	Application	₹
		Payment of Tax	35,000

3. Provision for taxation made during the year is ₹ 45,000 calculated as below. This amount will be added back to net profit for finding funds from operations.

Calculation of Provision for Taxation Made During the Year

Opening balance of provision for tax on 1-1-2005	40,000
Less: Tax paid during the year	35,000
	5,000
Closing balance of provision on 31-12-2005	50,000
Provision made during the year	45,000

OR

Dr. **Cr.**

Provision for Taxation A/c

To cash (tax paid)	35,000	By balance b/d	40,000
To balance c/d	50,000	By adjusted P/LA/c (Provision made–balancing figure)	45,000
	85,000		85,000

Note: It is suggested to students to adopt 'Prepare Account' approach to find out the hidden information so that double entry concept can be applied conveniently. More so, account preparation leaves no confusion about adding or subtracting the figures.

Illustration No. 8

Following are the Balance Sheet of a company as on 31-3-2003 and 2004:

(₹)

Liabilities	2003	2004	Assets	2003	2004
Share capital	61,000	74,000	Plant	38,000	43,000
Reserves	13,000	15,500	Building	50,950	48,020
P and L a/c	8,600	8,800	Stock	25,500	18,800
Creditors	28,000	24,000	Debtors	22,000	16,200
Bank loan	18,000	—	Cash	150	180
Prov. for tax	8,000	8,500	Bank	—	2,100
			Goodwill	—	2,500
	1,36,600	1,30,800		1,36,600	1,30,800

Additional Information:

(a) Dividend: ₹ 6,000 was paid.

(b) Provision: ₹ 9,000 for income-tax was made during the year.

(c) ₹ 3,600 was written off as depreciation on plant.

Prepare Fund Flow Statement.

(B.U., M.B.A., 2004–05)

Solution

Statement of Changes in Working Capital

	As on 31-3-2003	As on 31-3-2004	Increase in Working Capital	Decrease in Working Capital
Current Assets:				
Stock	25,500	18,800		6,700
Debtors	22,000	16,200		5,800
Cash	150	180	30	
Bank	—	2,100	2,100	
	47,650	37,280		

Contd...

Current Liabilities				
Creditors	28,000	24,000	4,000	
Bank loan	18,000	—	18,000	
Provision for tax	8,000	8,500		500
	54,000	32,500		
Working capital	–6,350	4,780		
Increase in working capital		11,130		11,130
			24,130	24,130

Dr. Plant and Machinery Account Cr.

To opening balance b/d	38,000	By depreciation	3,600
Bank (purchase of plant and machinery)	8,600	By closing balance c/d	43,000
	46,600		46,600

Dr. Building Account Cr.

To opening balance b/d	50,950	By depreciation (Balancing figure)	2,930
		By closing balance c/d	48,020
	50,950		50,950

Funds from Operations

Increase in profit (8,800 – 8,600)	200
Dividend paid	6,000
Depreciation on plant	3,600
Depreciation on building	2,930
Funds from operations	12,730

Funds Flow Statement for the Period Ended 31st March, 2004

Sources	
Issue of shares	13,000
Funds from operations	12,730
	25,730
Application	
Increase in working capital	11,130
Purchase of plant and machinery	8,600
Dividend paid	6,000
	25,730

- Creation of goodwill for ₹ 2,500 has increased reserves by ₹ 2,500.

Illustration No. 9

From the following comparative balance sheets of Lakshminarayan Ltd. and additional information, prepare Funds Flow Statement along with statement of working capital charges.

	31st March, 2002	31st March, 2001
Assets		
Cash	5,000	7,000
Machinery	15,000	20,000
Building	10,000	5,000
Debtors	10,000	8,000
Bills receivable	10,000	12,000
Stock	14,000	10,000
Prepaid expenses	1,000	2,000
Preliminary expenses	10,000	15,000
	75,000	**79,000**
Liabilities		
Equity share capital	30,000	20,000
P/L a/c	15,000	10,000
General reserve	5,000	3,000
Debentures	10,000	23,000
Creditors	5,000	6,000
Bills payable	3,000	11,000
Provision for tax	7,000	6,000
	75,000	**79,000**

Additional Information:

(a) Dividend paid ₹ 10,000.
(b) Depreciation on machinery ₹ 10,000.
(c) Depreciation on building ₹ 3,000.
(d) Tax paid ₹ 1,000.
(e) Provision for tax ₹ 5,000 has been made during the year 2002.

Solution

Statement of Changes in Working Capital

	As on 31-3-2001	As on 31-3-2002	Increase in Working Capital	Decrease in Working Capital
Current Assets:				
Cash	7,000	5,000		2,000
Debtors	8,000	10,000	2,000	
Bills receivable	12,000	10,000		2,000
Stock	10,000	14,000	4,000	
Prepaid expenses	2,000	1,000		1,000
	39,000	40,000		
Current Liabilities				
Creditors	6,000	5,000	1,000	
Bills payable	11,000	3,000	8,000	
Provision for tax*	6,000	7,000		1,000
	23,000	15,000		
Working capital	16,000	25,000		
Increase in working capital	**9,000**			**9,000**
	25,000	25,000	15,000	15,000

Funds from Operations

Increase in profit (15,000 –10,000)	5,000
Dividend paid	10,000
General reserve (5,000 – 3,000)	2,000
Depreciation on machinery	10,000
Depreciation on building	3,000
Preliminary expenses written off	5,000
Funds from operations	**35,000**

Dr. Plant and Machinery Account Cr.

To opening balance b/d	20,000	By depreciation	10,000
Purchase of machinery	5,000		
		By closing balance c/d	15,000
	25,000		25,000

Dr. Building Account Cr.

To opening balance b/d	5,000	By depreciation	3,000
Additions	8,000		
		By closing balance c/d	10,000
	13,000		13,000

Funds Flow Statement for the Period Ended 31st March, 2002

Sources	
Issue of shares	10,000
Funds from operations	35,000
	45,000
Application	
Increase in working capital	9,000
Purchase of plant and machinery	5,000
Additions to building	8,000
Dividend paid	10,000
Redemption of debentures	13,000
	45,000

* When 'Provision for Tax' is treated as a current liability, tax provision and payment of tax do not require any additional treatment. Treating 'Provision for Tax' as a current liability is the easiest way. In the absence of specific requirement in the question, students are advised to treat 'Provision for Tax' as a current liability.

Proposed Dividend

Treatment of Proposed Dividend is similar to Provision for Taxation.

Proposed dividend can be treated as current liability or appropriation of profits.

(i) **As Current Liability:** Dividend recommended for payment by Board of Directors is, normally, approved for payment at Annual General Meeting. Till it is approved, it is appropriation of profits and after approval, it is an obligation on the part of company to make payment. So, it is a current liability. **Students are advised to treat the amount of proposed dividend as current liability as the treatment is simple.** Show the amount as current liability in the Schedule of Changes in Working Capital. Information in respect of provision and its payment are to be ignored. Provision should not be added back to the net profits and payment should not be shown in application.

(ii) As Non-current Liability: As proposed dividend is an appropriation of profit, it is not a current liability. Hence, the amount is not to be included in the Schedule of Changes in Working Capital. The appropriation of dividend, made during the year, is to be added back to net profits to calculate funds from operations. Actual dividend payment is to be shown as application in Funds Flow Statement.

Treatment of proposed dividend is similar to provision for taxation.

Interim Dividend: The expression 'Interim Dividend' denotes dividend paid to shareholders of the company during the financial year, before the finalization of accounts. This is the dividend paid or declared between two Annual General Meetings. Interim dividend should be added back to the figure of net profits (or debited to Profit and Loss Adjustment Account) to arrive at Funds from Operations. However, if the closing balance in the profit and loss account is given after payment of interim dividend, this adjustment is not required. To ascertain whether the closing balance in the Profit and Loss Account is after or before payment of interim dividend, it is desirable to prepare the Profit and Loss Account and incorporate the adjustments to find out the picture. Interim dividend is to be shown as an application of funds.

Illustration No. 10

From the following balance sheets as on 31st March 2005 and 31st March 2006, prepare a Schedule of Changes in the working capital and Funds Flow Statement taking:

(i) the provision for tax and proposed dividend as current liabilities, and

(ii) the provision for tax and proposed dividend as non-current liabilities.

Balance Sheet

Liabilities	31-12-2005 ₹	31-12-2006 ₹	Assets	31-12-2005 ₹	31-12-2006 ₹
Share capital	1,00,000	1,50,000	Fixed assets	1,00,000	1,55,000
Profit and loss account	4,000	6,000	Current assets	13,000	14,500
Provision for tax	2,000	3,000			
Proposed dividends	1,000	1,500			
Sundry creditors	4,000	6,000			
Outstanding expenses	2,000	3,000			
	1,13,000	1,69,500		1,13,000	1,69,500

Additional Information:

1. Tax paid during 2006 ₹ 2,500
2. Dividend paid during 2006 ₹ 1,000

Solution:

(i) When provision for tax and proposed dividends are taken as current liabilities.

Schedule of Changes in Working Capital

Particulars	31-12-2005	31-12-2006	Effect on Working Capital	
			Increase(+) ₹	Decrease(–) ₹
Current assets	13,000	14,500	1,500	
Current liabilities				
Sundry creditors	4,000	6,000		2,000
Outstanding expenses	2,000	3,000		1,000
Provision for tax	2,000	3,000		1,000
Proposed dividends	1,000	1,500		500
Total current liabilities	9,000	13,500		
Net working capital (CA – CL)	4,000	1,000		
Decrease in working capital		3,000	3,000	
	4,000	4,000	4,500	4,500

Funds Flow Statement for the Year Ended 31-12-2006

Sources	₹	Application	₹
Increase in share capital	50,000	Purchase of fixed assets	55,000
Funds from operations	2,000		
Decrease in working capital	3,000		
	55,000		55,000

(ii) When provision for tax and proposed dividends are taken as non-current liabilities:

Schedule of Changes in Working Capital

Particulars	31-12-2005	31-12-2006	Effect on Working Capital	
			Increase(+) ₹	Decrease(–) ₹
Current assets	13,000	14,500	1,500	
Current liabilities				
Sundry creditors	4,000	6,000		2,000
Outstanding expenses	2,000	3,000		1,000
Total current liabilities	6,000	9,000		
Net working capital (CA – CL)	7,000	5,500		
Decrease in working capital		1,500	1,500	
	7,000	7,000	3,000	3,000

Provision for Tax

Dr.			Cr.
To cash (tax paid)	2,500	By balance b/d	2,000
To balance c/d	3,000	By P & L adjustment A/c (balancing figure)	3,500
	5,500		5,500

Proposed Dividend Account

Dr.			Cr.
To cash	1,000	By balance b/d	1,000
To balance c/d	1,500	By profit and loss adjustment A/c	1,500
	2,500		2,500

Profit and Loss Adjustment Account

Dr.			Cr.
To provision for tax	3,500	By balance b/d	4,000
To proposed dividend	1,500	By funds from operations (balancing figure)	7,000
To balance b/d	6,000		
	11,000		11,000

Funds Flow Statement for the Year Ended 31-12-2006

Sources	₹	Application	₹
Increase in share capital	50,000	Purchase of fixed assets	55,000
Funds from operations	7,000	Tax paid	2,500
Decrease in working capital	1,500	Dividend paid	1,000
	58,500		58,500

Illustration No. 11

The following information has been taken from the Balance Sheet of Tarkh & Company, Indore.

	31st March, 2005 ₹	31st March, 2006 ₹
Machinery	1,00,000	2,70,000
Accumulated depreciation	45,000	60,000
Profit and loss account	15,000	40,000

The following additional information is also available:

(i) A machine costing ₹ 15,000 was purchased during the year by issue of equity shares.

(ii) On January 1st 2005, a machine costing ₹ 25,000 (with an accumulated depreciation of ₹ 10,000) was sold for ₹ 22,000.

Find out sources/application of funds.

Solution

Machinery Account

Dr. Cr.

	₹		₹
To balance b/d	1,00,000	By sale of machinery A/c	25,000
To share capital	15,000	By balance c/d	
To cash—purchase of machinery (balancing figure)	1,80,000		2,70,000
	2,95,000		2,95,000

Adjusted Profit and Loss Account

Dr. Cr.

	₹		₹
To Accumulated depreciation A/c	25,000**	By balance b/d	15,000
To balance c/d	40,000	By machinery A/c (profit on sale)	7,000
		By funds from operations	43,000
	65,000		65,000

** represents depreciation provided during the year.

1. Purchase of machinery for ₹ 15,000 by issue of equity shares is neither a source nor an application of funds.
2. Sale of machinery ₹ 22,000 is a source of funds.
3. Funds from operations, ₹ 43,000, are a source of funds.
4. Purchase of machinery by cash, ₹ 1,80,000, is an application of funds.

Illustration No. 12

The following relevant information has been extracted from the following balance sheets:

	As on 31st December, 2005 ₹	As on 31st December, 2006 ₹
Equity share capital	6,00,000	10,00,000
Preference share capital	3,00,000	4,50,000

Additional Information:

1. Equity shares were issued during the year for the purchase of building for ₹ 2,50,000.
2. 9% Preference Share Capital value ₹ 1,75,000 was redeemed during the year.

Prepare necessary accounts and identify source/application of funds.

Solution

Equity Share Capital Account

Dr.			Cr.
To balance c/d	10,00,000	By balance b/d	6,00,000
		By building A/c	2,50,000
		By cash (issue of shares-balancing figure)	1,50,000
	10,00,000		10,00,000

9 % Preference Share Capital Account

Dr.			Cr.
To cash (redemption of shares)	1,75,000	By balance b/d	3,00,000
To balance c/d	4,50,000	By cash (issue of shares-balancing figure)	3,25,000
	6,25,000		6,25,000

1. Issue of equity shares against the purchase of building ₹ 2,50,000 is neither a source nor application of funds. Issue of shares for ₹ 1,50,000 is a source.
2. Redemption of preference shares ₹ 1,75,000 is an application of funds.
3. Issue of preference shares ₹ 3,25,000 is a source of funds.

Issue of Shares Other Than Cash: If shares are issued for cash, proceeds from the issue of shares are a source. If shares are issued for acquiring non-current assets like fixed assets, the transaction is totally ignored, as the transaction does not appear anywhere, in sources and application of funds. However, the typical question comes when shares are issued for acquiring current assets as well as non-current assets, how the transaction is to be presented. Total value of the amount of shares issued is to be shown as a source. The current assets acquired increase working capital and the increased working capital is shown as application of funds. The non-current assets acquired too are to be shown as application.

The following problem explains the method of presentation.

Illustration No. 13

Prepare statement showing changes in working capital and source & application of funds from the following information.

	March, 2005	March, 2006
Creditors	1,40,000	1,30,000
Bills payable	40,000	30,000
Bank overdraft	50,000	—
Income tax provision	75,000	65,000
Reserves	80,000	80,000
P & L account	84,000	28,000
Share capital	5,00,000	6,00,000
	9,69,000	**9,33,000**
Cash in hand	50,000	70,000
Cash at bank	1,00,000	1,20,000
Debtors	1,65,000	1,00,000
Prepaid expenses	4,000	3,000
Stock	1,50,000	1,00,000
Fixed assets	5,00,000	4,80,000
Goodwill	—	60,000
	9,69,000	**9,33,000**

The following information was obtained:

(i) In 2006, a dividend of ₹ 84,000 was paid.

(ii) Assets of another firm were purchased at ₹ 1,00,000, payable in 10,000 shares of ₹ 10 each. The assets included stock ₹ 10,000; fixed assets ₹ 30,000; and goodwill ₹ 60,000.

(iii) Income tax paid in 2006 was ₹ 10,000.

(iv) Net profit in 2006 was ₹ 28,000.

Solution

Statement Showing Changes in Working Capital

	As on 31.3.05	As on 31.3.06	Increase in working capital	Decrease in working capital
Current Assets:				
Stock	1,50,000	1,00,000		50,000
Debtors	1,65,000	1,00,000		65,000
Cash in hand	50,000	70,000	20,000	
Cash at bank	1,00,000	1,20,000	20,000	
Prepaid expenses	4,000	3,000		1,000
	4,69,000	3,93,000		

Contd...

Current Liabilities				
Creditors	1,40,000	1,30,000	10,000	
Bills payable	40,000	30,000	10,000	
Bills overdraft	50,000	--	50,000	
Income-tax provision	75,000	65,000	10,000	
	3,05,000	2,25,000		
Working capital	1,64,000	1,68,000		
Increase in working capital	4,000			4,000
	1,68,000	1,68,000	1,20,000	1,20,000

Fixed Assets Account

Dr. **Cr.**

To opening balance	5,00,000	By depreciation (balancing figure)	50,000
To Additions	30,000	By Balance c/d	4,80,000
	5,30,000		5,30,000

Income Tax Provision Account

Dr. **Cr.**

To cash	10,000	By balance b/d	75,000
To balance c/d	65,000		
	75,000		75,000

Funds from Operations (₹)

Net profits	28,000
Add: Depreciation	50,000
Funds from operations	78,000

Statement of Sources and Application of Funds

Sources		**Application**	
Funds from operations	78,000	Increase in fixed assets	30,000
Issue of shares	1,00,000*	Goodwill	60,000
		Cash dividends	84,000
		Increase in working capital	4,000
	1,78,000		1,78,000

Note: Balance in Profit and Loss Account at the end of 31st March, 2005 is ₹ 84,000. The amount is totally paid as dividend, hence shown as application. There is no balance left out for the previous year's profit. Net profit for the year 2006 is ₹ 28,000, which is the balance in the Profit and Loss Account at the end of March, 2006.

*This represents the total value of shares acquired in consideration of stock ₹ 10,000 included the current assets shown in Schedule of Changes in working capital and non-current assets acquired shown as application.

Tip to Students: When shares are issued for acquiring current and non-current assets, the whole transaction has to be taken.

Treatment of Investments

Investments: Treatment of investments depends on the nature of investments purchased, i.e. current assets or fixed assets. They can be temporary investments or permanent investments.

Temporary Investments: When a firm has temporary excess funds, it is normal to purchase temporary investments. They are to be treated as current assets. They find a place in Schedule of Changes in working capital and they are to be treated like any other current assets. Just like any other current assets, they do not appear in the Funds Flow Statement. **Dividend received on such investments is treated like business income.** Loss/profit on sale of such investments is like any other business loss/profit and is to be shown in Profit and Loss Account. If the amount is credited to Profit and Loss Account, it does not appear in Profit and Loss Adjustment Account, again, as no adjustment is needed.

Long-term or Non-current, Trade Investments: Trade investments are purchased with an intention to hold them for a long period. For example, if there is a long-term relationship between a buyer and seller, one or both the parties may acquire the shares of the other company as a long-term investment. Here, intention is not to book profits, if price appreciates, but to hold them for a long-period, at least till the relationship lasts. They are to be treated like fixed assets or non-current assets. As they are not current assets, they should not appear in the Schedule of Changes in Working Capital. If investments are purchased on the basis of 'cum-dividend', pre-acquisition dividend as and when received, subsequently, is to be credited to Trade Investment Account. Reason is the price of investments paid, includes the amount of dividend to be received later. Here, dividend has been declared and the due date for receipt of dividend has not yet lapsed. Investments are to appear at cost. For this reason, dividend declared but not received is to be credited to the Investment Account. Investment Account has to be prepared to find out investments purchased or sold and profit/loss on sale/purchase of investment, if any.

Purchase of investment is to be treated as application and sale as a source of funds. **Dividend received on these investments is not normal business income and is not to be credited to Profit and Loss Account.** This dividend amount is to be deduced from net profit to arrive at funds from operations. In case dividend is credited, the amount should be credited to Profit and Loss Adjustment Account to arrive at funds from operations.

The following problem **explains the** treatment of trade investments (fixed asset or non-current asset).

Illustration No. 14

From the following balance sheets of Beta Limited, make out:

(i) Statement of changes in Working capital, and

(ii) Funds Flow Statement.

Balance Sheets

Liabilities	2001 (₹)	2002 (₹)	Assets	2001 (₹)	2002 (₹)
Equity share capital	3,00,000	4,00,000	Goodwill	1,00,000	80,000
8% Redeemable preference share capital	1,50,000	1,00,000	Land & building	2,00,000	1,70,000
Capital reserve	—	20,000	Plant	80,000	2,00,000
General reserve	40,000	50,000	Investments	20,000	30,000
Profit & loss account	30,000	48,000	Sundry debtors	1,40,000	1,70,000
Proposed dividend	42,000	50,000	Stock	77,000	1,09,000
Sundry creditors	25,000	47,000	Bills receivable	20,000	30,000
Bills payable	20,000	16,000	Cash in hand	15,000	10,000
Liabilities for expenses	30,000	36,000	Cash at bank	10,000	8,000
Provision for taxation	40,000	50,000	Preliminary expenses	15,000	10,000
	6,77,000	8,17,000		6,77,000	8,17,000

Notes:

1. A piece of land has been sold out in the year 2002 and profit on sale has been credited to capital Reserve.
2. A machine has been sold for ₹ 10,000. The written down value of the machine was ₹ 12,000. Depreciation of ₹ 10,000 is charged on plant account in the year 2002.
3. The investments are trade investments. ₹ 3,000 by way of dividend is received including ₹ 1,000 from pre-acquisition of profit, which had been credited to investments account.
4. An interim dividend of ₹ 20,000 has been paid in the year 2002.

(M.B.A., B.U., Bhopal 2003)

Statement of Changes in the Working Capital

Particulars	2001	2002	Increase in Working Capital	Decrease in Working Capital
Current Assets				
Sundry debtors	1,40,000	1,70,000	30,000	
Stock	77,000	1,09,000	32,000	
Bills receivable	20,000	30,000	10,000	
Cash in hand	15,000	10,000		5,000
Cash at bank	10,000	8,000		2,000
	2,62,000	3,27,000		
Current Liabilities				
Sundry creditors	25,000	47,000		22,000
Bills payable	20,000	16,000	4,000	
Liabilities for expenses	30,000	36,000		6,000
Provision for taxation	40,000	50,000		10,000
	1,15,000	1,49,000		
Working capital	1,47,000	1,78,000	76,000	45,000
Increase in Working Capital	**31,000**			**31,000**
	1,78,000	1,78,000	76,000	76,000

Trade Investment Account

Dr. **Cr.**

To opening balance b/d	20,000	By dividend received (credited to this account)	1,000
To purchase of investments (balancing figure)	11,000	By closing balance c/d	30,000
	31,000		31,000

Plan Account

Dr. **Cr.**

To balance b/d	80,000	By depreciation	10,000
To machinery purchased (balancing)	1,42,000	By cash (sale of machine)	10,000
		By loss on sale of machine	2,000
		By balance c/d	2,00,000
	2,22,000		2,22,000

Proposed Dividend Account

Dr.			Cr.
To cash (payment of dividend)	42,000	By balance b/d	42,000
To balance c/d	50,000	By profit and loss account	50,000
	92,000		92,000

Adjusted Profit and Loss Account

Dr.			Cr.
To general reserve	10,000	By balance	30,000
To depreciation	10,000	By dividend on trade investments	2,000
To Interim dividend	20,000	By funds from operations	1,33,000
To Loss on sale of machine	2,000		
To Preliminary expenses written off	5,000		
To proposed dividend account	50,000		
To Goodwill written off	20,000		
To balance	48,000		
	1,65,000		1,65,000

Sources and Application of Funds

Sources		Applications	
Sale of land	50,000	Increase in working capital	31,000
Funds from operations	1,33,000	Payment of dividend	42,000
Sale of machine	10,000	Interim dividend paid	20,000
Dividend on trade investments	3,000	Redemption of 8% redeemable preference shares	50,000
Issue of equity shares	1,00,000	Purchase of machinery	1,42,000
		Purchase of trade investments	11,000
	2,96,000		2,96,000

Notes:

1. Dividend received on trade investments is ₹ 3,000. Out of ₹ 3,000, only ₹ 1,000 has been credited to Trade Investments Account. The balance amount ₹ 2,000 has been credited to Profit and Loss Account. This is the interpretation of the problem. Many think ₹ 3,000 totally has been credited to Trade Investments Account. But, this is not so. Many a time, students' loose full marks, as answer would be different for incorrect interpretation.
2. The second part is reasoning for crediting part of dividend to Trade Investments Account. When trade investment is purchased on the basis of 'cum dividend', pre-acquisition dividend, subsequently received, it is to be credited to Investment Account, as investment should appear at cost only.
3. Dividend received on investments (Fixed assets, non-current assets) is not operating income and so it is to be shown in Profit and Loss Adjustment Account for calculating funds from operations. In other words, dividend is not part of normal business income.
4. Proposed dividend has not been treated as current liability. It has been treated as appropriation of profit for better presentation. Interim dividend has been shown in application as the amount has been paid during the year. Another alternative way is to show proposed dividend as current liability. In that event, both proposed and interim dividends are not to be shown as application.

Illustration No. 15

The comparative balance sheets of Kalyan & Kishore Ltd. in a condensed form are indicated as under:

Liabilities	31-3-06 ₹	31-3-05 ₹	Assets	31-3-06 ₹	31-3-05 ₹
Share capital	4,00,000	3,60,000	Fixed assets	5,20,000	4,80,000
General reserve	60,000	1,10,000	*Less:* Depreciation	1,40,000	1,08,000
Profit & loss account	53,450	20,450		3,80,000	3,72,000
Sundry creditors	1,75,350	1,83,650	Investments	50,000	1,00,000
Proposed dividend	15,000	28,800	Debtors	1,67,800	1,18,300
Provision for tax	32,000	—	Stock	90,500	55,600
			Bank balance	47,500	49,800
			Preliminary expenses	—	7,200
	7,35,800	7,02,900		7,35,800	7,02,900

Additional Information

1. The net profit for the year 2005-06 (after providing depreciation ₹ 40,000, writing off preliminary expenses of ₹ 7,200 and making provision for tax ₹ 32,000) amounted to ₹ 58,000.
2. The company sold during the year an old machinery costing ₹ 9,000 for ₹ 3,000. The accumulated depreciation on the said machinery was ₹ 8,000.
3. A portion of company's investments became worthless and was written off to General Reserve during the year. The cost of such an investment was ₹ 50,000.
4. During the year, the company paid an interim dividend of ₹ 10,000 and the directors have recommended final dividend of ₹ 15,000 for the current year.

Treat proposed dividend as non-current liability and prepare the Schedule of Change in Working Capital and the Funds Flow Statement.

Solution

Schedule of Change in Working Capital

Particulars	As on 31-3-2005	As on 31-3-2006	Increase in Working Capital	Decrease in Working Capital
Current Assets				
Debtors	1,18,300	1,67,800	49,500	
Stock	55,600	90,500	34,900	
Bank Balance	49,800	47,500		2,300
Total Current Assets	2,23,700	3,05,800		
Current Liabilities				
Creditors	1,83,650	1,75,350	8,300	
Total Current Liabilities	1,83,650	1,75,350		
Working Capital (CA – CL)	40,050	1,30,450		
Net Increase in Working Capital	**90,400**			**90,400**
	1,30,450	**1,30,450**	**92,700**	**92,700**

Fixed Assets Account

Dr. **Cr.**

To opening balance b/d	4,80,000	By sale of old machinery account	9,000
To cash—purchase of assets (balancing figure)	49,000	By closing balance c/d	5,20,000
	5,29,000		5,29,000

Sale of Old Machinery Account

Dr. **Cr.**

To fixed assets account	9,000	By cash (sale amount)	3,000
To profit on sale of machinery	2,000	By depreciation account	8,000
	11,000		11,000

Depreciation Account

Dr. **Cr.**

To old machinery account	8,000	By opening balance b/d	1,08,000
To closing balance c/d	1,40,000	By depreciation for the year	40,000
	1,48,000		1,48,000

Profit and Loss Adjustment Account

Dr. **Cr.**

To proposed dividend (2006)	15,000	By opening balance	20,450
To interim dividend paid	10,000	By net profit for the year	58,000
To closing balance	53,450		
	78,450		78,450

Funds from Operations

Net profit for the year 1998	58,000	
Add:		
Depreciation	40,000	
Preliminary expenses written off	7,200	
Provision for tax	32,000	
		1,37,200
Less: Profit on sale of machinery		– 2,000
Funds from Operations		**1,35,200**

Source and Application of Funds

Sources	₹	Application	₹
Sale of old machinery	3,000	Purchase of assets	49,000
Funds from operations	1,35,200	Payment of dividends:	
Issue of share capital	40,000	Interim dividend	10,000
		Final dividend	28,800
		Increase in working capital	90,400
	1,78,200		1,78,200

Notes:

1. Profit and Loss Adjustment Account has been prepared to show that interim dividend and proposed dividend for the year 2006 have been appropriated.
2. The balance in the profit and loss account at the end of 2006 is after payment of interim dividend and provision for proposed dividend for the year 2006. To confirm that the closing balance in the Profit and Loss Account is after payment of interim dividend, Profit and Loss Adjustment Account is prepared and the adjustments have been incorporated.

Revaluation of Fixed Assets

Sometimes, fixed assets are revalued and profit or loss on such revalued assets is transferred to Profit and Loss Account. Such a change in the value of fixed assets is neither inflow nor outflow of funds.

At times, the profit on revaluation of the fixed asset may be credited to Capital Reserve Account. There is no inflow or outflow of funds as both the accounts are non-current. So, the transaction does not appear in Source and Application of Funds.

The following illustration explains the presentation.

Illustration No. 16

In the following Balance Sheet, a part of machinery costing ₹ 20,000 has been revalued at ₹ 30,000 and transferred to Profit and Loss Account. Show the necessary accounts.

Liabilities	2005	2006	Assets	2005	2006
			Machinery	1,50,000	2,50,000

Solution

Profit and Loss Adjustment Account

Dr. **Cr.**

		By machinery account (Profit on revaluation of machinery)	10,000

Machinery Account

Dr. Cr.

To balance b/d	1,50,000	By balance c/d	2,50,000
To profit and loss adjustment account (profit on revaluation of machinery)	10,000		
To cash—Purchase of machinery (balancing figure)	90,000		
	2,50,000		2,50,000

Funds Flow Statement

Sources		Applications	
		Purchase of machinery	90,000

Redemption of Debentures by Issue of Shares: If debentures are redeemed by cash, redemption of debentures is to be shown as application of funds. Instead of redeeming by cash, shares may be issued for redemption of debentures. As both the items are non-current, neither issue of shares nor redemption of debentures appears in Source and Application of Funds.

Illustration No. 17

You are given the balance sheets of Sandhya & Co., which are as under:

Liabilities	2005 ₹	2006 ₹	Assets	2005 ₹	2006 ₹
Equity share capital	2,00,000	2,50,000	Building	2,00,000	2,00,000
Share premium	—	5,000	Plant at cost	1,04,000	1,00,000
General reserve	50,000	60,000	Furniture at cost	7,000	9,000
Profit & loss account	10,000	17,000	Investments at cost	60,000	80,000
8% Debentures	70,000	50,000	Debtors	30,000	70,000
Provision for depreciation on plant	50,000	56,000	Stock	60,000	65,000
Provision for depreciation on furniture	5,000	6,000	Cash	30,000	45,000
Provision for taxation	20,000	30,000			
Sundry creditors	86,000	95,000			
	4,91,000	5,69,000		4,91,000	5,69,000

Equity shares were issued, at par, for redemption of debentures. A dividend of 10% on the share capital, at the end of the year, was paid.

A plant purchased for ₹ 4,000 (Depreciation ₹ 2,000) was sold for cash for ₹ 800 during the year. An item of furniture was purchased for ₹ 2,000. These were the only transactions concerning fixed assets during 2006.

Treat provision for tax as non-current liability.

Prepare Schedule of Changes in working capital and Funds Flow Statement.

Solution

Schedule of Changes in Working Capital

	2005 ₹	2006 ₹	Increase (+) ₹	Decrease (–)
Current Assets :				
Debtors	30,000	70,000	40,000	
Stock	60,000	65,000	5,000	
Cash	30,000	45,000	15,000	
	1,20,000	1,80,000		
Current Liabilities :				
Sundry creditors	86,000	95,000		9,000
	86,000	95,000		
Working capital	34,000	85,000		
Increase in Working Capital	**51,000**			**51,000**
	85,000	85,000	60,000	60,000

Plant Account

Dr. **Cr.**

	₹		₹
To balance b/d	1,04,000	By bank	800
		By P & L (loss on sale of plant)	1,200
		By provision for depreciation (on plant sold)	2,000
		By balance c/d	1,00,000
	1,04,000		1,04,000

Provision for Depreciation on Plant

Dr. **Cr.**

	₹		₹
To plant account (depreciation on plant sold)	2,000	By balance c/d	50,000
To balance c/d	56,000	By P & L A/c (depreciation charged for the year – balancing figure)	8,000
	58,000		58,000

Furniture Plant

Dr.			Cr.
To balance b/d	7,000	By balance c/d	9,000
To cash (balancing figure)	2,000		
	9,000		9,000

Provision for Depreciation on Furniture

Dr.			Cr.
To balance b/d	6,000	By balance c/d	5,000
		By P & L A/c (depreciation charged for the year – balancing figure)	1,000
	6,000		6,000

Adjusted Profit and Loss Account

Dr.			Cr.
To dividend paid	25,000	By balance b/d	10,000
To provision for taxation	30,000	By funds from operations (balancing figure)	82,200
To transfer to general reserve	10,000		
To plant (depreciation)	8,000		
To furniture (depreciation)	1,000		
To loss on sale of plant	1,200		
To balance c/d	17,000		
	92,200		92,200

Funds Flow Statement

Sources of Funds		Applications of Funds	
Share capital (including premium)	35,000	Purchase of furniture	2,000
Sale of plant	800	Dividend paid	25,000
Funds from operations	82,200	Investments purchased	20,000
		Tax paid	20,000
		Increase in working capital	51,000
	1,18,000		1,18,000

The increase in working capital in schedule of changes in working capital is confirmed with the increase in working capital in Funds Flow Statement.

Note: Shares for ₹ 20,000 were issued at par for redemption of debentures. This transaction does not find a place in Funds Flow Statement and Schedule of Changes in Working Capital as both the items are non-current.

6.11 FUNDS FLOW STATEMENT, INCOME STATEMENT AND BALANCE SHEET

Funds Flow Statement is not a substitute of an income statement, i.e. a Profit and Loss Account and a Balance Sheet. Their purposes are different. Funds flow statement is not competitive but complementary to these financial statements.

Differences Between Funds Flow Statement and Income Statement

Base	Funds Flow Statement	Income Statement
1. Purpose	Shows the means the funds were obtained and ways these funds were used.	Find out profit or loss of the organization.
2. Scope	Includes both capital and revenue items.	Only revenue items are considered.
3. Knowledge	Provides information on change in the working capital and changes in financial position.	Depicts the items of expenses and income to arrive at profit or loss in business.
4. Format	No prescribed format.	Prescribed format exists for organizatioos like insurance companies, banking companies and electricity companies.
5. Period	Prepared for short intervals.	Prepared yearly and sometimes half-yearly.
6. Preparation	Complementary to Income Statement. Income Statement helps the preparation of Funds Flow Statement.	Income Statement is not prepared from Funds Flow Statement.

Differences between Funds Flow Statement and Balance Sheet

Base	Funds Flow Statement	Balance Sheet
1. Purpose	Funds flow statement reveals the net increase or decrease in working capital and shows the reasons for the change. Dynamic in nature.	The purpose of Balance sheet is to reveal the financial position on a particular date. Static in nature.
2. Basis	It is prepared with the help of the balance sheets of two years and additional information.	It is prepared with the help of trial balance and additional information provided.
3. Publication	Not required to be published.	In the case of limited companies, Balance Sheet is published and is required to be circulated among the shareholders.
4. Period	Prepared occasionally.	Prepared at the end of the accounting period.
5. Preparation	Usually, schedule of changes in working capital is prepared, before preparing Funds Flow Statement.	No schedule of changes in working capital is prepared. Rather Profit and Loss Account is prepared, before the preparation of Balance Sheet.

6.12 LIMITATIONS OF FUNDS FLOW STATEMENT

Funds Flow Statement is an important tool for analysis and serves several useful purposes. However, its limitations cannot be ignored and they are:

1 It is not an original statement. It is only a rearrangement of data taken from the financial statements (Profit and Loss Account and Balance Sheet).

2. It is based on the financial statements and so the limitations of financial statement are equally applicable to them.

3. It is essentially historic in nature and projected statement cannot be prepared with much accuracy.

4. Funds Flow Statement is not a substitute for basic financial statements like Profit and Loss Account and Balance Sheet. At best, it can be a supplementary statement to explain the changes in the working capital.

Despite the above limitations, Funds Flow Statement serves the basic purpose of explaining the causes for changes in the financial position of the firm between two periods.

Check Your Understanding

(A) State whether the following statements are True or False

1. The term 'fund' in a Fund Flow Statement refers to working capital.
2. Loss on sale of machine should be added to net profit for calculating funds from operations.
3. Statement of change in financial position can be either funds flow statement or cash flow statement.
4. Income statements need not be prepared, but funds flow statements are required to be compulsorily prepared.
5. Basic financial statements (Profit and Loss account and Balance sheet) fail to show the movement and causes of changes in assets and liabilities during the year.
6. Statement of change in financial position identifies changes in assets, liabilities and the shareholders' funds over a given period.
7. Funds flow statement points out the sources from which additional funds have been received during the year and the uses to which funds have been applied.
8. In funds flow statement, if both the affected accounts relate to working capital only they appear.
9. As per existing legal requirement, in case of a listed company, it is not required to publish funds flow statement along with other financial statements.
10. Flow of funds takes place from transactions, when one account is current and the other is non-current.
11. A funds flow statement shows diversion of working capital for purchase of fixed assets.
12. Funds flow statement is a substitute to profit and loss account and balance sheet.

Answers

1. True 2. True 3.True 4. False 5. True 6. True 7. True 8. False 9. False 10. True. 11. True 12. False

(B) Objective Questions (Identify what is most appropriate)

1. Stock at the end results in the:
   (i) Application of fund (ii) Source of funds
   (iii) No flow of funds
2. Sale of investments indicate:
   (i) Source of funds (ii) Application of funds
   (iii) None of the above
3. Tax paid is:
   (i) Application of funds (ii) Source of funds
   (iii) No flow of funds
4. Which of the following will result in flow of funds:
   (i) Purchase of furniture on credit (ii) Writing of goodwill
   (iii) Depreciation of assets (iv) Appreciation in building
5. Net profit earned plus non-operating expenses is equal to:
   (i) Funds provided by operations (ii) Use of funds
   (iii) Sinking fund
6. Depreciation is a source of funds:
   (i) Yes (ii) No
   (iii) Both 'Yes' and 'No'
7. An increase in the share premium account is
   (i) An application of funds (ii) A source of funds
   (iii) No flow of funds
8. Increase in a fixed asset due to issue of shares is
   (i) Source of funds (ii) Use of funds
   (iii) None
9. By preparing provision for Taxation A/c, we can find out the missing figure of
   (i) Taxes paid during the year (ii) Taxes provided during the year
   (iii) Either of a. and b. above (iv) Neither of (i) and (ii) above
10. A company engaged in financial activities receives interest. Such interest is:
    (i) Operating income (ii) Non-operating income
    (iii) Loss from operation (iv) Non-operational charge
11. ... is not a current asset:
    (i) Book debts (ii) Short-term investment
    (iii) Long-term investment (iv) Stock

12. ... is not a current liability:
    (i) Sundry creditors
    (ii) Bank overdraft
    (iii) Outstanding expenses
    (iv) Long-term loan
13. X Ltd. has sales revenue of ₹ 2,000. Depreciation for the period is ₹ 3,000. Other operating expenses are ₹ 900. Net loss for the period is ₹ 500.

    What is the amount of funds generated by X Ltd from operations during the period?
    (i) 2,500
    (ii) 1,500
    (iii) 3,500
    (iv) 1,400

Answers

1. (ii), 2. (i), 3. (i), 4. (i), 5. (i), 6. (iii), 7. (ii), 8. (iii), 9. (iii), 10. (i), 11. (iii), 12. (iv), 13 (i).

(C) Identify the most appropriate answer

1. If depreciation on furniture is in the additional information, it will be posted...
    (i) At the debit side of adjusted profit and loss A/c
    (ii) At the credit side of plant A/c
    (iii) Neither of (i) and (ii) above
    (iv) At both (i) and (ii) above
2. Current liabilities are equal to:
    (i) Working capital + Current assets
    (ii) Working capital – Current assets
    (iii) Current assets – Working capital
    (iv) Current assets + Working capital
3. Inflow of funds does not take place due to:
    (i) Funds from operation
    (ii) Increase in capital
    (iii) Increase in working capital
    (iv) Sale of fixed assets
4. Increase in working capital is a:
    (i) Source of funds
    (ii) Application of funds
    (iii) Funds from operation
    (iv) Loss from operation
5. Vehicle sold for credit for a vehicle dealer results in:
    (i) Increases the working capital
    (ii) Decreases the working capital
    (iii) Does not change the working capital
6. Cash realisation from debtors increases working capital:
    (i) Yes
    (ii) No
    (iii) None of the above answers

Answers

1. (iv), 2. (iii), 3. (iii), 4. (ii), 5. (iii), 6. (ii)

(D) Fill in the blanks

1. Any gain on sale of non-current assets should be ________________ from the net profit for determining funds from operations.

2. Difference between Current Assets and Current Liabilities is known as ____________.
3. Funds flow refers to changes in ________________.
4. Depreciation is sometimes treated as ________________ funds.
5. Goods purchased on credit ________________ in flow of funds.
6. Increase in working capital is ________________ of funds.
7. Vehicle sold on credit is ________________ of funds.
8. Furniture sold for cash ________________ funds flow.

Answers

1. Deducted, 2. Working capital, 3. Working capital, 4. A source, 5. Does not result, 6. An application, 7. A source, 8. Increases.

Descriptive Questions

1. What is the need of Funds Flow Statement when the traditional financial statements, Profit and Loss Account and Balance Sheet are available? **(6.1 and 6.1.1)**
2. Explain the meaning importance and objectives of Funds Flow Statement. **(6.4)**
3. Describe the significance of Funds Flow Statement to the different users. **(6.5)**
4. Describe the need and limitations of Funds Flow Statement. **(6.1.1 and 6.12)**
5. What are the different sources and applications in a Funds Flow Statement? **(6.2, 6.6 and 6.8)**
6. "Depreciation can be taken as a source of funds in a limited sense". Illustrate with a suitable example. **(6.7)**
7. "Depreciation is an indirect source of funds under certain circumstances – Explain. **(6.7)**
8. Depreciation is a source to the extent of reduction of tax liability. Explain with a suitable example. **(6.7)**
9. Explain briefly the procedure and steps to be followed for preparing Funds Flow Statement. **(6.10)**
10. Differentiate between:
    (a) Funds Flow Statement and Income Statement **(6.11)**
    (b) Funds Flow Statement and Balance Sheet **(6.11)**

Short Questions /Answers

Q.1. When we have financial statements of Profit and Loss Account and Balance Sheet, what is the need of Funds Flow Statement, separately?

Ans. Financial statements like Profit and Loss Account and Balance Sheet are static statements. Profit and Loss Account shows the financial results in a consolidated manner, during a specific period, combining results of operating performance as well as non-operating performance. Firm may be in loss and the true picture may be concealed with the profits of non-operating activities.

Balance sheet shows the statement of assets and liabilities on a fixed date. It shows the financial position at the end of a specified period, but does not explain the causes for the changes during the period.

Funds Flow Statements show the operating results from operations and non-operations, separately. The way funds raised and deployed is explained in the funds flow statement.

Funds Flow Statement shows the sources and uses of funds. It also explains the causes and diversion of funds from short-term sources to long-term uses and vice versa. Reason for failure and success of business can be better understood with this statement. Funds Flow Statement gives a comprehensive picture, which the normal financial statements do not provide. So, there is a separate need for the funds flow statement.

Q.2. What are long-term sources?

Ans. Long-term sources are share capital, reserves, long-term loans and debentures, etc.

Q.3. What are short-term sources and when they are due for payment?

Ans. Short-term sources are creditors for goods and services, short-term working capital, provided by banks and outstanding expenses, etc. Even employees, technically, provide short duration credit as salaries are paid after the end of the month. Basically, these short-term funds are to be repaid in the normal course of business, as per payment terms normally within a period of one year.

Q.4. What is the golden rule in respect of long-term and short-term sources of funds? What is the consequence of diversion of funds?

Ans. The golden rule is that long-term funds are to be used for long-term purposes and short-term purposes. These funds can be used for purchase of fixed assets and a part for meeting working capital requirements. Long-term sources are permanent and remain in the business firm, relatively for a very long period. So, there is no pressure on these funds for repayment in a short period.

Short-term sources are to be used only for short-term uses, but not for long-term applications. Short-term sources, at times, are used for long-term purposes, such as purchase of fixed assets or luxurious vehicles, basically for those purposes, which are not to be used. When a firm uses short-term sources for long-term uses, there would be crunch of funds and difficulty is experienced in meeting short-term obligations. This situation leads to liquidity crunch and may even lead to insolvency in serious situations.

Q.5. What is 'Funds from Operations'? Why this is important? Illustrate with an example.

Ans. 'Funds from Operations' means net income from main business activity. Funds from non-operations is income from such activities carried on by the firm that do not relate to the main business.

Separate calculation is important as profit and loss account shows only net profit that includes net income from the main business activity and other activities carried on by the firm. Firm may be in loss from the main business activity and still profit and loss account may show profit due to non-operating income. Examples of non-operating income are rental income, income by way of dividend and interest on investments made by the firm. Real picture that the main business is in loss and corrective action is necessary may not be known to the firm as it only looks at the profit in Profit and Loss Account and be happy with the final result.

Preparation of Sources and Application of Funds Statement throws the real picture of business as operating income and non-operating income are shown separately.

Example: Hotel President carries on the business of boarding and lodging (main activity) and has let out its ground floor to State Bank of India. Its profit and loss account shows a profit of ₹ 3 lakhs. Management is happy.

When Sources and Application of Funds Statement is prepared for analysis, it is identified that the main business (boarding and lodging) is in net loss by ₹ 2 lakhs and it has been getting a rental income of ₹ 5 lakhs from State Bank of India, which has saved the firm from showing net loss. Analysis has given the recommendation that it is desirable to close the main business (boarding and lodging) to improve the profitability. Reason for loss has been identified—boarding and lodging business is in loss due to bad location of hotel. As the hotel is located in a lane, tourists do not prefer to visit and stay there. Had there been no main business (boarding and lodging), firm's Profit and Loss Account would have shown a net profit of ₹ 5 lakhs.

Q.6. What are non-operating expenses? How they are to be dealt with for calculating operating profits?

Ans. Expenses, which are not related with day-to-day affairs of the business are called non-operating expenses. To arrive at the operating income from business, both non-operating expenses as well as non-operating income are to be excluded from the net profits to ascertain operating profits, which is the resultant of the main activity of the business.

Q.7. What is the purpose of 'Schedule of changes in working capital'?

Ans. In the context of 'Source and Application of Funds Statement', the term 'Funds' mean 'working capital'. This statement shows the increase or decrease of working capital during a specified period. Further, this statement provides information for the causes or reasons for increase/decrease of working capital. From which sources, this working capital is raised or to what purposes there has been diversion of working capital is known from this statement.

In other words, the story behind the change in the financial position between the beginning and end of a period is known.

Interview Questions

Q.1. Which type of financial institutions sanction working capital needs of a firm? Which statement helps you in finding the diversion of working capital?

Ans. Commercial banks sanction working capital needs of a firm. From the "Sources and Application of Funds Statement", we can know if there is any diversion of working capital.

Q.2. State Bank of India, Gulmohar branch has sanctioned working capital of ₹ 10 lakhs to Smitha Jain & Co., running a garment shop on Thrilinga Road. The bank suspects that the borrowing firm is not utilizing the working capital limit for the purpose sanctioned by the bank. They want your advice. Which statement is to be called from

the company to find out whether there is any diversion of working capital? How the statement would help the bank? Explain.

Ans. Commercial banks sanction working capital needs of a firm.

State Bank of India, Gulmohar branch, should call for the submission of "Sources and Application of Funds Statement" to know if there is any diversion of working capital.

"Sources and Application of Funds Statement" contains the statement of changes in working capital. If there is diversion of working capital, statement of changes in working capital would show decrease in working capital. Reasons for decrease in working capital would be known. In other words, working capital would have been utilized for purchase of fixed assets or payment of dividends from accumulated profits, despite current year loss, resulting in its decrease.

From the "Sources and Application of Funds Statement" and 'Statement of Changes in Working Capital', bank can know about the diversion of working capital, if any, and its use/ application.

Q.3. Who are the users of the Funds Flow Statement and for what purpose this statement is used?

Ans. Funds Flow Statement is widely used by the financial institutions, banks and credit rating agencies. By preparing the statement, the user can know well, in advance, about the adequacy or otherwise of working capital position for proper planning.

Q.4. What is a non-operating profit and give an example?

Ans. Non-operating profit is that amount of profit, which is not connected with the regular business. Examples are loss on sale of assets, dividend income on trade investments and rent from building, not connected to the business.

Q.5. What is depreciation? What is its impact on cash?

Ans. Depreciation is decrease in the value of an asset due to wear and tear, passage of time, obsolescence, exhaustion and accident. It is a part of capital cost of fixed asset spread over the life of the asset. Depreciation is taken as an operating expense, while arriving at the true profits of a business. Depreciation is, simply, a book entry to arrive at book profits. Depreciation is a non-cash item. Depreciation does not result in any outgo of cash.

Q.6. Is depreciation a direct source of funds?

Ans. No. Depreciation is not a direct source of funds. Depreciation is an indirect source of funds to a limited extent. It depends upon circumstances. If the firm is in profits, depreciation acts as a tax shield in helping the firm for reducing tax liability. Income tax act permits depreciation as an admissible expenditure to the extent it is provided as per its rules. As a result, taxable profits and tax liability are reduced. So, to that extent, depreciation is a source. In consequence, depreciation is a source to the extent tax liability is reduced. Due to depreciation, profits available for distribution of dividend get reduced. So, more funds would be available to the business for expansion. In these circumstances, depreciation is a source. But, when the firm is in loss, question of tax payment does not rise. In those circumstances, depreciation is not a source. It can be said, with certainty, that depreciation is not a source of funds, directly. **So, depreciation is only an indirect source to a limited extent, under certain circumstances.**

Q.7. Explain the different meanings of the term "Funds"?

Ans. The term "Funds" has different meanings. Its popular meaning is 'working capital'. Based on this meaning, Funds Flow Statement is prepared. The second meaning—narrow meaning —is 'cash'. Based on this meaning, Cash Flow Statement is prepared. The third meaning, broad in nature, is 'Total Resources'. Based on this meaning, Statement of Total Financial Resources is prepared.

Q.8. What is meant by 'Operating Profit'? From which statement, you can find out this item? Explain the importance of the relevant statement in the context of operating profit?

Ans. Operating profit refers to profit from business operations. This is the business profit, after deducting all the expenses incurred for earning that profit. Operating profit does not include other incomes, not connected with the main business, and equally the expenses connected to earn such other incomes.

Operating profit can be found from the Statement of Sources and Application of Funds as this item is shown separately. At times, the firm may be in net profit, even though the business may be sustaining business losses, due to higher other incomes. Other incomes may be neutralizing the business loss. Normal Profit and Loss Account shows only the final profit or loss in a consolidated manner. It does not show that the business operations are in loss. As the real picture is not known, corrective action may be delayed or not known at all, till the business collapses. Only Statement of Sources and Application of Funds throws the real picture about the profit or loss from business and other operations, separately. Statement of Sources and Application of Funds exposes what profit and loss account may conceal.

Q.9. In what manner can 'Statement of Sources and Application of Funds' be utilized by financial institutions?

Ans. Normally, commercial banks sanction working capital limits. Before sanction, commercial bank wants to assess the needs and requirements of the working capital limits of the borrowers. After sanction, bank wants to ensure that there is no diversion of working capital limit for other purposes. Borrowers may use the working capital limits for the purchase of fixed assets and withdraw funds for personal use, against the terms of sanction. Banks can utilize the statement to find out any diversion of working capital limit.

Term lending institutions want to satisfy, before sanction, that the projects, proposed to be financed, would generate sufficient funds to service the debt. These institutions want to ensure that the borrower would have sufficient funds to pay the instalment and interest amounts, during the proposed repayment period.

Sources and Application of Funds, is used by the financial institutions to monitor end use of funds and repayment of the sanctioned loans.

CHAPTER 7

Cash Flow Statement

7.1 IMPORTANCE OF CASH

Cash is an important economic resource needed by every business. It is one of the most significant current assets of an organization. As the most liquid asset, cash is needed to make purchases of raw materials, payment of wages and meeting day-to-day expenses for every type of activity, including entertainment expenditure. Development of business and faster growth are dependent on adequate and timely availability of cash. **In fact, cash is needed to every business enterprise, just like blood to a human body.**

> **Firm may be profitable, yet, may experience difficulty in arranging timely payments. It may not have adequate liquid resources to make immediate payments, such as wages and salaries. It is due to poor management of cash.**

Though profits are earned, reason for insufficiency of cash could be of two types. Profits may not be realized in cash. Secondly, profits are diverted for the purchase of fixed assets. The classical example is shelling cash for a premium car from profits, beyond means and without planning, later searching cash for payment of daily wages.

Both adequacy and timely availability of cash are essential for the success of any firm's activities. Therefore, management of cash is of vital importance to any enterprise.

7.2 CASH FLOW STATEMENT

Meaning: Cash Flow Statement is a statement, which describes the inflows (sources) and outflows (uses) of cash and cash equivalents during a specified period. It is a summary of cash-book. **A Cash Flow Statement explains the causes of changes in cash position of a business enterprise between two balance sheet dates.** Cash flow statement is a tool that is available to the management to assess, monitor and control the liquidity available in the enterprise.

Cash Flow Statement is a summary of firm's cash receipts and cash payments during a period. The primary objective of cash flow statement is to provide information about a firm's cash inflows and outflows during the period of time, segregated into three categories: operating, investing and financing activities.

> **According to AS-3 (Revised), an enterprise should prepare and enclose the cash flow statement for the same period for which the financial statements are prepared, in the prescribed format, by the listed companies.**

The following terms, in the context of cash flow statement, are explained hereunder:

Cash means physical cash on hand and demand deposits in bank. Balance in a current account in bank comes under the category of demand deposits as the amount can be withdrawn on demand, without any limit.

Cash equivalents are short term, highly liquid investments that can be converted into known amounts of cash within a reasonable period, without subjecting to any significant risk. **Short-term deposits in a bank, government securities and treasury bills qualify the category of cash equivalents.** They are meant for meeting short-term obligations and not for long-term investment. They are to be converted into cash at short notice, without any significant risk at the time of conversion. Risk refers to financial risk, particularly the loss in value at the time of conversion. So, equity shares of even the reputed companies do not come into the category of cash equivalents though they are listed on stock exchange and are convertible into ready cash, within a short period say three or four days. The reason for non-inclusion is that there is no certainty about the amount of realization as they are subject to fluctuations in price. Preference shares that are subject to redemption, shortly, in a very good company fall into the category of cash equivalents as the amount of realization is predetermined and there is insignificant risk in respect of failure of the company.

> **Cash flows are both inflows and outflows of cash and cash equivalents. Flow of cash is said to have taken place, when a transaction changes availability of cash and equivalents, before and after happening of the transaction. If cash and cash equivalents increase, on account of transaction, it is called inflow of cash and if it decreases, it is said to be outflow of cash.**

Conversion of cash into cash equivalents and vice versa does not constitute cash flows because they are not part of operating, financing and investing activities. Cash management includes the investment of cash into cash equivalents and vice versa.

Definition: A Cash Flow Statement may be defined as "**a financial statement that summarizes the cash receipts and payments and net changes resulting from operating, financing and investing activities of an enterprise during a given period of time**".

Cash Flow Statement is a summary of sources of cash inflows and uses of cash outflows.

7.3 NEED OF CASH FLOW STATEMENT

Basic financial statements, i.e. Profit and Loss Account and Balance Sheet provide the essential basic information about the financial activities of the business. But, their utility is limited for analysis and planning purposes. To serve those needs, Funds Flow Statement is prepared to show the causes for changes in assets and liabilities from one period of time to the end of another period. **The question arises when the Funds Flow Statement is prepared, what is the need to prepare Cash Flow Statement separately?** Funds Flow Statement presents comprehensive picture of different components of working capital. However, working capital concept does not reveal the true picture of the availability of cash. In the Funds Flow Statement, cash and inventories are treated alike. All the components of working capital are treated, alike, in respect of availability from the viewpoint of cash. However, this is not the correct picture as their time and quality of realization is different from the viewpoint of cash. Debtors take less time for converting into cash, while inventories take more time for realization. Similarly, inventories may consist of dead stock that has not been written off. Debtors may have bad debts that are not yet removed. But, Funds Flow Statement does not recognize this basic difference in their nature. An enterprise may have more slow paying debtors and non-moving stocks, with little cash or its equivalents.

Due to comfortable working capital position, Funds Flow Statement does not throw the real picture about the inadequacy of cash. Only, when Cash Flow Statement is prepared, the real situation about the adequacy of funds, in the sense of cash, is known. From this angle, Cash Flow Statement is superior compared to Funds Flow Statement.

Where profit has gone?

At times, chief executives (often, this happens in state government undertakings), who do not have rudimentary finance background put this question, when their firm is in profit, why they should have the problem for cash at any time? Chief executives in state public sector undertakings, normally, know the functioning of state, which deals only with cash and are not aware of accrual system of accounting.

Profit is like water. If water is put in a jar, water takes the shape of a jar. If the same water is put in a bowl, it takes the shape of a bowl. In a similar manner, profit can be utilized for the purchase of fixed assets, current assets and, equally to reduce liabilities. Profit does not always assume the form of cash.

Let us assume, for a while that the firm is making cash sales only and there are no credit sales. Profit, received in the form of cash, can be utilized for the purchase of fixed assets. Then, one does not find adequate cash, if the entire profit is used for the purchase of fixed assets. Again, profit in the form of cash can be used for building up of stock. Now, profit is in the shape of inventory. It can be used for making credit sales and then it has assumed the position of debtors.

The same profit, received in cash, can be used for repaying creditors. Then creditors reduce. In other words, profit can be used for repayment of liabilities too. In such an event, there would be no change on the assets side of the balance sheet. Balance in Profit and Loss Account increases and sundry creditors go down to that extent.

Cash Flow Statement can explain the question where the profit has gone.

Firms prepare Cash Flow Statements for short periods for proper cash planning.

Legal Requirement: To underline the importance of the funds flow statement, the Institute of Chartered Accountants of India had issued Accounting Standard-3 (AS-3) in 1981 that was made applicable to every listed company. However, the accounting standard provided more flexibility in implementation as the term "Funds" was meant for cash and cash equivalents or working capital. **In other words, companies had been given the option to prepare Funds Flow Statement or Cash Flow Statement along with the financial statement.** So, many firms had provided the Funds Flow Statement along with the financial statements based on working capital concept. This had served the useful purpose in understanding the changes in assets and liabilities between two different dates.

However, this Accounting Standard had suffered the following limitations:

1. **Flexibility:** Many firms had prepared the statement on the basis of working capital, where as others prepared it on cash basis, due to flexibility of the Accounting Standard. **As inventories and prepaid expenses were treated similar to cash, while preparing on working capital basis, firm's ability to pay short-term obligations, as and when they fall due, could not be assessed.**
2. **No Standard Format:** AS-3 did not provide the standard format. As such, firms had adopted different methods for preparing the Funds Flow Statement. **Lack of uniformity had made the comparison difficult.**
3. **Lack of Adequate Disclosure:** Even the firms that had prepared the Cash Flow Statement had provided the information merely in respect of inflows and outflows. They did not disclose information in respect of Operating, Financing and Investment activities, separately.

AS-3 Revised: In view of the above limitations and recognizing the importance of Cash Flow Statement, in 1995, Securities and Exchange Board of India (SEBI) had amended clause 32 of the Listing Agreement requiring every listed company to give along with the balance sheet and profit and loss account, a cash flow statement in the prescribed format. The prescribed format requires the listed company to provide the information in respect of cash flows in respect of Operating, Financing and Investing Activities, separately. **AS-3 (Revised) issued in 1995 supersedes the requirement of AS-3, issued in 1981.**

> **Listed companies now do not have the option of either preparing funds flow statement or cash flow statement. Every listed company has to provide the Cash Flow Statement along with the financial statements in the prescribed format.**

Applicability: AS-3 (Revised) applies to the following enterprises:

(i) If turnover of the enterprise exceeds more than ₹ 50 crores in a financial year, even though it is not a listed company.

(ii) Listed companies—shares of those companies listed on Stock Exchange.

> **Cash Flow Statement of listed companies should be presented only under the indirect method, as prescribed in AS-3.**

7.4 OBJECTIVES OF CASH FLOW STATEMENT

1. **Cash Management:** Cash Flow Statement is a tool for short-term financial planning. By preparing the statement, a firm can know how much cash can be generated by its operations. **It helps the firm to plan to arrange for additional cash requirements in advance.**
2. **Cash Planning:** It helps in **planning repayment of loans, dividend policy, replacement of fixed assets and capital budgeting decisions.**
3. **Answers to Difficult Questions:** It explains the causes for financial difficulties. Even if the firm is profitable, firm experiences difficulty for cash. **The statement throws light on the intricate questions** like—'what happened to the net profits', where did the profits go? Why more dividends could not be paid, despite increase in profits'?
4. **Discloses Reasons for Success or Failure:** It is an **important technique for evaluating success or failure of cash planning.** The actual cash flow is compared with the projected cash flow. If the results are not as per expectation, reasons can be analyzed and corrective steps can be taken.

To appear in Cash Flow Statement, actual receipt or payment in cash or cash equivalents, is essential.

7.5 CLASSIFICATION OF CASH FLOWS

Cash flows as per Accounting Standard-3 are classified into three categories. They are:

1. **Cash Flows from Operating Activities:** Operating activities relate to the core business, carried on by the organization. Operating activities are the revenue producing activities of the enterprise, a core activity that are not investing and financing activities. **Revenue producing activity is the key activity in the cash flows.** They generally determine the net profit or loss of the organization.

   For example, for a pickle industry, the main operation is to buy fruits like mangoes, lemon and apples, take out the pulp, mix the necessary ingredients and bottle them as different varieties of pickles, with the help of human resources, plant and machinery, etc. Therefore, the cash flows incidental to purchase of fruits and ingredients, payment of wages to labour and salaries, packing charges is operating outflows. Receipts from sale of pickles are to be regarded as operating cash inflows.

2. **Cash Flows from Investing Activities:** Investing activities are the acquisition of long-term assets and other investments that are not included in cash equivalent. In other words, long-term assets, such as plant and machinery, land and building, etc. that are held by the firm for long-term production, not meant for sale, fall in this category. Short-term securities, temporary excess funds, are cash equivalents and so are not to be included in this category. However, trade investments that are intended for long-term are to be included in this category.

   Separate disclosure is necessary to know the amount spent in acquiring the resources—long term assets, such as plant and machinery and other fixed assets—intended to generate the future income and cash flows.

3. **Cash Flows from Financing Activities:** Financing activities are activities that result in changes in size and composition of owners' capital (including preference share capital in the case of company) and short-term and long-term debts of the firm.

   Separate disclosure is important and necessary, as it is useful to predict the claims of the providers of funds as well as anticipated repayments on the future cash flows.

   Inflows and outflows of these activities are:

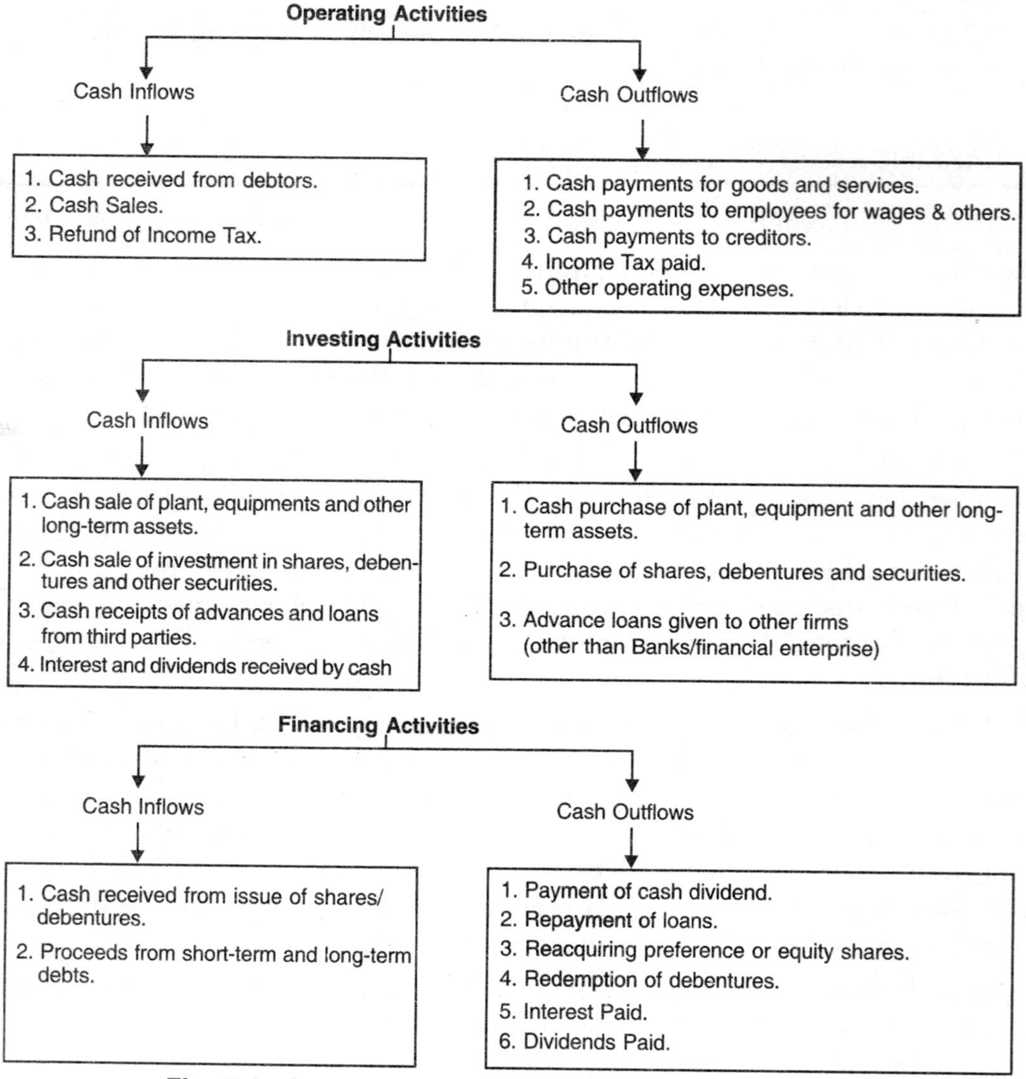

Fig. 7.1: Classification of cash flows and cash outflows

7.6 PROCEDURE FOR PREPARING CASH FLOW STATEMENT

Cash Flow Statement is prepared from the following three sources:

1. **Balance Sheet at the Opening and Closing Period:** If we are preparing cash flow statement for the financial year 2006, Balance Sheets for the years 2005 and 2006 are required. These balance sheets provide the information in respect of assets, liabilities and shareholders' funds.
2. **Profit and Loss Account of Current Year:** We need Profit and Loss Account or Income Statement for the year 2006. This statement provides information in respect

of operating, financing and investment activities. Interest/dividend paid is covered in the financing activity. Interest/Dividends received is an instance of investing activity.

3. **Additional Information:** Both the above statements do not provide all the information required. Additional information, such as purchase and sale of assets, payment of taxes, amount paid on redemption of debentures and funds raised in the form of shares, including share premium, etc. are needed for preparing cash flow statement. This information may be hidden which is to be explored.

Cash flow means both inflow and outflow of cash.

7.7 STEPS INVOLVED IN PREPARING CASH FLOW STATEMENT

The following steps are involved in its preparation:

Step 1: Calculate the increase or decrease in cash and cash equivalents by making a comparison of the opening and closing balance sheets.

Step 2: Calculate the net cash flow from operating activities by analyzing the Profit and Loss Account, Balance Sheet and other additional information. For this purpose, they are two methods—direct and indirect methods. They are explained, subsequently.

Step 3: Calculate the net cash flow from investing activities.

Step 4: Calculate the net cash flow from financing activities.

Step 5: Prepare a formal cash flow statement indicating the cash flows from operating, investing and financing activities.

Step 6: Make an aggregate of net cash flows from three activities and ensure that the total net cash flow is equal to the net increase or decrease in cash and cash equivalents, as calculated in Step 1.

Step 7: Report the non-cash transactions that do not involve cash and cash equivalents in a separate schedule to the cash flow statement. Examples are redemption of debentures in exchange of issue of shares and purchase of machinery against issue of share capital, etc.

7.8 CALCULATION OF CASH FROM OPERATIONS

Cash flows generated from operating activities is an important indicator about the operating capability of the enterprise to pay dividends, repay loans and make new investments, without recourse to external sources of financing.

This determines whether the firm can continue in the long run or not.

Separate Non-operation Items: The net effect of various transactions in a business is reflected in the form of net profit or net loss, shown in the Profit and Loss Account. A firm may be in net profit, even though the results from operations may be negative, due to non-operational gains. Similarly, firm may be in net loss, even though the firm has made operational profits, due to non-operational losses. To know whether the firm is operationally profitable or not, it is necessary to separate the non-operational expenses and income.

Replace Accrual System with Cash System: Net profit is not normally equal to net flow (difference of inflow and outflow). It is so because certain non-cash and non-operating items are charged to profit and loss account. While preparing profit and loss account, accrual system of accounting is followed as per the Generally Accepted Accounting Principles (GAAP). Whether sales are realized or not (credit sales), they are accounted for.

All revenues are taken into account, if they relate to the period whether they are actually received or not. Similarly, all expenses are charged to the profit and loss account, if they relate to the period, whether they are actually paid or not. Basic principle of accrual is followed both for expenses and revenues.

To calculate net flow from operating activities, it is necessary to replace revenues and expenses with the actual receipts and payments in cash.

Effect of Opening and Closing Stocks

The amount of opening stock is charged to Profit and Loss Account. It thus reduces net profit without reducing cash from operations. Similarly, closing stock increases the net profit, without increasing cash from operations. When net profit is taken as the base to arrive at cash from operations, they require adjustments.

The following illustration explains the concept more clearly.

Illustration No. 1

	₹
Opening stock	10,000
Purchases	25,000
Sales	30,000
Closing stock	15,000
Expenses (paid in cash)	3,000

Compute the net profit and cash from operations.

Solution

The amount of net profit can be computed as follows:

Profit and Loss Account (in Rupees)

Opening stock	10,000	Sales	30,000
Purchases	25,000	Closing stock	15,000
Expenses	3,000		
Net profit	7,000		
	45,000		45,000

The net profit for the year is ₹ 7,000. The cash from operations is computed as follows:

	Net profit for the year	7,000
Add	Opening stock	10,000
		17,000
Less	Closing stock	15,000
	Cash from operations	2,000

Alternatively, cash from operations can be calculated as under:

	Net profit	7,000
Less	Outflow of cash on account of increase in stock	–5,000
	Cash from operations	2,000

7.9 METHODS OF PREPARING CASH FLOW STATEMENTS

There are two methods of preparing Cash Flow Statement:

1. Traditional Method
2. Preparing under AS-3

1. Traditional Method: The traditional method does not have any standard format. There is no classification of inflow and outflow under operation, investment and finance activities separately.

2. Preparing under AS-3: The basic difference from traditional method is presentation of Cash Flow Statement. They are two methods of reporting cash flows from operating activities: the Direct Method and Indirect Method.

(A) Direct Method

Cash flows from operations include cash receipts from sale of goods and services, cash payments to suppliers of goods and services, other cash payments and receipts. Total cash receipts and payments are to be calculated. Only cash receipts and cash payments (known as cash flows) from operating activities are considered. Examples are:

(i) Cash receipts from the sale of goods and rendering of services;

(ii) Cash receipts from royalties, fees, commission and other revenue;

(iii) Cash payments to suppliers of goods and services;

(iv) Cash receipts and payments relating to insurance, taxes, claims, annuities and other benefits.

Under the direct method, actual receipt and payment in cash only are relevant.

Adjustments for depreciation, amortization of preliminary expenses and intangible assets like goodwill, discount on issue of shares and debentures are not required. Similarly, no adjustment is needed in respect of profit or loss on sale of assets because operating cash receipts and payments are directly reported in the Cash Flow Statement.

(B) Indirect Method

Under the indirect method, net profit is taken as base and is adjusted instead of individual items appearing in the Profit and Loss Account to arrive at cash from operations.

Net profit or loss is adjusted for the following:

1. Non-cash items, such as depreciation, writing off goodwill and preliminary expenses, etc.;
2. Changes during the period in inventories, operating receivables and payables; and
3. All other items which affect cash included in financing and investing activities, such as loss/gain on sale of fixed assets and loss/gain on sale of investments, etc.

> **Cash flow statement of listed companies should be presented only under the indirect method as prescribed in AS-3.**

Traditional Method: There is no standard format for showing the method of calculation of cash from operations (Traditional Method)

Calculation of Cash from Operations (Traditional Method)

	₹	₹
Net Profit for the year		—
Add: Non-cash expenses:		
Depreciation	—	
Goodwill written off	—	
Loss on sale of fixed assets	—	
Discount on shares/debentures written off	—	
Provision for taxation, etc.	—	—
Less: Non-cash incomes		
Profit on sale of fixed assets	—	(—)
Net profit, after adjustment of non-cash items		—
Changes in inventories, operating receivables and payables		
Add: Decrease in current assets	—	
Increase in current liability	—	
Less: Increase in current assets	—	
Decrease in current liabilities	—	—
Cash from operations		—

Calculation of Changes in Inventories, Operating Receivables and Payables

For example, decrease in debtors (current asset) indicates that cash has been collected, without affecting net profits in any manner, hence added.

Increase in creditors (current liability) occurs when credit purchases are made but not paid. This reduces the net profits and so is added to arrive at cash flows.

Increase in Debtors (current assets) occurs when credit sales are made, but not realized. This has already increased profits. So, deducted to arrive at cash flows.

Decrease in creditors (current liability) occurs when cash is paid, without any effect on net profits. So, deducted to arrive at cash flows.

Note: Students have to think what impact the transaction has created on net profits to decide—add or deduct—to arrive at cash flows.

7.10 CALCULATION OF CASH FLOWS FROM OPERATING ACTIVITIES

1. **Calculation of Cash Collected from Customers (sales made):** Sales figure in Profit and Loss Account/Income Statement includes cash sales and credit sales. We are to collect total cash collected from customers. This figure can be arrived at by adjusting credit sales with the opening and closing balance of debtors and bills receivable as follows:

Calculation of Cash Collected from Customers

Debtors and bills receivable at the beginning of the year	Xxx
Add: Credit sales	Xxx
Less: Debtors and bills receivable at the end of the year	Xxx
Cash collected from total credit sales	Xxx

2. **Cash Paid for Purchase of Inventory:** The figure in the Profit and Loss Account/ Income Statement shows the total purchases. Total purchases include both cash and credit purchases. The credit purchases are to be adjusted with the opening and closing balance of creditors and Bills Payable to arrive at the cash paid for purchase of inventory.

Calculation of Cash Paid to Creditors

Creditors and bills payable at the beginning of the year	Xxx
Add: Credit purchases	Xxx
Less: Creditors and bills payable at the end of the year	Xxx
Cash paid for total credit purchases	Xxx

3. **Cash Payments for Expenses:** Expenses in the Profit and Loss Account are charged on the accrual basis. There are outstanding expenses or prepaid expenses. They are to be adjusted to arrive on cash basis.

Cash Paid for Expenses—Adjustment of Prepaid Expenses

Expenses appearing in profit and loss account	Xxx
Add: Prepaid expenses in closing balance sheet	Xxx
Less: Prepaid expenses in opening balance sheet	Xxx
Cash paid for expenses	Xxx

Cash Paid for Expenses-Adjustment of Outstanding Expenses

Expenses appearing in profit and loss account	Xxx
Add: Outstanding expenses in opening balance sheet	Xxx
Less: Outstanding expenses in closing balance sheet	Xxx
Cash paid for expenses	Xxx

Let us explain with the following two examples:

(A) Salary expense in Profit and Loss Account is ₹ 30,000. Salary outstanding at the beginning of the year is ₹ 5,000 and salary outstanding at the close of the year is ₹ 3,000.

Here, cash paid for salary = Salary – outstanding salary at the year end + outstanding salary at the beginning of the year.

= 30,000 – 3,000 + 5,000

= 32,000

(B) Insurance premium appearing in Profit and Loss Account is 10,000. Premium prepaid at the beginning of the year is ₹ 2,000 and premium prepaid at the end of the year is ₹ 1,500.

Here cash paid for insurance = Insurance premium – Prepaid premium at the beginning + Premium paid at the end.

= 10,000 – 2,000 + 1,500

= 9,500

After arriving at the answer, students are advised to check the correctness calculating in a reverse manner, i.e. from cash to profit figure appearing in the Profit and Loss Account.

4. **Non-cash Items:** Certain non-cash expenses like depreciation, goodwill and preliminary expenses written off appear in the Profit and Loss Account. They are charged to arrive at true profits, though there is no outgo of cash. So, these items are to be added.

7.11 DIFFERENCES BETWEEN FUNDS FLOW STATEMENT AND CASH FLOW STATEMENT

The term 'funds' has a variety of meanings. In a narrow sense, it means cash. When Statement of Changes in Financial Position is prepared on cash basis, it is called Cash Flow Statement. When Statement of Changes in Financial Position is prepared on working capital basis, it is called Funds Flow Statement. Both the statements are similar in several respects, yet there are some differences between the Funds Flow Statement and Cash Flow Statement. The differences are as under:

Base of Difference	Funds Flow Statement	Cash Flow Statement
1. Meaning	It is a statement of changes in the financial position of business due to inflow and outflow of **funds**.	It is a statement of changes in the financial position of business due to inflow and outflow of **cash.**
2. Basis of concept	It is based on the wider concept of funds, i.e. working capital.	It is based on the narrower concept of funds, i.e. cash.
3. Basis of accounting	It is based on accrual system of accounting.	It is based on cash system of accounting.
4. Concerned with	A funds flow statement is concerned with changes in the working capital position, between two balance sheet dates.	A cash flow statement is concerned with changes in cash position between two balance sheet dates.
5. Schedule of changes in working capital	Schedule of Changes in Working Capital is prepared to show the changes in working capital.	No such statement is required/ prepared.
6. Purpose of preparation	This statement reveals sources and uses of funds. The difference between sources and uses indicate the increase or decrease in the working capital.	All inflows and outflows are classified in terms of operating, investing and financing activities. The net difference represents the net increase or decrease of cash and cash equivalents.
7. Usefulness	It is useful for long-term planning and financing.	It is more useful for short-term analysis and cash planning of the business.

7.12 LIMITATIONS

Despite a number of uses, Cash Flow Statement suffers from the following limitations:

1. **Ignores Basic Principles of Accounting:** Cash Flow Statement is prepared on the basis of cash accounting. It ignores the basic accounting concept of accrual basis.

2. **Not Suitable for Judging Profitability:** Cash Flow Statement is prepared ignoring non-cash charges, while preparing cash flow from operations. So, this statement is not suitable for judging profitability of a firm.
3. **Statement does not Reflect Real Liquid Position:** Purchases and payments can be postponed to present a better liquid position.
4. The cash balance reflected in the cash flow statement may not represent the real liquid position.
5. **Cannot be Equated with Income Statement:** Cash flow statement cannot be equated with Income Statement. An income-statement takes into account cash as well as non-cash items and, therefore, net cash flow does not necessarily mean net income of the business.

In spite of these limitations, cash flow statement has its own role to play. It is a useful tool for financial analysis. It is a useful supplementary instrument. It discloses the volume of cash flows in different segments of the business. It helps the management in knowing the amount of capital tied up in each segment of the business. It serves as a barometer in measuring the profitability and financial position of the business.

The following illustration explains the traditional method of calculating cash from operations:

Illustration No. 2

Following information is available from the books of Suresh Ltd. for the year ending 31 December, 2005 and 31 December, 2006.

	31-12-2005	31-12-2006
Profit made during the year	—	2,50,000
Income received in advance	500	400
Prepaid expenses	1,600	2,000
Debtors	80,000	20,000
Bills receivable	25,000	40,000
Creditors	45,000	65,000
Bills payable	13,000	5,000
Outstanding expenses	2,500	3,000
Accrued income	1,500	1,800

Calculate Cash Flow from operations for the year ending 31-12-2006.

Solution

Calculation of cash from operations for the year ending 31st December, 2006

		(₹)
Profit made during the year		2,50,000
Add:		
Decrease in Debtors	60,000	
Increase in creditors	20,000	
Increase in outstanding expenses	500	+ 80,500
		3,30,500
Less:		
Decrease in income received in advance	100	
Increase in prepaid expenses	400	
Increase in bills receivable	15,000	
Decrease in bills payable	8,000	
Increase in accrued income	300	– 23,800
Cash from Operations		3,06,700

Tip for Students: Students often experience difficulty, while dealing with outstanding expenses; income received in advance, liabilities, similar to creditors. Think that they are creditors; you would understand whether to add or deduct. Similarly, think accrued income and prepaid expenses as assets, similar to debtors for solving the problem.

Illustration No. 3

From the Balance Sheet of Dimpy Ltd. as at 31-3-2005 and 31-3-2006, prepare Cash Flow Statement:

(₹)

	31-3-2005	31-3-2006
Liabilities		
Equity share capital	4,00,000	4,50,000
Share premium	—	30,000
General reserve	45,000	65,000
Profit and loss	30,000	80,800
7% Debentures	—	70,000
Sundry creditors	85,000	90,700
Provision for taxation	22,500	40,500
Proposed dividend	30,000	35,000
	6,12,500	8,62,000
Assets		
Land and building	3,30,000	4,90,000
Plant and machinery	85,400	1,40,000
Furniture	5,500	6,500
Stock	82,400	95,700
Sundry debtors	75,000	85,500
Bank balance	34,200	44,300
	6,12,500	8,62,000

Additional Information

Details of depreciation written off on the following assets during the year are as under:

	₹
Land and building	60,000
Plant and machinery	50,000
Furniture	1,200

Solution

Calculation of Operating Profit, before Working Capital Changes

		(₹)
Profit and loss account (31-3-2006)		80,800
Add: Depreciation–Land and building	60,000	
Depreciation–Plant and machinery	50,000	
Depreciation–Furniture	1,200	
General reserve	20,000	
Provision for taxation	40,500	
Proposed dividend	35,000	+ 2,06,700
		2,87,500
Less: Profit and loss account (31-3-2005)		– 30,000
Operating profit, before working capital changes		2,57,500

Land and Building A/c

Dr. **Cr.**

To balance b/d	3,30,000	By depreciation	60,000
To bank (balancing figure)	2,20,000	By balance c/d	4,90,000
	5,50,000		5,50,000
To balance b/d	4,90,000		

Plant and Machinery A/c

Dr. **Cr.**

To balance b/d	85,400	By depreciation	50,000
To bank (balancing figure)	1,04,600	By balance c/d	1,40,000
	1,90,000		1,90,000
To balance b/d	**1,40,000**		

Furniture A/c

Dr. **Cr.**

To balance b/d	5,500	By depreciation	1,200
To bank (balancing figure)	2,200	By balance c/d	6,500
	7,7,00		
To balance b/d	6,500		7,700

Provision for Taxation A/c

Dr.			Cr.
To bank	22,500	By balance b/d	22,500
To balance c/d	40,500	By profit & loss A/c	40,500
	63,000		63,000
		By balance b/d	40,500

Proposed Dividend A/c

Dr.			Cr.
To bank	30,000	By balance b/d	30,000
To balance c/d	35,000	By profit & loss A/c	35,000
	65,000		65,000
		By balance b/d	35,000

Calculation of Cash from Operations

		(₹)
Operating profit, before working capital changes		2,57,500
Add: Increase in current liabilities		5,700
Sundry creditors (₹ 90,700 – ₹ 85,000)		
		2,63,200
Less: Increase in current assets		
Stock (₹ 95,700 – ₹ 82,400)	13,300	
Sundry debtors (₹ 85,500 – ₹ 75,000)	10,500	23,800
Cash inflow from operations		2,39,400

Cash flow statement for the year ended 31st March, 2006

		(₹)
Opening bank balance		34,200
Add Cash flow from operations	2,39,400	
Issue of equity shares	50,000	
Share premium	30,000	
Issue of 7% debentures	70,000	
		3,89,400
		4,23,600
Less:		
Additions to land and buildings	2,20,000	
Additions to plant and machinery	1,04,600	
Additions to furniture	2,200	
Payment of dividend	30,000	
Payment of tax	22,500	3,79,300
Closing bank balance		44,300

Proforma of Cash Flow Statement

As Per As – 3

Direct Method

Particulars	₹	₹
Cash Flows from Operating Activities		
Cash receipts from customers	–	
Cash payment to suppliers	(–)	
Cash paid to employees as salaries and wages	(–)	
Other operating expenses	(–) —	
Cash generated from operations	–	
Income tax paid	(–)	
	–	
Income tax refund	–	
Cash flow before extra-ordinary items	–	
Cash flow from extra-ordinary items	–	
E.g. Proceeds from earthquake disaster settlement	–	
Net cash flow from/used in operating activities		–
Cash Flows from Investing Activities		
Proceeds from sale of fixed assets	–	
Cash payment for purchases of fixed assets	(–)	
Interest received	–	
Dividend received	–	
Net cash flows from/used in investing activities		–
Cash Flows from Financing Activities		
Proceeds from issue of shares	–	
Proceeds from issue of debentures	–	
Proceeds from long-term borrowings	–	
Redemption of shares	(–)	
Redemption of debentures	(–)	
Repayment of long-term borrowings	(–)	
Interest paid	(–)	
Net cash flows from/used in financing activities		–
Net increase/decrease in cash and cash equivalents		–
Cash and cash equivalent at the beginning of the period		–
Cash and cash equivalents at the end of the period		–

Indirect Method

Particulars	₹	₹
Cash Flows from Operating Activities		
Balance of P & L A/c as per closing balance sheet	–	
Less: Balance of P & L A/c as per opening balance sheet	–	
OR		
Increase in the balance of P & L A/c	–	
OR		
Net Profit as per P & L A/c after appropriations	–	
Add: Appropriations during the year		
Transfer to general reserve	–	
Transfer to debenture redemption fund	–	
Transfer to dividend equalisation fund	–	
Proposed dividend	–	
Net profit for the year		
Add: Non-operating expenses	–	
Interim – Dividend paid	–	
Loss by fire	–	
Interest paid	–	
	–	
Less: Non-operating incomes	–	
Interest received	(–)	
Dividends received	(–)	
Operating net profit	–	
Add: Non-cash expenses		
Depreciation	–	
Loss on sale of fixed assets	–	
Loss on revaluation of fixed assets	–	
Loss on redemption of shares	–	
Loss on redemption of debentures	–	
Goodwill written off	–	
Preliminary expenses written off	–	
Discount on shares written off	–	
Discount on debentures written off	–	
Provision for taxation	–	
Less: Non-cash incomes		
Profit on sale of fixed assets	(–)	
Profit on revaluation of fixed assets	(–)	
Profit on redemption of debentures	(–)	
Profit on redemption of shares	(–)	
Operating profit before working capital changes	–	
Add: Decrease in current assets	–	
Less: Increase in current assets	(–)	
Add: Increase in current liabilities	–	
Less: Decrease in current liabilities	(–)	
Cash Generated from operations	–	
Less: Income tax paid	(–)	

Contd...

Add: Income tax refund	–	
Net cash from operating activities after income tax but before extra-ordinary items		
Add: Cash inflows from extra-ordinary items	–	
Less: Cash outflows from extra-ordinary items	–	
Net cash flows from/used in operating activities		–
Cash flows from investing activities		
Proceeds from sale of fixed assets	–	
Cash payment for purchase of fixed assets	(–)	
Interest received	–	
Dividend received	–	
Net cash flows from/used in investing activities		–
Cash flows from financing activities		
Proceeds from issue of shares	–	
Proceeds from issue of debentures	–	
Proceeds from long-term borrowings	–	
Redemption of shares	(–)	
Redemption of debentures	(–)	
Repayment of long-term borrowings	(–)	
Interest paid	(–)	
Dividend paid	(–)	
Net cash flows from/used in financing activities		–
Net increase/decrease in cash and cash equivalents		–
Cash and cash equivalent at the beginning of the period		–
Cash and cash equivalents at the end of the period		–

Presentation of Dividend and Interest

Normally, surplus cash is invested in shares and debentures, when funds can be spared for a long-period. Investment in shares and debentures is shown under 'cash outflows -investment activities'. As dividend and interest is a result of such investment, their receipt is also shown under 'Cash Inflows-Investment Activities'.

Similar treatment is given for payment of dividend and interest. Shares and Debentures are the normal means of rising finance. Issue of Shares and Debentures is shown under 'Cash Inflows-Financing Activities'. Payment of dividend and interest is related to those sources of finance, so payment of dividend and interest is shown under 'Cash Outflows-Financing Activities'.

Illustration No. 4

You are required to prepare cash flow statement from Balance Sheets of THEER & TARKH Company on 31st December, 04 and 31st December, 05 in the Traditional Method and AS-3.

Balance Sheets

Liabilities	31.12.2004 ₹	31.12.2005 ₹	Assets	31.12.2004 ₹	31.12.2005 ₹
Share capital	1,25,000	1,53,000	Cash	10,000	7,000
Capital reserve	—	25,000			
Creditors	40,000	44,000	Debtors	30,000	75,000
Mrs. A's loan	25,000	—	Stock	35,000	25,000
Loan from bank	40,000	50,000	Machinery	80,000	55,000
			Land	40,000	50,000
			Building	35,000	60,000
	2,30,000	2,72,000		2,30,000	2,72,000

During the year a machine costing ₹ 10,000, with accumulated depreciation of ₹ 3,000 was sold for ₹ 5,000. The provision for depreciation against machinery as on 31.12.2004 was ₹ 25,000 and on 31.12.2005 ₹ 40,000. Net profit for the year 2005 amounted to ₹ 45,000. Building has been revalued and credited to capital reserve account.

Solution

Cash Flow Statement (Traditional Method)

Cash balance as on 31.12.2004		₹ 10,000
Add: Sources:		
Cash from operations	₹ 34,000	
Loan from bank	10,000	+ 49,000
Sale of machinery	5,000	
Less: Applications:		
Purchase of land	10,000	
Mrs. A's loan repayment	25,000	
Drawings	17,000	– 52,000
Cash balance as on December 31, 2005		7,000

Working Notes

Cash from Operations & Working Capital Changes

Profit made during the year		₹ 45,000
Add: Depreciation on machinery	18,000	
Loss on sale of machinery	2,000	
Decrease in stock	10,000	
Increase in creditors	4,000	34,000
		79,000
Less: Increase in debtors		45,000
Cash from operations		34,000

Capital Account

Dr. **Cr.**

To cash-drawings (balancing figure)	17,000	By balance b/d	1,25,000
		By profit	45,000
To balance c/d	1,53,000		
	1,70,000		1,70,000
		By balance b/d	1,53,000

Machinery Account (at cost)

Dr. **Cr.**

To balance b/d	1,05,000 *	By bank	5,000
		By loss on sale of machinery	2,000
		By provision for depreciation	3,000
		By balance c/d	95,000
	1,05,000		1,05,000
To balance b/d	95,000		

Provision for Depreciation Account

Dr. **Cr.**

To machinery A/c	3,000	By balance b/d	25,000
To balance c/d	40,000	By P & L A/c (Depreciation charged – balancing figure)	18,000
	43,000		43,000
		To balance b/d	40,000

Note: Revaluation of Building is a non-cash item and so does not appear in Cash Flow Statement.

* Machinery at cost as on 31-12-2004 comprises of the following:

WDV on 31-12-2004:	80,000
Provision for depreciation till 31-12-2004	25,000
Machinery at cost as on 31-12-2004	1,05,000

Cash Flow Statement
(AS-3 (Revised) Method)

		₹	
I.	***Cash Flows from Operating Activities***		
	Net profit made during the year	45,000	
	Adjustments for depreciation	18,000	
	Loss on sale of machinery	2,000	
	Operating profit before working capital changes	65,000	
	Decrease in stock	10,000	
	Increase in creditors	4,000	
	Increase in debtors	(45,000)	
	Net cash flows from operating activities		34,000
II.	***Cash Flows from Investing Activities***		
	Sale of machinery	5,000	
	Purchase of land	(10,000)	
	Net cash flow from investing activities		(5,000)
III.	***Cash Flows from Financing Activities***		
	Loan from bank	10,000	
	Ms. A's loan repayment	(25,000)	
	Drawings	(17,000)	
	Net cash flow from financing activities		(32,000)
	Net increase (decrease) in cash and cash equivalent		(3,000)
	Cash and cash equivalents at the beginning of the period		10,000
	Cash and cash equivalents at the end of the period		7,000

Illustration No. 5

From the following Profit and Loss Account, you are required to compute cash from operations of Vikas & Co. who are engaged in the beauty products business. A part of their building taken on rent has been sublet to a hair dressing saloon.

What type is the income by way of rent from tenant? Do you think that it is desirable for the company to close the business, when the business is in profit?

Profit and Loss Account for the year ended December 2008

Dr.			Cr.
To salaries	52,000	By gross profit	52,000
Rent	25,000	Profit on sale of land	2,000
Electricity charges	12,000		
Depreciation	10,000	Rent from tenant	5,000
Loss on sale of machinery	2,000	Dividend on equity shares	84,200
Goodwill written off	6,000		
Preliminary expenses written off	2,000		
Proposed dividend	15,000		
Provision for taxation	3,200		
Net profit	16,000		
	1,43,20		1,43,200

Solution

Net profit		16,000
Add:		
Depreciation	10,000	
Loss on sale of machinery	2,000	
Goodwill written off	6,000	
Preliminary expenses written off	2,000	
Proposed dividend	15,000	
Provision for taxation	3,200	38,200
		54,200
Less: Non-operating income		
Profit on sale of land	2,000	
Rent from tenant	5,000	
Dividend on equity shares	84,200	91,200
Loss from operations		37,000

Rental income from the tenant ₹ 5,000 is non-operating income as this income is not connected to the main business carried on by Vikas & Co.

Net profit is ₹ 16,000, out of which non-operating income is ₹ 91,200. In other words, the beauty products business is in loss and the firm is in profit due to inclusion of non-operating income. If the beauty products business is closed, there would be a net profit of ₹ 53,000 (37,000 + 16,000). As the main business activity is in loss, it is desirable to close, if there is no possibility to convert the business into loss.

Illustration No. 6

From the following information, determine Cash Flow from operating activities by applying direct method.

Profit and Loss Account of Reshma Ltd., for the year ended March, 2009.

Dr.		Cr.	
To opening stock	15,000	By cash sales	5,000
Cash purchases	15,500	Credit sales	65,500
Credit purchases	10,000	Closing stock	15,000
Gross profit	45,000		
	85,500		85,500
To salaries	10,000	By gross profit	45,000
Insurance premium	3,000		
Depreciation	2,000		
Preliminary expenses written off	4,000		
Discount on issue of shares written off	1,000		
Net profit	25,000		
	45,000		45,000

Additional Information

	1-4-2008	1-4-2009
Debtors	5,000	6,000
Bills receivable	3,000	1,500
Creditors	8,000	3,500
Bills payable	2,000	1,000

Salaries and Insurance have been paid in cash. Opening cash balance has been ₹ 50,000.

What is the closing cash balance? In case, closing stock is ₹ 17,000, what would be the cash flow from operating activities?

Solution

Calculation of Cash from Operating Activities

1. Cash inflows from sales	Cash sales Collections from debtors & bills receivable	5,000 66,000	+ 71,000
2. Cash outflow towards Purchases	Cash purchases Payment to creditors and bills payable	15,500 15,500	– 31,000
3. Cash outflow for salaries			– 10,000
4. Cash outflow for Insurance premium			– 3,000
5. Cash from operating activities			27,000

Debtors' and Bills Receivable Account

To opening balance	8,000	By cash (collections)	
To credit sales	65,500	By closing balance	66,000
			7,500
	73,500		73,500

Creditors' and Bills Payable Account

Dr. **Cr.**

To cash (payments)	15,500	By opening balance	10,000
To closing balance	4,500	By credit purchases	10,000
	20,000		20,000

Calculation of Closing Cash Balance

Opening cash balance	50,000
Cash inflows from sales	+ 71,000
Cash outflow towards purchases	– 31,000
Cash outflow for salaries	– 10,000
Cash outflow for insurance premium	– 3,000
Closing cash balance	77,000

If closing stock is ₹ 17,000 instead of ₹ 15,000:

In case, closing stock is ₹ 17,000 instead of ₹ 15,000, cash flow from operating activities would be ₹ 25,000.

To become closing stock ₹ 17,000, purchases have to be more by ₹ 2,000. So, payments to creditors and bills payable would be more by ₹ 2,000 which would result in reduction of cash from operating activities by ₹ 2,000.

Note: Depreciation, preliminary expenses and discount on issue of shares does not result into any cash outgo, hence do not appear in cash flow statement.

Opening stock and closing stock are same; hence it does not have any effect on the Cash Flow Statement.

Illustration No. 7

Following are the summarized balance sheets of Cherry and Dimpy Ltd. as on 31st March 2005 and 2006, you are required to make the Statement of cash flow under the traditional method and AS-3 (revised method).

Liabilities	2005	2006
Equity share capital	2,00,000	2,50,000
General reserve	50,000	60,000
Profit and loss a/c	30,500	30,600
Bank loan (long term)	70,000	—
Sundry creditors	1,50,000	1,35,200
Provision for taxation	30,000	35,000
	5,30,500	5,10,800

Assets	2005	2006
Machinery	1,50,000	1,69,000
Land and building	2,41,800	2,28,200
Goodwill	—	5,000
Stock	74,000	20,000
Debtors	64,200	80,000
Bank	—	8,000
Cash	500	600
	5,30,500	5,10,800

Additional Information

During the year ended 31st March, 2006.

(i) Dividend ₹ 23,000 was paid.

(ii) Assets of another company were purchased for a consideration of ₹ 50,000 payable in shares for the purchase of the assets-stock : ₹ 20,000; Machinery ₹ 25,000.

(iii) Machinery was further purchased for ₹ 8,000.

(iv) Depreciation written off on machinery ₹ 12,000; Land & Buildings ₹ 13,600.

(v) Income tax provided during the year ₹ 33,000.

(vi) Loss on sale of machinery for ₹ 200 was written off to general reserve.

Solution

Machinery A/c

Dr.			Cr.
To balance b/d	1,50,000	By general reserve (loss on sale of machine)	200
To share capital a/c (purchase by issue of shares)	25,000	By depreciation	12,000
To cash (purchase of machinery)	8,000	By cash (sale of machine)- balancing figure	1,800
		By balance c/d	1,69,000
	1,83,000		1,83,000
To balance b/d	1,69,000		

Provision for Taxation A/c

Dr. **Cr.**

To bank (Tax paid)	28,000	By balance b/d	30,000
To balance c/d	35,000	By profit & loss a/c (tax provision)	33,000
	63,000		63,000
		By balance b/d	35,000

General Reserve Account

Dr. **Cr.**

To machinery account (loss on sale)	200	By balance b/d	50,000
To balance c/d	60,000	By profit and loss adjustment A/c (transfer of profit)	10,200
	60,200		60,200
		By balance b/d	60,000

Profit and Loss Adjustment Account

Dr. **Cr.**

To general reserve A/c	10,200	By opening balance b/d	30,500
To provision for taxation	33,000	By funds from operations (balancing figure)	91,900
To machinery (depreciation)	12,000		
To land and buildings-depreciation	13,600		
To dividend paid	23,000		
To closing balance c/d	30,600		
	1,22,400		1,22,400
		By balance b/d	30,600

Decrease in Stock

Opening stock		74,000
Closing stock	20,000	
Less: Stock acquired * in acquisition	20,000	Nil
Decrease in stock (Increase in cash)		74,000

Cash Flow Statement for the Year Ending 31st March, 2006

(Traditional Method)

Opening cash & bank balance		500
Sources:		
Funds from operations	91,900	
Sale of machinery	1,800	
Decrease in stock	74,000	
Uses:		+ 1,67,700
Increase in debtors	15,800	
Purchase of machinery	8,000	
Tax paid	28,000	
Dividends paid	23,000	
Decrease in creditors	14,800	
Repayment of bank loan	70,000	– 1,59,600
Closing cash & bank balance		8,600

Note: Acquisition of business –stock and machinery–in exchange of share is a non-cash transaction.

Cash Flow Statement

AS-3 (Revised Method)

Cash Flows from Operating Activities		
Net profit made during the year (100 +10,200 + 23,000 + 33,000)	66,300	
Adjustment for depreciation on land and building	13,600	
Adjustment for depreciation on machinery	12,000	
Operating profit before working capital changes	91,900	
Decrease in stock	74,000	
Increase in debtors	(15,800)	
Decrease in creditors	(14,800)	
Income tax paid	(28,000)	
1. Net Cash Flows from Operating Activities		1,07,300
Cash Flows from Investing Activities		
Sale of machinery	1,800	
Purchase of machinery	(8,000)	
2. Cash from Investing Activities		(6,200)
Cash Flows from Financing Activities		
Repayment of bank loan	(70,000)	
Dividend paid	(23,000)	
3. Cash Flows from Financing Activities		(93,000)
Net increase in cash and cash equivalents		8,100
Cash and cash equivalents at the beginning of the period		500
Cash and Cash Equivalents at the End of the Period		8,600

7.13 STATEMENT OF CHANGES IN FINANCIAL POSITION (TOTAL RESOURCES BASIS)

Here, the term "Funds" refer to all financial resources. The resources may be in any form—material, machinery, money and others—used in the business. The term 'funds' is used in the comprehensive way. This is a statement summarising the effect of changes in cash, along with other significant investment and financing activities, which do not involve cash.

Preparation: Preparation of this statement is similar to the preparation of cash flow statement. In cash flow statement, transactions like conversion of debentures into shares and issuance of bonus shares do not get reflected as they do not affect cash. In this statement, these types of transactions are shown under the head '**Financial Resources not Affecting Cash**' both under sources and uses in this statement, **additionally**. This is the only difference. This provides the comprehensive picture of total resources. There is no fixed standard format for presentation.

An illustration explains the concept better.

Illustration No. 8

From the following comparative balance sheets of Kishore & Co. Ltd, prepare the Cash Flow Statement on Total Financial Resources basis.

Comparative Balance Sheets for the year ended 31st March, 2005 and 2006

(₹)

	2005	2006
Current Assets		
Bank	65,000	1,65,000
Debtors	45,000	70,000
Inventory	90,000	62,000
Total current assets	2,00,000	2,97,000
Fixed Assets		
Goodwill	—	50,000
Land & building	2,00,000	2,50,000
Equipment	2,50,000	2,95,000
Less: Accumulated depreciation	(80,000)	(95,000)
Total net fixed assets	3,70,000	5,00,000
Total Assets	**5,70,000**	**7,97,000**

Current Liabilities		
Creditors	15,000	2,000
Salaries payable	22,000	60,000
Provision for tax	60,000	5,000
Proposed dividend	25,000	10,000
Total current liabilities	1,22,000	77,000
Long-term Liabilities		
Long-term loan	18,000	84,000
Debentures	1,30,000	1,06,000
Total long-term liabilities	1,48,000	1,90,000
Total liabilities	2,70,000	2,67,000
Shareholders' Equity		
Equity share capital	2,35,000	3,75,000
Share premium	25,000	65,000
Reserves and surplus	40,000	90,000
Net worth	3,00,000	5,30,000
Total Funds	**5,70,000**	**7,97,000**

The additional information is given below:

1. Debentures ₹ 24,000 were converted to share capital at par.
2. During the year, equipment costing ₹ 40,000 (accumulated depreciation ₹ 12,000) was sold for 32,000.
3. The company acquired another company for ₹1,00,000 for which equity shares were issued. Assets acquired were: Goodwill ₹ 50,000 and Building ₹ 50,000.
4. The company declared a cash dividend of ₹ 25,000.
5. The company issued additional shares, par value ₹ 100 per share, at a premium during the year.
6. Bonus shares were also issued at par for ₹ 10,000.
7. Payment of tax ₹ 60,000 was made and a new provision for ₹ 5,000 has been created.

Solution

Cash from Operations

(₹)

Net profit during the year		70,000
Add: Depreciation	27,000	
Decrease in stock	28,000	
Increase in salaries payable	38,000	
Provision for tax made	5,000	+ 98,000
Less: Profit on sale of equipment	4,000	
Decrease in creditors	13,000	
Increase in debtors	25,000	– 42,000
Cash from operations		1,26,000

Reserves and Surplus Account

Dr.			Cr.
To proposed dividend	10,000	By balance b/d	40,000
To share capital (bonus shares issue)	10,000	By profit and loss account (profit made during the year – balancing figure)	70,000
To balance c/d	90,000		
	1,10,000		1,10,000
		By balance b/d	90,000

Accumulated Depreciation Account

Dr.			Cr.
To sale of asset (depreciation on the asset sold)	12,000	By balance b/d	80,000
To balance c/d	95,000	By profit and loss account (depreciation provided)	27,000
	1,07,000		1,07,000
		By balance b/d	95,000

Equipment Account

Dr.			Cr.
To balance b/d	2,50,000	By sale of asset	40,000
To cash (purchase of new equipment - Balancing figure)	85,000	By balance c/d	2,95,000
	3,35,000		3,35,000
To balance b/d	2,95,000		

Equity Share Capital Account

Dr.			Cr.
To balance c/d	3,75,000	By balance b/d	2,35,000
		By reserves and surplus account (issue of bonus shares)	10,000
		By acquisition of company	1,00,000
		By cash (balancing figure)	6,000
		By debentures account (conversion of debentures into shares)	24,000
	3,75,000		3,75,000
		By balance b/d	3,75,000

Cash Flow Statement

Sources:		
Cash from operations	1,26,000	
Cash from issue of shares	6,000	
Cash from share premium	40,000	
Sale of equipment	32,000	
Receipt of long-term loan	66,000	
Financial Resources, not Affecting Cash – Sources:		
Issue of bonus shares from reserves and surplus	10,000	
Issuance of equity shares for purchase of goodwill and equipment	1,00,000	
Issuance of equity shares for conversion of debentures	24,000	
		4,04,000
Financial Resources Provided Uses:		
Purchase of equipment	85,000	
Payment of tax	60,000	
Payment of dividend	25,000	
Financial Resources, not affecting Cash – Uses		
Purchase of goodwill	50,000	
Purchase of equipment	50,000	
Issue of bonus shares from reserves and surplus	10,000	
Payment of debentures through issuance of equity shares	24,000	
Financial Resources Applied		**3,04,000**
Increase in bank balance		1,00,000

Check Your Understanding

(A) State whether the following statements are True or False

1. Every listed company has an option to prepare and enclose the Cash Flow Statement or Funds Flow Statement along with the financial statements.
2. Cash flow statement describes the inflows and outflows of cash.
3. Cash equivalents are short term, highly liquid investments that are readily convertible into cash.
4. As per AS-3 (Revised), cash flows resulting from the sale of fixed assets are classified as cash flows from investing activities.
5. Cash flow statement reveals the effects of transactions involving movement of cash.
6. Cash Flow Statement is a summary of cashbook.
7. Increase in provision for doubtful debts should be added back to net profit in order to find out cash from operations.

8. Funds Flow Statement and Cash Flow Statement serve the same purpose.
9. A Cash Flow Statement can very well be equated with an Income Statement.
10. Cash Flow Statement is based upon accrual basis of accounting.
11. The term "Funds means" "Current Assets" in case of a cash flow analysis.
12. Cash Flow Statement is a substitute of a cash Account.

Answers

1. False 2. True 3. True 4. True 5. True 6. True 7. True 8. False
9. False 10. False 11. False 12. False.

(B) Objective Questions (Identify what is most appropriate)

1. In the context of Cash Flow Statement, the term "Fund" refers to:
   (i) Working capital (ii) Cash and cash equivalents
   (iii) Total resources (iv) None
2. Cash from operations is equal to:
   (i) Net profit plus increase in outstanding expenses
   (ii) Net profit plus increase in debtors
   (iii) Net profit plus increase in stock
3. In the context of Cash Flow Statement, the term 'cash' is equivalent to:
   (i) Physical cash on hand
   (ii) Physical cash on hand and demand deposits in a bank
   (iii) Physical cash on hand and all types of deposits in a bank
4. Profit and Loss Account shows profit, while the actual business is in loss. Which of the following statements helps in knowing that the operating profit is negative and non-operating profit is positive, ending with final profit position?
   (i) Profit and loss account (ii) Balance sheet
   (iii) Source and application of funds (iv) Cash flow statement

Answers

1. (ii), 2. (i) 3. (ii), 4. (iii) Operating profit/loss and non-operating profit/loss are shown separately. So, actual position that the main business is in loss would be known.

(C) Match the following

Some of the situations are described hereunder. Match the statement that can provide relevant information:

Situation	Statement
1. Inability to pay more dividend, despite higher profits	Cash flow statement
2. Diversion of working capital for the purchase of fixed assets	Statement of working capital changes
3. Financial position on a specified date	Cash flow statement
4. Profit or loss made during a period	Where got, where gone statement
5. Inability to pay wages though long-term loan is taken	Funds flow statement
6. Diversion of short-term sources for long-term uses	Sources and application of funds
7. Causes for increase or decrease in working capital	Profit and loss account
8. Ability to pay instalment on principal and interest on long-term loan	Balance sheet

Solution

Situation	Statement
1. Inability to pay more dividend, despite higher profits	Sources and application of funds or funds flow statement or where got where got statement (different names)
2. Diversion of working capital for the purchase of fixed assets	Funds flow statement or sources and application of funds or where got, where gone statement (different names)
3. Financial position on a specified date	Balance sheet
4. Profit or loss made during a period	Profit and loss account
5. Inability to pay wages, though long-term loan is taken	Cash flow statement
6. Diversion of short-term sources for long-term uses	Funds flow statement or sources and application of funds or where got, where got statement (different names)
7. Causes for increase or decrease in working capital	Statement of working capital changes
8. Ability to pay instalment on principal and interest on long-term loan	Cash flow statement

(D) State the effect of each of the following transactions considered individually on funds (cash concept):

(a) Purchase of furniture for cash.

(b) Purchase of plant and machinery against a long-term loan payable.

(c) Issue of bonus shares, capitalizing profits.

Answer

Fund denotes 'cash'. Item (a) will result in decrease of cash, while items (b) and (c) will have no effect on cash.

(E) Fill in the Blanks:

1. Cash payments to suppliers for goods and services are classified under 'cash flows from ________ activities'.
2. Income from long-term investments is cash flow from ________ activities.
3. Decrease in debtors is ________ of cash.
4. Net cash flow is the difference of ________ and ________ of cash.

Answers

1. Operating 2. Investing 3. Inflow 4. Inflow, Outflow

Descriptive Questions

1. Explain the importance of cash. What is a Cash Flow Statement? **(7.1 and 7.2)**
2. Explain the need Cash Flow Statement and state its objectives. **(7.3 & 7.4)**
3. Describe the classification of cash flows from operating, investing and financing activities in a Cash Flow Statement. **(7.5)**
4. Explain the procedure of preparing Cash Flow Statement and method of calculating fund from operating activities. **(7.6, 7.7, 7.8 and 7.10)**
5. Describe different methods of preparing Cash Flow Statement. **(7.9)**
6. Differentiate between Funds Flow Statement and Cash Flow Statement. **(7.11)**
7. What is a Cash Flow Statement and describe the different steps involved in preparing Cash Flow Statement? **(7.2 and 7.7)**
8. Describe limitations of Cash Flow Statement. **(7.12)**

Short Questions & Answers

Q.1. What is the purpose of a Cash Flow Statement?

Ans. Cash Flow Statement is a summary of cash-book. It is a statement, which contains the inflows (sources) and outflows (uses) of cash and cash equivalents during a specified period. A Cash Flow Statement explains the causes of changes in the cash position of a business enterprise, between two balance sheet dates. The firm may be profitable, yet it may experience difficulty, even, to make payment of wages and salaries. The firm wants to understand, where the profit has gone and for what purposes, the profit amount has been utilized. This is possible with Cash Flow Statement. Through Cash Flow Statement, management can assess, monitor and control the available liquidity in the enterprise.

Q.2. Do you consider Cash Flow Statement better in utility as compared to Funds Flow Statement?

Ans. Yes, Cash Flow Statement is better in utility compared to Funds Flow Statement.

Funds Flow Statement shows an increase or decrease in the working capital and changes in assets and liabilities. However, the working capital concept does not reveal the true picture of availability of cash. In the Funds Flow Statement, cash and inventories are treated, alike. All the components of working capital are treated equally, in respect of availability from the viewpoint of time. However, this is not the correct position as their time and quality of realization are different from the viewpoint of cash.

Debtors take less time for converting into cash, while inventories take more time for realization. Similarly, inventories may consist of dead stock that has not been written off. Debtors may have bad debts that are not yet removed. Funds Flow Statement does not recognize this basic difference in their nature. An enterprise may have more slow paying debtors and non-moving stocks, with little cash or its equivalents. Due to comfortable working capital position, Funds Flow Statement does not throw the real picture about the inadequacy of cash. Only, when Cash Flow Statement is prepared, the real situation about the adequacy of funds, in the sense of cash, is known.

So, Cash Flow Statement is superior to Funds Flow Statement in respect of utility.

Q.3. Is it necessary to prepare and publish Cash Flow Statement?

Ans. It is necessary for a limited company to prepare and publish Cash Flow Statement, in case it is a listed company (shares of the company listed on the stock exchange) or its turnover exceeds rupees fifty crores, though not listed. In such circumstances, it is necessary for the concerned company to enclose the Cash Flow Statement to the financial statements—Profit and Loss Account and Balance Sheet. The Cash Flow Statement has to be in the prescribed format and should follow the guidelines of AS-3 (Revised). It should follow the format of indirect method of AS-3.

Q.4. What is meant by 'Flows' in the context of Cash Flow Statement?

Ans. The term 'Flows' mean inflows (receipts) and outflows (payments) of cash. Cash Flow Statement is a summary of cash book in a condensed form.

Q.5. Do you consider that inventory and receivables stand on the same level in respect of realization into cash?

Ans. No, inventory and receivables do not stand on the same level in respect of realization into cash. Receivables get realized faster into cash compared to inventory. In inventory, there are three components, raw materials, work-in-progress and finished products. Amongst the components of inventory, finished goods get realized quickly as they can be sold in the form they are. In the event of discontinuation of business, liquidation or any other unforeseen event, raw materials can be sold, but the same is not the case with work-in-progress. Work-in-progress is the most difficult component to be sold as only those firms who deal in that activity buy it. In consequence, there would be limited buyers for work-in-progress.

Interview Questions

Q.1. Board of Directors of Rishi Ltd. are worried why they cannot declare more dividend, when the profit and loss account of the company for the year 2008 shows higher profits, compared to the previous year, 2007. Equity shareholders have expected a higher rate of dividend in the light of substantial increase in profits. The directors do not find any reason why they cannot satisfy the increased expectations of the

shareholders. Which statement would help the Board of Directors to know the answer? Explain the probable reason for the situation.

Ans. Cash Flow Statement explains the reason why the company is not able to declare a higher rate of dividend, despite increase in profits.

Rishi Ltd. might have utilized the increase in profits for purchase of fixed assets, without leaving liquid funds in current assets. The company might not have planned for adequate liquid resources, for increased dividend rate, despite earning more profits. In the absence of adequate cash, the company is now not in a position to declare higher dividend. This may be the cause why the firm is not able to declare a higher rate of dividend to meet the expectations of the shareholders for higher dividend rate.

Q.2. Devendra & Ltd. is engaged in construction of a Multiplex at Bhopal. They have applied for a term loan of ₹ 2 crores to Hudco for building a shopping complex. They want to repay the loan over a period of ten years, after an initial moratorium period of three years as the construction would take around two years and rents from shopping complex can commence thereafter only.

Why Devendra & Ltd. cannot commence the payment of interest and instalments soon after the sanction of loan?

Which statement would satisfy Hudco that the company would be in a position to service the debt?

What points are to be verified by Hudco?

Ans. Devendra & Ltd. is engaged in construction of a Multiplex at Bhopal. As stated, the shopping complex takes around two years for construction and one more year is likely to be taken for renting the shops. For this reason, they want a moratorium period of three years. Moratorium means suspension of instalment and interest on the loan for a specified period.

Borrower can make payment only after the project is completed. Moratorium period is granted by the term lending institution as the borrowing institution would not have the capacity to repay as no profits would be made during the gestation period. Cash generation would not be there during moratorium period.

Cash Flow Statement shows the cash generation by way of rents from shopping complex. Hudco can verify the following:

- When the rental income, after meeting all expenses, would commence?
- Whether the excess cash amount would be adequate to meet the payment of interest and instalments over the loan period?

So, Hudco insists on the Cash Flow Statements for ten years (period of repayment of term-loan) to satisfy the cash generating capacity of the company for proper repayment of loan along with interest.

Q.3. What is meant by 'servicing of debt'?

Ans. Servicing of debt means ability to make payment of instalment and interest on loan as and when they fall due.

Q.4. I am CEO of Karan Preet Sabarwal Ltd. My profit and loss account shows increase in profit, compared to the last year. However, I experience lot of difficulty in making

even wage payments. Is there any way to find out why I experience cash crunch, despite profits? Explain the function of the statement that would help in?

Ans. Main problem is shortage of cash. Though profits are more, firm is not finding cash even to make wage payments. Cash Flow Statement (CFS) is the solution to find out where profit has been actually utilized. Profit is like water. If water is put in a jar, water takes the shape of a jar. If same water is put in a bowl, it takes the shape of a bowl. Profit might have been used for purchase of fixed assets. In such an event, cash flows from operating activities would be positive, while cash flows from investing activities would be negative. This shows diversion of profit for increase in fixed assets.

Amount of profit might have been used for acquisition of current assets, other than cash. Profit could have been used for repayment of liabilities too. Analysis of Cash Flow Statement (CFS) gives the information, where the profit has gone.

Funds Flow Statement too can explain the position about the application of profit towards the acquisition of fixed assets. However, approach of Funds Flow Statement is wider, while Cash Flow Statement (CFS) is more specific to highlight from the view point of cash, which is the main problem here.

Q.5. A potential investor wants to verify whether the company has diverted its profits for the purchase of fixed assets in the past year. How the investor can know the truth?

Ans. Enclosing Cash Flow Statement (CFS) to financial statements is a statutory obligation/ requirement for every listed company. Audited financial statements are public documents, which are, normally, kept on the company site. So, one can visit the website of the concerned company to see Cash Flow Statement of the company to find out the use of profits made in the past year.

CHAPTER 8

Cost-Volume Profit Analysis

8.1 INTRODUCTION

Decision-Making is the most important function of a manager. All the functions of management can be delegated to others. But, the final Decision-Making is the ultimate responsibility of the manager as it is the final outcome of thinking process.

8.2 DECISION-MAKING PROCESS

Decision-making is a selection process and concerned with selecting the best type of alternative. The decision taken is aimed at achieving the organizational goals. It is concerned with the detailed study of the available alternatives for finding out the best possible alternative. Decision-making is a mental process which is the outcome of constant thoughtful considerations. It leads to commitment which depends upon the nature of the decision, whether short-term or long-term.

Steps in Decision-Making Process

- Define the Problem or Specify the Objective
- Explore all Available Alternatives
- Analyze all Pros and Cons of Different Alternatives
- Select the Best Alternative
- Decision-Making is only a beginning, not the end in Process
- Implement Effectively
- Follow-Up untill Planned Result is achieved

Profit Planning

A firm's performance is measured by the profit it makes. Profits of a firm depend upon a large number of factors. But, the most important factors are costs of manufacture, volume of sales and selling price of the products.

> **The analytical techniques employed to study the inter-relationship of cost, volume and price and their impact on the behaviour of profit is known as 'Cost-Volume Profit Analysis'.**

In the short-run, profit planning can be made with the use of CVP analysis. It helps the management to achieve an ideal combination of costs and volume. This becomes possible with the understanding of the implications of variable cost, fixed cost and volume. It also helps the management in deciding the quantum of sales required to be made to avoid losses as well as reaching a particular level of sales to achieve the targeted amount of profit.

8.2.1 Behaviour of Fixed and Variable Costs

Fixed Costs: When a cost does not change with increase in volume, it is called Fixed Cost. Fixed costs are constant and do not change irrespective of the level of production. Examples are rent, insurance, depreciation and repairs. The total fixed cost is one and the same whether one unit is produced or one hundred units are produced, till the production does not exceed the capacity of machine. However, the unit fixed cost decreases as the volume of production increases. In the pictorial presentation of behaviour of fixed costs, unit fixed cost curve descends while total fixed cost is constant at all levels of production. In other words, unit cost decreases as and when volume increases. But, there is no change in fixed costs at different volume levels.

The graphical presentation of total fixed cost and unit fixed costs are shown as under:

Behaviour of Fixed Costs

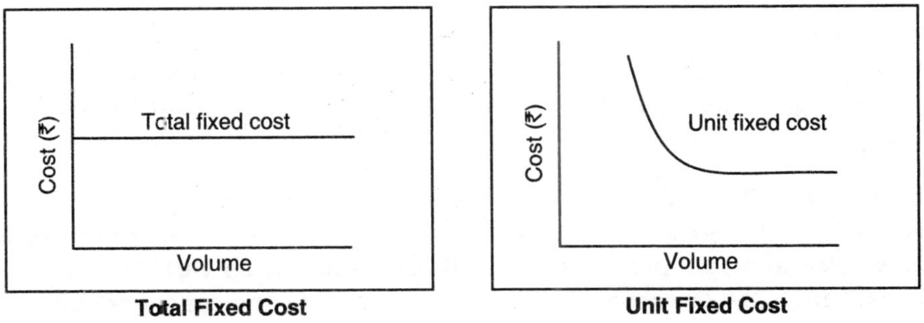

Variable Costs: When a cost changes in proportion to change in volume, it is called Variable Cost. The typical example is raw materials. If production increases, total cost of raw materials increases in the same proportion of level of production. If production is suspended or closed, cost of raw materials becomes zero. Mathematically, a linear relationship exists between a variable cost and volume. If volume increases or decreases by 20%, the cost of production varies in the same proportion. So, unit cost remains constant and total cost changes proportionally to volume.

The graphical presentation of total variable cost and unit variable cost are shown as under:

Behaviour of Variable Costs

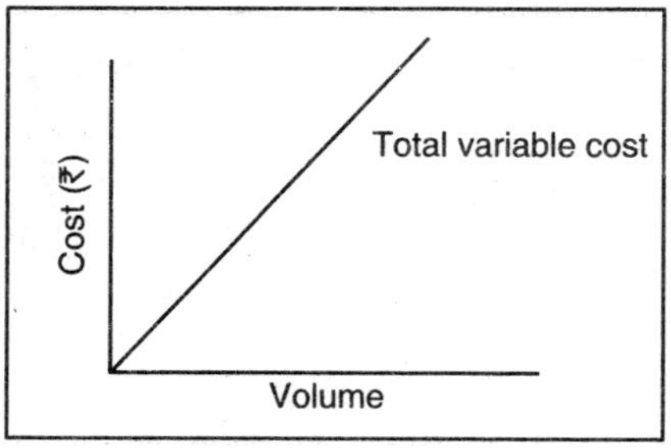

Total Variable Cost

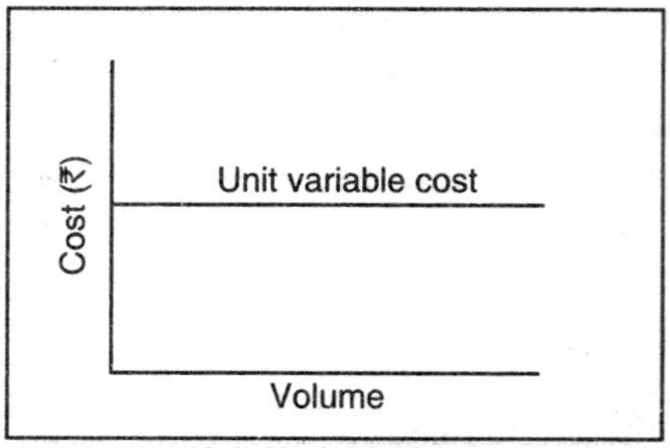

Unit Variable Cost

In CVP analysis, it is presumed that fixed cost and variable cost can be separated.

8.3 CVP ANALYSIS

Utility of CVP Analysis: CVP analysis studies the relationship of cost-volume-profit at different levels of output. This analysis is an important tool for profit planning. The three factors of CVP analysis– viz. Costs, Volume and Profit- are interconnected and dependent on one another. For example, profits depend upon the selling price. Selling price largely depends upon cost of production. Cost of production, in turn, depends upon volume of production. It is only the variable costs that vary directly with production, whereas fixed costs remain constant, regardless of the volume of production in the short-run.

In some quarters, there is an opinion that business firms, rarely, operate at their break-even point, and so its analysis is of very limited use to the management. This is incorrect. Also, many people consider CVP analysis and Break-even point as one and the same which is incorrect too.

> **The scope of CVP analysis is quite wide and BEP is only a part of it. Break-even analysis provides answer that how much sales are to be made to avoid losses. CVP analysis provides not only this answer, as BEP is a part of it but also provides answers in many other areas to the management.**

Understanding CVP relationship is important in financial decision making to a dynamic management. It provides right answers to the following questions such as:

- How much sales are required to avoid losses?
- What level of sales is required to achieve a targeted amount of profit?

- What will be the effect of change in price, cost and volume on profits?
- What will be the effect of change in sales mix on profits?
- What will be the new break-even point, if there is change in price, cost, volume or sales mix?
- Should we buy or manufacture some products or components?
- What will be the impact of plant expansion on the relationship of cost-volume-profit?
- Which product or product mix is most profitable and which one is least profitable?
- Should the sale of a product or an operation of a plant be discontinued?
- Is it desirable to shut down the plant temporarily?

These are some of the intricate questions for which management can find answers with the help of CVP analysis. All the above aspects have immense influence on profitability of the firm. CVP analysis is concerned with entire profit planning, as management's main thrust is to build a good level of profit at all times. This analysis provides the necessary insight to management to take suitable decisions for timely action. It is of great use for profit planning, cost control and decision-making.

8.4 CVP ANALYSIS AND BREAK-EVEN ANALYSIS

Many people think that break-even analysis and CVP analysis are one and the same. It is not so. **The Break-even analysis is the most widely known form of CVP analysis.** For this reason, many use both the terms interchangeably.

The purpose of CVP analysis is to examine the effect of change in cost, volume and price on profits. This is a comprehensive study. Break-even analysis is a part of CVP analysis.

8.5 BREAK-EVEN ANALYSIS

Break-even analysis establishes the relationship between revenues and costs with respect to volume. It indicates the level of sales at which total costs are equal to total revenues. Break-even analysis is a specific way of presenting information to management in a precise manner. Many a time, CVP analysis is popularly designated as break-even analysis. But, there is a narrow difference between the two.

> **CVP analysis is concerned with the entire profit planning, while the break-even analysis is one of the techniques used in that process.**

Break-even point: Break-even point is the point at which the firm makes no profit or loss. At break-even point, firm is in the stage of equilibrium. The equilibrium point is commonly known as break-even point. **Break-even point is that point where the revenue is just equal to total costs.** It is the point, where the firm makes neither profit nor loss. This is a zero position. After this level, if the firm makes production and sells above the variable cost, it earns profit. If the sales fall below this level, firm sustains loss. There are two approaches to calculate the break-even point. They are:

(A) Break-even Formulae Approach and

(B) Break-even Chart or Graphic Method of break-even Analysis

(A) Break-even Formulae Approach: The break-even point can be calculated in terms of units, value of sales volume and as a percentage of estimated capacity.

Break-even Situation

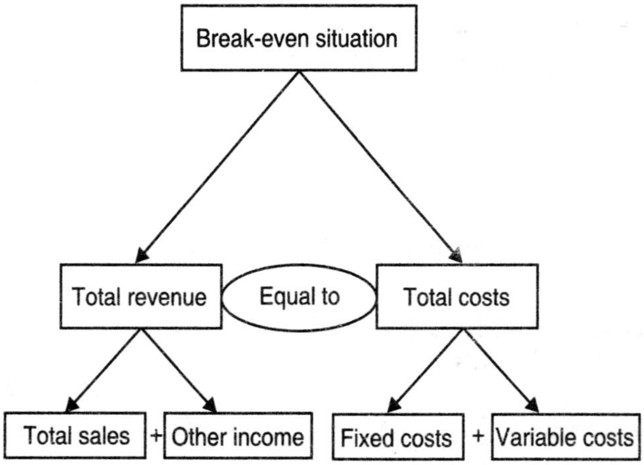

8.5.1 Contribution

When selling price per unit is more than its variable cost, the excess is called contribution. **Contribution is also known as 'Gross Margin'.**

To calculate total contribution, multiply unit contribution with number of units sold. Total contribution is the excess of total sales over total variable costs incurred by the firm. After covering variable costs, amount left out from total sales in the firm is contribution or gross margin. So, contribution covers total fixed costs and profit. If contribution does not cover fixed costs, the difference is loss sustained by the firm. Every firm looks to achieve break-even point at the earliest. After break-even level, whatever is sold and can leave in the form of contribution to the firm is a welcome decision. While making production and sales decisions, firm chooses that product which gives the highest contribution. Contribution is vital in profit planning decision-making. Firm is always concerned to choose that product which it can sell and achieve the highest amount of contribution. Contribution is important to finance manager as well as marketing manager to show impressive performance of the firm in terms of profitability.

The formulae for their calculation are

Contribution per unit = Selling price per unit – Variable cost per unit

Contribution per unit × Number of units sold = Total Contribution

Total Contribution = Total fixed costs + Profit

Profit = Total contribution – Total fixed costs

Loss = Total fixed costs – Total contribution

BEP in terms of Units: The break-even point, in terms of units, can be computed by dividing fixed costs by contribution per unit. The formula for break-even point (BEP), in terms of units, is as follows:

$$\textbf{BEP (units)} = \frac{\textbf{Total fixed cost}}{\textbf{Selling price per unit – Variable cost per unit}}$$

or

$$= \frac{\textbf{Total fixed cost}}{\textbf{Contribution per unit}}$$

The above formula is useful to find out break-even point in terms of number of units of sales.

From the above formula, it is evident that the selling price per unit should be higher than the variable cost per unit to have positive break-even point. Suppose, if variable cost is higher than the selling price, a negative sales volume can be calculated mathematically to arrive at break-even point. But it is of no help in real life situation.

No fixed costs situation: In case a firm has no fixed costs, what is its break-even point?

Under zero fixed cost situations, there would be only variable costs. When variable cost is equal to selling price, in the absence of fixed costs, no production situation is the first break-even situation. This is the safest situation for a firm. Even with production of one unit, selling price is equal to variable cost hence there is a break-even situation. Break-even situation continues whatever be the level of production in the absence of fixed costs as total costs are equal to total sales. It is rightly said when fixed costs are absent, every sales volume is a break-even point as revenue is equal to total costs at any sales volume.

BEP in terms of Rupees: The break-even point can be calculated from the following formula:

$$\textbf{BEP (in rupees)} = \frac{\textbf{Fixed cost}}{\textbf{P/V ratio}}$$

or

$$= \frac{\textbf{Total fixed cost}}{\textbf{1 – (Variable cost per unit/Selling price per unit)}}$$

or

= BEP (in terms of units) × Selling price per unit

8.5.2 P/V Ratio or Contribution Ratio

P/V Ratio is important for studying profitability of operations of a business. This ratio establishes the relationship between contribution and sales value. P/V ratio is useful to calculate the BEP in terms of rupees.

Break-even analysis is a useful device for profit planning.

The term 'P' represents Profit that is equivalent to contribution when calculating BEP, in terms of rupees. The term 'V' refers to Volume of sales.

$$\text{P/V Ratio or Contribution ratio} = \frac{\text{Contribution per unit}}{\text{Selling price per unit}}$$

or

$$= \frac{\text{Change in contribution} \times 100}{\text{Change in sales}}$$

or

$$= \frac{\text{Change in profit (loss)} \times 100}{\text{Change in sales}}$$

Profit-volume ratio (P/V Ratio) is also known as contribution ratio.

Importance of break-even point: In the initial period, firms operate at their break- even point. Even if break-even point is achieved, firms feel happy. Once that stage is over, firms plan for profit making. BEP is helpful in knowing level of sales to be made to achieve a particular level of profit for profit planning.

Profit planning is the greatest concern of every firm. BEP analysis helps the management in planning not only to achieve no loss, no profit situation at the earliest but is also of immense use in planning the required level of sales to achieve a planned level of profit.

"Business firms rarely operate at their break-even points. Therefore, the break-even analysis is of very limited use to the management." This is a wrong perception of break-even analysis. No doubt, this concept is of immense use to management in the initial stages of a firm as the management is concerned to achieve no loss, no profit situation at the earliest when the firm is not able to achieve profits. This concept is of high value in profit planning. With P/V ratio, one can understand the level of profits it can make at different sale levels. If the firm wants to achieve a particular level of profits, it can know from the very beginning and plan how much sales are to be achieved.

Illustration No. 1

Divya Sakally Ltd. produces a single product and its selling price is ₹ 40. Its variable cost per unit is ₹ 32. Its fixed costs are ₹ 2,40,000. What is its break-even point?

Solution

Selling price per unit = ₹ 40

Variable cost per unit = ₹ 32

Contribution per unit = 8

$$\text{BEP (units)} = \frac{\text{Fixed costs}}{\text{Contribution per unit}} = \frac{2,40,000}{8} = 30,000 \text{ units}$$

Proof:

Selling price per unit = ₹ 40

Variable cost per unit = ₹ 32

Contribution per unit = 8

Total contribution	= 30,000 units × 8 =	2,40,000
Fixed cost	=	2,40,000
Profit		Nil

ALTERNATIVELY

Total sales	30,000 × 40 =	12,00,000
Total variable cost	30,000 × 32 =	9,60,000
Contribution	30,000 × 8 =	2,40,000
Fixed costs		2,40,000
Profit		0

By proof, student can know that the answer obtained is correct.

To find out BEP in terms of rupees:

$$\text{BEP (in rupees)} = \frac{\text{Total fixed cost}}{1 - (\text{Variable cost per unit/Selling price per unit})}$$

$$\text{BEP (in rupees)} = \frac{2,40,000}{1-(32/40)}$$

$$= \frac{2,40,000}{8/40}$$

$$= 2,40,000 \times 40/8 = 12,00,000$$

Note to Students: There are various formulae to calculate the same result. It is advisable to remember simple formula. To facilitate students, required formulae to remember are put in bold.

Illustration No. 2

From the following data, find out the break-even point and P/V Ratio:

	₹
Fixed costs	60,000
Variable costs	1,20,000
Net profit	20,000
Sales	2,00,000

(B.U. MBA, 2009)

Solution

$$\text{Contribution} = \text{Sales} - \text{Variable costs}$$

$$= 2,00,000 - 1,20,000$$

$$= 80,000$$

$$\text{P/V Ratio} = \frac{\text{Contribution} \times 100}{\text{Sales}}$$

$$= \frac{80,000 \times 100}{2,00,000}$$

$$= 40\%$$

Break-even point is that point where the firm does not make any profit or loss. BEP is calculated as under:

$$= \frac{\text{Fixed cost}}{\text{P/V ratio}}$$

$$= \frac{60,000}{40\%}$$

$$= 1,50,000$$

BEP to achieve a desired amount of profit: P/V ratio requires a small change to calculate the desired amount of profit. In the numerator, the desired amount of profit is to be added to the fixed costs. The formula is

BEP (to achieve required amount of profit)

$$= \frac{\textbf{Total fixed cost + Desired profit}}{\textbf{P/V ratio}}$$

Illustration No. 3

Calculate sales required to earn a profit of ₹ 60,00,00 from the following data.

Fixed Expenses	= 1,20,000
Variable cost per unit:	
Direct Material	= ₹ 4
Direct Labour	= ₹ 2
Direct Overheads	= 50% of Direct Labour
Selling price per unit	= ₹ 14

Solution

		(₹)
Selling price per unit		14
Less: Direct Material Direct Labour Direct Overheads	4 2 1	7
Contribution per unit		7

$$\text{P/V Ratio} = \frac{\text{Contribution}}{\text{Sales}} \times 100$$

$$= \frac{7}{14} \times 100$$

$$= 50\%$$

$$\text{Sales required to earn a profit of ₹ 6,00,000} = \frac{\text{Fixed expenses + Desired profit}}{\text{P/V Ratio}}$$

$$= \frac{1{,}20{,}000 + 6{,}00{,}000}{0.5}$$

$$= 14{,}40{,}000$$

Required sales are ₹ 14,40,000 to make a profit of ₹ 6,00,000

Illustration No. 4

Find out the BEP in ₹ and units from the following information:

Sales is ₹ 1,00,000 (1,000 units), Variable cost is ₹ 50,000 and Fixed cost is ₹ 20,000.

Solution

(i) Contribution = Sales – Variable cost

= 1,00,000 – 50,000 = ₹ 50,000

P/V Ratio = Contribution/sales = 50,000/1,00,000 = 50%

$$\text{BEP in ₹} = \frac{\text{Fixed cost}}{\text{P/V Ratio}}$$

$$= \frac{20{,}000}{50{,}000/1{,}00{,}000}$$

= ₹ 40,000

(ii) Selling price per unit = Total Sales/No. of units sold = 1,00,000/1,000 = ₹ 100

$$\text{BEP in units} = \frac{\text{BEP sales in ₹}}{\text{Selling price per unit}}$$

$$= \frac{40{,}000}{100}$$

= 400 units

Importance of P/V Ratio: Management always remains interested to know which product is more profitable. Organization wants to reward the department which works efficiently and pull up that which does not work to its expected level. Higher the P/V Ratio, more will be the profit. Thus, aim of management is always to increase the P/V Ratio by identifying areas where actions are needed.

P/V Ratio indicates availability of margin on sales made. So, firm that enjoys higher P/V Ratio stands to gain when demand for the product grows.

Impact of costs on P/V Ratio: Basically costs are of two types, fixed costs and variable costs. P/V ratio is a relationship between contribution and selling price. Contribution is the difference between selling price and variable costs. A change in selling price, variable cost or both influences P/V ratio. However, if both variable costs and selling price change in a similar manner, say increase or decrease by 20% in both in same direction, P/V ratio does not change. Increase or decrease in fixed costs does not change P/V ratio. In other words, only change in selling price and variable costs change P/V ratio while fixed costs do not change P/V ratio. Fixed costs do not change P/V ratio as they are not considered for calculating P/V ratio.

Change in P/V Ratio: If selling price is reduced, P/V Ratio gets reduced. In consequence, break-even point becomes higher and margin of safety becomes lower. So, the effect of a price reduction is always to reduce P/V Ratio that raises break-even point and shortens margin of safety.

The above concept is explained with a simple example.

Milk-man teaches break-even point: Let us take the example of a milkman. He purchases milk packets @ ₹ 6 per packet and sells at ₹ 10. He distributes milk packets hiring a motorcycle and the fixed hire charge is ₹ 100 per day. So, contribution per packet is ₹ 4. At this stage, his P/V Ratio is 40% (contribution 4/selling price 10). If he sells 25 packets, he becomes break-even. If he sells 60 packets, his margin of safety is 35 packets (Actual sales 60–sales at break-even point 25).

Suppose, he reduces the selling price to ₹ 8 per packet and continues to sell 60 packets as earlier. Now, his P/V Ratio is 25% (contribution 2/selling price 8). As fixed cost is ₹ 100 and contribution is ₹ 2, break-even point is 50 packets. However, he continues to sell 60 packets so his margin of safety is reduced to 10 packets (Actual sales 60–sales at new break-even point 50).

Now, margin of safety is reduced to 10 packets, which was earlier 35 packets.

This explains reduction of selling price results in the following:

(i) Reduction of P/V Ratio (40% reduced to 25%)

(ii) Break-even point is increased (in place of 25 packets, 50 packets are needed) and

(iii) Margin of safety reduced (earlier 35 packets reduced to 10 packets)

This situation is explained through pictorial presentation.

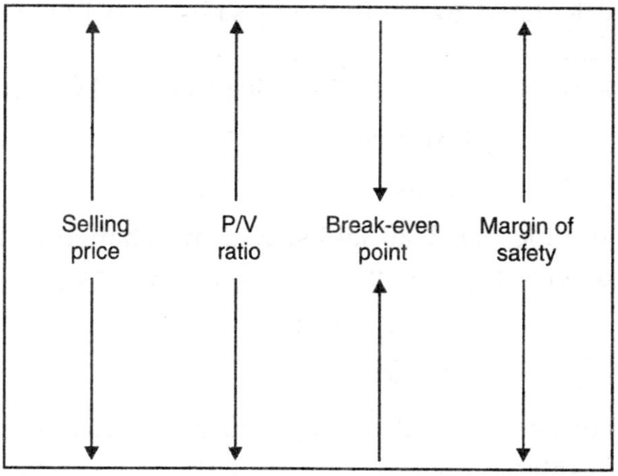

Impact of selling price on P/V ratio, BEP and margin of safety

8.5.3 Impact of P/V Ratio on Fixed Costs and Sales

P/V Ratio does not change even though there is an increase in fixed costs and sales. Reason, P/V Ratio is a ratio between variable cost and selling price per unit. Unless there is a change in variable cost or selling price per unit or both, P/V Ratio does not change. Once P/V Ratio and volume of sales are known, contribution can be calculated by multiplying sales with P/V Ratio.

Illustration No. 5

Chanchal & Co is engaged in manufacturing cosmetic products with brand name "Chanchal". Product's variable cost is ₹ 30, while its selling price is ₹ 40. Its fixed costs are ₹ 2 lakhs. If sales are ₹ 40 lakhs, what is its P/V Ratio and profit? If its sales get doubled, what is the impact on P/V Ratio and profits? Note that there is no change in fixed costs.

In case fixed costs and sales increase, whether P/V Ratio would change? Whether profits get double when sales are double, without any change in setting price? If not, explain reason.

Solution

$$\text{Selling price} = ₹\ 40$$

$$\text{Variable cost} = \frac{₹\ 30}{10}$$

$$\text{P/V Ratio} = \frac{\text{Contribution}}{\text{Selling price}}$$

$$= \frac{10}{40} = 25\%$$

Contribution is calculated by multiplying sales with P/V ratio.
If sales are ₹ 40 lakhs:
Contribution = 40,00,000 × P/V Ratio = 40,00,000 × 25% =10,00,000

Fixed costs	= 2,00,000
Profit	= 8,00,000

If sales become double, i.e. ₹ 80 lakhs, with no change in fixed costs:
Contribution = 80,00,000 × P/V Ratio = 80,00,000 × 25% = 20,00,000

Fixed costs	= 2,00,000
Profit	= 18,00,000

P/V ratio does not change with increase in sales. Increase of sales and fixed costs do not influence P/V ratio.

Reason: Profits are more than double, even though sales are double. Reason is fixed costs are constant and do not increase with the increase in sales.

Special features of P/V Ratio: The following are special features:

1. It helps management in ascertaining the total amount of contribution for a given volume of sales. Say, if sales are rupees four lakhs and P/V Ratio is 25%, its contribution is rupees one lakh. It is so simple and easy to calculate contribution.
2. Management can increase this ratio by increasing selling price or reducing variable cost of products.

3. P/V Ratio remains constant so long as the selling price and variable cost per unit remain constant or fluctuate in the same proportion.
4. This remains unaffected by any change in the level of activity. In other words, it remains the same, whether the sales are 1,000 units or 2,000 units.
5. This ratio also remains unaffected with any change in fixed cost, as they are not considered. It means even if the fixed cost increases or decreases, P/V ratio remains the same as fixed costs are not taken into account while calculating.

Uses or Advantages of Break-even Analysis: These are the following advantages of Break-even point:

1. **Know no Profit or Loss situation:** New firms cannot make profit in the beginning of their operations. At that stage, the focus of every firm is to achieve no profit, no loss situation.

> **Break-even analysis helps the firm to know amount of sales it has to make to achieve no loss, no profit situation. For new firms, it is the biggest challenge and this tool helps them in achieving that goal.**

2. **Determination of Break-even point in a Multi Product firm:** The above formula is of immense use to calculate break-even point even when the firm is engaged in multiple products. A Multi-product firm experiences difficulty to calculate break-even point in terms of any common unit. Such firms can calculate composite break-even point at the time of budgeting and actual sales in terms of total sales value.

   For example, budgeted sales are ₹ 10 lakhs while its sales at BEP are ₹ 6 lakhs. So, at the time of budgeting, the firm is aware that it can achieve BEP with a performance of 60% of budgeted sales. If the actual sales performance turns out to ₹ 5 lakhs, it becomes aware that it is short of ₹ One lakh sales only to achieve BEP.

3. **Ranking profitable products:** When firm is engaged in producing more than one product by calculating P/V ratio for each product, it can concentrate to produce that product, which has higher P/V Ratio as it gives more profitability. By leaving products that have less P/V Ratio, firm can concentrate on those products which are having higher P/V Ratio to boost profitability.
4. **Simple and easy tool to guide management:** Break-even analysis is easy to understand. Graphical presentation is possible. So, management can understand and appreciate which product is to be preferred for manufacture, based on contribution each product generates. At what capacity level, firm can achieve no profit–no loss situation is also known.
5. **Determination of selling price that gives a desired profit:** To achieve a particular level of profit, what should be the selling price of product? This information is helpful to the firm in determining selling price of the product.

6. **Determination of costs and revenues at different levels of output.**
7. **Impact of increase or decrease in fixed and variable costs on profits.**
8. **Study on effect of differential prices in different markets e.g. home market and foreign market on profits:** At times, firms receive export orders at prices lower than the prices quoted by them in the home market. This helps them in accepting or refusing the orders.

BEP in terms of Capacity: Many firms compute break-even point in terms of estimated sales or full capacity of the manufacturing unit. Dividing the break-even sales with estimated sales or full capacity sales would give the answer to know the capacity needed to achieve break-even point. If break-even sales are say, rupees ten lakhs and the estimated sales are rupees forty lakhs, then the break-even point is 25%.

$$\textbf{BEP (\% of capacity)} = \frac{\textbf{Sales at break - even point}}{\textbf{Estimated sales or full capacity sales}}$$

Alternatively, if the total contribution at the estimated sales or full capacity is known, it can be calculated directly.

$$\textbf{BEP (\% of capacity)} = \frac{\textbf{Total fixed cost}}{\textbf{Total contribution at the estimated sales}}$$

Illustration No. 6

There are two firms under the same management. Management wants to merge both the firms for better utilization.

	Firm A	**Firm B**
Capacity operation	100%	75%
Sales	₹ 400 lakhs	₹ 200 lakhs
Variable costs	₹ 200 lakhs	₹ 80 lakhs
Fixed costs	₹ 30 lakhs	₹ 20 lakhs

Calculate the following:

(i) What is the PV Ratio of individual firms and combined firm A & B?

(ii) What is the break-even point capacity for the merged firm A & B?

(iii) What would be profitability of working at 60% of the merged capacity?

Make calculations in lakhs (rupees).

Solution

	Firm A (at 100% capacity)	Firm B (at 100% capacity)	Combined firm A & B (at 100% capacity)
Sales	₹ 400 lakhs	₹ 200 lakhs	₹ 600 lakhs
Less: Variable costs	₹ 200 lakhs	₹ 80 lakhs	₹ 280 lakhs
Contribution	₹ 200 lakhs	₹ 120 lakhs	₹ 320 lakhs
P/V Ratio	$\frac{200}{400} \times 100 = 50\%$	$\frac{120}{200} \times 100 = 60\%$	$\frac{320}{600} \times 100 = 53.33\%$

$$\text{Break-even volume (in rupees) for combined firm A \& B} = \frac{\text{Fixed expenses}}{\text{Combined P/V ratio}}$$

$$= \frac{50 \text{ lakhs}}{93.76 \text{ lakhs}}$$

$$= 53.33\%$$

(i) Combined firm A & B can achieve break-even point by making a sale of ₹ 93.76 lakhs.

(ii) $$\text{BEP (\% of capacity)} = \frac{\text{Sales at break-even point}}{\text{Full capacity sales}}$$

$$= \frac{93.76 \text{ lakhs}}{600 \text{ lakhs}} \times 100 = 15.63\%$$

(iii) Profitability of working at 60% of the merged capacity

	₹
Sales	= 360 lakhs
Less: Variable costs	= 168 lakhs
Contribution	192 lakhs
Less Fixed costs	= 50 lakhs
Net profit	= 142 lakhs

Combined firm A & B achieves a profit ₹ 142 lakhs by working at 60% of its capacity.

Impact of Break-even point: When two firms working with same amount of sales and equal unit variable cost, with difference in fixed costs, which firm can withstand better? A firm enjoying lower break-even point is always at an advantage as its fixed costs get recovered early and can withstand better compared to a firm with higher break-even point.

(B) Break-even Chart or Graphic Method of Break-even analysis

The break-even point can be presented graphically. The pictorial presentation gives a better understanding of the relationship of cost, volume and profit. Graphical presentation gives immediate and clear understanding of instantaneous situations which always impresses the management.

The graphical chart of break-even analysis looks like this:

Break-even Chart

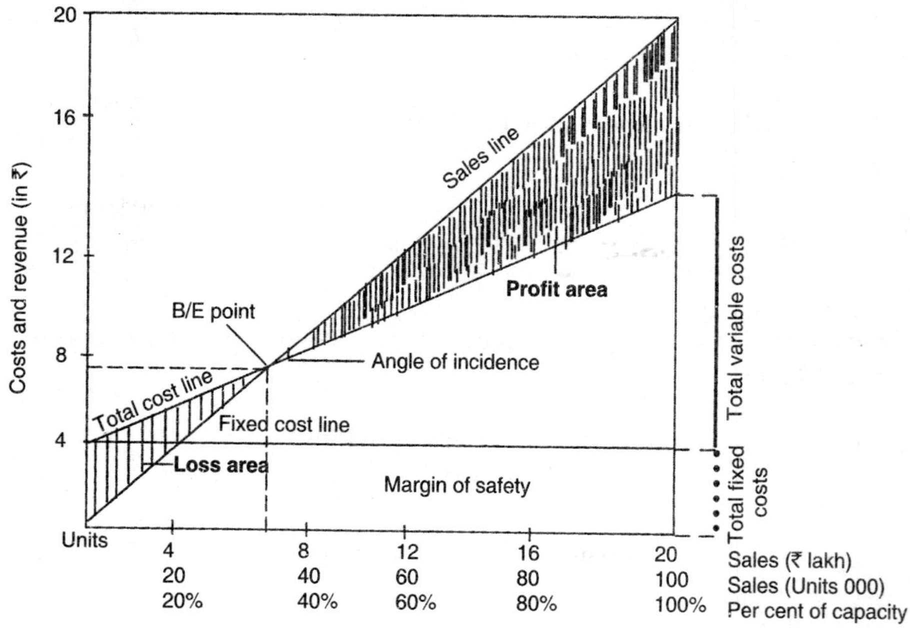

Following are the steps involved in preparing break-even chart:

1. Sales volume is plotted along the horizontal line i.e. X-axis. Sales volume may be expressed in terms of units, rupees or as a percentage of capacity.
2. Vertical line i.e. Y-axis is used to represent revenue, fixed costs and variable costs.
3. Both horizontal and vertical lines are spaced equally with same distance.
4. Break-even point is the point of intersection between Total cost line and Sales line.
5. Sales revenue at break-even point can be determined by drawing a perpendicular line to the X-axis from the point of the above intersection.
6. Total sales line and Total cost line intersect forming an angle, known as Angle of Incidence.

Why Total Cost Line starts at a higher point i.e. at the level of fixed cost? Even though, the production is zero, firm incurs fixed costs. In other words, fixed costs are permanent costs or non-reversible costs in the short run. So, total cost line is equal to fixed costs even at the nil production stage. For this reason, total cost line starts at the level of fixed costs.

8.5.4 Angle of Incidence

The break-even point is indicated where Total cost line and Total sales line intersect each other. The angle that is formed with their intersection is called 'Angle of incidence'. **Larger the angle of incidence, lower is the break-even point and vice versa.** A lower break-even point is an indication that the firm can withstand, even if sales fall. Firm does not go into loss immediately and remains atleast with a small amount of profit.

Area of Contribution: Profit area is shown on the right side where total sales line is in excess of the total cost line, while loss area is shown where the total cost line is above the total sales line. The variable cost is represented by the gap between total cost line and fixed cost line.

8.6 ADVANTAGES OR USES OF BREAK-EVEN CHART

Following are the advantages or uses of break-even chart:

1. It is simple to form. Even a layman can understand.
2. It helps management to take decisions as effect of changes in fixed cost and variable cost at various levels of output can be depicted in a meaningful manner. Effect of changes in selling price on profits can be better explained by graphical presentation.
3. Comparative study of various products' profitability is possible.
4. Break-even chart is a better managerial tool for forecasting, planning and control.
5. Besides determining break-even point, profit at various levels of output can also be determined.

8.7 ASSUMPTIONS OF BREAK-EVEN ANALYSIS

The break-even analysis is based on the following assumptions:

1. **Costs segregation:** It is based on the assumption that all costs can be segregated into fixed costs and variable costs.
2. **Constant selling price:** The selling price remains constant. In other words, selling price does not change with volume or other factors.
3. **Constant fixed costs:** Fixed costs are constant at all levels of activity. They do not change, with change in sales.
4. **Constant variable costs:** Variable cost per unit is constant. So, variable costs fluctuate directly in proportion to changes in volume of output. In other words, they change in direct proportion to sales volume.

5. **Synchronized production and sales:** It is assumed that production and sales are Synchronized. That is, inventories remain the same in opening stock and closing stock.
6. **Constant sales mix:** Only one product is manufactured. In case more than one product is manufactured, sales mix of products sold does not change.
7. **No change in operating efficiency:** There is no change in operating efficiency.
8. **No other factors:** Volume of output or production is the only factor that influences the cost. It is assumed that no other factors have any influence on break-even analysis.

8.8 LIMITATIONS OF BREAK-EVEN ANALYSIS AND BREAK-EVEN CHARTS

Break-even analysis depends on the assumptions made in a given situation. If the actual situation comes nearer to assumptions made, validity of break-even calculations would be higher.

Greater the deviations from the given assumptions, more imperfect and incorrect would be the break-even calculations. Limitations of break-even chart suggest that validity of break-even calculations depend on validity of assumptions made.

Despite many advantages, break-even analysis and charts suffer from the following limitations:

1. **Number of assumptions:** Break-even analysis is based on several assumptions and they may not hold good under all circumstances. Fixed costs are presumed to be constant, irrespective of the level of output; but it does not happen in practice. When production increases above the installed capacity, fixed costs change as new plant and machinery has to be installed for increased production. Variable costs do not vary in direct proportion to the change in volume of output due to law of diminishing returns. Selling price that is supposed to be constant also changes due to increased competition.
2. **Application in short run:** Break-even analysis is a short run analysis. For instance, variable costs are presumed to be constant. However, variable costs are likely to increase as the firm approaches full capacity. Reason is costly overtime as firm employs additional employees to meet short-term requirements. In long-run, cost analysis may not hold good as the assumptions may vary and situation may be totally different.
3. **Applicable for single product line:** This analysis is applicable for a single product only. If break-even point for each product is to be calculated, fixed costs have to be allocated to different products, a practical problem in real life. Otherwise, Composite BEP for the overall firm can only be calculated.

4. **No remedial action:** It does not suggest any remedy or action to management for solving the problem.
5. **Other factors ignored:** Other important factors such as amount of investment, problems of marketing and policies of government influence the firm. Break-even analysis does not consider them. This analysis focuses only on cost-profit - volume relationship.
6. **Limited information:** Break-even charts provide limited information. If we want to study the effect of changes in fixed costs, variable costs and selling prices on profitability, a number of charts have to be drawn. It becomes rather more complicated and difficult to understand.
7. **Static view:** More often, break-even chart presents a static view of the problem under consideration.

Despite these limitations, it has great application for the basic problem of understanding the inter-relationship of cost, volume and price on profits.

8.9 MARGIN OF SAFETY

The excess of actual or budgeted (expected) sales over break-even sales is known as 'Margin of safety'. It is the difference between actual sales minus break-even sales.

Margin of safety = Estimated sales – Sales at Break-even point

Above formula explains amount of safety to the firm. High margin of safety provides a lot of comfort to the firm as sales fall during recession period. Suppose, if the firm is able to break-even at a sale level of rupees ten lakhs while its actual sales are rupees forty lakhs, then its margin of safety is rupees thirty lakhs. It means if the sales fall by rupees thirty lakhs, still the firm does not incur loss. Higher the margin of safety, it is better for the firm. When two firms are compared, then the firm having higher margin of safety can withstand adverse conditions such as fall in demand for the product or even recession.

Margin of safety indicates the extent to which sales can fall, before the firm suffers a loss.

Margin of safety ratio can be calculated as under:

$$\textbf{Margin of safety ratio} = \frac{\text{Actual sales} - \text{Break-even sales}}{\text{Actual sales}} \times 100$$

As margin of safety is the volume of sales beyond the break-even sales point, all the sales above the break-even point give some profit, which can be calculated as:

Profit = Margin of safety × P/V Ratio

Or

$$\text{Margin of safety} = \frac{\text{Profit} \times 100}{\text{P/V Ratio}}$$

Size of margin of safety is an important indicator to show strength of business. If margin of safety is large, then that firm can withstand fall of sales and continue to be in some profit. If the margin of safety is thin, decline of sales would seriously affect profit of business and may run into losses.

Steps to improve Margin of Safety: Margin of safety can be improved by taking the following steps:

1. Increasing the level of production and sales.
2. Increasing the selling price.
3. Reducing fixed costs.
4. Reducing the variable cost.
5. Substituting profitable products with the unprofitable products.
6. Changing business mix to improve contribution and also dropping unprofitable products.

Illustration No. 7

Dheera Ltd. has the following information in respect of sales ₹ 10,00,000, variable cost ₹ 6,00,000 and fixed cost ₹ 50,000. Unit cost is ₹ 100. Calculate margin of safety, in rupees and units, and also break-even point in rupees.

Solution

(i) Statement of profit

Sales	= 10,00,000
Less: Variable cost	= 6,00,000
Contribution	= 4,00,000
Fixed costs	= 50,000
Profit	= 3,50,000

P/V Ratio = Contribution/Volume of sales

$$= \frac{4,00,000}{10,00,000}$$

$$= 40\%$$

$$\text{Margin of safety in rupees} = \frac{\text{Profit} \times 100}{\text{P/V Ratio}}$$

$$= \frac{3,50,000}{40\%}$$

$$= ₹\ 8,75,000$$

(ii) Margin of safety in units $= \dfrac{\text{Margin of safety in ₹}}{\text{Selling price per unit}}$

$= \dfrac{8{,}75{,}000}{100}$

$=$ 8,750 units

(iii) Break-even sales in ₹ $= \dfrac{\text{Fixed costs} \times 100}{\text{P/V Ratio}}$

$= \dfrac{50{,}000}{40\%}$

$=$ ₹ 1,25,000

Illustration No. 8

Cost accountant of Cherry & Ltd. finds that the ratio of variable cost to sales of the company is 80%. Break-even point occurs at 50% capacity of the plant and at that level, sales are ₹ 10,00,000.

Find out the sales at full capacity, if fixed costs are ₹ 1,00,000. Determine the profits at 80% and 100% of sales.

Solution

Ratio of variable cost to sales = 80%
P/V Ratio (Ratio of contribution to sales) = 20%
At break-even point, there is no profit or loss.
Fixed costs = 1,00,000

Sales at BEP $= \dfrac{\text{Fixed cost}}{\text{P/V Ratio}}$

Sales at BEP $= \dfrac{1{,}00{,}000}{20\%}$

$=$ 5,00,000

At this point, contribution is 1,00,000 (20% of ₹ 5 lakhs), equal to fixed costs.

(i) BEP occurs at 50% capacity and BEP is ₹ 5,00,000.

Sales at full capacity (100%) $= \dfrac{5{,}00{,}000 \times 100}{50}$

$=$ ₹ 10,00,000

(ii) Contribution at 80% capacity of the plant = Sales × P/V

= 8,00,000 × 20%

= 1,60,000

Profit at 80% of sales = Contribution – Fixed cost
= 1,60,000 – 1,00,000
= ₹ 60,000

(iii) Contribution at 100% capacity of the plant = Sales × PV
= 10,00,000 × 20%
= 2,00,000

Profit at 100% of sales = Contribution – Fixed cost
= 2,00,000 – 1,00,000
= ₹ 1,00,000

8.10 CASH BREAK-EVEN POINT

Many a time, it is difficult for industrial units to become break-even in the initial years. From this situation, the concept of Cash Break-even point has emerged. **The Cash break-even point may be defined as that point of sales volume where cash revenues are equal to cash costs.** In other words, if we eliminate non-cash items both from revenues and costs, cash break-even analysis can be computed. Depreciation is, generally a fixed cost. However, when plant and machinery is used for additional shifts, the additional depreciation is a variable cost. Reason for treating the additional depreciation as variable cost is that the firm can avoid additional shift at any time and in such circumstances this cost would not be incurred. There is no outgo of cash with both depreciation and additional depreciation, though they are costs. For this reason, to calculate cash break-even point, depreciation is deducted from fixed costs. The same argument holds good for additional depreciation too. Additional depreciation component, treated as variable cost, is also to be deducted from variable costs. Similarly, deferred expenses are to be excluded from fixed cost. In other words, accrual accounting is changed to cash accounting to calculate cash break-even point.

Thus, cash break-even point may be calculated as below:

$$\textbf{Cash break-even point (in terms of units)} = \frac{\textbf{Cash fixed cost}}{\textbf{Cash contribution per unit}}.$$

Illustration No. 9

From the following information, calculate cash break-even point.

	₹
Selling price per unit	60
Variable cost per unit	40
Additional depreciation, included in variable cost per unit	5
Fixed cost	1,50,000
Depreciation included in fixed cost	25,000

Solution

Cash fixed cost = 1,50,000 – 25,000

= 1,25,000

Cash contribution per unit = 60 – (40 – 5) = 25

Cash break-even point (in terms of units) $= \frac{\text{Cash fixed cost}}{\text{Cash contribution per unit}}$

$= \frac{1,25,000}{25}$

= 5,000 units

Cash break-even point (in sales value) = 5,000 × 60 = ₹ 3,00,000

8.11 MULTI PRODUCT BREAK-EVEN POINT (COMPOSITE BREAK-EVEN POINT)

If a firm produces more than one product, it is known as a Multi-product firm. As the firm produces various products, the relative proportion of sales of different products is called Sales mix or Product mix. In the case of a Multi-product firm, contribution of each product can be calculated by deducting variable cost from the individual revenue of the product. If contribution of all products is aggregated, firm's total contribution is arrived at. **Firms overall break-even point is calculated by dividing total contribution by total sales volume of the firm.**

Composite break-even point (in ₹) $= \frac{\textbf{Total fixed cost}}{\textbf{Composite P/V ratio}}$

or

$= \frac{\textbf{Total fixed cost}}{\textbf{Weighted average marginal contribution per unit}}$

Composite P/V Ratio $= \frac{\text{Total contribution} \times 100}{\text{Total sales}}$

P/V ratio of each product can be calculated without distributing fixed costs of firm over different products. So, it is not really important to calculate cost-volume-profit interrelations to allocate fixed costs to individual product lines. Even without allocating fixed costs, individual product contribution can be calculated to decide priority amongst different products to take advantage of the available production capacity for profit maximization.

Break-even point in a Multi-product firm can be calculated without allocating fixed costs to different products.

Illustration No. 10

The following data of Kish & Co. for the period ending 31st March, 2006 is as under:

(₹)

	Product A	Product B	Product C
Sales	10,00,000	4,00,000	6,00,000
Variable costs	6,00,000	2,80,000	4,00,000

Total fixed costs are ₹ 2,00,000. You are required to calculate contribution of each product, firm's composite break-even point, net profit and composite P/V Ratio.

Solution

(₹)

	Product A	Product B	Product C	Total
Sales mix	50%	20%	30%	100%
Sales revenue	10,00,000	4,00,000	6,00,000	20,00,000
Variable cost	6,00,000	2,80,000	4,00,000	12,80,000
Contribution	4,00,000	1,20,000	2,00,000	7,20,000
Fixed cost				2,00,000
Net profit				5,20,000
PV ratio	40%	30%	33.33%	36%
BEP for the firm (₹)				$\frac{\text{Total fixed cost}}{\text{P/V Ratio}} = \frac{2,00,000}{36\%} = 5,55,556$

To arrive at break-even point of a multi-product firm, multiply product mix of each product with its corresponding P/V ratio. Then aggregate P/V Ratio of all products, which becomes P/V Ratio of a multi-product firm. Once fixed cost is divided by aggregate composite P/V ratio, BEP of multi product firm is arrived at.

$$\text{Firm's P/V Ratio is 36\%. i.e. } \frac{7,20,000}{20,00,000}$$

This is the weighted average of P/V ratios for individual products i.e.

$$(40\% \times 50\%) + (20\% \times 30\%) + (30\% \times 33.33\%) = 36\%$$

Illustration No. 11

A factory is producing four products and their cost and revenue details are as under. In addition, there are common fixed costs amounting to ₹ 1,00,000.

	A	B	C	D
Fixed costs	1,20,000	1,00,000	80,000	60,000
Variable costs	2,00,000	3,00,000	4,00,000	5,00,000
Sales	6,00,000	8,00,000	9,00,000	12,00,000

Calculate composite BEP for the factory.

Solution

	A	B	C	D	Total
Sales	6,00,000	8,00,000	9,00,000	12,00,000	35,00,000
Variable costs	2,00,000	3,00,000	4,00,000	5,00,000	14,00,000
Contribution	4,00,000	5,00,000	5,00,000	7,00,000	21,00,000
Fixed costs	1,20,000	1,00,000	80,000	60,000	3,60,000
Common fixed cost					1,00,000
Aggregate fixed cost					4,60,000

$$\text{Composite P/V Ratio} = \frac{\text{Aggregate contribution}}{\text{Aggregate sales}}$$

$$= \frac{21,00,000}{35,00,000}$$

$$= 60\%$$

$$\text{Composite BEP} = \frac{\text{Aggregate fixed cost}}{\text{Composite P/V Ratio}}$$

$$= \frac{4,60,000}{60\%}$$

$$= ₹\ 7,66,667$$

Illustration No. 12

Apeksha Seethal Ltd is engaged in manufacture of beauty products. It plans to revise the existing sales mix in value. Details of sales and its operating costs are as under:

Brand name	% of existing sales	% of revised sales	% of operating costs in selling price
Beauty	40%	30%	30%
Handsome	30%	40%	40%
Fair	20%	10%	10%
Lovely	10%	20%	20%

Total budgeted sales (100%) are ₹ 10,00,000 per month. Operating costs do not change even in the revised sales mix.

Fixed costs are ₹ 6,00,000 per month.

Calculate the following:

(a) Calculate existing break-even point.

(b) After implementation of the changed business mix, calculate new break-even point, if fixed costs do not change. Do you recommend change in business mix?

(c) New break-even point, if fixed costs decrease by ₹ 1 lakh per month. Do you recommend the proposal?

Solution

(A) Computation of existing break-even point

	Beauty	Handsome	Fair	Lovely	Total
Sales	4,00,000	3,00,000	2,00,000	1,00,000	10,00,000
Less: Variable costs	1,20,000	1,20,000	20,000	20,000	2,80,000
Contribution	2,80,000	1,80,000	1,80,000	80,000	7,20,000

$$\text{Composite P/V Ratio} = \frac{\text{Total contribution}}{\text{Total sales}}$$

$$= \frac{7,20,000}{10,00,000} = 72\%$$

$$\text{BEP sales for existing business mix} = \frac{\text{Fixed cost}}{\text{P/V Ratio}}$$

$$= \frac{6,00,000}{72\%}$$

$$= ₹\ 8,33,333$$

(B) New break-even point with change in product mix (No change in fixed costs):

	Beauty	Handsome	Fair	Lovely	Total
Sales	3,00,000	4,00,000	1,00,000	2,00,000	10,00,000
Less: Variable costs	90,000	1,60,000	10,000	40,000	3,00,000
Contribution	2,10,000	2,40,000	90,000	1,60,000	7,00,000

$$\text{Composite P/V Ratio} = \frac{\text{Total contribution}}{\text{Total sales}}$$

$$= \frac{7,00,000}{10,00,000} = 70\%$$

$$\text{BEP sales for revised business mix} = \frac{\text{Fixed cost}}{\text{P/V Ratio}}$$

$$= \frac{6,00,000}{70\%}$$

$$= ₹\ 8,57,143$$

Recommendation: It is not recommended to change the business mix as contribution has decreased from ₹ 7,20,000 to ₹ 7,00,000 and in consequence firm has to make a sale of ₹ 8,57,143 instead of ₹ 8,33,333 to achieve break-even point.

(C) New break-even point, if fixed costs decreased by ₹ 1 lakh per month:

$$\text{BEP sales with decreased fixed costs} = \frac{\text{Fixed cost}}{\text{P/V Ratio}}$$

$$= \frac{5,00,000}{70\%}$$

$$= ₹\ 7,14,286$$

Recommendation: Firm can achieve break-even point by making sales of ₹ 7,14,286 instead of ₹ 8,33,333 In other words, break-even point is achieved even with reduced sales, hence recommended.

Illustration No. 13

You are required to calculate the break-even point from the following information:

Selling price per unit	₹ 20
Variable cost per unit	₹ 04
Fixed costs for the year	₹ 80,000
Estimated sales for the period	₹ 2,00,000

The number of units involved coincides with the expected volume of output.

Calculate the margin of safety percentage and margin of safety in terms of units and value. Also advice its impact, if there is a fall of demand in business.

(B.U. Bhopal, MBA-2002)

Solution

Selling price per unit	₹ 20
Variable cost per unit	₹ 04
Contribution per unit	₹ 16

$$\text{Break-even point} = \frac{\text{Fixed costs}}{\text{Contribution}}$$

$$= \frac{80,000}{16} = 5,000 \text{ units}$$

Estimated sales for the period = ₹ 2,00,000

Selling price per unit = ₹ 20

$$\text{So, number of units estimated to be sold} = \frac{\text{Estimated sales for the period}}{\text{Selling price per unit}}$$

$$= \frac{2,00,000}{20} = 10,000 \text{ units}$$

Estimated sales = 10,000 units

Sales at break-even point = 5,000 units

$$\text{Margin of safety ratio} = \frac{\text{Estimated sales} - \text{Break-even sales} \times 100}{\text{Actual sales}}$$

$$= \frac{10,000 - 5,000 \times 100}{10,000}$$

$$= 50\%$$

Margin of safety (in terms of units) = Estimated sales – sales at Break-even point

= 10,000 – 5,000 = 5,000 units

Margin of safety (in terms of rupees) = 5,000 × 20 = ₹ 1,00,000

$$\text{Margin of safety (in terms of capacity)} = \frac{\text{Sales at break-even point}}{\text{Estimated sales}}$$

$$= \frac{5,000}{10,000}$$

= 50% capacity

Break-even point is 50% of the estimated sales in terms of number of units.

So, margin of safety is 50%. Higher margin of safety indicates soundness of business. Even if there is some fall in sales, still the firm can withstand loss. If sales of the firm decline by ₹ 1,00,000 still firm would not suffer any loss.

Illustration No. 14

The sales and profits of a company during two periods were as follows:

Period	Sales	Profit
I	1,00,000	10,000
II	1,50,000	20,000

(1) Find out P/V ratio.

(2) What amount of sales will generate a profit of ₹ 40,000?

(3) What will be the profit, if the sales are ₹ 1,20,000?

(B.U. Bhopal–MBA, 2003)

Solution

(i) P/V Ratio $= \dfrac{\text{Change in profit} \times 100}{\text{Change in sales}}$

$= \dfrac{10,000}{50,000} \times 100$

$= 20\%$

(ii) Calculation of sales to generate a profit of ₹ 40,000:

P/V Ratio $= \dfrac{\text{Contribution}}{\text{Sales}}$

Contribution = Fixed cost + Profits

P/V Ratio $= \dfrac{\text{Fixed cost + Profit}}{\text{Sales}}$

Problem states that sales of ₹ 1,00,000 gives a profit of ₹ 10,000

So, $20\% = \dfrac{\text{Fixed cost} + 10,000}{1,00,000}$

$\Rightarrow \dfrac{20}{100} = \dfrac{\text{Fixed cost} + 10,000}{1,00,000}$

$\Rightarrow (0.2) \times 1,00,000 = \text{Fixed cost} + 10,000$

Fixed cost $= 20,000 - 10,000$

$= 10,000$

Desired sales × P/V Ratio = Contribution

Contribution = Fixed cost + Desired profit

Desired sales $= \dfrac{\text{Fixed cost + Desired profit}}{\text{P/V Ratio}}$

$= \dfrac{10,000 + 40,000}{\text{P/V Ratio}}$

$= \dfrac{50,000}{0.2}$

$= 2,50,000$

So, sales of ₹ 2,50,000 are needed to earn a profit of ₹ 40,000

(iii) Calculation of profit, if sales are ₹ 1,20,000

$$\text{P/V Ratio} = \frac{\text{Fixed cost + Profit}}{\text{Sales}}$$

$$0.2 = \frac{10,000 + \text{Profit}}{1,20,000}$$

$$(0.2) \times 1,20,000 = 10,000 + \text{Profit}$$

$$\text{Profit} = 24,000 - 10,000$$

$$= 14,000$$

If sales are ₹ 1,20,000, profit would be ₹ 14,000

Illustration No. 15

Vaishali Tiwari Ltd, engaged in manufacturing toys for children furnishes the following information.

Particulars	Year 2008	Year 2009
Sales	2,00,000	8,00,000
Profit / (loss)	(1,00,000)	2,00,000

Fixed costs of year 2008 are same in the year 2009.

Calculate the following:

(A) P/V Ratio

(B) Fixed cost for both the periods

(C) Break-even point for sales

(D) Profit if firm makes a sale of ₹ 6,00,000

Solution

	Sales	Profit
Year 2009	8,00,000	2,00,000
Year 2008	2,00,000	(1,00,000)
Increase or change	6,00,000	3,00,000

$$\text{(A) P/V Ratio} = \frac{\text{Change in profit} \times 100}{\text{Change in sales}}$$

$$= \frac{3,00,000 \times 100}{6,00,000} = 50\%$$

(B) Contribution = Sales × P/V Ratio

Contribution for Year 2008 = 2,00,000 × 50%
= 1,00,000

Fixed costs for year 2008 = Profit – contribution
= –1,00,000 – 1,00,000
= 2,00,000

As fixed costs are same in both the years, fixed cost is ₹ 2,00,000 for the year 2009.

(C) Break-even point for sales $= \frac{\text{Fixed cost}}{\text{P/V Ratio}}$

$= \frac{2,00,000}{50\%}$

= 4,00,000

(D) Profit, if firm makes a sale of ₹ 6,00,000

Contribution when firm makes a sale of 6,00,000 = 6,00,000 × 50%
= 3,00,000

Profit = Contribution – Fixed costs
= 3,00,000 – 2,00,000
= 1,00,000

Illustration No. 16

Farah Khan Ltd. has furnished you the following information:

Particulars	First half - Year 2009	Second half - Year 2009
Sales	7,00,000	10,50,000
Profit earned	70,000	3,00,000

Assume that the structure and fixed costs have remained constant in both the half years.

Find out

(A) P/V Ratio

(B) Fixed cost for both the periods

(C) Variable costs for both the periods

(D) Break-even point for sales

(E) Profit or loss when sales are 12,00,000

Solution

	Sales	Profit
First half	7,00,000	70,000
Second half	10,50,000	3,00,000
Increase or change	3,50,000	2,30,000

(A) P/V Ratio $= \dfrac{\text{Change in profit} \times 100}{\text{Change in sales}}$

$= \dfrac{2{,}30{,}000 \times 100}{3{,}50{,}000}$

= 65.71%

(B) Contribution = Sales × P/V Ratio

Contribution in first half year 2009 = 7,00,000 × 65.71%

= ₹ 4,59,970

Contribution – Fixed cost = Profit

Fixed cost = Contribution – Profit

= 4,59,970 – 70,000

= ₹ 3,89,970

As structure and fixed costs are constant, fixed costs in the second year is also ₹ 3,89,970

Contribution in second half year 2009 = 10,50,000 × 65.71%

= ₹ 6,89,955

(C) Variable costs = Sales – Contribution

Variable costs in the first half year = 7,00,000 – 4,59,970 = 2,40,030

Variable costs in the second half year = 10,50,000 – 6,89,955 = 3,60,045

(D) Break-even point for sales $= \dfrac{\text{Fixed cost}}{\text{P/V Ratio}}$

$= \dfrac{3{,}89{,}970}{65.71\%}$

= ₹ 5,93,471

(E) Contribution when sales are 12,00,000 = 12,00,000 × 65.71%

= 7,88,520

Profit = Contribution – Fixed costs

= 7,88,520 – 3,89,970

= 3,98,550

Illustration No. 17

Two firms, X Ltd and Y Ltd sell identical products in the same market. Their budgeted profit and loss accounts for the year ending on 30th June 2001 are as follows:

	X Ltd.		Y Ltd.	
Sales		4,00,000		4,00,000
Less: Variable cost	3,20,000		2,80,000	
Fixed cost	40,000	3,60,000	80,000	3,60,000
Net Profit		40,000		40,000

You are required to:

(a) calculate break-even point for each firm and

(b) state what shall be the likely effect on profits of the firms in conditions of

(i) increasing demand for the products

(ii) falling demand for the products. Explain with an example of 10% fall in sales for both the firms.

(c) Calculate the sales volume at which each business will earn ₹ 50,000 profit.

(B.U. Bhopal MBA- 2000)

Solution

(a)

		X Ltd.	Y Ltd.
Sales		4,00,000	4,00,000
Less: Variable cost		3,20,000	2,80,000
Contribution		80,000	1,20,000
Fixed cost		40,000	80,000
P/V Ratio	$\frac{\text{Contribution}}{\text{Sales}} \times 100$	$\frac{80,000}{4,00,000} \times 100$ = 20%	$\frac{1,20,000}{4,00,000} \times 100$ = 30%
Break-even point	$\frac{\text{Fixed cost}}{\text{P/V Ratio}}$	$\frac{40,000}{20\%}$ = 2,00,000	$\frac{80,000}{30\%}$ = 2,66,667

(b) (i) Effect on profits of the firms in conditions of increasing demand for the products:

P/V Ratio of X Ltd is 20% while it is 30% in case of Y Ltd. P/V Ratio indicates availability of margin on sales made. So, firm that enjoys higher P/V Ratio stands to gain, when demand for the product is growing. In case of high demand, Y Ltd will be in a position to earn higher profit because P/V ratio is higher.

(ii) Effect on profits of the firms in conditions of falling demand for the products:

Break-even point of X Ltd is 2,00,000 while it is 2,66,667 in case of Y Ltd.

Firm that has a low break-even point would be in a position to withstand even if there is a fall in sales. So X Ltd would have more profits compared to Y Ltd, if there is a corresponding fall in sales to both the firms.

Effect of fall in sales by 10% for both the firms

$$\text{Sales} = \frac{\text{Fixed Expenses + Desired Profit}}{\text{P/V Ratio}}$$

	X Ltd	Y Ltd
Sales	3,60,000	3,60,000
P/V Ratio	20%	30%
Fixed cost	40,000	80,000
Profit	3,60,000 x 20% = 40,000 + P P = 72,000 – 40,000 = 32,000	3,60,000 x 30% = 80,000 + P P = 1,08,000 – 80,000 = 28,000

(c) Sales volume at which each business will earn ₹ 50,000 profit

$$\text{Sales required to earn a profit of ₹ 50,000} = \frac{\text{Existing fixed costs + Existing profit}}{\text{P/V ratio}}$$

$$\text{X Ltd} = \frac{40{,}000 + 50{,}000}{20\%}$$

$$= 4{,}50{,}000$$

$$\text{Y Ltd} = \frac{80{,}000 + 50{,}000}{30\%}$$

$$= 4{,}33{,}333$$

Illustration No. 18

Bhavana Shukla Ltd wants to make a profit of ₹ 70, 000, after taxes. Its tax rate is 30 %. Firm's fixed costs are ₹ 2,00,000. Variable cost is ₹ 10 while its selling price is ₹ 50. Calculate the required volume of sales.

Solution

Selling price per unit	=	50
Variable cost per unit	=	10
Contribution		40

$$\text{P/V Ratio} = \frac{\text{Contribution}}{\text{Sales}} \times 100 = \frac{40}{50} \times 100 = 80\%$$

$$\text{Sales} = \frac{\text{Fixed Expenses} + \dfrac{[\text{Desired Profit, after taxes}]}{1 - \text{tax rate}}}{\text{P/V Ratio}}$$

$$= \frac{2{,}00{,}000 + \dfrac{[70{,}000]}{1 - 30\%}}{80\%}$$

$$= \frac{2{,}00{,}000 + 1{,}00{,}000}{80\%}$$

$$= 3{,}75{,}000$$

Firm has to achieve a sales level of ₹ 3,75,000 to make a profit ₹ 70,000, after taxes.

Illustration No. 19

Suresh Ltd is incurring an existing fixed cost of ₹ 12,000. Present P/V ratio is 40%. At this point, firm is even in break-even stage. Additional fixed costs are to be incurred to achieve additional sales. In case firm wants to achieve an increase of sales by ₹ 1,70,000, what would be the additional fixed costs the firm has to incur to achieve break-even stage with incremental sales?

Solution

$$\text{Present sales} = \frac{\text{Fixed costs}}{\text{P/V ratio}}$$

$$= \frac{12{,}000}{40\%}$$

$$= 30{,}000$$

Required sales (proposed sales) = Existing sales + Incremental sales

= 30,000 + 1,70,000 = 2,00,000

$$\text{Required sales} = \frac{\text{Existing fixed costs} + \text{Additional fixed costs}}{\text{P/V ratio}}$$

$$2{,}00{,}000 = \frac{12{,}000 + \text{Additional fixed costs}}{40\%}$$

$$2{,}00{,}000 \times 40\% = 12{,}000 + \text{Additional fixed costs}$$

Additional fixed costs = 80,000 – 12,000

= 68,000

Firm has to incur additional fixed costs ₹ 68,000 to achieve break-even stage with incremental sales of ₹ 1,70,000.

Illustration No. 20

The price structure of 1,000 units of a part of Motor Bike, Hero Honda, is as under:

	Per part (₹)
Material	120
Labour	40
Variable overhead	40
Fixed overhead	100
Selling price	400

Based on the above information, calculate the BEP sales at the current selling price and also desired sales if the selling price is reduced by (i) 10% and (ii) 20% for 1,000 units. However, the total profit should remain the same for both the options.

Solution

Total Variable costs

Material	= 120
Labour	= 40
Variable overhead	= 40
	200
Selling price per unit	= 400
Variable cost per unit	= 200
Contribution	200

$$\text{P/V Ratio} = \frac{\text{Contribution}}{\text{Selling price}} \times 100 = \frac{200}{400} \times 100 = 50\%$$

$$\text{Break-even point} = \frac{\text{Fixed cost}}{\text{P/V ratio}}$$

$$= \frac{100 \times 1{,}000}{50\%}$$

$$= ₹\ 2{,}00{,}000$$

Existing profit:

Sales 1,000 × 400 = 4,00,000

Variable costs 1,000 × 200 = 2,00,000

Fixed costs = 1,00,000

Profit 1,00,000

If selling price is reduced by 10%, selling price becomes ₹ 360.

To maintain same level of profit ₹ 1,00,000

New break-even point, if selling price is ₹ 360:

Selling price per unit = 360

Variable cost per unit = 200

Contribution 160

$$\text{P/V Ratio} = \frac{\text{Contribution}}{\text{Selling price}} \times 100 = \frac{160}{360} \times 100 = 44.44\%$$

$$\text{Required sales} = \frac{\text{Existing fixed costs + Existing profit}}{\text{P/V ratio}}$$

$$= \frac{1,00,000 + 1,00,000}{44.44\%}$$

$$= 4,50,045$$

If selling price is reduced by 10% and firm wants to maintain same level of profit ₹ 1,00,000, then the firm has to make total sales of ₹ 4,50,045.

If selling price is reduced by 20%, selling price becomes ₹ 320.

To maintain same level of profit of ₹ 1,00,000

New break-even point, if selling price is ₹ 320:

Selling price per unit = 320

Variable cost per unit = 200

Contribution 120

$$\text{P/V Ratio} = \frac{\text{Contribution}}{\text{Selling price}} \times 100 = \frac{120}{320} \times 100 = 37.5\ \%$$

$$\text{Required sales} = \frac{\text{Existing fixed costs + Existing profit}}{\text{P/V ratio}}$$

$$= \frac{1,00,000 + 1,00,000}{37.5\%}$$

$$= 5,33,333$$

If selling price is reduced by 20% and firm wants to maintain same level of profit ₹ 1,00,000, the firm has to make a total sales of ₹ 5,33,333.

8.12 ROLE OF BEP IN RECESSION TIMES

Recession times are tough to bear. Even, profitable firms experience the pinch of acute fall in sales, and consequently loose their edge in market. Effort of every firm is to sustain somehow through out recession period. Firms adopt different strategies to pass through difficult periods. During such periods, BEP plays an important role. Reengineering strategies to have foothold and increase their share in the market even entering into unexplored areas would be the need of the hour.

GLOOM BUSTERS–SUCCESS STORY OF INDIAN ENTERPRISE

—Live story from Hindustan Times (18th April, 2009)

Profit Waltzes in High-end Shoes

HIS FACTORIES are humming with activity; his sales force is buzzing with ideas; he is logging thousands of international air miles every month, his accountants are busy in counting the cash.

Indereshwar Singh Paul, 58, managing director of Drish Shoes, an export firm he started 19 years ago, has beaten the recession by taking the contrarian route. He has jumped in to make high-end shoes at low costs, and in the process, has even acquired two century-old high-street fashion brands in Germany, Manz and Fortuna, for unspecified prices.

Paul's three main production locations – a tannery in Jalandhar, Punjab, a leather finishing and shoe and accessory unit in Nalagarh, Himachal Pradesh, and a shoe production unit in Panchkula, Haryana – are working overtime to meet deadlines. And Drish Shoes, which he started in 1990 with ₹ 1.80 lakh, has set a target of expanding its 2008-09 sales of ₹ 115 crore by 30 per cent.

But less than a year ago, in July last year, the picture was not so rosy. "Our clients abroad were not lifting ready consignments. We were operating at less than 50 per cent capacity, and the future looked bleak," said Paul, who has studied at a Swiss business school. The global slow-down – recession still hadn't set in then – but it seemed that it would claim yet another Indian exporter as its victim.

Paul went against the grain. "I decided that I would not lay off any of the 1,700 people I employed," he said. Drish also decided to move up the value chain. And Paul was determined to do so, without increasing prices.

He approached Zara and Kickers, two leading European brands of high-end shoes with a compelling offer they couldn't refuse – he would supply them with high-end shoes at a price that was 40 per cent lower than what their Portugese and Spanish suppliers were offering.

India was not known as a supplier of high-end shoes–Zara and Kickers bought only low – quality products from Indian suppliers – and, in normal times, his approach would probably have been rebuffed. But these were not normal times. Both Zara and Kickers agreed – and Drish was back in business.

"We got large orders ..... Drish sold over three lakh pairs between October and April to these two brands. Now, we have orders to manufacture five lakh pairs of shoes over the next six months, resulting in 66 per cent increase in production," said Paul.

Paul decided to ride his luck. His back end, producing high quality shoes at a reasonable cost was in place. Why not buy a well-known brand in Europe and establish himself at the front end – facing the customer-as well?

It was an audacious plan, and the chances of failure were quit high. "You don't get a second chance to jump over a chasm. Either you cross it or you fall. I took a risk and succeeded," said Paul.

Identification of Problem and Strategy Solution

Problem: Operating at less than 50% of installed capacity and as a result not recovering fixed costs, resulting loss in operations. Firm is in loss.

Strategy: Moving up the value chain to produce high quality shoes, at reasonable prices, astronomically less than 40% the price offered by competitors, just to cover costs initially and later to capture market to improve the bottom – line.

Risk: Audacious plan

Circumstances: Recession

Result: Able to retain existing man power. Poised for expansion during recession. Effect of audacious decision on operating results not known.

Check Your Understanding

(A) Please state whether the following statements are True or False

1. CVP analysis helps the firm in understanding the impact of change in cost, volume and price on the behaviour of profit.
2. Break-even analysis is fundamentally a static analysis.
3. With the help of CVP analysis, it is possible to decide which product is most profitable and least profitable.
4. A higher margin of safety does not provide any additional comfort to firms during recession period.

5. Contribution is also known as Gross Margin.
6. At break-even point, contribution covers total fixed costs and leaves a little towards profit.
7. It is not possible to calculate break-even analysis of the firm, if the firm is engaged in producing and selling multiple products.
8. Fixed costs and variable costs do not behave in the same manner.
9. In break-even analysis, unit variable cost decreases as and when the volume of production increases.
10. A large margin of safety indicates that the business is sound and even if there is some fall in sales, there will be profit.
11. Angle of incidence is the angle between the sales line and the total cost line formed at the break-even point.
12. Margin of safety = $\frac{\text{Fixed expenses}}{\text{P/V Ratio}}$
13. P/V Ratio can be used to calculate BEP and ascertain required sales to achieve a desired level of profit.
14. P/V Ratio does not change with a change in fixed costs.
15. By reducing the fixed expenses, the P/V ratio of a product can be improved.
16. CVP analysis does not deal with break-even analysis.
17. To calculate BEP in a multi-product firm, it is necessary to allocate fixed costs among different products manufactured by the firm.
18. Depreciation is not treated as a cost for calculating cash break-even point.
19. If a firm does not produce anything and still incurs fixed costs, total cost line starts at zero level in terms of costs.

Answers

1. True	2. False	3. True	4. False	5. True	6. False	7. False	8. True
9. False	10. True	11. True	12. False	13. True	14. True	15. False	16. False
17. False	18. True	19. False.					

(B) Objective Questions (Identify what is most appropriate)

1. In the graphical presentation of break-even analysis, larger the angle of incidence ..... is the break-even point.

   (A) Lower (B) Higher (C) Similar

2. Angle of incidence is formed in break-even analysis when the intersection occurs between:

   (A) Fixed cost line and sales line

   (B) Total cost line and sales line

   (C) Fixed cost line and total cost line

3. If Margin of safety is ....., the firm cannot withstand if there is a large fall in sales.
   (A) Low (B) High (C) Does not exist
4. Margin of safety and break-even point are inter-connected
   (A) Yes (B) No (C) No relation exists
5. Break-even point would occur early to a firm, if fixed costs are ....
   (A) High (B) Low (C) Not relevant
6. P/V Ratio can be improved by reducing fixed costs.
   (A) True (B) False (C) No change
7. P/V Ratio can be increased by
   (A) Reducing variable cost (B) Increasing selling price
   (C) A & B (D) None
8. Break-even sales =
   (A) Variable cost + Fixed cost (B) Fixed cost – Variable Cost
   (C) Variable cost – Fixed cost (D) None
9. Profit Volume ratio =
   (A) Contribution/Sales (B) Sales/Contribution
   (C) $\dfrac{\text{Sales} - \text{Fixed Expenses}}{\text{Sales}}$ (D) Profit/Sales

Answers:

1. (A) 2. (B) 3. (A) 4. (A) 5. (B) 6. (B) 7. (C) 8. (A) 9. (A).

Descriptive Questions

1. What do you understand by the term cost-volume-profit relationship? Why is this relationship important in financial decision making? (B.U, Bhopal, MBA- 2003) (8.3)
2. What is CVP analysis? Explain its utility to management in decision-making process? (8.3)
3. 'Profit volume analysis' is a technique of analyzing the relationship of cost and profit at various levels of volume? Explain how such analysis helps the management in decision-making? (8.3)
4. 'Break-even point is the point at which total cost and revenue are just equal' – Discuss? (8.5,8.5.1and 8.5.2)
5. What is meant by contribution? How it is calculated? Discuss its role in the profit-decision making? (8.5.1 and 8.5.2)
6. "The break-even analysis is a useful device of profit planning." Do you agree? Discuss? (B.U., Bhopal, MBA - 2000) (8.5, 8.5.1 and 8.5.2)
7. Is CVP Analysis different from Break-even point? How would you compute Break-even point? (8.4, 8.5, 8.5.1 and 8.5.2)

8. "Business firms rarely operate at their break-even points. Therefore, the break-even analysis is of very limited use to the management." Is it correct? Discuss? (8.5, 8.5.1and 8.5.2)
9. Discuss P/V Ratio and its features and uses to assist management in break-even analysis to achieve the desired level of profit? (8.5 and 8.5.2)
10. Would it be really important for the cost-volume-profit interrelations to allocate fixed costs to individual product lines? Defend your answer? (B.U, Bhopal—2005) (8.5, 8.5.1, 8.5.3 and 8.11)
11. Discuss the advantages, assumptions and limitations of break-even analysis? (8.6, 8.7 and 8.8)
12. "Despite many advantages, the greater the deviations from the given assumptions, the more imperfect and incorrect would be the break-even calculations". –Discuss (8.6 to 8.8)
13. Write short notes on:
    (A) Margin of safety (8.9)
    (B) Angle of Incidence (8.5.4)
    (C) Cash break-even point (8.10)
    (D) Multi product break-even point (8.11)

Short Questions

Q.1. What is 'Break-even Point'? Explain its importance.

Ans. The 'Break-even Point' is that volume of sales at which total revenue is equal to total costs with zero profit. 'Break-even Point' is a situation where firm is neither in profit nor in loss. In other words, this is a 'no-profit, no-loss situation'. When organization is not able to earn profits, the best alternative for the firm is at least not to incur loss. So every organization would like to know at what level of production and sales, the organization would be able to achieve no-loss, no-profit situation. This is the greatest contribution of 'Break-even point'.

Q.2. Is 'Break-even Analysis' useful to achieve the target level of profit?

Ans. Yes. Organizations identify those products which yield the highest contribution. 'Break-even Analysis' helps the firm in selecting and ranking those products based on contribution to achieve the targeted level of profit.

Q.3. What is the importance of cash Break-even point?

Ans. In the present world of business, it is difficult for a new industrial unit to break-even in the initial years. In this scenario, concept of Cash Break-even Point has emerged.

Cash break-even point is that stage where cash costs is equal to cash revenues. Cash break-even point is reached first before BEP stage is achieved. In calculating cash break-even point, depreciation is excluded as it is a fixed cost and there is no outgo of cash. Similarly, additional depreciation–charged in the event of extra shift–would be excluded from variable costs. All firms strive to reach cash break-even point if they are not able to achieve BEP stage.

Q.4. What costs influence P/V ratio?

Ans. Basically costs are of two types, fixed costs and variable costs. P/V ratio is a relationship between contribution and selling price. Contribution is the difference between selling price and variable costs. A change in selling price, variable cost or both, influences P/V ratio. However, if both variable costs and selling price change in a similar manner, say increase or decrease by 20 % in both in same direction, P/V ratio does not change. Increase or decrease in fixed costs does not change P/V ratio. In other words, change in selling price and variable costs only change P/V ratio while fixed costs does not change P/V ratio as they are not considered for calculating P/V ratio.

Interview Questions

Q.1. What is the importance of P/V Ratio?

Ans. Contribution ratio is also called as P/V Ratio. This ratio shows the proportion of contribution (Selling price–Variable cost) to sales. Once P/V Ratio is known, contribution can be calculated by multiplying P/V Ratio with sales. So, contribution can be calculated at different volume of sales. Higher the contribution ratio, higher the profitability provided factors such as fixed costs and selling price remain same between two firms.

Q.2. How cash break-even point is different from break-even point?

Ans. Cash break-even point is that sales volume which covers cash expenses only during a particular period. Depreciation is treated as an expense for calculating break-even point. However, the same is not included in costs for calculating cash break-even point. In other words, non-cash items are excluded from costs and revenues to calculate cash break-even point. If the firm were not able to reach break-even point, the effort of the firm would be to achieve at least cash break-even point.

Q.3. Is it possible to calculate contribution at different volume of sales once P/V Ratio is known?

Ans. Yes, contribution can be calculated at different volume of sales with P/V Ratio. If volume of sales is multiplied with P/V Ratio, contribution is known at that sales level.

○○

CHAPTER

9

Leverages

9.1 INTRODUCTION

It is the duty of finance manager in every firm to estimate the requirement of funds and procure them at economic cost. There are various alternative sources to raise funds, however costs are different for each source. These sources may be broadly classified into two categories from investors point of view:

(A) Sources which carry a fixed rate of return like preference share capital, debentures etc.; and

(B) Sources which do not carry a fixed rate of return like equity share capital.

In respect of some funds, firm has to pay fixed cost like interest on debentures. However, if same amount of funds is raised through equity share capital, corresponding return to shareholders varies. The finance manager has to determine best mix of such funds or decide about capital structure of the concerned firm. The capital structure finally chosen influences risk and return of the firm.

Leverage analysis is a technique used by business firms to quantify risk-return relationship of different alternative capital structures.

9.2 MEANING OF LEVERAGE

The term 'leverage' is derived from 'lever', which indicates the means of lifting heavy objects. Leverage helps us in lifting heavy objects, which otherwise may not be possible. Stone cannot be moved if we apply force, directly. However with a small force in a particular direction, a heavy stone can be moved in a different direction. Classical example is crowbar, which is a mechanical leverage. The crowbar is a means to achieve the objective of lifting or removing the stone from existing place to the desired place.

We exert pressure at one point for lifting a stone to receive force or power at a second point. See the magic of leverage, the same stone does not move if we push it, directly.

In Layman's language, leverage is an instrument or equipment which helps in moving an object from one place to another by applying some force.

The dictionary meaning of the term 'Leverage' refers to "an increased means of accomplishing some purpose".

This concept of 'leverage' is valid in business too. In business, leverage is the means for increasing profits. Christy and Roden define leverage as the tendency for profits to change faster than sales. In the area of finance, the term 'leverage' has a special meaning.

Basically, there are two types of leverages—Operating Leverage and Financial Leverage.

Fixed costs are classified as:

(i) those elements of operating expenses such as selling, and administrative expenses such as salaries, rent etc; and

(ii) those non-operating expenses such as interest payment, which are also relatively fixed in nature.

There are fixed costs associated with production of goods and services. Fixed costs are incurred while producing goods and services. Operating leverage deals with the use of fixed operating costs by the firm, like administrative costs, depreciation, selling and advertisement expenses etc. Financial leverage deals with the use of fixed financing costs. Financial leverage occurs due to existence of fixed financing costs. Both the types of leverages influence the level and variability of firm's after tax earnings. In other words, their objective is to magnify the earnings per equity share.

In financial management, the term 'leverage' is used to describe firm's ability to use fixed operating costs or fired financing costs to magnify earnings or returns to the owners of firm. Finance manager in a firm uses leverage to influence risk and return of equity shareholders.

Definition: James Horne has defined leverage as "the employment of an asset or funds for which the firm pays a fixed cost or fixed return".

Concept of Leverage: The term leverage in general refers to relationship between two interrelated variables. In financial matters, one financial variable influences another variable. Those financial variables may be cost, sales revenue, earnings before interest and Tax (EBIT), output, earnings per share etc. In leverage analysis, emphasis is made on the measurement of relationship of two variables, rather than on measuring those variables.

$$\text{Leverage} = \frac{\text{\% Change in dependent variable}}{\text{\% Change in independent variable}}$$

For example, a firm has increased sales promotion expenses from ₹ 2,000 to ₹ 2,500 i.e. an increase of 25%. This has resulted in increase of sales from ₹ 40,000 to ₹ 60,000 i.e. an increase of 50%. The leverage between promotional expenses and sales can be expressed as:

$$\text{Leverage} = \frac{\text{\% Change in sales (dependent variable)}}{\text{\% Change in sales promotion expenses (independent variable)}}$$

$$= \frac{0.50}{0.25} = 2$$

This means that % increase in sales is twice that of increase in sales promotional expenses. If one hundred rupees sales promotional expenses were incurred, sales would increase by rupees two hundred.

9.3 TYPES OF LEVERAGES

Leverage is of three types:

(i) Operating Leverage,

(ii) Financial Leverage and

(iii) Combined Leverage.

9.4 OPERATING LEVERAGE

Operating leverage refers to use of fixed costs in the operation of a firm. Operating leverage results due to the presence of fixed costs (rent, salaries, insurance etc). Sales change but fixed costs do not change with sales. On account of fixed costs, the operating profit changes disproportionately with sales. In other words, increase or decrease in operating profit does not occur proportionately with sales.

A firm is said to have higher degree of operating leverage if it employs a higher proportion of fixed costs and smaller proportion of variable costs in its cost structure. On the other hand, a firm has a low operating leverage when it employs a greater proportion of variable costs and a lesser proportion of fixed costs. Thus, **degree of operating leverage depends upon proportion of fixed element in the cost structure.**

Operating leverage is defined as the firm's ability to use fixed operating costs to magnify effect of changes in sales on operating profits.

Factors that influence operating leverage: Operating leverage in firm is a function of three factors:

1. The amount of fixed costs.
2. The contribution margin.
3. The volume of sales.

A firm does not have operating leverage if ratio of fixed costs to total costs is nil. In such a situation, a given percentage of increase in sales produces the same percentage of operating profits i.e. EBIT.

There is no operating leverage, if there are no fixed costs.

Presence of fixed costs on assets (depreciation) and fixed expenses (like selling and advertisement expenses, Administrative expenses etc) cause operating leverage. However, fixed borrowing costs are not to be included for calculation of operating leverage. If the firm does not have fixed assets and fixed costs, it will not have operating leverage at all.

Operating leverage is calculated as under:

$$\textbf{Operating leverage} = \frac{\textbf{Contribution}}{\textbf{EBIT}}$$

Importance of operating leverage: Operating leverage plays an important role in determining operating profits of a firm. If the operating leverage of a firm is high, the operating profits of the firm are more sensitive. Sales change over periods, but operating profits do not behave in the same manner. Change in operating profits would be more than the change in sales. Operating profits behave in this manner due to composition of fixed costs in the cost structure of the firm.

Firm that has higher operating leverage is more sensitive in terms of operating profits for a similar change in sales. If operating leverage is high, fluctuations in profits will be more in response to changes in volume of sales. It means operating profits would increase as well as decrease more than the change in sales depending on leverage of the firm. For these reasons, if a choice is to be made between operating leverage and operating profits, it is desirable to choose operating profits in comparison to operating leverage.

Significance of Operating Leverage: Analysis of operating leverage is useful to a finance manager. The significance of operating leverage is as under:

1. **Tells about the impact of change in sales:** Operating leverage tells the impact of sales on income. Depending on the operating leverage, a given percentage of increase in sales results in a higher percentage of increase in operating income and net profit. This multiplier effect depends on the operating leverage of the firm. Conversely, a decline in sales may wipe out the operating profit or even turn into loss.
2. **Measurement of business risk:** If the fixed costs are higher, the operating leverage as well as operating risk of the firm would be higher. So, EBIT would be more sensitive for a given change in sales. The business risk refers to the variability of the firm's EBIT.
3. **Production planning:** Degree of operating leverage is useful in production planning. A firm may plan to replace labour with machinery to save wages which is a variable cost. But, this step would increase fixed costs. Such a situation increases DOL. Any method of production which increases DOL is justified, if

the probability of increase in sales is more, which would help the firm to improve earnings.

4. **Impact on break-even point:** If operating leverage is higher, break-even point would also be higher. If break-even point of firm is high, margin of safety would be low.

   Important point to be noted is that when operating leverage is said to be high, it is only a comparison of the firm with industry to the category it belongs to.

   Utility: The operating leverage indicates the impact of change in sales on operating income. Suppose operating leverage of a firm is 2, it means if sales increases by 100%, operating income would increase by 200%.

> **Operating leverage causes operating risk. Operating risk is that risk which the firm is not able to cover fixed operating costs.**

Option of Higher operating leverage or higher operating profit: If choice is to be made between higher operating leverage and higher operating profit, it is better to choose for a firm to have higher operating profit rather than having higher operating leverage. Reason being a firm having higher operating leverage is more vulnerable in case sales decline due to high fixed costs. In consequence, that firm suffers more loss. More so, a higher operating profit would lead to greater income.

Illustration No. 1

Determine operating leverage of the following firms and state which firm's operating profit (EBIT) is more sensitive to change in sales?

	Firm A	Firm B	Firm C
Sales	1,00,000	1,10,000	1,95,000
Operating costs:			
Fixed costs (FC)	70,000	20,000	1,40,000
Variable costs (VC)	20,000	70,000	30,000

Solution

	Firm A	Firm B	Firm C
Sales	1,00,000	1,10,000	1,95,000
Less: Variable costs (VC)	20,000	70,000	30,000
Contribution	80,000	40,000	1,65,000
Fixed costs	70,000	20,000	1,40,000
Operating profit (EBIT)	10,000	20,000	25,000
Operating leverage $= \frac{\text{Contribution}}{\text{EBIT}}$	$\frac{80,000}{10,000}$ = 8	$\frac{40,000}{20,000}$ = 2	$\frac{1,65,000}{25,000}$ = 6.6

Conclusion: Operating leverage shows sensitivity of the firm – change of operating profit to change in sales. Firm A has the highest operating leverage (8), compared to B (2) and C (6.6). So, firm A's operating profit is more sensitive to change in sales.

Now, we compare two firms with similar data. Let us see how operating profit behaves, when sales and total costs of two firms are one and the same, howsoever with a difference in composition of fixed costs and variable costs.

Illustration No. 2

Calculate operating leverage of both the following firms, whose total costs are same. Explain how and why both the firms would behave in terms of operating profit, if there is an increase of 50% in sales?

(₹ in lakhs)

	Firm A	Firm B
Sales	120	120
Operating costs:		
Fixed costs (FC)	80	20
Variable costs (VC)	20	80
Total operating costs	100	100

Solution (₹ in lakhs)

	Firm A	Firm B
Sales	120	120
Less: Variable costs (VC)	20	80
Contribution	100	40
Fixed costs	80	20
Operating profit (EBIT)	20	20
$\text{Operating leverage} = \dfrac{\text{Contribution}}{\text{EBIT}}$	$\dfrac{100}{20}$ = 5	$\dfrac{40}{20}$ = 2

Operating leverage of firm A is high (5) as compared to firm B (2).

If there is an increase of 50% sales: (₹ in lakhs)

	Firm A	Firm B
Sales	180	180
Less: Variable costs (VC)	30	120
Contribution	150	60
Fixed costs	80	20
Operating profit (EBIT)	70	40

Conclusion: Sales and total costs of both firms A and B are same. Sales of both firms have increased similarly by 50%. However, operating profit of firm A has increased by 250% (from 20 lakhs to 70 lakhs), while operating profit of firm B has increased only by 100% (from 20 lakhs to 40 lakhs).

Reason: Reason is difference in their operating leverage. Firm A's operating leverage is 5, while it is only 2 in case of firm B. Firm A' s profits have increased by 250% (increase in sales 50% × leverage 5). Firm B's profits have increased by 100% (increase in sales 50% × leverage 2). Firm that would have higher operating leverage is more sensitive to increase in operating profit for a similar increase in sales, compared to a firm that has lower operating leverage.

Illustration No. 3

The installed capacity of Chandu & Co is 1,000 units. Actual capacity utilized is 800 units. Selling price per unit is ₹ 20. Variable cost is ₹ 15 per unit. Calculate operating leverage in the following situations:

(A) When fixed costs are ₹ 2,000

(B) When fixed costs are ₹ 3,000

(C) When fixed costs are ₹ 4,000

Establish operating leverage if sales increase by 100% in situation C with no change in fixed costs.

Solution

Statement showing operating leverage

	Situation A	Situation B	Situation C	
			1,000 units	2,000 Units (Increase of sales by 100%)
Sales	20,000	20,000	20,000	40,000
Variable cost	15,000	15,000	15,000	30,000
Contribution (Sales – variable cost)	5,000	5,000	5,000	10,000
Fixed cost	2,000	3,000	4,000	4,000
Operating profit or EBIT (Contribution – fixed cost)	3,000	2,000	1,000	6,000
Operating leverage $= \frac{\text{Contribution}}{\text{EBIT}}$	$\frac{5,000}{3,000}$ = 1.67	$\frac{5,000}{2,000}$ = 2.5	$\frac{5,000}{1,000}$ = 5	

Interpretation: In situation C, when sales have increased by 100%, operating profit has gone up from ₹ 1,000 to 6,000. Operating profit has increased by ₹ 5,000. In other words, there is an increase of 500% operating profit for 100% increase in sales as its operating leverage is 5 at the time of increase in sales.

9.4.1 Degree of Operating Leverage

The degree of operating leverage may be defined as percentage change in operating profit resulting from a percentage change in sales. It is calculated at a particular level of sales. It can be presented as a formula as under:

$$\textbf{Degree of operating leverage} = \frac{\%\ \text{change in EBIT}}{\%\ \text{change in sales}}$$

$$= \frac{\Delta\ \text{EBIT/EBIT}}{\Delta\ \text{Sales/Sales}}$$

Where Δ (called delta) is change.

Contribution = Sales – Variable cost

EBIT = Contribution – Fixed cost.

Here, operating profit and EBIT mean the same.

Illustration No. 4

Arvind Joshi & Co is providing the following cost information of its company:

Sales are ₹ 3 lakhs in the previous year and ₹ 4 lakhs in the current year.

Variable cost is 60% of sales.

Find out percentage of change in sales and operating profit (EBIT) when:

(1) Fixed costs are not there.

(2) Fixed costs are ₹ 80,000 (leverage situation). What is the degree of operating leverage?

(3) Is it possible to conclude that fixed costs play an important role in magnifying the earnings of the firm? Explain with reason.

Solution

(1)

Situation: No Fixed Costs	Previous year (₹)	Current year (₹)	% change
Sales	3,00,000	4,00,000	33%
Less: Variable cost	1,80,000	2,40,000	33%
Contribution / Profit from operations	1,20,000	1,60,000	33%

Conclusion: Increase in operating profits and sales (33%) are the same. There is no operating leverage as there are no fixed costs.

(2)

Situation: Fixed Costs Exist	Previous year (₹)	Current year (₹)	% change
Sales	3,00,000	4,00,000	33%
Less: Variable cost	1,80,000	2,40,000	33%
Contribution	1,20,000	1,60,000	33%
Fixed costs	80,000	80,000	
Profit from operations (EBIT)	40,000	80,000	100%

$$\text{Degree of operating leverage} = \frac{\%\text{ of change in EBIT}}{\%\text{ of change in sales}}$$

$$= \frac{100}{33} = 3$$

1. **Situation: No fixed costs:** When there are no fixed costs, percentage of change in sales and percentage of changes in operating profit are one and the same i.e. 33%.
2. **Situation: Fixed costs exist:** When there are fixed costs, there is leverage to the firm. Operating leverage of the firm is 3. Operating profits increases (100%); i.e., three times to sales (33%). In other words, due to operating leverage, for every 100% of increase in sales, operating income would increase by 300%.
3. **Role of Fixed Costs:** Fixed costs play an important role in magnifying the earnings of the firm: Often it is presumed that sales and operating profits increase or decrease in the same per cent. This does not happen, if there are fixed costs. So we can conclude fixed costs help in magnifying earnings of the firm. **Reason, fixed costs do not increase even if there is increase in sales.** As a result, operating profits increases (100%) while increase in sales (33%). Actual increase in operating profits depends on the degree of leverage of the firm.

   Operating leverage arises when there are fixed costs in the firm's cost structure. Fixed operating costs do not include debt cost, which is a fixed financial cost. Fixed costs include costs such as depreciation, administrative costs, selling and advertisement expenses etc.

Favourable and Unfavourable Leverage: Operating leverage may be favourable or unfavourable.

In case, contribution exceeds fixed costs, there is favourable operating leverage. In a reverse situation when fixed cost exceeds contribution, operating leverage is termed as unfavourable operating leverage.

High Degree Operating Leverage: If a firm has a high degree of operating leverage, the percentage of change in operating income will be more than the percentage of change in sales. In other words, a small percentage of increase in sales results in a higher percentage of increase in operating income. As operating income (EBIT) is affected, increase or decrease also results in net income. Similarly, when the sales of a firm fall, a smaller percentage of fall in sales results in a larger percentage of fall in operating income.

A high operating leverage factor indicates presence of automated production processes as heavy costs are normally involved in fixed assets.

9.4.2 Operating Leverage is a Double-Edged Sword

Operating profit of a highly leveraged firm would increase at a faster rate for any given increase in sales. However if sales fall, the firm with a higher operating leverage would suffer more loss than the firm with no or low operating leverage. This is a very risky situation.

Operating leverage is a double-edged sword

Typical Examples: A retail firm and an airline are typical examples of low and high operating leverage. Proportion of fixed costs in the total cost structure is low in a retail firm as amount of investment is more on inventory with a small investment in furniture and other fixed assets to support the business. So to a retail firm, a small increase in sales does not produce a bigger increase in operating profit. To an airline, amount of fixed costs in the total cost structure is very high. Firm with high degree of operating leverage is more vulnerable to change in sales. So profit is highly sensitive to increase in revenue and passengers carried in an airline. Percentage increase in revenue to an airline firm produces a higher percentage of operating profit. This is the reason why unsold tickets are sold at a cheap rate when the flight is about to depart to increase the operating profit.

Even if the flight leaves with empty seats, there would be no reduction in fixed costs. So any additional revenue even at reduced fares is always welcome. A retail firm and an airline are typical examples of low and high operating leverage respectively.

Illustration No. 5

Gangadhar & Co Ltd has provided the following information. Its capacity is 2,000 units.

Sales	1,000 units
Selling price	₹ 150
Cost of raw materials per unit	₹ 20
Wages per unit	₹ 10
Variable overhead expenses per unit	₹ 20
Depreciation	₹ 20,000
Administrative cost	₹ 5,000
Interest	₹ 10,000
Selling & Advertisement cost	₹ 25,000

1. Calculate operating leverage and Degree of operating leverage.
2. If sales change (both increase and decrease) by 50%, what will be the effect on EBIT?
3. Prove that operating leverage is a double-edged sword.

Solution

Sales (1,000 x 150)		1,50,000
Less: Variable costs		
Cost of raw materials (1,000 x 20)	20,000	
Wages (1,000 x 10)	10,000	
Variable overhead expenses (1,000 x 20)	20,000	50,000
Contribution		1,00,000
Less: Fixed costs		
Depreciation	20,000	
Administrative cost	5,000	
Selling & Advertisement cost	25,000	50,000
EBIT		50,000

$$\text{Operating leverage} = \frac{\text{Contribution}}{\text{EBIT}}$$

$$= \frac{1{,}00{,}000}{50{,}000}$$

$$= 2$$

EBIT at various sales levels

	–50%	Base	+ 50%
Sales (in units)	500	1,000	1,500
Sales revenue	75,000	1,50,000	2,25,000
Less: Variable costs	25,000	50,000	75,000
Contribution	50,000	1,00,000	1,50,000
Less: Fixed costs	50,000	50,000	50,000
EBIT	Zero	50,000	1,00,000

$$\text{Degree of operating leverage} = \frac{\text{\% of change in EBIT}}{\text{\% of change in sales}} = \frac{+100\%}{+50\%} = 2$$

or

$$= \frac{-100\%}{-50\%} = 2$$

1. Both operating and degree of operating leverage are 2. In other words, both formulae give same result.
2. An increase of sales by 50% (from 1,000 units to 1,500 units) results into an increase of EBIT by 100% (from ₹ 50,000 to ₹ 1,00,000). On the other hand, fall in sales by 50% (from 1,000 units to 500 units) leads to a decrease of EBIT by 100% (from ₹ 50,000 to zero). On both sides, multiplier effect in 2 as DOL is 2.
3. Operating leverage is a double-edged sword: When a firm has fixed operating costs, an increase in sales volume results in a more than proportionate increase in EBIT. Similarly, a fall in the level of sales has an exactly opposite effect. Thus operating leverage has worked in both directions. % of increase or decrease in EBIT depends on the degree of leverage.

9.4.3 Impact of Market Conditions on Operating Leverage

Periods of rising prices or inflation: During periods of inflation, sales of all firms rise. When sales rise, the firms with high degree of operating leverage benefit more in terms of increased profit. The percentage of increase in operating profit and net income would be more than the percentage of increase in sales. Similarly, when sales fall during depression or declining prices, the firms with high operating leverage lose more. Indeed, during the later periods, high operating leverage becomes a nuisance.

Firms having low operating leverage neither make money during inflation nor lose in the times of depression due to their special feature of low operating leverage.

Normal conditions: When market conditions are normal, firm that has high degree of operating leverage would benefit more, if sales increase. Suppose operating leverage is 3. For every 100% increase in sales, operating profit increase by 300%. On the other hand, if sales dip, its operating profit would dip by similar percentage too. However, as market conditions are normal, stable growth in sales can be expected. Firm that has high degree of operating leverage can gain advantage. **So, it is desirable for a firm to have high degree of operating leverage under normal market conditions.**

High degree of operating leverage is a boon during inflation period while it is a curse during depression or period of declining prices.

Impact of technology: Whenever a company has to face the choice of technology, the company that opts capital-intensive technology incurs high fixed costs and low variable costs. On the other hand, low automated technology firms having low automated production processes would have less fixed costs and high variable costs. Capital-intensive firms have higher operating leverage and so are more vulnerable if there is a decline in sales. On the other hand, low automated firms have lower operating leverage and are not so vulnerable.

9.4.4 Operating Leverage and Degree of Operating Leverage

It is possible to calculate operating leverage based on one year's financial statements. Sensitivity of the firm can be understood by calculating operating leverage. However, for calculating degree of operating leverage (degree of sensitivity) we need financial statements of two periods as degree of operating leverage involves comparison of data over different periods.

Tip to Students: Use operating leverage formula when one year data is given. Use degree of operating leverage formula when data of two years or two periods are given. Degree of operating leverage is a more precise way of calculation.

Sensitivity of operating leverage: Operating leverage is related to the level of sales. As and when sales level changes, operating leverage also changes. The sensitivity of the firm to a change in sales as measured by DOL will be different at each level of output or sales. So, it is necessary to indicate the level of output at which DOL is measured.

Operating leverage measures sensitivity of firm in terms of impact of change of sales on operating profit. Sensitivity of the firm is not constant but changes as and when sales change.

9.5 FINANCIAL LEVERAGE

A firm would raise funds at the initial set up and subsequent expansion or diversification plans. Funds may be raised through two sources: in the form of owners' equity and external equity.

Owner's equity is share capital and reserves. External equity could be long-term loans and debentures. Various means which are used to raise funds represent the capital structure of the firm.

Financing is a crucial matter in every business and as a general rule there should be a proper mix of debt and equity capital.

> **The use of long-term interest/fixed dividend bearing securities such as debt and preference share capital along with equity share capital is called financial leverage. The process of magnifying equity shareholders' earnings through use of low cost debt is known as financial leverage or 'Trading Equity'.**

Purpose of Financial Leverage: The financial leverage is employed by a company to earn more on the fixed charge funds (debentures, long-term loan etc) than their costs. The surplus increases the return on total equity. An example will clear the picture better. For example, if a company borrows ₹100 at 10% per annum and earns 15% return (that is, ₹15 per annum), after paying interest 10%, the balance 5% (₹5 per annum) belongs to equity shareholders. In case, firm is able to earn only 8% per annum, the deficit 2% reduces the earnings of the equity shareholders. Thus, financial leverage provides the potential of increasing equity shareholders' earnings as well as creating risks to them. And so, it is called a double-edged sword.

Computation of Financial Leverage: Financial Leverage is computed with the following formula:

$$\text{Financial leverage} = \frac{\text{Operating profit (EBIT)}}{\text{Profit before tax}}$$

There is no financial leverage if quotient does not exceed one. Financial Leverage exists if the quotient is more than one.

Financial leverage is defined as the firm's ability to use fixed financial charges to magnify the effect of changes in operating profits on earnings per shares (EPS).

Financial Risk: Financial risk refers to the situation when the firm is not able to recover fixed financial costs. This is the primary risk. If the firm cannot recover the fixed financial payments, it can be technically forced into liquidation. Therefore, the very existence of the business is at stake. Second risk lies in the variability of earnings per share (EPS) caused by financial leverage. Financial risk also causes fluctuations in earnings. If there is no borrowing, there is no financial risk. Financial risk has arisen due to composition of the means of financing. If the means of financing change, risk may increase or decrease. If expansion is made through total debt, existing risk increases. On the other hand, if total equity is used for expansion, existing risk decreases.

If there are no fixed financial charges, there is no financial risk at all.

Means of financing play a vital role in influencing risk to a firm.

Aggressiveness of Firm: Financial leverage indicates risk the firm has assumed in respect of fixed financial costs. Higher financial leverage shows risky attitude of the firm while lower financial leverage shows cautious approach. If financial leverage is neither too high nor too low, it is an indication that the firm is adopting a balanced approach.

Level of leverage of the firm, be it operative leverage or financial leverage, is to be compared with leverage of the other firms in the same industry or industry leverage to understand aggressiveness of the firm.

Illustration No. 6

Geeta Kashyap & Co has an EBIT of ₹ 60,000. Firm is totally financed by 5,000 equity shares. Tax rate is 40%. Calculate earnings per share. Discuss the impact of financial leverage in case EBIT changes by 50%. Analyse consequences of change in EBIT.

Solution

	Case I (Increase of EBIT by 50%)	Base	Case II (Decrease of EBIT by 50%)
EBIT & PBT*	90,000	60,000	30,000
Less: Taxes 40%	36,000	24,000	12,000
Earnings available to equity shareholders	54,000	36,000	18,000
Number of equity shares	5,000	5,000	5,000
Earning per share	10.8	7.2	3.6
Financial leverage = EBIT / PBT	90,000 / 90,000 = 1	60,000 / 60,000 = 1	30,000 / 30,000 = 1

* EBIT & PBT is one and the same as there is no interest in the absence of borrowing.

Analysis

1. **Financial leverage:** Even though EBIT has increased and decreased by 50%, there is no change in the financial leverage as there is no borrowing. Financial leverage occurs only when there is fixed financial charge.
2. **EPS:** EPS has also changed in the same direction of EBIT by 50%. When EBIT has increased by 50%, EPS also has increased by 50% (from 7.2 to 10.8). Similarly when EBIT has decreased by 50%, EPS also has decreased by 50% (from 7.2 to 3.6).

Illustration No. 7

Rashmi & Co has three financial plan options. It has to choose one of the following financial plans. Calculate financial leverage in each case. Record your observations and interpret different financial options. Indicate final option.

(₹)

	Option A	Option B	Option C
Capital Structure:			
Equity share capital	10,000	6,000	8,000
Debt	6,000	10,000	8,000
	16,000	16,000	16,000
Operating profit (EBIT)	2,000	2,000	2,000
Interest 12% on debt in			

Solution

(₹)

	Option A	Option B	Option C
Operating profit (EBIT)	2,000	2,000	2,000
Less:			
Interest 12% on debt	720	1,200	960
Profit before tax	1,280	800	1,040
Financial leverage = $\frac{\text{Operating profit}}{\text{Profit before tax}}$	$\frac{2,000}{1,280}$ =1.56	$\frac{2,000}{800}$ = 2.5	$\frac{2,000}{1,040}$ =1.92

Observation: Capital structure, consisting of equity share capital and debt, is same ₹ 16,000 in all the three options – A, B and C. Operating profit is also same in all the three options. However, composition of debt and equity is different in capital structure.

Interpretation: Option B has the greatest financial leverage. This indicates the existence of fixed interest bearing securities is the highest in option B in the capital structure of company. Risk is more, in case earnings fall below the cost of debt. However, equity shareholders would be more benefited with increased earnings as the fixed commitment in the form of interest on debt is fixed and does not change with earnings of the company.

Option A has the least financial leverage. Risk is the least, in case earnings fall below the cost of debt.

Option C is balanced as its financial leverage is in between the two options–A and B.

Final Choice: Final choice of the firm depends on the risk appetite of the firm. If firm is more aggressive, it opts B option. It chooses option A if it is least aggressive. Firm chooses option C if it wants to adopt a cautious and balanced approach.

Tip to Students: Do not write any specific option is good. Choice depends on the aptitude of the management of the firm.

Measures of Financial Leverage: Debt ratio, debt-equity ratio and interest coverage ratio are the measures of financial leverage, which have already been discussed in detail in the Ratio Analysis. In the capital structure of the company, if use of fixed interest/ dividend bearing securities is greater than equity share capital of the company, the leverage is said to be larger. In a reverse case, the leverage is said to be smaller.

9.5.1 Degree of Financial Leverage

The degree of financial leverage is defined as:

$$\textbf{Degree of financial leverage} = \frac{\textbf{\% Change in EPS}}{\textbf{\% Change in EBIT}}$$

Income Tax Shield: Financial leverage is caused due to use of fixed interest charge funds. Interest charges are also tax deductible. This income tax shield increases earnings of equity shareholders.

Utility: Financial leverage helps finance manager considerably in designing capital structure of the firm. **Financial leverage shows impact of operating income on EPS in the same direction.** Assume financial leverage is 2. It indicates if operating income increases by 10%, EPS increases by 20% (2 × 10%). If operating income decreases by 20%, EPS decreases by 40% (2 × 20%).

9.5.2 Relationship between Financial Leverage and Financial Risk

For a given degree of variability of EBIT, variability of EPS and ROE increases with more financial leverage.

Variability of EPS by financial leverage is called financial risk.

The financial risk of two firms differs when the assets are financed differently. Financial risk arises when assets are financed by debt. A totally equity financed firm does not have financial risk. Financial risk is avoidable if firm decides to finance all assets totally with equity.

Financial leverage and degree of financial leverage: Financial leverage is calculated with reference to a position at the end of a particular period, say March, 2008. Degree of financial leverage is calculated with reference to change that has occurred over a period; say from year 2008 to 2009.

Tip to Students: Use formula of financial leverage when data of one year is given. Use formula of degree of financial leverage, when data of two years is given.

9.5.3 Computation of Profit Before Tax when Share Capital consists of Preference Share Capital

Why dividend to preference shareholders is to be grossed up, while computing PBT for financial leverage? When share capital consists of preference shares, amount of preference dividend is to be grossed up (as per tax rate applicable to the company) and deduct it from EBIT to arrive profit before tax. Reason being preference dividend is paid from profits, after payment of taxes. If tax rate is 30% and ₹10 lakhs are 7% preference share capital, preference dividend ₹ 70,000 is available only after payment of tax. As we are to calculate profit before tax for the formula, this amount requires adjustment. So if 70% (profit after tax) is ₹ 70,000, then 100% (profit before tax) would be ₹ one lakh. So, ₹ one lakh is to be deducted from operating profit (EBIT).

Students often have put up this question to me as this point is not clear to many and books on finance are silent without any explanation. In the formula for financial leverage, the denominator is 'Profit before tax'. If a company has preference shareholders along with equity shares, it is legally binding to the company to pay dividend first to preference shareholders. Dividend amount to preference shareholders is after tax. We are to arrive at profit before tax. So applying tax rate, dividend to preference shareholders before tax is to be arrived for deduction from EBIT.

The above type of adjustment (grossing up) is not necessary for interest on debentures. Reason being that interest is payable before tax, unlike dividend to preference shares, which is payable after tax.

Illustration No. 8

The capital structure of Gopal & Ganga Ltd consists of the following securities:

10% Preference share capital	₹ 1,00,000
Equity share capital (FV ₹ 10)	₹ 1,00,000

Operating profit is ₹ 80,000. Company is in a tax bracket of 50%.

Calculate financial leverage of the above company.

What would be new financial leverage if operating profits of the company increase by 50%? Calculate earnings per share and interpret the results.

Solution

Computation of PRESENT Financial Leverage

	(₹)
Operating profit (EBIT)	80,000
Less: Preference dividend (after grossing up)	20,000 *
Profit before tax (PBT)	60,000
Present financial leverage $= \dfrac{\text{Operating profit (EBIT)}}{\text{Profit before tax}}$	
$= \dfrac{80,000}{60,000}$	
$=1.33$	

* Dividend to Preference shareholders, before tax

Computation of NEW Financial Leverage

	(₹)
Operating profit	1,20,000
Less: Preference dividend (after grossing up)	20,000
Profit before tax (PBT)	1,00,000
New financial leverage $= \dfrac{\text{Operating profit (EBIT)}}{\text{Profit before tax}}$	
$= \dfrac{1,20,000}{1,00,000}$	
$= 1.2$	

Computation of PRESENT Earnings per Share (EPS)

	(₹)
Operating profit (EBIT)	80,000
Less: Tax @ 50%	40,000
Profit, before distribution of dividend to Preference and Equity shareholders	40,000
Dividend to preference shareholders	10,000
Earnings available to equity shareholders	30,000
Earnings per share $= \frac{30,000}{10,000}$	3

Computation of New Earnings per Share (EPS)

	(₹)
Operating profit (EBIT)	1,20,000
Less: Tax @ 50%	60,000
Profit, before distribution to Preference and Equity shareholders	60,000
Dividend to preference shareholders	10,000
Earnings available to equity shareholders	50,000
Earnings per share $= \frac{50,000}{10,000}$	5

Interpretation: The existing financial leverage is 1.33.

$$\text{Degree of financial leverage} = \frac{\%\text{ change in EPS}}{\%\text{ change in EBIT}} = \frac{67\%}{33\%} = 1.33$$

It means if EBIT changes by 1%, EPS would change by 1.33%.

Problem states that EBIT has increased by 50%. As financial leverage is 1.33, EPS should increase by 1.33 × 50% i.e. 67%.

Here, EPS has increased from 3 to 5 (increase of 2). So, EPS has increased by 2/3 or 67%.

9.6 MIX OF OPERATING LEVERAGE AND FINANCIAL LEVERAGE

Both operating leverage and financial leverage are quantitative tools to measure return to owners. The right combination is a great challenge to the management. A proper combination of both operating leverage and financial leverage is indeed a blessing for firm's growth, while an improper combination is a curse.

Now, question arises what is right mix? There is no right mix; it all depends on the risk-bearing capacity and approach of the firm. A high operating leverage indicates presence of high fixed costs due to heavy investment in fixed assets. A high financial leverage is an indication that it's financing is largely by debt capital. The fixed costs and fixed interest charges bring a greater business and financial risk to the firm respectively. A firm with fluctuating earnings cannot afford to take such risk. So a firm must make all possible efforts to combine the operating and financial leverage to suit its risk-bearing capacity.

The ideal situation is to have a low operating leverage and high financial leverage, provided firm has enough profitable opportunities.

A firm with high operating leverage should not have a high financial leverage. If the firm opts to have low operating leverage and low financial leverage, it shows the cautious policy of the management and, of course, the firm may be losing certain profitable business opportunities in this process.

Finally, the mix of financial and operative leverage shows the aggressive, cautious or prudent policy of management.

Operating leverage is concerned with the presence of fixed costs in the cost structure. Emphasis of operating leverage is to increase operating profits. Financial leverage is concerned with the employment of fixed cost funds in the capital structure of the firm. Its concentration is on increasing earnings per equity share.

Operating leverage deals with the use of fixed operating costs by the firm. Financial leverage deals with the use of fixed financing costs.

Difference between operating leverage and financial leverage: Employment of fixed costs creates operating leverage. For calculating fixed costs, financial costs are not considered. Employment of fixed cost funds creates financial leverage.

Common factor: Both operating leverage and financial leverage have one common factor. Both are double-edged swords. In boom times, equity shareholders of company would be benefited while recession would be a great disadvantage to them.

A proper combination of both operating leverage and financial leverage is a blessing for firm's growth while an improper combination may prove to be a curse.

Both operating leverage and financial leverage are double edged–swords, which greatly benefit equity shareholders in boom times while they would adversely affect the firm in recession period.

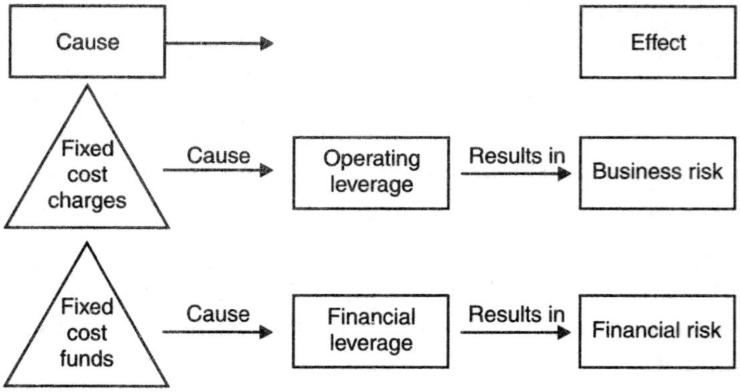

Operating Leverage and Financial Leverage – Cause and Effect

9.6.1 Relationship between Operating Leverage and Financial Leverage

In operating leverage, EBIT is determined by sales level. However, in the case of financial leverage EBIT determines the level of EPS. That is why EBIT is called linking point in leverage study.

EBIT is a linking point between operating leverage and financial leverage.

Operating Leverage	Financial Leverage
Sales	**EBIT**
Less: Variable expenses	Less: Interest
Contribution	Profit before tax
Less: Fixed costs	Less: Tax
EBIT	Profit after tax
	Divided by number of equity shareholders
	Earning per share (EPS)

In the above, the left hand side deals with operating leverage starting with sales and ending with EBIT. The right hand side deals with financial leverage starting with EBIT and ending with earning per share (EPS). The linking point is EBIT, which is the end in operating leverage while it is starting point in financial leverage. Finally, the aim of sale is to improve earning per share.

9.6.2 Combined effect of Operating Leverage and Financial Leverage

Following table shows various combinations of operating leverage and financial leverage and their combined effect.

Operating leverage	Financial leverage	Combined effect
High	High	This combination is a very dangerous policy, desirable to avoid.
Low	Low	This combination shows cautious policy and 'not assuming risk' nature of firm.
High	Low	This combination neutralises adverse effect of high operating leverage with low financial leverage.
Low	High	This combination is an ideal situation. Firms can plan this combination to follow aggressive debt policy.

9.7 TRADING ON EQUITY

Every firm makes its own decisions about the quantum of funds to be borrowed. When the amount of debt is relatively large in relation to capital, the company is said to be trading on equity. If the amount of debt is comparatively low in relation to equity, the company is said to be trading on thick equity.

The aim of a finance manager is to increase revenue available to equity shareholders. A finance manager has to perform 'Finance Function' as well as 'Investment Function'. Funds are needed for investment in projects. The required funds can be raised by way of equity alone or through combination of debt and equity. The mix adopted for debt and equity in the capital structure of the organization is significant. **The process of magnifying the shareholders' earnings through the process of debt is called 'Trading on Equity'; otherwise also known as Financial Leverage or Financial Gearing.** The objective is to give a high rate of return to equity shareholders above general rate of earning on capital employed in the company to compensate them for the risk they bear. **The term 'Trading on Equity' is used for the financial leverage only when the financial leverage is favourable.** In other words, the quotient (financial leverage) should be more than one. Financial leverage could be positive as well as negative, but trading on equity is always positive.

Financial leverage shows the impact on EPS. Trading on equity shows impact on ROE.

Impact of Financial Leverage on Shareholders' Return: Interest is a fixed commitment, which must be paid irrespective of earnings. The preference share capital also bears a fixed rate of dividend. However, the dividend to preference shareholders is paid only when there is a surplus in earnings. If earnings from debt were more than cost, the leverage would be positive or favourable. If earnings made by fixed cost funds is more than their cost (interest and/or preference dividend), the residual would be available to the equity shareholders. As the surplus earnings belong to the equity shareholders, earnings per share (EPS) increase and also return on equity (ROE) also increases. On the contrary, if cost of debt is more than earnings of debt, leverage would be negative or unfavourable. Then, earnings of equity shareholders get reduced and in turn return on equity and earnings per share also goes down.

Earning on other's shoulders: Suppose, you have an opportunity of earning 20 per cent on an investment of ₹ 100 for one year. If you invest your own money, your return is 20 per cent. On the other hand, you have an opportunity to borrow, say ₹ 50 at 10% interest from your friend and put your money for the balance ₹ 50 only. You continue to get a total earning of ₹ 20 as earlier out of which you have to pay ₹ 5 as interest to your friend. Still, you are left with ₹ 15 on your investment of ₹ 50, which gives you a return of 30%. You have earned more at the cost of your friend.

As long as return on investment (ROI) is greater than cost of debt, financial leverage is favourable. Otherwise, it gives a negative impact. Borrowing is resorted to maximize the earning of the equity holders. The additional gain is for the risk taken by equity shareholders to pay committed interest to the debenture debt holders irrespective of the return to them.

Let us take one more example to explain. Investment is ₹ 100 which is raised through equity ₹ 50 and balance ₹ 50 by debentures. Return expected is 18%. If actual return happens 28% or 6%, return available to equity shareholders would be as under:

Sources of investment	Amount	Forecast return & (yield to different sources)	If actual return more than forecast - (yield to different sources)	If actual return less than forecast - (yield to different sources)
		18 %	**28 %**	**6 %**
8 % Debentures	50	4 (8%)	4 (8%)	4 (8%)
Equity (Owners' funds)	50	14 (28%)	24 (48%)	2 (4%)
Total Investment	100	100	100	100
Return on Equity		**28%**	**48%**	**4 %**

Observation: Debentures holders get the fixed return irrespective of the earnings. However, return to equity shareholders changes, depending on the actual earnings position.

Impact of financial leverage: Favourable and unfavourable impact to equity shareholders can be presented in the following way.

ROI > Cost of Debt	↑	ROE & EPS
ROI < Cost of Debt	↓	ROE & EPS

Double-edged weapon: So long as return on investment is greater than cost of debt, return on equity goes up. Return on equity goes down, when the return on investment falls lower than the cost of debt.

> **The use of the term 'Trading on Equity' is derived from the fact that it is the owner's equity that is used as a basis to raise debt.**

That is, equity is traded upon. The supplier of debt has limited participation (fixed interest) in the company's profits and therefore insists upon protection in earnings and protection in values which is represented by ownership equity.

The finance manager has to bear in mind both return and risk while finalizing mix for raising funds. When economic conditions are good and EBIT is increasing, EPS would grow faster with increased debt in the capital structure. However, when economic conditions turn unfavourable and EBIT starts falling, pace of EPS fall would be greater than the falling rate of EBIT. **Financial Leverage is a double-edged sword.** The finance manager has to remember its double-edged impact and design the capital structure suitably.

Effect of Leverage

Favourable	ROI > i
Unfavourable	ROI < i
Neutral	ROI = i

Where 'i' = interest or cost of debt

Example to illustrate Financial Leverage is a double-edged sword:

	Company X	Company Z
Equity share capital of ₹ 10 each	20,00,000	8,00,000
10 % debentures	2,00,000	14,00,000
Total capital employed	22,00,000	22,00,000
Earning before interest and taxes (EBIT)- **40 %** on capital employed **(ROI)**	8,80,000	8,80,000
Less: Interest on debentures	20,000	1,40,000
Profit before Tax (PBT)	8,60,000	7,40.000
Less: Tax @ 30%	2,58,000	2,22,000
Profit after tax (PAT)	6,02,000	5,18,000
Earning available to equity shareholders	6,02,000	5,18,000
Number of equity shares	2,00,000	80,000
Earning per share (EPS)	3.01	6.47
Return on equity (ROE)	30.1%	65%

Both companies X and Z have same amount of investment i.e. 22,00,000 and their return on investment is the same 40%. $\left(\frac{8,80,000}{22,00,000}\times 100\right)$

Interesting point is that their EPS are totally different. In fact, EPS of company Z is more than double as compared to company X. What is the real reason? The difference in EPS is due to their diverse capital structure. i.e. difference in financing the total capital employed.

Company Z has relied more on fixed return source of funds. Company Z is earning 40% on total funds but paying only 10% interest. The difference between the return and cost along with benefit of tax on interest (Tax shield) has increased earnings of equity the shareholders.

Let us see what would happen to EPS if EBIT **increases** by similar 50% to both companies:

	Company X	Company Z
Equity share capital of ₹ 10 each	20,00,000	8,00,000
10% Debentures	2,00,000	14,00,000
Total capital employed	22,00,000	22,00,000
Earning before interest and taxes (EBIT)- **60%** on Capital employed **(ROI)**	13,20,000	13,20,000
Less: Interest on debentures	20,000	1,40,000
Profit before tax (PBT)	13,00,000	11,80,000
Less: Tax @ 30%	3,90,000	3,54,000
Profit after tax (PAT)	9,10,000	8,26,000
Earning available to equity shareholders	9,10,000	8,26,000
Number of equity shares	2,00,000	80,000
Return on equity	45.5%	103.3 %
Earning per share (EPS)	4.55	10.33
Increase of EPS	51.16%	59.65%

Let us see what would happen to EPS if EBIT **decreases** by similar 50% to both companies:

	Company X	Company Z
Equity share capital of ₹ 10 each	20,00,000	8,00,000
10% Debentures	2,00,000	14,00,000
Total capital employed	22,00,000	22,00,000
Earning before interest and taxes (EBIT)- **60%** on Capital employed **(ROI)**	13,20,000	13,20,000
Less: Interest on debentures	20,000	1,40,000
Profit before tax (PBT)	13,00,000	11,80,000
Less: Tax @ 30%	3,90,000	3,54,000
Profit after tax (PAT)	9,10,000	8,26,000
Earning available to equity shareholders	9,10,000	8,26,000
Number of equity shares	2,00,000	80,000
Return on equity	45.5%	103.3 %
Earning per share (EPS)	4.55	10.33
Increase of EPS	51.16%	59.65%

$$\textbf{Financial Leverage} = \frac{\text{EBIT}}{\text{Profit before tax}}$$

	X	Z
	$\frac{8,80,000}{8,60,000}$	$\frac{8,80,000}{7,40,000}$
Financial Leverage	= 1.02	= 1.19

Financial Leverage of Z Company is higher than X Company. So, when there is an increase of 50% in EBIT, EPS of Z Company has increased by 59.65%, while X Company has increased on a lower side by 51.16%. However, when fall of EBIT has been by 50%, again. EPS of Z Company has fallen by 59.65%, while fall of X Company has been 51.16% only. Due to higher financial leverage, percentage of increase as well as fall of EPS in Z Company is higher than X Company. This proves financial leverage is a double-edged sword.

9.8 SIGNIFICANCE OF FINANCIAL LEVERAGE

Financial leverage is employed to plan ratio between debt and equity so that earnings per share are magnified. The significance of financial leverage is as under:

1. **Planning Capital Structure:** Financial leverage helps in planning capital structure. The capital structure is concerned with raising of long-term funds, both from shareholders and long-term creditors. The structure has implication of cost and risk that are to be borne in mind while finalizing the capital structure.
2. **Profit Planning:** Earning per share is affected by degree of financial leverage. If profitability of the concern is increasing, fixed costs will help in increasing availability of profits to equity shareholders. When profits decline and do not cover interest on debt, sufferers will be equity shareholders. Therefore, financial leverage is important for profit planning.

9.9 LIMITATIONS OF FINANCIAL LEVERAGE / TRADING ON EQUITY

These are the following limitations of financial leverage/trading on equity:

1. **Double-edged weapon:** Trading on equity is a double-edged weapon. It can be successfully used to increase earning per share as long as return on investment is higher than cost of fixed-charge funds. If cost of debt is more than return on the investment, then it will work adversely and hence cannot be employed.
2. **Beneficial only to companies having stable earnings:** Trading on equity is beneficial only to companies having stable earnings. This is so because interest on debentures, a recurring expenditure, has to be paid irrespective of profits.

If company does not have profits in lean years, it cannot pay. So unless company is assured of stable profits, it should not borrow and resort to financial leverage to take advantage.

3. **More debt increases risk and interest rate:** Every rupee of extra debt increases interest burden and along with it risks too. After a certain stage, it becomes difficult for the company to borrow, without paying higher interest rate and offering additional securities. Payment of higher interest rate reduces profitability and makes financial leverage not workable.
4. **Restrictions and covenants from financial institutions:** To prevent excessive borrowing and contain risk, financial institutions stipulate stringent conditions while sanctioning loans. This makes the ceiling for borrowing even if company wants to borrow and funds are available, without higher interest rate.

9.10 RELATIONSHIP BETWEEN OPERATING LEVERAGE AND FINANCIAL LEVERAGE

Operating Leverage and Financial Leverage are interrelated. The formulae for operating leverage and financial leverage are as under:

$$\text{Degree of Operating leverage} = \frac{\%\text{ change in EBIT}}{\%\text{ change in sales}}$$

$$\text{Degree of Financial leverage} = \frac{\%\text{ change in EPS}}{\%\text{ change in EBIT}}$$

EBIT is dependent on sales. In turn, EPS is dependent on EBIT. **An ideal combination in a firm is to have low operating leverage and high financial leverage, provided opportunities are available to utilize borrowed funds, profitably.** Lower operating leverage indicates low fixed costs and in consequence break-even point would be low and margin of safety would be high. High financial leverage gives benefit of a higher percentage of EPS for a given change in EBIT.

9.11 DISTINCTION BETWEEN OPERATING LEVERAGE AND FINANCIAL LEVERAGE

Operating leverage is concerned with the change of operating income with change in sales, while financial leverage is concerned with change in earning per share with the change in operating income. High degree of operating leverage indicates large business risk and high degree of financial leverage shows large financial risk. High operating leverage, with high financial leverage, constitutes a very large risky situation.

The ideal situation is to have a high financial leverage and low operating leverage, provided profitable opportunities exist.

Basic objective of both the leverages is to improve profitability of firm and earning per share. Both are to remain within the limits, comparable to the industry.

The basic differences between operating leverage and financial leverage are as under:

Operating leverage	Financial leverage
1. Operating leverage is associated with investment activities of the company.	1. Financial leverage is associated with financing activities of the company.
2. Operating leverage is based on the use of fixed operating expenses of the company.	2. Financial leverage is based on the use of fixed financial costs of the company.
3. Calculation of operating leverage OL = Contribution/Operating profit.	3. Calculation of financial leverage FL = Operating profit / Profit before tax
4. A percentage change of operating profits occurs due to a percentage change of sales.	4. A percentage change of taxable profits occurs due to a percentage change of EBIT.
5. Trading on equity is not possible with operating leverage.	5. Trading on equity is possible with financial leverage.
6. Operating leverage depends on variable cost and fixed cost.	6. Financial leverage depends on operating profit.
7. Tax rate and interest rate do not affect operating leverage.	7. Financial leverage change due to tax rate and interest rate.

9.12 COMBINED LEVERAGE (COMPOSITE LEVERAGE)

Both financial and operating leverages magnify earnings of equity shareholders. **Operating leverage affects operating profit, which is the result of production and sales. On the other hand, financial average is the result of financing decisions.** High financial leverage may be offset by low operating leverage or vice versa. The combined leverage focuses the attention on the entire income of the concern.

Computation: Combined leverage is computed as under:

Combined leverage = Operating leverage × Financial leverage.

$$= \frac{\text{Contribution}}{\text{EBIT}} \times \frac{\text{EBIT}}{\text{Profit before tax}}$$

$$= \frac{\textbf{Contribution}}{\textbf{Profit before tax}}$$

Alternatively

$$\frac{\%\ \text{Change in EBIT}}{\%\ \text{Change in sales}} \times \frac{\%\ \text{Change in EPS}}{\%\ \text{Change in EBIT}}$$

$$= \frac{\textbf{\% Change in EPS}}{\textbf{\% Change in sales}}$$

Operating leverage deals with business risk while financial leverage deals with financial risk. Firm has to look for overall risk or total risk, which is business risk plus financial risk. The total risk is reflected by combined leverage.

The effect of change in sales on EPS is known as combined leverage.

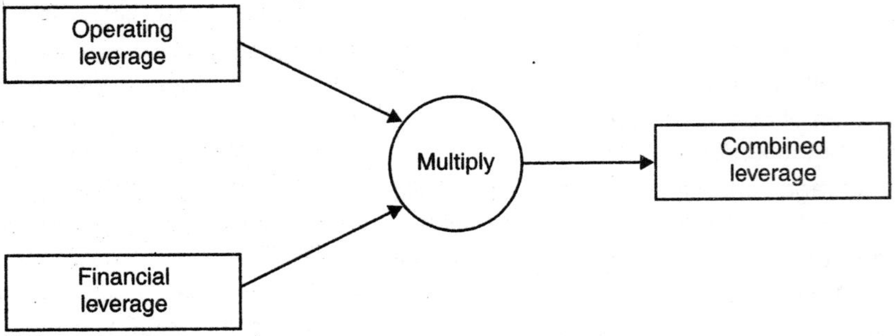

Formation of Combined Leverage

Illustration No. 9

Calculate degree of operating leverage, financial leverage and combined leverage for the following firms and interpret the results:

	P	Q	R
Output (Units)	3,00,000	75,000	5,00,000
Fixed costs (₹)	3,50,000	7,00,000	75,000
Unit variable cost (₹)	1.0	7.50	0.10
Interest expenses	25,000	40,000	Nil
Unit selling price	3.0	25.00	0.50

(B.U. MBA-2004)

Solution

	P	Q	R
Unit selling price	3.00	25.00	0.50
Unit variable cost	1.00	7.50	0.10
Number of units	3,00,000	75,000	5,00,000
Total sales	9,00,000	18,75,000	2,50,000
Total variable cost	3,00,000	5,62,500	50,000
Total contribution	6,00,000	13,12,500	2,00,000
Fixed cost	3,50,000	7,00,000	75,000
EBIT	2,50,000	6,12,500	1,25,000
Interest	25,000	40,000	Nil
Profit before tax	2,25,000	5,72,500	1,25,000

(Contd...)

Operating leverage = $\frac{\text{Contribution}}{\text{EBIT}}$	$\frac{6,00,000}{2,50,000}$ = 2.4	$\frac{13,12,500}{6,12,500}$ = 2.14	$\frac{2,00,000}{1,25,000}$ = 1.6
Financial leverage = $\frac{\text{EBIT}}{\text{Profit before tax}}$	$\frac{2,50,000}{2,25,000}$ = 1.11	$\frac{6,12,500}{5,72,500}$ = 1.07	$\frac{1,25,000}{1,25,000}$ = 1.00
Combined leverage = Operating leverage × financial leverage	2.4 × 1.11 = 2.667	2.14 × 1.07 = 2.29	1.6 × 1.0 = 1.6

Interpretation: Operating leverage, financial leverage and combined leverage are the highest for firm 'P' amongst all firms. This indicates P is exposed to the highest business risk as well as financial risk. The management of P is highly aggressive. A high operating leverage and financial leverage is a very risky situation to the firm.

If the firm's sales increase by 100%, the EPS increases by 266%. Equally, if sales fall by 100%, EPS also falls, similarly.

R is exposed to the lowest risk of the above categories. This position indicates that the management of R is cautious.

The following pictorial presentation shows the cause and impact of different leverages.

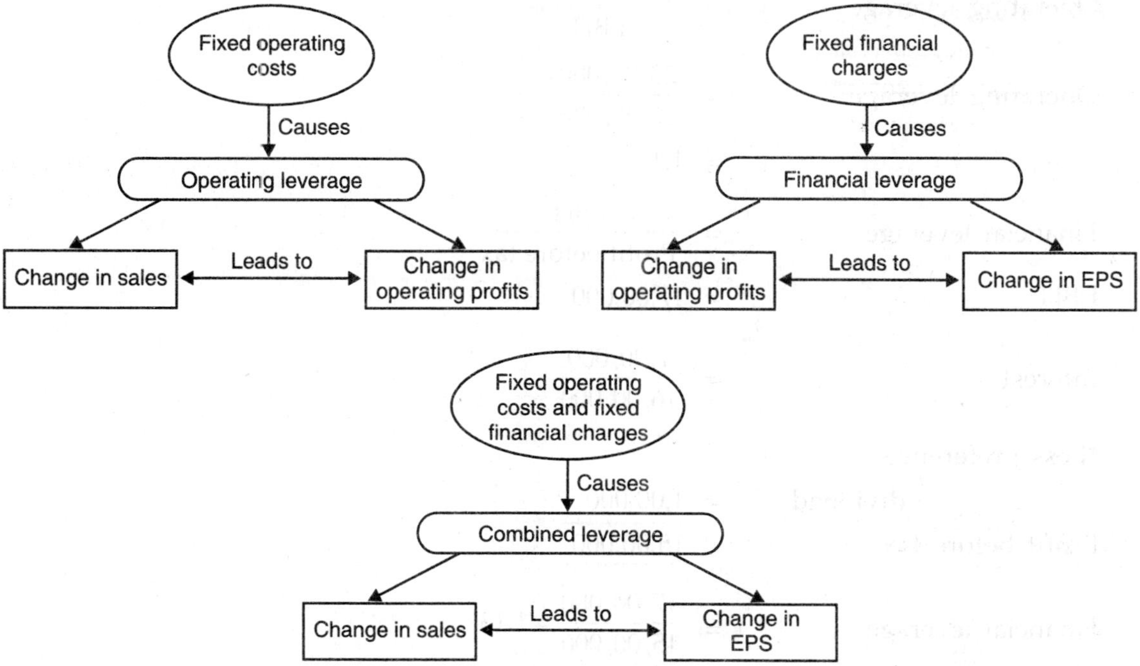

Impact of Operating Leverage, Financial Leverage and Combined Leverage

Illustration No. 10

Consider the following data of ABC Company

	₹
Selling price per unit	60/-
Variable cost per unit	40/-
Fixed Cost	3,00,000
Interest burden	1,00,000
Tax Rate	50%
Preference dividend	50,000

Calculate the 3 leverages, if number of units sold are 1,00,000.

Solution

Contribution per unit = 60 − 40 = 20

Total contribution = 20 × 1,00,000

= 20,00,000

EBIT = Contribution − Fixed Cost

= 20,00,000 − 3,00,000 = 17,00,000

$$\text{Operating leverage} = \frac{\text{Contribution}}{\text{EBIT}}$$

$$\text{Operating leverage} = \frac{20,00,000}{17,00,000}$$

= 1.18

$$\text{Financial leverage} = \frac{\text{EBIT}}{\text{Profit before tax}}$$

EBIT = 17,00,000

Interest = 1,00,000

16,00,000

*Less preference dividend = 1,00,000

Profit before tax 15,00,000

$$\text{Financial leverage} = \frac{17,00,000}{15,00,000} = 1.13$$

Combined leverage = Operating leverage × Financial leverage

$= 1.18 \times 1.13 = 1.33$

Or Combined leverage $= \frac{\text{Contribution}}{\text{PBT}}$

$= \frac{20,00,000}{15,00,000}$

$= 1.33$

* Preference dividend is ₹ 50,000. Tax rate is 50%. **Preference dividend is paid from profits available after payment of tax.** For the formula, we are to calculate corresponding amount of preference dividend, before tax. Pre-tax amount ₹ 100 is equal to post-tax amount ₹ 50. So dividend, after tax, ₹ 50,000 is equal to ₹ 1,00,000, before tax (grossed up).

Illustration No. 11

The following information has been given in respect of a company:

Particulars	₹
1. Equity share capital (divided into shares of ₹ 10 each)	10,00,000
2. Debentures (14%)	30,00,000
3. Selling price per unit	50
4. Variable cost per unit	30
5. Fixed costs	12,00,000

The company is producing at present 1,00,000 units. Now, the management of company plans to increase output by 25%. Tax rate for the company is 40%.

On the basis of the above information, you are required to make out the following calculations for the existing as well as the planned level of output.

(A) Operating leverage

(B) Financial leverage

(C) Earnings per share

Analyse and interpret the results.

(B.U. MBA-2003)

Solution

	Present Production	Planned Production
Production (in units)	1,00,000	1,25,000
Total sales realization	50,00,000	62,50,000
Total variable cost	30,00,000	37,50,000
Contribution	20,00,000	25,00,000
Fixed cost	12,00,000	12,00,000
EBIT	8,00,000	13,00,000
Interest	4,20,000	4,20,000
Profit, before tax	3,80,000	8,80,000
Tax @ 40%	1,52,000	3,52,000
Profit, after tax	2,28,000	5,28,000
Operating leverage = $\frac{\text{Contribution}}{\text{EBIT}}$	$\frac{20,00,000}{8,00,000}$ = 2.5	$\frac{25,00,000}{13,00,000}$ = 1.92
Financial leverage = $\frac{\text{EBIT}}{\text{Profit, before tax}}$	$\frac{8,00,000}{3,80,000}$ = 2.11	$\frac{13,00,000}{8,80,000}$ = 1.48
Earning per share = $\frac{\text{Profit, after tax}}{\text{Number of equity shares}}$	$\frac{2,28,000}{1,00,000}$ = 2.28	$\frac{5,28,000}{1,00,000}$ = 5.28

Analysis and Interpretation: The company has increased production and sales by 25%. The operating leverage is 2.5. In other words, if sales increases by 100%, operating profit would increase by 250%. So EBIT has increased by ₹ 5 lakhs from 8 lakhs to 13 lakhs 62.5% (25% × 2.5). This has happened as fixed costs have not increased.

However, EPS has increased from 2.28 to 5.28 i.e. an increase of 131.57% $\left\{\frac{(5.28 - 2.28) \times 100}{2.28}\right\}$. This is the combined effect of operating leverage and financial leverage (combined leverage). In other words, for every 25% increase of sales, EPS would increase by 131.57%.

Illustration No. 12

Consider the following data of XYZ Ltd.

	₹
Selling price per unit	60
Variables cost per unit	40
Fixed cost	3,00,000
Interest burden	1,00,000
Tax rate	50%
Preference dividend	50,000

Calculate the three types of leverages, if the number of units sold is 10,000.

Solution

	₹
Sales (10,000 × ₹ 60 per unit)	6,00,000
Less: Variable cost (10,000 × 40)	4,00,000
Contribution	2,00,000
Less: Fixed cost	3,00,000
EBIT	– 1,00,000
Less: Interest	– 1,00,000
PBT	– 2,00,000

$$\text{Operating leverage} = \frac{\text{Contribution}}{\text{EBIT}} = \frac{2,00,000}{-1,00,000}$$

$$= -2$$

$$\text{Financial leverage} = \frac{\text{EBIT}}{\text{PBT}} = \frac{-1,00,000}{-2,00,000} = 0.5$$

$$\text{Combined leverage} = \text{Financial leverage} \times \text{Operating leverage}$$
$$= 0.5 \times (-2) = -1$$

Note: EBIT (operating profit) is negative. So, tax liability does not arise. In the absence of profits, preference dividend is not considered.

Illustration No. 13

The capital employed in a business has been financed as below:

	(₹)
Equity share capital	6,00,000
7% Preference share capital	4,00,000
6% Debentures	8,00,000
Reserves and surplus	2,00,000
Total	20,00,000

The company earns a profit of ₹ 4,00,000 before interest and tax.

Test for 'Trading on Equity' and explain the principles of 'Trading on Equity' by above illustration. Tax rate is 30%.

(B.U. MBA-2003)

Solution

Trading on equity exists when the financial leverage of the company is favourable i.e. when the quotient of financial leverage is more than one. So, it is necessary to determine financial leverage of the above company.

EBIT	=	4,00,000
Interest	=	48,000
Profit before tax		3,52,000
Dividend to Pref. shares (grossed up)		40,000 *
Profit before tax		3,12,000

* Dividend due to preference shareholders ₹ 28,000 is grossed up as tax rate is 30%.

$$\text{Financial Leverage} = \frac{\text{EBIT}}{\text{PBT}} = \frac{4{,}00{,}000}{3{,}12{,}000} = 1.28$$

As financial leverage is positive and more than one, there is 'Trading on equity' [Alternatively

$$\text{Capital Gearing Ratio} = \frac{\text{Funds bearing fixed interest/dividend}}{\text{Funds not bearing fixed interest/dividend}}$$

$$= \frac{\text{Debentures + Preference share capital}}{\text{Equity share capital + Reserves and surplus}}$$

$$= \frac{12{,}00{,}000}{8{,}00{,}000}$$

$$= 1.5$$

As the capital-gearing ratio is more than one, the capital structure is "high geared". There should be "Trading on equity".]

$$* \text{ Return on Investment} = \frac{\text{EBIT}(1 - \text{T})}{\text{Capital employed}}$$

$$= \frac{4{,}00{,}000\,(1 - 30\%)}{20{,}00{,}000}$$

$$= \frac{2,80,000}{20,00,000}$$

$$= 14\%$$

ROI is greater than cost of debt, debenture (6%) as well as fixed dividend bearing security, preference share capital (7%). This establishes that the concerned firm is having trading on equity.

Calculation of ROE

EBIT	=	4,00,000
Interest	=	48,000
Profit before tax		3,52,000
Tax @ 30 %		1,05,600
Profit after tax		2,46,400
Dividend to Pref. shares		28,000
Profit due to equity shareholders		2,18,400

Rate of Return on

$$\text{Equity Shareholders' funds (ROE)} = \frac{\text{Profit available to equity shareholders}}{\text{Shareholders' funds}}$$

$$= \frac{2,18,400}{8,00,000}$$

$$= 27.3\%$$

Return on investment is 14% while return on equity is 27.3%. This is due to trading on equity. In this case, trading on equity is beneficial to equity shareholders.

Trading on equity is beneficial to equity shareholders as long as the return on investment is greater than cost of debt. In a reverse situation, when return on investment falls below cost of debt, return on equity goes down. Trading on equity is a double-edged sword.

Note:

*1. For calculating return on investment, normally, EBIT (operating profit before tax) is taken. However, company is concerned with tax management too as tax involves outgo of funds. Tax is an inevitable expenditure for earning profits.

2. In case, tax rate is not given in the problem, tax rate is to be assumed to explain the benefit of tax on interest, as interest is tax deductible.

It is to be noted that the profits available to equity shareholders of a company, having a high financial leverage or capital gearing ratio, will be subject to wider fluctuations as compared to a company, which has a low financial leverage or capital-gearing ratio. This is because after making payment of interest and dividend to fixed income bearing securities, the entire balance belongs to the equity shareholders which would be distributed among the equity shareholders.

Illustration No. 14

Given below are Income Statements of three firms P, Q and R:

	P ₹	Q ₹	R ₹
Sales revenue	9,00,000	18,75,000	2,50,000
Less: Variable expenses	3,00,000	5,62,500	50,000
Contribution	6,00,000	13,12,500	2,00,000
Less: Non-variable expenses	3,50,000	7,00,000	75,000
EBIT	2,50,000	6,12,500	1,25,000
Less: Interest	25,000	40,000	Nil
EBT	2,25,000	5,72,500	1,25,000
Less: Tax @ 40%	90,000	2,29,000	50,000
PAT	1,35,000	3,43,500	75,000
Less: Dividend: On preference shares	37,500	43,500	25,000
On equity shares	75,000	2,00,000	15,000
Addition to retained earnings	22,500	1,00,000	35,000

Calculate degree of operating leverage, financial leverage and combined leverage for these firms and interpret the result. **(DAVV, MBA, 2005)**

Solution

Type of leverage	P	Q	R
Operating leverage = $\frac{\text{Contribution}}{\text{EBIT}}$	$\frac{6,00,000}{2,50,000}$ = 2.4	$\frac{13,12,500}{6,12,500}$ = 2.14	$\frac{2,00,000}{1,25,000}$ = 1.6
Profit before tax	2,25,000	5,72,500	1,25,000
Preference dividend, before tax (grossed up)	– 62,500	–72,500	– 41,667
PBT for financial leverage	1,62,500	5,00,000	83,333
Financial Leverage = $\frac{\text{EBIT}}{\text{Profit before tax}}$	$\frac{2,50,000}{1,62,500}$ = 1.54	$\frac{6,12,500}{5,00,000}$ = 1.23	$\frac{1,25,000}{83,333}$ = 1.50
Combined Leverage = Operating Leverage x Financial Leverage	2.4 × 1.54 = 3.70	2.14 × 1.23 = 2.63	1.6 × 1.50 = 2.4

Interpretation: Operating leverage, financial leverage and combined leverage are the highest in P amongst the three firms. So, business risk (fluctuations in earnings) and financial risk (need to pay fixed interest, irrespective of profit) are the highest in P. So, change in % operating profit would be more than the % change in sales, due to high operating leverage. Similarly, % change in earning per share (EPS) would occur more than the % change in operating profit (EBIT). Hence, business risk and financial risk are the highest to P, compared to Q and R.

R has the lowest operating leverage, financial leverage and combined leverage amongst the three firms. So business risk and financial risk are the least in this firm, compared to P and Q.

Q is balanced in respect of risk, as operating leverage, financial leverage and combined leverage are neither the highest nor the least amongst the three firms.

Illustration No. 15

In the case of Illustration No. 13, calculate ROE and EPS if there is an increase and decrease of earning by 50% and draw relationship between financial leverage and ROE and EPS.

Solution

(₹)

	Existing Capital structure	Changed capital structure I (50% increase in operating profits)	Changed capital structure II (50% decrease in operating profits)
Equity share capital	6,00,000	6,00,000	6,00,000
7% preference share capital	4,00,000	4,00,000	4,00,000
6% debentures	8,00,000	8,00,000	8,00,000
Reserves and surplus	2,00,000	2,00,000	2,00,000
Total capital employed	20,00,000	20,00,000	20,00,000
Calculation of EPS			
EBIT	4,00,000	6,00,000	2,00,000
Less: interest	48,000	48,000	48,000
Profit before tax	3,52,000	5,52,000	1,52,000
Tax @ 30%	1,05,600	1,65,600	45,600
Profits after tax	2,46,400	3,86,400	1,06,400
Less: dividend to preference shares	28,000	28,000	28,000
Profits after tax, available to equity shareholders	2,18,400	3,58,400	78,400

(Contd...)

No. equity shares (assumed face value ₹ 10)	60,000	60,000	60,000
Earnings per share $\frac{\text{PAT}}{\text{No. of equity shares}}$ Increase/decrease in EPS	3.64	5.97 (64%)	1.31 (–64%)
Calculation of financial leverage			
EBIT	4,00,000	6,00,000	2,00,000
Less: interest	48,000	48,000	48,000
Profit before tax	3,52,000	5,52,000	1,52,000
Less: preference dividend (grossed up) *	– 40,000	– 40,000	– 40,000
Earning before tax (for calculation of financial leverage	3,12,000	5,12,000	1,12,000
Financial leverage = $\frac{\text{EBIT}}{\text{Earning before tax}}$	$\frac{4,00,000}{3,12,000}$ = 1.28	$\frac{6,00,000}{5,12,000}$ = 1.17	$\frac{2,00,000}{1,12,000}$ = 1.79
Return on equity = $\frac{\text{profit after tax, available to equity shareholders}}{\text{Equity shareholders' Funds}}$	$\frac{2,18,400}{8,00,000}$ = 27.3%	$\frac{3,58,400}{8,00,000}$ = 44.8%	$\frac{78,400}{8,00,000}$ = 9.8%
increases/decrease in ROE		(64%)	(–64%)

* Preference dividend is ₹ 28,000. Tax rate is 30%. We are to calculate total liability to the company in respect of dividend and tax on account of preference shareholders. The above preference dividend amount is after tax. We are to calculate corresponding amount before tax. For a pre-tax amount of ₹ 100, post tax amount is ₹ 70. So for post-tax amount of ₹ 28,000, corresponding pre-tax amount is ₹ 40,000 (grossed up).

Comments

When the financial leverage is beneficial, it is called 'trading on equity'. Trading on equity shows the impact on 'Return on equity'. As firm is having financial leverage of 1.28 at the existing earning level, its Return on equity is 27.3 while it is paying only 6% and 7% to debenture holders and preference shareholders respectively. The equity shareholders are benefited with the financial leverage. Financial leverage is 1.28. Due to this financial leverage, ROE has increased from 27.3% to 44.8%. However, when there is a fall of 50% in earnings, ROE has fallen from 27.3% to 9.8%.

Financial leverage is a double-edged sword. In other words, when EBIT increases ROE and EPS increase by a higher percentage. Similarly when EBIT falls, ROE and EPS fall by a greater percentage than EBIT.

When EBIT has gone up by 50%, both ROE and EPS have increased by 64%. Similarly, when the EBIT has fallen by 50%, both ROE and EPS have decreased by 64%. (50% × 1.28).

Financial leverage shows the impact on EPS. Trading on equity shows the impact on ROE.

Illustration No. 16

A Ltd. has equity share capital of ₹ 5,00,000 divided into shares of ₹ 100 each. It wishes to raise further ₹ 3,00,000 for expansion cum modernization plans. The company plans the following financing schemes.

(i) All equity stock.

(ii) ₹ one lakh in equity shares and ₹ two lakhs in 10% debentures.

(iii) All debt at 10% p.a.

(iv) ₹ one lakh in equity shares and ₹ two lakhs preference capital with rate of dividend at 8%.

The company's earnings before interest and tax (EBIT) are ₹ 1,50,000. The corporate rate of tax is 50%.

You are required to determine earning per share (EPS) in each plan and comment on the implications of financial leverage.

If the company suffers a loss of ₹ 70,000, discuss the impact of leverage under all the four plans.

Solution

	Plan I ₹	Plan II ₹	Plan III ₹	Plan IV ₹
Earnings before interest and tax	1,50,000	1,50,000	1,50,000	1,50,000
Less: Interest	----	20,000	30,000	-----
	1,50,000	1,30,000	1,20,000	1,50,000
Less: Tax @ 50%	75,000	65,000	60,000	75,000
Earnings after tax	75,000	65,000	60,000	75,000
Less: Preference dividend @ 8%	----	-----	----	16,000
Earnings available for equity stockholders	75,000	65,000	60,000	59,000
No. of equity shares	8,000	6,000	5,000	6,000
Earnings per share	₹ 9.375	₹ 10.83	₹ 12	₹ 9.83

Comments

In the four plans of fresh financing, Plan III is the most leveraged of all as highest component of debt is used in expansion cum modernization. In this case, additional financing is done by raising loans @ 10% interest. Plan II has fresh capital stock of ₹ one lakh and ₹ two lakhs from loans. Plan IV does not have fresh loans but preference capital has been raised for ₹ two lakhs.

The earnings per share is highest in Plan III i.e. ₹ 12. This plan depends upon entire fixed cost funds and thus has benefited equity shareholders by increasing their share in profits. Plan II is the next best scheme where EPS is ₹ 10.83. In this case too, ₹ 2 lakhs are raised through fixed cost funds. Even in Plan IV where preference capital of ₹ 2 lakhs is issued, it is better than Plan I where entire expansion is made through equity shares ₹ 3 lakhs.

The analysis of this information shows that financial leverage has helped in improving earnings per share for equity shareholders. It helps to conclude that higher the ratio of debt to equity, the greater the return for equity stockholders.

Impact of Leverage on loss of ₹ 70,000:

	Plan I ₹	Plan II ₹	Plan III ₹	Plan IV ₹
Loss before interest and tax	– 70,000	– 70,000	– 70,000	– 70,000
Add: interest	---	20,000	30,000	----
Loss: after interest	– 70,000	– 90,000	– 1,00,000	– 70,000
No. of Equity shares	8,000	6,000	5,000	6,000
Loss per share	₹ 8.75	₹ 15	₹ 20	₹ 11.67

Comments

Loss per share is the highest in Plan III because it has the higher debt-equity ratio while it is the lowest in Plan I because all additional funds are raised through equity capital. The leverage with plan III will have an adverse impact on earnings, if firm suffers losses because fixed cost securities are the highest that will magnify the losses.

Conclusion

The plan that has the highest financial leverage would be the most advantageous so long as operating profits are increasing. However, if firm starts incurring losses, that plan will magnify the losses per share.

Illustration No. 17

The following information has been given in respect of a company:

S. No.	Particulars	₹
1	Equity share capital (dividend into shares of ₹ 10 each)	10,00,000
2	Debentures (14 %)	30,00,000
3	Selling price per unit	50
4	Variable costs per unit	30
5	Fixed costs	12,00,000

The company is producing at present 1,00,000 units. Now the management of the company plans to increase output by 25%. The tax rate for the company is 40%.

On the basis of above information, you are required to make out the following calculations for the existing as well as the planned level of output.

(a) Operating leverage

(b) Financial leverage

(c) Earnings per share

(BU, MBA, 2003)

Solution

	Existing level	Proposed level (25 % increase)
Production	1,00,000 units	1,25,000 units
Sales @ ₹ 50	50,00,000	62,50,000
Variable cost @ ₹ 30	30,00,000	37,50,000
Contribution	20,00,000	25,00,000
Less: Fixed costs	12,00,000	12,00,000
EBIT	8,00,000	13,00,000
Less: Interest on debentures	4,20,000	4,20,000
Profit before tax (PBT)	3,80,000	8,80,000
Tax @ 40 %	1,52,000	3,52,000
Profit after tax	2,28,000	5,28,000
Operating leverage $= \frac{\text{Contribution}}{\text{EBIT}}$	$\frac{20,00,000}{8,00,000} = 2.5$	$\frac{25,00,000}{13,00,000} = 1.92$
Financial leverage $= \frac{\text{EBIT}}{\text{PBT}}$	$\frac{8,00,000}{3,80,000} = 2.11$	$\frac{13,00,000}{8,80,000} = 1.48$
Earnings per equity share $= \frac{\text{Profit after tax}}{\text{Number of equity shares}}$	$\frac{2,28,000}{1,00,000} = 2.28$	$\frac{5,28,000}{1,00,000} = 5.28$

Illustration No. 18

Find out the financial leverage from the following data and analyze.

Selling price	₹ 10
Variable cost	₹ 6
Number of units sold	20,000
9% interest on a loan of	₹ 2,00,000
Tax rate	40%

Calculate profit after tax.

In case, the company has 9% preference share capital in place of loan, what is the financial leverage?

Explain the reasons for the difference in financial leverage in both the alternatives. Does source of funds influences financial leverage? Draw conclusion based on the above data.

Solution

Selling price	₹ 10
Variable cost	₹ 6
Contribution	4

Total contribution = Contribution per unit × Number of units sold

= 4 × 20,000

= 80,000

There are no fixed costs, hence EBIT = 80,000

EBIT	80,000
Interest	18,000
PBT	62,000
Tax @ 30%	18,600
PAT	43,400

$$\text{Financial leverage} = \frac{\text{EBIT}}{\text{PBT}}$$

$$= \frac{80{,}000}{62{,}000}$$

$$= 1.29$$

In case, company has company has 9% preference share capital in place of loan, financial leverage is:

EBIT	80,000
Dividend to preference shareholders (gross)	30,000*
PBT	50,000

$$\text{Financial leverage} = \frac{80{,}000}{50{,}000}$$

$$= 1.6$$

Financial leverage is more (1.6) in case the firm has preference share capital in place of long-term loan (1.29). Firm does not enjoy tax benefit on dividend payable to preference shares while interest is admissible for tax benefit. Due to this reason, financial leverage is more, in case preference share capital is used in place of long-term loan.

Conclusion: Source of funds used in business influences financial leverage, in particular when one source enjoys tax benefit while the other does not.

* Dividend to preference shareholders (net) is ₹ 18,000. Dividend does not enjoy tax benefit unlike interest. So, company has to pay income-tax on dividend component too. So, total liability to company is both dividend as well as tax on it. So, the net amount (18,000) has to be grossed up which becomes 30,000.

Check Your Understanding

(A) State whether the following statements are True or False

1. In financial management, the term 'leverage' is used to describe the firm's ability to use fixed cost assets or funds to magnify the return to its owners.
2. The use of debt funds in a profit making and tax paying business does not improve the return to equity shareholders.
3. A firm's use of fixed-charge securities like debentures and preference shares in its plan of financing assets is called Financial Leverage.
4. Financial leverage occurs when a firm borrows funds.
5. A high operating leverage factor indicates presence of automated production processes.
6. If a firm's fixed costs were higher the operating leverage as well as operating risk of the firm would be higher.
7. A totally equity financed firm also has financial risk.
8. Earning per share is affected by degree of financial leverage.
9. The ideal situation is to have a low operating leverage and high financial leverage, provided the firm has enough profitable opportunities.
10. If Company A has an operating leverage of '3' and company B has operating leverage of '4'; company B has less amount of business risk.
11. A high break-even point would indicate a high operating leverage.
12. Higher degree of operating leverage indicates larger business risk and higher degree of financial leverage shows larger financial risk.
13. Financial leverage shows the impact on EPS while trading on equity shows the impact on ROE.
14. High degree of operating leverage is a boon for a firm during inflation as well as depression periods.
15. EBIT is a linking point between the operating leverage and financial leverage.

Answers

1. True 2. False 3. True 4. True 5. True 6. True 7. False 8. True
9. True 10. False 11. True 12. True 13. True 14. False 15. True

(B) Fill in the blanks:

i. Financial leverage is also known as .... , when it is positive.

ii. Firms that have a high ratio of fixed costs to variable costs are said to operate with a high degree of........

iii. A firm will have favourable leverage if its .... is more than the debt cost.

iv. A management would be considered too cautious if both operating leverage and financial leverage are kept ....

v. Operating Leverage x Financial Leverage = ...

vi. The shareholders of a company, which has a high financial leverage stand to gain when the company's return on investment (ROI) is .... as compared to .... of debt.

vii. Financial leverage indicates disproportionate change in taxable income as a result of change in ....

viii. If a firm can obtain funds at an interest rate lower than it's internal rate of return, rate of return on equity capital increases, which is known as ....

Answers:

i.	Trading on Equity	ii.	Operating leverage	iii.	ROI
iv.	Low	v.	Combined leverage or total leverage		
vi.	Higher, cost, vii. EBIT	viii.	Financial leverage/trading on equity.		

(C) Objective Questions (Identify what is most appropriate)

1. If a profit making and tax paying firm borrows at a rate of interest lower than the return on capital employed, the return on equity will be ... than/to return on capital employed.

   (A) equal (B) more (C) lower

2. Financial leverage always improves the total return on capital employed.

   (A) Yes (B) No certainty (C) No

3. Other things being constant, if firm A has more operating leverage than firm B, then a given percentage of decline in sales will cause a larger percentage of decline for firm A than for firm B in

   (A) EBIT (B) Net Income

   (C) Both EBIT and net income (D) Neither EBIT nor net income

4. Other things being constant, if firm A has more financial leverage than firm B, then a given percentage of increase in operating income causes a large percentage of increase of.... for firm A, compared to firm B.

   (A) EBIT (B) Net income (C) Neither (A) nor (B)

   (D) Both (A) and (B) (E) EPS

5. Financial leverage is different from operating leverage in that the former is concerned with

   (A) capital structure (B) uncertainty of markets

   (C) inefficient finance manager (D) None of these

6. In general, financial leverage is more favourable whenever return on asset exceeds
   (A) total cost of capital (B) cost of debt
   (C) cost of equity share capital (D) net return after taxes
7. Highly leveraged companies are advantageous in industries where sales are
   (A) increasing around a trend line (B) relatively stable
   (C) relatively unstable (D) expected to decline
   (E) relatively uncertain with increasing margin
8. The term trading on equity is generally used for .... financial leverage.
   (A) unfavourable (B) favourable (C) indifferent
9. The variability of. ...caused by the financial leverage is called financial risk.
   (A) contribution (B) EPS (C) EBIT
10. Operating leverage affects earnings ...interest and tax while financial leverage affects earnings ... interest and tax.
    (A) before, after (B) after, before
    (C) before, before (D) after, after
11. Highly automated firms contains high
    (A) Financial leverage (B) Operating leverage (C) Combined leverage
12. Which of the following ratios is the best indicator of the degree of financial leverage used by a firm?
    (A) Current ratio (B) Debt to equity ratio.
    (C) Return on assets (D) Return on sales.

Answers

1. (B) 2. (B) 3. (C) 4. (E) 5. (A) 6. (B) 7. (B) 8. (B) 9. (B) 10. (A) 11. (B) 12. (B).

Descriptive Questions

1. What do you understand by the term 'Leverage'? Define operating leverage. Explain its significance and impact on profits? **(9.1, 9.2 and 9.4)**
2. What is Operating Leverage? Would you like to have higher operating leverage or higher operating profit, if you have to choose only one of those? Why? **(9.4)**
3. Would you prefer high degree of operating leverage or low degree of operating leverage under normal market conditions? Why? **(9.4 and 9.4.3)**
4. A retail firm and an airline are typical examples of low and high operating leverage, respectively. Discuss. **(9.4 and 9.4.1)**
5. "High degree of operating leverage is a boon during inflation period, while the same is a curse during depression or period of declining prices"–Discuss. **(9.4.3)**
6. Explain the concept of 'Financial Leverage'. Show the impact of financial leverage on earnings per share. **(9.5)**

7. In what manner is financial leverage related to operating leverage? Discuss with an example. **(B.U. MBA 2003) (9.6, 9.6.1 and 9.6.2)**
8. Compare the nature of financial leverage with operating leverage. **(9.10 and 9.11)**
9. What is financial leverage? Describe the circumstances to be present in a firm for financial leverage. **(9.5)**
10. Explain the importance of right mix of operating leverage and financial leverage to a firm. **(9.6)**
11. 'Trading on Equity is a double-edged sword'–Explain with a suitable example. **(9.7)**
12. 'Financial Leverage is a double-edged sword'–Explain and illustrate with a suitable example, taking hypothetical data. **(9.7)**
13. Leverages are double-edged weapons and should be used with care. Explain this statement and show practical uses of operating leverage and financial leverage. **(9.4.2 and 9.7)**
14. Write short notes on:

    (A) Combined Leverage **(9.12)**

    (B) Significance and limitations of Financial Leverage. **(9.8 and 9.9)**

Short Questions

Q.1. What do you understand by leverage?

Ans. The term 'leverage' is derived from 'Lever', which indicates some means of lifting heavy objects. Leverage allows us to do things which otherwise are not possible. This concept of 'leverage' is valid in business too. In financial management, term 'leverage' is used to describe firm's ability to use fixed cost assets or funds to magnify earnings or returns to owners of the firm. The finance manager uses leverage to determine the best mix of funds to influence risk and return of equity shareholders.

Q.2. What is operating leverage? Explain consequence of a higher operating leverage to a firm.

Ans. Operating leverage refers to the proportion of fixed costs in the cost structure. Fixed costs do not change with change in sales but they remain same. Since fixed costs remain same irrespective of sales, percentage of change in operating profit will be more than percentage change in sales. Suppose, operating leverage of a firm is 3, what is its consequence? For a change of 100% in sales, operating profit (EBIT) would increase by 300%. Similarly if sales fall by 100%, operating profit falls by 300%. Higher operating leverage is a boon in boom times but a great curse during recession period as sales of a firm normally falls with a general decline in demand.

Q.3. Explain 'Business risk' and 'Financial risk' briefly.

Ans. The main factors or causes for business risk are uncertainty of sales and production costs. The consequence is volatility of operating income (EBIT). Change in operating income would be more than the change in sales. High fixed costs cause this situation.

The cause for financial risk is the presence of fixed financial costs. It influences earnings per equity share (EPS). Financial risk is due to the presence of high fixed return funds such as debentures and long-term loans. Here, firm has to pay fixed interest irrespective of profits.

In nutshell, business risk causes greater change in operating profits (EBIT) while financial risk causes greater change in EPS.

Q.4. Financial leverage of a company is three. Describe its consequence to that firm in a sagging economy.

Ans. The characteristic of a slow down in economy is fall in sales. People do not get new jobs and firms try to reduce man power to cut costs. Due to reduction of sales, firms experience reduced operating profits. When financial leverage of a firm is three, it indicates that there is a heavy fixed commitment of interest to the company, which it cannot reduce in the short run. If operating profits falls by 100%, EPS would fall by 300%. No firm is flexible in respect of fixed interest costs as they cannot be reduced in the short run. Firm that has high financial leverage would experience more difficulty compared to firms with lower operating leverage.

Q.5. What is the utility and importance of 'Leverage' to a finance manager?

Ans. 'Leverage' plays an important role in increasing earning per share, which influences market price of a share. Every one is interested that the price of share is up in the market. A proper combination of both operating leverage and financial leverage is a blessing for firm's growth, while an improper combination may prove to be a curse. During recession period, in particular, if combination were not in proper/proportion, adverse effects would be more severe. It is duty of finance manager to bring such a combination of operating leverage and financial leverage that suits the risk-bearing capacity of the firm.

Q.6. Sudhanshu & Co is not enjoying any long-term borrowing for its business. However, to meet its working capital requirements, the firm is enjoying a cash credit limit of ₹ 10 lakhs from Canara Bank, Gulmohar branch. Is there any financial leverage to the firm?

Ans. No. Sudhanshu & Co is not having any long-term commitment in the form of interest burden. Fixed financial costs are a primary requisite for financial leverage. Interest in a cash credit account is always under control of firm as it can stop utilizing the limit any time unlike interest on a debenture or a long-term a loan, which is a permanent burden once taken. As firm is not having any long-term borrowing, there is no financial leverage.

Interview Questions

Q.1. Explain difference between operating leverage and financial leverage.

Ans. Employment of fixed costs creates operating leverage. Employment of fixed return funds creates financial leverage.

Q.2. What is the cause of operating leverage?

Ans. Fixed operating costs cause operating leverage.

Q.3. What are different leverages? Which one is better?

Ans. Leverages are of three types—operating leverage, financial leverage and combined leverage, last is derived from both. An ideal combination to a firm is to have low operating leverage and high financial leverage provided opportunities are available to utilize borrowed funds profitably.

Q.4. State the main advantage of high operating leverage.

Ans. A high operating leverage results in higher operating profits than the corresponding increase in volume of sales. Firm that is having high operating leverage stands to gain in boom times.

Q.5. Which type of firms are worst affected during slowdown in a market witnessing fall in sales?

Ans. When market is undergoing slowdown in sales, firm that would have high operating leverage stands to lose more compared to other firms in the same industry.

Q.6. What is the cause of financial leverage?

Ans. Fixed financial charges cause financial leverage.

Q.7. What is a debt-free company? Does it enjoy the advantage of financial leverage?

Ans. A debt-free company is one which is free from debts. All its fixed assets, are totally financed from long–term sources. As there is no permanent debt, debt-free company does not enjoy any advantage of financial leverage. Financial leverage has the advantage as well as disadvantage. To a debt-free company, both would not be there.

Q.8. What is the advantage to a debt-free company during recession times?

Ans. The greatest advantage to a debt-free company is in times of recession. During recession almost every company would experience fall in sales. All debt companies experience difficulty in servicing debt due to fixed commitment of interest obligations. When profits are under pressure, debt companies face problems to pay interest obligations while such problems would not exist with debt-free companies.

Q.9. What is meant by servicing debt?

Ans. Debt carries a fixed interest obligation. Interest is to be paid by a company irrespective of profits. Payment of interest at the stipulated interest rate at the prescribed periodical intervals—monthly, quarterly or half-yearly or annually is called servicing of debt.

Q.10. What is the advantage in having financial leverage?

Ans. Financial leverage brings the benefit of increasing earnings per share as long as the return on investment is higher than cost of debt. It is a great temptation to a finance manager to employ debt in improving earnings per share.

Q.11. What are the adverse effects of high operating leverage?

Ans. High operating leverage results in greater fluctuations in operating profits i.e. EBIT. During recession, demand decreases resulting in a reduced volume of sales. Consequently, fall in operating profits would be greater than the fall in sales.

Q.12. Name the ill effect of high financial leverage.

Ans. Wide fluctuations in earnings per equity share are likely to occur due to high financial leverage. This is the ill effect of high financial leverage.

Q.13. If combined leverage of a firm is high compared to other firms in the same industry, what does it indicate?

Ans. It indicates that the concerned firm is highly aggressive. Its earnings per share would be highly volatile.

OO

CHAPTER 10

Instruments of Long-term Finance

10.1 INTRODUCTION

Joint stock companies have become the common forms of business in modern times. They enjoy the powers of a legal entity which enable them to carry on the business like a normal person. Finance is said to be the life-blood of any enterprise. Without finance, no enterprise can accomplish its objectives. Capital required for any business enterprise can be classified under two main categories. They are:

(A) Fixed Capital and

(B) Working Capital

Here, in this chapter, we deal with fixed capital. Fixed capital is provided by long-term securities. The two long-term securities available to a company are shares and debentures. Shares include Equity shares and Preference shares. Equity shares provide ownership status to investors. Debentures are a form of loan capital. Those who provide funds through debentures are only lenders. Long-term finance is also provided by term lending institutions too in the form of term loans. Different means of long-term finance enjoy merits and demerits, differently. What are those merits and demerits and why both types of securities are needed? Let us discuss.

10.2 KINDS OF OWNERSHIP SECURITIES

The Companies Act, 1956 permit issue of two types of shares. They are Equity shares and Preference shares. What is the need for a company to issue two types of shares? All investors are not alike. Some investors prefer higher returns, even uncertain, and, in turn, are prepared to take risk. Another category of investors wishes to have regular returns, though it may be relatively low. Company may need to issue two types of shares to tap the required funds. Only one type may not serve all the requirements of the company adequately, and different types serve the investors' requirements suitably.

10.3 EQUITY SHARES

Equity shares were earlier known as ordinary shares or common shares. Equity shareholders are the real owners of the company as they have the voting rights and enjoy decision-making authority on important matters related to the company.

The equity shareholders' return is in the form of dividend, depends on the profits of the company and capital gain/loss, at the time of their sale.

They enjoy higher returns, if the company performs well and may not get any dividend, at all, if the company does not perform well or when the Board of Directors do not recommend any dividend for payment. **Therefore, equity shares are known as 'variable income security'.** They are the last one to get repayment in the event of liquidation of the company.

10.4 FEATURES OR CHARACTERISTICS OF EQUITY SHARES

Equity shares enjoy a number of special characteristics which distinguish it from other securities. They relate to their rights and claims, which are:

1. **Claim on Income:** Equity shareholders enjoy their claim on the residual income of the company. Residual income is that part of income which is left in the business after meeting all the expenses, interest on debentures, taxes and preference dividend, if any. This income may be split into two parts: dividend and retained earnings. If income is distributed to shareholders, it is called dividend. If the income is not distributed, it remains with the company in the form of retained profits. Additionally, the shareholders stand to benefit in the form of enhanced value, capital gain, when the shares are sold. So, residual income benefits the shareholders immediately in the form of dividend, or later by way of capital gains. Dividend is not tax deductible to the company.

   Distribution of dividend is the discretionary right or prerogative of the Board of Directors. Even if the profits are sufficient and, in fact, even if the profits increase as compared to the earlier year, still the equity shareholders cannot legally compel the company to declare dividend. Thus, equity share is not an assured security from the investors' point of view as they are not sure of dividend rate. More so, capital gains/loss depends on the market value at the time of their sale. So, equity shares are risky security, too.

Though equity shareholders cannot compel the company to increase the rate of dividend, they can reduce the dividend, recommended by Board of Directors, in the interests of the company.

2. **Claim on Assets:** Equity shareholders have a residual claim on the ownership of company's assets. In the event of liquidation of a company, the claims of creditors are paid first, later to preference shareholders, if any, and balance goes to the equity shareholders. Company, normally, goes into liquidation, when the going is not good; and so, the equity shareholders may not get back much of their investment. So, equity shares provide cushion to absorb losses, in the event of liquidation of the company.

3. **Right to Control or Voting Rights:** Equity shareholders are the real owners of the company. They have a voting right in the working of the company. The Board of Directors, appointed by the equity shareholders in the Annual General Meeting, exercise real control over the company. So, equity shareholders exercise an indirect control over the company. But, such control is, often, weak due to their indifference in casting their voting rights. More so, they are scattered. Most of the shareholders do not attend even the annual general meeting and even if they attend, they care more for the gifts that the company distributes rather than participating seriously in the proceedings of the meetings.

4. **Pre-emptive Rights:** As and when a public limited company wants to issue fresh equity shares, they are to be offered first to the existing shareholders. This is known as pre-emptive right. The purpose is to enable the shareholders to continue to have proportionate share of ownership. For example, if a shareholder has 5% ownership, he has to be offered 5% of the new shares to be issued. The shareholders' option to purchase a stated number of new shares at a specified price, determined by Board of Directors, during a given period is called 'Rights'. Rights are valuable to the existing shareholders as the company issues shares, normally at a price, lower than the market rate. This right is made available to prevent the management to issue shares to persons of their choice. This right protects the shareholders from dilution of their holding (financial interest) as well as to retain their control. If the shareholders do not want to exercise their rights, they can sell them too for a price, as they are valuable.

5. **Limited Liability:** Another distinct feature 'liability' of the equity shareholder is limited to the face value of the shares. In case the shareholder has paid the full amount of the face value, he is no more liable even if the company goes into liquidation and its liabilities are more than its assets. In case of sole proprietorship or partnership firm, liability is unlimited. This limited liability feature attracts even otherwise, unwilling investors to invest in a limited company. This enables the firm to raise the risky funds in the market by issuing equity shares.

10.4.1 Pros and Cons of Equity Financing

Equity capital is the most important form of long-term source of financing. Its merits and demerits are as under:

Merits

1. **No Outflow of Cash:** It is a permanent source of capital. The company need not have any fear of redemption, with the outflow of cash. These funds are available till the company goes into liquidation.
2. **Borrowing Base:** What a company can borrow depends on its capital base. Lenders feel confident to lend, looking to the capital base and they lend in proportion to the company's equity capital.
3. **No obligation to Pay Dividend:** There is no fixed obligation to pay dividend. In case of financial difficulties, it can reduce or even suspend payment of dividend.
4. **Real Owners and Gainers:** They are the real owners of the company as they have the voting right. In case of profits, they are the real gainers by way of increased dividend as well as appreciation of market price.

Demerits

1. **Cost:** Cost of equity shares is the highest to a company as dividend is not tax deductible. More so, floatation costs are also high compared to debt. Floatation costs are those costs which are incurred by the company incidental to the issue of shares.
2. **Trading on Equity:** Trading on equity is possible when debt is issued along with equity shares. But, trading on equity is not possible when the total requirements of the company is met by equity share capital alone. Trading on equity magnifies the earnings of equity shares.
3. **Risk:** From the view-point of investors, equity is more risky compared to debt as there is no certainty of return. So, investors want higher return to invest in equity shares. It is more difficult and costly for the company to raise funds through equity.
4. **Earnings Dilution:** If company raises funds through equity and its earnings do not increase in the proportion of the additional issue of shares, the earnings per share gets diluted.
5. **Ownership Dilution:** Pre-emptive right enables the existing shareholder to buy new shares and maintain the proportionate ownership. For maintaining control, additional funds are needed. In case of financial difficulty to invest, the existing control is likely to be lost. This is the threat with a closely held company.

10.4.2 Bonus Shares

Bonus shares are issued to reward the existing equity shareholders. Companies make abnormal profits but do not want to increase the dividend rate to conserve cash to meet the expansion plans. To satisfy the expectations of the eager shareholders who anticipate a higher dividend rate, companies issue bonus shares. Expansion plans require liquidity and increased dividend rate result in outgo of cash. Bonus shares are a solution to reward the shareholders, without foregoing liquidity. With the issue of bonus shares, there is no cash outgo.

Balance in share premium, general reserves or profit and loss account or capital reserves are utilized for issue of bonus shares. Amount from these accounts is transferred to equity share capital account and in this process, bonus shares are issued. This is a book adjustment. Bonus shares are the children of equity shares. Only existing equity shareholder are benefited. If a bonus issue of 1 : 4 is made, it means existing equity shareholder who is holding four shares get one bonus share. Consequent on bonus shares, normally, market price of the existing share falls. Number of equity shares would increase immediately but profits do not increase in the same proportion, immediately. As a result, there would be no change in the wealth of existing equity shareholders. There is no change in the net worth of company. Net worth remains the same both before and after issue of bonus shares. When profits increase in the same proportion of issue of bonus shares, company would be in a position to maintain the same dividend rate.

Bonus shares are free shares issued to existing equity shareholders. So, announcement of bonus is normally welcomed by the equity market. Price of equity shares immediately flares if market expectations are fulfilled, but falls later after the issue of bonus shares. Key for the market price is to what extent the company fulfils the expectations of market.

10.4.3 Rights Shares

As and when a company issues new equity shares, the new shares are to be offered to the existing equity shareholders. The existing equity shareholders enjoy the right to receive the offer first. Purpose behind this right is to protect the interests of equity shareholders and prevent the company to offer new shares to outsiders, depriving the existing equity shareholders. This helps the existing equity shareholders to retain their proportionate holding and control. Normally, company offers the new equity shares at a rate lower than the prevailing market price. So, equity shareholders who do not want to exercise the rights can sell the rights in the market and make profit for the difference between the market price and price at which the share offered.

10.5 PREFERENCE SHARES

As the very name suggests, preference shares have certain preferences compared to equity shares. They enjoy preference in respect of payment of dividend. Whenever company has surplus profits, before payment of dividend to the equity shareholders, dividend is to be paid to preference shareholders. The second preference relates to repayment in the event of liquidation of the company. After paying outside creditors, preference share capital is returned, before repaying to equity shareholders.

Preference shareholders enjoy the twin preferences in respect of dividend payment and repayment of principal amount, in the event of liquidation, compared to equity shareholders.

10.5.1 Features

Preference shares have several features. They are:

1. **Claims on Income and Assets: Preference share is a senior security compared to equity share:** It has a prior claim on the company's income and repayment. Dividend is to be paid on preference shares, before payment on equity shares. Similarly, repayment is to be made to preference shareholders, in preference to equity shareholders, in the event of liquidation of the company.
2. **Fixed Dividend:** The dividend rate is fixed in the case of preference shares. Dividend payment to preference shareholders is not a legal obligation on the part of the company. However, companies honour payment of dividend, when they make adequate profits. Otherwise, company's image would be adversely affected. The important point to be noted is that company cannot pay dividend to equity shareholders without paying dividend to preference shareholders. This indirectly forces the company to declare and pay dividend to preference shareholders, as management of every company wants to keep equity shareholders in good humour by declaring suitable dividend, dependant on profits of company.
3. **Cumulative Dividend:** Dividend is cumulative in case of cumulative preference shares. This is the position unless a contrary intention is specified at the time of issue of these shares. This is a protective right to the preference shareholders as the dividend in arrears is to be paid to them, before declaring dividend to equity shareholders. Preference shareholders cannot force the company to pay dividend and non-payment does not result in liquidation of company. As they do not have the enforcing right to pay dividend, cumulative feature is valuable to them.
4. **Voting Rights:** Preference shareholders do not have any voting right in the management of the company. However, they have a right to vote in respect of those matters that affect them directly. In case dividend is in arrears for two consecutive years, preference shareholders can nominate a member on the board of the company.

5. **Maturity:** Preference shares are perpetual. They are not repaid, similar to equity shares in the normal course. Their money is returned in the event of liquidation, after payment of debenture holders. However, in case of redeemable preference shares, the amount is returned on the due date as per the terms of issue.
6. **Hybrid form of security: In the real sense, preference share capital is a hybrid form security, as it carries some of the features of equity share as well as debenture**. Preference share is similar to equity share, as non-payment of dividend does not compel the company to go into liquidation. Payment of dividend is not obligatory. However, dividend paid is not tax deductible. Similar to debenture, preference share has a fixed rate of dividend, just like a fixed rate of interest. They cannot claim a share in the residual profits of the company.

Preference shares are a hybrid form of security to a joint stock company as they enjoy some of the features of both the equity shares and debentures.

10.5.2 Advantages of Preference Shares

Preference shares provide a number of advantages, both to the company as well as to its investors.

(A) Company's Point of view: The company has the following advantages by issuing preference shares:

1. **No Legal Obligation:** Preference dividend is payable, if the company has distributable profits only. Hence, there is no legal obligation or committed financial burden to the company.
2. **Fixed Dividend:** The preference dividend is restricted to the stated amount, specified at its issue time. Preference shareholders cannot participate in the surplus profits of the company.
3. **Long-term Capital:** There is no threat of cash outflow to the company as the capital is permanent. In case of redeemable preference shares only, they are to be redeemed at the end of specified period out of the proceeds of fresh issue of shares or accumulated profits of the company.
4. **Cost of Capital:** As an instrument of financing, the cost of capital of preference shares is less than that of equity shares.
5. **Trading on Equity:** Company can take advantage of trading on equity, when the return on investment is higher than the dividend rate. Raising funds through this source magnifies the earning of the equity shares, paying a fixed rate of dividend to preference shareholders. **This is a risk-free leverage advantage with preference share capital**. Even, default in payment of dividend does not force the company into insolvency.
6. **Enhances Creditworthiness/Borrowing Ability:** As preference share capital is generally regarded as part of net worth, it enhances creditworthiness of the

firm. Preference shares strengthen the financial position of the company. In consequence, it enhances the ability of the company to borrow more.

7. **No Dilution of Control:** Preference shares carry voting rights only if the matter, directly affects their interests. Under normal circumstances, they do not enjoy voting rights and, so, there is no threat of dilution of control from preference shareholders.
8. **No Assets are Pledged:** No specific assets are pledged, while issuing preference shares. So, company's mortgageable assets are not disturbed in any manner.

> **Trading on capital is possible with preference share capital, when the return on those funds is higher than the cost of capital, which in turn magnifies the return of equity shareholders.**

(B) Investors' Point of view: Investors enjoy the following advantages:

1. **Fixed Rate of Dividend:** In case of cumulative preference shares, even if the company has made loss in one year, dividend for that year has to be paid from the subsequent year's profits. In the case of non-cumulative preference shares, this is not the case. Dividend need not be paid for the year of loss.
2. **Superior Security over Equity Shares:** Preference shareholders enjoy preference for payment of dividend and return of funds, compared to equity shares. So, investors prefer to invest in preference shares.
3. **Voting Rights:** Preference shareholders can exercise voting rights on those resolutions that directly affects their rights.

10.5.3 Disadvantages of Preference Shares

Inspite of many advantages, they suffer from the following shortcomings.

(A) Company's Point of view

1. **Costly Source:** Investors expect a higher return, compared to rate of interest on debentures, as risk with preference share capital is greater. So, preference share capital is costlier compared to debentures.
2. **Tax Disadvantage:** Dividend on preference shares is not tax deductible, while interest payment on debentures or debt enjoys tax shield or advantage.
3. **Affects Creditworthiness:** There is no legal obligation to the company for payment of preference dividend. However, non-payment affects the creditworthiness of the company. If preference shares are cumulative, company has to pay the dividend to them, before the dividend is paid to equity shares.

(B) Preference Shareholders' Point of view

1. **At Management's Mercy:** As preference shareholders do not have any voting rights, normally, they remain at the mercy of management for dividend as well as redemption of share capital.
2. **Lower Return:** Compared to equity shares, the return is always lower.

3. **No Charge on Assets:** Assets are charged to debentures. Such charge of assets is not available to the preference shares, and so, they rank after debentures, in case of liquidation of the company.

10.6 DEBENTURES

A company may raise long-term finance by issuing debentures. A debenture is a long-term promissory note for raising loan capital. Those who invest in debentures are called debenture holders. **An alternative form of debenture is Bond, in India.** Public sector companies in India, mostly issue bonds.

A debenture holder is a creditor of a company. Company pays the debenture holders interest and principal as per the terms of debentures issued. The interest that is paid is a charge to the profit and loss account. Debentures are, normally, secured by a floating charge on the assets of the company.

10.6.1 Features of Debentures

Debenture or Bond is a creditorship security, with a fixed rate of interest and fixed maturity period. **Debentures provide low risk capital to the company.** The salient characteristics of debentures are as follows:

1. **Interest Rate:** The interest rate is fixed and does not change during the tenure of debenture, irrespective of the profit/loss of the company. Interest is calculated on the face value of the debenture. Interest is tax deductible to a company. However, interest is an income and taxable in the hands of the debenture holder.
2. **Maturity:** Debentures are issued for a specific period of time. Normally, they provide long-term finance. Debentures are, normally, issued for a period of 7 to 10 years. They are to be redeemed on the specific date.
3. **Claim on Income:** Interest is to be paid to the debenture holder irrespective of the earnings of the income. Company is under a legal obligation to pay interest. Default in payment of interest empowers the debenture holder to move a petition in a court of law for the winding up of the company.
4. **Claim on Assets:** In the event of liquidation, debenture holders are to be repaid first, before repayment is made to preference and equity shareholders. Debentures may have a specific charge or floating charge on the assets of the company. In that event, they are secured creditors. The sale proceeds of the assets pledged to them go towards repayment of principal and interest to them. In case, the sale proceeds are inadequate, they stand as unsecured creditors for the balance amount. For the balance, they rank paripasu (standing on the same footing), along with unsecured creditors. In other words, for the balance amount, they rank equally along with unsecured creditors.

5. **Control:** As debenture holders are creditors of the company, they do not have any voting right and cannot participate in the management of the company. They enjoy only a prior claim in repayment, over equity and preference shareholders.
6. **Call Feature:** Debentures may provide a call feature. **Call feature enables the company to redeem the debentures before the due date of redemption.** Company invokes the call feature, when the interest rate payable on debenture is high and the current interest rate is low. To save costs, company redeems the debentures before the due date. Normally, call price is higher than the issue price. As company is gaining, it does not mind to share some of its gain with the debenture holders.
7. **Indenture or Trust Deed:** Indenture or trust deed is a legal agreement between the company issuing debentures on one hand, and the trustees representing debenture holders on the other hand. The trust deed provides the specific terms in respect of the description of debentures, security available, rights of debenture holders and of the issuing company and responsibilities of the trustees. It is the responsibility of the trustees to protect the rights of the debenture holders by enforcing the responsibilities of the company that has issued debentures. Normally, a financial institution or insurance company is appointed as a trustee.

Debentures are attractive to investors as well as company. To investors, they are secured. Interest paid on debentures is low and, more so, tax deductible to company, hence they are the most cost effective means of financing.

10.6.2 Pros and Cons of Debentures

(A) Debentures have a number of advantages as long-term source of finance:

1. **Less Costly:** It involves less cost to the company as investors are prepared to invest in debentures, accepting a lower rate of return compared to equity. Reason is investors consider debentures relatively less risky investment. To the company, interest is tax deductible, and so, the effective cost to the company is lower compared to preference and equity share capital.
2. **No Dilution:** Debenture holders do not enjoy any voting rights and so there is no threat of dilution of ownership or control.
3. **Fixed Payment of Interest:** Debenture holders are entitled to a fixed interest rate, specified in the debenture. They cannot claim any extra share in the earnings of the company. So, cost to the company is fixed.
4. **Advantage during Inflation:** Real interest cost declines during the period of inflation.
5. **Trading on Equity:** When the return on investment is more than the cost of debt, it is beneficial to the company to issue debentures as it can trade on equity and magnify the earnings of the equity shareholders. So, it is advantageous for a company to mix debentures in its capital structure, while raising funds in the market.

6. **Flexibility:** Debentures provide flexibility in the capital structure as company can redeem debentures, as and when it has surplus funds and desires to do so. Normally, companies reserve this right in the form of 'call option' at the time of issue to take advantage of the falling interest rates in the market.
7. **Easy to Raise Funds:** Even in depression period, when the market sentiment is low, it is relatively easy for the company to raise funds through debentures. Investors appreciate the advantage of certainty of income, with low risk during those periods.

(B) Limitations of Debentures: Despite the above advantages, debentures have limitations too. They are:

1. **Obligatory Payments:** Payment of interest is a legal obligation, even if the company is not in profits. Redemption of debentures is to be made on the due date. Default may force the company to go into liquidation.
2. **Financial Risk:** To a firm that has fluctuating sales and earnings, it increases the financial leverage and financial risk.
3. **Cash Outflows:** Debentures are to be redeemed at one time or other. As and when redeemed, cash outflow occurs. Even if a sinking fund is created to meet the redemption outflow, annual cash outflow occurs.
4. **Restrictive Covenants:** They are the restrictive conditions contained in the debenture indenture. For example, a condition can be incorporated in the indenture that the total borrowing by a company cannot exceed a specified limit. So, the restrictive covenants limit the operating flexibility of the company in future.
5. **Not Possible to All Companies:** Interest is a fixed commitment. It is not desirable for companies that do not have stable earnings or who deal in products with elastic demand to issue debentures. Similarly, companies that cannot offer assets as security cannot use this source of financing.
6. **Stamp Duty:** Stamp duty increases the cost of financing.

10.7 DIFFERENCES BETWEEN SHARES AND DEBENTURES

Out of the three long-term instruments of finance – equity shares, preference shares and debentures, debentures are the least risky. Debentures carry a fixed rate of interest, which is to be paid by the company, irrespective of profits. Normally, debentures are secured. Companies offer collateral security to debenture holders to make them comfortable from the view-point of security. As they are secured, even, if the company fails and, finally goes into liquidation, debenture holders get back their money from the proceeds of their collateral security. Debenture holders are unlikely to suffer from the financial failure of the firm, in case they are secured and enough money is realized at the time of sale. In other words, debenture holders get regular return, in the form of interest and safety of funds even if things go wrong with the company.

As far as preference shareholders are concerned, they enjoy preference in respect of dividend and return of money, before equity shareholders are paid dividend and their original investment, respectively. So, preference shares are lesser risky compared to equity holders.

Equity shares bear the highest risk as there is no guarantee of dividend payment. If a company does not make profits, equity shareholders do not get any dividend at all. When company goes into liquidation, generally, equity shareholders hardly get back their money, as most of the money would have disappeared from the company towards losses by that time.

From the view-point of the investors, debentures are least risky, lesser risky are preference shares and highest risky are equity shares.

The differences between the two corporate securities are as under:

Nature of Difference	Shares	Debentures
1. Type of Capital	Part of owned capital.	Part of loan capital.
2. Type of Security	Ownership security	Creditorship security, also known as debt capital.
3. Return	Dividend on equity shares is variable, which depends on the profits of the company. Preference shares get the stated fixed rate of dividend.	Interest is fixed and it depends on contractual terms.
4. Impact on Profit and Loss	Appropriation of Profit.	Fixed expense. Charge on profit and loss account.
5. Voting Rights	Equity shares enjoy voting rights on all matters of the company. Preference shareholders enjoy voting rights on those matters that affect their interests only.	No say in management. No Voting Rights.
6. Redemption	Equity shares are not redeemable during the life of the company. Redeemable Preference shares are redeemed at the end of the specified period.	Redeemed at the end of the specified period, stated in the indenture.
7. Priority of Repayment	At the time of liquidation, first outside liabilities are repaid. Then, Preference shares are returned. If balance is left, it goes to equity shares.	Enjoy priority in repayment, over share capital.

10.8 TERM LOANS

Companies can raise long-term finance through term loans, in addition to share capital and debentures. They are obtained for financing large expansion, diversification or modernization projects. Term loans are meant for meeting medium-term and long-term financial needs.

Term lending financing is also known as project financing.

The major advantage of a term-loan is that it is for a fixed period. Repayment of the instalment can be paid back from the profit generations of the company. More so, interest liability is fixed and cannot be varied so the profitability of the project is not affected for a long-term.

10.8.1 Features

1. **Purpose:** The purpose is mostly to meet the capital expenditure.
2. **Documentation:** When shares and debentures are issued, company issues share certificates and debenture certificates respectively to the investors. In case of term loan, agreement is entered between the company and the financial institution that sanctions the term loan. The term loan document specifies all conditions of sanction, security, interest as well as repayment etc.
3. **Maturity:** Medium-term loans are for periods ranging from one to five years and long-term loans are granted for periods beyond five years.
4. **Repayment Schedule:** Normally, loans are repaid through instalment system. Interest is charged on the outstanding balance. So, interest burden declines over the years. Company has to pay interest as well as instalment amount fixed in the agreement.

   Term loan granted is meant for capital expenditure because the project may not generate revenues immediately. Certain period is needed for completion of the project and start generating revenues, which is called 'gestation period'. During this period, payment of interest as well as instalment are suspended by the financial institution, which is known as moratorium period. This aspect is also specified in the agreement.
5. **Security:** Term loans are always secured. The assets purchased through the term loan constitute the security. This is called primary security. The company's current and future assets also generally secure term loans. This is called secondary security.
6. **Direct Negotiation:** A company directly negotiates term loan for project finance with the term lending institution. Thus, term loan is a Private Placement. It saves the company underwriting commission and floatation costs. The advantages of term loan are ease of negotiation and low cost of raising funds.

7. **Restrictive Covenants:** In addition to security, the lender may also like to protect its financial interests. This is done through restrictive covenants, incorporated in the agreement while sanctioning term-loan. The restrictive covenants can be categorized as follows:
   (A) **Asset-related Covenants:** Lender may impose a condition on the borrower to maintain certain minimum current ratio. Additional charge on assets may be prohibited, without the approval of the lender.
   (B) **Liability-related Covenants:** The company may be restrained from further borrowings or not allowed to repay the existing loans, without its approval.
   (C) **Cash Flow Related Covenants:** Lenders may be restrained to declare dividend beyond a specified percentage; or further capital expenditure is not to be incurred without its consent.
   (D) **Management Related Covenants:** At the time of sanction, financial institution may stipulate a condition, to appoint its nominee director on the Board of Directors. Certain conditions may be incorporated in the agreement about the appointment of suitable personnel to manage the affairs of the company and their competence. The nominee director has to protect the interests of the lending institution, contributing to the company's policies and sound financial management.

10.9 BOOK BUILDING

Book building is a common practice in developed countries and has recently been making inroads into emerging markets as well, including India.

Book building is essentially a process used by companies for raising capital through Public Offerings–both Initial Public Offers (IPOs) and Follow-on Public Offers (FPOs) to aid price and demand discovery. It is a mechanism where during the period for which the book for the offers are open, the bids are collected from investors at various prices, which are within the price band specified by the issuer. The process is directed towards both the institutional as well as the retail investors. The issue price is determined after the bid closure, based on the demand generated in the process. Example: Larsen And Toubro Limited (Indian conglomerate) has used book building process to sell its stake (approx: 12%) in Mahindra-Satyam Ltd.

Process: During the fixed period of time for which the subscription is open, the book runner collects bids from investors at various prices, between the floor price and the cap price. Bids can be revised by the bidder before the book closes. The process aims at tapping both wholesale and retail investors. The final issue price is not determined until the end of the process when the book is closed. After the closure of the book building period, the book runner evaluates the collected bids on the basis of certain evaluation criteria and sets the final issue price.

Main advantage of book building is that it avoids under-pricing to the company. Volatility in price is avoided, after issue is made. In simple words, company takes the gain of what the speculative buyer can expect.

If demand is high enough, the book can be oversubscribed. In this case, the green-shoe option is triggered.

Check Your Understanding

(A) State whether the following are True or False

1. If company distributes income to shareholders, it is called dividend and if not distributed, it remains with the company in the form of retained profits.
2. A company normally goes into liquidation when it's going is not good and equity shareholders get back their full investment.
3. The Board of Directors appointed by the equity shareholders in the Annual General Meeting exercise control over the company.
4. Preference share is often considered to be a hybrid security.
5. Payment of dividend to preference shareholders is not a legal obligation on the part of the company, similar to equity shareholders.
6. Debentures are ownership securities.
7. Equity shareholders have a residual claim on the assets and profits of the company.
8. Debenture or Bond is a creditorship security with a fixed rate of interest and fixed maturity period.
9. The company's future assets, generally, secure term loans, which is called primary security.
10. The effective cost of debentures to a company is low, compared to preference and equity shares.
11. Preference shares are entitled to fixed dividend, though level of earnings is very high to a company in a particular year, unlike equity shareholders.
12. Company cannot declare dividend to equity shareholders, without paying dividend to preference shareholders.
13. If no mention is made, preference shares are cumulative in character in respect of dividend.

Answers

1. True 2. False 3. True 4. True 5. True 6. False 7. True 8. True
9. False 10. True 11. True 12. True 13. True.

(B) Objective Questions (Identify what is most appropriate)

1. This security is known as variable income security.

(A) Debentures (B) Preference shares

(C) Equity shares (D) Term-loan

2. Real ownership of a company rests with
   (A) Board of Directors (B) Equity shareholders (C) Preference shareholders
3. Preference share is a ... security, compared to equity share, in respect of repayment.
   (A) senior (B) junior (C) equal

Answers

1. (C) 2. (B) 3. (A).

Descriptive Questions

1. Describe the main types of securities, which are considered useful for meeting long-term financial requirements of industries? **(10.2, 10.3, 10.4, 10.5, 10.5.1, 10.6 and 10.6.1)**
2. What do you understand by long-term finance? Critically examine the importance of instruments of long-term finance? **(10.2, 10.3, 10.4, 10.5, 10.5.1, 10.6 and 10.6.1)**
3. Examine the usefulness of Debentures as an instrument of long-term finance? **(10.6 and 10.6.1)**
4. Why a preference share is called hybrid security? Explain the advantages and disadvantages of preference shares from the view-point of company and investors? **(10.5, 10.5.1, 10.5.2 and 10.5.3)**
5. What are term loans? What are their features? **(10.8 and 10.8.1)**
6. What are the features of equity shares and explain their pros and cons? **(10.3, 10.4 and 10.4.1)**
7. Bring out the differences between shares and debentures? **(10.7)**
8. 'From the view-point of the investors, debentures are least risky, lesser risky are preference shares and highest risky are equity shares'. Discuss. Bring out the differences between any two different instruments of long-term finance? **(10.7)**
9. Write short notes on
   (A) Restrictive covenants **(10.8 and 10.8.1–Point No. 7)**
   (B) Indenture **(10.6.1–Point No. 7)**
   (C) Pre-emptive rights **(10.4–Point No. 4)**
   (D) Book Building **(10.9)**

Short Questions

Q.1. Why a company issues debentures instead of shares?

Ans. Debentures carry a fixed interest rate. Even if the company earns higher profits, debenture holders are entitled only to that fixed interest rate. When the return on investment (ROI) is greater than the cost of debt (interest on debentures), the residual profits goes to the benefit of equity shareholders. In other words, the earnings of the equity shareholders are increased. More so, interest on debentures is tax deductible. So, the effective cost to company by issue of debentures is lesser than the actual interest rate paid to them.

Dividend paid to share holders, be preference or equity shares, is not tax deductible. So, debentures are a cheaper source of long-term finance to a company. So, a company prefers to raise long-term funds, by issuing debentures, compared to shares.

Q.2. What is 'pre-emptive right'? Why equity shareholders are given this right?

Ans. As and when a limited company wants to issue additional equity shares in the market, the new shares are to be issued first to the existing equity shareholders. This right of receiving the offer by existing equity shareholders to subscribe for additional equity shares, as and when issued, is called 'pre-emptive right'. If this right were not given, proportion of ownership of the existing equity shareholders may be diluted. Even loss of control may also occur. Normally, company issues the new equity shares at a price lesser than the prevailing market price. So, it is just logical that the existing equity shareholders are to be benefited from the issue of additional equity shares.

Q.3. Explain the preferences 'Preference Shares' enjoy? Why they are so named?

Ans. Preference Shares carry preference in two respects–payment of dividend as well as repayment of their investment. Dividend is to be paid to preference shares, before it is paid to equity shares. In the event of liquidation, investment made by preference shareholders is to be repaid first, before equity shareholders are paid. As they enjoy certain preferences compared to equity shareholders, they are named as 'Preference Shares'.

Q.4. How preference shares provide a risk-free leverage to a company?

Ans. Preference shareholders are only entitled to a fixed rate of dividend. If the return of investment (ROI) is higher than the rate of dividend payable on preference shares, the residual profit goes to the benefit of equity shareholders. In this process, the earnings of equity shareholders are magnified. In case company is in loss, there is no obligation to the company to pay dividend to preference shareholders, unlike interest to debenture holders. Borrowing by issuing preference shares is advantageous to a company, with no risk attached to it. So, a company enjoys risk-free leverage by issuing preference shares.

Q.5. Name any three long-term finance instruments and state their risk profile from the view-point of investors?

Ans. Debentures, preference shares and equity shares are the most popular forms of long-term finance instruments. Debentures are the most attractive instruments to investors as they carry fixed interest rate. Companies normally provide collateral security, while issuing them in the market. So, there is certainty of return in the form of interest as well as greater safety of funds, so far as investors are concerned. Preference shares are the second best as there is preference in respect of payment of dividend. They get back their investment before money is returned to equity shareholders, if there are adequate funds to cover their interests. Equity shareholders are the highest risky instruments as there is no guarantee for payment of dividend. Generally, they do not get back much of their money when the company goes into liquidation as liquidation often is the last choice if there is no possibility for its revival.

Q.6. 'From the view-point of the investors, debentures are least risky, lesser risky are preference shares and highest risky are equity shares'—Explain.

Ans. Out of the three long-term instruments of finance – equity shares, preference shares and debentures, debentures are least risky. Debentures carry a fixed rate of interest, which is to be paid by the company, irrespective of profits. Normally, debentures are secured. Companies offer collateral security to debenture holders to make them comfortable from the view-point of security. As they are secured, even if the company fails and finally goes into liquidation, debenture holders normally get back their money from the proceeds of their security. Debenture holders get the assured interest amount even if the company incurs loss. In other words, debenture holders get regular return in the form of interest and safety of funds, if things go wrong with the company.

As far as preference shareholders are concerned, they enjoy preference in respect of dividend and return of money, before equity shareholders are paid dividend and their original investment, respectively. So, preference shares are lesser risky compared to debenture holders.

Equity shares are the highest risky as there is no guarantee of dividend. If a company does not make profits, equity shareholders do not get any dividend at all. When company goes into liquidation, generally equity shareholders hardly get back their money as most of the money would have disappeared from the company towards losses by that time.

Q.7. Why preference shares are called as 'hybrid security'?

Ans. Preference shares enjoy the twin features of both equity shares as well as debentures. Like equity shares, there is no compulsion for payment of dividend by the company. Non-payment of dividend does not make the company to go into liquidation. Similar to debentures, there is only a fixed commitment to pay the agreed interest rate, though the company makes heavy profits. So, preference shares are called as a hybrid security as good features of both the instruments – equity shares as well as debentures-are available in one instrument to the company.

Q.8. Whether preference shares are the real owners of a limited company and why a company prefers to raise funds in this form?

Ans. No, preference shares are not real owners of the company. Only equity shareholders are the real owners of the company. Owner has to assume risk. Preference shareholders do not assume any risk, unlike equity shareholders. Preference shareholders are paid dividend, before dividend is paid to equity shareholders. Similarly, in the event of winding up of a company, their money is paid first, before payment is made to equity shareholders. However, for computation of net worth, preference shares are also included, as their investment in the company is not temporary but for a very longer duration. There is no risk from their end, even in the event of non-payment of dividend, if there are no profits.

Interview Questions

Q.1. What is a 'Debenture'?

Ans. Debenture is a type of borrowing by a company. It is one of the long-term sources of finance, adopted by a company, generally for purchase of fixed assets and meeting working capital requirements. Normally, debentures are secured by way of a fixed charge on the fixed assets of the company. Debenture certificate is issued to the purchaser, which spells out the terms and conditions of issue such as interest, security and period of redemption etc.

Q.2. What is a 'floating charge'?

Ans. Assets covered by a 'floating charge' can change, from time to time. Company is allowed to sell those assets in the ordinary course of business. Floating charge is generally provided on the current assets of the company. For example, a company may give floating charge on its stock and debtors to the financing institution. Company can sell the stock, either for cash or credit, and also utilize the collections from debtors for further purchase of goods to carry on the business. In other words, company is not prevented from dealing with such assets covered by a floating charge, for any normal business activities. However, as and when company does any activity in contravention of the agreement entered with the lender, and if lender initiates any action, floating charge crystallizes and company is not allowed to deal with such assets covered by the floating charge.

Q.3. What is 'project financing'?

Ans. Companies approach term lending institutions for securing sanction of term loans for purchase of fixed assets. This method of financing is called 'project financing'.

Q.4. What is a book building and state its main advantage?

Ans. Book building is a process of determining the price at which an Initial Public Offering will be offered. Investors indicate the price they are willing to pay per share. When the book is closed, the issue price is determined by an underwriter by analyzing these values. The main advantage is that it avoids under-pricing and volatility in price, after issue is made.

Q.5. What is meant by greenshoe option?

Ans. A greenshoe option is a clause in the underwriting agreement of an IPO, which allows selling additional shares. Usually, it is 15% of the shares originally offered to the public. Company takes the benefit if the demand exceeds expectations and the stock trades above its offering price. It is also known as the over-allotment provision.

It gets its name from the Green Shoe company, which is the first company to allow such an option.

Q.6. What is meant by sweat equity shares? What is its aim in issue of such shares?

Ans. Sweat equity shares refer to equity shares given to the company's employees on favourable terms, in recognition of their work. They usually take the form of giving options to employees to buy shares of the company, so that they become part-owners and participate in the profits, apart from earning salary. The aim of ESOP (Employee stock option plan) or sweat equity is simple: retain your best employees by offering a good enough carrot.

Q.7. What is meant by 'ASBA' and state the benefits to an investor?

Ans. ASBA stands for 'Application Supported by Blocked Amounts'. This is a new initiative taken by the capital markets regulator, Securities and Exchange Board of India (SEBI).

All along, for securing allotment of shares, investor has to part with the funds from his bank account. Now, ASBA process ensures that only the requisite amount of funds is debited to the investor's bank account, that too, only on allotment of shares. In this mechanism, the need for refunds is completely avoided.

The ASBA process shall be available in all public issues made through the book building route.

❍ ❍

CHAPTER 11

Investment and Capital Structure Decisions

11.1 INTRODUCTION

Funds are needed by all business enterprises for investment at every stage, from formation to expansion. If funds are inadequate, the business suffers. Growth that is possible does not happen. On the other hand, if proper sources of funds are not arranged and managed properly, the whole organization suffers. Even a profitable firm may turn to loss making, or even become sick, if correct source of funds are not identified and tapped properly.

Estimation of funds is necessary, but formation of capital structure is more important. Funds can be raised in two ways; first through the ownership securities i.e. equity shares and preference shares, and secondly through borrowing securities i.e. debentures and/or bonds. While raising funds, two factors are important, one is quantum and the other is mix. Quantum is important estimation of funds for current as well as future needs to run the business smoothly, without stress and strain. More importantly, every firm has to maintain a proper mix of both these types of securities so that their cost and risk associated with those securities are minimum. A judicious combination of debt and equity affects cost of capital as well as value of the firm. Effort of every firm is to design the capital structure in the right mix of equity and debt to achieve lower cost of capital, in turn improving the value of the firm.

Capital structure shows the mix of different securities used by the firm. In other words, capital structure deals with the composition of funds which is important to increase profitability and also minimizing risk to the firm.

11.2 CAPITALIZATION, CAPITAL STRUCTURE AND FINANCIAL STRUCTURE

The terms Capitalization, Capital Structure and Financial Structure do not mean the same.

Capitalization refers to the total amount of securities issued by a company. The different securities are equity share capital, preference share capital and debentures.

> **Capitalization refers to the total amount of long term-funds raised by the company.**

Capital structure refers to the proportionate amount that makes up capitalization. In other words, capital structure refers to the break up of the securities raised by the company. Capital structure may be defined as mix of long-term sources of funds–Equity share capital, Preference share capital, reserves and surplus long-term debt and debentures.

> **'Capitalization' deals with the total amount of securities issued by a company, while 'Capital Structure' relates to its mix. Capitalization is a quantitative aspect of financial planning of a firm, while capital structure is concerned with the qualitative aspect.**

Financial structure refers to the way the firm's assets are financed. In other words, it includes both long-term as well as short-term sources of funds. Financial structure means the entire liabilities side of the balance sheet of the company. Thus, capital structure is only a part of financial structure.

> **Financial structure refers to both long-term and short-term funds, while capitalization refers to only long-term funds.**

Example: For example, the funds raised by a company are:

(₹ in lakhs)

Nature of Funds	Amount	Break-up
Equity shares	4	50%
Preference shares	2	25%
Debentures	2	25%
Capitalization	**8**	**100%**
Reserves	1	
Short-term borrowing from bank	1	
Total	10	

Capitalization: ₹ 8 lakhs. This is the total long-term fund raised.

Capital Structure: Proportionate amount of capitalization (50% equity shares, 25% preference shares and 25% debentures).

Some authors include retained earnings and reserves too for the purpose of capital structure.

Financial Structure: ₹ 10 lakhs. This represents all the financial resources, short-term as well as long-term.

A brief comparative chart makes the position more clear.

	Capitalization	Capital Structure	Financial Structure
MEANING	Capitalization refers to the **TOTAL** amount of securities issued by a company.	Capital structure refers to the **PROPORTIONATE AMOUNT** of securities that makes up capitalization.	Financial structure refers to the **WAY OF FINANCING** firm's assets.
COMPOSITION & EMPHASIS	**TOTAL** of securities are equity share capital, preference share capital and debentures.	**BREAK UP** long-term securities raised by the company.	Includes **BOTH** long-term and short-term securities.

11.3 FORMS OR PATTERN OF CAPITAL STRUCTURE

The capital structure of a company may take any one of the following forms:

(A) Equity Share Capital

(B) Equity and Preference Share Capital

(C) Equity Share Capital and Debentures

(D) Equity Share Capital, Preference Share Capital and Debentures.

11.4 IMPORTANCE OF CAPITAL STRUCTURE

The term 'Capital structure' refers to the mix of different sources of long-term funds such as equity share capital, preference share capital and long-term debt like long-term loans, debentures etc. The choice of an appropriate capital structure depends upon a number of factors such as nature of business, regularity of earnings the business can maintain, conditions of market, and finally, attitude of investors at the time of fund raising etc.

Borrowing is Cheap Compared to Equity: Amongst the different determinants in designing the capital structure, the most important factor is 'mix of debt and equity' in the capital structure. Raising of funds through debt is cheaper compared to equity. This is because interest on debt is an admissible expenditure. In other words, it is allowed as an expense while computing profits for income-tax. Payment of dividend is only an appropriation of profit. Dividend paid on equity is not allowed for income tax. In simple language, interest is an expense, while dividend is not from the viewpoint of income-tax.

Role of Debt in Capital Structure: There is a basic difference between debt and equity. Debt is a liability. Interest on debt is a fixed commitment which has to be paid, irrespective of the profits of the company. Dividend is payable to shareholders, only if there are profits after payment of tax. So, there is no commitment for payment of dividend to equity shareholders.

The principal attraction of debt is its tax benefit. Due to tax benefit, the real cost of debt to the company becomes low than its visible cost. Let us explain this concept through an example. Suppose, a company is in the tax bracket of 50% and pays an interest of 12% on its debentures. As it is expenditure under the Income Tax Act, the effective cost comes to only 6%. If funds were raised through equity, the cost would have been 12% as dividend is not an expense.

Above all, debt is also risky beyond a certain point. If the proportion of debt in the capital structure increases, risk of the firm increases that may lead to the insolvency of the company in adverse situations.

Indian corporate sector uses long-term borrowings over short-term borrowings. The changed trend is that they try to substitute short-term debt for long-term borrowings.

Importance of Mix: The mix in capital structure has great implications. It is true that the mix of capital structure does not influence the total earnings of the firm, but definitely, mix has a great impact on the individual earnings of equity shareholders. Let us see how the mix works.

Suppose a firm has an equity share capital of ₹ 1 lakh, consisting of shares of ₹ 10 each. When it is earning ₹ 20,000, its return is 20% (ignoring tax). Now, the company plans to go for expansion involving ₹ 1 lakh. It has two options of raising funds, through equity or debentures. It has decided to raise the funds by issuing 8% debentures as this option is profitable. As the available funds have gone up by 100%, earnings are also presumed to increase in a similar manner, and so, profits are now ₹ 40,000. Company pays interest of ₹ 8,000 on debentures, leaving ₹ 32,000 to equity shareholders. So, now their return is 32% against earlier 20% (ignoring tax). The return to equity shareholders has increased by 60%, without any additional stake, due to use of debt.

Double-edged Sword: What is the reason for increase in return? It is simple. The cost of debt is lower than the return on investment. In consequence, the earnings of the equity shareholders are magnified. This is called **'Trading on Equity' or 'Financial Leverage' or 'Financial Gearing'.** This concept has already been explained in detail in the Chapter No. 9- Leverages (Para no. 9.7). Financial Leverage also behaves in an adverse manner, negative way, too. If the return on investment falls below the cost of debt, then the earnings of equity shareholders decreases compared to its earlier earnings. This situation may happen in recession or falling prices. That's why financial gearing is also called as Double-edged sword.

11.4.1 Approach to Establish an Appropriate Capital Structure

As and when firm is raising funds for expansion, it has to choose the mode of financing out of the different options available. The options or routes of financing are–equity, preference share capital, debt or a combination of the three, in different proportions. How to select the mode of financing or the route which would be more rewarding to the firm? **EBIT-EPS Approach is the method followed by the firms to answer the above question.**

> **Capital structure that gives highest earnings per equity share is the one that is ideal to a company. Determination of optimum capital structure is a formidable task. It is the constant endeavour of every company to achieve that level. However, what can be achieved in operational terms is an appropriate capital structure, depending on the particular facts of a company. An appropriate capital structure should provide room for flexibility, not only in obtaining funds but also in refunding them.**

The above approach establishes the impact of different methods of financing on equity shareholders' value, reflected in the revised EPS under the different methods of financing. When EPS is at its peak, the value of the equity share would be at its highest level. For this reason that route of financing is to be chosen because the value of a firm is reflected by its equity share price. When ROI is greater than the fixed charge funds, be it debt or preference share capital, ROE increases and in consequence, EPS increases. Firm has to make up its mind; looking to the increased risk it may be exposed to once the route is accepted.

The following illustration explains the concept of EBIT-EPS approach.

Illustration No. 1

The following capital structure is available in Farah Khan & Co Ltd:

Equity share capital (Face value ₹ 100)	₹ 5,00,000
Retained earnings	₹ 2,00,000
General Reserve	₹ 2,00,000
8% Preference share capital	₹ 50,000
12% Debentures	₹ 50,000

Following sources have been identified for raising finance for meeting its expansion programme:

Equity share capital	₹ 4,00,000
14% debentures	₹ 1,00,000

Return on investment is 15%. Calculate existing EBIT and proposed EBIT.

Solution

Existing capital structure:	
Equity share capital	₹ 5,00,000
Retained earnings	₹ 2,00,000
General Reserve	₹ 2,00,000
8% Preference shares	₹ 50,000
12% Debentures	₹ 50,000
Total	**₹ 10,00,000**
Present EBIT 15% on ROI ₹ 10,00,000	₹ 1,50,000
Additional Capital Structure:	
Equity Share capital	₹ 4,00,000
14% debentures	₹ 1,00,000
Total	₹ 5,00,000
Proposed EBIT 15% on ROI ₹ 5,00,000	₹ 75,000
Total EBIT (1,50,000 + 75,000)	₹ 2,25,000
After expansion, EBIT of the firm is estimated at	₹ 2,25,000.

Illustration No. 2

A firm has an all-equity capital structure consisting of 1,00,000 equity shares of ₹10 per share. The firm wants to raise ₹ 2,50,000 to finance its investments and is considering three alternative methods of financing:

(i) to issue 25,000 equity share at ₹ 10 each,

(ii) to borrow ₹ 2,50,000 at 8% interest rate,

(iii) to issue 2,500 Preference shares of ₹ 100 each, at 8% dividend rate.

(a) If the firm's earnings before interest and tax after additional investment are ₹ 3,12,500 and the tax rate is 50 per cent, which choice is to be made? Comment on the outcome of choice.

(b) Explain the effect on EPS, if EBIT decreases to ₹ 75,000.

(c) Draw conclusion in respect of relationship between EBIT and EPS.

Solution

EPS UNDER DIFFERENT FORMS OF FINANCING

	Equity Financing ₹	Debt Financing ₹	Preference Financing ₹
EBIT	3,12,500	3,12,500	3,12,500
Less : Interest	0	20,000	0
PBT	3,12,500	2,92,500	3,12,500
Less : Taxes @ 50%	1,56,250	1,46,250	1,56,250
PAT	1,56,250	1,46,250	1,56,250
Less : Preference dividend	0	0	20,000
Earning available to equity shareholders	1,56,250	1,46,250	1,36,250
Equity shares outstanding	1,25,000	1,00,000	1,00,000
EPS	1.25	1.46	1.36

(a) The firm is able to maximize the earnings per share, when it uses debt financing. Though the rate of preference dividend is equal to the rate of interest, both at 8%, EPS is high in case of debt financing. Reason, interest charges are tax deductible, while preference dividends are not. This is an interesting point in mix of financing. **Change of form of financing has increased EPS.**

Higher is the ratio of debt to equity, the greater would be the return to the equity shareholders.

(b)

EPS UNDER DIFFERENT FORMS OF FINANCING (REDUCED EBIT)

	Equity Financing ₹	Debt Financing ₹	Preference Finance ₹
EBIT	75,000	75,000	75,000
Less : Interest	0	20,000	0
PBT	75,000	55,000	75,000
Less : Taxes @ 50%	37,500	27,500	37,500
PAT	37,500	27,500	37,500
Less : Preference dividend	0	0	20,000
Earning available to equity shareholders	37,500	27,500	17,500
Equity shares outstanding	1,25,000	1,00,000	1,00,000
EPS	0.30	0.27	0.17

With the use of debt financing, EPS has been the highest with 1.46, when EBIT has been at a high level of ₹ 3,12,500. When EBIT has fallen to ₹ 75,000, EPS with debt financing has fallen to 0.27. EPS under debt financing has not fallen below preference share financing as interest paid is eligible for tax benefit, while dividend on preference shares is not eligible for tax benefit.

(c) Relationship between EBIT and EPS: With increasing levels of EBIT, EPS will increase at a faster rate with a high degree of leverage. However, if a company is not able to earn a rate of return on its assets higher than the interest rate (or the preference dividend rate), debt (or preference financing) will have an adverse impact on EPS. EPS decreases, drastically, in such an event. Use of Fixed charge funds such as debentures or preference share capital acts as a double-edged sword. So, these funds have to be used very judiciously.

Conclusion: It can be concluded that if the level of EBIT is greater and its probability in the downward fluctuation is lower, it is more beneficial to employ debt in the capital structure.

Illustration No. 3

Vijay & Co Ltd plans to raise a total capital of ₹ 4,00,000 . Company has three option plans:

Plan A : No debt, all equity shares

Plan B : 40% debt (10%), 40% Preference shares (12%) and 20 % Equity shares

Plan C : 70% debt (10%) and 30% Equity shares.

Face value of equity shares and Preference shares is ₹ 10, in all plans. Rates in bracket indicate the fixed return on debt and preference shares.

The company estimates its earnings before interest and tax (EBIT) would be ₹ 80,000. Tax rate is 50%.

Which plan is profitable to implement?

Solution

Alternative Financial Plans

(Amount in ₹)

	Plan A	Plan B	Plan C
Capital structure	4,00,000	4,00,000	4,00,000
Equity share capital (Face value ₹ 10)	4,00,000 (No. of shares 40,000)	80,000 (No. of shares 8,000)	1,20,000 (No. of shares 12,000)
Preference share capital (Face value ₹ 10)	---	1,60,000 (No. of shares 16,000)	---
Debentures (Face value ₹ 10)	---	1,60,000 (No. of debentures 16,000)	2,80,000 (No. of debentures 28,000)
EBIT	80,000	80,000	80,000

Contd...

Less : Interest on debt (10%)	---	16,000	28,000
Earnings before tax (EBT)	80,000	64,000	52,000
Less: Tax (50%)	40,000	32,000	26,000
Profit after Tax (PAT)	40,000	32,000	26,000
Less: Preference share dividend (12% on preference share capital ₹ 1,60,000)	--	19,200	---
Profits available for equity shareholders	40,000	12,800	26,000
No. of equity shares	40,000	8,000	12,000
EPS Profits available to equity shareholders / No. of equity shares	₹ 1	₹ 1.6	₹ 2.17

Recommendation: PLAN C is recommended as EPS is the highest amongst all three option plans. Increased portion of debt (70%) is advantageous to the company as interest on debt is tax deductible.

Illustration No. 4

The existing **capital structure** of Pooja Purvatkar & Co Ltd is as under:

Equity share capital (F.V. ₹ 10)	₹ 6,00,000
Retained earnings	₹ 2,00,000
10% Preference shares	₹ 3,00,000
8% Debentures	₹ 2,00,000

The company requires a sum of ₹ 5,00,000 to finance its expansion programme. It is considering the following three option plans:

(i) Issue of 40,000 equity shares (F.V. ₹ 10) at a premium of ₹ 2.50

(ii) Issue of 10% Preference shares, at par

(iii) Issue of 8% Debentures.

EBIT, after expansion, would be ₹ 8,00,000. Tax rate is 50%.

It is estimated that P/E ratio of equity share in the above three options of financing would be 12, 8 and 6 respectively.

Which of the alternative plan would you consider to be the best, amongst the three options given?

Solution

Market plan that produces the highest market price is the best as market price of a share is a barometer for judging the success of any company's plans. So, it is necessary to find out estimated price per share.

ESTIMATED MARKET PRICE PER SHARE

(Under Various Financing Plans)

(₹)

	Plan (i)	Plan (ii)	Plan (iii)
EBIT	8,00,000	8,00,000	8,00,000
Less: Interest on debentures	16,000	16,000	56,000
Earnings before Tax (EBT)	7,84,000	7,84,000	7,44,000
Less: Tax (50%)	3,92,000	3,92,000	3,72,000
Profit after Tax (PAT)	3,92,000	3,92,000	3,72,000
Less: Preference share dividend	30,000	80,000	30,000
Profits available for equity shareholders	3,62,000	3,12,000	3,42,000
No. of equity shares	1,00,000	60,000	60,000
EPS Profits available for equity shareholders / No. of equity shares	3.62	5.2	5.7
P/E Ratio (P/E Ratio = Market Price per Share / EPS)	12	8	6
Market Price per Equity Share = EPS x (P/E ratio)	3.62 x 12 = ₹ 43.44	5.2 x 8 = ₹ 41.6	5.7 x 6 = ₹ 34.2

Recommendation: Market price of equity share in plan (i) is ₹ 43.44 which is the highest amongst three plans. **So, plan (i) is recommended.**

Illustration No. 5

Ankita Soni & Co Ltd plans to expand their existing business, with a new factory. Its existing equity share capital (Face value ₹ 10) is ₹ 5 lakhs. 10% Debentures outstanding are ₹ 3 lakhs. Funds requirement of new factory is ₹ 20 lakhs. Company has three alternative plans to raise debt requirements, 8 lakhs, 12 lakhs and 20 lakhs. Balance amount would be raised by equity.

Cost of borrowing for additional funds is as under:

Up to ₹ 5,00,000	— 10%
Up to ₹ 12,00,000	— 12%
Up to ₹ 25,00,000	— 14%

Existing EBIT is ₹ 10 lakhs. New factory would yield an EBIT of ₹ 30 lakhs, additionally. Company's policy is to maintain a debt equity ratio, not exceeding 3 : 1 and is prepared to take maximum advantage of debt.

Assume a tax rate of 50%. Work out the EPS, meeting the objective of the firm. Recommend the scheme selected.

Solution

	(₹ in lakhs)
Existing capital structure:	
Equity share capital	= 5
10% Debentures	= 3
	8
New capital structure	20
Total long-term sources	28

Maximum permitted debt equity ratio is 3:1. So, maximum debt can be ₹ 21 lakhs. Additional debt is to be raised within the above ceiling. Balance amount would be met by equity. Effort of the company is to maximize EPS, taking advantage of the permissible debt equity ratio of 3 : 1 to the maximum limit.

STATEMENT SHOWING EPS UNDER DIFFERENT SCHEMES

(₹)

	Scheme I	Scheme II	Scheme III
Additional Debt	8,00,000	12,00,000	18,00,000 *
Total Earnings before interest and tax (EBIT) – ₹ 10 lakhs + ₹ 30 lakhs	40,00,000	40,00,000	40,00,000
Total interest (Existing interest on debentures + interest on proposed debt, based on applicable slab the additional debt falls in) **	1,26,000 (30,000 + 96,000)	1,74,000 (30,000 + 1,44,000)	2,82,000 (30,000 + 2,52,000)
Earning before tax (EBT)	38,74,000	38,26,000	37,18,000
Tax @ 50%	19,37,000	19,13,000	18,59,000
Earnings after tax (EAT)	19,37,000	19,13,000	18,59,000
Fund requirement of new factory (A)	20,00,000	20,00,000	20,00,000

Contd...

Debt component for new factory (B)	8,00,000	12,00,000	18,00,000
Additional equity share capital for new factory (A – B)	12,00,000	8,00,000	2,00,000
Existing equity share capital	5,00,000	5,00,000	5,00,000
Total equity share capital	17,00,000	13,00,000	7,00,000
No. of equity shares	1,70,000	1,30,000	70,000
EPS (EAT / No. of equity shares)	$\frac{19,37,000}{1,70,000}$ = 11.39	$\frac{19,13,000}{1,30,000}$ = 14.72	$\frac{18,59,000}{70,000}$ = 26.56

* Debt component cannot exceed ₹ 21 lakhs as maximum permissible debt is ₹ 21 lakhs to maintain debt equity ratio of 3:1. Existing debt (debentures) is ₹ 3 lakhs. So, balance amount available in the form of debt is only ₹ 18 lakhs.

** All additional funds would be borrowed at one time, not in instalments, hence applicable slab rate for total borrowing is considered.

Recommendation: In scheme III, EPS of ₹ 26.56 is the highest. So, plan III is recommended for starting the new factory. Scheme III meets the objective of the firm to maximize EPS and also to maintain maximum debt equity ratio of 3 : 1.

Illustration No. 6

Sumit Mathur Ltd, with net operating earnings of ₹ 3,00,000, is attempting to evaluate a number of possible capital structures as given below. Which capital structure will you recommend, and why?

Capital structure	Debt in capital structure (₹)	Cost of debt (K_1) %	Cost of equity (K) %
1	3,00,000	10.0	12.0
2	4,00,000	10.0	12.5
3	5,00,000	11.0	13.5
4	6,00,000	12.0	15.0
5	7,00,000	14.0	18.0

Solution

Particulars	Capital structure plans having debts of various amounts				
	I	II	III	IV	V
EBIT (in ₹)	3,00,000	3,00,000	3,00,000	3,00,000	3,00,000
Less interest (K_1 x B)	– 30,000	– 40,000	– 55,000	– 72,000	– 98,000
Net income (NI) for equity holders	2,70,000	2,60,000	2,45,000	2,28,000	2,02,000
K_e (equity capitalisation rate)	0.12	0.125	0.135	0.150	0.180
S (market value of equity)	22,50,000*	20,80,000	18,14,815	15,20,000	11,22,222
B (market value of debt)	3,00,000	4,00,000	5,00,000	6,00,000	7,00,000
Total market value (S + B) = V	25,50,000	24,80,000	23,14,815	21,20,000	18,22,222
Overall cost of capital $= \frac{(EBIT)}{V}$	11.76%	12.10%	12.95%	14.15%	16.46%

$* \ \frac{100 \times 2{,}70{,}000}{12}$

Recommendation: Capital structure I, having debts of ₹ 3,00,000, is recommended. Reason is its overall cost of capital which is the lowest.

11.5 CAPITAL GEARING

Capital gearing ratio analyses the capital structure of the company. This is the ratio between fixed charge bearing securities and non-fixed charge bearing securities. Preference share capital, debentures and long-term loans are fixed charge bearing securities, while equity share capital and reserves are non-fixed charge bearing securities. Interest and dividend are fixed on debentures and preference shares respectively, irrespective of the level of profits of the company. Balance amount of profit only belongs to equity share holders. So, dividend on equity share capital is dependent on the balance profits of the company, which normally changes from year to year.

Capital gearing ratio is calculated as under

$$\frac{\textbf{Preference share capital + Debentures + Long-term debts bearing fixed interest}}{\textbf{Equity share capital + Reserves and Surplus}}$$

If preference share capital and other fixed interest bearing loans exceed equity share capital and free reserves, the company is said to be highly geared. In such a case, the capital gearing is more than one and the firm is said to be highly geared. On the other hand, if preference share capital and other fixed interest bearing loans are less than the equity share capital and free reserves then the company is said to be low geared. In the low-geared firms, capital gearing is less than one. In case, both are equal, the firm is said to be even-geared.

Significance of Capital Gearing: Capital gearing is of immense importance for every company. As the fixed charge bearing securities carry a fixed amount of commitment in the form of interest and dividend, only the balance amount of profits belong to the equity shareholders. In case of low-geared firms, the amount of interest and dividend would be low as the aggregate amount of preference share capital and debentures as low, compared to equity share capital. So, the amount of divisible profits would be high to equity shareholders. Whereas in case of high-geared firms, the amount of interest and dividend would be high as the proportion of debentures and preference share capital exceeds equity share capital. So, the amount of profit available to equity shareholders would be low. Proper gearing of a firm is important for its smooth running.

Comparison of Capital Gearing with Automobile: The capital gearing in the financial structure of a business is rightly compared with the gears of an automobile. To start the vehicle, we start with a low gear i.e. first gear and when the vehicle picks up the speed, we move into the higher gear i.e. second gear. Finally, when we want to pick up the real speed, we move the vehicle into the next higher gear i.e. third gear. Similar is the functioning of capital gearing in a business enterprise. Company is initially commenced with equity share capital only. After a couple of years, debt is introduced in the form of debt or issue of preference share capital. When the company totally stabilises and picks up momentum, a higher mix of fixed charge bearing funds in the form of preference share capital and debt is used to avail the advantage of financial leverage and magnify the earnings of equity shareholders.

Capital gearing is important not only to equity shareholders but also to creditors, debenture holders and financial institutions that have lent money to the firm.

A higher capital gearing is an indication that it is burdened with more debt and preference shares that result in a fixed commitment/payment, irrespective of profits. This would turn risky in case of a reduction in profits, in particular during recession times. Lenders have to be very careful while dealing with a highly geared firm.

11.5.1 Capital Gearing and Trade Cycles

Company can use the technique of capital gearing successfully during different conditions of inflation and deflation. Depending on the situation, company has to change the technique either to high gear or low gear, from time to time.

1. **During Inflation or Boom Period:** During boom, companies enjoy high profits. So, the interest on debt and rate of dividend on preference shares is always lower than the return on investment. To take advantage of the situation, firms borrow more and they adopt the policy of high gear. In consequence, the

earning per equity share increases. **It is desirable that companies should adopt the policy of high gear during inflation or boom periods to magnify the earning per equity share.**

> **Capital structure is more of permanent character, while boom and depression may not sustain for long, continuously. This is the risk in designing the capital structure and so, wisdom of management is always put to test in forecasting the future economic trends.**

2. **During Deflation or Depression Period:** Profits dip during the periods of depression. Companies experience difficulty to pay the fixed interest on debt or dividend on preference shares. So, a cautious approach is desirable to be adopted during that period. It is prudent for companies to raise equity funds as there is no commitment to pay fixed rate of dividend. During the periods of deflation, companies have to adopt the policy of low gear.

Illustration No. 7

Calculate the capital gearing ratio from the following information. Comment on the ratio, if the firm is passing through the period of inflation and planning expansion.

	(₹)
Equity share capital	7,00,000
7% Preference share capital	2,00,000
11% Debentures	4,00,000
Long-term loan from MPSFC (term lending institution)	3,00,000
Reserves and surplus	4,00,000
Current liabilities	10,00,000

Solution

Capital gearing ratio is

$$= \frac{\text{Preference share capital + Debentures + Long-term debts bearing fixed interest}}{\text{Equity share capital + Reserves and Surplus}}$$

$$= \frac{2{,}00{,}000 + 4{,}00{,}000 + 3{,}00{,}000}{7{,}00{,}000 + 4{,}00{,}000}$$

$$= 0.82$$

Capital gearing is 0.82. As the capital gearing is less than one, the firm is low geared. During the inflation period, profits of the firm remain high and so company does not experience difficulty to meet the fixed interest/dividend obligations. Firm can use more debt to improve the earning per equity share. In case, the firm is planning expansion, more debt is to be used in capital structure to improve the return on investment.

Check Your Understanding

(A) State whether the following statements are True or False

1. Capital structure refers to the mix of different sources of long-term funds such as equity share capital, preference share capital and long-term debt like long-term loans, debentures etc.
2. The terms 'Capitalization' and 'Capital structure' mean one and the same.
3. The term 'Capital gearing' is used to describe the relationship between equity share capital including reserves and surpluses to preference share capital and other fixed charge bearing securities.
4. In case of low-geared firms, the aggregate amount of preference share capital and debentures is more than equity share capital and free reserves.
5. Capital gearing does not affect dividend pattern of equity shareholders.
6. It is prudent for companies to have low gear during the period of inflation and high gear during depression.
7. Capital structure is not different from financial structure.
8. To retain control over company, debt is preferred to equity.
9. It is ideal to achieve optimum capital structure, but what operationally possible is only appropriate capital structure.

Answers

1. True 2. False 3. True 4. False 5. False 6. False 7. False 8. True 9. True.

(B) Objective Questions (Identify what is most appropriate)

1. Capital gearing refers to the relationship between equity capital and ______.
   (A) Preference share capital (B) Reserves and Surplus
   (C) Fixed charge bearing securities (D) None of the above
2. It is better for a company to remain in ______ during the period of depression.
   (A) Low gear (B) High gear
   (C) Neutral gear (D) None of the above
3. Capital structure deals with the ______ of long-term funds.
   (A) Mix (B) Quantum
   (C) Quantum and composition (D) None of the above
4. Capitalization refers to the total amount of ______ raised by the company.
   (A) Long-term funds (B) Short-term funds
   (C) Short-term and long-term funds (D) None of the above

Answers

1. (C) 2. (A) 3. (A) 4. (A).

Descriptive Questions

1. Define the capital structure. Distinguish between Capitalization, Capital Structure and Financial Structure. **(11.1 and 11.2)**
2. Detail the different forms of capital structure and explain their importance. Illustrate the role of debt in capital structure as a means to increase the return on equity and magnify the earnings of equity shareholders, with suitable examples. **(11.3 and 11.4)**
3. Discuss the concept of capital gearing and explain its significance. What type of technique has to be adopted by prudent companies during various phases of trade cycle? **(11.5 and 11.5.1)**
4. Discuss the approaches to establish an appropriate capital structure **(11.3 and 11.4.1)**

Short Questions

Q.1. Explain the difference between capitalization, capital structure and financial structure?

Ans. Capitalization refers to the aggregate of long-term sources of finance. Long-term sources of finance are equity share capital, preference share capital, debentures and long-term loans. Capital structure relates to the mix of those long-term sources. In other words, the former relates to the **total** of long-term sources, while the later refers to its **mix.** Financial structure is the total of long-term and short-term sources of finance.

Q.2. Which method of capital structure is recommended? Justify the choice, with reasons.

Ans. Capital structure that gives the highest earning per equity share is the best choice. Capital structure contains both equity and debt. Equity share capital does not have any fixed commitment in respect of dividend as it is payable out of profits only. Fixed rate of dividend is payable on preference shares. In case of debt i.e., debentures and long-term loans, they carry fixed interest rate, with a fixed burden and commitment to the company, irrespective of profits to the company.

Dividend is not tax deductible, while interest is. In consequence, normally capital structure with total equity does not provide the highest EPS. Hence, capital structure containing debt is preferred. Another reason is that debentures bear lower interest rate compared to the higher expectations of equity shareholders. Higher composition of debt is preferable as it gives higher EPS. However, higher proportion of debt in capital structure attracts higher interest rate on debt due to higher risk. So, a balance between the two i.e. equity and debt, is needed. A combination of debt and equity that provides the highest EPS is the most preferred capital structure.

Q.3. How capital structure is important to the existing and potential investor?

Ans. Any investor looks for profits and capital appreciation before buying an equity share. If capital structure contains debt, profits would be high as debt is tax deductible. More so, interest on debt is lower than the dividend expectations of equity shareholders. However, debt is risky, too. So, a proper combination of debt and equity in the capital structure gives higher net profits to a company. If net profits are high, EPS of the company would be high. If EPS is high, market value of equity share would be high, which benefits all the equity shareholders.

Capital structure is also a long-term decision and the decisions would have long-term implications on profits of the company. Potential investor is interested in future prospects and profits of the company. Capital structure plays a pivotal role in determining the earnings available to equity shareholders. Hence, before investing in a company, potential investor looks to the composition of capital structure that determines his future earnings and appreciation. So, capital structure is important to the existing as well as potential investor.

Interview Questions

Q.1. What is meant by 'Capital Structure' and state its importance?

Ans. Capital Structure relates to the mix of long-term securities. Mixture consists of debt and equity. Debt can be used to magnify the earnings of equity shareholders, when the return on investment is higher than the cost of debt. Capital Structure plays an important role in deciding the risk profile of any firm.

Q.2. Which type of capital structure is ideal to a company?

Ans. Capital structure that gives highest EPS (earnings per equity share) is ideal to a company.

Q.3. Is it necessary to have a balanced Capital Structure for every firm?

Ans. Yes, it is desirable to have a balanced Capital Structure. However, the mix of Capital Structure depends on the risk profile of the organization. If the firm is aggressive, firm would have a higher component of debt in its capital structure.

❍ ❍

CHAPTER 12

Time Value of Money

12.1 INTRODUCTION

Time value of money is the basis of financial management. Focus of financial management is wealth maximization of the equity shareholders of the company. All the financial decisions i.e. the investment decision, the financing decision and dividend decision involve evaluation of various alternatives. For example, a finance manager is evaluating the proposal of replacement of machinery for which two alternatives are received. Machine A is costly but has long life of 10 years, with low returns in the first two years and high returns in the later period. Machine B has a life of 5 years, with equal returns throughout the life; costing less than machine A. Repair costs during their life time are different too. In other words, their cost, life, scrap value, annual benefits, repair etc are different. In consequence, series of cash inflows and outflows would be different. In such a situation, how a finance manager can decide correctly from the financial angle? The concept of 'Time Value of Money' guides the finance manager to take the right financial decisions.

12.1.1 Concept of Time Value of Money

The concept 'Time Value of Money' is based on the fact that the money has a time value i.e. a rupee today is much more valuable than a rupee that would be received tomorrow. An ice cream today or tomorrow, the immediate answer from any child would be for an ice cream today itself. Even a child prefers today's enjoyment over tomorrow's fulfilment.

The English proverb "A bird in hand is worth two in bush" possibly gives the correct understanding of the concept "Time Preference for Money" or simply "Time Value of Money".

12.2 MONEY HAS TIME VALUE

Money has a time value. These are the following reasons in its support:

1. **Uncertainty and Risk:** Future is always uncertain and risky. Outflows are in our control as payments to others are to be made by us. There is no certainty for future cash inflows. Inflows are dependent on others convenience. People prefer to receive immediately than waiting for the uncertain tomorrow. There is risk too that the other party (creditor) may become insolvent or whereabouts may be unknown tomorrow.
2. **Present Needs are More Important:** Generally individuals prefer current consumption. Even, a child wants an ice cream today rather than tomorrow.
3. **Reinvestment Opportunities:** An individual or firm invests money for returns. An investor can profitably employ a rupee received today to give him a higher value to be received tomorrow, or after a certain period.
4. **More Purchasing Power in Inflationary Economy:** In an inflationary economy, today's rupee has more purchasing power to buy, rather than the same amount of money can buy at a later date.

From the above, it is evident that money received today is more valuable than the money that may be received tomorrow. Often, individuals or firms encounter difficulty in comparing inflows and outflows as they occur at different periods of time.

The logical solution to compare different cash inflows and outflows is to recognize the principle of time value of money and make appropriate adjustments for time.

In the absence of suitable adjustment for non-comparable cash flows, faulty financial decisions are likely to occur. Time value of money is of vital importance to reach a proper financial decision.

The following examples clarify the concept more clearly.

Example 1: A loan of ₹ 5,000 is given at an interest rate of 10% per annum. At the end of one year, the individual receives back ₹ 5,500. So, ₹ 5,000 at the beginning of the year is equivalent to ₹ 5,500 received at the end of the year.

Example 2: A project needs an initial investment of ₹ 1,00,000. The return is spread over a period of eight years @ ₹ 15,000 annually. The question is whether the project is to be accepted or rejected. The outflow is at the 'Zero year', initially. It means that the investment of ₹ 1 lakh is to be made in the beginning. The inflows would be at different future periods. The firm has to ascertain the current value of the future annual returns or inflows, at the desired rate of interest or return. If the discounted value of the future inflows exceeds the initial investment, or at least equals the initial investment, then only the project is accepted, otherwise rejected.

Example 3: A firm has an option to receive two types of returns for an initial investment of ₹ 20 lakhs. The first option is to receive annual return of ₹ 5 lakhs for a period of seven years, commencing from the end of the first year. The second one is to receive a return of ₹ 10 lakhs for five years, commencing from the end of the third year of investment. The firm can make the correct choice only when the present value of the inflows of both options is calculated.

12.2.1 Time Preference Rate and Required Rate of Return

The time preference for money is generally expressed by an interest rate. This rate will be positive, even in the absence of risk. Unless inducement is offered, no one would like to part present preference for future receipt. When an individual is offered a choice to receive ₹ 100 today, or ₹ 110 at the end of one year, what is offered extra is a compensation for parting with money for the time. Here, this rate of return 10% is for the time, and not for risk. The individual is indifferent between the receipt of ₹ 100 today and ₹ 110 at the end of one year, because he considers these two amounts to be equivalent in value.

Time preference for money is expressed as interest rate, which is free from risk.

Risk Factor: But, there is risk too, when money is parted with as there is uncertainty of time of receipt, or even for its actual return. So, one expects compensation for the risk taken. **Higher the risk, the return expected is higher.** So, required rate of return has to compensate for time as well as risk too. It can be expressed as:

Required Rate of Return = Risk free rate + Risk premium

The risk-free rate compensates for time, while risk premium compensates for risk. The required rate of return may also be called opportunity cost of capital of comparable risk. In other words, risk premium increases when the risk is great. This is the reason why higher interest is charged when money is lent to a film producer as production of a movie is highly risky and return of money also depends on the success or failure of the movie. The purpose for which money is utilized also influences the interest rate. This is the reason why speculative business has to pay higher interest, in comparison to a stable business.

Time Preference Rate is based on no risk, compensation for time only. The classical example is bank deposit, where there is no risk for return of money. Required rate of return involves compensation for time as well as risk. Example is money lent to a third party, where compensation is required for time as well as risk assumed.

Time Preference Rate is compensation for time alone, while Required Rate of Return is compensation for time as well as risk involved with the transaction. Return for time is constant; however, return for risk varies with the degree of risk involved in the transaction.

12.3 IMPORTANCE OF TIME VALUE OF MONEY IN FINANCIAL MANAGEMENT

The objective of financial management is wealth maximization rather than the profit maximization as the later ignores the principle of 'Time value of money'. All financial decisions recognize the importance of this concept 'Time value of money'. When assets are purchased, funds outgo occurs immediately, while returns in the form of 'inflow' occur in future period. Similarly, when funds are borrowed, 'inflow' is immediate, while 'outflow' by repayment happens later. If these inflows and outflows are just identical, no financial decision will take place as no one likes to part current sacrifice for future uncertain receipt. It is necessary that there should be some compensation for present sacrifice. When assets are purchased, the inflow has to be more than the outflow. In the same way, outflow has to be more than the inflow, if funds are to be raised. How the inflow and outflow can be matched? The logical answer is to make necessary adjustments for the flows that will happen in future to compare them with the current flows, so that financial decisions do not go wrong. This is recognition of time value of money, which is the basis for financial decisions. In this process, the owner's equity is maximized, when the net present worth is created from such financial decisions.

Time Value of Money or Time Preference for Money means the same. This is one of the central ideas of finance for decision-making.

12.4 TECHNIQUES OF TIME VALUE OF MONEY

There are two techniques for adjusting time value of money. They are:

(A) Compounding Technique

(B) Discounted or Present Value of Technique.

12.5 COMPOUNDING TECHNIQUE

Every one wants to have money, immediately rather than at a later date. However, he may accept to wait, if he is duly compensated for the waiting time. If an individual is offered ₹ 100 immediately or ₹ 110 after one year, he may opt the later choice, provided his preference is for an interest rate of 10%. In other words, to him the later preference is more attractive, as ₹ 100 today and ₹ 110 at the end of one year are, at least the same. It means one has to receive, in future, more for a rupee than received, today.

In case of this concept, the interest earned on the initial principal becomes a part of principal, at the end of the compounding period. For example, if ₹ 100 is invested for a period of two years at an interest rate of 10% per annum, at the end of first year, the return is ₹ 10. This interest ₹ 10 becomes part of the principal amount at the beginning of the next year and interest is calculated on ₹ 110. Along with interest ₹ 11

(10 % interest on ₹ 110), the total amount at the end of the second year becomes ₹ 121. **This is the yearly compounding of interest.** This compounding procedure continues for an indefinite period.

The general equation used to calculate the compounded value at the end of 'n' years is as under:

$$A = P(1 + i)^n$$

Where A = Amount at the end of period 'n'
P = Principal at the beginning of the period
i = Interest rate
n = Number of years

Computation of this formula is cumbersome, manually, if the number of years is very large. The other alternative is to use compound value tables. These tables are available for a wide range of combinations of 'i' and 'n'.

Note: Many textbooks work out the problems, simply, with annuity tables. Annuity tables are not given to students, in the question paper. Life is not so simple for students in examinations. To assist the students in the right way for examination, problems are worked as if help of annuity tables are not available.

12.5.1 Multiple Compounding Periods

Interest may be compounded monthly, quarterly and half yearly. The above formula used for annual compounding requires suitable adjustment. If compounding is quarterly, annual interest rate is to be divided by 4 and number of years is to be multiplied by 4. Similarly, if monthly compounding is to be made, annual interest rate is to be divided by 12 and number of years is to be multiplied with 12.

The formula to calculate the compounded value is:

$$A = P(1 + i/m)^{m \times n}$$

Where m = number of times for which compounding is to be done.

With annuity table, compounded value can be calculated even if the compounding is done on half yearly, quarterly or monthly interest basis. If 12% interest per annum for 5 years on quarterly basis is to be calculated, then annuity table – 3% interest (dividing 12% by four) and for 20 years period (multiplying 5 by four) – provides the compounding interest on quarterly basis. Similar procedure can be adopted for half yearly and monthly interest.

The term compounded value is also referred as terminal value i.e. value at the end of the period.

Illustration No. 1

Calculate the compound value when ₹ 10,000 is invested for 3 years and interest 10% per annum is compounded on quarterly basis.

Solution

The formula to calculate the compounded value is:

$$\mathbf{A = P\ (1 + i/m)^{m \times n}}$$

$$A = 10{,}000(1 + 0.10/4)^{3\times 4}$$

$$= 10{,}000(1 + 0.025)^{12}$$

$$= ₹\ 13,\ 448.89$$

Illustration No. 2

Rama Gopal has given ₹ 10,000 each to both daughters Radhi and Dheera to invest. Both have chosen to invest in post office, but in different schemes prevailing at that time. Radhi has invested her amount in NSC, which gives ₹ 16,010 at the end of six years. Dheera has made her investment in KVP which doubles at the end of 8 years 7 months. Find out the annual compounded interest rate of both the investments. Whose investment decision is wise?

Ignore income-tax implication. Calculate interest on an annual compounded basis.

Solution

Here, principal amount and maturity amount and period of investment are given. Interest rate is to be ascertained.

So, the relevant formula is

$$\mathbf{A = P\ (1 + i)^n}$$

Where A = Amount at the end of period 'n'

P = Principal at the beginning of the period

i = Interest rate

n = Number of years

Radhi's interest rate:

$$16{,}010 = 10{,}000\ (1 + i)^6$$

$$(1 + i)^6 = \frac{16{,}010}{10{,}000} = 1.60$$

$$1 + i = 1.081$$

$$i = 1.081 - 1 = 0.081 = 8.1\%$$

Dheera's interest rate:

$$20{,}000 = 10{,}000\,(1 + i)^{8.58}$$

$$(1 + i)^{8.58} = \frac{20{,}000}{10{,}000} = 2$$

$$10{,}000$$

$$1 + i = 1.084$$

$$i = 1.084 - 1 = 0.084 = 8.4\%$$

Conclusion: In case of Radhi, investment has yielded an interest rate of 8.1% on an annual compounded basis, while it is 8.4% in case of Dheera. So, Dheera is wise in her investment decision.

12.6 ANNUITY

The term 'Annuity' means a fixed amount, either receipt or payment, at regular intervals for a specified period. Annuity is an equal instalment evenly spread over a specified period. The relevant point is that annuity could be a payment or receipt. Importance is a series of equal cash flows occurring over equally spaced periods in time. Both amount and period are to be constant. The classical example for annuity is the instalment amount in a recurring deposit with a bank. Here, the instalment is fixed and the same amount is paid over a period at regular intervals. Other example is equated monthly instalments when a housing loan is taken. Insurance premium paid on the insurance policy, be it monthly, half-yearly or yearly, is also an annuity. Even if the house is taken on rent for a period of one year, even the fixed rent paid every month is also an annuity. **If the instalment differs from month to month or period to period, this is not called annuity.**

Features of Annuity: Following are the features of an annuity:

- Fixed instalment amount.
- Amount can be payment or receipt.
- For a specified period.
- Amount cannot be changed during the specified period.

12.6.1 Compound Value of Annuity

The value of annuity at the end of the specified period is called compound value of annuity. So, compound value of annuity includes the total instalments paid and interest accrued on those instalments. Interest compounding may be annual, half-yearly or monthly, depending on the terms of the contract agreed.

Formula for Compound value of Annuity is given below:

$$F_n = A\left[\frac{(1+i)^n - 1}{i}\right]$$

Where F_n = Future value of annuity
A = Annuity
i = Interest rate

A depositor has deposited equal instalment of ₹ 1,000 every year for a period of five years, carrying an interest rate of 10% per annum. For calculating the compounding value of annuity, annuity table gives compound value of annuity of one rupee at 10% for five years – 6.105. That is to be multiplied with the constant amount ₹ 10,000 to arrive at the compound value of annuity.

Illustration No. 3

Mr. X deposits ₹ 1,000 at the end of every year for 4 years and the deposit earns a compound interest of 10% per annum. Calculate the amount at the end of 4th year.

Solution

$$F_n = A\left[\frac{(1+i)^n - 1}{i}\right]$$

Where F_n = Future value of annuity
A = Annuity
i = Interest rate

$$\text{Value at the end of four years} = 1{,}000\left[\frac{(1+0.10)^4 - 1}{0.10}\right]$$

$$= 1{,}000\left[\frac{0.4641}{0.10}\right]$$

$$= 1{,}000 \times 4.641 = 4{,}641$$

Illustration No. 4

Padmini deposits ₹ 20,000 in Bank of India on quarterly basis. Banks pays an interest rate of 8% p.a., compounded on quarterly basis. How much she would get at the end of two years?

Solution

Problem is concerned with calculation of compound value of annuity, at the end of specified period.

Formula for calculation is

$$F_n = A\left[\frac{(1+i)^n - 1}{i}\right]$$

Where F_n = Future value of annuity

A = Annuity

i = Interest rate

$$\text{Value at the end of two years} = 20{,}000\left[\frac{(1+0.02)^{4\times 2} - 1}{0.02}\right]$$

$$= 20{,}000\left[\frac{0.171}{0.02}\right]$$

$$= ₹\ 1{,}71{,}659$$

12.7 SINKING FUND

The purpose of sinking fund is to create a fund, when a big liability is to be repaid at the end of a known period; like redemption of debentures that involves a huge cash outflow to the firm. The purpose can be, even replacement of a fixed asset, at the end of its useful or economic life. Here, the events which are likely to happen are known in the beginning. So, the firm plans and earmarks a fixed amount every year, so that there would be no difficulty to meet the payment. If such planning is not made, normal operations of the business are likely to be affected. Normally, the annual payment is invested outside the business in certain safe investments where the return is fixed, like a bank deposit or Government securities that mature with interest at the end of the period.

The formula for sinking fund is reciprocal of the compound value annuity. The formula is as under:

$$\mathbf{A = FV\left[\frac{i}{(1+i)^n - 1}\right]}$$

Where A = Annuity

FV = Future value

Illustration No. 5

A company has issued debentures of ₹ 50 lakh to be repaid after 7 years. How much should the company invest in a sinking fund, earning 12 per cent per annum, in order to repay debentures?

Solution

Sinking fund:

$$FV\left[\frac{i}{(1+i)^n - 1}\right]$$

$$= 50{,}00{,}000\left[\frac{0.12}{(1+0.12)^7 - 1}\right]$$

$$= 50{,}00{,}000\left[\frac{0.12}{2.210 - 1}\right]$$

$$= 50{,}00{,}000 \times \frac{0.12}{1.210} = ₹\ 4{,}95{,}867.77$$

Illustration No. 6

Rupa has been working as senior executive. She plans to have a lump sum amount of ₹ 10 lakhs at the end of her retirement. She is due to retire at the end of 5 years. She is prepared to save regularly, every year. Her savings would yield an interest rate of 10% p.a., compounded on an annual basis. Advise her about her savings she has to make?

Solution

Sinking fund required is ₹ 10 lakhs, at the end of 5 years on retirement.

Problem is concerned with calculation of annuity. In this case, annuity is the annual payment she has to make to receive the above lump sum amount.

$$A = FV\left[\frac{i}{(1+i)^n - 1}\right]$$

Where A = Annuity

FV = Future value

$$= 10{,}00{,}000\left[\frac{0.1}{(1+0.10)^5 - 1}\right]$$

$$= 10{,}00{,}000\left[\frac{0.1}{0.61051}\right]$$

$$= ₹\ 1{,}63{,}797$$

12.8 COMPOUND VALUE OF ANNUITY DUE

The concepts of compound value and present value of annuity are based on the assumption that series of payments are made **at the end of the year**. A series of fixed payments starting **at the beginning of the year** for a specified number of years is called

Annuity Due. When a fridge is purchased, first instalment is to be paid immediately, and subsequent instalments in the beginning of each period. Its calculation is as under:

$$F_n = A\left[\frac{(1+i)^n - 1}{i}\right] \times (1+i)$$

Where F_n = Future value of annuity

A = Annuity

Illustration No. 7

Mr. Rao deposits ₹ 5,000 at the beginning of each year for 5 years in a bank and the deposit earns a compound interest at 8% per annum. Calculate the amount at the end of the five-year period?

Solution

Formula for calculating the annuity due is as under:

$$F_n = A\left[\frac{(1+i)^n - 1}{i}\right] \times (1+i)$$

Where F_n = Future value of annuity

A = Annuity

$$= 5{,}000\left[\frac{(1+0.08)^5 - 1}{0.08}\right] \times (1+0.08)$$

$$= 5{,}000 \times \frac{0.4693 \times 1.08}{0.08}$$

$$= 5{,}000 \times 5.87 \times 1.08 = ₹\ 31{,}679$$

12.9 DIFFERENCE BETWEEN ANNUITY AND ANNUITY DUE

When the cash flow or instalment occurs at the end of each period, it is called regular annuity or deferred annuity. When the cash flow or instalment occurs at the beginning of each period, it is called Annuity Due. In other words, both Annuity and Annuity Due have similar 'n' cash flows, however, the date of cash flows is different that make the valuation methods different.

Illustration No. 8

Your father has promised to give you ₹ 1,00,000 in cash on your 25th birthday. Today is your 16th birthday. He wants to know the following things:

(a) If he decides to make annual payments into a fund after one year, how much cash will each have to be, if the fund pays 8 per cent per annum?

(b) If he decides to invest a lump sum in the account after one year and let it compound annually, how much will be the lump sum?

(c) If in (a) the payments are made in the beginning of the year, how much will be value of annuity?

Solution

(a) Sinking fund concept is to be applied to know the annual payment. Formula to know the annual payment is:

$$A = FV\left[\frac{i}{(1+i)^n - 1}\right]$$

where A = Annuity

FV = Future value = ₹ 1,00,000

i = Interest rate = 8%

n = Number of years = 9 Years.

$$A = 1{,}00{,}000 \times \left[\frac{0.08}{(1+0.08)^9 - 1}\right]$$

$$= 1{,}00{,}000 \times \frac{0.08}{1.999 - 1}$$

$$= 1{,}00{,}000 \times \frac{0.08}{0.999} = ₹\ 8{,}008$$

Father has to contribute ₹ 8,008 every year, commencing from his 17th birthday. He has to contribute for 9 birthdays as 16th birthdays are already over.

(b) Compound value of a lump sum : $P\ (1 + i)^n$

Where P = Principal at the beginning of the period

$$1{,}00{,}000 = P\ (1 + 0.08)^8$$

$$= P \times 1.8509$$

$$P = \frac{1{,}00{,}000}{1.8509} = ₹\ 54{,}027$$

Father would be investing ₹ 54,027 at the end of 17th birthday, so that the amount would earn interest for a period of 8 years and gives ₹ 1,00,000 at the end of 25th birthday.

(c) As payments are made at the beginning of each year, it is a problem related to 'Annuity Due'. In annuity, instalment is paid at the end of the period, while instalment is paid in the beginning of the period in the case of 'Annuity Due'. The first payment would be made on the first day of 17th year.

$$F_n = A\left[\frac{(1+i)^n - 1}{i}\right] \times (1+i)$$

Where F_n = Future value of annuity = ₹ 1,00,000

A = Annuity

i = Interest rate = 8%

n = Number of years = 9 Years.

$$1{,}00{,}000 = A\left[\frac{(1+0.08)^9 - 1}{0.08}\right] \times (1+0.08)$$

$$= A \times [12.49] \times 1.08$$

$$= A \times 13.49$$

$$= A = ₹\,7{,}413$$

Father has to contribute ₹ 7,413 at the beginning of each year, commencing from 17th birthday.

Note: In 'Annuity', instalment is paid at the end of the year, while in 'Annuity Due', instalment is paid at the beginning of the year. Hence, instalment amount in 'Annuity Due' is always lower compared to 'Annuity', if other aspects are similar.

12.10 DOUBLING PERIOD

We want to calculate the period that is needed to double the amount, once the interest rate is given. This is called Rule of 72.

$$\text{Doubling period} = \frac{72}{\text{Rate of Interest}}$$

Illustration No. 9

If you deposit an amount of ₹ 5,000 at 8 per cent rate of interest, in how many years will this amount double? Work out the problem by using Rule of 72.

Solution

For calculating the double period, the formula is

$$\text{Doubling period} = \frac{72}{\text{Rate of Interest}}$$

$$= \frac{72}{8}$$

$= 9$ years

12.11 EFFECTIVE RATE OF INTEREST IN CASE OF MULTI-PERIOD COMPOUNDING

There are different bases for compounding such as yearly, half-yearly, quarterly and monthly basis.

Effective interest rate brings all the different bases of compounding on a single platform for comparison to select the beneficial base.

The question is which works out highest interest amount? When interest is compounded on half-yearly basis, interest amount works out more than the interest calculated on yearly basis. Quarterly compounding works out more than half-yearly basis. Monthly compounding works out more than, even, quarterly compounding. So, **if compounding of interest is more frequent, then the total amount of interest per year works out more.** If principal amount is compounded daily, it works out the highest.

If interest rate is equal, then there is no problem. Compounding frequently gives more interest. When interest rates are different, it is not easy to choose, at a glance.

Now, we want to equate them for comparison. Suppose, an option is given as follows:

Basis of Compounding	Interest Rate
Yearly	10
Half-yearly	9.5
Quarterly	9
Monthly	8.5

Now, the question is which basis of compounding is to be accepted to get the highest interest rate. The answer is to calculate 'Effective Interest Rate'. Effective interest rate brings all the different bases of compounding on a single platform, for comparison and to choose.

Actual interest rate realised is called 'Effective Rate of Interest'.

Effective interest rate (EIR) can be calculated in case of Multi-period compounding by using the following formula:

$$\text{EIR} = [1 + i/m]^m - 1$$

Where EIR = Effective interest rate

i = Nominal interest rate (Yearly interest rate)

m = Frequency of compounding, per year

Take yearly interest rate (nominal interest rate) as the base and find out the comparable rate of interest for half-yearly, quarterly and monthly basis and select that which is attractive.

Illustration No. 10

(i) A company offers 12% rate of interest on deposits. What is the effective rate of interest, if the compounding is done:

(A) Half-yearly

(B) Quarterly

(C) Monthly

(ii) As an alternative, the following rates of interest are offered for choice. Which basis gives the highest rate of interest that is to be accepted?

Basis of Compounding	Interest Rate
Yearly	12
Half-yearly	11.75
Quarterly	11.50
Monthly	11.25

Solution

(i) The formula for calculation of effective interest is as below:

$$EIR = [1+i/m]^{m} - 1$$

Where EIR = Effective interest rate

i = Nominal interest rate (Yearly interest rate)

m = Frequency of compounding per year

n = number of years

(A) When the compounding is done on half-yearly basis:

$= [\ 1 + 0.12/2]^{2} - 1$

$= 0.1236 = 12.36\%$

(B) When the compounding is done on quarterly basis:

$= [\ 1 + 0.12/4]^{4} - 1$

$= 0.1255 = 12.55\%$

(C) When the compounding is done on monthly basis:

$= [\ 1 + 0.12/12]^{12} - 1$

$= 0.1268 = 12.68\%$

Basis of Compounding	Interest Rate	Effective Interest Rate
Yearly	12	12%
Half-yearly	12	12.36%
Quarterly	12	12.55%
Monthly	12	12.68%

(ii) All options are brought to a common platform of interest rate on annual basis for comparison.

When the compounding is done on half-yearly basis:

$$= [\ 1 + 0.1175/2]^2 - 1$$
$$= 0.1201 = 12.01\%$$

When the compounding is done on quarterly basis:

$$= [\ 1 + 0.1150/4]^4 - 1$$
$$= 0.1192 = 11.92\%$$

When the compounding is done on monthly basis:

$$= [\ 1 + 0.1125/12]^{12} - 1$$
$$= 0.1184 = 11.84\%$$

Basis of Compounding	Interest Rate Offered	Effective Interest Rate works out to
Yearly	12	12%
Half-yearly	11.75	12.01%
Quarterly	11.50	11.92%
Monthly	11.25	11.84%

Out of all, interest rate of 11.75% on half-yearly compounding works out to be the highest effective interest rate i.e. 12.01%. So, this option is to be accepted.

Illustration No. 11

Calculate effective interest rate on the following and decide the best investment that yields the highest interest rate, amongst them:

Post office MIS scheme, monthly interest	= 8% p.a.
ICICI Bank Deposit, quarterly interest	= 8.25% p.a.
HDFC Ltd, half-yearly interest	= 8.50% p.a.

Solution

Formula for calculation of Effective Interest Rate (EIR) is as below

$$EIR = (1 + i/m)^m - 1$$

i = Nominal interest rate (yearly interest rate)

m = Frequency of compounding per year

Post office MIS scheme, monthly interest = 8% p.a.

$$\begin{aligned} EIR &= (1 + i/m)^m - 1 \\ &= (1 + 0.08/12)^{12} - 1 \\ &= 1.08292 - 1 \\ &= 8.29\% \end{aligned}$$

ICICI Bank Deposit, quarterly interest = 8.25% p.a.

$$\begin{aligned} EIR &= (1 + i/m)^m - 1 \\ &= (1 + 0.0825/4)^4 - 1 \\ &= 1.0851 - 1 \\ &= 8.51\% \end{aligned}$$

HDFC Ltd, half-yearly interest = 8.50% p.a.

$$\begin{aligned} EIR &= (1 + i/m)^m - 1 \\ &= (1 + 0.0850/2)^2 - 1 \\ &= 1.0868 - 1 \\ &= 8.68\% \end{aligned}$$

Comparative interest table for decision-making

Name of Institution	Interest Rate	Compounding	Effective Interest Rate (EIR)
Post office MIS scheme	8% p.a.	Monthly	8.29%
ICICI Bank Deposit	8.25% p.a.	Quarterly	8.51%
HDFC Ltd Deposit	8.50% p.a.	Half-yearly	8.68%

Recommendation: HDFC Ltd Deposit is recommended as its interest rate 8.68% is the highest amongst the three different options.

12.12 PRESENT VALUE OF A PERPETUITY OR INFINITE LIFE ANNUITY

Annuity is a receipt or payment for a specific period, while Perpetuity is for an indefinite period. Perpetuity is an infinite life annuity. Both are different concepts. Pension to a freedom fighter is perpetuity. In other words, the payment is made to him as long as the freedom fighter is alive. The formula for calculating the present value of an infinite life annuity is by simply dividing the regular receipt by interest rate.

$$V_o = \frac{R}{i}$$

Where V_o = Present value of perpetuity

R = Regular receipt

i = Interest rate

Illustration No. 12

Calculate the present value of ₹ 2,000 received in perpetuity for an infinite period, taking the discount rate of 10%.

Solution

$$V_o = \frac{R}{i}$$

Where R = Regular receipt

i = Interest rate

$$= \frac{2{,}000}{0.10} = 20{,}000$$

12.13 DISCOUNTING OR PRESENT VALUE TECHNIQUE

Present value is the exact opposite of compound of future value. In case of compounding, we calculate the value of money at the end of the period; while in case of present value concept, we estimate the present worth of a future payment/instalment. Future value shows the amount receivable of present money on a future date. Principal amount always appreciates with interest. So, the future value is always higher than the present money. In case of present value, we calculate the value of future money receivable as on date, so it would be always lower than the future amount.

The present value approach is based on the concept that money has opportunity cost for money, lying idle.

The formula for calculating discounting value is

$$V_o = \frac{V_n}{(1+i)^n}$$

Where V_o = Present value

V_n = Future value at the end of 'n' period

Illustration No. 13

X has an option to receive the value today for a debenture with face value ₹ 1,000 and carrying interest rate of 10% per annum. The debenture falls due for payment after three years. Calculate the present value today.

Solution

The formula for calculating discounting value is

$$V_o = \frac{V_n}{(1+i)^n}$$

Where V_o = Present value

V_n = Future value at the end of 'n' period

$$\text{Present value} = \frac{1000}{(1+0.10)^3}$$

$$= \frac{1000}{1.331}$$

$$= ₹\ 751.31$$

12.14 SERIES OF CASH FLOWS

There are two types of calculating series of cash flows. They are:

(A) Present value of Series of Cash Flows

(B) Future value of Series of Cash Flows

12.15 PRESENT VALUE OF SERIES OF CASH FLOWS

In a business situation, investment is made today and returns are spread over a future period. One would like to know whether the investment is desirable or not. Cash flows may be uniform or changing at periodical intervals. In other words, the following formula is useful to calculate the present value of annuity, where the cash flow is constant or cash flows vary from period to period. For this, series of future cash flows are to be adjusted for the present value.

The present value of series of cash flows can be calculated by the following formula.

$$PV = \frac{A_1}{(1+i)} + \frac{A_2}{(1+i)^2} + \frac{A_3}{(1+i)^3} \cdots\cdots\cdots \frac{A_n}{(1+i)^n} = \frac{A_t}{(1+i)^t}$$

Where PV = Sum of individual present values of cash flows

A_1, A_2, A_3 = Cash flows for periods 1,2,3 etc

i = Discount rate

t = Time period

If the discounted value of the future inflows is more than the initial investment amount, investment proposal is to be accepted; otherwise, the proposal is to be rejected.

Illustration No. 14

Annuity received is ₹ 500 per annum. Calculate the present value for the annuity received for four years, if the discounting factor is 10%.

Solution

$$PV = \frac{A_1}{(1+i)} + \frac{A_2}{(1+i)^2} + \frac{A_3}{(1+i)^3} \dots\dots\dots \frac{A_n}{(1+i)^n}$$

Where PV = Sum of individual present values of cash flows

A_1, A_2, A_3 = Cash flows for periods 1,2,3 etc

i = Discount rate

n = time period

$$PV = \frac{500}{(1+0.10)} + \frac{500}{(1+0.10)^2} + \frac{500}{(1+0.10)^3} + \frac{500}{(1+0.10)^4}$$

$= 454.54 + 413.22 + 375.66 + 341.51$

$=$ ₹ 1,584.93

Illustration No. 15

For the following future cash flows, calculate the present value, assuming the time value of money is 10%.

(i) Decide its acceptance, in case initial investment is ₹ 7,000.

(ii) In case the initial investment is ₹ 8,000, what is the decision for acceptance or rejection?

(₹)

Year	Cash flows
1	1,000
2	2,000
3	3,000
4	4,000

Solution

We are to calculate the present value for the future cash flows.

Formula for calculating the present value of future cash flows is:

$$PV = \frac{A_1}{(1+i)} + \frac{A_2}{(1+i)^2} + \frac{A_3}{(1+i)^3} \dots\dots\dots \frac{A_n}{(1+i)^n}$$

Where PV = Sum of individual present values of cash flows

A_1, A_2, A_3 = Cash flows for periods 1,2,3 etc

i = Discount rate

n = Time period

$$PV = \frac{1,000}{(1+0.10)} + \frac{2,000}{(1+0.10)^2} + \frac{3,000}{(1+0.10)^3} + \frac{4,000}{(1+0.10)^4}$$

$$= 909.09 + 1,652.89 + 2,253.94 + 2,732.05$$

$$= ₹\ 7,547.97$$

Conclusion:

(i) The present value of future cash flows is ₹ 7,547.97. Proposal is acceptable as the present value of future cash flows is more than the initial investment ₹ 7,000.

(ii) Present value of the future cash flows ₹ 7,547.97 is less than the initial investment ₹ 8,000, so the proposal is to be rejected.

Illustration No. 16

A and B have been receiving the following remittances, over a period of five years.

	Year - I	Year - II	Year - III	Year - IV	Year - V	Total
A	4,000	5,000	3,000	6,000	2,000	20,000
B	2,000	5,000	4,000	3,000	6,000	20,000

Discount rate is 12%. Calculate present value of series of cash flows, received in the form of remittances. Decide who is better paid off?

Solution

We are to calculate the present value of the future series of cash flows.

Relevant formula is

$$PV = \frac{A_1}{(1+i)} + \frac{A_2}{(1+i)^2} + \frac{A_3}{(1+i)^3} \cdots\cdots\cdots \frac{A_n}{(1+i)^n}$$

Where PV = Sum of individual present values of cash flows

A_1, A_2, A_3 = Cash flows for periods 1,2,3 etc

i = Discount rate

n = Time period

$$\text{Present value of } A = \frac{4,000}{(1+0.12)} + \frac{5,000}{(1+0.12)^2} + \frac{3,000}{(1+0.12)^3} + \frac{6,000}{(1+0.12)^4} + \frac{2,000}{(1+0.12)^5}$$

$$= \frac{4,000}{1.12} + \frac{5,000}{1.2544} + \frac{3,000}{1.4049} + \frac{6,000}{1.5735} + \frac{2,000}{1.76234}$$

$$= 3,571.43 + 3,985.96 + 2,135.38 + 3,813.16 + 1,134.88$$

Present value of A = ₹ 14,640.81

$$\text{Present value of B} = \frac{2{,}000}{(1+0.12)} + \frac{5{,}000}{(1+0.12)^2} + \frac{4{,}000}{(1+0.12)^3} + \frac{3{,}000}{(1+0.12)^4} + \frac{6{,}000}{(1+0.12)^5}$$

$$= \frac{2{,}000}{1.12} + \frac{5{,}000}{1.2544} + \frac{4{,}000}{1.4049} + \frac{3{,}000}{1.5735} + \frac{6{,}000}{1.76234}$$

= 1,785.71 + 3,985.97 + 2,847.18 + 1,906.58 + 3,404.64

Present value of B = ₹ 13,930.08

A is better paid off with ₹ 14,640.81, compared to B with ₹ 13,930.08.

12.16 FUTURE VALUE OF SERIES OF CASH FLOWS

Earlier, we have considered the future value of a single payment made at the time zero. At times, different cash flows may occur at different periods of time. We may like to know the future value of series of payments made at the end of the period.

Formula for future value at the end is

$$V_n = R_1 (1+i)^{n-1} + R_2(1+i)^{n-2} + R_3(1+i)^{n-3} + \ldots\ldots(R_{n-1})(1+i) + R_n$$

Where V_n = Future value at the end of period 'n'

R_1 = Payment after period 1

R_2 = Payment after period 2

R_3 = Payment after period 3

R_n = Payment after period 'n'

i = Interest rate

Illustration No. 17

Calculate the future value at the end of five years of the following series of payments at 10% interest rate:

(₹)

At the end of Year	Cash Flow
1	1,000
2	2,000
3	3,000
4	2,000
5	1,500

Solution

$$V_n = R_1 (1+i)^{n-1} + R_2(1+i)^{n-2} + R_3(1+i)^{n-3} + \ldots\ldots(R_{n-1})(1+i) + R_n$$

Where V_n = Future value at the end of period 'n'

R_1 = Payment after period 1

R_2 = Payment after period 2

R_3 = Payment after period 3

R_n = Payment after period 'n'

i = Interest rate

$$= 1{,}000(1+0.10)^4 + 2{,}000(1+0.10)^3 + 3{,}000(1+0.10)^2 + 2{,}000(1+0.10) + 1500$$

$$= 1{,}464 + 2{,}662 + 3{,}630 + 2{,}200 + 1{,}500 = ₹11{,}456$$

Check Your Understanding

(A) State whether the following statements are True or False

1. Value of money received today is more than the value of the same amount of money received tomorrow.
2. Discounting technique is also known as compounding technique.
3. An annuity is a series of receipts or payments of unequal amounts.
4. There is no difference between simple interest and compound interest value of money.
5. Time value of money and time preference for money mean the same.
6. Cash flows of different years in absolute amounts are comparable.
7. The term 'annuity' does not necessarily apply to annual cash flows; it can even apply to monthly or quarterly cash flows occurring at equal intervals.
8. If cash flows occur at the end of the each period, the annuity is called regular annuity or deferred annuity.
9. Annuity and perpetuity are two different concepts.
10. Even if the instalment differs from month to month or period to period, this is still called annuity.
11. Effective interest rate brings all the different bases of compounding such as yearly, half-yearly, quarterly and monthly on a single platform for comparison to select the beneficial base.
12. Rule of 72 is useful to calculate period required for doubling principal amount, in the absence of interest rate.
13. Instalment amount in 'Annuity' and 'Annuity Due' is same for the same lump sum amount at the end of a specified period.
14. To calculate the present value, future series of cash flows are discounted at the appropriate rate.
15. Present value is the exact opposite of compound of future value.

Answers:

1. True 2. False 3. False 4. False 5. True 6. False 7. True 8. True
9. True 10. False 11. True 12. False 13. False 14. True 15. True.

(B) Objective Questions (Identify what is most appropriate)

1. Formula for sinking fund is
   (A) same as compounding annuity formula
   (B) reciprocal of compound value of annuity
   (C) reverse of effective interest rate formula
   (D) none of the above
2. Discounting technique is
   (A) slightly different from compounding technique
   (B) exactly opposite to compounding technique
   (C) same as compounding technique
   (D) none of the above
3. Formula for Compound value of a sum is
   (A) $A = P(1 + i)^n$ (B) $A = P(1 - i)^n$
   (C) $A = C(1 + i)^n$ (D) none of the above

   Where P = Principal
   i = Interest rate
   n = Number of years
   A = Amount at the end of 'n' number of years
4. Effective Interest Rate means
   (A) simple interest rate (B) compound interest rate
   (C) a single common interest rate for comparison between half-yearly, quarterly and monthly interest rates.
   (D) none of the above
5. Cash flows of two years, in absolute amounts are
   (A) comparable (B) different
   (C) same (D) none of the above
6. When interest is compounded on half-yearly basis, interest amount works out .... than the interest calculated on yearly basis.
   (A) less (B) more
   (C) same (D) none of the above
7. The value of money in hand today is ... than money receivable in future.
   (A) same (B) more
   (C) less (D) none of the above

Answers

1. (B) 2. (B) 3. (A) 4. (C) 5. (B) 6. (B) 7. (B).

Descriptive Questions

1. "A rational human being has a time preference for money." What are the reasons for such preference and illustrate with suitable examples? **(12.1.1 and 12.2)**
2. "Individuals have a time preference for money". State the reasons for such a preference. **(12.1.1 and 12.2)**
3. 'Generally individuals show a time preference for money.' Give reasons for such a preference and explain the relation between time preference rate and required rate of return. **(12.1.1,12.2 and 12.2.1)**
4. "The financial manager should take into consideration the time value of money in order to take correct financial decisions." Elucidate and explain importance in financial management. **(12.1.1,12.2 and 12.3)**
5. What is the relevance of "Time Value of Money in financial decision making?" **(12.1 and 12.1.1)**
6. Define

   (A) Compound value of annuity **(12.6.1)** (B) Required Rate of Return **(12.2.1)**
7. Write short notes on:

   (A) Annuity **(12.6)** (B) Effective Interest Rate **(12.11)**

   (C) Present and Future Value of cash flows **(12.15 and 12.16)**

   (D) Multiple compounding periods **(12.5.1)** (E) Sinking Fund **(12.7)**

Short Questions

Q.1. "A bird in hand is worth two in bush". How do you relate this statement to "Time Value of Money" in diverse financial decisions?

Ans. By nature, human beings are rationale and so prefer current consumption. That is the meaning of the proverb "A bird in hand is worth two in bush". No one would like to sacrifice present benefit, if only same benefit is assured later. One wants more, which is known as 'interest', value for waiting period. Money received at different periods does not carry the same value. In the concept of "Time Value of Money", money received at different periods is discounted to arrive at present value of money to understand whether money, today, is preferable or money receivable at a later date. Compenzation for time delay is interest. Unless suitable return is received for the waiting period, no financial decision is taken. In the absence of 'Time Value of Money', no financial decision takes place.

Q.2. Explain the term 'Annuity'. Give some examples.

Ans. Annuity is a series of equal receipts or payments occurring over a specified number of periods. Here, a fixed amount is paid or received, at regular interval, for a specified period. Annuity should be equal amount. The important point is amount can be either a receipt or payment. Annuity can be insurance premium, housing loan instalment or recurring deposit instalment paid at the end of every month. Annuity amount should not change from month to month and has to be constant for the whole specified period.

Q.3. Name the plan that helps the company to ascertain annual amount it has to set apart for replacement of an expensive fixed asset, whose life is to end after fifteen years?

Ans. 'Sinking Fund Plan' helps the company to ascertain the amount, it has to set apart every year for replacement of an expensive fixed asset, at the end of fifteen years. The annual amount can be calculated, once interest (return) the funds secure on a regular basis is known. Here, normally funds set apart, are invested outside the business which yield return. Investments would be disposed off at the time when the expensive asset needs replacement. This would not affect liquidity of the company at the time of replacement of asset. The idea of creation of sinking fund is to avoid disturbances to normal business operations by replacement of an expensive fixed asset.

Interview Questions

Q.1. What is meant by 'Time Value of Money?

Ans. 'Time Value of Money' is based on the concept that the money has a time value. 'Today rupee is more valuable than tomorrow rupee' is the underlying idea of this concept.

Q.2. State the difference between 'Annuity' and 'Annuity Due'.

Ans. 'Annuity' is the fixed sum received or paid at regular intervals, at the **end** of each period, while in an 'Annuity Due', receipts or payments occur at the **beginning** of the period. Amount is constant in both annuity and annuity due, but the payment occurs at the end of specified period (month/quarter etc.) in the former, while it occurs at the beginning in the later.

❍ ❍

CHAPTER 13

Basic Concepts of Standard Costing

13.1 INTRODUCTION

Aim: The aim of this chapter is to provide a basic idea on standard costing.

Cost figures in general can be divided into two broad categories viz. Historical Costs and Standard Costs. Historical costs are available after they are incurred. Such cost figures may have some value once they are analyzed. By analysis inefficiencies and deficiencies in production may be detected. By the time, the analysis under historical costs is made damage would have already occurred. Analysis can be done only after completion of period, and in consequence, the exercise would not be effective to correct past errors; though it is necessary to learn lessons for not repeating the same mistakes in future.

Standard cost is a predetermined cost, cost of production is determined in advance.

From management's point of view 'What a product should have costed' is more important than 'What did it cost?'

Standard costs are compared with actual costs to find out differences between the two. The differences or variances so obtained are analyzed to determine efficiency of operations so that necessary remedial and timely action may be taken.

To plan what should be the cost before production is the underlying idea of Standard Costing.

Management is always concerned to plan costs before they are actually incurred to exercise required control. The important techniques for exercising cost control are standard costing and budgetary control.

Standard costing is superior as compared to historical costing or actual costing. Historical costing is just post-mortem of expenditure incurred. So, this is not indeed an effective tool for cost control.

13.2 MEANING AND DEFINITION OF STANDARD COSTING

Standard: The word 'Standard' means criterion. Standard is a predetermined measurable quantity under defined set of conditions.

Standard Cost: Standard cost is a scientifically predetermined cost, which is arrived at assuming a particular level of efficiency in utilization of material, labour and indirect services.

When the actual figure is compared against standard, one can measure level of efficiency achieved by seeing how much actual cost differs from the standard that was set.

When costing is used for purpose of cost control, the technique is known as standard costing.

Through standard costing system, management is able to control variances in materials, labour and controllable expenses on quantity, efficiency and cost basis (in terms of money). Standard costs are widely used as they serve as an effective management tool of cost control.

Standard costing is a managerial device to determine efficiency and effectiveness of cost performance.

Definition: The costing terminology of the Institute of Cost and Management Accounts, London defines Standard Costing as:

"Standard Costing is the preparation of standard costs and applying them to measure the variances from actual costs and analyzing the causes of variations with a view to maintain maximum efficiency in production".

Standard cost has also been referred as cost plan for a single unit. This thinking is not merely an estimate or guess work, but it is based on certain assumed conditions of efficiency, economic and other factors.

From the above definition, technique of Standard Costing can be divided into the following:

1. Determination of standard costs under each element of cost-material, labour and overheads. In other words, preparation of standard cost sheet is the first step.
2. Finding out actual costs.
3. Comparison of actual costs with standard costs to ascertain and measure variances.
4. Analyse variances.
5. Presentation of information to appropriate levels of management for remedial action to control costs for achieving improved or better performance.

13.3 STEPS INVOLVED IN IMPLEMENTING STANDARD COSTING

Following are the steps involved in standard costing for achieving planned results and efficiency:

(A) Determination of standard cost

(B) Recording actual cost

(C) Comparison of standard cost with actual cost

(D) Finding out reasons for variance

(E) Reporting variance to the concerned for corrective action

13.4 UTILITY OF STANDARD COSTING

The system of standard costing is useful in all types of industries. But it is more commonly used in industries producing standardized products, which are repetitive in nature.

Standard Costing is a valuable aid in cost control.

Application of standard costing: Standard costing can be applied in industries producing standardized products, which are repetitive in character. Examples are fertilizers, bricks, sugar, cement etc.

In jobbing industries, jobs undertaken are different from one another. Setting standards in such job industries may prove to be expensive. So it is not worthwhile to develop and employ a full system of standard costing. Implementation of partial standard costing in such industries is a better idea. Certain processes or operations may be repetitive and introduction of standard costing can be applied only to those areas.

It is not possible to apply standard costing in jobbing industries because each job undertaken is different and setting standard for each job may be difficult.

The product in such industries may not be of a repetitive nature. Still, there are several operations or processes in the jobbing industries, which are of a repetitive nature or character. Standards can be set up for such repetitive-nature of operations or processes. In this way, the benefit of standard costing can be derived even in jobbing industries.

13.5 PRELIMINARIES FOR ESTABLISHMENT OF STANDARD COSTING

Standard costing is the most effective method available for controlling performance and cost.

The following preliminaries are necessary for establishment of standard costing:

(A) Study of technical aspects of factory

(B) Organization chart

(C) Establishment of cost centres

(D) Setting right standards

(E) Allocation and apportionment of overheads

(F) Training of staffs

It is presumed that there would be no power failures and breakdown in machinery.

(A) Study of technical aspects of factory

This involves study of various methods of manufacture and different processes involved. For setting right standard, understanding different processes and ascertaining reasons for previous years defects and their respective costs incurred for their rectification is very important. Previous years records are to be studied carefully to understand normal efficiency in each production process.

> **Study of technical aspects of factory is very important since standard cost should be based on actual situation in factory and areas of improvement that can reasonably be expected in the existing conditions.**

(B) Organization chart

Lines of authority and responsibility have to be defined clearly so that responsibility may be assigned as and when required.

(C) Establishment of cost centres

> **A cost centre is a location, person or item of equipment at which costs may be gathered, ascertained and used for purpose of cost control.**

Costs can be gathered at every stage of machine for control. Establishment of cost centre is necessary for fixing responsibilities of unfavorable variances for corrective action, and rewarding wherever favourable variances are shown.

(D) Setting right standard

Setting right standard is a big challenge. The challenge set should be attainable and also give spirit and enthusiasm to all staff in organization to achieve.

Different firms may fix different standards. Even the same firm may fix different standards at different periods of time. This is due to change in circumstances.

Standards may be classified as under:

(i) **Theoretical or Ideal Standard:** A standard based on ideal working conditions is said to be ideal standard. This standard is based on assumption of perfect performance. In this standard, it is assumed that there will be the most desirable conditions of performance. It does not consider possibility of loss due to wastage of materials or time. These standards provide no scrap, no idle time and no rest period. It is also presumed that there would be no breakdown in machinery, and moreover, total devoted performance of workers. It assumes no inefficiencies in manufacturing process. In nutshell, ideal standard presumes that there would be perfect working conditions. This standard is not likely to be achieved as ideal conditions of performance do not prevail. It is therefore a theoretical standard. Ideal conditions do not exist in real world. Once standards are fixed with ideal working conditions, they can never be achieved in real life. In consequence, there would be no incentive for workers to put in their best efforts as they know from the beginning that the standards fixed are never achievable. One Professor told his students "ideal standards are like dreams of Sophia Lorens – distant, desirable and rarely attainable".

The ideal standard breeds or creates frustration among employees because such standard is never attained.

Ideal standard sets a goal, which is always aimed at. However, in actual practice it is not attainable. So no body pays serious attention to achieve such standards. In fact setting up of this standard becomes a farce.

(ii) Basic Standard: It is a standard which is established for use over a longer period of time. Basic standard is set up for some base year. This standard is not changed on the basis of change in prices of materials and labour rates.

This is useful to help forward planning. They remain unaltered over a period of time. They are not adjusted to current market conditions. In other words, prices fixed in base year are applied to all the years for quantity of materials or number of labour hours. Thus this type of standard is not suitable from cost control view-point. They serve purpose of statistical data at the most. However, they may be suitable for those items of cost which are fixed in nature such as rent, managerial salaries etc.

Variances calculated on this basis at best helps in studying trends in manufacturing costs over a longer period of time.

(iii) Expected or Attainable Standard: This is the standard which is anticipated to be attained under conditions and circumstances prevailing within the organization.

Attainable standard is based not on ideal conditions but on expected performance.

In fixing attainable standard, allowance is also made for some unavoidable normal wastage and other inevitable inefficiencies. This standard is considered to be more realistic than the ideal standard because this standard is based on realities. To achieve attainable standard, certain amount of effort is needed. Attainable standard offers a challenge to achieve. All employees feel this standard as a goal to achieve or even to excel. Hence, this type of standard is best suited from control point of view. Application of attainable standard exposes real variances for exercising control.

Expected standard is based on anticipated performance, ideal from control view-point, as it reveals real deviations from actual performance.

This is an effective tool for cost control. In short, this is a standard which is anticipated to be achieved during a specified budget period.

13.5.1 Fixation of Standards

It is important to note that standard set should neither be too high nor too low. Nobody takes interest in standards if they are too high because such standards are not capable of being achieved easily. Low standards, on the other hand, does not encourage or induce to put in more efforts because they can be achieved very easily without incremental efforts. As a general rule, standards should be such that they are attainable, if workers put some more conscious efforts or become more efficient.

Success of standard costing depends upon fixation of right standard costs.

Thus, every possible effort should be made for establishing each element of cost i.e. raw materials, labour and overhead charges.

Just like a budget committee, there should be a standard committee entrusted with responsibility of setting standard costs. The committee should consist of all functional heads such as production manager, purchase manager, finance manager, sales manager, cost accountant and other functional heads, if any. As all functional departments are involved in fixation of standards, standards would be a collective decision of the organization. As all departments are involved in fixation of standards, there would be concerted effort from all concerned to achieve them.

Amongst all persons, cost accountant plays an important role in setting standards and plays a key role in control to achieve the main objectives of standard costing.

The role of cost accountant is vital to co-ordinate activities of committee so that standards set are as accurate as possible.

(E) Allocation and apportionment of overheads

Existing methods and policies regarding allocation and appropriation of overheads should be reviewed in light of standard costing principles.

(F) Staff training

Staff concerned should be given proper training before introduction of standard costing.

13.6 VARIANCE ANALYSIS

The Institute of Cost and Management Accountant terminology defines a variance as "the difference between a standard cost and the comparable cost incurred during a given period".

Variance is the difference between the actual and standard fixed. Variance may be related to materials, labour and overheads. Overheads relate to indirect materials, indirect labour and other indirect expenses such as insurance, lighting, rent etc. Once the difference is found out, reasons are to be analyzed.

> **Finding out difference between standard and actual cost component and analyzing reasons for difference is called variance analysis.**

Purpose of Variance Analysis: Variance analysis is the process of analyzing variances by subdividing total variance in such a manner that management can assign responsibility for departure from the standard performance. Variance analysis is the foundation for standard costing.

> **The purpose of variance analysis is to enable management to improve operations, increase efficiency, utilize resources more effectively and reduce costs.**

Standard costing is very important in controlling performance to achieve planned profits.

There are a number of reasons which give rise to variances and the analysis will help to locate reason and person or department responsible for it. For purpose of control, reasons of variance must be calculated immediately, causes must be inquired into, and remedial measures are timely taken.

The deviation of total actual cost from total standard costs is known as total cost variance. Analysis of variances may be done in respect of each element of cost and sales namely:

1. Direct Material Variances.
2. Direct Labour Variances.
3. Overhead Variances.
4. Sales Variances.

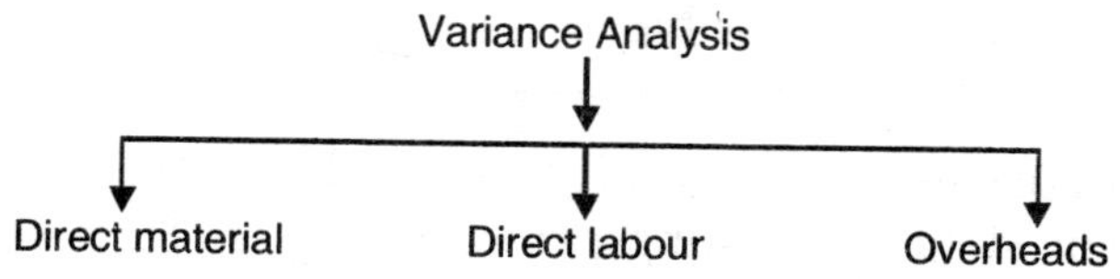

Variance analysis—types of variances

Favourable and Unfavourable Variance: When actual cost is less than standard cost or actual profit is more than standard profit, it is known as favourable variance or credit variance.

When actual cost exceeds standard cost, it is called unfavourable or adverse variance or debit variance.

Controllable and Uncontrollable Variances: If variance can be identified to a specific person, it is said to be controllable variance. Material used in excess of standard quantity results in controllable variance. Here, concerned person can take remedial action so it is a controllable variance.

If variance is due to factors beyond control of an individual action then the variance is said to be uncontrollable variance. Fluctuations in demand and supply and increase in the labour rate of workers belonging to a particular industry fall in the category of uncontrollable variance as they cannot be controlled by human action. No person or department can be held responsible for uncontrollable variance.

13.7 MATERIAL COST VARIANCE

Material cost variance is difference between standard cost of direct materials specified for the output achieved and actual cost of direct materials used. It is important that entire calculation is to be made for the actual production but not for planned production. It is calculated as under:

$$\text{Material Cost Variance} = \text{Standard Cost} - \text{Actual Cost}$$

$$\text{MCV} = \text{SC} - \text{AC}$$

or

$$\left[\text{Material cost variance} = \begin{Bmatrix}\text{Standard} \\ \text{quantity}\end{Bmatrix} \times \begin{Bmatrix}\text{Standard} \\ \text{price}\end{Bmatrix} - \begin{Bmatrix}\text{Actual} \\ \text{quantity}\end{Bmatrix} \times \begin{Bmatrix}\text{Actual} \\ \text{price}\end{Bmatrix}\right]$$

$$\text{MCV} = (\text{SQ} \times \text{SP}) - (\text{AQ} \times \text{AP})$$

It should be noted that the standard quantity must relate to the actual production.

Material cost variance is the sum of Material quantity (usage) variance and Material price variance.

Illustration No. 1

A furniture company uses sunmica tops for dining tables. It provides following data:

Standard quantity of sunmica per dining table	4 sq. fit.
Standard price per sq. ft. of sunmica	₹ 5
Planned production of dining tables	1,200
Actual production of dining tables	1,000
Sunmica actually used	4,300 sq. ft.
Actual purchase price of sunmica per sq. ft.	₹ 5.50

Calculate material cost variance.

Solution

Material cost variance will be calculated as under:

$$\begin{aligned} \text{MCV} &= (\text{SQ} \times \text{SP}) - (\text{AQ} \times \text{AP}) \\ \text{MCV} &= (4{,}000 \times 5) - (4{,}300 \times 5.5) \\ &= 20{,}000 - 23{,}650 \\ &= 3{,}650 \text{ (A)} \end{aligned}$$

13.7.1 Material Usage (or Quantity) Variance

This is that portion of material cost variance, which is due to the difference between the standard quantities specified and the actual quantity used. Its formula is as under:

$$\text{Material Usage Variance} = \begin{Bmatrix} \text{Standard} & - & \text{Actual} \\ \text{quantity} & & \text{quantity} \end{Bmatrix} \times \begin{matrix} \text{Standard} \\ \text{price} \end{matrix}$$

$$\text{MUV} = (\text{SQ} - \text{AQ}) \times \text{SP}$$

Material usage variance is the difference between standard and actual quantity multiplied by the standard price.

Illustration No. 2

Using the data given in Illustration No. 1, calculate material usage variance.

Solution

Material usage variance will be calculated as under:

$$\begin{aligned} \text{MUV} &= (\text{SQ} - \text{AQ}) \times \text{SP} \\ &= (4{,}000 - 4{,}300) \times 5 \\ &= ₹\ 1{,}500\ (\text{A}) \end{aligned}$$

Reasons for material usage variance

Some or all the following reasons may cause the material usage variance:

1. Use of defective or sub-standard materials, causing spoilage.
2. Carelessness in use of materials, resulting excessive consumption.
3. Pilferage of materials.
4. Faulty workmanship.
5. Defect in plant and machinery, causing excessive consumption of materials.
6. Change in design or specification of product.
7. Change in quality of materials.
8. Use of material mixture, other than standard mix.
9. Use of substitute or non-standard materials.
10. Yield from materials in excess of or less than standard yield.
11. Faulty material processing.

Responsibility: Normally, foreman of that machine that has caused variance is responsible for not exercising effective supervision over the concerned worker. But, department head or production manager is responsible for this variance as a whole.

13.7.2 Material Price Variance

This is "that portion of the material cost variance which is due to the difference between the standard price specified and the actual price paid". It is calculated by the following formula:

Material price variance = (Standard price − Actual price) × Actual quantity.

$$MPV = (SP - AP) \times AQ$$

Material price variance is the difference between standard and actual price multiplied by actual quantity.

Illustration No. 3

Using the data given in Illustration No. 1, calculate material price variance.

Solution

The material price variance will be calculated as follows:

$$MPV = (SP - AP) \times AQ$$

$$MPV = (5 - 5.50) \times 4{,}300$$

$$= ₹\ 2{,}150\ (A)$$

Reasons for material price variance

This variance usually arises due to the following reasons:

1. Change in basic prices of materials.
2. Failure to purchase standard quality, thereby resulting in a different price being paid.
3. Uneconomical size of purchase orders leading to lower/higher quantity discount.
4. Not availing cash discounts when standards set are based on such discounts.
5. Bad purchasing.
6. Change in transportation costs.
7. Rush purchases from uneconomical markets.
8. Purchase of a substitute material on account of non-availability of the material specified.
9. Change in rates of excise duty, purchase tax etc.
10. Off-season purchasing especially for certain seasonal products like jute, cotton etc.

Responsibility: Normally, purchase manager is responsible for material price variance. However, he cannot be held responsible for variance due to general change in market prices as this situation is obviously outside his control. Similarly, purchase of smaller quantity may be due to shortage of finances, which is a financial matter beyond his control.

The algebraic sum of material price variance and material usage variance should be equal to material cost variance.

Thus:

MCV = MPV + MUV

MCV = ₹ 2,150 (A) + ₹ 1,500 (A)

MCV = ₹ 3,650 (A)

Illustration No. 4

You have gathered the following information in respect of a product 'Y'.

Standard output	1,200 units
Actual output	1,000 units
Standard quantity for standard output	1,200 kg.
Actual quantity used	1,100 kg.
Standard price	₹ 7.00 per kg.
Actual Price	₹ 7.50 per kg

Calculate material cost variance.

Solution

Material cost variance is to be made for actual production but not for planned production. The actual production (output) is 1,000 units. So, entire calculation is to be made for 1,000 units.

Standard output (production) = 1,200 units

Standard quantity to be used = 1200 kg

So, for one unit of production (output), standard quantity to be used is one kg.

Actual output = 1,000 units

Standard quantity to be used = 1,000 kg

Actual quantity used = 1,100 kg

MCV = (SQ × SP) – (AQ × AP)

= (1,000 × 7) – (1,100 × 7.50) = 7,000 – 8,250

= 1,250 (Adverse variance)

13.8 LABOUR COST VARIANCE

The analysis and computation of labour cost variance is quite similar to material variances.

Labour cost variance is the difference between standard direct labour costs specified for the activity achieved and actual direct labour cost incurred. The entire calculation is to be made for actual production, but not for planned production.

It is calculated as under:

Labour cost variance = Standard cost – Actual cost

LCV = SC – AC

or

LCV = (Standard hours × Standard rate) – (Actual hours × Actual rate)

LCV = (SH × SR) – (AH × AR)

Illustration No. 5

Standard time and rate for unit component "Z" are given below:

Standard hours per unit	15
Standard rate	₹ 4 per hour

The actual data and related information are as under:

Planned production	1,200 units
Actual production	1,000 units
Actual hours	15,300 hours
Actual rate	3.90 per hours

Calculate Labour Cost Variance.

Solution

Labour Cost Variances = (SH for actual output × SR) – (AH × AR)

= (15,000 × 4) – (15,300 × 3.90)

= 60,000 – 59,670

= ₹ 330 (F)

Labour cost variance is sum of Labour time (or efficiency) variance and Labour rate variance.

13.8.1 Labour Time (or Efficiency) Variance

This is "that portion of the labour cost variance which is due to the difference between labour hours specified and the actual labour hours expended".

This variance is calculated as under:

Labour efficiency variance = (Standard hours – Actual hours) × Standard rate

LTV or LEV = (SH – AH) × SR

Labour efficiency time variance is the difference between standard and actual time valued at standard rate.

Tip to Students: This is similar to material quantity variance. Here instead of quantity of materials, labour hours are taken into account. The formula is just similar.

Illustration No. 6

Using the data given in Illustration No.4, calculate labour efficiency variance.

Solution

$$\begin{aligned} LEV &= (SH - AH) \times SR \\ &= (15{,}000 - 15{,}300) \times 4 \\ &= ₹\ 1{,}200\ (A) \end{aligned}$$

Reasons for labour efficiency variance

One or more of the following reasons usually causes this variance:

1. Poor working conditions e.g. inadequate lighting and ventilation, excessive heating, etc.
2. Defective tools and plant and machinery.
3. Inefficient workers.
4. Incompetent supervision.
5. Use of defective or non-standard materials, which requires more or less time than the standard time for processing.
6. Time wasted by factors like waiting for materials, tools etc. or machine breakdown.
7. Insufficient training to workers.
8. Change in method of operation.
9. Non-standard grade workers.

13.8.2 Labour Rate Variance

This is "that portion of the labour cost variance which is due to the difference between the standard rate specified and the actual rate paid." Its formula is as under:

$$\text{Labour Rate Variance} = (\text{Standard rate} - \text{Actual rate}) \times \text{Actual hours}$$

$$LRV = (SR - AR) \times AH$$

Labour rate variance is difference between standard and actual rates of wages multiplied by actual hours.

Tip to Students: This is similar to material price variance. Here instead of price of materials rate per hour is taken into account. The formula is just similar.

Illustration No. 7

Using the data given in Illustration No. 4, calculate Labour Rate Variance.

Solution

$$\begin{aligned} \text{LRV} &= (\text{SR} - \text{AR}) \times \text{AH} \\ &= (4 - 3.90) \times 15{,}300 \\ &= ₹\ 1{,}530\ (\text{F}) \end{aligned}$$

13.8.3 Reasons for Labour Rate Variance

Usual reasons are:

1. Change in basic wage rates.
2. Use of a different method of wage payment.
3. Employing workers of different grades from standard grades specified.
4. Unscheduled overtime.
5. New workers not being paid at full rates.

Responsibility: Often labour rate variance is an uncontrollable variance as this is usually determined by demand and supply conditions in the labour market, backed by a negotiable strength of trade union. Where this variance is due to use of a grade of labour other than that specified, acceptable explanation is non-availability of the labour grade specified. But when a foreman carelessly employs a wrong grade of labour on a job, he may be held responsible.

The algebraic sum of labour rate variance and labour efficiency variance is equal to labour cost variance.

Thus,

$$\begin{aligned} \text{LCV} &= \text{LRV} + \text{LEV} \\ ₹\ 330\ (\text{F}) &= ₹\ 1{,}530\ (\text{F}) + ₹\ 1{,}200\ (\text{A}) \\ &= 330\ (\text{F}) \end{aligned}$$

13.9 OVERHEAD VARIANCE

Overhead costs are the operating costs of a business, which cannot be identified or allocated but which can be apportioned to or absorbed by cost centers or cost units. According to terminology of cost accountancy (ICWA) overhead is defined as "the aggregate cost of indirect material cost, indirect wages (indirect labour cost) and indirect expenses". Thus overhead costs are important to management for cost control. Under standard costing, overhead rates are predetermined in terms of either labour hours or production units. The actual labour hours or actual units produced are multiplied by the standard overhead rate to determine the standard overheads cost. Standard overhead cost so calculated is then compared with actual overhead cost to find out the variance, if any, so as to take corrective measures. Overhead cost variance can thus be defined as difference between standard cost of overhead allowed for actual output and actual overhead cost incurred.

13.10 ADVANTAGES OF STANDARD COSTING

The following are the advantages of standard costing:

1. Help to management

Functions of management are planning, coordination, organization, motivation and control. Standard costing helps management in performing its functions in the following manner:

(A) Planning: Activities are studied carefully before hand and standards are fixed on an attainable basis with effort. This is a useful exercise in business planning. Standard costing instills in management a habit of thinking in advance.

(B) Coordination: Standards are fixed for different functions such as purchasing, selling, production, accounting etc. Coordination is achieved between different functions through standard costing.

(C) Organization facilitates delegation of authority: Shortfalls are to be identified for corrective actions. So, organization chart is prepared which establishes responsibilities of executives. With the help of organization chart, authority is defined and responsibility for corrective action is identified in the very beginning. This facilitates better achievement of results as authority and responsibility go hand in hand for better performance.

(D) Motivation: Standards fixed are to be achieved or excelled by concerned staff, maintaining quality of product. Plans can be formulated to reward achievers with suitable incentives. The incentive system motivates employees to achieve or even excel levels expected of them. This increases efficiency and productivity.

(E) Control: By comparing actual performance with standards fixed, immediate remedial action can be taken on the basis of variances revealed. Standard costing is an important technique of cost control. Cost control is more effective when standards are constantly reviewed and prompt action is taken on those lines.

The most important advantage of Standard Costing is that it facilitates cost control.

2. Measurement of efficiency

Standard cost provides a yardstick to measure efficiency or inefficiency. This makes possible the application of the principle 'Management by Exception'. Operations that meet standard performance or reaches closely are ignored. Management's attention is drawn to those distinct areas where action is essentially needed.

3. Fixing prices and formulating policies

Prices may be fixed by adding standardized margin of profits to standard cost. It enables management to quote prices for potential orders to push sale of products. This serves as a valuable aid to management in formulation of pricing policies.

4. Facilitates control and decision-making

Variance analysis provides ready means for interpretation of information and decision-making to exercise control in the areas where attention is required. Ready reports serve as a guide for immediate action.

5. Eliminates wastages

By fixing standards, certain wastes such as material wastages, idle time and machine hours etc. can be reduced.

6. Inventory valuation

Standard costing simplifies valuation of inventory. This ensures uniform valuation of stock–raw materials, work-in-progress and finished goods over a period. The difference between standard and actual cost is transferred to a variance account.

7. Creates cost consciousness

Targets are set for employees to achieve them. Additionally, standard costing creates cost consciousness amongst employees irrespective of their level in the whole organization.

8. Economical and simple

Standard costing is simple and economical in implementing costing system. It results in reduction of paper work in accounting and needs lesser number of forms and records. This results in reduction of costs.

9. Price quotations

Standard costing is useful to prepare cost estimates. Quotations can be sent to secure orders and increase business.

In short, standard costing is widely used as it is a very effective managerial tool for cost control.

13.11 LIMITATIONS

Standard costing suffers from certain limitations. These are:

1. **Difficult to establish standard costs:** It is difficult to establish standard costs. Inaccurate standards do more harm than good. Inaccurate and unreliable standards may give misleading results and may not enjoy the confidence of users.
2. **Changing conditions:** A business may not be able to keep standards up-to-date. Business conditions is never static. Standards too have to change with changing times. If firms ignore to revise standards suitably, damage would occur and even the current level of progress may not be sustained. Firms may not always revise standards as it is a difficult and costly affair.
3. **Morale and motivation may be affected:** If standards are set too high, it may have an adverse effect on morale and motivation of employees. Staff may not be able to cope up with the changed system.

4. **Expensive:** Operation of standard costing system is a costly affair for small concerns.
5. **Unsuitable for job orders:** Standard costing is expensive and unsuitable in job order industries and units engaged in manufacturing non-standardized products. For example, in a repair workshop, for each repair job undertaken, standards have to be set. Setting standards for each individual job is quite expensive and impractical.

Check Your Understanding

(A) State whether the following statements are True or False

1. Standard costing is not superior as compared to historical costing.
2. Standard costing is more widely applied in process and engineering industries.
3. Standards in standard costing are arrived on the basis of past performance.
4. Establishment of cost centre is necessary for fixing responsibilities for unfavourable variances.
5. Ideal standard is useful to help forward planning in standard costing.
6. Attainable standard reveals real variances for exercising control.
7. Cost Accountant does not play an important role in setting standards in standard costing.
8. As a general rule in standard costing, standards should be such that these are attainable, if workers put some more efforts or become more efficient.
9. Success of standard costing depends upon fixation of standard costs.
10. Attainable standards represent achievable targets with conscious efforts.
11. In jobbing industries, standard costing can be applied to all operations.
12. Standard costing is a valuable aid in cost control.
13. Variance analysis is the foundation of standard costing.
14. Variance is always negative.
15. When actual cost is more than standard cost, it is called adverse variance.
16. Standard costing is very important in monitoring performance and achieving planned profits.
17. Attainable standards fixed under standard costing do not allow any wastage, and so they are highly theoretical.
18. Historical cost means predetermined cost.
19. In jobbing industries, standard costing cannot be applied in any of the operations as they are not repetitive and their nature differs.
20. Standard costing is widely used as it is a very effective managerial tool of cost control.
21. Specific person or department can be held responsible for uncontrollable variance.
22. Ideal standard is based on assumption of perfect performance achievable in normal course of events.
23. Standard costing and budgetary control are complementary to each other.

24. Variances are divided into two categories, controllable variance and uncontrollable variance.
25. Ideal standards do not create frustration among employees as they are easy to achieve.
26. Standard costs are fixed by trade association of the concerned industry.
27. Study of technical aspects of a factory has no relation to introduction of standard costing.
28. Management can control inefficiencies on the fronts of quantity as well as costs through standard costing.
29. A cost center is a location, person or item of equipment at which costs may be gathered, ascertained and used for the purpose of cost control.
30. Standard costs are compared with actual costs to find out the differences between the two to analyze and determine efficiency of the operations so that necessary remedial action may be taken immediately.
31. Unfavourable variances are always uncontrollable.
32. Variance analysis is the difference between standard cost and comparable actual cost for a given period.

Answers:

1. False	2. True	3. False	4. True	5. False	6. True	7. False	8. True
9. True	10. True	11. False	12. True	13. True	14. False	15. True	16. True
17. False	18. False	19. False	20. True	21. False	22. False	23. True	24. True
25. False	26. False	27. False	28. True	29. True	30. True	31. False	32. True

(B) Objective Questions (Identify what is most appropriate)

1. Variance is
   (A) The sum of total cost and standard cost.
   (B) The standard cost.
   (C) The difference between standard cost and actual cost.
   (D) None of the above.
2. Under standard costing, cost of product is determined on the basis of
   (A) Historical cost (B) Variable cost
   (C) Fixed cost (D) Predetermined cost after technical assessment
3. Variances can be divided into following categories:
   (A) controllable and uncontrollable variances
   (B) favourable and unfavourable variances
   (C) both A and B
   (D) none of the above
4. Which is the best standard to be adopted in implementing standard costing?
   (A) Ideal standard (B) Attainable standard
   (C) Base standard (D) Marginal standard

5. Technique of evaluating deviations of actual cost from standard cost is called
   (A) trend analysis (B) variance analysis
   (C) regression analysis (D) linear programme
6. Standard costing is useful for all of the following except
   (A) valuation of closing stock
   (B) application of 'Management by exception' principle
   (C) cost control
   (D) maintenance of accounts
7. The formula for material cost variance is:
   (A) (SP × SQ – AP × AQ) (B) (SP × AP – SQ × AQ)
   (C) (AP × AQ – SP × SQ) (D) (SP × AQ – AP × SQ)
8. Material cost variance is the sum of
   (A) Material quantity variance and Material yield variance
   (B) Material quantity variance and Material price variance
   (C) Material mix variance and Material yield variance
   (D) Material price variance and Material mix variance
9. Labour efficiency variance is
   (A) (SH – AH) × SR (B) (SH + AH) × SR
   (C) (AH – SH) × SQ (D) (AH + SH + SQ)

Answers:

1. (C) 2. (D) 3. (C) 4. (B) 5. (B) 6. (D) 7. (A) 8. (B) 9. (A).

Descriptive Questions

1. Explain terms "Historical Cost" and "Standard Cost". **(13.1)**
2. What is standard costing? In what type of industries, standard costing can be applied? **(13.2 and 13.4)**
3. Explain the different steps in the implementation of standard costing. **(13.3)**
4. Write the preliminaries required for introducing a standard costing system in an organization. **(13.5)**
5. Explain the meaning of variance analysis and give a brief note on it. **(13.6)**
6. What is meant by 'Variance Analysis'? Whether all variances can be controlled? **(13.6)**
7. Describe material cost variance and labour cost variance. **(13.7, 13.7.1, 13.7.2, 13.8, 13.8.1 and 13.8.2)**
8. Write the advantages and limitations of standard costing. **(13.10 and 13.11)**
9. Standard costing can be applied in every industry–Discuss. **(13.2 and 13.4)**

Short Questions

Q.1. What is a cost centre?

Ans. A cost center is a location, person or item of equipment at which costs may be gathered, ascertained and used for the purpose of cost control.

Q.2. What is meant by overheads and state the role of standard costing in controlling overhead variances?

Ans. Overheads are the aggregate cost of indirect material cost, indirect wages (indirect labour cost) and indirect expenses. Overhead costs are important for the management to achieve cost control as they are significant costs. Under standard costing, overhead rates are predetermined in terms of either labour hours or production units. The actual labour hours or actual units produced are multiplied by the standard overhead rate to determine the standard overheads cost. Standard overhead cost so calculated is then compared with actual overhead cost to find out the variance, if any, so as to take corrective measures.

Q.3. In what type of industries, standard costing is applied and state the main utility of standard costing?

Ans. Standard costing is useful in all types of industries. But, it is more commonly used in industries producing standardized products, which are repetitive in nature. So standard costing is more widely applied in process and engineering industries. Examples of industries where standard costing can be usefully employed are: bricks, cement, fertilizers, paper, electronic lamps, sugar and tobacco products etc. Standard costing is a valuable aid in cost control.

Interview Questions

Q.1. What is the purpose of standard costing?

Ans. Main purpose of standard costing is to plan for determining costs before they are actually incurred. Management of every firm would be more interested to know what a product should cost rather than knowing how much it has costed them to make.

Q.2. Explain the meaning of variance analysis.

Ans. The difference between the standard and actual cost component is called variance. Finding out the reasons for difference is called variance analysis.

❍ ❍

CHAPTER 14

Budget and Budgetary Control

14.1 INTRODUCTION

A business organization needs a future plan to survive and ensure effective functioning to achieve the targets it wants to achieve. Costs are to be controlled to maximize profits. Budgeting is a useful device, widely used in the business for planning and control in the direction of monitoring costs and achieving targeted profits.

Modern Management wants something more to make the concern successful. Modern Management wants:

(A) All operations should be forecasted and planned in advance as far as possible.

(B) Compare actual results with the planned action for exercising control.

For the above two functions of Planning and Control, two new techniques are applied viz. Standard Costing and Budgetary Control.

Planning is a management function. In this competitive environment, the business enterprise becomes successful only with planning. Plans are framed to achieve better results. However, planning for its own sake is of no use. Plans should work to achieve the results planned. This is possible through co-ordination as all the tasks cannot be performed in isolation. Where more than one individual is involved, only co-ordination can bring the required results. For this to happen, control is needed.

Management is termed efficient, if maximum results are achieved with minimum costs, resources and efforts.

To achieve the anticipated targets, Planning, Co-ordination and Control are the three important tasks of management, achieved through budgeting and budgetary control.

14.2 MEANING OF BUDGET AND BUDGETING

A budget is a plan expressed in quantitative and monetary terms. In the language of business, a budget is a formal expression of the expected incomes and expenses for a definite future period. So, budget is a monetary and/or quantitative expression of business plans and policies, prepared in advance, and to be pursued in the future.

Definition: According to Certified Institute of Management Accountants, **"A budget is a financial and/or quantitative statement, prepared prior to a defined period of time, of the policy to be pursued during that period for the purpose of attaining the objective".**

> **Budget is a systematic plan for utilization of all types of resources at its command. It acts as a barometer of a business as it measures the success from time to time, against the standard set for achievement.**

Budgeting is a technique of formulating budgets.

Need of Budget: A budget is prepared to have effective utilization of resources and for the realization of objectives as efficiently as possible.

Characteristics of a Budget: The main characteristics of a budget are:

(A) A comprehensive business plan showing what the enterprise wants to achieve.

(B) Prepared in advance.

(C) For a definite period of time.

(D) Expressed in quantitative form, physical or monetary terms, or both.

(E) For achieving a given objective.

(F) A proper system of accounting is essential.

(G) System of proper fixation of authority and responsibility has to be in place.

14.3 MEANING AND NATURE OF BUDGETARY CONTROL

Budgetary control is the process of determining various budgeted figures for the enterprise and then comparing the actual performance with the budgeted figures for calculating the variances, if any. In this process, first budgets are prepared. Second, actual results are recorded. Third, comparison is made between the actual with the planned action for calculating the variances. Once the discrepancies are known, remedial measures are to be taken at proper time. Then only, planned results can be achieved.

> **A budget is a means and budgetary control is the end result.**

Definition of Budgetary Control: The Chartered Institute of Management Accountants, London, defines the Budgetary Control as

"The establishment of budgets relating to the responsibilities of executives to the requirements of a policy, and the continuous comparison of the actual with the budgeted result, either to secure by individual action the objective of the policy or to provide a basis for its revision".

Thus, establishment of budgetary control involves the following:

1. Establishment of budgets.
2. Continuous comparison of actual expenses with the budgets for achievement of targets, and fixing the responsibility to avoid failure to achieve the budget figures.
3. Revision of budgets in the light of changed circumstances.

The position of budgetary control can be likened or compared with the navigation of a ship across the seas. The navigating officer works out the course in advance and records the happening of the position of the ship from hour to hour in a log-book. To navigate the ship across the seven seas safely, the captain wants the navigating officer to check his ship's position constantly against the predetermined one. If the ship is off its course, the navigating officer must report immediately to the captain for prompt action to regain the course. Valuable lessons are learnt by the captain of the ship from a study of the factors that have caused misadventure in the past. Exactly, same is with the industrial ship.

What the modern management requires for day to operating purposes is detailed forecasts and immediate reporting of variances, with explanations of the reasons for variations.

This facilitates the management to take the required corrective action by the persons who have been made responsible, but contributed for the deviation/failure.

14.4 OBJECTIVES OF BUDGETARY CONTROL

The main objectives of budgetary control are as under:

1. Planning: Budgetary control forces the management at all levels to plan, in time, all the activities to be done during the future period. If planning is done properly, better results can be achieved.

2. Co-ordination: Normally, employees are efficient. If they are not considered efficient, they would not have been recruited, at all. Most of the employees can work very efficiently individually, but they fail to deliver better or improved results when they work as a group. This culture, inability to work in a group, collectively and cohesively, is more evident in Indian workforce. They work individually very well, but as a group their collective performance does not become the aggregate of individual outputs. Majority of the functions in an organization cannot be done in isolation. The functions, be it production or marketing, are to be performed in a greater co-ordination for smooth completion and better results. Budget exercise develops team spirit amongst the employees to work in a coordinated manner. The role of Budgetary Control is immense in integrating the activities of different departments.

> **Budgetary Control forces executives to think and think as a group.**

3. Communication: A budget is a communicating device. Budget cannot be achieved without communicating to the concerned, what is expected of him to be achieved. The approved budget shows, in detail, the plans of management which are communicated to the concerned departments. This would help them to give adequate understanding and knowledge of the programmes and policies, but also the restrictions to which the organization is expected to adhere to. For example, maximum amount that can be spent on advertisement, maintenance will be brought to the knowledge of the executives for exercising restraint and achieving the results.

4. Control: Control refers to that action which is necessary to bring the performance according to the original plan. Control is possible with pre-determined standards laid down in the budget. Budgetary control becomes possible with continuous comparison of actual performance with that of budget to find out the variances and report them for necessary corrective action.

> **Standard Costing and Budgetary Control are complementary to each other for achieving improved performance in an organization.**

14.5 REQUISITES FOR SUCCESSFUL BUDGETARY CONTROL SYSTEM

The following requisites are essential for effective budgetary control system:

1. **Determination of the Objectives:** There should be clear perspective of the objectives to be achieved through the budgetary control system. In most of the cases, the basic objective is to achieve desired/increased profits. To achieve, the following problems are to be sorted out:

   (A) **Laying down the Plan** for implementation to achieve the objectives,

   (B) Bringing **co-ordination** amongst the different departments; and

   (C) **Controlling** each function so as to bring the best possible results.

The steps needed to be followed to achieve the above are explained further, here.

2. **Proper Delegation of Authority and Responsibility:** The first step is to have a clear organizational chart explaining the authority and responsibility of each individual executive. **There should be no uncertainty regarding the point when the jurisdiction of one authority ends and that of another begins.**

3. **Proper Communication System:** The flow of information should be quick so that the budgets are implemented. **Two-way communication is important.** What is required to be achieved and how it is to be achieved should reach the lowest

level. Similarly, upward communication in respect of implementation difficulties should reach the top level to sort out, without loss of time. The performance reports at the various levels help the management in monitoring, leading to the achievement of the budgeted goals.

4. **Participation of All Employees:** Budget preparation and control are done at the top level. However, involvement of all persons, including at the lower level, is necessary in framing the budget and its implementation for the success of budgetary control. In practice, budgets are executed at the lower level. With experience, they can offer practical suggestions that can lead to success.

> **The success of Budgetary Control depends more on the active participation of all employees of the organization.**

5. **Flexibility:** Future is uncertain. Despite the best planning and foresight, still there may be occurrences that may require adjustments. Budgets should work in the changed circumstances. **Flexibility in budgets is required to make them work under changed circumstances.**
6. **Motivation:** Human beings execute Budgets. **There should be incentive in achieving the required targets.** All persons should be motivated to improve their working to achieve the goals set in the budgets.

14.6 ESSENTIAL STEPS FOR INSTALLATION OF BUDGETARY CONTROL SYSTEM

In order to have effective Budgetary Control System, it is appropriate to take the following steps:

1. **Budget Manual:** This is a written document specifying the objectives and procedures of budgetary control. **It spells out the duties and responsibilities of executives.** The budget manual defines the sanctioning powers of various authorities.
2. **Budget Centres:** A budget centre is that part of organization for which the budget is prepared. **Budget centre can be a department, section of a department or any other part of department.** Budget centres are necessary for the purpose of ascertaining cost, performance and its control.
3. **Budget Committee:** In a large concern, all the functional heads are the members of the budget committee. They discuss their respective budgets and finalise the budget after collective decisions. **The committee is responsible for its execution and achievement of the goals set.**
4. **Budget Officer:** The chief executive appoints budget officer, who is conversant with the functioning of various departments. All budgets are presented to the budget officer who places before the budget committee for its approval, after making the necessary changes. The actual performance of each department is communicated to the budget officer. He determines the variances, analyses the

reasons and reports to the top management to take the necessary actions to remove the deviations. The variances are reported to the concerned departments too, for necessary action.

> **As the convenor of the budget committee, the main function of Budget officer is co-ordination to ensure achievement of the budgeted targets.**

5. **Functional Budgets: Separate functional budgets have to be prepared.** Examples are Production Budget, Sales Budget, HR Budget, Cash Budget, Capital Expenditure Budget and R & D Budget.
6. **Budget Period: A budget period is the length of the period for which budget is prepared.** Normally, budgets like purchases and sales budgets are prepared for one year. However, a capital expenditure budget is prepared for a longer period i.e., 3 to 5 years.
7. **Determination of Key Factor:** Budgets are prepared for all the functional areas such as production, sales, purchases, finance, human resources and research and development. These activities are inter-connected and inter-dependent and so the budgets are. For example, raw material supply may be limited. So, production and sales budgets are prepared based on the purchase budget. To some of the firms, finance may be a constraint. Then, all other budgets are prepared based on the availability of finance.

> **A factor, which influences all other budgets, is known as key factor or principal factor.**

A better co-ordination brings better performance, even while facing constraints.

The influence of key factor may neither be permanent nor may the same factor be constant. Limited supply of raw materials may be the key factor till an alternative source of supply for that material is found. When the raw material supply problem is eased, another factor may create the problem and become key factor. After raw materials problem is solved, sales may become a problem and become a key factor due to change in trends. The management would be constantly endeavouring to remove the problems associated with key factor for better performance.

14.7 ADVANTAGES OF BUDGETARY CONTROL

The following are the advantages of budgetary control system:

1. **Profit Maximization**: The resources are put to best possible use, eliminating wastage. Proper control is exercised both on revenue and capital expenditure. To achieve this, proper planning and co-ordination of various functions is undertaken. So, the system helps in reducing losses and increasing profits.
2. **Co-ordination:** Co-ordination between the plans, policy and control is established.

The budgets of various departments have a bearing on each other as activities are inter-related. As the size of operations increases, co-ordination amongst the different departments for achieving a common goal assumes more importance. This is possible through budgetary control system.

As all the personnel in the management team are involved and coordinated, there is bound to be maximum profits.

Budgetary control system acts as a friend, philosopher and guide to the management.

3. **Communication:** A budget serves as a means of communicating information throughout the organization. A sales manager for a district knows what is expected of him. Similarly, production manager knows the amount of material, labour and other expenses that can be incurred by him to achieve the goal set to him. So, every department knows the performance expectation and authority for achieving the same.

4. **Tool for Measuring Performance:** Budgetary control system provides a tool for measuring the performance of various departments. The performance of each department is reported to the top management.

   The system helps the management to set the goals. The current performance is compared with the pre-planned performance to ascertain deviations so that corrective measures are taken, well at the right time.

   It helps the management to economise costs and maximize profits.

5. **Economy:** Planning at each level brings efficiency and economy in the working of the business enterprise. Resources are put to optimum use. All this leads to elimination of wastages and achievement of overall efficiency.

6. **Determining Weaknesses:** Actual performance is compared with the planned performance, periodically, and deviations are found out. This shows the variances highlighting the weaknesses, where concentration for action is needed. Action at the right point brings required results.

7. **Consciousness:** Budgets are prepared in advance. So, every employee knows what is expected of him and they are made aware of their responsibility. So, they do their job uninterrupted for achieving what is set to him to do.

8. **Timely Corrective Action:** The deviations are reported to the attention of the top management as well as functional heads for suitable corrective action, in time. In the absence of budgetary control, deviations would be known only at the end of the period. There is no time and opportunity for necessary corrective action.

9. **Motivation:** Success is measured by comparing the actual performance with the planned performance. Suitable recognition and reward system can be introduced to motivate the employees at all levels, provided the budgets are prepared with adequate planning and foresight.

10. **Management by Exception:** The management is required to exercise action only when there are deviations. So long as the plans are achieved, management need not be alerted. This system enables the introduction of 'Management by Exception' for effective delegation and control.

11. **Overall Efficiency:** Every one in the management is associated with the preparation of budget. So, there is involvement from the top functionaries and each one knows how the targets fixed can be achieved. Budgets approved by the Budget Committee, represents the collective decision of the organization. With the implementation of budgetary control, there would be over all alertness and improved working in all the departments, with better coordination.

> **Budgetary Control acts like an impersonal policeman to bring all round efficiency in performance.**

12. **Optimum Utilization of Resources:** As there is effective control over production, the resources of the organization would be put to optimum utilization.

14.8 CLASSIFICATION OF BUDGETS

Budgets can be classified on the basis of time, function and flexibility.

(A) Classification on the Basis of Time: Budgets can be long-term and short-term. Long-term budgets relate to a period ranging from 5 to 10 years. Only the top level knows these budgets and lower level would not be aware of them. These budgets are prepared for certain areas of the enterprise such as capital expenditure and research and development. Short-term budgets are for one or two years. Generally, budgets are prepared to coincide with the financial year so that comparison of the actual performance with budgeted estimates would facilitate better interpretation and understanding.

(B) Classification on the Basis of Function: Budgets are divided on the basis of different functions performed in the organization. They are Sales Budget, Production Budget, Purchase Budget, Direct Labour Budget, Overheads Budget, Cash Budget and, finally, Master Budget.

> **The Master or Final Budget is a summary budget, which incorporates all functional budgets in a summarized form.**

(C) Classification on the Basis of Flexibility: There are two types of budgets on the basis of flexibility.

(i) Fixed Budgets: The budget is prepared on the basis of fixed level of activity. For example, budget is prepared to achieve a production level of 70,000 units with sales of 50,000 units. In other words, **a fixed budget remains unchanged, irrespective of the change in volume or level of activity.** It is presumed that the forecast and the actual level of activity, both production and sales, would be one and the same. In other words, if the budget is prepared for a particular quantity of production and sales, at a particular cost and selling price, the same should happen. Then only, this type of budgeting would be useful. Where static conditions occur, this is useful. In practical life, it does not happen on account of changes that cannot be anticipated or foreseen. It is not practically possible to anticipate the likely production and sales, accurately. Due to this limitation, fixed budgets are not followed, where the forecast cannot be done accurately, both for production and sales.

(ii) **Flexible Budgets:** Flexible budget is a good budgeting technique as well as tool of control.

> **Flexible budgets are prepared where the level of activity cannot be estimated with accuracy. Preparation of Flexible budgets is normally adopted in real life working.**

This type of budget is prepared for a range of production activity say 15,000 to 25,000 units.

> **A flexible budget recognizes the difference between fixed, semi-fixed and variable cost and is designed to change in relation to the change in level of activity.**

The flexible budgets will be useful, where the level of activity changes and cannot be estimated at the time of preparation of budget.

14.9 DIFFERENCE BETWEEN FIXED AND FLEXIBLE BUDGET

Basis of Difference	Fixed Budget	Flexible Budget
1. Level of Activity	It is based on a single level of activity.	It is based on more than one level of activity.
2. Assumptions	Assumes that conditions and level of activity remain constant.	Assumes that level of activity may change.
3. Cost Classification	Costs are not classified according to their nature.	Costs are classified as per their nature i.e. fixed, semi-fixed and variable.
4. Comparison	If the level of activity changes, budget and actual performance cannot be compared.	If there is a change in the level of activity, budget can be recast to make it possible for comparison.
5. Adjustment	Fixed budget is not able to provide any automatic adjustment, when the volume of production/sales changes.	Flexible budget is automatically geared to changes in production/ sales activity.
6. Utility	A fixed budget has limited utility and it may give misleading results, when level of activity changes.	Flexible budget provides wider acceptance to several organisations as it provides a reliable basis for changed level of activity.

Illustration No. 1

With the following data for a 60% activity, prepare a budget for Pankaj Kumar Tiwari & Co. having production at 80% and 100% capacity:

Production at 60% activity	600 units
Material	₹ 100 per unit
Labour	₹ 40 per unit
Expenses	₹ 10 per unit
Factory Expenses	₹ 40,000 (40% fixed)
Administration Expenses	₹ 30,000 (60% fixed)

Solution

Production Budget at 80% capacity and 100% capacity

	80% capacity	100 % capacity
Production activity	**800 units**	**1,000 units**
Variable Cost:		
Materials @ ₹ 100 per unit	80,000	1,00,000
Labour @ ₹ 40 per unit	32,000	40,000
Expenses @ ₹ 10 per unit	8,000	10,000
Factory Expenses @ ₹ 40 per unit*	32,000	40,000
Administration Expenses @ ₹ 20 per unit*	16,000	20,000
Total Variable Cost	**1,68,000**	**2,10,000**
Fixed Cost:		
Factory Expenses	16,000	16,000
Administration Expenses	18,000	18,000
Total Fixed Cost	**34,000**	**34,000**
Total Cost	**2,02,000**	**2,44,000**

* Factory and Administrative expenses are divided into fixed and variable costs at the level given. For example, at 600 units fixed cost in factory expenses is ₹ 16,000, so balance ₹ 24,000 is variable cost for 600 units (₹ 40 per unit).

Illustration No. 2

The expenses for the production of 5,000 units in Rahul Talreja & Co are given as follows:

	Per Unit ₹
Materials	50
Labour	20
Variable overhead	15
Fixed overhead (₹ 50,000)	10
Administrative expenses (5% Variable)	10
Selling expenses (20% fixed)	6
Distribution expenses (10% fixed)	5
Total cost of sales per unit	116

You are required to prepare a budget for the production of 7,000 units and 9,000 units.

Solution

Production Budget for 7,000 units and 9,000 units

(₹)

Production Activity	7,000 units	9,000 units
Variable Cost:		
Material cost ₹ 50 per unit	3,50,000	4,50,000
Labour ₹ 20 per unit	1,40,000	1,80,000
Variable overhead ₹ 15 per unit	1,05,000	1,35,000
Administrative expenses @ 50 p per unit *	3,500	4,500
Selling expenses @ ₹ 4.80 per unit **	33,600	43,200
Distribution expenses @ ₹ 4.50 per unit ***	31,500	40,500
Total Variable Cost	**6,63,600**	**8,53,200**
Fixed Cost:		
Fixed overheads	50,000	50,000
Administrative expenses	47,500	47,500
Selling expenses	6,000	6,000
Distribution expenses	2,500	2,500
Total Fixed Cost	**1,06,000**	**1,06,000**
Total Cost of Sales	**7,69,600**	**9,59,200**

Note: *In the problem, expenses per unit are calculated on the production level of 5,000 units. So, administrative expenses were ₹ 10 per unit when the production level was 5,000 units. So, total administrative expenses were ₹ 50,000. Out of which, 5% was variable cost (₹ 0.50 per unit) and balance 95% was fixed cost, which works out to ₹ 47,500. Fixed costs ₹ 47,500 are constant, whatever be the level of activity.

** Total Selling Expenses are ₹ 30,000. Out of which, 20% were fixed costs, which works out to be ₹ 6,000. Balance amount is variable cost ₹ 24,000, which works out to be ₹ 4.80 per unit.

*** Total Distribution costs were ₹ 25,000. Out of which 10% were fixed costs, which works out to ₹ 2,500. Balance amount was variable cost ₹ 22,500, which works out to be ₹ 4.50 per unit.

Illustration No. 3

Prepare a Production Budget for each month and summarized Production Budget for the six months period ending 31st Dec., 1989 from the following for product X.

(i) The units to be sold for different months are as follows:

July, 1989	1,100
August	1,100
September	1,700
October	1,900
November	2,500
December, 1989	2,300
January, 1990	2,100

(ii) There will be no work in progress at the end of any month.

(iii) Finished units equal to half the sales for the next month will be in stock at the end of each month (including June 1989).

(iv) Budgeted production and production cost for the half-year ending 31st December, 1989 are as follows:

Production units	11,100
Direct materials per unit	₹ 10
Direct wages per unit	₹ 4
Total factory overheads apportioned to product	₹ 44,400

Solution

Summarized Production Budget for the period ending 31st Dec., 1989 for product X

(in terms of units)

Month (Year 1989)	Opening Stock	Production	Sales	Closing Stock
June				550*
July	550	1,100	1,100	550*
August	550	1,400	1,100	850
Sept	850	1,800	1,700	950
Oct	950	2,200	1,900	1,250
Nov	1,250	2,400	2,500	1,150
Dec	1,150	2,200	2,300	1,050
Total		11,100	10,600	

* First arrive at closing stock based on the next month sales, and the balancing figure is production.

Summarized Production Budget for the period ending 31st Dec., 1989 for product X.

(in ₹)

Month (Year 1989)	Production (in units)	Direct Materials ₹ 10 per unit	Direct Wages ₹ 4 per unit	Total Factory Overheads Apportioned @ ₹ 4 per unit	Total
July	1,100	11,000	4,400	4,400	19,800
August	1,400	14,000	5,600	5,600	25,200
Sept	1,800	18,000	7,200	7,200	32,400
Oct	2,200	22,000	8,800	8,800	39,600
Nov	2,400	24,000	9,600	9,600	43,200
Dec	2,200	22,000	8,800	8,800	39,600
Total	11,100	1,11,000	44,400	44,400	1,99,800

Illustration No. 4

Following are the budget estimates of a repairs and maintenance department, which are to be used to construct a flexible budget for the ensuing year:

(₹)

Details of Cost	Planned at 6,000 Direct Hours	Planned at 9,000 Direct Hours
Employee salaries	28,000	28,000
Indirect Repair Material	42,000	63,000
Miscellaneous cost	16,000	20,500

(i) Prepare a flexible budget for the department, up to activity level of 10,000 direct repair hours, using increment of 1,000 hours.

(ii) What would be the budget allowance for 9,500 direct repair hours?

(B.U. MBA-2002)

Solution (i)

Flexible Budget of Repairs and Maintenance Department

Details of Cost	Planned Activity (Direct Hours)					
	6,000 hours	7,000 hours	8,000 hours	9,000 hours	9,500 hours	10,000 hours
Fixed Cost Employee salaries	28,000	28,000	28,000	28,000	28,000	28,000
Variable Cost Indirect Repair Material (@ ₹ 7 per hour)	42,000	49,000	56,000	63,000	66,500	70,000
Semi-fixed cost Miscellaneous cost*	16,000	17,500	19,000	20,500	21,250	22,000
Total Cost	86,000	94,500	1,03,000	1,11,500	1,15,750	1,20,000

* ₹ 16,000 is fixed cost and ₹ 4,500 is variable cost for 3,000 direct hours; hence ₹ 1.50 is the variable cost per direct hour.

(ii) At 9,500 hours, for the incremental increase of 500 hours, the cost increases by ₹ 4,250 due to the following:

Variable Cost

Indirect Repair Material (@ ₹ 7 per hour) = 500 × 7 = 3,500

Semi-fixed cost

Miscellaneous cost (@ ₹ 1.50 per hour -Variable cost component) = 500 × 1.50 = 750

Total incremental cost 4,250

Illustration No. 5

The following are the costs, at 50% capacity:

	₹
Fixed expenses	1,49,500
Semi variable expenses	89,500
Variable expenses	2,67,000

Sales are as under:

Capacity	60 %	80 %	100 %
Product A	2,00,000	3,80,000	5,00,000
Product B	3,10,000	3,00,000	3,50,000

Semi variable costs remain constant between 40% and 70% capacity. They increase by 10% between 70% and 85% capacity, and increase by 15% of the above figures when the capacity is between 85% and 100% capacity. Assume that all items produced are sold.

Prepare a flexible budget based on the above information at 60%, 80% and 100% capacity. Interpret the results.

Solution

Flexible Budget at Different Capacities

Capacity	60%		80%		100%	
Sales						
Product A	2,00,000		3,80,000		5,00,000	
Product B	3,10,000		3,00,000		3,50,000	
		5,10,000		6,80,000		8,50,000
Fixed costs	1,49,500		1,49,500		1,49,500	
Variable costs	3,20,400		4,27,200		5,34,000	
Semi Variable costs	89,500		98,450		1,02,925	
Total Costs		5,59,400		6,75,150		7,86,425
Profit / Loss		– 49,400		4,850		63,575

Interpretation: Fixed costs are constant irrespective of the level of production. Increased sales result in profit, which has happened when the level of capacity increased from 60% (Loss) to 80% (Profit). This profit level has significantly increased when the capacity of 100% is achieved.

Variable costs are proportionate and do not influence the level of capacity.

Semi variable costs contain a portion of fixed costs as well as variable costs. Benefit of fixed costs in the range would be available when the plant achieves that capacity.

Conclusion: When costs contain fixed costs in the aggregate costs, loss would result at a lower level, but it results into profit when higher capacity is utilized.

Illustration No. 6

Koralla Ranga Rao & Co Ltd is engaged in manufacturing a specialized product. The demand for the product is not certain, so they decided to prepare a flexible budget. Firm's optimum selling capacity is 6,000 units per annum and the following is its cost structure:

	₹	₹
Fixed cost		25,550
Variable costs:		
Direct materials	12,000	
Direct labour	9,000	
Power	4,500	
Repairs etc	6,000	
Miscellaneous	18,000	
		49,500
		75,050

Assume that selling price of the unit is ₹ 25 per unit. Financial cost would be ₹10 per unit. One machine is needed for production of 4,000 units and its relative depreciation is ₹ 4,000 per machine.

Prepare a flexible budget at 50%, 80% and 100% capacity and determine the net profit at different levels of production and sales for the year ending March 2009.

You can assume that whatever is produced is sold.

Solution

Flexible Budget of Korall Ranga Rao & Co. Ltd. for the year ending March 2009.

(₹)

Particulars	At 100% Capacity (6,000 units)		At 80% Capacity (4,800 units)		At 50% Capacity (3,000 units)	
Fixed Cost	25,550		25,550		25,550	
Depreciation*	8,000		8,000		4,000	
Total Fixed Costs		33,550		33,550		29,550
Variable Costs:						
Direct Materials per unit ₹ 2	12,000		9,600		6,000	
Direct labour per unit ₹ 1.50	9,000		7,200		4,500	
Power per unit ₹ 0.75	4,500		3,600		2,250	
Repairs etc per unit ₹ 1	6,000		4,800		3,000	
Miscellaneous per unit ₹ 3	18,000		14,400		9,000	
Financial cost per unit ₹ 10	60,000		48,000		30,000	
		1,09,500		87,600		54,750
Total Cost		1,43,050		1,21,150		84,300
Sales @ ₹ 25 per unit		1,50,000		1,20,000		75,000
Profit (+) / Loss (–)		+ 6,950		– 1,150		– 9,300

* For production of every 4,000 units, one machine is needed. Whenever the production capacity exceeds 4,000 units - till 8,00 units - another machine is needed. Depreciation is a fixed cost.

Illustration No. 7

Gopi Conservative Ltd is preparing their budget for the year 2009. In the preparation of budget, they would like to consider all sorts of possibilities and incorporate them in the budget.

Their variable costs per unit are ₹ 10 per unit. Fixed costs are ₹ 30,000 per annum.

Their considered estimates for the year are as under:

(A) If the worst possible happens, the firm would sell 8,000 units at ₹ 12 per unit.

(B) If the best possible happens, the firm would sell 15,000 units at ₹ 20 per unit.

(C) It is most likely that the sales would be 3,000 units above the worst possible level, at a price of ₹ 18 per unit.

(D) There is 25% probability for the possibility of worst to happen, a 15% probability for the best to happen and a 60% probability that the most likely outcome to occur.

Prepare the budget for the pessimistic level, most likely level and the optimistic level.

Calculate the expected level of profit for the year 2009.

Solution

Particulars	Pessimistic Level (8,000 units) ₹	Most likely Level (11,000 units) ₹	Optimistic Level (15,000 units) ₹
Selling Price per unit	12	18	20
(i) Sales	96,000	1,98,000	3,00,000
(ii) Variable cost (₹ 10 per unit)	80,000	1,10,000	1,50,000
(iii) Contribution (i) – (ii)	16,000	88,000	1,50,000
(iv) Fixed costs	30,000	30,000	30,000
(v) Profit / (Loss) (iii) – (iv)	(14,000)	58,000	1,20,000

Statement showing Expected Value of Profit

Estimate	Profit (Loss)	Probability	Expected Value
Pessimistic	(14,000)	0.25	(3,500)
Most likely	58,000	0.60	34,800
Optimistic	1,20,000	0.15	18,000
Expected value of profit			49,300

14.10 PREPARATION OF CASH BUDGET

A cash budget is an estimate of cash receipts and disbursements during a future period. The anticipated cash receipts from various sources are taken into account. Similarly, the amount to be spent on various heads, both revenue and capital, are taken into cash budget. In short, it is a summary of cash intake and outlay.

Illustration No. 8

Prepare a Cash-Budget of Vipin & Company for April, May and June 2003 in a columnar form using the following information:

Month, 03	Sales	Purchases	Wages	Expenses
January (Actual)	80,000	45,000	20,000	5,000
February (Actual)	80,000	40,000	18,000	6,000
March (Actual)	75,000	42,000	22,000	6,000
April (Budgeted)	90,000	50,000	24,000	7,000
May (Budgeted)	85,000	45,000	20,000	6,000
June (Budgeted)	80,000	35,000	18,000	5,000

You are further informed that:

(a) 10% of the purchases and 20% of the sales are for cash;

(b) The average collection period of the company is ½ month and the credit purchases are paid off regularly after one month;

(c) Wages are paid half monthly, and the rent of ₹ 500 included in expenses is paid monthly;

(d) Cash and Bank Balance as on April, was ₹ 15,000 and the company wants to keep it at the end of every month approximately this figure, the excess cash being put in fixed deposits in the bank.

(B.U. MBA-2003)

Solution

(₹)

Cash Budget For the months from April to June, 2003			
	April	**May**	**June**
Receipts			
Opening Balance of Cash at Bank	15,000	15,000	15,000
Cash Sales	18,000	17,000	16,000
Collections from Debtors	66,000	70,000	66,000
Total Receipts	**99,000**	**1,02,000**	**97,000**
Payments			
Cash purchases	5,000	4,500	3,500
Payments for credit purchases	37,800	45,000	40,500
Wages	23,000	22,000	19,000
Expenses	6,500	5,500	4,500
Rent	500	500	500
Total Payments	**72 ,800**	**77,500**	**68,000**
Cash Balance left	26, 200	24,500	29,000
Fixed Deposit placed	11,200	9,500	14,000
Closing cash balance	15,000	15,000	15,000

Calculation of Cash Sales and Realization of Credit Sales				
Month	**Total Sales**	**Cash Sales (20% of Total Sales)**	**Credit Sales (80% of Total Sales)**	**Collections during Month**
March (Actual)	75,000	15,000	60,000	Current month 30,000 + previous month 32,000 = 62,000
April (Budgeted)	90,000	18,000	72,000	Current month 36,000 + Previous month 30,000 = 66,000
May (Budgeted)	85,000	17,000	68,000	Current month 34,000 + Previous month 36,000 = 70,000
June (Budgeted)	80,000	16,000	64,000	Current month 32,000 + Previous month 34,000 = 66,000

Calculation of Payments for Purchases				
Month	**Total Purchases**	**Cash Purchases (10% of Total Purchases)**	**Credit Purchases (90% of Total Purchases)**	**Payments for Credit Purchases**
March (Actual)	42,000	4,200	37,800	36,000
April (Budgeted)	50,000	5,000	45,000	37,800
May (Budgeted)	45,000	4,500	40,500	45,000
June (Budgeted)	35,000	3,500	31,500	40,500

Calculation for Payment of Wages				
Month	**Total Wages**	**Payment for Current Month's Wages (50%)**	**Payment for Previous Month's Wages***	**Total Payment of Wages**
March (Actual)	22,000	11,000	9,000	20,000
April (Budgeted)	24,000	12,000	11,000	23,000
May (Budgeted)	20,000	10,000	12,000	22,000
June (Budgeted)	18,000	9,000	10,000	19,000

* Wages are paid half-monthly. So, wages relating to the second half of the previous month are paid on the first of next month.

Illustration No. 9

From the following forecast of income and expenditure, prepare a cash budget for the months January to April 2001:

Months	Sales (Credit)	Purchases (Credit)	Wages	Manufacturing Expenses	Administrative Expenses	Selling Expenses
2000 Nov	30,000	15,000	3,000	1,150	1,060	500
2000 Dec	35,000	20,000	3,200	1,225	1,040	550
2001 Jan	25,000	15,000	2,500	990	1,100	600
Feb	30,000	20,000	3,000	1,050	1,150	620
March	35,000	22,500	2,400	1,100	1,220	570
Apr	40,000	25,000	2,600	1,200	1,180	710

Additional information is as follows:

1. The customers are allowed a credit period of 2 months.
2. A dividend of ₹ 10,000 is payable in April.

3. Capital expenditure to be incurred: Plant purchased on 15th January for ₹ 5,000, a Building has been purchased on 1st March and the payments are to be made in monthly instalments of ₹ 2,000 each.
4. The creditors are allowing a credit of 2 months.
5. Wages are paid on the 1st of the next month.
6. Lag in payment of other expenses is one month.
7. Balance of cash in hand on 1st January, 2001 is ₹ 15,000.

(B.U. MBA-2002)

Solution

	January, 2001	February, 2001	March, 2001	April, 2001
Opening Balance	15,000	23,985	31,795	33,975
Sales	30,000	35,000	25,000	30,000
Total Receipts	**45,000**	**58,985**	**56,795**	**63,975**
Payments				
Purchases	15,000	20,000	15,000	20,000
Wages	3,200	2,500	3,000	2,400
Manufacturing expenses	1,225	990	1,050	1,100
Administrative expenses	1,040	1,100	1,150	1,220
Selling expenses	550	600	620	570
Capital * expenditure instalment (Plant)		2,000	2,000	1,000
Capital * expenditure instalment (Building)				2,000
Dividend				10,000
Total Payments	**21,015**	**27,190**	**22,820**	**38,290**
Closing balance	**23,985**	**31,795**	**33,975**	**25,685**

* Problem states '₹ 2,000 each'. Key word is 'each'. So, instalment payments are applicable for both plant and building. Instalment is payable in monthly instalments, so first instalment is to be paid after 30 days only.

Illustration No. 10

Varun Ltd. has approached the bank for overdraft with the following data. Prepare a cash budget for the period from April to June, 2009, indicating the extent of overdraft the company may require at the end of each month:

Month	Sales	Purchases	Wages
Jan, 2009	1,80,000	2,00,000	20,000
Feb,2009	2,60,000	3,00,000	40,000
Mar,2009	3,00,000	2,60,000	60,000
April,2009	4,00,000	4,20,000	80,000
May,2009	4,20,000	4,00,000	1,00,000
June, ,2009	4,80,000	4,60,000	1,20,000
July,2009	5,00,000	4,00,000	1,20,000

(A) 50% of credit sales are realized in the month following the sales and the remaining 50% in the second month following.

(B) 75% of purchases are cash purchases. Balance is credit purchases. Creditors are paid in the month following the month of purchase.

(C) Monthly rent payment is ₹ 5,000.

(D) Overheads are 10% of purchases, paid in cash in the same month.

(E) Advance income tax is paid in the month of June is ₹ 25,000.

(F) Bonus payable to workers, due at the end of April, 2009 is ₹ 1,20,000, out of which ₹ 1,00,000 is paid in May, 2009 and balance ₹ 20,000 in July, 2009.

(G) Plant and machinery costing ₹ 50,000 is purchased in April, 2009. However, payment could be made in May, 2009, while its installation expenses ₹ 5,000 are paid in June, 2009.

(H) Interest on 12% of 50,000 debentures is realized in April every year.

(I) Existing overdraft with bank on 1st April, 2009 is ₹ 20,000.

Bank has stipulated the condition that the amount of overdraft at the end of June, 2009 is not to exceed ₹ 5,00,000, while the outstanding can exceed in between. For any excess amount, directors have agreed to give a loan to the company at the end of June, 2009, if necessary.

Show the amount of outstanding debtors and creditors at the end of June, 2009.

Solution

Cash Budget of Varun Ltd. from April to June, 2009

Particulars	April, 2009	May, 2009	June, 2009
Receipts:			
Collections from debtors	2,80,000	3,50,000	4,10,000
Interest on debentures	6,000		
Loan from directors			27,000
Total receipts (A)	2,86,000	3,50,000	4,37,000
Payments:			
Opening balance of overdraft	20,000	1,61,000	4,11,000
Cash Purchases	3,15,000	3,00,000	3,45,000
Payments for credit purchases	65,000	1,05,000	1,00,000
Rent	5,000	5,000	5,000
Overheads	42,000	40,000	46,000
Advance income -tax			25,000
Bonus		1,00,000	
Plant and machinery		50,000	
Installation expenses for plant and machinery			5,000
Total Payments (B)	4,47,000	7,61,000	9,37,000
Closing balance of overdraft (A–B)	1,61,000	4,11,000	5,00,000

Collections from Sales:

Month	Sales	Collections
Feb, 2009	2,60,000	
Mar, 2009	3,00,000	1,30,000 + 90,000 = 2,20,000
April, 2009	4,00,000	1,30,000 + 1,50,000 = 2,80,000
May, 2009	4,20,000	1,50,000 + 2,00,000 = 3,50,000
June, 2009	4,80,000	2,00,000 + 2,10,00 = 4,10,000

Outstanding debtors at the end of June, 2009:

May: 2,10,000

June: 4,80,000

6,90,000

Payments for Purchases:

Month	Purchases	Cash Purchases (75%)	Credit Purchases (25%)	Payments for Credit Purchases
Feb, 2009	3,00,000	2,25,000	75,000	
Mar, 2009	2,60,000	1,95,000	65,000	75,000
April, 2009	4,20,000	3,15,000	1,05,000	65,000
May, 2009	4,00,000	3,00,000	1,00,000	1,05,000
June, 2009	4,60,000	3,45,000	1,15,000	1,00,000

Outstanding creditors at the end of June, 2009: 1,15,000

14.11 LIMITATIONS OF BUDGETARY CONTROL

Budgetary control is a sound technique of control but is not a perfect tool. Despite many good points, it suffers from the following limitations:

1. Uncertainty of Future: The budgets are prepared for the future periods with certain assumptions. In fixed budget, it is assumed that the planned level of activity as anticipated would happen in future. There is no certainty that all the assumptions will prevail in future. With the change in assumptions, the situation in future changes. Due to this, the utility of budgetary control reduces.

2. Problem of Co-ordination: The success of budgetary control largely depends upon effective co-ordination. The performance of one department depends on the performance of the other department. To ensure necessary co-ordination, organization appoints a budget officer. All organizations cannot afford the additional expenditure involved with the appointment of a budget officer, separately. In case, budget officer is not appointed, lack of co-ordination results in poor performance.

3. Not a Substitute for Management: Budgetary control helps in decision-making, but is not a substitute for management. A budgetary programme can be successful, if there is proper administration and supervision.

4. Discourages Efficiency: Every person is given a target to achieve. So, every one is concerned only achieving the target of his own. This is the common tendency. Even capable and competent people too would concentrate just to achieve their individual targets. So, budgets may turn into managerial constraints unless suitable award or incentive system is introduced. In the absence of award system to recognise efficiency and exceptional talents, budgets may dampen the people with initiative and enthusiasm.

5. Timely Revision Required: Budgets are prepared on certain assumptions. When those conditions do not prevail, it becomes inevitable to revise the budget. Such frequent revision of budgets reduces the reliability and value. Revision of budgets involves additional expenditure too.

6. Conflict among Different Departments: For the success of budgetary control, co-ordination of the different departments is essential. Every department is concerned with the achievement of the individual department's goal, not concerned with the final goal of the enterprise. In this process, each department tries to secure maximum fund allocation and this creates conflict among different departments.

7. Depends upon Support of Top Management: The success of budgetary control depends upon the support of top management. If the top management is not enthusiastic for its success, the budgetary control collapses. So, the whole-hearted interest of top management is highly essential for its implementation, in its true spirit, to make it workable and successful.

14.12 COMPARISON OF STANDARD COSTING WITH BUDGETARY CONTROL

Standard Costing and Budgetary Control both aim at maximising efficiency and controlling costs. They are useful tools to management. However, they differ in the following aspects.

Base	Budgetary Control	Standard Costing
1. Coverage	It covers all the functions of a business such as purchases, production, sales, finance, capital expenditure and research and development etc. In other words, it has a macro-approach.	Standard costs are, basically, developed for the manufacturing function i.e. production. In other words, it has a micro-approach.
2. Objective	Objective is to delegate responsibility and ensure performance, without sacrificing control.	Objective is to enable the management to fix standards, control variances and value closing stock.
3. Application	It can be implemented in all industries.	It is not possible to implement in all types of industries. It cannot be applied in jobbing activity in all operations.
4. Scope	It is more extensive as it covers all the departments or operations of the business, as a whole.	It is more intensive in application as it calls for detailed analysis of variances. Concentration is on various elements of cost like raw materials, labour and overheads.
5. Implementation	It can be implemented even in parts. To certain areas or departments, it can be implemented, while leaving rest of the areas. For example, it can be implemented in the sales department alone.	It cannot be operated in parts. It has to cover all items of expenses, without leaving any item.

Contd...

6. Emphasis	Emphasis is on Limits. Targets are to be achieved.	Emphasis is on Standards. Costs should not exceed the standards set.
7. Projection	It is based on the past actual records and suitably adjusted to future trends and expectations. It is a projection of financial accounts.	It is based on the technical assessments. It is a projection of cost accounts.
8. Variances	Budgetary control deals with total variances. The variances are calculated for the different departments or the organization as a whole.	Variances are calculated for different elements of costs i.e. material, labour and overheads. Further, they are analyzed in detail for their causes.
9. Orientation	It is more management oriented.	It is more engineering oriented.
10. Relationship	Budgetary control can be applied, even without the help of standard costing.	To establish standard costing, some form of budgeting is needed to forecast the level of output and prescribed set of working conditions in which standard costs would be used.
11. Difference in Advantages	It aims in policy determination and facilitates introduction of 'Delegation of Authority'.	Standard costs are used in various management decisions, price fixing and valuation of closing stock etc.

Both standard costing and budgetary control are complementary to each other. Both should be used to achieve maximum efficiency.

Check Your Understanding

(A) State whether the following statements are True or False

1. A budget is a means and budgetary control is the end result.
2. To achieve the anticipated targets, Planning, Co-ordination and Control are the three important tasks of management, achieved through budgeting and budgetary control.
3. A key factor or principal factor does not influence the preparation of all other budgets.
4. Budgetary control does not facilitate introduction of 'Management by Exception'.
5. Generally, budgets are prepared to coincide with the financial year so that comparison of the actual performance with budgeted estimates would facilitate better interpretation and understanding.
6. A flexible budget is one which changes from year to year.
7. A flexible budget recognizes the difference between fixed, semi-fixed and variable cost and is designed to change in relation to the change in level of activity.
8. Sales budget, normally, is the most important budget among all budgets.
9. The principal factor is the starting point for the preparation of various budgets.
10. A budget manual is the summary of all functional budgets.

11. Budgeting is a technique for formulating budgets.
12. Budgets are blueprints for action.
13. Standard Costing and Budgetary Control are not complementary to each other for achieving improved performance in an organization.
14. On the basis of budget, next year's financial statements, profit and loss account and balance sheet can be drawn up.
15. A flexible budget is quickly recast based on changed volumes of activity.
16. A budget is nothing but an estimate based on the past records.
17. Budget is drawn by the accountant of the organization.
18. The Master Budget is a summary budget, which incorporates all functional budgets in a summarized form.
19. Raw materials supply can be a key factor.
20. Standard costing can operate without the support of budgetary control in any manner.
21. Standard costing cannot be introduced when budgetary control is in operation.
22. Normally, sales budget is prepared first and the other budgets are coordinated with it.
23. Materials Budget and Purchase Budget mean one and the same.
24. A fixed budget is preferable to flexible budget.
25. Budgetary control has a macro-approach, while standard costing has a micro-approach.
26. Before the functional budgets are prepared, master budget is prepared.

Answers

1. True	2. True	3. False	4. False	5. True	6. False	7. True	8. True
9. True	10. False	11. True	12. True	13. False	14. True	15. True	16. False
17. False	18. True	19. True	20. False	21. False	22. True	23. False	24. False
25. True	26. False						

(B) Objective Questions (Identify what is most appropriate)

1. The basic difference between a fixed budget and flexible budget is that a fixed budget
   (A) is concerned with a single level of activity, while flexible budget is prepared for different levels of activity.
   (B) is concerned with fixed costs, while flexible budget is concerned with variable costs.
   (C) is fixed while flexible budget changes.
   (D) None of the above
2. A flexible budget requires a careful study of
   (A) Fixed, semi-fixed and variable expenses
   (B) Past and current expenses
   (C) Overheads, selling and administrative expenses.
   (D) None of the above

3. Sales budget is a
   (A) Expenditure budget (B) Functional budget
   (C) Master budget (D) None of the above
4. The budget that is prepared first of all is
   (A) Master budget (B) Budget, with key factor
   (C) Cash budget (D) Capital expenditure budget
5. The difference between fixed cost and variable assumes significance in the preparation of the following budget
   (A) Master budget (B) Flexible budget
   (C) Cash budget (D) Capital budget
6. Materials becomes key factor, if
   (A) quota restrictions exist (B) insufficient advertisement prevails
   (C) there is low demand (D) there is no problem with supplies of materials
7. Which of the following is a long-term budget?
   (A) Master budget (B) Flexible budget
   (C) Cash budget (D) Capital budget
8. Which of the following is not a potential benefit of using a budget?
   (A) Enhanced co-ordination in firm's activities
   (B) More motivated managers
   (C) Improved interdepartmental communication
   (D) More accurate external financial statements
9. Which of the following is not an element of master budget?
   (A) Capital expenditure budget (B) Production schedule
   (C) Operating expenses budget (D) All of the above
   (E) None of these
10. Budgets are shown in ...., terms
   (A) Qualitative (B) Quantitative
   (C) Materialistic (D) Both (B) and (C)

Answers

1. (A) 2. (A) 3. (B) 4. (B) 5. (B) 6. (A) 7. (D) 8. (D) 9. (B) 10. (D).

Descriptive Questions

1. How Budget fulfils the needs of Modern Management? Explain the meaning of 'Budget' and describe its characteristics. (14.1 and 14.2)

2. Explain 'Budget' and 'Budgeting'. Describe the characteristics of Budget. (14.2)
3. What does Budgetary Control mean? Discuss, in brief, the objectives and advantages of budgetary control. (14.2 to 14.4, and 14.7)
4. Discuss the essentials of a good budgetary control system. Explain briefly the steps in setting up of a budgetary control system so that its working efficiency is ensured. (14.5 and 14.6)
5. Explain the classification of Budgets. (14.8)
6. Bring out the differences between Fixed and Flexible Budget (14.8-Point C and 14.9)
7. Detail the advantages and limitations of Budgetary Control. (14.7 and 14.11)
8. Compare Standard Costing with Budgetary Control and bring out the differences between them. (14.12)

Short Questions

Q.1. What is 'Budgetary Control' and how this is achieved?

Ans. A budget is a quantitative financial statement, prepared prior to a defined period of time. Budgetary control is a technique of exercising control to achieve the desired objective of the firm. In this process, budget having a key factor is prepared first. Based on that budget, all other budgets are prepared. Later, actual results are compared with the budgets and variances are found out for action to be exercised. Person who has contributed the shortfall is the proper person who can take the corrective action.

Q.2. What is the importance of Budgetary Control in the current context?

Ans. Organizations are becoming big, with increasing volumes of production associated with complex problems. Delegation of authority is necessary for achieving the results, bringing co-ordination between the different departments. At the same time, fixation of responsibility and initiating corrective action are essential. Budgetary control is an important tool to execute the principle of 'Management by Exception'. Top management would be concerned only when the actual result is off the planned action. Corrective action is to be initiated, in time, to achieve the planned result, without loss of time and resources. In this light, budgetary control is essential in the current context.

Q.3. What is a key factor in the context of Budgetary Control? What is its importance?

Ans. A factor, which influences all other budgets, is known as key factor or principal factor. A key factor is a limiting factor in any organization. First, the key factor in the organization is identified. Budget related to that key factor is prepared first. For example, raw materials may be a key factor to a particular firm, where there is shortage of raw materials. In such an event, the firm first prepares the raw materials budget and based on that budget, all other budgets are prepared.

Q.4. What types of budgets are normally prepared and justify the reason?

Ans. Normally, flexible budgets are prepared as production/sales level and selling price can not be estimated, with total accuracy. Flexible budget meets the requirements, even if the actual production/sales level changes, compared to the original estimates. In other words, flexible budget is, automatically, geared to changes in production/sales activity. The other type– fixed budget – can work only if the planned production/sales levels do not change. As this is not likely to happen in practical life, fixed budgets are not prepared.

Interview Questions

Q.1. What is a budget?

Ans. A budget is a plan expressed in quantitative and monetary terms. In the language of business, a budget is a formal expression of the expected incomes and expenses for definite future period.

Q.2. What is the objective of budgetary control?

Ans. The objective of budget and budgetary control is to reduce costs and maximize profits.

Q.3. Why a flexible budget is preferred in comparison to a fixed budget?

Ans. A flexible budget is the most ideal form of budgeting as it would suit different levels of production and sales. Despite best planning, in the light of growing uncertainties, it is rather difficult to predict the demand for any product, with certainty. Flexible budget overcomes the disadvantage of a fixed budget and would meet the different levels of production and changing conditions of sales.

Q.4. What is meant by 'Key factor'?

Ans. A key factor or principal factor is that factor which influences all other budgets. In other words, performance of all budgets depends on the key factor. For example, raw materials supply is a constraint to a particular firm. Performance of all budgets depends on the adequate availability of raw materials. So, budget that has the key factor is to be prepared first.

Q.5. How a cash budget helps in planning the cash requirements?

Ans. Cash budget helps the company to forecast receipts and payments, and plan accordingly for any shortfall by means of temporary overdraft from the bank. In case, the cash shortfall is of permanent nature, firm can approach the bank, well in advance, for permanent borrowing. In case, there is a surplus fund, it can arrange temporary investment. Cash is vital for every firm and so there should be no sudden surprises to the firm. Firm requires time to arrange funds, if the shortfall is of a permanent nature, as bank requires time to process the application of the firm.

Q.6. What is a Master Budget?

Ans. Master Budget is a summary budget, which incorporates all functional budgets in a summarized form. After preparation of all the functional budgets, then 'Master Budget' is prepared. Master budget is a consolidated plan of overall proposed operations developed by management for the company, covering a definite period of time, normally a year.

CHAPTER 15

Zero-Base Budgeting

15.1 INTRODUCTION

Budget is a detailed plan of operations for some future period. A budget is a representation of quantification of firm's objectives. In budgeting, use of *i.e.,* **Zero-Base Budgeting (ZBB)** as a managerial tool has increasingly become popular since the early 1970s. This new technique has been introduced in USA by Peter Pyhrr of Texas Instruments in 1969. ZBB has been gaining acceptance in business world as a tool in integrating managerial functions of planning and control. Initially, the former President of America, Jimmy Carter had developed this technique, when he had been working as the Governor of Gorgia for controlling state expenditure.

15.2 CONCEPT

Zero-base budgeting, as the name suggests, examines or reviews a programme or function from zero or scratch. It is the latest technique of budgeting. It is a management tool in which all activities are re-evaluated each time a budget is prepared and justification of expenditure is made for past as well as new projects. ZBB also means construction of a budget, based on fundamental reappraisal of objectives, methods and resources. In a liberal sense, it means constructing a budget without referring to what has been done in the past. In traditional budgeting, figures of previous years are taken as base and additions are made for current year. But, in Zero-base budgeting, even running projects are to be justified for continuation. If past projects were allowed to continue, without justification, the past inefficiencies would continue automatically. So, manager has to justify why he wants to continue to spend. In other words, reviewer proceeds with the assumption that nothing is to be allowed. The manager proposing the activity has to justify that the activity is essential and amount sought is reasonable, taking into account the volume of activity. Nothing is allowed simply because it was done in the past. It means writing on a clean slate.

Term 'Zero-base budgeting' means starting from the scratch.

Where ZBB is more appropriate: An accurate budget can be framed when a relationship between inputs and outputs can be established. In all activities, relationship between inputs and outputs cannot be established. In such areas, it is difficult to develop standard costs. Where it is difficult to compare resource allocation with output, ZBB is more appropriate in decision-making for allocation of funds and controlling their continuation with continuous monitoring.

In ZBB, every manager has to justify essentiality of the new projects for their starting and continuation of previous projects every year. Equally, the concerned manager has to justify amount of spending, thereon, is reasonable.

Definition: The Institute of Cost and Management Accountants (ICMA) defines ZBB as **"a method of budgeting whereby all activities are re-evaluated each time a budget is formulated. Each functional budget starts with the assumption that the function does not exist and is a zero cost. Increments of cost are compared with increments of benefits culminating in the planned maximum benefits for a given budgeted cost".**

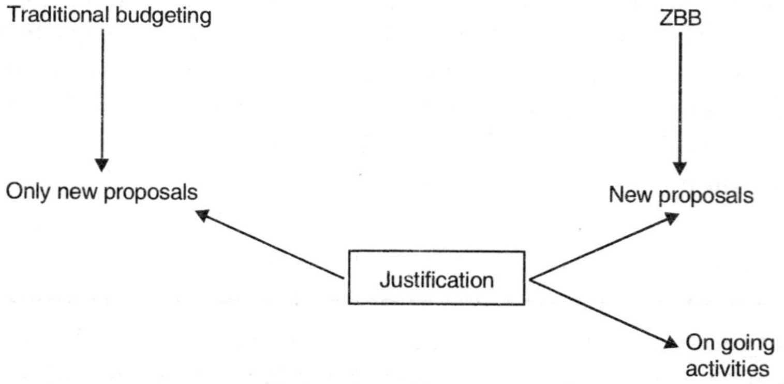

Traditional budgeting Vs ZBB

15.3 DIFFERENCE BETWEEN TRADITIONAL BUDGETING AND ZERO-BASE BUDGETING

Superiority of zero-base budgeting: Zero-base budgeting is superior to conventional budgeting. Zero-based budgeting is a technique of planning and decision-making which reverses the working process of traditional budgeting. In traditional or incremental budgeting, departmental managers justify only increases over the previous year budget and what has been already spent is automatically sanctioned. No reference is made to the previous level of expenditure. By contrast, in zero-based budgeting, every department function is reviewed comprehensively and all expenditures must be approved, rather than only increased amounts. Zero-based budgeting requires the budget request be justified in complete detail by each division manager starting from the zero-base. The zero-base is indifferent to whether the total budget is increasing or decreasing.

The following differences between the two explain superiority of zero-base budgeting over conventional budgeting:

Traditional Budgeting vs Zero-base budgeting		
	Traditional Budgeting	**Zero-Base Budgeting**
1. Emphasis	Lays emphasis on 'How much'.	Lays emphasis on 'Why'.
2. Focus	Focus is on increase or decrease in expenditure.	Focus is towards achievement of objectives based on 'cost benefit analysis'.
3. Communication	Communication is usually vertical.	Communication is usually both vertical and horizontal.
4. Approach	Past is taken for granted and never questioned for continuation.	Past is questioned and justification needed for continuation and fund allocation.

Zero-base budgeting can be applied successfully in state government spendings.

15.4 STEPS FOR PREPARATION OF ZERO-BASE BUDGETING

The following steps are involved in Zero-base budgeting:

A. **Determining Objectives:** Determination of objectives is the first step. The objective can be cost reduction in staff overheads or dropping those projects that do not fit in overall organizational objectives or focus.

B. **Extent of Coverage:** It relates to decision whether zero-base budgeting is to be introduced in all areas or certain select areas on trail basis.

C. **Developing Decision Units:** The next step is to develop decision units for which cost benefit analysis is proposed. Decision Unit can be a functional department, a programme, a product-line or sub-line. Each decision unit must be independent so that they can be dropped, if required, without affecting others. Then only they come under consideration. Decision is to be taken, whether the units are to be continued or dropped. If cost benefit analysis is favourable, only then decision unit can be implemented, otherwise can be dropped.

A ZBB decision unit can be described as a cost or budget center. These could be responsibility centers, cost centers, profit centers, investment centers, program categories or program elements. They must be independent for continuation or discontinuation.

Decision units should have the following characteristics:

A. A specific manager should be clearly responsible for operation of the program.

B. It must have well defined and measurable impacts.

C. It must have well defined and measurable objectives.

If the decision unit is dropped, no further thinking is needed about those activities.

D. **Developing Decision Packages:** After identification of appropriate decision units, next step is 'decision packages'. This is the most important step involved in ZBB process. Decision package is a document for each decision unit that describes objectives or purposes of the decision unit and actions that could be taken to achieve them. Such document is called "Decision Package". Decision package shows alternative ways of performing its functions so as to enable management to choose the best alternative.

In other words, a decision package can be described as a set of documents which identifies and describes activities of the decision units in such a way that the management can evaluate and rank them against other activities competing for limited resources, and decide whether to approve or disapprove them.

Benefit should be more compared to its comparative cost. Cost benefit analysis is foundation of ZBB, which helps in ranking projects.

After decision for selection of units, the concerned manager of activity is given freedom to come out with alternatives to achieve. He does cost-benefit analysis and selects the best course of alternative. He summarizes plans and resources required to achieve. A decision manager generally prepares and submits 3 to 5 such packages.

For developing a decision package, it is desirable to get answers for following questions:

1. What are the alternatives to do an activity?
2. What are actual costs and benefits associated with each choice?
3. If an activity is dropped for execution by the firm, can it be executed by an outside agency and at what cost?

E. **Ranking:** Rank decision packages in the order of priority, keeping the objective in mind and cost benefit analysis.

F. **Allocation of Resources:** After ranking those projects, project that exhaust the resources are accepted and others are rejected. In other words, all those projects up to the cut off point of resources are accepted.

Zero-Base Budgeting is an extension of the cost benefit analysis method to the area of corporate budgeting.

15.5 BENEFITS OF ZERO-BASE BUDGETING

ZBB is a revolutionary concept. The benefits are as under:

1. **Proper Allocation of Funds:** Funds are scarce. Priority in allocation of funds is made on cost benefit analysis.
2. **Systematic Evaluation:** Manager has to justify demand for resources every year. So, it provides organization a systematic way to evaluate different programmes and operations undertaken. For the ongoing projects too, review is made every year. Funds allocation for the ongoing projects is made, if there is justification to continue further.

   In other words, there is no difference between new projects and ongoing projects from the view-point of allocation of funds.
3. **Links Budgets with Goals of Enterprise:** Those projects that do not fit within the overall goals of the enterprise are not continued even if they were commenced. Goal oriented approach of the enterprise would be developed.
4. **Zero-Base Approach:** Zero is taken as the base every time. Only those activities and programmes that are essential are undertaken which improves overall efficiency of the enterprise. Alternative courses of action are always studied. Economies are achieved, eliminating wastages. Focus of the management lies on analysis and decision-making
5. **Optimum Use of Resources:** As cost benefit analysis is the guiding principle in fixing priorities, resources are used to optimum advantage the of organization.
6. **No Incremental Approach:** Normally, budgets are based on incremental approach. The usual feature of functional heads is to seek information from the accounts department for the previous year's expenditure, add 'something' for current year and try to justify the increase. This incremental approach is not possible with zero-base budgeting. Manager has to justify their activities and funds requested.
7. **Most Appropriate for Non-Manufacturing Areas:** Zero-Base Budgeting is very appropriate for the staff and support areas (non-manufacturing areas). In these areas, the output of these areas is not directly related with final output of the organization.

> **Within the business world, ZBB can be applied to research and development, data processing, quality control, marketing and transportation, legal staff and personnel office.**

Example: A separate training department is functional in an organization. Utility of continuation of department may be studied in comparison to conducting training outside organization. Training is a non-manufacturing area and its discontinuation within the organization and providing diverse types of training to staff, outside firm, may be more ideally suitable while reducing the costs to the enterprise.

15.6 LIMITATIONS OF ZERO-BASE BUDGETING

In spite of the many advantages, it suffers from the following limitations:

1. Computation of cost benefit analysis is essential for ZBB. This is not possible in respect of non-financial matters.
2. System of ZBB has no scope to adjust for changes. So, ZBB has no scope in flexible budgeting.
3. ZBB involves lot of time and cost of operating is also high.
4. Formulation of decision package is a difficult process and all managers may not have the necessary expertise. It is also difficult to define decision units and decision packages as it is time-consuming and exhaustive.

15.7 CONCLUSION

To conclude, zero-base budgeting is not a panacea for all evils. But it can certainly overcome the weaknesses of the conventional budgets and improves the usefulness of budgeting process.

Check Your Understanding

(A) State whether the following statements are True or False

1. Zero-base budgeting is the latest technique of budgeting.
2. In Zero-base budgeting, focus of management is on analysis and decision-making.
3. There is no difference between conventional budgeting and zero-base budgeting.
4. In Zero-base budgeting, zero is taken as base.
5. Zero-base budgeting allows continuation of ongoing projects, without any review and justification.
6. Non-manufacturing areas are suitable for implementation of zero-base budgeting.
7. Cost benefit analysis is foundation for Zero-base budgeting.
8. Zero-base budgeting cannot be applied in Government departmental budgets.
9. A budget is a detailed plan of operations for some future period.
10. Zero-base budgeting is a new technique in which all activities are re-valuated each time budget is prepared.
11. A budget is nothing but an estimate.
12. ZBB can be used in non–manufacturing activities such as selling and administration activities.

Answers

1. True 2. True 3. False 4. True 5. False 6. True 7. True 8. False
9. True 10. True 11. False 12. True.

(B) Fill in the Blanks

1. Zero-Base Budgeting overcomes the weaknesses of ....
2. Zero-Base Budgeting is ideal for implementation in ....

Answers

1. Conventional/traditional budgeting. 2. Non-manufacturing areas/Government budgets.

(B) Objective Questions (Identify what is most appropriate)

1. A budget that gives summary of all functional budgets is

   (A) Master budget (B) Flexible budget (C) Capital budget (D) Fixed budget

2. Which of the following is a long-term budget?

   (A) Cash budget (B) Capital expenditure budget (C) Sales budget (D) Production budget

3. Cost classification into variable cost and fixed cost has a special significance in preparation of

   (A) Cash budget (B) Master budget (C) Flexible budget (D) Fixed budget

4. Under flexible budgeting

   (A) planned activity level is adjusted to actual activity level before the budget comparison is prepared.

   (B) planned activity level and actual activity level should be same before the budget comparison is prepared.

   (C) reporting is made as per convenience.

   (D) budget standards are varied according to will.

5. Fixed budget is concerned with

   (A) fixed costs only (B) variable costs only

   (C) both fixed and variable activity levels (D) fixed level of activity

6. Zero-Base Budgeting is concerned with the justification of

   (A) New projects

   (B) Old projects

   (C) All projects, irrespective whether they are old or new

   (D) None of the above

7. Zero-Base Budgeting is based on

   (A) Cost-benefit analysis

   (B) Risk and return approach

   (C) Interest on capital vs. borrowed funds

   (D) Return on investment method

8. The main theme of Zero-Base Budgeting is concerned with
   (A) Evaluation of new projects.
   (B) Justification of all projects from scratch.
   (C) Elimination of those projects where funds are not adequate.
   (D) Ranking of those projects based on their returns.
9. In Zero-Base Budgeting, this is the beginning for approval.
   (A) Minimum
   (B) Zero
   (C) Past expenditure
   (D) Expenditure projected
10. Zero-Base Budgeting can be applied in this area only.
   (A) Training
   (B) Governmental activities
   (C) Research and development activities
   (D) All the above
11. Zero-Base Budgeting is superior to conventional budgeting in this aspect.
   (A) Justification of every project and expenditure whether it is existing or new
   (B) Justification of all new projects
   (C) Justification of old projects only for their continued viability
   (D) Elimination of old projects, if funds are insufficient

Answers

1. (A) 2. (B) 3. (C) 4. (A) 5. (D) 6. (C) 7. (A) 8. (B) 9. (B) 10. (D) 11. (A)

Descriptive Questions

1. What is meant by Zero-Base Budgeting? What are the different steps involved in it and how is it useful to the business? Explain its limitations. **(15.2, 15.4 to 15.6)**
2. Justify how Zero-Base Budgeting is superior to conventional budgeting. **(15.1, 15.2, 15.3 and 15.5)**
3. What do you mean by Zero-Base budgeting? How does it overcome weaknesses of conventional budgeting? **(15.1, 15.2, 15.3 and 15.5)**

Short Questions

Q.1. How Zero-Based Budgeting is superior to traditional incremental budgeting?

Ans. Zero-Based Budgeting is a technique of planning and decision-making which reverses the working process of traditional budgeting. In traditional incremental budgeting, departmental managers justify only increases over the previous year budget. What has been already spent is automatically sanctioned. No reference is made to the previous level of expenditure. By contrast, in Zero-Based Budgeting, every department function is reviewed comprehensively and all expenditures must be approved, rather than only increased amounts. Zero-Based Budgeting requires the budget request be justified in complete detail by each division manager starting from the zero-base. The Zero-Base Budgeting is indifferent to whether the total budget is increasing or decreasing.

Interview Questions

Q.1. What is 'Zero-Base Budgeting'? State its utility.

Ans. 'Zero-Base Budgeting' is the latest technique of budgeting. 'Zero' is taken as the base and past is not allowed as base for consideration or justification. The objective of Zero-Based Budgeting is to "reset the clock" each year. This is a managerial tool where every manager has to justify each rupee of expenditure on the basis of cost-benefit analysis. This is applicable to new as well as on-going projects/activities. This is more applicable in non-manufacturing areas such as research and development, training, legal, staff and support areas. This type of budgeting is ideal in governmental activities.

Q.2. How 'Zero-Base Budgeting' is superior compared to conventional budgeting?

Ans. 'Zero-Base Budgeting' presupposes that budget is to be prepared from the scratch. In other words, no presumption of expenditure is permitted and even existing expenditure is to be substantiated by every one in the organization. Existing inefficiencies are not allowed to be accrued. In other words, fresh thinking and justification eliminates accrual of inefficiencies. Even existing project is not allowed to continue without sufficient justification for its continuation. This provides fresh approach for thinking, which does not exist in a conventional budgeting.

❍ ❍

CHAPTER 16

Methods of Capital Budgeting

16.1 INTRODUCTION

Acquisition and purchase of fixed assets involve capital budgeting decisions. Basically, capital expenditure is always huge and return of funds to firm normally takes a very long period. A capital expenditure may be defined as an expenditure the benefit of which is spread over a period exceeding one year. The main feature of a capital expenditure is that the big expenditure is incurred at one period of time while benefits of expenditure are spread at different points of time in future.

Capital expenditure involves exchange of current assets to acquisition of fixed assets.

Some of the examples of capital expenditure are:

(A) Purchase or acquisition of permanent assets such as machinery, building, goodwill etc.

(B) Cost of improvement, additions, expansion or alteration in fixed assets.

(C) Cost of replacement of fixed assets.

(D) Research and Development expenditure.

Capital expenditure decisions are also called as long-term investment decisions.

16.2 DEFINITION AND MEANING OF CAPITAL BUDGETING

Definition: Investment decisions of a firm related to acquisition of fixed assets are generally known as capital budgeting or capital expenditure decisions. Capital budgeting is concerned with allocation of firm's scarce financial resources in long-term projects whose benefits occur over a future period.

Capital budgeting may be defined as firm's decision to invest current funds in long-term assets to get benefits spread over future years.

The characteristics of capital budgeting or long-term investment decisions are:

(A) Exchange of current assets for future benefits.

(B) Investment of funds in non-flexible and long-term assets or activities.

(C) Huge funds are involved.

(D) Future benefits or cash flows occur over a series of years.

(E) Decisions are irreversible without substantial financial loss.

(F) Significant impact on profitability of concern.

16.3 NEED AND IMPORTANCE OF CAPITAL BUDGETING

Investment decisions are of great importance to any concern. These decisions involve commitment of a large sum of money. They greatly affect profitability of the enterprise. These decisions are difficult to make.

The need, significance or importance of these decisions is due to the following reasons:

1. **Large Investments:** Funds are limited and opportunities are abundant. Capital expenditure decisions involve commitment of large sums of money. If funds are committed to one project, other projects are denied. So a great deal of planning is necessary before capital expenditure is made.
2. **Growth and Profitability:** The direction of growth is set by the capital expenditure. If the expenditure goes in right direction, organization gets a boost in profitability. If the decision proves wrong, it is fatal for its growth, or at times, even the existing profitable concern may suffer due to their heavy financial implications. Thus capital budgeting decisions determine future destiny of company for a very long period.
3. **Irreversible Nature:** Most investment decisions are irreversible. Once these assets are acquired, their disposal is difficult as there is no ready market and often results in heavy losses. Due to this long-term implication, decisions are taken after careful planning. More often decisions cannot be reversed without substantial financial loss.
4. **Difficult to Forecast Cash Flows:** Impact of investment decision is not limited for one year. Its influence spreads over a series of years. Future is uncertain, and so, it is difficult to forecast its impact over life of asset, totally and correctly. It is difficult to estimate future cash flows accurately. Economic, political, social and technological forces cause uncertainty of cash inflows.

5. **Risk:** Long-term commitment of funds changes risk profile of firm. Adoption of a profitable investment increases earnings per share and causes a change in earning pattern. As future is uncertain, there is no guarantee for continuation of same earnings.

Thus investment decisions shape basic character of a firm.

16.4 TYPES OF INVESTMENT DECISIONS

They are many ways to classify investments. One way of classification is as follows:

1. **Expansion and Diversification: A company may add capacity to its existing capacity, which is known as expansion.** If present capacity of an enterprise is 10,000 mt. of urea and it decides to manufacture another 5,000 mt. by adding a new plant, it is expansion. A firm engaged in soft drinks invests in a package manufacturing; it is diversification as it has not engaged in packing activity earlier.
2. **Replacement and Modernization: The main objective of modernization and replacement is to improve operating efficiency and reduce costs.** A cement manufacturing company may replace an existing semi-automatic with fully automatic machine. This reduces costs and increases profitability while revenue remains unchanged. However, substantial modernization and replacement with modern technological improvements expands revenues as well as reduces costs.

Another classification may be as follows:

(A) **Mutually exclusive investments: Mutually exclusive investments serve same purpose but compete with each other.** The best example is when a stone crusher is planning to replace its existing manual operations either with semi-automatic machine or fully automatic machine. Both the machines are simultaneously not needed. One of them serves the purpose.

(B) **Independent investments: Independent investments do not compete with each other but serve different purposes.** For example, a company may plan to purchase additional machinery for increasing production and vehicle for improved transportation and reduction of costs. Both these investments do not compete with each other. One purchase does not dispense another. Depending on availability of funds and profitability planned, company can undertake both investments.

(C) **Contingent investments:** Contingent investments are dependent investments. **The choice of one investment necessitates undertaking one or more investments.** When a company plans to start a new factory in a remote and backward area, it may have to invest in houses and roads to attract employee force to join and remain to work. The total expenditure will be treated as one investment. Factory cannot run successfully without required infrastructure. This includes suitable housing and schooling to employees to live and work in a conducive atmosphere under congenial working conditions.

16.5 INVESTMENT EVALUATION CRITERIA

A finance manager is faced with several investment opportunities. There are several investment techniques.

The essential property of a sound investment evaluation criterion is it should maximise shareholders' wealth.

So, finance manager should have clear understanding of features of a sound investment evaluation criterion for proper selection.

Evaluation criteria for choice: The following are sound characteristics or criteria for choice of an investment decision:

- All cash flows over life of project are to be considered.
- Criteria should be clear and objective to separate a good project from a bad one.
- Help in ranking projects according to their profitability.
- Should recognize the fact that bigger cash flows are preferable to smaller ones and early cash flows are better than later ones.
- Should help to choose among mutually exclusive projects that maximise the shareholders' wealth.
- Should be applicable to all conceivable projects for selection.

16.6 CAPITAL BUDGETING OR INVESTMENT TECHNIQUES

Capital Budgeting techniques are broadly divided into two categories. They are discounted and non-discounted techniques.

(A) Discounted techniques
- Net Present Value (NPV)
- Internal Rate of Return (IRR)
- Profitability Index (PI)
- Discounted Payback Period (DPB)

(B) Non-Discounted techniques:
- Payback Period (PB)
- Accounting Rate of Return (ARR)

16.7 NET PRESENT VALUE METHOD

The Net Present Value technique explicitly recognizes time value of money. This technique recognizes cash flows arising at different time periods differ in value and is comparable only when their present values are found out.

> **The best method for evaluation of investment proposals is the 'Net Present Value Method' or discounted cash flow technique.**

16.7.1 Steps for Calculation of NPV

1. Cash flows of different investment projects are to be forecast based on realistic assumptions.
2. Choose the appropriate discount rate.
3. The appropriate discount rate is firm's opportunity cost of capital. This is equal to the rate of return expected by investors on investments of equivalent and comparable risk. Investors want compenzation for time as well as risk they assume. This is the meaning of 'Required Rate of Return'.
4. Cash flows are to be discounted applying the discount rate to arrive at present value of cash flows.
5. Net Present Value should be found out by subtracting the present value of future cash outflows from the present value of the cash inflows.
6. Accept the Project, if NPV is positive. (i.e. NPV > 0); otherwise, reject.

Formula for calculation of NPV: The formula for calculating NPV is as under:

$$\text{Net Present Value} = \frac{C_1}{(1+k)} + \frac{C_2}{(1+k)^2} + \ldots + \frac{C_n}{(1+k)^n} - C_0$$

$$= \sum_{t=1}^{n} \frac{C_t}{(1+k)^t} - C_0$$

Where, Σ = Sigma (sum)

C_1 and C_2 = Net cash inflows in year 1 and 2 to ... n years

k = Appropriate discount rate (cost of capital)

C_0 = Initial cost of investment

t = Assumes values from 1 to n

In case present value factors (PVF) are given, cash flows of the different years are multiplied with the respective present value factors to arrive at the present values of cash flows.

Importance of Net Present Value: NPV is a true measure of firm's profitability. When different independent projects compete, projects can be ranked in the order of net present value for selection. The NPV method can also be used to select between mutually exclusive projects.

Acceptance Rule: A project may be accepted, if NPV is positive. The net present value would be positive if the project generates cash flows at a rate higher than its cost of capital.

Positive NPV increases the value of firm's share price and contributes to maximization of shareholders' wealth.

A zero NPV implies that the project generates enough cash flow at a rate just equal to its opportunity cost of capital.

Thus, NPV acceptance rules are:

- Accept if NPV > 0
- Reject if NPV < 0
- May Accept or Reject if NPV = 0

16.7.2 Advantages of NPV Method:

The advantages of NPV method for evaluating investment proposals are as follows:

1. **Recognition of Time Value of Money:** NPV method recognizes time value of money. This is suitable for evaluation of investment proposals whether cash flows, both inflows and outflows, are uniform or uneven.
2. **All cash flows considered:** It takes into account all cash flows arising during total life of projects and true measure of profitability can be evaluated.
3. **Profitability objective:** It takes into consideration the objective of maximum profitability.
4. **Value Additivity Principle:** It satisfies value-additivity principle (i.e. NPV of two or more projects can be added).

16.7.3 Limitations of NPV

1. In practice, it is difficult to obtain estimates of future cash flows due to uncertainty of future.
2. It is difficult to measure precisely the discount rate.
3. When alternative projects with unequal lives are evaluated, caution must be exercised.
4. Equally caution is necessary when firm has constraint of funds. Even if alternative project's NPV were higher, that firm would not be in position to select due to higher commitment of funds of that project.
5. As compared to the easy traditional method of Payback period, this is difficult to calculate and understand.

Illustration No. 1

Della Ltd. is considering a proposal for ₹ 8,00,000 and inflows from investment are as under:

Year	Cash flows (before tax)
1	Nil
2	2,00,000
3	2,50,000
4	8,25,000
5	3,80,000

Discount rate is 15%. Tax rate is 30%. The present value factor for 15% is as under:

Year	1	2	3	4	5
Factor	0.87	0.76	0.66	0.57	0.50

Adopt net present value method for evaluating the investment proposal and make recommendation.

Solution

Year	Cash Flows (before tax)	Cash Flows (after tax)	PV Factor	Present Value
1	Nil	Nil	0.87	-
2	2,00,000	1,40,000	0.76	1,06,400
3	2,50,000	1,75,000	0.66	1,15,500
4	8,25,000	5,77,500	0.57	3,29,175
5	3,80,000	2,66,000	0.50	1,33,000
Total	16,55,000	11,58,500		6,84,075

Recommendation: Outflow is ₹ 8,00,000 and net present value of future outflows is ₹ 6,84,075 at a discount rate of 15%. Hence, the investment proposal is not acceptable.

Illustration No. 2

Calculate NPV of the following project requiring an initial cash outlay of ₹ 20,000 which has no scrap value after 6 years. The net profits after depreciation and taxes for each year is ₹ 6,000 for six years. Assume the present value of an annuity of Re. 1 for 6 years at 8% per annum is ₹ 4.623.

Solution

Calculation of Net Present Value

Initial Cash Outlays = ₹ 20,000

Present Value of Cash Inflows = ₹ 6,000 × 4.623

= ₹ 27,738

Net present value (NPV) = Present value of cash inflows – Present value of cash outflows

= ₹ 27,738 – ₹ 20,000 = ₹ 7,738

Comments: It is accepted for investment as present value of cash inflows is excess over present value of cash outflows by ₹ 7,738.

Illustration No. 3

Out of the following options, which option a rational person chooses?

(A) Option to receive ₹ 2,000 today.

(B) Option to receive ₹ 4,500 at the end of eighth year.

Cost of capital is 10%.

Solution

Cash Flows (₹)	Discount Factor 10%	Net Present Value
2,000	1.00	2,000
4,500	0.467*	2,102

* This is the present value of Re. 1 at 10% received at the end of eighth year.

Option to receive ₹ 4,500 at the end of eighth year is more valuable by ₹ 102. Hence that option is to be chosen.

Illustration No. 4

Inflows and outflows of Jollyyappa & Co. for an investment proposal considered are as under:

Year	Inflows	Outflows
0	--	1,00,000
1	50,000	25,000
2	95,000	
3	60,000	
Scrap value at the end of third year	5,000	

Company accepts investment proposal, if return on investment is 10%. What is company's decision?

Solution

Calculation of NPV

Year	Inflows	Discount Factor	Present Value
1	50,000	0.909	45,450
2	95,000	0.826	78,470
3	60,000	0.751	45,060
Scrap value at the end of third year	5,000	0.751	3,755
Present value of Cash Inflows			1,72,735
Present value of Cash Outflows *			1,22,725
Net Present Value			50,010

Present value of Outflows*

Year	Outflows	Discount Factor	Present Value
0	1,00,000	1	1,00,000
1	25,000	0.909	22,725
Present value of Cash Outflows			1,22,725

Recommendation: Proposal is to be accepted as net present value of inflows is more than outflows by ₹ 50,010 at a discount rate of 10%, which is the requirement of company.

Illustration No. 5

A machine purchased six years ago for ₹ 1,50,000 has been depreciated to a book value of ₹ 90,000. It originally had a projected life of 15 years and zero salvage value. A new machine will cost ₹ 4,30,000 and results in a reduced operating cost of ₹ 30,000 per year for next nine years. The old machine can be sold for ₹ 50,000. Cost of capital is 10%. The new machine will also be depreciated on a straight line basis, similar to existing machine, over its nine year's life with ₹ 25,000 – salvage value. The company's tax rate is 55%.

Decide whether old machine should be replaced? **(B.U. MBA-2004)**

Solution

Incremental Net Investment or net initial outflow

Cost of the proposed machine	=	4,30,000
– Current scrap value of existing machine	=	50,000
Incremental net investment (Net outflow)		3,80,000

Incremental Annual Cash Inflows

	Existing Machine	Proposed Machine
Depreciation of existing machine $= \frac{\text{Depreciated value}}{\text{Balance life of asset}}$ $= \frac{90{,}000}{9}$ Depreciation of new machine $= \frac{\text{Cost} - \text{salvage value}}{\text{life of asset}}$ $= \frac{4{,}30{,}000 - 25{,}000}{9}$	10,000	45,000
Reduction in operating cost		–30,000
Eligible for tax benefit	10,000	15,000
Tax Benefit @ 55%	5,500	8,250
Net tax benefit 8,250 – 5,500		2,750
Savings in annual operating cost		30,000
Increase in annual inflow		32,750

NPV of proposal (cost of capital 10%)

= Present value of inflows – Present value of outflows

$$\text{Net Present Value} = \frac{C_1}{(1+k)} + \frac{C_2}{(1+k)^2} + \dots + \frac{C_n}{(1+k)^n} - C_0$$

C_1 and C_2 = Net cash inflows in year 1 and 2 ... n

k = Appropriate discount rate (cost of capital)

C_0 = Initial cost of investment

$$= \frac{32{,}750}{(1.10)} + \frac{32{,}750}{(1.10)^2} + \frac{32{,}750}{(1.10)^3} + \frac{32{,}750}{(1.10)^4} + \frac{32{,}750}{(1.10)^5} + \frac{32{,}750}{(1.10)^6} + \frac{32{,}750}{(1.10)^7} +$$

$$\frac{32{,}750}{(1.10)^8} + \frac{32{,}750}{(1.10)^9} - 3{,}80{,}000$$

= 29,773 + 27,066 + 24,606 + 22,369 + 20,335 + 18,487 + 16,806 + 15,278 + 13,889 –3,80,000

= 1,88,609 –3,80,000 = ₹ –1,91,391

By replacing existing machine with new machine, there would be a loss of ₹ 1,91,391 with a cost of capital @ 10%. So, it is not desirable to replace the existing machine.

Tutorial Note: In case, the problem gives PVAF value:

NPV = 32,750 × PVAF (present value of annuity factor of 10% for 9 years) –3,80,000

= 32,750 × 5.759 –3,80,000

= ₹ 1,88,609 –2,00,000

= ₹ –1,91,391

Illustration No. 6

Sumithra plans to start a project costing ₹ 25,000. The project generates cash inflows of ₹ 9,000, ₹ 8,000, ₹ 7,000, ₹ 6,000 and ₹ 5,000 over a period of five years. The required rate of return is assumed to be 10%. Give recommendation. At the end of fifth year scrap value is ₹ 1,000. Find out NPV of the project.

Solution:

The following table gives us NPV of the project:

(₹)

Year	Cash inflows	Discounted Factor	Present Value of Cash Inflows
(1)	(2)	(3)	(2 × 3) = (4)
1	9,000	0.9091	8,181
2	8,000	0.8264	6,611
3	7,000	0.7513	5,259
4	6,000	0.6830	4,098
5	5,000	0.6209	3,104
Net present value of cash inflows			27,253

Net Present Value = Present value of cash inflows – Present value of cash outflows

= ₹ 27,253 – ₹ 25,000 = ₹ 2,253

Comments: The NPV of the project is positive since present value of cash inflows ₹ 27,253 is greater than present value of cash outflows of ₹ 25,000. Project would be accepted for investment.

Treatment of depreciation: Depreciation is an expense. As a result, profit is arrived at after its deduction. However, there is no outgo of cash. For calculation of inflow, tax is to be deducted from profits but depreciation is to be added.

Let us explain with an example.

Illustration No. 7

Randheer & Co. are planning for a project costing ₹ 5,50,000, which has a life of 10 years. At the end of its life, its scrap value is likely to be ₹ 50,000. The firm cut-off rate for capital budgets is 12%. The project is expected to yield an annual profit, after tax, ₹ 1,00,000. Depreciation is charged on straight line basis. At 12% per annum, present value of rupee received annually for 10 years is ₹ 5.65. Value of one rupee received at the end of tenth year is ₹ 0.322. Ascertain NPV of the project.

Solution

Calculation of NPV	₹
Annual Profit, after Tax	1,00,000
Add: Depreciation $\frac{5,00,000^*}{10}$	50,000
Cash flows, after tax (for years 1 to 10)	1,50,000
Present value factor for 10 years at 12% = 5.65	
Total Present Value (1,50,000 × 5.65) – A	8,47,500
Cash flow in 10th year (scrap value)	50,000
Present value factor for money in tenth year = 0.322 (50,000 × 0.322) – B	16,100
Present value of cash inflows in ten years (A + B)	8,63,600
Less: Present value of cash outflow	5, 50,000
Net Present Value (NPV)	3,13,600

Since the NPV of the project is positive, it can be accepted for investment.

* Depreciation is charged on the original cost ₹ 5,50,000 – scrap value ₹ 50,000. Depreciation does not involve outgo of cash; hence added to arrive at cash inflows.

Illustration No. 8

Kalyan & Co. Ltd. is planning for installing a special machine for ₹ 2,50,000. As the machine is of special category, total amount is to be paid in advance. Machine would be supplied after one year. Firm would incur ₹ 10,000 towards installation charges for machine supplied, which is one year after advance payment.

From the date of advance payment, inflows are as under:

Second year	₹	50,000
Third year	₹	1,00,000
Fourth year	₹	3,00,000
Fifth year	₹	1,75,000

At the end of fifth year, scrap value of the machine is ₹ 10,000.

Discount rate is 12%. Calculate net present value. Give recommendation.

Solution

NPV of proposal (discount rate 12%)

= Present value of inflows – Present value of outflows

$$\text{Net Present Value} = \frac{C_1}{(1+k)} + \frac{C_2}{(1+k)^2} + \ldots + \frac{C_n}{(1+k)^n} - C_0$$

C_1 and C_2 = Net cash inflows in year 1 and 2 ... n

k = Appropriate discount rate (cost of capital)

C_0 = Initial cost of investment

$$= \frac{50{,}000}{(1.12)^2} + \frac{1{,}00{,}000}{(1.12)^3} + \frac{3{,}00{,}000}{(1.12)^4} + \frac{1{,}75{,}000}{(1.10)^5} - \left[2{,}50{,}000 + \frac{10{,}000^*}{(1.12)}\right]$$

$$= \frac{50{,}000}{1.2544} + \frac{1{,}00{,}000}{1.4049} + \frac{3{,}00{,}000}{1.5735} + \frac{1{,}75{,}000}{1.7623} - \left[2{,}50{,}000 + \frac{10{,}000^*}{(1.12)}\right]$$

= 39,860 + 71,179 + 1,90,658 + 99,302 – [2,50,000 + 8,928]

= 1,42,071

* Installation expenses ₹ 10,000 are incurred at the end of first year. So, this amount is also discounted to present net value.

Recommendation: At a discount rate of 12%, net present value of the proposal is 1,42,071. As net value of the proposal is positive and it has met the required discount rate, proposal is accepted.

16.7.4 Effect of Working Capital in Capital Budgeting Proposals - Treatment

Capital budgeting decision proposals are undertaken to increase firm's sales and profits. More production and sales are to be made to achieve higher profits. More production needs more inventory and higher level of sales results in more book debts (accounts receivable). A part of increase in current assets would be offset by increase in liabilities in the form of increased credit from suppliers. It is evident that there is a need for working capital along with capital budgeting proposals.

Capital budgeting decisions involve funds for working capital too. Working capital is to be treated as outflow. Working capital is blocked in current assets and gets realized on recovery of proceeds from sales. In other words, working capital does not disappear in a profitable firm as cash is finally converted into cash at the end of project. So, discounted value of working capital at end of the project is to be considered as inflows.

Number of years for which working capital amount would be blocked is to be calculated to find out the relevant discount factor. For example if working capital is introduced at the beginning of first year in a project of five years, working capital is blocked for a period of five years. However, if the same amount of working capital is introduced at the end of first year, amount is blocked for a period of four years only. So, relevant discount factor depends on the number of years working capital amount is blocked.

Illustration No. 9

Mirza & Co. is considering an investment proposal. It has two alternatives. Both alternatives need machinery investment of ₹ 1,75,000. Their cash inflows are as under:

(₹)

Year	Cash Inflows	
	Machinery A	Machinery B
1	30,000	20,000
2	70,000	10,000
3	90,000	40,000
4	40,000	75,000
5	20,000	90,000
Total	2,50,000	2,35,000

Their working capital requirements are not same. Machinery A needs ₹ 50,000 and ₹ 36,000 is required for machinery B at the beginning of first year.

The company requires a return on capital 10%. On the rate of return, company has a consistent policy and does not want to reconcile with a lower return of capital.

Advise about the acceptance of equipment.

Solution

Present Value of Inflows

Year	Discount factor of 10%	Machinery A		Machinery B	
		Cash Inflows	Present Value	Cash Inflows	Present Value
1	0.909	30,000	27,270	20,000	18,180
2	0.826	70,000	57,820	10,000	8,260
3	0.751	90,000	67,590	40,000	30,040
4	0.683	40,000	27,320	75,000	51,225
5	0.621	20,000	12,420	90,000	55,890
Working capital Machinery A – 50,000 Machinery B – 36,000	0.621		31,050		22,356
Total			2,23,470		1,85,951

Present Value of Outflows

	Machinery A – Cash Outflows	Machinery B – Cash Outflows
	1,75,000	1,75,000
	50,000	36,000
Total	2,25,000	2,11,000

Net Present Value

	Machinery A	Machinery B
Present value of inflows	2,23,470	1,85,951
Present value of outflows	2,25,000	2,11,000
Excess of outflows	1,530	25,049

Recommendation: On the basis of the required return of 10%, both machinery A and B are not acceptable.

Illustration No. 10

Vijaya Lakshmi & Co. has an investment opportunity for ₹ 5,00,000. Investment amount has to be spent in the following schedule:

At the beginning of first year: ₹ 3,00,000

In second year: ₹ 2,00,000

Working capital required to be tied up during whole project of ten years is ₹ 10,000. Project would not have cash flows during the first five years.

The following are the expected cash flows, after tax, before depreciation.

Year	Cash Flows, after Depreciation, before Tax	Depreciation	PV factor
1	Nil	Nil	0.909
2	Nil	Nil	0.826
3	Nil	Nil	0.751
4	Nil	Nil	0.683
5	Nil	Nil	0.621
6	6,00,000	20,000	0.564
7	7,00,000	15,000	0.513
8	8,00,000	12,000	0.467
9	3,00,000	10,000	0.424
10	2,00,000	8,000	0.386

Tax rate is 30%.

Cost of capital is 10%.

Advise about acceptability of project.

Solution

Calculation of Inflows

Year (1)	Cash Flows, after Depreciation, before Tax (2)	Tax @ 30 % (3)	Depreciation (4)	Cash Flows, before Depreciation, after Tax (2 + 4 –3)	Relevant PV Factor for Years Left	Net Present Value
6	6,00,000	1,80,000	20,000	4,40,000	0.564	2,48,160
7	7,00,000	2,10,000	15,000	5,05,000	0.513	2,59,065
8	8,00,000	2,40,000	12,000	5,72,000	0.467	2,67,124
9	3,00,000	90,000	10,000	2,20,000	0.424	93,280
10	2,00,000	60,000	8,000	1,48,000	0.386	57,128
Return of working capital at the end of 10th year	10,000				0.386	3,860
Total						9,28,617

Calculation of Outflows

Year	Investment	Working Capital	Total Out Flow	Relevant PV Factor	Net Present Value
1	3,00,000	10,000	3,10,000	1.000	3,10,000
2	2,00,000		2,00,000	0.826	1,65,200
					4,75,200

Net Present Value

Present value of inflows	9,28,617
Present value of outflows	4,75,200
Net present value	4,53,417

Recommendation: Project is to be accepted at it has positive NPV.

Illustration No. 11

Chandam Guy & Co., engaged in extracting iron ore from open pits, is considering a new technological process that needs capital investment. It extracts 10,000 tons per annum. Till now, it has been cleaning dirt from iron ore and selling it in the market.

Firm plans to refine 40% iron ore extracted and sells it to improve profits. Refining cost per ton is ₹100. Yield of refined output is 60% of input processed. Refined output is sold at an additional price of ₹ 500 per ton.

For refined processing, additional capital equipment needed is ₹ 10,00,000. Life of equipment is five years and company adopts written down method for providing depreciation @ 20%.

Additional working capital ₹ 20,000 is needed at the end of first year.

Required return on investment is 12% p.a. Tax rate is 30%. Ignore capital tax.

Recommend whether the capital proposal is to be accepted or rejected in light of the required return on investment on capital proposal.

Solution

Present Value of Cash Outflows

Particulars	Amount	Discount Factor @ 12%	Present Value
Capital equipment	10,00,000	1	10,00,000
Working Capital at the end of first year	20,000	0.797*	15,940
Total			10,15,940

* Discount factor for four years as working capital is invested at the end of first year.

Depreciation Schedule

Year	Original cost / Written down value	Depreciation @ 20% on WDV
1	10,00,000	2,00,000
2	8,00,000	1,60,000
3	6,40,000	1,28,000
4	5,12,000	1,02,400
5	4,09,600	81,920

Present Value of Cash Inflows

Particulars	First Year	Second Year	Third Year	Fourth Year	Fifth Year
Revenue from processing ** (2,400 x 500) = 12,00,000 Less: Processing Costs 4,00,000 (4,000 x 100)	8,00,000	8,00,000	8,00,000	8,00,000	8,00,000
Depreciation	2,00,000	1,60,000	1,28,000	1,02,400	81,920
Earning before taxes (EBT)	6,00,000	6,40,000	6,72,000	6,97,600	7,18,080
Less: Tax @ 30%	1,80,000	1,92,000	2,01,600	2,09,280	2,15,424
Earning after tax (EAT)	4,20,000	4,48,000	4,70,400	4,88,320	5,02,656
Add: Depreciation	2,00,000	1,60,000	1,28,000	1,02,400	81,920
Cash inflows	6,20,000	6,08,000	5,98,400	5,90,720	5,84,576
Discount Factor	0.893	0.797	0.712	0.636	0.567
Discounted value of cash inflows	5,53,660	4,84,576	4,26,061	3,75,698	3,31,455
Total Discounted value of cash inflows	21,71,450				
Discounted value of working capital ₹ 20,000 at a discount factor of 0.636 applicable for 4 years ***	12,720				
Present Value of cash inflows	21,84,170				

** Iron ore allocated for refinement is 40% of ore extracted (10,000 tons), so 4,000 tons is allocated for refinement. Yield of refined output is 60% of input processed. So 60% of 4,000 tons is 2,400 tons available for sale as refined output.

*** Working capital is blocked for a period of 4 years only as it is introduced at the end of first year.

Net Present Value

Present value of cash inflows	21,84,170
Present value of cash outflows	10,15,940
Net present value	11,68,230

Recommendation: Net present value is ₹ 11,68,230 at a discount rate of 12%. So capital proposal meets the requirement of the company in respect of return on investment, hence accepted.

In the above problem, only incremental costs and incremental revenues are to be considered to find out whether additional investments is feasible or not at the required rate of return.

16.8 INTERNAL RATE OF RETURN METHOD

The internal rate of return (IRR) method is another discounted cash flow technique which takes into account magnitude and timing of cash flows. IRR is simple to understand in case of one-period project. For example, a deposit of ₹ 1,000 in a bank would get ₹ 1,100 after one year if rate of return is calculated as under:

$$\text{Rate of Return} = \frac{1{,}100 - 1{,}000}{1{,}000} = 10\%$$

Formula for rate of return on an investment is

$$r = \frac{C_1 - C_0}{C_0}$$

Where r = **Rate of return**

C_1 = **Single cash flow after one year**

C_0 = **Initial investment**

In the above equation, 'Rate of Return' can be defined as that rate which equates the investment outlay with the present value of inflow received at the end of one year. This also implies that the rate of return is the discount rate that makes NPV = 0.

In IRR technique, future cash flows are discounted in such a way that their total present value of inflows is just equal to present value of the total outflows. The time schedule of occurrence of the future cash flows is known but the discount rate is not known. The discount rate is ascertained by the trial and error method where the present value of future inflows is equal to the present value of outflows, which is known as 'Internal Rate of Return'. In simple words, future inflows are discounted to become equal to the present value of outflows and the discount rate is IRR.

Future inflows are discounted to become equal to the present value of outflows. The discount rate when both become equal is called 'IRR'.

Formula for Calculation: The formula for calculation of IRR in case of series of cash flows is as under:

$$C_0 = \frac{C_1}{(1+r)} + \frac{C_2}{(1+r)^2} + \frac{C_3}{(1+r)^3} + \ldots + \frac{C_n}{(1+r)^n}$$

It may be noted that the IRR equation is the same as the one used for the NPV method. The difference is the required rate of return 'k' is assumed to be known in NPV method, while in the IRR method, the value of 'r' has to be determined at which the present value of inflows becomes equal to present values of outflows.

Discount rate (k) is known in NPV method, while it is required to be ascertained in Internal Rate of Return by trial and error method.

Trial and Error Method: The value of 'r' can be determined through trial and error method. If the calculated present value of discounted inflows is higher than the present value of the outflows, a higher discount rate should be tried. In case, the present value of discounted inflows is lower than the present value of the outflows, a lower discount rate is to be tried. This process has to be repeated till both discounted values of inflows and outflows become equal. Only through the process of trial and error method, correct discount rate can be calculated.

Acceptance Rule: In order to take a decision about acceptance or rejection of the project, the IRR is to be compared with the required rate of return (k) fixed by the management of each firm, which is also known as cut-off rate or hurdle rate. In case IRR is greater than the cut-off rate, that project would be accepted. If IRR is lower than the cut-off rate, that project would be rejected. In case IRR is equal to required rate of return, that project may be accepted or rejected. In other words firm is indifferent about its acceptance or rejection.

> **The virtue of IRR rule in capital budgeting is that it does not require the availability of required rate of return.**

Symbolically, it can be presented as under:

- Accept if IRR > k
- Reject if IRR < k
- May Accept or Reject, if IRR = k

Evaluation of IRR-Merits: Let us evaluate IRR against the principles of sound investment evaluation criteria. The merits of IRR can be summarised as under:

1. **Recognition of time value:** IRR method recognizes time value of money. All cash flows happening at different periods of time are adjusted to make them comparable.
2. **All cash flows:** All cash flows occurring over entire life of project are considered for calculating rate of return.
3. **Shareholders' wealth maximization:** It is consistent with the objective of shareholders' wealth maximization.
4. **Proposal selection:** It helps in selecting proposals, which are expected to earn more than the required rate of return.
5. **More practical:** Since IRR is expressed as a percentage, it is easy to compare IRR of different projects and make proper selection in ranking order.
6. **Based on cash flows:** The IRR is based on cash flows rather than accounting profit. Hence, IRR is more justified.

Drawbacks of IRR: Though IRR has qualities of sound investment evaluation criterion, still this technique suffers from the following disadvantages:

1. Its calculation is complicated based on trail and error method.
2. It is based on the assumption that future cash outflows are reinvested at a rate equal to IRR. Practically, it is not essential that every firm would have reinvestment opportunities.

3. In evaluating mutually exclusive projects, the IRR rule may give misleading results in a number of situations.
4. IRR violates value-additivity principle. It means IRR of two or more projects cannot be added, unlike NPV method.

16.9 NPV VERSUS IRR

The NPV and IRR are closely related investment criteria.

Superiority of IRR over NPV: In the following respects, IRR may be considered to be superior to NPV:

1. **Basis:** IRR gives percentile result while NPV gives result in absolute amount.
2. **Required Rate of Return:** For calculating IRR, required rate of return is not a pre-requisite, while it is a must for NPV.

Superiority of NPV over IRR: NPV is superior to IRR for the following reasons:

1. NPV shows the expected increase in wealth of shareholders.
2. The NPV of different projects are additive while the IRRs can not be added.
3. NPV gives better ranking as compared to IRR.

Comparison between NPV and IRR: Both are modern techniques of capital budgeting and take 'time value of money' into account. Still there are certain basic differences between them.

Basis	NPV	IRR
1. Cash flows	Cash flows are discounted at pre-determined discount rate based on cost of capital.	Cash flows are not discounted at predetermined rate and arrived at by trial and error method.
2. Reinvestment	Cash flows are presumed to be re-invested at the cut off rate.	Cash flows are presumed to be reinvested at the internal rate of return.

Similarity between NPV and IRR: It must be remembered that both NPV and IRR methods show same results in respect of independent investment proposals, which do not compete with one another.

Different Results: In case of mutually exclusive projects, projects compete with each other and acceptance of one project automatically excludes acceptance of other. Both (NPV and IRR) may give contradictory results when evaluating mutually exclusive projects for the following reasons:

(A) Requirement of cash outlays for projects may be different. One project may require more funds, while the other may demand less.

(B) The projects have unequal lives.

(C) The projects have different patterns of cash inflows.

Illustration No. 12

Project cost is ₹ 3,50,000. Its life is three years. Cash inflows are ₹ 50,000 in first year, ₹ 1,00,000 in second year and ₹ 3,00,000 in third year. Firm's cut off rate for internal rate of return as a policy is 12%.

Advise acceptance of proposal based on internal rate of return method.

Solution

$$C_0 = \frac{C_1}{(1+r)} + \frac{C_2}{(1+r)^2} + \frac{C_3}{(1+r)^3} + \ldots + \frac{C_n}{(1+r)^n}$$

C_0 = initial investment

C_1 to C_n are cash flows

r is required rate of return

$$3{,}50{,}000 = \frac{50{,}000}{(1.12)} + \frac{1{,}00{,}000}{(1.12)^2} + \frac{3{,}00{,}000}{(1.12)^3}$$

$$= \frac{50{,}000}{1.12} + \frac{1{,}00{,}000}{1.2544} + \frac{3{,}00{,}000}{1.4049}$$

$$= 44{,}643 + 79{,}719 + 2{,}13{,}538$$

$$= 3{,}37{,}900$$

Initial investment ₹ 3,50,000 is greater than the discounted value of cash flows ₹ 3,37,900 at 12% IRR. So, let us take a lower return of 11.5% to try whether initial investment would be equal to discounted value of inflows.

$$3{,}50{,}000 = \frac{20{,}000}{(1.115)} + \frac{50{,}000}{(1.115)^2} + \frac{1{,}00{,}000}{(1.115)^3}$$

$$= \frac{50{,}000}{1.115} + \frac{1{,}00{,}000}{1.243} + \frac{3{,}00{,}000}{1.386}$$

$$= 44{,}843 + 80{,}451 + 2{,}16{,}450$$

$$= 3{,}41{,}744$$

Even with 11.5% IRR, discounted value of inflows is lower than the initial investment. It would be observed with lower IRR %, discounted value of cash inflows are increasing. With IRR lesser than 11.5%, discounted value of inflows would be equal to initial investment. Firm requires 12% IRR as a policy. Hence proposal is rejected.

16.10 PAY BACK METHOD

The Payback Method (PB) is one of the most popular and widely recognized traditional method of evaluating investment proposals.

Payback method is defined as the number of years required to recover original cash outlay invested in a project.

If project gives constant annual cash inflow, payback period can be calculated by dividing cash outlay by annual cash inflow.

Equal cash inflows: The formula for calculation of payback period when cash inflows are constant is as follows:

$$\text{Payback Period} = \frac{\text{Initial Investment}}{\text{Annual cash inflow}} = \frac{C_0}{C}$$

Unequal cash inflows: In case of unequal cash inflows, payback period can be found out by adding up all cash inflows until the total is equal to the initial cash outlay.

So, payback method is useful when cash flows are equal or unequal.

Acceptance rule: On account of simplicity, many firms follow payback method as an 'Accept or Reject' criterion as well as a method for ranking projects. First the management sets standard payback period. If the calculated payback period is below standard payback period project is accepted. In case calculated payback period is more than standard period, project is rejected. It is a very simple ways of decision-making. For example, if standard payback period is 3 years fixed by the management and the payback period calculated is 2 years, then the project is accepted. In case payback period is, say 4 years, the project is rejected. So, this is a very simple operation. If there is more than one project for consideration, all projects are ranked according to payback period. The project that has the shortest payback period is ranked first and the project that has the longest period is placed at the last. Thus, if a firm has to choose among the mutually exclusive projects, project with shorter payback period is selected.

Evaluation of payback method: If we analyze payback method against standard investment evaluation criterion, the outcome is as follows:

Merits: It has the following advantages:

1. **Simple to Operate:** The most significant merit is its simplicity to understand and easy to calculate. Its simplicity is considered as a virtue, which is evident from its popularity with business executives.
2. **Calculation Costs Low:** Its calculation costs are less while the other sophisticated techniques require lot of analyst's time and even use of computers.
3. **Risk of Obsolescence High:** This method is ideally suitable in those industries where risk of obsolescence is high. There is no guarantee that the same technology would continue in future. In such industries, projects that have shorter payback period only are to be financed.

Demerits: In spite of its simplicity, it suffers from the following limitations:

1. **All cash flows not considered:** Cash inflows throughout the total life of projects are not considered. It fails to take into account the cash inflows after the payback period. In other words, if standard payback period is say 5 years, cash inflows

occurring after 5 years, though available, are ignored. It is not an appropriate method for measuring profitability of project as it ignores an important principle of 'Time Value of Money'.

2. **Equal weightage to all cash flows:** It fails to consider the pattern of cash inflows i.e. magnitude and timing of cash flows. It gives equal weightage to all the cash inflows, though they may happen at different periods of time.
3. **No rational in fixing standard period:** The firm may experience administrative difficulty to fix the standard payback period as there is no rational in fixing period.
4. **Not consistent with shareholders' wealth maximization:** The payback period is not consistent with the maximization of the shareholders' wealth.

Illustration No. 13

Delhi Machinery Manufacturing Company wants to replace the manual operations by new machine. There are two alternative models of X and Y for the new machine. Using payback period, suggest the most profitable investment. Ignore taxation.

(₹)

	Machine X	Machine Y
Original investment	9,000	18,000
Estimated life of machine (Years)	3	5
Estimated savings in scrap	500	800
Estimated savings in wages	6,000	8,000
Additional cost of maintenance	800	1,000
Additional cost of supervision	1,200	1,500

(B.U. MBA- 2004)

Solution

	Machine X	Machine Y
Estimated savings in scrap and wages	6,500	8,800
Less: Estimated additional costs on maintenance and supervision	2,000	2,500
Net savings	4,500	6,300
Depreciation (cost – scrap value) / Life of asset X = 8,500 / 3 Y = 17,200 /5	2,833	3,440
Net gain	1,667	2,860
Add: Depreciation	2,833	3,440
Annual inflow	4,500	6,300
Payback period (years) Investment / Annual cash inflow	9,000 / 4,500 2 years	18,000 / 6,300 2.86 years

Conclusion: Under payback method, machine that gives the earliest recovery of outlay is selected. Management has not fixed any standard period. Machine X has 2 years payback period while payback period of Y is 2.86 years. So, Machine X has to be selected based on payback method.

Illustration No. 14

In case tax rate is 30%, work out the above illustration.

Solution

	Machine X	Machine Y
Estimated savings in Scrap and Wages	6,500	8,800
Less: Estimated additional costs on maintenance and supervision	2,000	2,500
Net savings	4,500	6,300
Depreciation (Cost – Scrap value)/Life of asset X = 8,500 / 3 Y = 17,200 /5	2,833	3,440
Net gain, before tax	1,667	2,860
Tax @ 30%	500	858
Net savings, after tax	1,167	2,002
Add: Depreciation	2,833	3,440
Annual inflow	4,000	5,442
Payback period (years) Investment Annual cash inflow	9,000 4,000	18,000 5,442
	2.25 years	3.31 years

Conclusion: Under Payback method, machine that gives the earliest recovery of outlay is selected. Management has not fixed any standard period. Machine X has 2.25 years payback period while for Y same is 3.31 years. So, Machine X has to be selected based on Payback Method.

Illustration No. 15

Prameela Ltd is conducting its manufacturing activity by manual operations. The company plans to replace the manual operations by machine. There are two alternative machine models A and B. From the following data, decide which machine is more profitable? In case company decides to adopt payback method for evaluating its investment project, what would be its decision? If the decision from the former is changed, justify the change.

Particulars	Machine A	Machine B
Estimated life of the machine	10 years	20 years
Cost of machine	₹ 3,20,000	₹ 5,50,000
Estimated savings in scrap	₹ 20,000	₹ 50,000
Estimated reduction in consumption of direct materials	₹ 40,000	₹ 60,000
Estimated savings in direct wages	₹ 20,000	₹ 25,000
Additional cost of overheads	₹ 10,000	₹ 12,000
Estimated increase in consumption of indirect materials	₹ 10,000	₹ 30,000
Tax rate	30%	30%

Solution

Calculation of Net Profit

Particulars	Machine A (₹)	Machine B (₹)
Savings:		
Estimated savings in scrap	20,000	50,000
Estimated reduction in consumption of direct materials	40,000	60,000
Estimated savings in direct wages	20,000	25,000
Total additional savings	80,000	1,35,000
Additional costs:		
Additional cost of overheads	10,000	12,000
Estimated increase in consumption of indirect materials	10,000	30,000
Depreciation (cost of asset – scrap value) / life of asset	30,000	25,000
Total additional costs	50,000	67,000
Additional operating profit, before tax	30,000	68,000
Tax @ 30%	9,000	20,400
Net profit	21,000	47,600

Calculation of Payback Period

Particulars	Machine A (₹)	Machine B (₹)
Net profit	21, 000	47,600
Depreciation	30,000	25,000
Annual inflow	51,000	72,600
Cost of machine	3,20,000	5,50,000
Payback period (years) Investment / Annual cash inflow	$\frac{3,20,000}{51,000}$ = 6.27 years	$\frac{5,50,000}{72,600}$ = 7.57 years

Recommendation on basis of profitability: Out of the two alternatives A and B machines, B is more profitable by ₹ 26,600 (47,600 – 21,000). On the basis of profitability, Machine B is recommended.

Recommendation on basis of payback method: Shorter payback period is the main criterion for selection of a project under payback method. On the basis of payback method, Machine A takes 6.27 years while Machine B takes 7.57 years for recovery of investment on the project made. So, on the basis of payback method, Machine A is recommended.

Final conclusion: All methods do not give same result. In payback method, emphasis is on recovery, not profitability. So, decision is changed.

Illustration No. 16

Amit Saxena & Company is considering an investment of ₹ 1,00,000 in a project. The following are the income forecasts, after depreciation and tax: first year ₹ 10,000, second year ₹ 40,000, third year ₹ 60,000, fourth year ₹ 20,000 and fifth year Nil.

From above information you are required to calculate:

(1) Payback Period.

(2) Discounted Payback Period at 10% interest factor.

In case, management decides that the investment is to be recovered within a 3 year period, which method is recommended for acceptance of the proposal?

Solution

1. Calculation of Payback Period

(₹)

Year	Annual cash inflows	Cumulative cash inflows
1.	10,000	10,000
2.	40,000	50,000
3.	60,000	1,10,000
4.	20,000	1,30,000
5.	Nil	1,30,000

The above table shows that at the end of third year, cumulative cash inflows exceeds the investment by ₹ 1,00,000. Thus the Payback Period is as follows:

$$\text{Payback Period} = 2 \text{ Years} + \frac{1{,}00{,}000 - 50{,}000}{60{,}000}$$

$$= 2 \text{ Years} + \frac{₹\ 50{,}000}{₹\ 60{,}000}$$

$$= 2 \text{ Years} + 0.833 = 2.833 \text{ Years}$$

2. Calculation of Discounted Payback Period at 10% Interest Rate.

Year	Cash Inflows	Discounting Present Value Factor at 10%	Present Value of Cash Inflows (2 x 3)	Cumulative Value of Cash Inflows
(1)	(2)	(3)	(4)	(5)
1	10,000	0.9091	9,091	9,091
2	40,000	0.8265	33,060	42,151
3	60,000	0.7513	45,078	87,229
4	20,000	0.6830	13,660	1,00,889
5	Nil	0.6209	Nil	1,00,889

It is observed that by the end of fourth year, investment ₹ 1,00,000 is recovered because the discounted cumulative cash inflows of ₹ 1,00,889 exceeds the original cash outlay of ₹ 1,00,000. The discounted payback period is calculated as follows:

$$\text{Payback Period} = 3 \text{ Years} + \frac{1{,}00{,}000 - 87{,}229}{13{,}660}$$

$$= 3 \text{ Years} + \frac{12{,}771}{13{,}660}$$

$$= 3 \text{ Years} + 0.935 = 3.935 \text{ Years}$$

Illustration No. 17

A company has to choose one of the following two projects. Both projects have a life of 5 years and profits before tax are to be depreciated on straight line basis. The tax rate is 50 per cent. At zero year is the outflow and rest of the following are inflows.

Year	X (₹)	Y (₹)
0	30,000	30,000
1	8,400	8,400
2	9,600	9,000
3	14,000	8,000
4	16,000	10,000
5	4,000	20,000

Use payback period as the criterion for project selection.

(B.U., MBA, 2008)

Solution

Here, initial outlay for project X and Y is ₹ 30,000. Life of the project is five years, so depreciation is ₹ 6,000.

Year	Project X						Project Y					
	Profit before depreciation	Dep.	Profit after dep.	Tax 50%	Profit / Loss after tax	Inflows	Profit before depreciation	Dep.	Profit after Dep.	Tax 50%	Profit / loss after tax	Inflows
(1)	(2)	(3)	(4)	(5)	(6)	(7) (3 + 6)	(8)	(9)	(10)	(11)	(12)	(13) (9 + 12)
1	8,400	6,000	2,400	1,200	1,200	7,200	8,400	6,000	2,400	1,200	1,200	7,200
2	9,600	6,000	3,600	1,800	1,800	7,800	9,000	6,000	3,000	1,500	1,500	7,500
3	14,000	6,000	8,000	4,000	4,000	10,000	8,000	6,000	2,000	1,000	1,000	7,000
4	16,000	6,000	10,000	5,000	5,000	11,000	10,000	6,000	4,000	2,000	2,000	8,000
5	4,000	6,000	–2,000	Nil	–2,000	4,000	20,000	6,000	14,000	7,000	7,000	13,000

Payback Period in Project X

In project X, cumulative inflows at the end of three years are 25,000. In the fourth year, the inflows are 11,000. In payback method, inflows should be equal to the initial investment. So, Payback period is in between 3 and 4 years.

So, actual payback period is $3 + \left[\frac{5{,}000 \times 12}{11{,}000}\right] = 3$ years 5.45 months.

Payback Period in Project Y

In project Y, cumulative inflows at the end of four years are 29,700. In fifth year, inflows are 13,000. In payback method, inflows should be equal to initial investment. So, payback period is in between 4 and 5 years.

So, actual payback period is $4 + \left[\frac{300 \times 12}{13{,}000}\right] = 4$ years and 0.28 months.

Recommendation: Payback period of X is low compared to Y. So, firm has to choose project X under payback method.

Check Your Understanding

State whether the following statements are True or False

1. Capital expenditure decisions are also called as long-term investment decisions.
2. Net Present Value is arrived at by deducting present value of outflows (investment) from present value of cash inflows.
3. Capital rationing and capital budgeting mean the same thing.
4. Net present value method takes into account earnings over entire life of project.
5. Mutually exclusive investments do not serve the same purpose.

6. Contingent investments are dependent investments and the choice of one investment necessitates undertaking one or more investments.
7. Positive NPV does not contribute to maximization of shareholders' wealth.
8. NPV method is not suitable for evaluation of investment proposals when the cash flows, both inflows and outflows, are uneven.
9. The Internal Rate of Return (IRR) method, a discounted cash flow technique, takes into account the magnitude and timing of cash flows.
10. Both NPV and IRR methods show the same results in respect of independent investment proposals, which do not compete with one another.
11. In payback method, firm chooses that investment which has a longer payback period.
12. Capital investment decisions are generally of irreversible nature.
13. Acquisition and purchase of fixed assets involve capital budgeting decisions.
14. The greatest difficulty with Net Present Value method is to select the appropriate discount rate.
15. Net Present Value method can be applied for capital budgeting decisions without any discount rate.
16. Payback method is useful when cash flows are equal or unequal.
17. Shorter payback period is the main criterion for selection of a project under payback method.
18. Discounted cash flow technique gives weightage to different cash flows over life of the fixed asset for a proper choice in evaluating capital budget decisions.

Answers

1. True	2. True	3. False	4. True	5. False	6. True	7. False	8. False
9. True	10. True	11. False	12. True	13. True	14. True	15. False	16. True
17. True	18. True.						

Descriptive Questions

1. What is Capital Budgeting? Detail its significance for a firm. **(16.1 to 16.3)**
2. What do you mean by Capital Investment Decision? Write its importance. **(16.1 to 16.3)**
3. Explain in detail the classification of capital expenditure and their evaluation criteria for selection. **(16.4 and 16.5)**
4. What is Net Present Value Method? Why it is regarded as best method for evaluation of investment proposals. **(16.7, 16.7.1 to 16.7.3)**
5. "The virtue of the IRR rule is that it does not require the availability of the required rate of return." Comment. **(16.8)**
6. Write a note on different methods of Capital Budgeting. Choose any three methods and analyze their strength and weakness against the standard evaluation criteria. **(16.6 to 16.8 and 16.10)**
7. Compare Net Present Value and Internal Rate of Return. **(16.9)**
8. 'Payback method is a traditional capital budgeting technique and simple to calculate'. Why this method is not universally applicable in all capital budgeting decisions? **(16.10)**
9. Name capital budgeting techniques. **(16.6)**

Short Questions

Q.1. What is a capital budgeting decision and state its importance to a firm?

Ans. Acquisition and purchase of fixed assets involve capital budgeting decisions. Basically, they are long-term decisions and have severe impact over future life of a firm. The fixed assets, in a sense, represent true earning assets of a firm. They are acquired for generating profits and are for long-term use. They involve single outlay or series of cash outlays over a period in return for anticipated future benefits. They have a bearing on competitive position of a company and determine its future destiny. Secondly, company commits itself to sizable amount of fixed costs in terms of wages, supervisor's salary, building rent and so on. If investment turns out to be unsuccessful in future or yields lesser profits than anticipated, firm has to bear fixed costs almost permanently unless firm decides to write off the investment completely. Thirdly, once decisions are made, they are not easily reversible without significant financial loss. Sale of fixed assets—profit generating assets–before their end of life normally results in monetary loss. So, every firm would consider all aspects carefully, in particular long-term profitability and other implications involved before taking any decision in respect of long-term fixed assets.

Q.2. Why capital proposals are to be ranked for final selection?

Ans. Economic resources are scarce, and so, all investment proposals compete with each other for selection. Generally, all firms allocate a certain amount, periodically, for investment purposes. For final selection and execution, all investment proposals are ranked in a descending order according to rate of return for achieving maximum profitability.

Q.3. Explain suitability of 'Payback Method' for evaluating investment proposals.

Ans. Period required to payback investment amount is calculated in 'Payback method'. Investment proposals whose payback is within the fixed predetermined period only are ranked for selection. Those proposals in order of payback period that exhaust the allocated funds for investment are selected. Under this method, focus is given for getting back the investment amount early within payback period fixed for ranking of proposals. The greatest merit of the method is its simple and easy nature to calculate. However, the greatest drawback of this method is cash flows occurring in the predetermined period only are considered for evaluation. As all cash flows occurring during the whole life of the asset are not considered, it is likely that the proposal selected may not be the maximum profitable one.

Payback method is a proper method to those firms which experience difficulty to lock funds for a long period. Where risk of obsolescence is very high, payback method is the most appropriate method to recover capital costs at the earliest before the relevant technology used becomes outdated.

Q.4. Out of NPV and IRR methods, which is more suitable for evaluating capital investment proposals?

Ans. Both NPV and IRR methods consider magnitude and timing of all cash flows occurring over the entire life of fixed asset. Objective of both the methods is to achieve shareholders' wealth maximization. Required rate of return is necessary for calculating NPV while this is derived by trial and error method in IRR.

NPV method shows value addition of wealth in absolute amount while IRR method does not allow. IRR method shows comparative returns in percentage.

Interview Questions

Q.1. What is 'Capital Budgeting'? Why they are important to a firm?

Ans. Investment decisions related to acquisition of fixed assets are known as capital budgeting or capital expenditure decisions. Capital budgeting involves planning for acquisition of capital assets. These decisions assume high importance as impact of most of decisions are of long-duration and irreversible, without substantial monetary loss.

Q.2. What is capital rationing?

Ans. Capital rationing is a situation when a firm experiences constraint on availability of funds for acquisition of capital assets. It is an act or practice of limiting a company's investment.

Q.3. How capital rationing is made?

Ans. Capital rationing occurs when a company's management places a cap (maximum amount) on new investments it can make over a given period of time. There are two methods of capital rationing. One is forbidding investments over a certain amount. The other is increasing cost of capital while weighing merits of investments. This ensures that capital projects are not accepted unless they are very highly profitable. Capital rationing is most common when a company has not enjoyed good returns on investments in the recent past. Capital rationing also occurs when company has excess production capacity on hand.

Q.4. What is 'Capital asset pricing model'?

Ans. Capital asset pricing model is an economic theory that describes relationship between risk and expected return. It serves as a model for pricing of risky securities. The CAPM asserts that the only risk that is priced by rational investors is systematic risk because that risk cannot be eliminated by diversification.

The CAPM states that the expected return of a security or a portfolio is equal to the rate on a risk-free security plus a risk premium.

Q.5. What is meant by mutually exclusive projects and explain with an example?

Ans. When two or more projects compete with each other for selection to serve the same purpose, they are called mutually exclusive projects. Only one among the competing projects would be selected. For example, manual crusher and mechanical are two methods used in crushing stones. In case, a firm chooses manual crusher, proposal for mechanical crusher is rejected.

Q.6. What is 'Internal Rate of Return Method'?

Ans. Internal Rate of Return Method is a discounted cash flow technique for evaluating different investment proposals. Future cash flows, both inflows and outflows, occurring during the life of the asset are discounted to become equal to arrive at the discount rate in IRR method. The calculated IRR is compared with the required rate of return (k). In case IRR is greater than k, the proposal is accepted.

Q.7. Which is the easiest and popular method in capital budgeting?

Ans. Payback method is the most popular method in capital budgeting as it is simple and easy to calculate. As this method provides emphasis on recovery of capital investment at the earliest, it is very popular.

Q.8. Which method of capital budgeting is followed in those industries where obsolescence risk rate is high?

Ans. Payback method is ideally suitable in those industries where risk of obsolescence is high. When there is no guarantee for continuation of the same technology in future, it is necessary to recover the capital outlay at the earliest. In such industries, projects that have shorter payback period only are to be financed.

Q.9. Which method of capital budgeting is appropriate for recovery of capital cost in a short period?

Ans. Payback method is appropriate capital budgeting technique for recovery of capital cost in a short period.

Q.10. Which is the best method for evaluating a capital project? Justify.

Ans. Net present value method and internal rate of return are the best methods to evaluate a capital project. Both are discounted techniques. All cash flows occurring during life of asset are considered while ranking proposals. Time Value of Money is given due weightage in selection. Net present value method is appropriate if discount rate is known, while internal rate of return can be followed if discount rate is not known but can be calculated by trial and error method.

CHAPTER

17

Cost of Different Sources of Raising Capital

17.1 INTRODUCTION

An investment proposal requires a certain required rate of return for acceptance. Unless proposal meets the required return, it is not accepted. This is a decision criterion to accept or reject a proposal. Such a rate is known as 'Cost of capital'. Cost of capital is also important in designing capital structure of a company.

17.2 COST OF CAPITAL

Fixed assets of a company are financed by long-term sources of finance. Sources of long-term finance are equity share capital, preference share capital and debentures. Providers of these sources expect a certain return to invest in a company. If they do not get the expected return, they prefer to invest elsewhere. To attract funds from these sources as well as retaining them, every company has to pay the required rate of return to these different sources. Return these investors get in turn becomes cost of capital to company.

Return is compensation for sacrificing current consumption.

Cost of capital is the minimum rate of return expected by investors, the suppliers of capital. In other words, it is a price for obtaining capital. It is a compensation for time and risk. Investors are of different categories—equity shareholders, preference share-holders and debenture holders. They provide different sources of finance. Their risks are different. Debentures are paid interest whether firm makes profit or not. They get back their money before payment is made to preference and equity shareholders. They get a fixed interest rate. However, debenture holders are exposed to risk of default in payment. Since cash flows of a company are uncertain, there is probability for default in payment of principal as well as interest. Still their risk is the lowest amongst different long-term sources of finance. Risk and return always go hand in hand. If risk is greater, one expects a higher return. Here their risk is the lowest. So they can expect the lowest rate of return amongst the different securities of a company. In other words, cost to company on funds raised through debentures is the lowest. Preference shares carry a fixed dividend but dividend is subordinated to interest on debentures. Return of funds to them is also only after repayment of debentures. Looking to the relatively higher risk, expectations of preference shareholders are higher than debenture holders. So cost on preference shares is more to company compared to debentures. Equity shareholders are residual claimants in profits as well as return of money. Their risk is the greatest and so cost to company is the highest amongst all sources of finance.

Importance: Concept of cost of capital is very important in financial management. Decision to invest in a particular project depends on cost of capital. **The minimum return expected from a project is its cost of capital.** It is a cut off rate. If the return is above or equal to the cut-off rate, then only investment is made. If return is below the cut-off rate, no investment is made. To achieve the objective of wealth maximization, the return has to be more than cut off rate.

Cost of capital to a company is the minimum return expected by different group of investors who invest their money in the form of shares, debentures or term loans. If company does not earn this minimum return, investors will be tempted to pull their funds out of the company. They withdraw their investment from that company and prefer to invest elsewhere. The company concerned would not be able to retain the investment, let alone attract fresh investment, at current market rate and in consequence, market price of the concerned company's equity share falls. At the reduced market price, company may receive the investment. In fact, cost of capital is the minimum rate of return, which will maintain market value of the shares at its present level.

Definition: According to Solomon Ezra, "Cost of capital is the minimum required rate of earnings or the cut-off rate of capital expenditure".

From the above definition, there are three basic aspects of cost of capital:

1. **Cost of capital is not cost as such:** It is not cost to the firm. In fact, it is the minimum rate of return that a firm requires.
2. **Minimum rate of return:** The rate of return is that minimum, expected by investors, which maintains market value of the shares.
3. **Composition:** The return should contain three components:
   (A) Normal return at zero risk
   (B) Premium for business risk; and
   (C) Premium for financial risk on account of pattern of capital structure

Symbolically, cost of capital may be represented as:

K = Normal return at zero risk level

+

Premium for business risk

+

Premium for financial Risk

Where K = Cost of Capital

17.3 SIGNIFICANCE OF COST OF CAPITAL

Cost of capital plays a crucial role in financial management in the following areas:

(A) Capital Budgeting Decisions: Cost of capital helps management in taking decisions about selection of capital expenditure projects. It is a cut-off or discount rate for evaluating desirability of investment projects. In capital budgeting, according to present value method, project would be accepted only if present value of expected future returns is more than or equal to initial capital or investment, otherwise project may be rejected. The present value is calculated by discounting future cash flows at cut-off rate, which is the cost of capital. The discount rate is cost of capital or cut-off rate. Discount rate is also known as implicit cost, which equates present value of cash inflows with present value of cash outflows. So, cost of capital is taken as a decision criterion in capital budgeting matters. Hence, cost of capital concept is highly useful in capital budgeting decisions.

(B) Designing Debt Policy: Financing firm's assets is a crucial problem in every business. There should be a proper mix of debt and equity in financing assets of the company. When return on investment is greater than cost of debt, earning on equity share is magnified. While designing capital structure of firm, management has to keep in mind to maximize the value of share in stock exchange. This becomes possible when the cost of capital is at its minimum and value of the firm is at its maximum. So, measurement of cost of capital from various sources of finance is essential in designing and planning capital structure.

(C) Measurement of Financial Performance: The actual profitability of project is compared to the overall cost of capital of funds used. If actual profitability of project is more than the projected and actual cost of capital, performance of management is said to be satisfactory. When two managers are to be compared, ranking becomes possible with this concept.

17.4 CONCEPT OF COST OF CAPITAL: OPPORTUNITY COST

Decision-making is a process of choosing alternatives. Consider an individual having two investment opportunities, investing in 8 per cent 6 year postal certificates and another 6 year fixed deposit in a nationalised bank that fetches an interest rate of 9 per cent. Government assures payment in respect of both securities. Looking to the higher interest rate, now the choice is made to deposit in a bank. By investing in a bank, the individual has foregone the alternative opportunity of investing in postal deposit that gives him 8 per cent interest. So, individual has incurred an opportunity cost. In this case, the cost is 8% for the individual. **The opportunity cost is the rate of return foregone on the next best alternative investment opportunity of comparable risk.** So, the required rate of return on an investment project is an opportunity cost. In other words, the minimum return required to invest in a project is the return foregone on the next best alternative, which is called opportunity cost.

Opportunity cost of capital and cost of capital mean the same.

17.5 RISK-RETURN RELATIONSHIP OF VARIOUS SECURITIES

Investors have numerous investment opportunities. Their returns as well as risks are different. Risk and return always go hand in hand. Why return in postal deposit is low compared to interest rate on a debenture? Postal deposit is a risk-free security while debenture is not. As risk is more with a debenture, return is also high compared to postal deposit. Return in an equity share is still high because the risk is higher than the postal deposit as well as debenture. It may be observed that the required return of any security is composed of two rates—a risk-free rate and risk premium. A risk free rate is compensation for time value and its risk-premium at that point is zero. Bank deposits and government securities are examples of risk-free securities. Investors expect a higher return on risky securities. Higher the risk of a security, higher is risk-premium, and therefore, a higher required rate of return is needed.

The risk-return relationship for various securities is shown in the following Fig.:

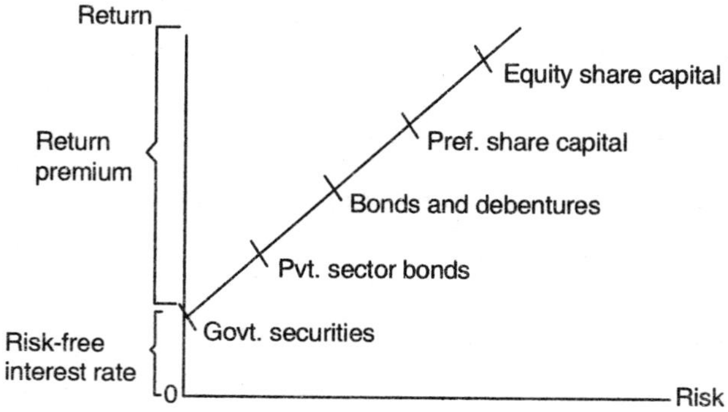

Risk-return relationship of different types of securities

17.6 DETERMINING COST OF DEBENTURE

Debt includes all interest-bearing borrowings. Cost of debt to company is the return (yield) which lenders expect from their investment. A company can raise debt in various ways. It can borrow funds from financial institutions or public in the form of public deposits or debentures. A debenture is issued at par, discount or premium. The contractual rate of interest forms the basis for calculating the cost of any debt. **Contractual rate of interest on a debenture is called as coupon rate.** For example, if interest rate of debentures is 12%, coupon rate is 12%. Though debenture is issued at discount or premium, interest is paid on the face value of the debentures.

So, for calculation of interest rate, face value of debenture is to be multiplied with interest rate or coupon rate.

Interest = Face value of the debenture x Interest rate

When the debenture is issued at par and to be redeemed at par, cost of debt (before –tax) simply is the contractual rate of interest. If face value of a 10% debenture is ₹100 and is issued at par and also to be redeemed at par, what is cost of debt (before-tax)? It is ₹ 10.

In other words, when the debenture is issued at par and also to be redeemed at par, the cost of debt and interest rate mean the same. However, the cost of debt (before-tax) would be different if the debenture is issued/redeemed at discount and premium.

Interest tax shield: Interest paid on debt is tax deductible. In consequence, the actual cost of debt (interest amount less tax there on) would be lower. In other words, indirectly the government is bearing a part of interest cost. As a result of interest tax shield, after-tax cost to firm is substantially lower than the rate of return required by investors. The before-tax cost of debt (k_d) should be adjusted for tax effect as follows:

$$\textbf{After-tax cost of debt} = k_d\,(I-T)$$

Where k_d = Before tax cost of debt

T = Corporate tax rate

If interest rate is 15% on debenture and the tax rate is 35%, after-tax cost of debenture would be:

$$k_d\,(I - T) = 0.15(1 - 0.35) = 0.0975 \text{ or } 9.75\%$$

In other words, actual cost of debt to company is 9.75% while return to its investors is 15%. The difference between the two, in fact, is not borne by company, but by government in the form of reduced tax.

It is to be noted that the tax benefit would be available if the firm is profitable and is paying taxes. A loss-making firm is not required to pay taxes. So, it would not gain any tax benefit associated with the payment of interest. So, cost of capital for a loss-making firm is its true cost of debt i.e. before tax-cost. In other words, effective cost of debt to a profit-making firm and loss-making firm is not the same.

For calculation of average cost of capital, the 'after-tax cost' of debt must be used, not the 'before tax cost' of debt.

17.7 DETERMINING COST OF PREFERENCE CAPITAL

Dividend paid on preference shares is not tax deductible, so tax benefit is not available. Dividend payment is only an appropriation of profit, not a charge on Profit and Loss Account. More so, payment of preference dividend is discretionary on the part of company. In other words, there is no legal obligation for payment of preference dividend. So one may be tempted to think that preference capital does not have cost. It is not true. **The cost of preference capital is a function of dividend expected by the investors.**

A company with intention not to pay dividend, never issues preference capital. Preference shareholders enjoy a prior claim on profits. So, only after payment of preference dividend, dividend to equity shareholders can be paid. Moreover, non-payment of dividend to preference shareholders, when profits are available, would adversely affect company's image. Preference shareholders would have voting rights in the event of default of dividend payment. In case of default in payment of dividend to preference shareholders, market value of the equity shares would be affected. Though there is no legal obligation, company defaults in payment of dividend on preference capital only when it does not make profits. The default can also happen if company's cash position is tight.

Cost of Irredeemable Preference Share: The irredeemable preference share is treated as perpetual security. The cost of irredeemable preference share is computed by the following equation:

$$**k_p = \frac{PD}{P_o}$$

Where k_p = Cost of preference share

PD = Annual preference dividend

P_o = Net proceeds on issue of preference shares

$$\text{*Cost of Preference share} = \frac{\text{Annual preference dividend}}{\text{Net proceeds on issue of preference shares}}$$

Note: For students, it is easy to remember the one star* type of definition as it gives meaning to remember rather than the two stars** definition as it contains a formula that is difficult to remember.

Illustration No. 1

A company issues 12 per cent irredeemable preference shares. The face value per share is ₹ 100. If the share is issued at a discount of ₹ 5, what is the cost of preference share? What is the cost price, if the share is issued at a premium of ₹ 5?

Solution

Issue price ₹ 95

$$k_p = \frac{PD}{P_o}$$

$$= \frac{12}{95} = 0.126 = 12.63$$

Issue price ₹ 105

$$k_p = \frac{PD}{P_o}$$

$$= \frac{12}{105} = 0.114 = 11.42$$

17.8 DETERMINING COST OF EQUITY CAPITAL

Equity shares are the residual/last claimants of company. After payment of interest on debentures, income-tax and dividend on preference shares, the balance of profits belongs to equity shareholders. There is no fixed commitment to a company in respect of equity dividend. Dividend to equity shareholders is decided by board of directors which is finally approved by equity shareholders in annual general meeting. Simply, equity shares do not bear a fixed commitment; it does not mean that equity share capital is a cost-free capital.

Potential investors invest in equity shares anticipating dividend over a period of holding and appreciation in the form of capital gain at the time of sale. Once future dividends over a period and sale value of shares are discounted, present value of future stream is arrived at. The discount rate at which the discounted value of future stream becomes equal to current market price of equity shares is the required rate of return of investors which becomes the cost of capital to company.

The cost of equity can be calculated by following methods:

(A) Dividend Yield Method

According to this method, cost of equity capital is calculated on the assumption that investors give prime importance to dividends and risk of the firm remains unchanged. This method does not consider the growth in dividends in future and does not consider capital gains. This method is useful for a company that has stable dividend policy over a period of time.

$$K_E = \frac{\textbf{Dividend per share}}{\textbf{Market price per share}} \times 100$$

Where K_E = Cost of equity capital

Illustration No. 2

ABC Ltd. has disbursed dividend of ₹ 25 on each equity share of ₹ 10. The current market price of equity share is ₹ 60. Calculate the cost of equity as per dividend yield method.

Solution

$$K_E = \frac{\text{Dividend per share}}{\text{Market price per share}} \times 100$$

$$\text{Cost of equity capital} = \frac{25}{60} \times 100 = 41.67\%$$

(B) Dividend Yield Plus Growth in Dividend Method

When a company follows a constant dividend rate method with a fixed perpetual growth rate in dividend, this method is used to compute the cost of capital. In this method, an allowance for future growth in dividend is added to the current dividend yield. This method recognizes that the current market price of a share reflects expected future dividends.

The formula for calculation is

$$K_E = \frac{\textbf{Dividend}}{\textbf{Market price}} \times \textbf{100 + Growth rate}$$

Illustration No. 3

XYZ LTD's shares are quoted in stock exchange trading at ₹ 120 each. Next year's dividend is expected to be ₹ 30 per share and the subsequent dividends are expected to grow at an annual rate of 5% of the previous year's dividend. What is the cost of Equity shares?

Solution

$$K_E = \frac{\text{Dividend}}{\text{Market price}} \times 100 + \text{Growth rate}$$

$$= \frac{₹\,30}{₹\,120} \times 100 + 5\% \quad = 30\%$$

(C) Earning Yield Method: This method is adopted when following conditions are satisfied:

(i) When earnings of the company are expected to remain constant in future,

(ii) When all expected profits would be distributed, without leaving any profits for retention i.e. pay-out ratio is 100% or retention ratio is zero,

(iii) When new equity capital is expected to earn the same current rate of earnings; and

(iv) Market price is likely to be influenced only by earnings per share and not by any other factors.

Formula for calculation is:

$$K_E = \frac{\text{EPS}}{\text{Market value per share}}$$

Illustration No. 4

Rani Ltd's shares are currently trading at a price of ₹ 70 with outstanding shares of ₹ 5,00,000. Their expected profit after tax for the coming year is ₹ 84 lakhs. Calculate the cost of capital based on earning yield method.

Solution

$$K_E = \frac{\text{EPS}}{\text{Market value per share}}$$

$$\text{Earning per share} = \frac{84{,}00{,}000}{5{,}00{,}000} = 16.8$$

$$K_E = \frac{16.8}{70} \times 100 = 24\%$$

(D) Cost of Capital based on Net Worth: Based on average net worth, cost of capital is calculated. Following is the formula for calculation of cost of capital based on net worth:

$$K_E = \frac{\textbf{Dividend}}{\textbf{Average net worth}} \times 100$$

Illustration No. 5

The balance sheet of Srinivas Ltd. as on 31-3-2006 is given below:

(₹ lakhs)

Capital and Liabilities			Assets	
5,00,000 equity share of ₹ 10 each		50	Land	70
Share premium		10	Buildings	40
General reserve as on 1-4-2005	20		Plant & Machinery	130
Added during the year	10	30	Current assets	60
P/L Appropriation A/c as on 1-4-2005	15			
Added during the year	5	20		
Term loans		15		
Current liabilities and provisions		175		
		300		300

For the year 2005-06, company has declared a dividend of 24% p.a. Calculate cost of capital based on net worth of company.

Solution

$$\text{Dividend Paid} = 50,00,000 \times \frac{24}{100} = ₹\ 12,00,000$$

Calculation of Net Worth

(₹ lakhs)

Particulars	1.4.2005	31.3.2006
Equity Share capital	50	50
Share premium	10	10
General reserve	20	30
P & L appropriation A/c	15	20
Total	95	110

$$\text{Average Net worth} = \frac{95 + 110}{2}$$

$$= ₹\ 1,02,50,000$$

$$\text{Cost of Capital} = \frac{\text{Dividend}}{\text{Average net worth}} \times 100$$

$$= \frac{12,00,000}{1,02,50,000} \times 100 = 11.7\%$$

17.9 COST OF RETAINED EARNINGS

Retained earnings are that profit which is not distributed to equity shareholders but retained in business. Retained profits normally are a substantial amount used in the business. Does it have any cost? Yes, it has cost. Before we explain this, let us understand the meaning of implicit cost and explicit cost.

Explicit cost: The explicit cost of capital of a particular source can be defined in terms of dividend or interest paid by firm. There is an explicit flow of funds in the form of return to its investors. If debt in the form of debenture is raised, interest is paid. Dividend at a fixed rate is paid on preference capital. There is some expected dividend on equity shares. These payments refer to explicit capital.

Implicit cost: Firm does not pay anything on retained profits. Then where is the cost? If retained profits are distributed to shareholders, shareholders could invest somewhere or other. If they invest elsewhere, they would get some return. By not distributing profits and retaining in business, equity shareholders have foregone their expected return. So, cost of retained earnings is the return foregone by the investors on the amount of profit not distributed to them but kept in the business.

The opportunity cost of the retained earnings is the rate of return on dividends foregone by equity shareholders.

Check Your Understanding

State whether the following statements are True or False

1. Cost of capital is the minimum rate of return required by investors.
2. Cost of capital is taken as a decision criterion in capital budgeting decisions.
3. Cost of capital is equal to normal return at any risk level.
4. According to present value method in capital budgeting, project would be accepted only if the present value of the expected future returns is more than or equal to the initial cost of capital or investment, otherwise the project may be rejected.
5. Implicit cost is the discount rate, which equates present value of cash inflows with present value of cash outflows.
6. Risk and return do not go hand in hand.
7. Dividend on preference shares is a charge on profit and loss account and so is tax deductible.
8. Contractual rate of interest on a debenture is called as its coupon rate.
9. When debenture is issued at par and also to be redeemed at par, cost of debt and interest rate are one and the same.
10. In case of default in payment of preference dividend, market value of equity shares of the company would be affected.
11. Equity share capital is a cost-free capital.
12. Cost of capital comprises both business and financial risks.

Answers

1. True 2. True 3. False 4. True 5. True 6. False 7. False 8. True
9. True 10. True 11. False 12. True.

Descriptive Questions

1. What do you understand by cost of capital? Explain its significance. **(17.1 to 17.3)**
2. Explain Risk-Return relationship of various securities through pictorial presentation. **(17.5)**
3. How cost of debentures and preference capital is calculated? **(17.6 and 17.7)**
4. Explain the different methods of cost of equity capital. **(17.8)**
5. Write short notes on:
   (A) Opportunity cost **(17.4)**
   (B) Cost of retained earnings **(17.9)**

Short Question

Q. Distinguish between business risk and financial risk.

Ans. Business risk refers to variability of earnings (operating income) due to fluctuations in sales. Business risk is associated with operational efficiency of firm. Financial risk refers to the proportion of debt and equity with which the firm is financed. Risk increases with usage of more debt in its capital structure. Financial risk can be controlled by controlling usage of debt, hence this risk is described as controllable risk. Both the risks are unsystematic risks as both are peculiar to a firm or industry.

❍ ❍

CHAPTER 18

Weighted Average Cost of Capital

18.1 INTRODUCTION

Majority of joint stock companies use a combination of funds, like owners' funds and borrowed funds to carry on business operations. Different sources of finance such as debentures, preference share capital, equity share capital and retained earnings have their individual cost of capital, dependent on the risk each one carries. The composite cost of capital lies in between the least and the most expensive funds. This approach enables maximization of profits and wealth of the equity shareholders by investing funds in projects earning in excess of the overall cost of capital.

18.2 SPECIFIC COST OF CAPITAL

The cost of each source of capital is known as specific cost of capital. Amongst different sources, debt is cheap due to tax deductibility. Preference share capital is dearer compared to debt as dividend is not admissible for deduction under Income Tax Act. Amongst the different sources of capital, equity is the costliest as the risk is maximum.

Weighted average cost of capital is also known as Overall Cost of Capital or Composite Cost of Capital or Average Cost of Capital.

18.3 IMPORTANCE OF OVERALL COST OF CAPITAL

What is the need of calculating overall cost of capital when the specific cost of capital is known? Let us take an example to explain. A company's internal rate of return (IRR) for project A is 10% and has an option to finance the entire project with debt whose cost is 8%. The company has accepted the project as its IRR is more than cost of debt. Later in the same year, another project B has come up for its consideration with the same level of risk, similar to project A. For funding the second project, debt funds are not forthcoming. So, company has explored the option to finance through equity. Equity is available at 12%. Using the component cost of capital as cut-off rate, company has rejected the proposal to go ahead with project B as cost of equity is higher than the IRR of that project. Is it a right decision? The firm is associating method of financing (equity) with investment project (Project B). The firm's cost of capital is not the same thing as the project's cost of capital. Firm represents aggregate of projects undertaken by it. Therefore, firm's overall cost of capital, also known as weighted average cost of capital, is the right approach to decide. The firm is not appreciating the aspect that various sources of capital are related to each other. With increasing usage of debt, risk of firm increases. Firm's decision to use debt reduces the future capacity of firm to use debt more and makes it more costly compared to the earlier situation. So, greater usage of debt enhances firm's risk. More so, equity is always dearer compared to debt. Reason is it increases risk to equity shareholders with uncertainty of earnings. Over a long run, every firm has to maintain a balance between debt and equity to have balanced or target capital structure. It is generally agreed that cost of capital should be used in the composite or overall sense. This is known as weighted average cost of capital.

For calculating overall cost of capital, use of weighted average is more appropriate and not the simple average as proportions of various sources of funds in the capital structure of a firm are different.

18.4 CALCULATION OF OVERALL COST OF CAPITAL

Once specific cost of capital of each of the above long-term sources is ascertained, next step is to calculate overall cost of capital. The overall cost of capital may be defined as the rate of return that must be earned by firm in order to satisfy the requirements of different investors. What is its importance? The overall cost of capital is of utmost importance.

The overall cost of capital is used as discount rate or cut-off rate in evaluating capital budgeting proposals.

The overall cost of capital should take care of the relative proportion of different sources in the capital structure of the firm. The formula for calculation is as follows:

$$\mathbf{WACC = k_e * w1 + k_d * w2 + k_p * w3}$$

Where WACC = Weighted average cost of capital

k_e = Cost of equity capital

k_d = After tax cost of debt

k_p = Cost of preference capital

w1 = Proportion of equity in capital structure

w2 = Proportion of debt in capital structure

w3 = Proportion of preference capital in capital structure

For calculating overall cost of capital, the following steps are involved:

(i) Different long-term sources of finance are to be identified.

(ii) Find out the proportion of each source in its capital structure.

(iii) Their individual proportionate weight is to be multiplied with the respective cost.

(iv) The aggregate is the overall cost of capital.

The critical assumption is that the firm will raise capital in the same specified proportions.

We now illustrate the mechanics of computation of the weighted average of cost of capital.

Illustration No. 1

A firm has the capital structure and after tax costs for the different sources of funds used are as under:

Source of funds	Amount (₹)	Proportion A	After tax cost
Debt	15,00,000	25	5
Preference shares	12,00,000	20	10
Equity shares	18,00,000	30	12
Retained earnings	15,00,000	25	11
Total	60,00,000	100	38

You are required to compute the weighted average cost of capital.

(B.U. MBA, 2009)

Solution

Weighted average of cost of capital:

Source of funds (A)	Amount (₹) (B)	Proportion A (C)	After tax cost (D)	Weighted average of cost of capital (C × D)
Debt	15,00,000	25	5	1.25
Preference shares	12,00,000	20	10	2.00
Equity shares	18,00,000	30	12	3.60
Retained earnings	15,00,000	25	11	2.75
Total	60,00,000	100	38	9.60

The overall cost of capital is 9.6%

Illustration No. 2

The following is the capital structure of XYZ Ltd.

(₹)

Source	Amount	Interest rate / Dividend
Equity share capital	25,000	11%
Preference share capital	20,000	10%
Retained earnings	10,000	8%
Debentures	20,000	10%

Tax rate is 50%. Calculate the overall cost of capital.

Solution

$$WACC = k_e * w1 + k_d * w2 + k_p * w3$$

Where WACC = Weighted average cost of capital

k_e = Cost of equity capital

k_d = After tax cost of debt

k_p = Cost of preference capital

w1 = Proportion of equity in capital structure

w2 = Proportion of debt in capital structure

w3 = Proportion of preference capital in capital structure

Source	Amount	Cost of capital	Amount × Cost of capital
Equity share capital	25,000	0.11	2,750
Preference share capital	20,000	0.10	2,000
Retained earnings	10,000	0.08	800
Debentures	20,000	0.05*	1,000
Total	75,000		6,550

$$WACC = \frac{6,550}{75,000} \times 100 = 8.73\%$$

* Interest payable on debentures is 10%. However, tax-rate is 50%. So after-tax cost is 5%.

The weighted average cost of capital of the firm can, alternatively, be calculated as under:

Source	Amount	Cost of capital	Amount × Cost of capital
Equity share capital	25,000	0.11	2,750
Preference share capital	20,000	0.10	2,000
Retained earnings	10,000	0.08	800
Debentures	20,000	0.05*	1,000
Total	75,000		6,550

$$\text{WACC} = \frac{6{,}550 \times 100}{75{,}000} = 8.73\%$$

* Interest payable on debentures is 10%. However, tax-rate is 50%. So, after-tax cost is 5%.

The weighted average of capital of the firm can, alternatively, be calculated as under:

Source (1)	Amount (2)	Proportion (3)	Cost of capital (after tax) (4)	Proportion x Cost of capital (after tax) (3 x 4)
Equity share capital	25,000	33	11	3.64
Preference share capital	20,000	27	10	2.70
Retained earnings	10,000	13	08	1.04
Debentures	20,000	27	5*	1.35
Total	75,000	100		8.73 8.73 %

18.4.1 Book Value vs Market Value Weights

The weighted cost of capital can be computed by using book value or market value as the basis. If there is a difference between the book value and market value, the weighted average cost of capital would also differ. The market value weights are sometimes preferred to the book value weights as the market value represents the true value to the investors. However, the market value weights suffer from the following limitations:

1. Due to frequent fluctuations in market rates, it is very difficult to determine the market value weights.
2. With the use of market value weights, equity capital gets greater importance.

Illustration No. 3

XYZ company supplied the following information and requested you to compute the cost of capital based on book values and market values.

Source of finance	Book value (₹)	Market value (₹)	After tax cost (%)
Equity capital	10,00,000	15,00,000	12
Long-term debt	8,00,000	7,50,000	7
Short-term debt	2,00,000	2,00,000	4
Total	20,000,000	24,50,000	

(B.U., MBA, 2008)

Solution

Cost of Capital based on Book values

Source of finance	Book value (₹)	Proportion	After tax cost	Weighted cost proportion x After tax cost
Equity capital	10,00,000	0.5	0.12	0.060
Long-term debt	8,00,000	0.4	0.07	0.028
Short-term debt	2,00,000	0.1	0.04	0.004
	20,000,000	1.0		0.092
Weighted average cost of capital (Based on book values)				9.2%

Cost of Capital based on Market values

Source of finance	Market value (₹)	Proportion	After tax cost	Weighted cost proportion x After tax cost
Equity capital	15,00,000	0.612	0.12	0.073
Long-term debt	7,50,000	0.306	0.07	0.021
Short-term debt	2,00,000	0.082	0.04	0.003
Total	24,50,000			0.097
Weighted average cost of capital (Based on book values)				9.7%

Illustration No. 4

You are required to determine the weighted average cost of capital of Ankita Soni Ltd using (i) book value weights and (ii) market value weights. The following information is available to you for your perusal.

	₹
10% Debentures (₹ 100 per debenture)	6,00,000
9% Preference share capital (₹ 10 each)	1,00,000
Equity share capital (₹ 10 per share)	3,00,000
Total	10,00,000

All the above securities are traded in the market. Recent prices of debentures are ₹ 95, preference shares are ₹ 8 and equity shares are ₹ 20. Cost of equity share capital is 15%.

Solution

Computation of weighted average cost of capital (Based on book value weights)

Source	Book value (₹)	Cost of capital	Book value × Cost of capital
10% Debentures	6,00,000	0.10	60,000
9% Preference share capital	1,00,000	0.09	90,000
Equity share capital	3,00,000	0.15	45,000
Total	10,00,000		1,95,000

$$\text{WACC} = \frac{1,95,000}{10,00,000} \times 100$$

$$= 19.5\%$$

Computation of weighted average cost of capital (Based on market value weights)

Source	Market value (₹)	Cost of capital	Book value × Cost of capital
10% Debentures (6,000 x 95)	5,70,000	0.10	57,000
9% Preference share capital (10,00 x 8)	80,000	0.09	72,000
Equity share capital (30,000 x 20)	6,00,000	0.15	90,000
Total	12,50,000		2,19,000

$$\text{WACC} = \frac{2,19,000}{12,50,000} \times 100$$

$$= 17.52\%$$

18.5 CAPITALIZATION

The term 'Capitalization' is different from capital. Capital represents equity share capital and preference share capital which appear in the balance sheet of a company.

The term 'Capitalization' is used in the context of companies only, and not in relation to sole proprietorship and partnership concerns. **In common parlance, capitalization refers to the par value of securities i.e. shares and debentures plus any other reserves kept to meet the long-term and permanent needs of the company.**

Market capitalization: Company's shares, currently outstanding, when multiplied by its market price gives market capitalization of that company. In other words, market capitalization refers to the market value of equity shares. Number of equity shares is multiplied with market value of equity share to arrive at market capitalization of the concerned company. Market capitalization changes with the market value of equity shares.

Value of capitalization: According to earnings theory of capitalization, capitalization of a company depends upon its earnings and expected fair rate of return on its capital invested. If a company is making net profit of ₹ 5 lakhs and its fair rate of return is 10%, capitalization of the company will be

$$5,00,000 \times \frac{100}{10} = ₹\ 50,00,000$$

Illustration No. 5

The following is the capital structure of Farah Khan Ltd.

Source	Amount	Specific cost of capital
Equity Share Capital (1,00,000 shares of ₹ 10 each)	₹ 10,00,000	12%
Preference Share Capital (20,000 Preference shares of ₹ 10 each)	₹ 2,00,000	10%
Retained earnings	₹ 5,00,000	12%
11% Debentures (Face Value ₹ 100)	₹ 8,00,000	11%

Presently, the debentures are traded at ₹ 96, preference share capital at par and equity shares at ₹ 12 per share. Find out weighted average cost of capital, based on book value weights and market value weights. Out of the two above, which one is better? Justify.

Solution

1. WACC based on book value weights:

Source	Book Value (₹)	Cost of capital	Book Value × Cost of capital
Preference share capital	2,00,000	0.1	20,0000
Equity share capital	10,00,000	0.12	1,20,000
Retained earnings	5,00,000	0.12	60,000
11 % Debentures	8,00,000	0.11	88,000
Total	25,00,000		2,88,000

$$\text{WACC} = \frac{2,88,000}{25,00,000} \times 100$$

$$= 11.52\%$$

Alternative Way of Calculations

Source	Book value (₹)	Weights	Cost of capital	Weighted Cost of capital
Preference share capital	2,00,000	0.08	0.1	0.0080
Equity share capital	10,00,000	0.40	0.12	0.0480
Retained earnings	5,00,000	0.20	0.12	0.0240
11% Debentures	8,00,000	0.32	0.11	0.0352
Total	25,00,000	1.0		0.1152

So, WACC based on book values is 11.52%

2. WACC based on market value weights:

Source	Market value (₹)	Cost of capital	Market value × Cost of capital
Preference share capital	2,00,000*	0.1	20,000
Equity share capital	8,00,000	0.12	96,000
Retained earnings	4,00,000*	0.12	48,000
11 % Debentures	21,68,000*	0.11	84,480
Total	7,68,000		2,48,480

$$\text{WACC} = \frac{2{,}48{,}480}{21{,}68{,}000} \times 100$$

$$= 11.46\%$$

***Calculation of Market Values:**

Total market value of equity shares = 1,00,000 × 12 = ₹ 12,00,000

Out of ₹ 12,00,000, equity share capital proportion is ₹ 12,00,000 (2/3) = ₹ 8,00,000 and the portion of retained earnings is ₹ 12,00,000 (1/3) = ₹ 4,00,000.

(Retained earnings totally belong to the equity shareholders. Market value of equity shares is also influenced by the amount of retained earnings available to them. Equity share capital and the retained earnings are in the ratio of 2:1 in the capital structure. So, market value of equity share capital ₹ 12 lakhs (1,00,000 × 12) is to be allocated to equity share capital and retained earnings in the same proportion of 2:1.)

Total market value of preference shares = 20,000 × 10 = ₹ 2,00,000

Total market value of debentures = 8,000 × 96 = ₹ 7,68,000

Alternative way of calculation of WACC based on market value weights:

Source	Market Value (₹)	Weights	Cost of capital	Weighted Cost of capital
Preference share capital	2,00,000	0.092	0.1	0.0092
Equity share capital	8,00,000	0.369	0.12	0.0443
Retained earnings	4,00,000*	0.185	0.12	0.0222
11% Debentures	7,68,000	0.354	0.11	0.0389
Total	21,68,000	1.000		0.1146

So, WACC based on market values is 11.46%.

Better method: WACC, based on market value is better compared to WACC based on book values. The former reflects market value of securities which is proximate to the actual amount to be received from sale.

Check Your Understanding

State whether the following statements are True or False

1. The overall cost of capital may be defined as the rate of return that must be earned by the firm in order to satisfy the requirements of different investors.
2. For calculation of the average cost of capital, before-tax cost of debt must be used.
3. The terms capital and capitalization convey the same meaning.
4. It is generally agreed that the cost of capital should be used in the composite or overall sense, which is known as weighted average cost of capital.

Answers

1. True 2. False 3. False 4. True.

Descriptive Questions

1. Explain the concept and method of calculating the weighted average cost of capital. **(18.1 to 18.4)**
2. Distinguish the difference between capital and capitalization. **(18.5)**

Short Question

Q. What is the importance of weighted average cost of capital?

Ans. Majority of joint stock companies use a combination of funds, like owners' funds and borrowed funds to carry on business operations. Different sources of finance such as debentures, preference share capital, equity share capital and retained earnings have their individual cost of capital dependent on the risk each carries. The composite cost of capital lies in between the least and most expensive funds.

When debt is used, risk of the company increases. Let us take an example to explain. A company's internal rate of return (IRR) for project A is 10% and has an option to finance the project with debt, whose cost is 8%. The company has accepted the project as its IRR is more than the cost of debt. Later in the same year another project B has come up for its consideration with the same level of risk similar to project A. For funding the second project, debt funds are not forthcoming. So company has explored the option to finance through equity. Equity is available at 12%. Using the component cost of capital as the cut-off rate, company has rejected the proposal to go ahead with project B as the cost of equity is higher than the IRR of that project. Is it a right decision? The firm is associating the method of financing (equity) with the investment project (Project B). The firm's cost of capital is not the same thing as the project's cost of capital. Firm represents the aggregate of the projects undertaken by it. Therefore firm's overall cost of capital is also known as weighted average cost of capital, is the right approach to decide. On the basis of overall cost of capital, firm has to decide whether to accept the project or not.

Interview Question

Q. What is 'interest tax shield'?

Ans. Interest paid on debt is an admissible expenditure under the Income Tax Act. In other words, interest on debt reduces tax liability. Tax advantage with interest on debt is known as 'interest tax shield'.

❍ ❍

CHAPTER 19

Optimum Capital Structure

19.1 INTRODUCTION

Debt in capital structure is profitable. Reason is its tax deductibility. If debt is so profitable, why companies are not totally financed by debt? As debt is risky compared to other forms of financing such as preference and equity share capital, proportion of debt financing is contained. There are several considerations for limiting debt. What are those considerations that prevent to have major debt component in financing, even sacrificing higher profits? Why companies try to achieve optimum capital structure? There is no mathematical formula to achieve optimal capital structure; then what issues govern to achieve the optimum capital structure? Let us discuss them.

19.2 CONCEPT AND SIGNIFICANCE OF OPTIMUM CAPITAL STRUCTURE

The optimum capital structure may be defined as **"The capital structure or combination of debt and equity that leads to the maximum value of firm"**. So, optimum capital structure is that relationship of debt and equity, which maximizes the value of the company's equity share in the stock exchange. Normally, every firm uses debt and equity in financing its assets. In case, company's borrowing helps it in increasing its market value of equity share in the stock exchange, it can be said that the company is moving towards its optimum capital structure. However, if use of borrowing results in fall of market value of its equity share in stock exchange, it can be said that the company is moving away from its optimum capital structure.

The optimum capital structure is obtained when market value of equity share is maximum while its average cost of capital is minimum. So, objective of every firm is to select that type of financing or debt-equity mix, which leads to maximize market value of its equity share in stock exchange.

Considerations

The following considerations should be kept in mind while achieving the goal of optimum capital structure.

(A) **Borrow when cheap:** Company should borrow as long as its cost of debt is lower than its return on investment. **If interest paid on debentures / long term loans or dividend payable on preference share capital is lower than its return on investment, it is preferable to borrow.** It increases the market value of share. So, every effort has to be made to take possible advantage of leverage.

(B) **Advantage of income tax:** Interest paid on borrowing is eligible for tax benefit. So, effective cost of debt goes down in comparison to other forms of financing. **Tax advantage comes with borrowing.**

(C) **Avoid perceived high risk:** Beyond a point, increased debt financing is attached with undue risk. If shareholders perceive amount of debt in capital structure is excessive, price of its equity share may drop. **The finance manager should not therefore, borrow whether risky or not, if the investors perceive borrowing as an excessive risky proposition.** Investors' perception is likely to depress the market price of equity share of that company. So, firm should avoid undue financial risk attached with borrowing.

(D) **Flexible structure:** The flexibility of capital structure refers to the ability of the firm to raise additional capital funds, whenever needed to finance viable and profitable investment opportunities. The capital structure should enable the firm to take advantage of opportunities that may come up due to changing conditions. **Precisely, it means firm should have always untapped borrowing power.** It facilitates to take advantage of the favourable government policies or capital market.

When capital market is conducive, firm should raise additional funds through equity market rather than the issue of debt; raising debt is relatively easy as compared to equity.

Continuous Process: Achieving balanced or optimum capital structure practically is a difficult task. The board of directors or chief operating officer develops capital structure, which is most advantageous to the company. As many factors affect determination of the capital structure, judgement of the person who is making the capital structure decision plays an important role. Two similar companies may have different capital structure if the decision-makers differ in their judgement.

The capital structure decision is a continuous process and has to be taken whenever firm needs additional finances.

Whenever company needs to raise finance, it involves a capital structure decision. At that time, it has to decide the quantum of finance to be raised as well as the sources from which it has to be raised.

19.3 OPTIMAL CAPITAL STRUCTURE–A DIFFICULT TASK

There are two extremes in financing, one is 0% debt financing and the other is 99.99% debt financing because 100% debt financing is not possible. Between these two extremes, particular debt-mix finance is to be decided. As already stated, there is no mathematical formula or method to determine the optimal capital mix. This is a formidable task. This is not possible to achieve overnight. At optimum capital structure, value of equity share of the relative company is at its maximum and average cost of capital is at its minimum. As long as the return on investment is more than the cost of debt, every rupee of borrowing brings in more profits. Then why firms do not have more debt content in their capital structure? **The simple reason is debt brings risk. Once investors perceive the risk, they may retreat from the share market and in consequence, share price of that company may fall.** However, if they consider the risk is reasonable and would bring in more profits, instead of share price declining, it may as well increase on account of investors' speculation. Share market is highly complex and does not work on theories as capital markets are never perfect. The exact optimal capital structure may be impossible, and therefore, every effort is to be made to achieve the best approximation to optimum capital structure. The capital structure so arrived may not be optimum but appropriate in those circumstances.

> **Optimum capital structure is a hypothetical concept. So, some people prefer to use the term 'sound or appropriate capital structure' in place of 'optimum capital structure' as the former appears to be more realistic.**

Let us see what optimal capital structure requires.

19.4 ESSENTIAL FEATURES OF AN APPROPRIATE CAPITAL STRUCTURE

A capital structure will be considered to be appropriate if it possesses the following features:

(A) Profitability: The capital structure of a company should facilitate it to be most profitable. **The most profitable capital structure is one when its cost of financing is at its minimum and earning per share is at peak.**

(B) Risk: Use of excessive debt threatens solvency of the firm. To a point, debt does not add significant risk, and to that extent, debt should be used. Beyond that level, debt should be avoided. So, the content of debt should not, therefore, increase the financial and business risk beyond the manageable limits.

> **While designing the capital structure, finance manager has to design capital structure of a company in such a manner that their cost and risk are minimum.**

(C) Flexibility: The capital structure should be flexible. Flexibility means the capital structure should always have an untapped borrowing power, which can be used in conditions that may arise due to favourable capital market, government policies etc. The structure should be such that it can be maneuvred to meet the changing requirements and conditions. The company should not borrow to its maximum extent. Whenever firm finds profitable opportunities, it should be in a position to take advantage. **Borrowing scope should be left to avail profitable opportunities.**

(D) Capacity: The capital structure should be within the debt capacity of the company. The debt capacity depends on its ability to generate future cash flows. In other words, **borrowing should be commensurate with the company's ability to generate future cash flows.** The firm should be in a position to meet its obligations in paying the loan and interest charges as and when they fall due.

(E) Control: The firm should so devise its capital structure that it involves minimum risk of loss of control. When additional funds are raised, controlling interest of existing owners gets diluted automatically unless they invest additional funds, suitably. A management concerned to retain control may prefer to issue debt rather than equity. Capital structure normally reflects management's philosophy. Redeemable debentures, even if excessive, do not dilute control; but convertible debentures will result in dilution of control as and when converted into equity shares. Preference shareholders would get the voting right if dividend is not paid for two consecutive years preceding the date of meeting. In such an event, composition of the board of directors may change that may result in reduced level of control. More so, owners of closely held companies are always concerned with the dilution of control.

Conflicting Approach: The above mentioned points are general principles of an appropriate capital structure. Some of the features are conflicting with each other. For example, raising funds through debt is cheap and so complies with the principle of profitability. However, debt is risky and so goes against the principles of conservatism and solvency.

Degree of Emphasis: Companies give different degrees of emphasis to the above features. For example, a company may give more importance to control and may not raise additional funds even needed if promoters of company are not in a position to contribute and retain their existing control. Raising finance from public may result in loss of control. Another company may be concerned with solvency alone and may be willing to lose existing control to save company from its existing financial difficulties. Further, relative importance of these requirements may change with shifting conditions.

Conflicting Interests: The finance manager is responsible to design appropriate capital structure, which is most advantageous to the interests of different groups that may be conflicting. Equity shareholders are owners of the company. Therefore, their interest is primary and due consideration has to be given to them. However, there are other interested groups such as customers, employees, society and the government. So due consideration is also required to be given to them.

Final Compromise: The prudent finance manager should try to have the best out of the circumstances within which the company is operating. **The fact remains that the finance manager has to make a satisfactory compromise to suit the management's desires and prevailing trends in the capital market when market is tapped for raising funds.**

19.5 FACTORS DETERMINING CAPITAL STRUCTURE

The factors that determine capital structure are of different importance and not possible to rank. The influence of the individual factors depends on preferences of the management. Importance of factors also changes over a period of time.

The 'Essential features' detailed above also determine the structure. Following are the **additional factors**:

1. **Financial Leverage or Trading on Equity:** The use of long-term fixed interest bearing debt and preference share capital along with equity share capital is called financial leverage. **Financial Leverage is the most important factor that determines capital structure.** Financial leverage is used as long as cost of debt is lower than return on investment. The use of debt increases return on equity and magnifies earnings per share. Leverage can also operate adversely if expected rate of earnings of firm falls below the cost of debt. Interest on long-term debt is fixed with a commitment over a long period. In the light of inherent greater risk with financial leverage, caution is required in planning capital structure.
2. **Stability of Sales and Growth:** If sales of a firm are fairly stable, earnings of firm would reasonably be constant. **If there is no great risk for decline in earnings, firm can utilize financial leverage to its optimum advantage.** When there is assured growth, firm can plan to utilize borrowing for expansion without much risk. Such type of firms can plan to use more debt in their capital structure for increased earnings.
3. **Cost of Capital:** Every rupee invested in business has a cost. Cost of capital is the minimum return expected by its suppliers. There are different sources of finance. Amongst the different sources, long-term debt is the cheapest. The reasons for its cheapness are
   (A) Fixed interest rate.
   (B) Long-term debt is, normally, secured by those assets for which finance is sanctioned. Suppliers get **priority for repayment of principal and interest** on debt compared to preference share capital and equity share capital. So, they would be willing to invest at a lower cost.
   (C) Admissibility of interest as an expense under Income Tax Act, so it's effective cost becomes the lowest.

Preference share capital has a legal obligation for a fixed rate of dividend. Dividend paid to preference shareholders is not an admissible expense under the tax. So, cost of preference share capital is higher than the cost of debt. Equity share capital is costlier compared to preference share capital. Reason is equity share capital does not have any fixed obligation for payment of dividend. So, comparatively equity share capital is dearer to preference share capital.

Preference share capital is cheaper than equity share capital while long-term debt is still cheaper in terms of cost implication. While formulating capital structure, every effort has to be made to keep the overall cost of capital lowest to boost up the earning per equity share.

4. **Cash flow ability to service debt:** This ability is measured through fixed charges coverage ratio. This is calculated by

$$\frac{\textbf{Earning before interest and tax}}{\textbf{Fixed interest charge}}$$

Comparison of an existing coverage ratio with the future ratio after the anticipated borrowings gives an idea about the risk the firm would be exposed to. If future cash flows grow in line with increased amount of borrowing, firm would be able to service the debt without difficulty. **In case interest coverage ratio falls after borrowing, this would be an indicator that the changed capital structure would create problems to that firm.**

Cash flows are more important than absolute amount of profit. Firms with stable and growing cash flows can employ more debt in comparison to those firms with unstable and lesser ability firms.

5. **Nature and size of business: Nature and size of business also influence the capital structure.** For example, a public utility concern, electricity-generating unit, requires more funds on account of heavy investment in fixed assets. These types of concerns enjoy regular and assured cash flows so they can afford more debt. Similarly big firms can raise funds through debt as investors consider them less risky. Small firms, not well known in the market, experiences more difficulty to raise funds through debt, and so have to rely considerably upon owners' funds for financing.

6. **Legal requirements:** The promoters of the company have to comply with legal requirements while deciding about capital structure of the company. For example, banking companies are not allowed to issue any other type of securities other than equity share capital for raising funds. SEBI governs regulatory framework. Approval of SEBI is to be obtained, where needed, for capital issue, which is accorded only after the stipulated guidelines are complied with. Such approval is not necessary while raising a long-term loan from financial institution. So, **finance manager has to take into account the legal and regulatory framework while designing the capital structure.**

7. **Capital market conditions and market sentiment:** Capital market conditions play an important role for raising funds in the market. Capital market conditions always do not remain the same. There are boom and depression periods. **Choice of securities is influenced by market conditions.** During the period of depression, investors are cautious and do not intend to take risk. So, they prefer investment in debentures as they consider them less risky. In times of boom, market sentiment is always high; and so, preference is towards investment in equity shares as the market considers investment in shares would be more profitable with anticipated appreciation in market value at a faster pace. So, depending upon capital market conditions and sentiment, companies have to plan their capital structure for raising funds.
8. **Corporate tax rate: High corporate tax rate compels companies to raise funds through debt as interest on debt is an admissible expenditure, so taxable profits would be low.** In consequence, tax liability would be low. On the other hand, dividend on shares is not an admissible expenditure. So, companies give lower preference for raising funds through equity for tax planning.

19.6 BALANCED CAPITAL STRUCTURE

In capital structure, debt is used to improve profitability. The advantage of debt is that it saves tax since interest is tax deductible. On the other hand, its disadvantage is that it can cause financial distress if there is a major fall in earnings when debt component is heavy. What is a financial distress? Financial distress arises when the fixed obligations of firm affect firm's normal operations. For example, if a firm has to dispose off some of its fixed assets to meet its fixed financial obligations, the firm is said to be in distress. One extreme form of financial distress is its liquidation when it is not able to meet its financial obligations. Therefore, a trade-off is necessary between tax advantage and cost/risk of financial distress.

> **Decision for a source of fund is to be taken in the totality of capital structure i.e. in the light of resultant capital structure after the proposed issue of capital or debt.**

Conclusion: In designing the appropriate capital structure of a firm, major policy decision is in determining the appropriate level of debt. The firm's debt capacity may be best defined, not as the maximum amount which the lenders or debt investors are willing to lend or its legal capacity, but the amount of debt the firm should use to maximize the value of firm.

No standard form of capital structure can be prescribed which would take care of all situations, at all times. The financing mix must be tailored to suit the requirements, situations and positions of the firm. Capital market conditions, expectations of the investors, legal and changing regulatory framework and above all, the operating efficiency of the firm are to be judiciously factored in designing the capital structure.

So, every company aims at balanced capital structure to take maximum advantage within the manageable limits.

Illustration No. 1

Determine the optimum capital mix of Radhi & Company Ltd., out of the following alternative situations, which have different proportions of equity and debt. Assign reason for the choice made.

Situations	Equity	Debt	Cost of equity (Ke) %	After tax, cost of debt %
1	2,00,000	6,00,000	16	12
2	6,00,000	2,00,000	10	8
3	4,00,000	4,00,000	12	10

Solution

Situations	Percentage of		Cost of		Percentage Total Cost
	Equity	Debt	Equity	Debt	
1	25	75	16	12	4 + 9 =13
2	75	25	10	8	7.50 + 2 = 9.50
3	50	50	12	10	6 + 5 = 11

Recommendation: The above table shows the capital mix in the three different situations. Out of the three above situations, situation 2 is recommended. At this level, composite cost of capital is the least. In this mix, equity would be 75% and debt 25%. Least composite cost is the factor for choice.

Illustration No. 2

In considering the most desirable capital for Neeraj Singh Ltd., following estimates of cost of debt and equity (after tax) have been made at various levels of debt-equity mix.

Debt as % of total capital employed	Cost of debt	Cost of equity %
0	7.0	15.0
10	7.0	15.0
20	7.0	15.5
30	7.5	16.0
40	8.0	17.0
50	8.5	19.0
60	9.5	20.0

You are required to determine the optimal debt equity mix for the company by calculating composite cost of capital. Justify the choice made.

Solution

Situations	Percentage of		Cost of		Percentage total cost
	Equity	Debt	Equity	Debt	
1.	100	0	15.0	7.0	15 + 0 = 15
2.	90	10	15.0	7.0	13.5 + 7 = 20.5
3.	80	20	15.5	7.0	12.4 + 1.4 = 13.8
4.	70	30	16.0	7.5	11.2 + 2.25 = 13.45
5.	60	40	17.0	8.0	10.2 + 3.2 = 13.4
6.	50	50	19.0	8.5	9.5 + 4.25 = 13.75
7.	40	60	20.0	9.5	8 + 5.7 = 13.7

Recommendation: Total cost is the lowest at 13.4% when the firm employs 60% equity and 40% debt.

Hence, composition of 60% equity and 40% debt is to be accepted by the firm.

Illustration No. 3

Cherry & Dimpy Ltd. maintains 50% debt-to-asset ratio. Their fixed assets are ₹ 10 lakhs. Three alternative current assets policies are under consideration—30%, 40% and 50% of projected sales. Interest rate is 10% on all debts. The company expects to earn 16% before interest and taxes (EBIT) on sales of ₹ 40 lakhs. Effective tax rate is 40%. What is the expected return on equity under each alternative? Decide the capital structure of the choice.

Solution

Expected return on equity under different alternatives may be ascertained as follows:

	Current assets 30% of projected sales	Current assets 40% of projected sales	Current assets 50% of projected sales
Sales	40,00,000	40,00,000	40,00,000
Fixed assets	10,00,000	10,00,000	10,00,000
Current assets	12,00,000	16,00,000	20,00,000
Total Assets (A)	22,00,000	26,00,000	30,00,000
Debt to assets ratio	50%	50%	50%
So, debt (B)	11,00,000	13,00,000	15,00,000

Contd...

Interest @ 10%	1,10,000	1,30,000	1,50,000
EBIT @ 16% of sales	6,40,000	6,40,000	6,40,000
- interest	1,10,000	1,30,000	1,50,000
Profit before tax	5,30,000	5,10,000	4,90,000
- Tax @ 40%	2,12,000	2,04,000	1,96,000
Profit after tax	3,18,000	3,06,000	2,94,000
Equity share capital (AB)	11,00,000	13,00,000	15,00,000
Return on equity Profit after tax / Equity share capital	28.91%	23.54%	19.6%

Return on equity is the highest when current assets are 30% of projected sales. So, capital structure with equity of ₹ 11 lakhs and debt of ₹ 11 lakhs is to be accepted.

Equity capitalization rate: The equity capitalization rate is that capitalization rate that reflects the relationship between the income of the property and the equity investment committed to the property. If income on an equity share (Face value ₹ 100) is ₹ 20 and its market price is ₹ 150, equity capitalization rate is 13.33% (20/150 × 100).

Illustration No. 4

Sumit Mathur Ltd., with net operating earnings of ₹ 3,00,000 is attempting to evaluate a number of possible capital structures as given below. Which capital structure will you recommend and why?

Capital structure	Debt in capital structure (B) (₹)	Cost of debt (K1) %	Cost of equity (K) %
1	3,00,000	10.0	12.0
2	4,00,000	10.0	12.5
3	5,00,000	11.0	13.5
4	6,00,000	12.0	15.0
5	7,00,000	14.0	18.0

Solution (₹)

Particulars	Capital Structure Plans having Debts of Various Amounts				
	I	II	III	IV	V
EBIT	3,00,000	3,00,000	3,00,000	3,00,000	3,00,000
Less interest (K1 x B)	–30,000	–40,000	–55,000	–72,000	–98,000
Net income (NI) for equity shareholders	2,70,000	2,60,000	2,45,000	2,28,000	2,02,000
Ke (equity capitalisation rate)	0.12	0.125	0.135	0.150	0.180
S (market value of equity)	22,50,000*	20,80,000	18,14,815	15,20,000	11,22,222
B (market value of debt)	3,00,000	4,00,000	5,00,000	6,00,000	7,00,000
Total market value (S + B) = V	25,50,000	24,80,000	23,14,815	21,20,000	18,22,222
Overall cost of Capital (KO) = $\frac{\text{(EBIT)}}{V}$	11.76%	12.10%	12.96%	14.15%	16.46%

$$\frac{\text{Net income (NI) for equity share holders}}{\text{*Equity capitalization rate}} \times 100$$

$$2{,}70{,}000 \times \frac{100}{12} = 22{,}50{,}000$$

Recommendation: Capital structure having debts of ₹ 3,00,000 (capital structure 1) is recommended as cost is the lowest. Reason is its overall cost of capital is the lowest.

19.7 ARBITRAGE PROCESS

Arbitrage by definition is a financial transaction that makes an immediate profit, without involving any risk. Arbitrage process refers to a two type related actions or steps simultaneously undertaken in order to derive some benefit. The simultaneous action is buying by a speculator in one market and selling in another market or selling one security and buying another security belonging to the same industry. Investor can take advantage of savings in investment or enjoy increased earnings from the same amount of investment through arbitrage process.

Here is an example where the investor can change the investment from a no-risk company to a risk-bearing company and make savings in funds in terms of investment, while retaining same level of income.

Illustration No. 5

Theer Ltd. and Tarkh Ltd. are engaged in the same nature of business and identical in all respects in terms of EBIT with ₹ 2,00,000, except the former has 12% debentures ₹ 4,00,000. Equity capitalization is 12% for Theer Ltd. and 10% for Tarkh Ltd. Calculate total value and overall capitalization rate of Theer Ltd. and Tarkh Ltd.?

Show the arbitration process by which an investor having shares worth ₹ 5,00,000 in Tarkh Ltd. will be benefited by switching over to company Theer Ltd.

Solution

(i)

(₹)

	Theer Ltd.	Tarkh Ltd.
Net operating income (EBIT)	2,00,000	2,00,000
Interest	48,000	-------
Earnings to equity shareholders	1,52,000	2,00,000
Equity capitalization rate	0.12	0.10
Market value of equity	12,66,667	20,00,000
Market value of debt	4,00,000	----
Total value of the firm	16,66,667	20,00,000
Overall capitalization rate	**12%**	**10%**

(ii) Arbitrage process:

Investor having shares worth ₹ 5,00,000 out of the total worth of equity of ₹ 20,00,000 is holding 25% shares in Tarkh Ltd.

Investor's current position in Tarkh Ltd:

	₹
Dividend income (25% of ₹ 2,00,000)	50,000
Total income from Tarkh Ltd.	**50,000**
Market value of investment in Tarkh Ltd.	5,00,000

He sells the investment in Tarkh Ltd. for ₹ 5,00,000 and buys 25% of equity shares and debentures in Theer Ltd.

In Theer Ltd, 25% of equity shares of ₹ 12,66,667 is ₹ 3,16,667 and 25% of debentures is ₹ 1,00,000.

Dividend income 25% of ₹ 1,52,000	= 38,000
12% Interest on ₹ 1,00,000	= 12,000
Total income from Theer Ltd.	**50,000**

Market value of investment in Theer Ltd:

Equity shares	₹ 3,16,667
Debentures	₹ 1,00,000
Total investment	₹ 4,16,667

Investor is able to maintain the same amount of income of ₹ 50,000. However, he has saved his investment by ₹ 83,333 (5,00,000 – 3,16,667 – 1,00,000)

19.8 RELEVANT RATIOS FOR ANALYSING CAPITAL STRUCTURE

The following ratios are relevant for analyzing capital structure.

Ratio Name	Formula	Purpose
1. Debt equity ratio	Total Debt / Net Worth	To measure long-term solvency as well as debt equity financing policy of business.
2. Financial leverage ratio	EBIT / Profit before tax	To find out the impact of operating income on shareholders' income.
3. Capital gearing ratio	Preference share capital + Debentures + Long-term debts bearing fixed interest / Equity share capital + reserves and surplus	To ascertain the influence of fixed-charge bearing securities in financing pattern of business.
4. Fixed charges coverage ratio	Earning before depreciation, Interest and Tax / Fixed interest charge	A test for firm's debt servicing capacity.

Check Your Understanding

(A) State whether the following statements are True or False:

1. Achieving an optimum capital structure, practically, is a difficult task.
2. Preference share capital is cheaper to equity share capital, while long-term debt is still cheaper in terms of cost implication.
3. The board of directors or chief operating officer develops the capital structure, which is most advantageous to the company.
4. Equity share capital is described as fixed charge bearing securities.
5. Raising funds through debt is dearer as compared to equity.
6. When additional funds are raised, the controlling interest of the existing owners gets diluted automatically unless they invest additional funds suitably.
7. The term 'capital structure' includes financial structure.
8. The optimum capital structure is obtained when the market value per equity share is the maximum.
9. Arbitrage process helps the investor to magnify earnings or save investment.
10. Capital structure is the mix of preference and equity share capital.
11. Increased use of debt increases financial risk of equity shareholders.

Answers

1. True 2. True 3. True 4. False 5. False 6. True 7. False 8. True
9. True 10. False 11. True.

(B) Objective Questions (Identify what is most appropriate)

1. Fixed cost bearing securities should be mixed with equity when the rate of earnings is ________ than the rate of interest of company.

   (A) More (B) Less (C) Equal

2. The optimum capital structure is obtained when the market value per equity share is at ________

   (A) maximum (B) minimum (C) zero

3. If use of borrowing results in fall of market value of share in stock exchange, it can be said that the company is ________ from its optimum capital structure.

   (A) moving away (B) moving towards (C) moving towards or moving away

Answers

1. (A) 2 (A) 3 (A)

Descriptive Questions

1. Explain the concept and significance of optimum capital structure. What do you mean by flexibility of capital structure? **(19.2)**
2. 'Optimum capital structure is a hypothetical concept'—Explain your views on the above statement. **(19.2 and 19.3)**
3. What do you understand by a balanced capital structure? Why should a company aim at balanced capital structure? **(19.2, 19.3 and 19.6)**
4. Discuss the essential features of an appropriate capital structure. **(19.4)**
5. If debt is a cheaper source of finance, then why every firm is not a 99% debt firm? **(19.1 and 19.3)**
6. What ratios would you like to compute to analyze the capital structure. **(19.8)**

Interview Questions

Q.1. Define capital structure.

Ans. Capital structure refers to the mix of long-term equity funds and long-term debt. Examples of long-term equity funds are equity share capital, preference share capital, reserves, retained profits. Examples of long-term debt are long-term loans, debentures etc.

Q.2. Who decides capital structure?

Ans. The board of directors or chief operating officer develops capital structure which is most advantageous to the company. Developing capital structure is a continuous process.

Q.3. What is the important factor in designing appropriate capital structure?

Ans. In designing appropriate capital structure of a firm, major policy decision is in determining the appropriate level of debt.

Q.4. When optimum capital structure is obtained?

Ans. Optimum capital structure is obtained when the overall cost of capital is the lowest.

CHAPTER 20

Valuation and Rates of Return

20.1 INTRODUCTION

Assets are broadly divided into two categories. They are real assets and financial assets. For example, physical assets like building and machinery are real assets. Securities like equity shares, preference shares and debentures are financial assets. The fundamental concepts of risk and return determine the value of real assets as well as financial assets.

How bonds and shares are valued? Earnings per share (EPS) and Price-earnings (P/E) ratios play a significant role in valuation of financial securities. These have been discussed, already, in chapter 'Ratio Analysis'.

20.2 CONCEPT OF VALUE

Definition of value: Value is defined as 'worth estimated by any standard of purchasing power, especially by the market price, or the amount of money agreed upon as an equivalent to the utility and cost of anything'. In other words, it is estimated at the time of purchase and compared with its market price for decision-making.

The concept 'Value' has different meanings. They are:

Book Value: Book value is an accounting concept. Assets are recorded at historical cost in books of accounts. Depreciation is provided on fixed assets and the depreciated value (cost minus depreciation provided) is shown in financial statements. Intangible assets (goodwill and preliminary expenses etc) are amortised. Amortisation means writing off an intangible asset investment over the projected life of asset. Writing off is made so that the burden is evenly spread over a specified period. Acquisition cost minus amortisation is shown as book value. The difference between the assets and liabilities is equal to net worth or shareholders' funds. To arrive at book value per share, net worth is to be divided by number of equity shares outstanding. **Book value reflects historical cost, not realisable value.**

Replacement Value: Replacement value is the amount that company has to spend to acquire the same asset in present existing condition. In times of inflation, replacement value is always higher than the book value of the asset that is already depreciated.

Liquidation Value: Liquidation value is the value one would get from the assets, after termination of business. As business is closed, assets do not get much value. In other words, sale value would be highly less than the book value. As a result, there would be a great loss on their sale. Intangible assets such as goodwill get nothing as the business is closed.

Going Concern Value: Going concern value is the amount that a company could realise, if sold when the business is still on as a whole. It has to be an operating business but not a business, which is proposed to be sold as the going is not good. More important the business has to be sold as a whole, not piecemeal. In such an event, value that can be realised is normally higher than the liquidation value. Even intangible assets command value even though not shown in financial statements due to prosperous condition of business. Realisable value depends on the condition of business. If the business is making super profits, realisable value would be highly significant while it would be highly low, in case the business is running at a low key.

Market Value: Market value of an asset or security is the price at which it is bought or sold in market. Market value of a share is higher than its book value if business is profitable. A number of factors influence the market value of a share. Most important is future term trend of the share in market. In other words, what market considers about potentialities of the share in future is more important rather than today's condition of business. In an ideal situation when capital market is efficient market price reflects intrinsic value of a share.

20.3 FEATURES OF BOND/DEBENTURE

A bond or debenture is a long-term debt instrument. Government sector companies or public sector companies normally issue bonds. They do not issue debentures. **Bonds are generally secured.** Private sector companies issue debentures as well as bonds. They may be secured or unsecured.

Recently, State Bank of India has issued 'SBI Bonds' to meet capital adequacy requirements. The bonds that have been issued are for a minimum period of 10 years. Here, the bonds are for meeting the capital requirements of the bank, but not as borrowings. These bonds are not secured.

Features: The features of a bond or debenture, in general, are as under:

1. **Face Value:** Face value is the value written on the face of instrument. This is also called par value. A bond/debenture is issued at face or par value, which

is normally ₹ 10, ₹ 100 or ₹ 1,000. Interest is paid on face value whether bonds/debentures are issued at par, premium or discount.

2. **Interest Rate:** Interest rate is fixed. Interest rate is mentioned specifically on face of certificate. Interest is tax deductible to the organisation that issues. Interest is paid quarterly, half-yearly, annually or at time of redemption. Interest rate is also called coupon rate.
3. **Maturity:** A bond/debenture is issued for a specified period of time. It is repaid on maturity. However, irredeemable debentures are perpetual and they are not redeemed by company that issues.
4. **Redemption Value:** The value, which a bondholder/debenture holder gets on maturity, is called redemption value. It can be redeemed at par, premium or discount.
5. **Market Value:** A bond/debenture may be traded in stock exchange. It can be bought or sold at market value. Market value may be different from par value or redemption value.
6. **Risk:** The risk in holding a government bond is generally lower than the risk associated with the debenture issued by a company. But, of late, the experience related to repayment with state government companies where bonds are guaranteed even by the concerned state governments has been bad. Government has not come forward to make payment on due date when there has been default in payment by government companies. It is better to hold a bond or debenture issued by a good private sector company rather than state government bond, if other factors such as interest rate and maturity period etc. are same.

20.4 VALUATION OF SECURITIES

Present value concept helps investor in decision making for buying or selling securities. If the present value is more than current market price, he chooses to buy. In case, the present value is less than current market price, the investor prefers to sell securities to make a profit. The basis for this decision-making is the required rate of return that the investor wishes to have and forecast about behaviour of future return. In case of debentures and preference shares, the return is fixed while dividend in the case of equity shares is only a planned estimate on which the decision is taken.

20.5 CALCULATION OF PRESENT VALUE-BOND, WITH A MATURITY PERIOD

A bond or debenture is normally issued for a specified period. Till date of maturity holder gets interest periodically. At the end of specified period, holder gets maturity value as per terms of instrument. Every investor wants to have certain rate of return. If the bond or debenture is quoted at a particular rate, investor wants to know whether the bond or debenture is worth buying at that rate or not. In other words, he wants to buy if face value (in case of direct issue) or market value satisfies his required rate of return. Present Value concept gives him the answer for taking decision. By comparing the present value of bond with current market value, it can be determined whether the bond is overvalued or undervalued. Accordingly, investor can decide whether to buy or sell security.

Formula for calculating present value of a debenture is

$$B_o = \frac{INT_1}{(1+k_d)} + \frac{INT_2}{(1+k_d)^2} + \ldots\ldots + \frac{INT_n}{(1+k_d)^n} + \frac{B_n}{(1+k_d)^n}$$

Where B_o = Present value of a bond/debenture

INT = Amount of interest

k_d = Required rate of return on bond (%)

B_n = Maturity value in period 'n'

n = Number of years to maturity

Illustration No. 1

Devendra Yadav is considering to purchase a five year, ₹ 1,000 par value bond bearing a coupon rate of 7 per cent. The investor's required rate of return is 8 per cent. The bond is quoted at ₹ 950. The bond will be redeemed at par value. Advise him for purchase.

Solution

The bond gives him interest of ₹ 70 per annum for a period of 5 years.

$$B_o = \frac{INT_1}{(1+k_d)} + \frac{INT_2}{(1+k_d)^2} + \ldots\ldots + \frac{INT_n}{(1+k_d)^n} + \frac{B_n}{(1+k_d)^n}$$

Where B_o = Present value of a bond/ debenture

INT = Amount of interest

k_d = Required rate of return on bond (%)

B_n = Maturity value in period 'n'

n = Number of years to maturity

$$= \frac{70}{(1+0.08)} + \frac{70}{(1+0.08)^2} + \frac{70}{(1+0.08)^3} + \frac{70}{(1+0.08)^4} + \frac{70}{(1+0.08)^5} + \frac{1000}{(1+0.08)^5}$$

$$= \frac{70}{1.08} + \frac{70}{1.1664} + \frac{70}{1.2597} + \frac{70}{1.3605} + \frac{70}{1.4693} + \frac{1000}{1.4693}$$

$$= 65 + 60 + 56 + 51 + 48 + 681 = 961$$

The bond is worth buying for ₹ 961 with the required return of 8% . It is available at ₹ 950 in market. So, it is worth buying.

Illustration No. 2

Deepali Murjani is already having 15% bonds (F.V. ₹ 100), issued by HDFC Ltd., presently quoted at ₹ 105. The tenure of the bond is five years out of which two years have passed by. If her required rate of return is 12%, is it desirable for her to buy or sell the bonds?

Solution

Tenure of bond is 5 years, out of which 2 years completed and so the bond is yet to run a further period of 3 years.

The formula for calculating the present value of the bond is

$$B_o = \frac{INT_1}{(1+k_d)} + \frac{INT_2}{(1+k_d)^2} + ... + \frac{INT_n}{(1+k_d)^n} + \frac{B_n}{(1+k_d)^n}$$

Where B_o = Present value of a bond/ debenture

INT = Amount of interest

k_d = Required rate of return on bond (%)

B_n = Maturity value in period 'n'

n = Number of years to maturity

$$= \frac{15}{(1+0.12)} + \frac{15}{(1+0.12)^2} + \frac{15}{(1+0.12)^3} + \frac{100}{(1+0.12)^3}$$

$$= \frac{15}{1.12} + \frac{15}{1.2544} + \frac{15}{1.4049} + \frac{100}{1.4049}$$

= 13 + 12 + 11 + 71

= ₹ 107

HDFC Ltd. bond is presently quoted at ₹ 105 while its value is ₹ 107 at the required rate of return 15%. Hence, it is desirable for Deepali Murjani to buy those bonds, as present market rate is lower than its value.

20.5.1 Bond Value in Case of Half-Yearly, Quarterly, Monthly Interest

The above formula works if return is paid on an annual basis. Return can be calculated on monthly, quarterly, half-yearly basis. In such a case, the formula requires a small change. To calculate return on quarterly basis, k_d is to be divided by four and n is to be multiplied by four. Interest amount is to be divided by four to show quarterly interest in place of INT_1 and INT_2 etc. For half yearly basis, this exercise is to be done by two and for monthly return, it is to be done by twelve.

Illustration No. 3

Apekha Jain is holding 12% bonds (F.V. ₹ 1,000), issued by Infosys Ltd., and presently quoted at ₹ 976 in the market. Interest is payable on half-yearly basis. The tenure of the bond is three years, out of which one year has already completed. Bond is repayable with a premium of 10%. If her required rate of return is 16%, is it desirable for her to sell the bonds?

Solution

The formula for calculating the present value of the bond, if interest is paid on yearly basis is:

$$B_o = \frac{INT_1}{(1+k_d)} + \frac{INT_2}{(1+k_d)^2} + \ldots\ldots + \frac{INT_n}{(1+k_d)^n} + \frac{B_n}{(1+k_d)^n}$$

Where B_o = Present value of a bond/debenture

INT = Amount of interest

k_d = Required rate of return on bond (%)

B_n = Maturity value in period 'n'

n = Number of years to maturity

Tenure of the bond is 3 years out of which 1 year is already completed and so the bond is yet to run a further period of 2 years (four half years). As interest is payable on half-yearly basis, the changed formula is as under:

$$= \frac{6}{(1+0.08)^2} + \frac{6}{(1+0.08)^4} + \frac{6}{(1+0.08)^6} + \frac{6}{(1+0.08)^8} + \frac{1{,}010}{(1+0.08)^8}$$

$$= \frac{6}{1.17} + \frac{6}{1.36} + \frac{6}{1.59} + \frac{6}{1.85} + \frac{1{,}010}{1.85}$$

= ₹ 5 + 4 + 4 + 3 + 546

= ₹ 562

Bond is quoted at ₹ 976 and its current value is ₹ 562 with the required return of 16%. As market value is more than its current value, it is desirable to sell.

20.5.2 Relationship between Interest Rate and Required Rate of Return

Interest rate is always fixed, calculated on par value of bond/debenture. Required rate of return depends on expectations of investor and risk profile of the investment instrument according to the perception of investor. When the required rate of return is more than the interest rate, the investor would be willing to pay a lesser price for the instrument in the market than its par value. As the interest amount is fixed, lesser investment amount gives higher return to satisfy his higher required rate of return. However, when the required rate of return is less than the interest rate, the investor would be ready to buy the bond/debenture at a higher price than its par value.

20.5.3 Perpetual Bonds

Bonds, which never mature are known as perpetual bonds. Perpetual bonds are rarely found in practice. In respect of these bonds, interest is received infinitely.

Formula for calculation of present value is

$$B_o = \frac{INT}{k_d}$$

Where B_o = Present value of a bond/debenture

INT = Amount of interest

k_d = Required rate of return on bond (%)

Illustration No. 4

If a 7% perpetual bond of ₹ 1,000 that gives interest monthly is quoted at ₹ 900 and your required rate of return is 8%. Is it worth buying?

Solution

$$B_o = \frac{INT}{k_d}$$

Where B_o = Present value of a bond/debenture

INT = Amount of interest

k_d = Required rate of return on bond (%)

$$= \frac{70/12}{0.08/12}$$

$$= \frac{5.83}{0.0067} = ₹\ 870$$

Bond is giving monthly interest. Both interest amount of ₹ 70 and interest rate of 0.08 (8%) are divided by 12 as they are for one year.

The bond is quoted at ₹ 900. So bond is not worth buying.

20.6 YIELD TO MATURITY (YTM)

From the date of purchase till date of maturity, the average return investment instrument gives over the entire period of holding to investor is called 'Yield to Maturity'. When investment instruments are purchased in market, market price may be more or less than the par value of instrument. 8% debenture with a face value of ₹ 100, redeemable after 3 years, is quoted at ₹ 105. In such a situation, investor would like to know the return he would get on the investment he makes. In other words, we are required to calculate the investment's 'Internal Rate of Return', when coupon rate (interest rate the instrument carries), market price of investment and cash flows are known.

Internal Rate of Return is also known as 'Yield to Maturity'. Yield to Maturity provides the answer about return investor would get, if purchase price is different from par value.

This concept is of real practical utility when investor has to take a decision and choice is to be made between alternative investment options. When the bond is quoted in the market and his required rate of return is also known, yield to maturity helps the investor to buy or sell.

If debt is issued, at par, interest rate paid by firm becomes the return to the investor. If debt is issued or quoted at discount/premium, the actual yield to the investor is to be calculated with the following formula:

$$= \frac{C + \frac{M - P}{n}}{\frac{M + P}{2}}$$

Where C = Annual interest rate (coupon rate)

P = Purchase price

M = Maturity or par value of bond

n = Number of years remaining to maturity

Tip to Students: For calculation of 'yield to maturity', another simple way is, add the annual interest amount to the annual average return available at the time of redemption. Divide by the average of redemption value and purchase price.

$$\frac{\text{Interest amount per year + Average annual return on redemption}}{\text{Average investment}}$$

Illustration No. 5

A deep discount bond is available in market at ₹ 700 and would be redeemed at ₹ 1,100. Period required for redemption is five years. Calculate 'yield to maturity'.

Solution

The actual yield to the investor is to be calculated with the following formula:

$$= \frac{C + \frac{M - P}{n}}{\frac{M + P}{2}}$$

Where C = Annual interest rate (coupon rate)

P = Purchase price

M = Maturity or par value of bond

n = Number of years remaining to maturity

$$= \frac{0 + \dfrac{1{,}1000 - 700}{5}}{\dfrac{1{,}100 + 700}{2}}$$

$$= \frac{80}{900}$$

$$= 8.9\%$$

Note: In a deep discount bond, no interest is paid annually. It is issued at a discount and redemption at face value or with premium. Difference between issue price and redemption amount is interest for the period instrument issued. Hence, annual interest is zero.

Alternatively

Annual interest	0
Add: Average annual return (400/5)	80
Total	80
Divide with Average investment	900
YTM $\left(\frac{80}{900} \times 100\right)$	8.9%

Illustration No. 6

10% bond of XYZ company Ltd (F.V. ₹ 1,000) is currently traded at ₹ 910. Maturity of bond is after 3 years at par value. Calculate yield to maturity. Required rate of return is 18%. Do you recommend purchase at that rate?

Solution

The actual yield to the investor is to be calculated with the following formula:

$$= \frac{C + \dfrac{M - P}{n}}{\dfrac{M + P}{2}}$$

Where
- C = Annual interest rate (coupon rate)
- P = Purchase price
- M = Maturity or par value of bond
- n = Number of years remaining to maturity

$$= \frac{100 + \dfrac{1{,}000 - 910}{3}}{\dfrac{1{,}000 + 910}{2}}$$

$$= \frac{130}{955}$$

$$= 13.61\%$$

Yield to maturity is 13.61%, which is less than the required rate of return 18%. Hence, it is not recommended for purchase.

Illustration No. 7

Sudhir Ltd has issued 12% bonds having F.V. of ₹ 1,000 at 5% discount for 10 years. Bonds would be redeemed at 10% premium. Calculate from the view-point of investor:

(i) Yield to Maturity.

(ii) In case, investor purchases at ₹ 1,050 in the market and pays ₹ 30 towards brokerage, what is yield to maturity when redemption is due after 5 years?

Solution

Relevant formula for calculation of yield to maturity is as under:

$$= \frac{C + \frac{M - P}{n}}{\frac{M + P}{2}}$$

Where C = Annual interest rate (coupon rate)

P = Purchase price

M = Maturity or par value of the bond

n = Number of years remaining to maturity

(i)
$$= \frac{120 + \frac{1,100 - 950}{10}}{\frac{1,100 + 950}{2}}$$

$$= \frac{135}{1025} = 13.17\%$$

Yield to Maturity from the view-point of investor is 13.17%.

(ii)
$$= \frac{120 + \frac{1,100 - 1,080^*}{5}}{\frac{1,100 + 1,080}{2}}$$

$$= \frac{124}{1,090} = 11.38\%$$

Yield to Maturity from the view-point of investor is 11.38%.

* Includes purchase price 1,050 and brokerage 50

Illustration No. 8

Venkat has invested ₹ 50,000 in Tata Deposit Certificate. Interest is payable @ 8% on yearly basis. At the time of purchase, postal agent has parted 0.75% from his commission amount, at the time of investment to Venkat. Tata Company pays 5% bonus at the time of maturity, which is at the end of 6 years. Calculate Yield to Maturity.

Solution

Agent has paid ₹ 375 (0.75% on ₹ 50,000) from his commission. So actual investment by Venkat is ₹ 49,625 (50,000 – 375). Company pays 5% bonus at the time of maturity, so ₹ 2,500 is the additional return, which is to be spread over a period of 6 years to get annual return.

Relevant formula for calculation of yield to maturity is as under:

$$= \frac{C + \frac{M - P}{n}}{\frac{M + P}{2}}$$

Where C = Annual interest rate (coupon rate)

P = Purchase price

M = Maturity or par value of the bond

n = Number of years remaining to maturity

$$= \frac{4{,}000 + \frac{(52{,}500 - 49{,}625)}{6}}{\frac{(52{,}500 + 49{,}625)}{2}}$$

$$= \frac{4{,}479.16}{51{,}062.50}$$

$$= 8.77\%$$

Illustration No. 9

Bhavana Shukla is planning to invest for long-term and two instruments have come for her consideration. Choose the instrument when her minimum required rate of return is 18%.

(i) Deep discount bond is available at ₹ 875 and would be redeemed after 5 years at ₹ 1,600.

(ii) 16% debenture (Face value ₹ 100) is quoted at ₹ 95 and would be redeemed at the end of 5 years.

Solution

'Yield to Maturity' is to be calculated and compared with the required rate of return for decision-making.

Relevant formula for calculation of yield to maturity is as under:

$$= \frac{C + \frac{M - P}{n}}{\frac{M + P}{2}}$$

Where
C = Annual interest rate (coupon rate)
P = Purchase price
M = Maturity or par value of the bond
n = Number of years remaining to maturity

(i)
$$= \frac{0 + \frac{(1{,}600 - 875)}{5}}{\frac{(1{,}600 + 875)}{2}}$$

$$= \frac{145}{1{,}237.50}$$

$$= 11.72\%$$

(ii)
$$= \frac{16 + \frac{(100 - 95)}{5}}{\frac{(100 + 95)}{2}}$$

$$= \frac{17}{97.5}$$

$$= 17.44\%$$

Recommendation: Both the instruments do not yield the required rate of return of 18%. Hence, she has to consider other investment instruments.

20.7 PRESENT VALUE OF PREFERENCE SHARES

The holders of the preference shares get a fixed rate of dividend on a continuous basis. They enjoy preference over equity shareholders in respect of dividend receipt. Preference shares may be issued with or without a maturity period. A company can also issue convertible preference shares. After the stated period, preference shares get converted into equity shares.

The formula for calculating the value of irredeemable preference share is

$$P_o = \frac{PDIV}{k_p}$$

Where P_o = Value of Preference share

PDIV = Preference dividend

k_p = Required Return on Preference share

Similar to bonds, it is relatively easy to estimate cash outflows associated with irredeemable preference shares as dividend is constant. It may be observed that the above formula is similar to the calculation of the value of the perpetual bond.

Illustration No. 10

A Company has issued irredeemable preference shares with a face value of ₹ 100 carrying a dividend rate of 9%. The value of the preference share is ₹ 82. What is the yield on the preference share?

Solution

$$P_o = \frac{PDIV}{k_p}$$

Where P_o = Value of preference share

PDIV = Preference dividend

k_p = Required return on preference share

$$k_p = \frac{PDIV}{P_o}$$

$$= \frac{9}{92} = 0.11 \text{ or } 11\%$$

The yield on the preference share is 11%.

20.7.1 Redeemable Preference Share

Value of redeemable preference shares is calculated, based on the following formula, which is similar to redeemable debentures. We need to know

(i) stream of future dividends at a fixed rate of dividend

(ii) maturity payment at the time of redemption and

(iii) required rate of return.

$$P_o = \frac{D_1}{(1+k_p)} + \frac{D_2}{(1+k_p)^2} + \text{........} + \frac{D_n}{(1+k_p)^n} + \frac{RV}{(1+k_p)^n}$$

Where P_o = Present value of a preference share

D = Amount of dividend

k_p = Required rate of return on preference share (%)

RV = Redemption value of preference share

n = Life of preference share

Illustration No. 11

Tisco Ltd has issued 10% redeemable preference shares (Face value of ₹ 100), which are due for redemption at the end of 3 years at ₹105. Required rate of return is 12%. Present market value of preference share is ₹ 110. Is it desirable to sell?

Solution

The formula for calculation of present value of preference share is

$$P_o = \frac{D_1}{(1+k_p)} + \frac{D_2}{(1+k_p)^2} + \ldots\ldots + \frac{D_n}{(1+k_p)^n} + \frac{RV}{(1+k_p)^n}$$

Where P_o = Present value of a preference share

D = Amount of interest

k_p = Required rate of return on preference share (%)

RV = Redemption value of preference share

n = Life of preference share

$$= \frac{10}{(1+0.12)} + \frac{10}{(1+0.12)^2} + \frac{10}{(1+0.12)^3} + \frac{105}{(1+0.12)^3}$$

$$= \frac{10}{1.12} + \frac{10}{1.2544} + \frac{10}{1.4049} + \frac{105}{1.4049}$$

$$= 8.92 + 7.97 + 7.12 + 74.73$$

$$= ₹\ 98.74$$

As the market value of redeemable preference share (₹ 110) is more than its present value (₹ 98.74), it is desirable to sell.

20.8 PRESENT VALUE OF EQUITY SHARE

Valuation of equity shares is relatively difficult. There are two types of difficulties. The rate of dividend on equity shares is not constant. More so, it is not known in advance for calculating present value. Secondly, dividend is discretionary and not compulsory. In case of debentures and preference shares, rate of interest and dividend are certain. It is therefore easy to forecast those cash flows. But, it is not the case with the equity shares. The earnings on equity shares are generally likely to grow. This feature of variable and uncertain dividend on equity shares makes the calculation of value of equity share rather difficult.

Dividend Capitalisation Model

Dividend capitalisation model is a basic valuation model for equity shares valuation. The value of an equity share is a function of cash flows in the form of dividends expected by investors and risk associated with the cash inflows. So value of an equity share is the present value of its future stream of dividends plus the present value of expected price at the time of sale.

(A) **One-Period Valuation Model:** Suppose an investor wants to hold the share for a period of one year. The value of the share for him will be the present value of the expected dividend at the end of one year plus the present value of the expected sale price at the end of one year.

The formula for calculation is

$$P_o = \frac{D_1}{1+k_e} + \frac{P_1}{1+k_e}$$

Where P_o = Current value of share

D_1 = Expected dividend at the end of first year

P_1 = Expected price at the end of first year

k_e = Required rate of return on equity

Illustration No. 12

Kalyan is planning to buy equity shares HCL Ltd. for holding them for a period of one year and then sell it. The expected dividend at the end of one year is ₹ 8 and the expected sale proceeds at the end of one year are ₹ 300. Determine the value of share to the investor assuming the expected required return is 20%. If the current market price is ₹ 225, is it worth buying?

Solution

$$P_o = \frac{D_1}{1+k_e} + \frac{P_1}{1+k_e}$$

Where P_o = Current value of share

D_1 = Expected dividend at the end of first year

P_1 = Expected price at the end of first year

k_e = Required rate of return on equity

$$= \frac{8}{(1.20)} + \frac{300}{(1.20)} = \frac{308}{(1.20)}$$

$$= ₹\ 257$$

The present value of equity share is ₹ 257. They are available at ₹ 225. So, they are worth buying.

(B) **Two-Period Valuation Model:** Suppose investor wants to hold the share for two years then the formula would be:

$$P_o = \frac{D_1}{1+k_e} + \frac{D_2}{(1+k_e)^2} + \frac{P_2}{(1+k_e)^2}$$

Where P_o = Current value of share

D_1 = Expected dividend at the end of first year

D_2 = Dividend at the end of the second year

P_2 = Expected selling price at the end of second year

k_e = Required rate of return on equity

Illustration No. 13

Mr. Kishore is planning to buy equity shares of TCS Ltd and wants to hold them for two years and then sell. The expected dividend at the end of first year is 8% and 9% at the end of second year. The expected selling price at the end of second year is ₹ 900. Calculate value of shares today, taking the required rate of return as 18%. The shares are now quoted at ₹ 780. Advise about their buying.

Solution

$$P_o = \frac{D_1}{1+k_e} + \frac{D_2}{(1+k_e)^2} + \frac{P_2}{(1+k_e)^2}$$

Where P_o = Current value of share

D_1 = Expected dividend at the end of first year

D_2 = Dividend at the end of the second year

P_2 = Expected selling price at the end of second year

k_e = Required rate of return on equity

$$= \frac{8}{(1.18)} + \frac{9}{(1.18)^2} + \frac{900}{(1.18)^2}$$

$$= \frac{8}{1.18} + \frac{9}{1.3924} + \frac{900}{1.3924}$$

= 7 + 6 + 646 = ₹ 659

For the required return, the shares are worth buying for ₹ 659 and the current market rate is ₹ 780. So, they are not worth buying.

(C) **'n'-Period Valuation Model:** Similarly, if the shareholder wants to retain for 'n' years, the formula for calculating present value of share is

$$P_o = \frac{D_1}{(1+k_e)} + \frac{D_2}{(1+k_e)^2} + \frac{D_n}{(1+k_e)^n} ...+ \frac{P_n}{(1+k_e)^n}$$

Here, **'n'** refers to the years' of holding equity shares.

Assumptions: Valuation of equity shares based on dividend requires the following assumptions:

1. The dividends are payable annually.
2. The first dividend is received after one year from the date of purchase/acquisition.
3. Sale of equity share occurs only at the end of a year and at ex-dividend terms.

Check Your Understanding

(A) State whether the following statements are True or False

1 Present value concept helps investor in taking a decision to buy or sell securities, once the required rate of return is known.

2. Bonds that mature at a specified period are known as perpetual bonds.
3. Present value concept compares present value of the bond with current market value, to determine whether the bond is overvalued or undervalued for decision making.
4. The value of an equity share is the present value of its future stream of dividends and its selling price.
5. Physical assets like building and machinery are financial assets.
6. The difference between the assets and liabilities is equal to net worth or shareholders' funds.
7. Replacement value is the amount that company has to spend to acquire the same asset in the existing condition.
8. Liquidation value is the value one would get on assets when the business is in progress.
9. Market value of a share is always lower than the book value, if the business is profitable.
10. When the capital market is efficient market price reflects the intrinsic value of a share.
11. Debentures are always secured.
12. Bonds/debentures can be redeemed at par, premium or discount.
13. When bond is quoted in the market and required rate of return is also known, 'yield to maturity' formula helps investor to make decision in respect of buy or sell of the concerned investment instrument.
14. Yield to maturity is the average rate of return that an investor earns on an investment asset, if held till maturity.
15. Coupon rate is the interest rate with which the bond is issued.
16. Value of bond is always equal to its par value.

17. When required rate of return is more than interest rate, investor would buy the investment instrument at a price more than its par value.

Answers

1. True	2. False	3. True	4. True	5. False	6. True	7. True	8. False
9. False	10. True	11. False	12. True	13. True	14. True	15. True	16. False
17. False.							

(B) Objective Questions (Identify what is most appropriate)

1. Amortization means writing off
   (A) Fixed asset (B) Current asset
   (C) Intangible asset (D) None of the above
2. When net worth is dividend by number of shares outstanding, this is arrived at.
   (A) Book value (B) Replacement value
   (C) Liquidation value (D) Going concern value
3. The amount that the company has to spend to acquire the same asset in the present existing condition is called as
   (A) Book value (B) Replacement value
   (C) Liquidation value (D) Going concern value
4. Face value of a 10% bond is ₹ 100 which is issued at a discount of ₹ 5. Presently, it is quoted at ₹ 110 in the market. Annual interest amount paid by the company on each bond is
   (A) ₹ 11 (B) ₹ 10
   (C) ₹ 9.5 (D) ₹ 105
5. Coupon rate means
   (A) Face value of a bond (B) Market rate of a bond
   (C) Interest rate specified on the face of a bond
   (D) Interest yield received by the investor
6. Par value means
   (A) Market value of a bond (B) Face value of a bond
   (C) Issue price of a bond (D) Redemption value of a bond
7. If the present value of a security is less than its current market price, investor does this to make a profit.
   (A) Buy that security (B) Sell that security
   (C) Hold that security (D) Does nothing with that security
8. This concept helps the investor to buy or sell the security comparing to its current market price.
   (A) Present value concept (B) Market value concept
   (C) Intrinsic value concept (D) Nominal value concept

9. If the required rate of return of the investor is more than interest rate shown on face of the security, the investor would be willing to purchase only if
   (A) Market price is more than the face value of security.
   (B) Market price is less than the face value of security.
   (C) Market price and face value of security are same.
   (D) Face value of security has no relevance in purchase decision.
10. Yield to maturity means
   (A) Average rate of return investor gets over the investment period.
   (B) Minimum rate of return investor gets over the investment period.
   (C) Maximum rate of return investor gets over the investment period.
   (D) Interest rate shown on the face of instrument.

Answers

1. (C) 2. (A) 3. (B) 4. (B) 5. (C) 6. (B) 7. (B) 8. (A)
9. (B) 10. (A)

Descriptive Questions

1. Explain the concept 'Value' and its meaning. **(20.2)**
2. Distinguish between bond and debenture and explain their features. **(20.3)**
3. Explain the method of calculating present value of equity shares based on dividend capitalisation model that helps in decision making for buying or selling. **(20.7)**

Interview Questions

Q.1. What is a 'Deep Discount Bond'? Who has issued them first?

Ans. 'Deep Discount Bond' does not carry any interest, but is sold by issuer company at deep discount from its final maturity (nominal value). The difference amount is interest from the date of issue till its maturity. The Industrial Development Bank of India (IDBI) has issued the 'Deep Discount Bonds' for the first time in the Indian capital market at ₹ 2,700 against its nominal value of ₹ One lakh, payable after 25 years.

Q.2. What is 'Yield to Maturity'?

Ans. From date of purchase till date of maturity, the average return investment instrument gives over its entire period of holding to investor is called 'Yield to Maturity'. It consists of interest yield plus a positive or negative capital gains yield.

Q.3. In what manner 'Yield to Maturity' helps investor in decision-making?

Ans. 'Yield to Maturity' is the average return available to investor, calculation based on total annual interest and appreciation/fall in value over entire period of holding. It helps investor in decision making as the expected 'Yield to Maturity' is compared with the required rate of return investor wishes to make.

Q.4. What is meant by 'Dividend Yield'? What is its significance?

Ans. Dividend yield means amount of dividend per share as a percentage of market price of the concerned share. Investors who buy income shares are interested to know the amount of dividend they would get as regular income on investment they make. Even if company makes profits but does not declare suitable dividend as expected by market, there would be an immediate fall of price in market.

Short Questions

Q.1. What is meant by 'Book Value'? Is it a proper basis for valuing equity shares?

Ans. Book value is arrived by dividing the firm's ownership by the number of equity shares. Firm's ownership is calculated by two methods. First method is subtracting all the liabilities from the value of assets. Second method is the sum of all equity shareholders' funds *i.e.* equity share capital + accumulated profits – all accumulated losses. An implied assumption in book value valuation is that the assets are expected to realise an amount equal to the value stated in the balance sheet.

Book value is based on accounting information and thus can be easily calculated. However book value lacks sophistication as value of fixed assets is based on the historical figures, most of which may be outdated. So, book value is not a proper basis for valuing equity shares.

Q.2. What is coupon rate?

Ans. Coupon rate is the interest rate with which the investment instrument is issued. Interest is payable on its par value of the instrument as per terms of issue. This rate is fixed. On a 7% bond, face value is ₹ 1,000, 7% is the coupon rate and interest amount is ₹ 70. Payment schedule of interest can be annual, half-yearly, quarterly or monthly basis.

Q.3. What is the difference between growth shares and income shares?

Ans. Investors normally buy equity shares for regular income in the form of dividend and capital appreciation on their sale. Growth shares are those which offer greater opportunities for capital gain. In these cases, companies follow the policy of lower dividends and retain higher profits in the form of retained earnings. They follow the higher retention policy to provide a higher growth rate.

To provide regular earnings to its shareholders, some companies follow the policy of declaring high dividend rate and retain a low portion of profits as retained earnings. Shares of these companies are described as 'Income shares'.

Aspirations of shareholders are different. Depending on their individual requirements, shareholders purchase and retain growth shares and income shares.

Q.4. What is the relationship between interest rate and required rate of return?

Ans. Interest rate is based on terms of issue of bond/debenture. This amount is fixed. Required rate of return depends on expectations of investors, depending on risk profile of the investment instrument. If the required rate of return is more than the interest rate, the value of bond would be less than the par value of the bond and vice versa. In other words, the investor would be willing to pay lesser amount than its par value to buy. However investor would get interest amount on its par value. So, he would get a higher return that would be equal to the required rate of return.

CHAPTER

21

Short-term Financing and Investments

21.1 INTRODUCTION

Short-term finance means availability of funds for a period of one year or less than that period. The basic purpose of short-term financing is to meet working capital requirements of corporate sector. There are two main types of short-term financing: trade credit and bank borrowing.

21.2 TYPES OF SHORT-TERM FINANCING

21.2.1 Trade Credit

Meaning: Trade credit refers to credit received by a customer from supplier of goods in normal course of business. When a retailer buys goods from a wholesaler, retailer is the customer to whom credit is extended by wholesaler. In India, buying goods on credit is a normal feature. This is a major source of short-term financing. In many areas of business unless credit is extended, business cannot sustain. Very few trades are lucky that do not extend credit and make a good business. In that trade, there are no credit sales and all sales are made on cash basis. For example, a retailer dealing in cooking gas does not provide any credit as this is a cash and carry business. Trade credit basically depends on nature of business.

In trade credit, payments are deferred. Small traders still heavily depend on trade credit as they continue to experience difficulty in securing borrowing from banks, though credit is made liberal by banks. Small traders cannot raise the needed finance by other means.

> **Trade credit is mostly an informal arrangement and granted on open account basis.**

Normal procedure is, supplier sends goods with an agreed understanding for credit period. Payment is received by retailer or wholesaler within the allowed credit period. Buyer accepts invoice and so in effect acknowledges debt. There is no other formal legal document. Once a link is established between wholesaler and retailer and payment is regularly made as per terms of the invoice, the former supplies goods for an increased amount as and when business of retailer increases. To a wholesaler, credit extended to retailers appears as 'Sundry debtors' in its balance sheet. In the balance sheet of retailer, trade credit is shown in the form of sundry creditors. In U.S.A., trade creditors are called 'accounts payable'.

Bills of Exchange: Bills of exchange provide an easy route to extend trade credit. When supplier of goods is less sure of receiving payment on due date, supplier draws the bill of exchange on the buyer to document transaction fool-proof method and buyer accepts the bill of exchange for payment on due date. In other words, **trade credit is documented in the form of bill of exchange.** For wholesaler, the bill of exchange becomes 'bills receivable' and the same document becomes 'bills payable' to retailer. In the accounts of wholesaler, bills receivable appears in place of sundry debtors. Bills payable takes the place of sundry creditors in the accounts of retailer.

The greatest advantage with bill of exchange is its self-maturing character as due date is certain and buyer cannot dodge payment unlike book debt.

Supplier is also in a position to discount bills receivable with his banker and can raise finance to meet his working capital needs. Even when there is no doubt of creditworthiness of buyer, seller may adopt this mode of payment through bill of exchange when he wants to have the option of raising finance through discounting bills of exchange. In case, bill of exchange is not executed between supplier and buyer, supplier can raise finance from bank in the form of hypothecation of book-debts. In other words, discounting bills of exchange and hypothecation of book-debts are the different routes available for meeting working capital needs.

Credit Terms: Credit terms refer to those terms under which supplier sells on credit to buyer. There are two important terms and they are 'due date' and 'cash discount'. Due date is the date on which buyer has to make payment for goods received. On the due date, supplier can expect payment. Credit terms refer to the length of credit period. Cash discount is granted to customers for early payment of debt. Cash discount is an incentive provided by supplier to buyer for early payment, before due date. The typical way of expressing credit period and cash discount in an invoice is '2/15, net 30 days'. This means 2% cash discount would be given, if buyer makes payment within 15 days from date of invoice. If the buyer does not want to avail cash discount, he can avail credit period of 30 days. Buyer can make payment at the end of 30 days from date of invoice.

Benefits and Costs of Trade Credit: Trade credit is a spontaneous source of financing. When volume of business grows, amount of credit also automatically increases. Suppose buyer is in habit of receiving credit for 30 days and his daily purchases are ₹ 10,000 per day. If his business increases and makes purchases for ₹ 15,000 per day, his trade credit has increased from ₹ 3,00,000 (30 × 10,000) to ₹ 4,50,000 (30 × 15,000). In an informal way, buyer receives extra credit as he has been making prompt payment at the end of 30 days.

Advantages: The major advantages of trade credit are as under:

Easy Availability: Unlike other sources of finance, trade credit is easier to obtain. Market practice in a particular trade normally determines credit period.

> **Trade credit depends on nature of business and no lengthy negotiation is necessary to obtain normal trade credit period.**

1. On this trade credit, many small firms survive. In many trades, it is an accepted way of conducting business. Even a new shop gets trade credit after a couple of transactions. It is not possible to secure borrowing from banks in initial periods. Even for a new company, trade credit is easier to secure and highly difficult to raise finance in capital market.
2. **Flexibility: Flexibility is a unique feature of trade credit.** If business expands, more purchases are made and with higher purchases, more trade credit is received. In contrast, when business declines automatically firm makes lower purchases and with it, lesser trade credit is received.
3. **Informality:** Trade credit is informal. **No legal documents are involved.** Generally no formal agreement is entered into while extending trade credit.

> **Trade credit is not free. Funds have economic cost and this cost is passed on to buyer by supplier of goods in price. This fact is evident as there is always a difference in cash price and credit price.**

Cost of Trade Credit: Is trade credit a free source of finance? Many think trade credit does not have any additional cost. It is wrong. Supplier of trade credit has to borrow more funds, paying interest, if trade credit is to be extended. This cost of credit is passed on by supplier via increased price to buyer. It is common knowledge cash purchase attracts a lower price, compared to purchase on credit.

21.2.2 Accrued Expenses

Accrued expenses represent a liability for services already received and yet to be paid. Here, payment is permitted after services are received. The classical example is salaries payable to staff. In case of salaries and wages, employees render their services and so benefit of services is received by the firm immediately while payments are made at the end of month. So even employees too provide a source of spontaneous short-term finance to the organization they work. Electricity and telephone are other examples where services are received first and payments are made at the end of specified duration normally end of month. In case of corporate taxes, they are paid quarterly while profits are made as and when sales are made. In this way, even government has provided credit to business firms in respect of their cash sales! When bill for payment is not received and accounts are to be finalised, provision for accrued expenses is made in accounts to reflect true and fair profit and financial position in financial statements.

Accrued expenses represent spontaneous and interest-free source of financing. The longer the period of payment, higher the benefit firm derives. However due to legal constraints and practical difficulties, firm cannot postpone their payment indefinitely. Till their payment, firm enjoys benefit as short-term financing.

21.2.3 Deferred Income

Deferred income represents funds received in advance for services to be rendered in future. The receipts improve liquidity of firm. However firms that have great demand for their products and services, enjoying good reputation in market, can only get the benefit of deferred income. Manufacturers and contractors engaged in producing or constructing costly goods, involving considerable length of time for manufacture or construction, demand advance money before accepting orders. In turn-key projects or where goods are to be made for a specific requirement, advance payments are insisted. This avoids possibility for cancellation of sale after commencement of execution of order. Normally, clause remains in those contracts that advance payment made would be forfeited on cancellation of the contract. These advances are adjusted when goods and services are supplied. Till supply of services, amount stands as a liability in the books of recipient. This is a cost-free source of finance and really useful in business.

21.3 FACTORING

Accounts receivable is another name for book debts. Factor is an institution which offers credit against receivables and provides services relating to management of debts arising from credit sales. Factor provides credit against receivables and in this process firm gets funds immediately for credit sales made. Management services relate to maintenance of sales ledger, collection of book debts (Accounts Receivable), rendering advisory services to their clients and protection from bad debts. Factoring may be on recourse basis where risk of bad debts is borne by client firm or on a non-recourse basis where risk of bad debts is borne by factor.

In spite of many services offered by factoring, following are the limitations of factoring:

(i) High cost of factoring compared to other short-term finance.

(ii) Firms availing factoring services are viewed as weak.

(iii) Once a buyer defaults in payment, factor takes a tough stance and may not agree to provide credit against sales made to the same buyer. This action may force the firm to discontinue sales, resulting in reduced sales.

21.4 BANK FINANCE FOR WORKING CAPITAL

Banks are main institutions that provide working capital, which is a short-term source of finance. Bank credit is the most important source for working capital. There are various forms of bank finance for short-term requirements. They are discussed hereunder:

(A) Cash Credit

Cash credit is the most popular form of credit with borrowers for meeting working capital requirements. Bank considers firm's sales and production plans to sanction a particular working capital limit, which is called 'sanctioned limit' in a cash credit account. In case of seasonal industries, bank sanctions peak credit limit to meet working capital requirements during season which is always higher in comparison to the limit sanctioned for non-peak period. So, bank sanctions separate limits for peak and non-peak periods as working capital requirement is maximum during peak season. These cash credit limits are against security of current assets such as stocks and book-debts.

Margin: Bank does not finance 100% of current assets. Banks stipulate margin. The drawing power (amount that can be drawn) is calculated after deducting the required margin from value of stocks. Borrower has to submit stock statement monthly as per terms of sanction, declaring physical stocks and their value on a specified date. If margin requirement is 30%, bank lends only up to 70% of value of stocks. The amount so calculated is called 'drawing power' and borrower is allowed to draw to the extent of the drawing power. Based on value of stocks, drawing power is calculated. Against stocks of ₹ 80,000, borrower can avail drawing power of ₹ 56,000 (80,000 –30% of 80,000).

Additional Temporary Over Drawings: Bank allows borrower to draw beyond sanctioned limit for temporary periods. This would be allowed if stocks cover borrowing with the stipulated margin. An example would clarify the picture better.

	₹
Sanctioned limit	1,00,000
Stocks	1,50,000
Margin	20%
Drawing power	1,20,000
Outstanding balance	90,000

In the above situation, borrower has approached bank for a temporary over drawings of ₹ 20,000. Normally, bank allows ₹ 10,000 only i.e. up to the sanctioned limit. As stocks cover additional drawings with required margin, bank can permit over drawings for a temporary period, normally, not exceeding 30 days. Once the over drawings are allowed, the outstanding balance becomes ₹ 1,10,000 (90,000 + 20,000), which is in excess of sanctioned limit but covered by the drawing power.

Ideal Form for Business: The greatest convenience of cash credit account is its flexibility. Borrower can deposit sale proceeds daily to reduce the outstanding balance in cash credit account and can draw as and when needed to the maximum extent of drawing power or cash credit limit, which ever is lower. Interest is charged on the outstanding balance only. In other words, borrower is required to pay interest for amount utilised only and not on the total sanctioned limit.

In loan account, this facility of withdrawing money again does not exist. Once deposited into loan account, the amount is not available for withdrawal as the money is deemed towards closure of loan account. This feature in cash credit account is the greatest convenience to borrowers. On account of this convenience, the actual interest rate on sanctioned limit would work out lower than the interest rate offered by bank, as no borrower requires money on a continuous basis. Moreover, there is no commitment charge for the limit not utilised. By virtue of margin, bank is secured even if value of stocks falls to the extent of margin.

Period of Sanction: Cash credit limits are normally sanctioned for one year. At the end of year, limits are reviewed. Technically advances are repayable on demand. However, bank recalls advance only when conduct of the account is not satisfactory.

Pledge/Hypothecation: Cash credit facility can be sanctioned either in the form of pledge or hypothecation of goods. In case of pledge, goods are kept in the godowns, under lock and key of bank. So possession of goods and control thereon is with bank, not borrower. As and when payment is made, goods are released, even proportionately to borrower. Normally, banks sanction this facility to new borrowers or when their credit worthiness is not fully known. However borrower does not enjoy total convenience with pledge facility as physical possession of goods is with bank. As and when borrower wants to sell the goods, proportionate amount is to be deposited into pledge account. While pledge provides almost total safety to bank, this facility is not practically convenient to borrower. However, pledge facility is good enough to new borrowers or where goods are stored for a long period in non-season for selling in season. In case of hypothecation, possession of goods is with borrower and can deal with goods in the manner he likes, even selling goods without bank's prior approval. However, borrower is required to deposit sale proceeds of goods into the cash credit—hypothecation account. As goods are in total possession of borrower and can deal with them in the ordinary course of business, bank assumes more risk while sanctioning hypothecation limit. So, hypothecation facility is extended to such type of borrowers only whose creditworthiness is well known to bank.

Cash credit is a common form of financing for meeting working capital requirements, which affords the greatest flexibility to borrower with economic cost. Hypothecation facility affords more flexibility to borrower compared to pledge.

(B) Overdraft

Banks sanction regular overdraft limits normally against security of fixed deposit receipts, shares, life insurance policy, postal certificates etc. Interest is charged on amount utilised. Cheque facility is made available in overdraft account. Cash credit is a normal feature in business while overdraft facility is normally availed by professionals for their working capital requirements. In addition to permanent overdraft limit, bank sanctions temporary overdraft in current account of customers as and when cheques received are in excess of balance in current account. This is a temporary arrangement.

(C) Purchase or Discounting of Bills

Banks often experience difficulty to check and control diversion of funds i.e. utilisation for purposes other than sanctioned. In that context, this form of finance is ideal as banks can control better in respect of utilisation as well as monitoring the end use of funds.

Bank sanctions the limit against bills of exchange drawn by the supplier on its buyers. Supplier can avail the limit for bills drawn on his buyers, covering supply of goods made. If the bill of exchange is payable on demand, it is purchased by bank. If the bill of exchange is drawn on acceptance basis, bank discounts the bill accepted by buyer of goods. Buyer has to make payment on the due date. In both the cases, working capital is provided by bank, by purchasing or discounting bills, as the case may be. Bank credits customer's account after deducting their commission. Borrower can avail the limit for goods sold only as invoice and documentary proof of dispatch goods such as railway receipt or motor receipt are necessary to submit to bank. Through accompanying documents, bank can ensure utilisation of limit for working capital purposes only.

The greatest convenient feature of this advance is its self-liquidating character. Once buyer makes payment, advance sanctioned against the bill is recovered. The amount sanctioned for working capital is normally divided between stocks and bills.

> **Purchase or discounting of bills finance has a self-liquidating character with greater control for banks to monitor utilisation of finances for working capital requirements.**

Banks can monitor utilisation of limit in this scheme better as chances for abuse of cash credit limit are more. Diversion of funds for other purposes is difficult in bill scheme. To encourage bills as an instrument of working capital, Reserve Bank of India had introduced the new bill market scheme in 1970. However, the scheme has failed to work.

(D) Letter of Credit

The purpose of letter of credit is that payment is assured to supplier of goods or services by bank. Here, responsibility for payment is assumed by bank and so supplier is not concerned with the creditworthiness of the buyer. In case payment is not made by customer, bank makes payment to the party in whose favour the letter of credit is opened. So, bank assumes risk for default in payment by the opener of letter of credit. Simply, creditworthiness of the buyer is not relevant to the supplier once letter of credit is opened. In other words, creditworthiness of borrower is substituted by creditworthiness of bank.

Letter of credit is a non-fund based limit. It means there is no outgo of funds when letter of credit is opened by bank in favour of customer. Bank opens letter of credit in favour of financially sound customers. While sanctioning letter of credit limit, banks normally stipulate margin from customers at the time of opening of letter of credit.

Additional Working Capital through Letter of Credit

Borrower may face a difficult situation when its cash credit limit for working capital is exhausted and suppliers are unwilling to give further trade credit. This situation occasionally happens in practical life. Many a time, sanctioned letter of credit limit may remain unutilised. In such circumstances, borrower can utilise the letter of credit limit for working capital purposes by requesting bank to open letters of credit in favour of suppliers. Even an unwilling supplier would gladly accept to supply goods on credit, if letter of credit is opened in his favour by bank as he is assured of payment in the event of default in payment by buyer. Supplier is confident with letter of credit as there would be no default in payment by bank. So, buyer can negotiate with suppliers for credit duration and open letter of credit on 'Documents against Acceptance' basis. Once bill of exchange is accepted, buyer can get possession of RR/LR as the case may be. Taking delivery of goods, buyer can sell goods and make payment on the due date of bill of exchange. This is an ingenious way of utilising a non-fund based limit for working capital purposes.

Margin-Earmarking from Cash Credit Account: Normally banks insist on cash margin for opening letter of credit. This margin amount is kept in a short-term deposit, which attracts low interest rate while the funds drawn from cash credit bear a higher interest rate. Instead of depositing cash margin, one can intelligently request the bank to earmark margin amount from the cash credit limit. Bank reduces the drawing power in cash credit account to the extent of margin on letter of credit and allows only reduced drawing power for operations of business. By this exercise, interest can be saved. This is one more way for finance manager to boost up profitability.

The author humbly submits that he had successfully negotiated with unwilling suppliers in times of working capital crunch situations to accept letter of credit with 'documents on acceptance' basis and could overcome working capital constraints. Request for earmarking from cash credit limit towards margin was also accepted by bank that has improved profitability of organization.

(E) Working Capital Loan

Working capital loan is normally sanctioned by banks for adhoc or temporary requirements of customers, not earlier foreseen. This is an additional sanction in excess of cash credit limit sanctioned. Once repayment is made loan account would be closed. In other words, customer cannot utilise this mode of finance on a continuous basis like cash credit account. Banks charge higher interest rate for extending this type of facility, compared to normal cash credit limit extended to same borrower. Other circumstance, bank opens a separate working capital loan account if the existing cash credit limit is reduced. The excessive outstanding balance in the cash credit account is transferred to working capital loan account and fixes suitable repayment schedule for its closure.

21.5 COMMERCIAL PAPER

Commercial paper is an unsecured instrument issued in the form a promissory note. They are issued by the highly rated corporate firms to diversify their sources of short-term financing. Equally they provide an outlet to invest the temporary excess funds by individual, corporate sector and non-corporate sector in safe and liquid instruments to secure higher returns compared to the interest rates offered by banks on short-term deposits. Even non residents and foreign institutional investors can invest in commercial paper. As the gamut of investors is more, commercial paper provides the real opportunity to raise finances from varied types of investors.

Commercial paper is an important money market instrument for raising short-term finance at a cheap interest rate.

> **Commercial paper is an ideal route to raise funds as well as investing excess short-term funds.**

Recent Importance: With the recent reduction in interest rates, importance of commercial paper has diminished, of late. However, corporate sector still finds issue of commercial paper cheap and has again regained its erstwhile importance to raise finances at a lower interest rate compared to the rates of interest charged on loans by banking sector.

The Indian economy has started witnessing the unprecedented increasing trends on inflation from the middle of the year 2006. In consequence, bank interest rates have been hardening more significantly from the year 2007. Increase in interest rates, offered by banks, is also in consequence of different stringent initiatives taken by RBI. The different measures are increase of credit reserve ratio and statutory liquidity ratio to contain or control the galloping inflation trends, prevailing more than 6% during the year 2010. So, commercial paper has regained its importance to work as a potent weapon to raise short-term finances by highly rated companies to improve their bottom line. In other words, commercial paper has become attractive as an alternative way to finance short-term requirements, instead of borrowing from banks.

Reserve Bank of India stipulates conditions for issue of commercial paper from time to time.

Conditions are as under, updated till 1st July, 2010:

(i) Eligibility: A corporate would be eligible to issue CP provided: (a) the tangible net worth of the company, as per the latest audited balance sheet, is not less than ₹ 4 crores; (b) company has been sanctioned working capital limit by bank/s or all-India financial institution/s; and (c) the borrowal account of the company is classified as a Standard Asset by the financing bank/s/institution/s.

(ii) **Rating Requirements: All eligible participants have to obtain the credit rating from CRISIL, ICRA or CARE or any other recognised credit rating agency.** The minimum credit rating required for issue of commercial paper is P-2 of CRISIL or any other equivalent rating from other rating agencies.

(iii) **Minimum Investment and Denomination:** Amount that can be invested by a single investor cannot be less than ₹ 5 lakhs (Face Value). Commercial paper can be issued in denomination of ₹ 5 lakhs or multiples there of.

(iv) **Maximum Limit:** CP can be issued within the overall umbrella limit fixed by the RBI, i.e., issue of CP together with other instruments, viz., term money borrowings, term deposits, certificates of deposit and inter-corporate deposits, all put together should not exceed 100 per cent of its net owned funds, as per the latest audited balance sheet.

(v) **Aggregate Limit:** The aggregate amount of CP from an issuer shall be within the limit as approved by its Board of Directors or the quantum indicated by the Credit Rating Agency for the specified rating, whichever is lower. Banks and financial institutions have the flexibility to fix working capital limits duly taking into account the resource pattern of companies' financing including CPs. **Earlier, commercial bank that sanctioned working capital limit was required to reduce the cash credit limit of the borrower to the extent of the issuance of commercial paper. Now, there is no need for the concerned commercial bank to reduce the sanctioned cash credit limit of the concerned company, automatically, after issuance of commercial paper. Commercial bank has the freedom to fix the working capital limits of the borrower.**

(vi) **Issuing and Paying Agent (IPA):** Only a scheduled bank can act as an IPA for issuance of CP.

(vii) **Period of Rising Subscription:** Commercial paper has to be raised within two weeks from the date of opening the issue for subscription.

(viii) **Maturity:** Maturity runs between a minimum of 7 days and maximum of one year from the date of issue.

(ix) **Interest:** Commercial paper is issued at a discount to its maturity value. The difference amount between the issue price and maturity amount is the return to the investor.

(x) **Credit Enhancement:** Commercial paper (CP) is a 'stand alone' product. However, banks have the flexibility to provide credit enhancement by way of stand-by assistance, based on their commercial judgement. In other words, in case of default in payment by the issuer, responsibility would be cast on the bank that has provided credit enhancement. This credit enhancement provides the necessary cushion to the investor's confidence to invest. It may be made clear that the credit enhancement is not compulsory for the issue of commercial paper. The issuer normally seeks the credit enhancement when the credit rating for the commercial paper is not adequate, though enough to issue commercial paper to attract the investors' response to raise finance at a cheaper interest rate. This credit enhancement strengthens the rating of the commercial paper.

The commercial paper market has ballooned from ₹ 44,000 crore in March, 2009 to ₹ 67,000 crore by June-end and ₹ 80,000 crore by mid-August, 2009 as interest rates in the debt market have fallen below bank rates at 4 to 5 per cent.

These conditions change from time to time and the conditions existing at the time of issue govern the issue of commercial paper.

Cheaper interest rate is the attraction for issue of commercial paper. Investors would generally invest in commercial paper issued by sound and creditworthy companies. Commercial paper gives higher interest rate compared to interest rate offered by banks on short-term deposits.

21.6 PUBLIC DEPOSITS

Acceptance of deposits by manufacturing companies and non-banking financial companies has been the unique feature of Indian financial system. The restrictive credit policy of Government of India has not allowed the companies to enjoy liberal credit, without regulations. To fill the substantial credit gap existing in the market, the corporate sector has explored the avenue of attracting deposits from public. When the corporate sector has offered higher interest rate than the interest rate prevailing in banks and post offices, the public has been tempted to invest their savings in corporate deposits. In fact, the public savings have found their way towards corporate deposits, in preference to the banking channels. Corporate sector too has found an easy way to get the money they wanted to have, without restrictions and regulations. Though they have been offering higher interest rate, still the effective cost to the company has been lower than the total cost incidental on their borrowing from the banks. Even the Public Sector (Government Companies) too has started accepting deposits.

Government Regulation: In that scenario to regulate acceptance and protect the interests of depositors, Government of India has framed the Companies (Acceptance of Deposits) Rules, 1975 in exercise of the powers conferred under section of 58 A of Companies Act. These rules relate to the maximum amount that a company can accept in the form of deposits, interest rate and other features to protect the interests of depositors. The company deposits are unsecured in their character and many investors have overlooked this important aspect while investing, attracted by the higher interest rate alone. Several investors have burnt their fingers and lost their hard earned savings. Despite the rules for acceptance of deposits still many depositors are yet to receive their money back from non-banking finance companies as well as manufacturing companies despite maturity of deposits and expiry of several years thereafter.

Under the current provisions, interest on public deposits is not exempted from income-tax in the hands of depositors.

21.7 SHORT-TERM INVESTMENTS

Cash is the most liquid asset held for business operations. Excess cash, amount in excess of the operating cash balance, is held for two reasons. When business is seasonal, firm would have excess cash during non-peak season. Other reason is to hold cash for precautionary motive i.e. for meeting unforeseen contingencies and unpredictable financial needs. However efficient the finance manager may be, cash flows can not be predicted with certainty. So, company would experience the need to park excess cash balance in short-term investments.

Need of short-term investments: Idle cash does not earn anything. The excess cash balance is temporarily invested in marketable securities, which can be considered as near moneys.

Features of Marketable Securities: Cash is parked in marketable securities for a temporary period.

The primary criterion in selection of marketable securities is quickest convertibility into cash.

If conversion into cash takes time, the very purpose of holding excess cash is defeated. Conversion should be immediate. While converting into cash there should be no financial loss for the original investment. The investment should yield certain gain, which is only secondary. In choosing investment opportunities firm is guided by the following principles or selection criteria.

Safety: It is the desire of every firm to make maximum gain while investing. But, risk and return always go hand in hand. This cardinal principle should not be forgotten. If the firm looks for return, risk would exist. The risk referred here is default risk. Risk may relate to principal or interest or both.

> **In choosing investment opportunity, default risk should be zero both in respect of principal and return that is assured at the time of investment.**

So, the finance manager does not have the option other than choosing low-return investments. Low-risk securities always earn lower return. The finance manager should not be tempted to invest the excess balance in risky securities. Once this primary objective is forgotten, selection goes wrong.

Maturity: Maturity refers to the period when the principal amount is realised. Interest may be paid during the period of security or at maturity. The price of a long-time security fluctuates more widely. Longer the maturity, the price variation would be higher. So, **selection should be made for short-term securities to avoid fluctuations in price realisation.**

Liquidity and Marketability: Liquidity refers to the ability to convert into cash, immediately without any significant loss of value. Marketability refers to the convenience and speed of conversion into cash. So, securities should be selected that have a ready market so that they are realisable before maturity, if necessary.

Return or Yield: Other things equal, firm should go for those securities that give the highest return. However, this criterion should be the last in selection and return should not influence the selection at any time. Restraint is necessary for the finance manager in selection process.

21.7.1 Avenues of Investment

The following are the different types of short-term investment opportunities available in India for investing surplus cash:

1. **Treasury Bills: Treasury bills are Government securities.** They are issued by Reserve Bank of India on behalf of the Central Government. There is no default risk with them as issue is made by Government. Normally, treasury bills are issued at a discount and redeemed at their face value. The difference is the return for investment in treasury bills. They are issued in bearer form and purchaser's name does not appear on the bills. So, they are easily transferable. Secondary market exists for sale so they are highly liquid. However, return is very low due to safety and backing of the Government for repayment.
2. **Bank Deposits:** Excess cash balance can be placed with banks in the form of deposits. The minimum period for short-term deposit is 14 days. As failure of banks is highly remote, there is no risk virtually with bank deposits. In case of need, they can be cancelled before maturity and funds are available immediately. However, if the deposit does not run for a minimum period of 14 days, no interest is paid on cancellation.
3. **Commercial Paper:** Commercial papers are short-term and unsecured securities issued by highly creditworthy large companies. CP is a negotiable instrument that makes it a marketable security. Detailed coverage has been already made above.
4. **Inter-corporate Deposits:** Inter-corporate lending/borrowing or deposits are a popular form of investment. Excess funds are placed with the sister/associate companies or outside companies of high repute and creditworthiness. Risk default is very high, but returns are attractive.

As they are unsecured in nature, the credit worthiness of borrower should be beyond question. Section of 370 of Companies Act has placed certain restrictions on inter-corporate deposits, which are to be complied with. The intention of the legislature is to provide a cap and diversification of risks. The main provisions are as follows:

(A) A company can not lend more than 10% of its net worth (aggregate of equity and free reserves) to a single company.

(B) The total lending of a company can not exceed 30% of its net worth, without passing a special resolution and obtaining the approval of the Central Government for such lending.

5. **Money Market Mutual Funds: Money markets are the financial markets in which funds are borrowed and loaned for short periods (less than one year).** Money market instruments are forms of debt that mature in less than one year and are very liquid.

The fund so raised by the money market mutual funds would be invested in the money market instruments such as call money, treasury bills, re-discounted bills, GOI securities, and certificates of deposits and commercial papers, with ratings of PI and above.

Money Market Mutual Funds like Unit Trust of India and private players like Kothari Pioneer invest the funds received in short-term marketable securities such as treasury bills, commercial and call money. Investors can withdraw the money at short-notice or over the counter and so highly liquid. They offer attractive yields. The key features are they are easy to trade, liquidated easily and no tax is deducted at source.

Check Your Understanding

(A) State whether the following are True or False

1. Trade credit refers to the credit received by a customer from supplier of goods in the normal course of business.
2. Trade credit is mostly an informal arrangement and is granted on open account.
3. Cash discount is offered as and when cash sale is made.
4. Trade credit is a spontaneous source of financing that is made available increasingly with expansion of business.
5. Trade credit does not involve any additional cost to the buyer while it is an easy source of finance.
6. Accrued expenses are an asset.
7. Technically, cash credit advance is repayable on demand but bank does not recall the advance, if the conduct of account is satisfactory.
8. Commercial paper is an important money market instrument for raising short-term finances at a cheap interest rate.
9. Commercial paper is unsecured in character.
10. Public deposits are always secured.
11. Cash credit, pledge is more convenient to a borrower compared to hypothecation type.
12. Treasury bills are government securities.
13. Commercial paper is a secured instrument.

Answers

1. True 2. True 3. False 4. True 5. False 6. False 7. True 8. True
9. True 10. False 11. False 12. True 13. False.

(B) Objective Questions (Identify what is most appropriate)

1. The basic purpose of short-tem financing is to meet the following requirements.
   (A) Purchase of fixed assets
   (B) Working capital
   (C) Bridge loan
   (D) Meeting share issue expenses

2. The following credit is called as 'Trade credit'.
   (A) Free credit received
   (B) Credit received by a retailer from a wholesaler of goods in normal course of business.
   (C) Credit received from bank
   (D) Credit for which interest is paid, separately

3. The following is a major source of short-term financing.
   (A) Trade credit
   (B) Working capital
   (C) Finance for purchase of fixed assets
   (D) Letter of credit

4. If credit is extended to a retailer by a wholesaler, the amount appears in the balance sheet of a wholesaler as
   (A) Sundry debtor
   (B) Sundry creditor
   (C) Bills payable
   (D) Accounts payable

5. When supplier is not certain of receipt of payment from buyer, the transaction is documented in the following form.
   (A) Sundry debtors
   (B) Bills receivable
   (C) Bills payable
   (D) Bill of exchange

6. Accounts receivable is also known as
   (A) Sundry debtors
   (B) Sundry creditor
   (C) Bills receivable
   (D) Bills payable

7. Accounts payable is also known as
   (A) Sundry debtors
   (B) Sundry creditor
   (C) Bills receivable
   (D) Bills payable

8. The greatest advantage with this instrument is its self-maturing character.
   (A) Bill of exchange
   (B) Sundry creditors
   (C) Bills receivable
   (D) Bills payable

9. When the buyer accepts bills of exchange, this form is replaced in the books of buyer.
   (A) Bills receivable in place of sundry creditor.
   (B) Bills receivable in place of sundry debtor.
   (C) Sundry creditor is replaced by bills payable.
   (D) Sundry debtor is replaced by bills receivable.

10. On acceptance of bill of exchange, this happens in the books of supplier.
    (A) Sundry creditor is replaced by bills receivable
    (B) Bills receivable in place of sundry debtor
    (C) Sundry creditor is replaced by bills payable
    (D) Bills payable is replaced by sundry creditor

11. When a credit sale takes place, the term 'credit terms' refer to this.
    (A) Period taken by buyer for repayment.
    (B) Length of credit period allowed by supplier to buyer for making payment.
    (C) Period allowed by supplier to buyer to avail discount.
    (D) Period of default in payment.
12. When goods are sold by supplier to buyer, the term 'cash discount' arises when this happens.
    (A) Goods are sold for cash. (B) Goods are sold on credit.
    (C) Goods are sold in bulk. (D) Goods are returned, after selling on credit.
13. When goods are sold by supplier to buyer, the term 'trade discount' arises when this happens.
    (A) To sell goods in bulk.
    (B) To sell goods for cash.
    (C) To lure buyer for early payment.
    (D) To make buyer not to return goods.
14. This institution offers trade credit and provides services relating to management of book debts.
    (A) Commercial bank (B) Term lending institution
    (C) Factor (D) Financial institution
15. If an invoice states '1/15, net 30', it means
    (A) Credit period of 15 to 30 days, with a cash discount of 1%.
    (B) Cash discount of 1%, if payment made within 15 days while normal credit period is 30 days.
    (C) Pay within 30 days and avail 1% discount or return goods within 15 days.
    (D) Pay within 15 days and avail 1% discount or return goods within 30 days.
16. The nature of 'accrued expenses' is
    (A) Asset appearing in balance sheet
    (B) Short-term source of finance
    (C) Long-term source of finance
    (D) Expense appearing on profit and loss account
17. This is a normal form of bank finance to meet working capital requirements.
    (A) Cash credit-pledge (B) Cash credit-hypothecation
    (C) Term loan (D) Bridge loan
18. This is a spontaneous source of short-term financing.
    (A) Bank credit (B) Trade credit
    (C) Bridge loan (D) Accrued expenses
19. This is not a short-term source of finance.
    (A) Trade credit (B) Temporary bank borrowing
    (C) Accrued expenses (D) Debenture

20. Calculate drawing power in a cash credit account based on this:

    Value of stocks : ₹ 2,00,000

    Margin : 20%

    (A) 2,00,000 (B) 1,85,000
    (C) 1,60,000 (D) 2,20,000

21. Determine the outstanding balance that a bank can permit in a borrower's cash credit account, based on the following:

    Sanctioned limit : ₹ 1,20,000

    Margin : 25%

    (A) ₹ 1,20,000 (B) ₹ 1,00,000
    (C) ₹ 90,000 (D) ₹ 1,45,000

22. Calculate the amount that can be withdrawn by a borrower in his cash credit account based on the following:

    Sanctioned limit: ₹ 1,00,000

    Margin: 30%

    Outstanding balance: ₹ 20,000 (Dr. balance in bank's books)

    (A) ₹ 50,000 (B) ₹ 1,00,000
    (C) ₹ 80,000 (D) ₹ 1,20,000

23. Identify non-fund based limit.

    (A) Loan (B) Overdraft
    (C) Cash credit (Pledge) (D) Letter of credit

24. Two way operation, deposit as well as withdrawal, is not possible to a borrower in this borrowing method.

    (A) Loan (B) Overdraft
    (C) Cash credit (Hypothecation) (D) Guarantee

25. Supplier insists on a buyer to make the following arrangement to ensure certainty of payment.

    (A) Bill of exchange (B) Letter of credit
    (C) Cash credit (Pledge) (D) Cash credit (Hypothecation)

26. This is the greatest advantage with a cash credit account to the borrower.

    (A) Interest is payable on outstanding balance
    (B) Interest is payable on sanctioned limit
    (C) No interest on this account
    (D) No stocks need to be maintained to borrow

27. In a cash credit (pledge) account, stocks remain in possession of the following person.

    (A) Borrower
    (B) Lock and key in a godown, under control of bank
    (C) Third party who is known to both borrower and bank
    (D) No need of stocks to avail this facility

28. To check diversion of funds, monitor better control on their utilization and ensure self-liquidating character of advance, banks prefer to give this facility to the borrowers.
    (A) Loan (B) Overdraft
    (C) Cash credit (Hypothecation) (D) Purchase or discounting of bills
29. Bank can ensure utilization of funds with this document while sanctioning bill purchase limit to a borrower.
    (A) Invoice (B) Rail receipt or motor receipt
    (C) Bill of exchange (D) Copy of order placed by buyer
30. A limited company should have this minimum tangible net worth to issue commercial paper.
    (A) ₹ 4 crores (B) ₹ 10 crores
    (C) ₹ 15 crores (D) No minimum is fixed
31. A company can issue commercial paper up to this maximum level
    (A) 50% of fund based limit (B) 75% of fund based limit
    (C) 100% of fund based limit (D) 100% of net owned funds
32. The primary requirement while choosing a short-term investment is this.
    (A) High return (B) Long maturity
    (C) Quickest convertibility into cash (D) None of the above
33. The following agency issues treasury bills.
    (A) Reserve Bank of India on behalf of Central Government
    (B) Public sector (C) Private sector
    (D) Any agency
34. In a cash credit account, bank charges interest on this.
    (A) Sanctioned limit (B) Outstanding balance
    (C) Value of stocks (D) Margin

Answers

1. (B)	2. (B)	3. (A)	4. (A)	5. (D)	6. (A)	7. (B)	8. (A)
9. (C)	10. (B)	11. (B)	12. (B)	13. (A)	14. (C)	15. (B)	16. (B)
17. (B)	18. (B)	19. (D)	20. (C)	21. (C)	22. (A)	23. (D)	24. (A)
25. (B)	26. (A)	27. (B)	28. (D)	29. (B)	30. (A)	31. (D)	32. (C)
33. (A)	34. (B)						

Descriptive Questions

1. Detail the different sources of short-term finance and explain whether these forms of finance involve any additional cost to the buyer. **(21.1, 21.2, 21.2.1 to 21.2.3)**
2. Explain the importance and advantages of trade credit as a source of working capital. Whether provision of this source involves any cost to the provider and who bears it, finally? **(21.1 and 21.2.1)**
3. Describe the different types of short-term finance provided by commercial banks for meeting working capital requirements. Is there a way to utilise non-fund based limit for working capital purposes? **(21.4)**

4. Enumerate the various facilities available for meeting working capital requirements, identify the ideal facility of borrowing for business and justify. **(21.4)**
5. What is factoring and explain its limitations? **(21.3)**
6. Explain the criteria that a firm should use in choosing short-term investments and detail the available avenues of investment. **(21.7 and 21.7.1)**

Short Questions

Q.1. Why role of 'liquidity' is important in selection of short-term marketable securities?

Ans. Liquidity refers to the ability to convert into cash immediately, without any significant loss of value.

When a firm has short-term surplus funds, it invests in marketable securities. Its intention of investment is to meet unforeseen needs. Here, purpose is quick availability of funds when needed and return is secondary or incidental. So, the marketable securities should be quickly realisable, without loss of original investment amount when the sudden need arises. Immediate realisation of securities and no loss are the most important features in selection of short-term marketable securities.

While investing surplus funds in short-term investments, liquidity plays the most important role as funds should be available as and when needed at short notice. Firm should not be tempted to invest unless the securities fulfil the primary feature of liquidity.

Q.2. Explain how cash credit account is the most cost effective form of working capital finance for a firm?

Ans. In a cash credit account, borrowing firm can withdraw funds for purchase of goods, services and meeting working capital needs. Firm is allowed to deposit sale proceeds into the same cash credit account. Firm can draw and deposit as many times as it wishes. On account of continuous withdrawal and deposit, the outstanding balance in the cash credit account would be changing from day to day. In consequence, borrower normally does not avail the whole sanctioned limit all days throughout year. Bank charges interest on the outstanding balance on daily product basis. As a result, total interest amount charged to the cash credit account would be lower than the interest rate applicable to the total sanctioned limit for the whole year. By this, borrowing firm would have the flexibility to draw funds as and when needed, paying lower effective interest rate. Cash credit facility is always cheap as compared to a loan.

Q.3. 'There is no guarantee that a borrower utilises the cash credit limit for working capital purposes, alone.' Is it right? Name the alternative form of finance by which bank can better monitor utilization of funds for working capital by borrower?

Ans. Banks cannot monitor the daily utilisation of cash credit limit, once sanctioned. By sanctioning 'Bills purchase limit', banks can regulate better utilization of working capital by borrowers. In bills purchase limit, borrowing firm draws bill of exchange on the buyer of goods or services and discounts the bill with the bank for funds. It is necessary to enclose invoice and supporting proof for goods, like railway receipt/lorry receipt for the goods sold to avail bills purchase limit. By this procedure, utilization of funds can be better monitored by banks. Abuse of working capital is greatly reduced in bills purchase/discount limit compared to cash credit account. More so, bills are self-liquidating in their character and so borrower has to frequently approach the bank for continuous utilisation of limit which may not happen with a cash credit account, if borrower draws funds and does not deposit sale proceeds.

Q.4. What is the basic difference between pledge and hypothecation? Which is operationally more flexible?

Ans. Both pledge and hypothecation are different forms to avail a cash credit limit. In pledge, goods are kept in a godown, keys remain with the bank and bank exercises total control over possession of goods. Unless borrowing firm deposits the proportionate amount of value of goods, bank does not release goods pledged. In a cash credit hypothecation account, possession of the goods lie with the borrower and firm can also sell the goods without the approval of bank. However, borrowing firm has to deposit sale proceeds into the cash credit account. Hypothecation provides more flexibility of operation to borrowers compared to pledge.

Q.5. When banks offer working capital facilities, what is the need of factoring services?

Ans. Banks provide working capital against stock and book debts. Factoring services provides not only working capital against receivables but also offer wider range of incidental management services connected with receivables.

Factor is an institution that provides a wider range of services apart from providing working capital credit against receivables. Their services relate to management of debts arising from credit sales. Factor provides credit against receivables and in this process firm gets funds immediately for credit sales made. Management services relate to maintenance of sales ledger, collection of book debts (Accounts Receivable), rendering advisory services to their clients and protection from bad debts. Factoring may be on recourse basis where risk of bad debts is borne by client firm or on a non-recourse basis where risk of bad debts is borne by factor. Factor services are comprehensive while role of banks in providing working capital is limited to provision of credit, alone.

Q.6. What is the difference between a loan and cash credit account?

Ans. In a loan account, borrower cannot withdraw funds deposited, again, for use. However, in a cash credit account, funds deposited can be withdrawn again to the extent of the sanctioned limit or drawing power, whichever is lower. In other words, cash credit account provides deposits as well as withdrawals upto the drawing power in account, which is based on stocks and margin. Cash credit account provides more flexibility to a borrower compared to a loan account. The effective interest rate in a cash credit account is normally lower than the loan account as no borrower requires the whole sanctioned limit throughout year.

Interview Questions

Q.1. Name the most important characteristics of 'Marketable securities'.

Ans. Liquidity and marketability are the most important characteristics of 'Marketable securities'.

Q.2. Name the most popular form of working capital management.

Ans. Banks sanction cash credit limit to firms for meeting working capital requirements. This is the most popular form of working capital arrangement between banks and borrowing firms.

Q.3. Which form of cash credit is most convenient to a borrower?

Ans. Cash credit-hypothecation form is most convenient to a borrower as he can deal with the goods hypothecated to bank in the ordinary course of business. In other words, firm can sell the goods without approval of bank but has to deposit the sale proceeds into cash credit account. More so, bank charges interest on the actual outstanding balance in cash credit account, not on total limit, which works out very economical to borrowers.

Q.4. What is the meaning of 'Trade credit'?

Ans. Trade credit is an informal arrangement where seller provides credit to the buyer for goods purchased. Trade credit is a spontaneous source of financing. This form of finance is very common in trade.

Q.5. Why bank insists on margin for sanction of cash credit limit?

Ans. Bank does not provide 100% finance for working capital needs. The borrower provides margin. Borrower provides margin from his own sources. Margin ensures commitment of borrower to the business for which borrowing is sought. If margin is 25%, bank provides funds of ₹ 75 and balance of ₹ 25 is provided by the borrower from his own sources. If bank provides 100% of stock value, there would be no financial stake of the borrower.

Q.6. What are Money Markets?

Ans. Money markets are the financial markets in which funds are borrowed and loaned for short periods (less than one year). They provide the opportunity to park funds at good yields, with the option of liquidating them when needed at short notice.

CHAPTER 22

Management of Working Capital

22.1 INTRODUCTION

Working capital may be regarded as lifeblood of a business enterprise. It is closely related to the day-to-day operations of business. Every business needs funds for two purposes—purchase of fixed assets and meeting working capital needs. Long-term funds are required for creation of production facilities such as plant and machinery, land, building and furniture etc. Investment in these assets represents that part of firm's capital, which is permanently blocked on a permanent or fixed basis and is called fixed capital. The form of these assets does not change in the normal course.

Funds are also needed for purchase of raw materials, payment of wages and other day-to-day expenses etc. These funds are known as working capital. Funds invested in these assets keep revolving fast. These assets are converted into cash and again cash is converted into current assets. So, working capital is also called revolving or circulating capital. These assets change form on a continuous basis. In other words, **working capital refers to that part of firm's capital, which is required for financing short-term or current assets such as cash, debtors, inventories and marketable securities etc.**

22.2 MEANING OF WORKING CAPITAL

The term 'working capital' refers to

(i) Those current assets, which are **convertible into cash, within a period of one accounting year** and

(ii) Those **funds needed for meeting day-to-day operations.**

22.3 CONCEPTS OF WORKING CAPITAL

There are two concepts of working capital—gross and net.

Gross working capital: Gross working capital refers to firm's investment in total current assets of enterprise. Current assets are those which can be converted into cash within an accounting year (or operating cycle). They include cash, debtors, bills receivable, stock, prepaid expenses and marketable securities etc. In a broader sense, working capital refers to gross working capital.

Net working capital: In a narrow sense, working capital refers to net working capital. **Net working capital is the difference between current assets and current liabilities.** Current liabilities are those claims of outsiders which are expected to mature for payment within an accounting year. They include creditors, bills payable, bank overdraft/cash credit account and outstanding expenses.

If payment to current liabilities is delayed, firm gets availability of funds to that extent. So, a part of funds required to maintain current assets is financed by the current liabilities. The firm is required to invest in current assets to that extent not financed by the current liabilities.

If current assets are in excess of current liabilities, net working capital is positive. A negative working capital occurs when current liabilities exceed current assets.

Treatment of Bank overdraft/cash credit account: Bank overdraft/cash credit account is treated as current liability as sanction of bank is for one year. It is a different matter bank renews these facilities on a continuous basis at the request of borrower on submission of the required data and particulars. Some authors treat bank overdraft/cash credit account as permanent borrowing, not as current liability, as those funds remain with firm on a continuous basis. As already discussed in Ratio Analysis, in detail, we consider bank overdraft/cash credit account, as a current liability as firm has to repay at the end of one year as the official written sanction of bank is available for one year only.

Gross and Net working capital not exclusive: The two concepts, gross working capital and net working capital, are not exclusive. It means both have equal significance or importance from management's view-point. The gross working capital concept is a financial or going concern concept while net working capital is an accounting concept of working capital. A finance manager must consider both the aspects as they provide different interpretation.

Gross Working Capital Concept: Gross working capital requires consideration from two angles:

(A) How to optimize investment in current assets?

There are two danger points in respect of working capital, excessive or inadequate investment in current assets. Both are equally dangerous.

The basic objective of working capital management is to manage firm's current assets and current liabilities in such a way that working capital is maintained at a satisfactory level.

What is a satisfactory level? **The working capital should be neither more nor less, but just adequate.** Cash is tied in current assets. Funds involve costs. If investment in current assets is excessive, profitability will be greatly affected. If investment in current assets is inadequate, firm experiences difficulty in meeting the current obligations as and when they fall due for payment. Inadequate working capital threatens solvency of firm due to inability to pay current obligations, in time. Both profitability and solvency are equally important. So, management should be prompt to initiate the necessary action to keep working capital adequate to the changing needs of business.

Moreover, different components of working capital are to be balanced. If inventory level is too high in total current assets due to slow moving stocks, it does not provide any cushion in the form of liquidity. Similar is the case with high proportion of accounts receivable, which are difficult to recover. If cash and bank balances are more in total current assets, they are idle and do not contribute to profitability.

It is important to maintain proper level of current assets in the aggregate as well as their individual proportion to optimize investment in current assets.

(B) How should current assets be financed?

The second aspect is arranging funds for financing current assets. Working capital requirement is not static. Its requirement keeps on changing. If business increases, more working capital is needed. If the same business shrinks, idle funds arise. Thus finance manager should have adequate knowledge to tap the different sources of working capital funds at short notice as well as investment avenues, where idle funds may be temporarily invested.

Net Working Capital Concept: Current assets are financed by current liabilities to a large extent. The balance amount of working capital, not financed by current assets, is financed from long-term sources of firm. Long-term sources are shareholders' funds and long-term borrowings. Net working capital, excess of current assets over current liabilities, measures firm's liquidity. This also gives an idea about the buffer available to current liabilities. It indicates margin of protection available to short-term creditors. Net working capital gives more assurance to creditors.

Creditors look for higher net working capital for their safety and promptness in payments. In all net working capital indicates financial soundness of firm. But, higher working capital eats profitability.

To finance manager, net working capital concept is also important to send signals of safety to creditors.

22.4 IMPORTANCE OF WORKING CAPITAL

Cash inflows and outflows are never synchronized. Cash inflows occur with realization of current assets such as stock and debtors. Their realizations are highly unpredictable as the inflows depend on outsiders' actions. Outflows are related with payments to creditors, bills payable and outstanding expenses. They are more predictable and controllable as they depend on the behaviour of firm. However efficient the finance manager may be, certainty of both cash inflows and outflows cannot be predicted with total accuracy. To meet the gap between cash inflows and outflows, working capital is needed.

> **Cash flows are unpredictable. The more these cash flows are predictable, lesser amount of working capital is needed.**

If these cash flows are uncertain, higher amount of working capital is essential for the enterprise.

22.4.1 Need for Working Capital

Every enterprise is not fortunate enough to conduct its business with total cash sales. Credit sales are common in almost every form of business. To support credit sales, working capital is needed in the form of current assets. Working capital is required to carry on day-to-day business activities. While every firm requires working capital, its quantum differs from business to business dependent on nature of activity the firm is engaged in. A retail firm may require lower amount of working capital while a wholesale firm needs more. Similarly, where gestation period is long for production the manufacturing firm requires more amount of working capital. It needs no further emphasis that the requirement of working capital is vital for every business, more so when the objective of each firm is wealth maximization. The amount of working capital depends on operating cycle involved in conversion of sales into cash or the total period needed for converting cash into cash again as cash is the starting for business while cash again is the end point of transaction.

Working Capital Level: It is a conventional rule to maintain level of current assets twice the level of current liabilities. In other words, **current ratio should be 2:1.** However, this is only a crude rule. It all depends on the quality of current assets. If the current assets are totally realizable and qualitative, even a lesser current ratio may be adequate and the firm may not experience any difficulty in meeting current obligations. If the current assets consists more slow moving stocks and more time taking debtors, even a higher ratio may not put the firm at ease for making payments, in time. **The mix of current assets is more important then its mere quantity.**

22.4.2 Impact of Excess or Paucity of Working Capital

Every firm must have sufficient working capital. It should be neither excessive nor inadequate. Both situations are risky and may have dangerous consequences.

Consequences of excessive working capital: If investment in working capital is more than the required level, it may result in unnecessary accumulation of inventories. Funds have costs. So, it is equally applicable to the money tied in working capital. Firm is paying unnecessary costs. If more raw materials are held than needed and firm maintains more finished stocks than the market demands/needs, firm's profitability is affected.

1. **Delays in collections from debtors:** If there is no urgency for funds, certain easy nature prevails in the firm that would result in slackness for collections from debtors. This is also an indication of defective credit policy.
2. **Extending liberal credit:** Firm tends to extend liberal credit to its customers more than the market practice without any corresponding benefit to the firm. Credit may be provided to those customers who do not deserve the credit.
3. **Adverse influence on performance of management:** Several departments may function in a haphazard and lazy manner without the professional approach that would affect overall performance of the management of firm.

Impact of inadequate working capital: Firms would have insufficient working capital to support their operations. Such a situation may result in:

1. **Idle fixed assets:** Fixed assets require raw materials to function with full capacity. In the absence of adequate working capital, fixed assets may not be optimally utilized, resulting in reduced profits.
2. **Loss of business opportunities:** Despite having capacity to manufacture and potentialities to make profits, firm may lose its existing business opportunities just for not having the required working capital support.
3. **Frequent stoppages:** Stoppage of machinery due to lack of raw materials may result in halt of production that may finally result in lower profits.
4. **Growth may stagnate:** Commensurate increase in working capital is required to support growth of a firm. Firm may not be able to register even the normal growth that is prevalent in industry. In consequence, growth may come to a halt.
5. **Loss of goodwill:** Goodwill of the firm may be affected if it is not in a position to meet the current liabilities as and when they fall due for payment.
6. **Cash discounts are lost:** It is customary in trade to extend cash discounts to buyers, who are given credit, to encourage early payments. Normally, cash discount works out profitable to buyers than cost of funds borrowed. However, if the firm is already struggling even to make normal payments in time, it is impossible for such firm to avail such attractive offers in the absence of comfortable working capital position.

It is necessary for each firm to build up a suitable policy and monitor periodically. It has to decide:

(i) What should be the total and individual current assets to the expected sales level?

(ii) Financing pattern of the working capital needs of the firm.

Working capital should be a judicious mix: Working capital should be a judicious mix of long-term and short-term funds for financing its current assets. The permanent component of current assets should be financed by long-term sources such as equity share capital, preference share capital, debentures, long-term loan and retained earnings. Each firm should decide the mix of short-term and long-term funds depending on their availability and risk the firm is prepared to assume. There is no hard and fast rule for deciding the exact quantum of working capital as the requirements of business fluctuates. Similarly, there is no specific rule how the current assets are to be financed. But, one thing is clear. There should be proper judicious mix and whatever funds are raised, they should be put to productive use.

22.5 ESTIMATION OF WORKING CAPITAL REQUIREMENT - METHODS

Estimation Process: Estimation of working capital is essential for smooth running of business. Every firm has to estimate its working capital requirements in advance for proper planning. Only then it can divide into permanent and temporary working capital and plan to raise the funds according to the category. Firm has different approaches to estimate working capital requirements.

22.5.1 Methods of Working Capital Requirement

1. **Operating cycle:** The most appropriate method for calculating working capital requirement is the concept of operating cycle.

In operating cycle method, working capital requirement is expressed in terms of length of operating cycle, i.e. number of days.

Efficiency of working capital management is evaluated in terms of actual days against the original operating cycle planned or anticipated. If actual operating cycle is higher than the planned operating cycle, it shows more working capital is tied up.

> **Lesser operating cycle against the planned operating cycle is a prima facie sign of efficiency in working capital management.**

2. **Working Capital in terms of Amount:** Working capital is expressed in terms of amount based on current assets and current liabilities holding period. The basis is the operating cycle but working capital amount is expressed in terms of amount. This method is popular with the banks as banks would like to know the working capital requirement in terms of amount for sanctioning working capital limits.

3. **Working capital as a percentage of Net Sales:** The assumption is working capital requirement is directly related to sales volume of firm. If sales increase, need

of working capital also increases. There are three steps involved in estimation of working capital requirement:

Estimation of current assets as a percentage of net sales

Estimation of current liabilities as a percentage of net sales

Difference between the two above is the net working capital as a percentage of net sales.

4. **Working capital as a percentage of Fixed Assets or Total Assets:** For proper utilization of fixed assets, it is necessary to have supporting capital in the form of gross working capital (current assets) or net working capital (current assets – current liabilities). Then only fixed assets can be utilized in an efficient and optimal way. Mere fixed assets do not generate profits. To provide service to customers, current assets are also needed.

> **No movie normally can be made without a hero and heroine. In the picture of a successful organization, if fixed assets are hero, working capital is heroine. There should be suitable mix between the two.**

Instead of fixed assets, total assets can be the basis too for calculating working capital requirement.

Amongst the different methods, working capital in terms of amount based on operating cycle is the most popular form.

22.6 OPERATING CYCLE

The operating cycle may be defined as time duration starting from procurement of goods or raw materials and ending with sales realization in the form of cash. The length and nature of operating cycle may differ from one firm to another depending upon the size and nature of the firm. Basically, this is the length of period required to procure resources such as materials, power etc. and convert into cash. In other words, time taken to convert cash into cash is called operating cycle. The operating cycle of a manufacturing firm, typically, involves three phases:

- **Acquisition of resources** such as raw material, labour, power and fuel etc.
- **Manufacture of the product** which includes conversion of raw material into work-in-process into finished products.
- **Sale of the product** either for cash or credit sales. Credit sales result into debtors or accounts receivable.

The operating cycle can be presented in a pictorial form.

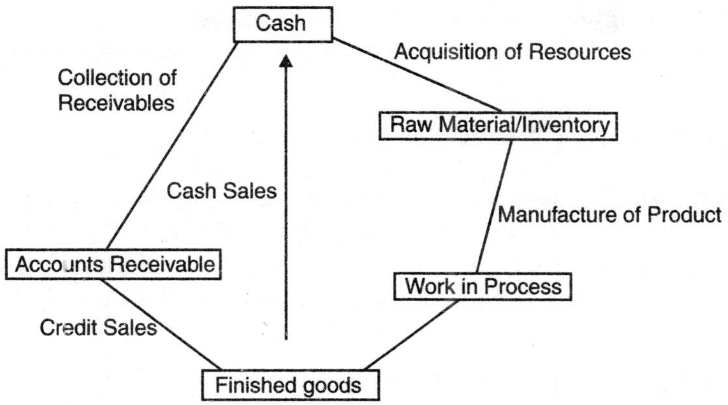

Operating Cycle in a manufacturing firm

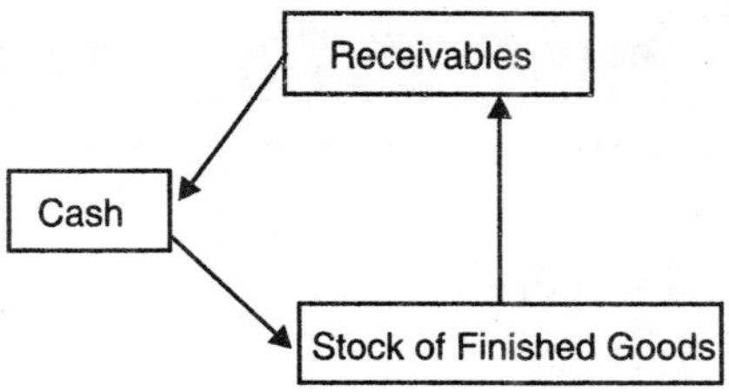

Operating Cycle in a non-manufacturing firm

The length of the operating cycle is the sum of:

(i) **Inventory Conversion Period:** The inventory conversion period includes raw materials conversion period, work-in-process conversion period and finished goods conversion period. So, it is the total period required for converting raw materials into finished goods.

(ii) **Debtors Conversion Period:** It is the period required for collecting credit sales into cash.

The aggregate of Inventory conversion period and debtors' conversion period is known as 'Gross Operating Cycle'. Firms are able to purchase raw materials on credit and also postpone payments for services such as wages, rent etc. and the period is known as 'Payables Deferral Period'. The difference between gross operating cycle and payables deferral period is known as 'Net Operating Cycle'.

When cash sales are involved the length of the operating cycle is short as there is no debtors' conversion period.

Estimation of Working Capital with Operating Cycle: With operating cycle method, working capital can be calculated in the form of length of operating cycle i.e. number of days. As depreciation is a non-cash expense, depreciation is to be excluded from expenses to compute cash operating cycle. Actual operating cycle would be compared with the anticipated operating cycle to evaluate performance of working capital management. If net operating cycle increases, requirement of working capital would increase and vice versa.

The method of calculation of operating cycle is as under:

Gross Operating Cycle = Inventory Conversion Period + Debtors' Conversion Period

Inventory Conversion Period (ICP) is the sum of Raw Materials Conversion Period (RMCP), Work-in-Process Conversion Period (WIPCP) and Finished Goods Conversion Period (FGCP).

$$\text{ICP} = \text{RMCP} + \text{WIPCP} + \text{FGCP}$$

Net Operating Cycle is the difference between the gross operating cycle and payables deferral period.

Net Operating Cycle = Gross Operating Cycle – Payables Deferral Period

The formulae for calculation of the different components are:

$$\text{Raw materials conversion period} = \frac{\text{Average raw materials held}}{\text{Total raw material consumption}} \times 365$$

Average is calculated by averaging total of opening and closing balance of raw materials stock held by firm.

$$\text{Work-in-progress conversion period} = \frac{\text{Average work-in-progress}}{\text{Total cost of production}} \times 365$$

$$\text{Finished goods conversion period} = \frac{\text{Average finished goods}}{\text{Total cost of goods sold}} \times 365$$

$$\text{Debtors' conversion period} = \frac{\text{Average debtors}}{\text{Total credit sales}} \times 365$$

$$\text{Payables deferral period} = \frac{\text{Average debtors}}{\text{Total credit purchases}} \times 365$$

Importance of operating cycle: If operating cycle is long, more working capital would be tied up in the operations of firm. Effort of every firm is to reduce the length of operating cycle so that working capital requirement is reduced. Once working capital requirement is reduced, firm can improve profitability. Length of operating cycle can be reduced by decreasing production cycle period and collection period of debtors. It means reducing the production period of a product and accelerating collections from credit sales.

Difference between net operating cycle and cash conversion cycle: If depreciation is excluded from expenses in the computation of operation cycle, the net operating cycle represents cash conversion cycle.

In other words, if the cost structure of a company does not have depreciation, cash conversion cycle and net operating cycle mean the same.

Illustration No. 1

From the following data, calculate cash conversion cycle.

Average raw materials period	: 90 days
Average work-in-progress period	: 15 days
Average period of holding finished goods	: 30 days
Average collection period of accounts receivables	: 50 days
Average period of credit received from suppliers	: 25 days

Solution

Cash conversion cycle or net operating cycle is calculated as under:

Cash conversion cycle: Gross operating cycle – Payables deferral period

Gross operating cycle = Inventory conversion period + Debtor's conversion period

= 90 + 15 + 30 + 50 = 185 days

Cash conversion cycle: 185 – 25 = 160 days

Illustration No. 2

Abhishekh & Co is engaged in making garments for kids. It provides the following information and requests you to calculate its operating cycle.

	₹
Sales	3,00,000
Inventory:	
Opening	40,000
Closing	30,000
Receivables:	
Opening	80,000
Closing	60,000
Cost of goods sold	2,60,000

Solution

1. Finished goods holding period

$$\frac{\text{Average finished goods stock}}{\text{Total cost of sales}} \times 365 = \frac{35,000 \times 365}{2,60,000} = 49 \text{ Days}$$

Average stock = (opening stock + closing stock)/2

= (40,000 + 30,000)/2

= 35,000

2. Debtors holding period

$$\frac{\text{Average debetors}}{\text{Credit sales}} \times 365 = \frac{70,000 \times 365}{3,00,000} = 85 \text{ Days}$$

Where average debtors = (Opening debtors + closing debtors)/2

= (80,000 + 60,000)/2 = 70,000

3. Gross operating cycle (1+2) = 134 days

Illustration No. 3

Shankar & Co is engaged in manufacturing toys. Following data of the company is made available:

	₹
Opening stock	4,000
Average stock	10,000
Cost of sales	80,000
Total purchases	2,50,000
Credit purchases	2,00,000
Creditors' holding	40 days
Opening creditors	3,000
Debtors' holding	45 days
Opening debtors	5,000
Cash sales	50,000
Total sales	1,80,000

Calculate operating cycle and number of operating cycles in a year. Also find out the missing figures—closing stock, closing debtors and closing creditors.

Solution

Gross operating cycle of Shankar & Co:

1. **Finished goods holding period**

$$\frac{\text{Average finished goods stock}}{\text{Total cost of sales}} \times 365 = \frac{10,000 \times 365}{80,000} = 46 \text{ Days}$$

Average stock = (opening stock + closing stock)/2

10,000 = (4,000 + Closing stock)/2

Closing stock = 20,000 – 4,000 = 16,000

2. **Debtors holding period**

$$\frac{\text{Average debtors} \times 365}{\text{Credit sales}} = \frac{\text{Average debtors} \times 365}{1,30,000} = 45 \text{ Days}$$

$$\text{Average debtors} = \frac{45 \times 1,30,000}{365} = 16,027$$

Average debtors = (Opening debtors + Closing debtors)/2

= (5,000 + Closing debtors)/2 = 16,027

Closing debtors = (2 × 16,027) – 5,000 = 27,054

3. **Gross Operating Cycle (1+2) = 91 days**
4. **Creditors holding period**

$$\frac{\text{Average creditors} \times 365}{\text{Credit purchases}} = \frac{\text{Average creditors} \times 365}{2,00,000} = 40 \text{ Days}$$

$$\text{Average creditors} = \frac{2,00,000 \times 40}{365} = 21,918$$

Average creditors = (Opening creditors + Closing creditors)/2

= (3,000 + Closing creditors)/2 = 21,918

Closing creditors = (2 × 21,918) – 3,000 = 40,836

Net Operating Cycle (3 – 4) = 51 days

Number of operating cycles in a year = $\frac{365}{51} = 7.15$

Illustration No. 4

Anuradha & Co. wants to know its cash conversion cycle and the relevant data of firm is as under:

	₹
Sales	2,50,000
Total purchases	2,20,000
Cash purchases	20,000
Cost of sales	2,15,000

	Finished goods	Debtors	Creditors
Opening balance	25,000	50,000	40,000
Closing balance	20,000	60,000	45,000

Solution

Cash conversion cycle means net operating cycle.

Gross operating cycle of Anuradha & Co:

1. **Finished Goods**

$$\frac{\text{Average finished goods stock} \times 365}{\text{Total cost of sales}} = \frac{22,500 \times 365}{2,15,000} = 38 \text{ days}$$

Where average finished stock = (Opening stock + Closing stock)/2

= (25,000 + 20,000)/2 = 22,500

2. **Debtors**

$$\frac{\text{Average debtors} \times 365}{\text{Credit sales}} = \frac{55,000 \times 365}{2,50,000} = 80 \text{ days}$$

Where Average Debtors = (Opening Debtors + Closing Debtors)/2

= (50,000 + 60,000)/2 = 55,000

3. **Gross operating cycle (1+2)= 118 days**

4. **Creditors**

$$\frac{\text{Average creditors}}{\text{Credit purchases}} \times 365 = \frac{42{,}500 \times 365}{2{,}00{,}000} = 78 \text{ days}$$

Where average creditors = (Opening creditors + Closing creditors)/2

= (40,000 + 45,000)/2 = 42,500

Cash conversion cycle (Net Operating Cycle) (3 – 4) = 40 days

Illustration No. 5

Anisha Ltd. is engaged in manufacturing ready-made garments. The following data relates to garments industry:

	Days
Raw materials holding period	30
Credit provided by suppliers	–10
Work-in-progress holding period	8
Finished goods holding period	30
Debtors' collection period	30
	88 Days

Using the following data, calculate working capital cycle of Anisha Ltd., and offer your comments, briefly. Draw tentative conclusion.

	(₹ In thousands)
Opening stock—Raw materials	200
Total purchases—Raw materials	3,000
Cash purchases—Raw materials	500
Closing stock—Raw materials	100
Average work-in-progress	70
Average finished goods stock	90
Average debtors	200
Average creditors	120
Total sales	5,000
Cash sales	800
Cost of sales	3,200**

Solution

Operating cycle of Anisha Ltd.

1. **Raw material**

$$\frac{\text{Average stocks of raw material}}{\text{Total raw materials consumption}^*} \times 365 = \frac{150 \times 365}{3,100} = 18 \text{ days}$$

Where average stock of raw materials = (Opening stock + Closing stock) /2
= (200 + 100) /2 = 150

* Total raw material consumption = Opening stock + Total purchases – Closing stock
= 200 + 3,000 –100
= 3,100

2. **Work-in-progress**

$$\frac{\text{Average work-in-progress}}{\text{Total cost of production}^{**}} \times 365 = \frac{70 \times 365}{3,200} = 8 \text{ days}$$

3. **Finished Goods**

$$\frac{\text{Average finished goods stock}}{\text{Total cost of production}^{**}} \times 365 = \frac{90 \times 365}{3,200} = 10 \text{ days}$$

4. **Debtors**

$$\frac{\text{Average debtors}}{\text{Credit sales}} \times 365 = \frac{200 \times 365}{4,200} = 17 \text{ days}$$

5. **Gross operating cycle**

(1 + 2 + 3 + 4) = 53 days

6. **Creditors**

$$\frac{\text{Average creditors}}{\text{Credit purchases}} \times 365 = \frac{120 \times 365}{2,500} = 18 \text{ days}$$

7. **Net Operating Cycle (5 – 6)** = 35 days

** Cost of sales is also cost of production, in the absence of selling and administrative costs.

Comments: For Anisha Ltd., the net operating cycle is 35 days. Firm's operating cycle is lower compared to the industry, which is 88 days. The following points deserve consideration:

1. **Raw materials:** Holding of the firm is 18 days, while industry's average is 30 days. Firm may not be getting adequate supplies as it is taking longer period of credit – 18 days against the stipulated credit period of 10 days allowed by suppliers. As suppliers are unwilling to provide credit, raw materials holding is low.
2. **Work-in-progress:** This period is 8 days, which is in line with the average of the industry.
3. **Finished goods:** Period of holding for finished goods is 10 days, which is substantially lower than the industry period of 30 days. This confirms that the firm is experiencing difficulty in getting and maintaining adequate stock of finished goods.
4. **Debtors:** Firm is giving a credit period of 17 days, while the whole industry extends a credit facility of 30 days. Firm may be giving lower credit due to inadequacy of working capital. Lower operating cycle is a supporting point that the firm's working capital is low. Firm may be deliberately extending a lower credit period due to working capital inadequacy. Firm may be missing business opportunities due to provision of lower credit period.
5. **Creditors:** Firm is delaying payments to its creditors. It is taking a longer credit period of 18 days against the credit period allowed 10 days. For this reason, probably, firm is not getting adequate supplies of raw materials. No supplier would provide more credit than the market practice. More so, no credit comes freely too.

Tentative Conclusion: Firm is experiencing working capital problem as its net operating cycle is grossly lower (35 days) than the operating cycle of the industry (88 days). Shorter credit period to buyers and lower stock holding of raw materials are also pointers in this direction. Firm has to increase its working capital requirement from its long-term sources.

Illustration No. 6

Adarsh & Co. Ltd deal in sports goods. Their profit and loss account and balance sheet for the year ended on 31st March, 2009 are given below. Calculate working capital requirement using operating cycle method.

Trading and Profit and Loss Account of Adarsh & Co. Ltd.
for the year ended 31st March, 2009

Particulars	₹	Particulars	₹
To Opening stock:		By Cash sales	1,20,000
Raw Materials	20,000	Credit sales	8,80,000
Work-in-progress	5,000	By Closing stock	
Finished goods	10,000	Raw materials	40,000
To Credit purchases	6,00,000	Work-in-progress	6,000
To Cash purchases	1,50,000	Finished goods	25,000
To Wages	50,000		
To Manufacturing expenses	60,000		
To Gross profit c/ d	1,76,000		
	10,71,000		10,71,000
To Administrative expenses	6,000	By Gross profit c/ d	1,76,000
Selling expenses	60,000		
Distribution expenses	10,000		
Net Profit	1,00,000		
	1,76,000		1,76,000

Balance Sheet of Adarsh & Co. Ltd. as on 31st March, 2009

Liabilities	₹	Assets	₹
Share capital		Fixed assets	6,42,000
(Equity share capital - F.V. ₹ 10 each)	4,00,000	Closing stock:	
		Raw materials	40,000
Profit and loss account	1,00,000	Work-in-progress	6,000
Debentures	2,00,000	Finished goods	25,000
Creditors	40,000	Debtors	30,000
Bills payable	20,000	Bills receivable	12,000
		Cash and bank	5,000
	7,60,000		7,60,000

Opening debtors and opening bills receivable are 25,000 and 35,000 respectively while opening creditors and opening bills payable are 15,000 and 12,000.

Solution

1. Raw material

$$\frac{\text{Average stocks of raw material}}{\text{Total raw materials consumption *}} \times 365 = \frac{30,000 \times 365}{7,30,00} = 15 \text{ days}$$

Where average raw material = (20,000 + 40,000)/2 = 30,000

Raw materials consumed = 20,000 + 6,00,000 + 1,50,000 – 40,000

= 7,30,000

2. Work-in-progress

$$\frac{\text{Average work-in-progress}}{\text{Total cost of production}} \times 365 = \frac{5,500 \times 365}{8,39,000} = 2 \text{ days}$$

Where average work-in-progress = (5,000 + 6,000)/2 = 5,500

Total cost of production = 5,000 + 7,30,000* + 50,000 + 60,000 – 6,000

= 8,39,000

* Raw materials consumption

3. Finished Goods

$$\frac{\text{Average finished goods stock}}{\text{Total cost of sales}} \times 365 = \frac{17,500 \times 365}{9,00,000} = 7 \text{ days}$$

Where average finished goods = (10,000 + 25,000)/2 = 17,500

Total cost of sales = 10,000 + 8,39,000** + 6,000 + 60,000 + 10,000 – 25,000 = 9,00,000

**Total cost of production

4. Debtors

$$\frac{\text{Average debtors + Average bills receivable}}{\text{Credit sales}} \times 365 = \frac{25,500 \times 365}{8,80,000} = 11 \text{ days}$$

Where average debtors + Average bills receivable are (25,000 + 35,000 + 30,000 + 12,000)/4 = 25,500

5. Gross Operating Cycle

$$(1 + 2 + 3 + 4) = 35 \text{ days}$$

6. Creditors

$$\frac{\text{Average creditors} + \text{Average bills payable}}{\text{Credit purchases}} \times 365 = \frac{21{,}750 \times 365}{6{,}00{,}000} = 13 \text{ days}$$

Where average creditors/Average bills payable are

$$= (15{,}000 + 12{,}000 + 40{,}000 + 20{,}000)/4$$
$$= 21{,}750$$

7. Net Operating Cycle (5 – 6) = 22 days

Illustration No. 7

From the following information extracted from the books of Mukesh Ltd., compute the operating cycle:

		(₹ In thousands)
Total sales		820
Cash sales		200
Credit purchases		480
Cash purchases		100
Cost of goods sold		400
Opening stock of inventory		20
Closing stock of inventory		30
Debtors:	Opening	50
	Closing	60
Creditors:	Opening	30
	Closing	20

Solution

$$\text{Average inventory} = \frac{\text{Opening stock} + \text{Closing stock}}{2}$$
$$= \frac{20{,}000 + 30{,}000}{2}$$
$$= 25{,}000$$

Inventory conversion period

$$\frac{\text{Average inventory}}{\text{Total cost of sales}} \times 365 = \frac{25{,}000 \times 365}{4{,}00{,}000} = 23 \text{ days}$$

Average Debtors $= \frac{\text{Opening debtors} + \text{Closing debtors}}{2}$

$= \frac{50,000 + 60,000}{2}$

$= 55,000$

Debtors conversion period

$= \frac{\text{Average debtors}}{\text{Credit sales}} \times 365 = \frac{55,000 \times 365}{6,20,000} = 32 \text{ days}$

Average Creditors $= \frac{\text{Opening creditors} + \text{Closing creditors}}{2}$

$= \frac{30,000 + 20,000}{2}$

$= 25,000$

Creditors conversion period

$= \frac{\text{Average creditors}}{\text{Credit purchases}} \times 365 = \frac{25,000 \times 365}{4,80,000} = 19 \text{ days}$

Gross Operating cycle:

Inventory conversion period + Debtors conversion period – Creditors conversion period

= 23 + 32 – 19

= 36 days

Illustration No. 8

Dimpy Ltd. has obtained the following data concerning the average working capital cycle for other companies in the same industry:

Raw material holding period	20 days
Credit received	– 40 days
Work-in-progress holding period	15 days
Finished goods stock holding period	40 days
Debtors' collection period	60 days
	95 days

Using the following data, calculate the current working capital cycle for Dimpy Ltd. Briefly comment on the policies of the firm in respect of working capital management. Give suggestions for improving profitability, if the data provides any clues.

	(₹ In thousands)
Credit sales	5,000
Total cost of sales	4,000
Cost of production	3,000
Purchases	3,500
Total raw materials consumed	600
Average raw material stock	80
Average work-in-progress	85
Average finished goods stock	180
Average creditors	700
Average debtors	350

Solution

Operating cycle of Dimpy Ltd:

1. **Raw materials conversion period**

$$\frac{\text{Average stock of raw materials}}{\text{Total raw materials consumption}} \times 365 = \frac{80 \times 365}{600} = 49 \text{ days}$$

2. **Work-in-progress conversion period**

$$\frac{\text{Average work-in-progress}}{\text{Total cost of production}} \times 365 = \frac{85 \times 365}{3,000} = 10 \text{ days}$$

3. **Finished goods conversion period**

$$\frac{\text{Average finished goods stock}}{\text{Total cost of sales}} \times 365 = \frac{180 \times 365}{4,000} = 16 \text{ days}$$

4. **Debtors**

$$\frac{\text{Average debtors}}{\text{Credit sales}} \times 365 = \frac{350 \times 365}{5,000} = 26 \text{ days}$$

5. **Gross operating cycle**

(1 + 2 + 3 + 4) = 101 days

6. **Creditors**

$$\frac{\text{Average creditors}}{\text{Credit purchases}} \times 365 = \frac{700 \times 365}{3,500} = 73 \text{ days}$$

Credit period granted by creditors = 73 days

7. **Net operating cycle** (5 – 6) = 28 days

Comments: Dimpy Ltd.'s operating cycle is 28 days, which is very much below the industry's average of 95 days. No doubt, a lower operating cycle involves a lower investment in net current assets. However, the following points deserve specific consideration about the individual elements of working capital. This is necessary to find out the business opportunities, the firm may be missing to improve the overall efficiency of the business:

(a) The stock holding of raw materials is 49 days, considerably higher than average of 20 days for the industry. There is heavy accumulation of stocks. So, there is a need to review stock control procedures.

(b) The period of credit availed from creditors is 73 days against the average of 40 days. There is abnormal delay in making payments to creditors. So, Dimpy Ltd. is delaying the payments to creditors highly beyond the normal credit period of the industry. This factor of abnormal delay is an indication of inadequacy of working capital. Although this is an additional source of finance, it may result in a higher cost of raw materials or loss of goodwill among the suppliers. When suppliers are aware of the abnormal delay in payment schedule, they may be charging a higher price to compensate the interest loss. Abnormal period of credit is never free in business.

(c) The finished goods stock holding is 16 days, which is below the average of 40 days for the industry. This may be due to high demand for the firm's goods or efficient stock control. A low finished goods stock is likely to reduce sales as it can cause delivery delays. Another reason may be, firm may not be maintaining the total range of stocks and concentrating only on the fast moving goods. This may be a reason for missing the sales opportunities, otherwise available.

(d) Debts are collected more quickly than average. The firm is extending a credit period of 26 days only against the average of 60 days. The company might have shortened the period of credit extended deliberately due to working capital inadequacy. May be, the firm could have offered heavy cash discounts for early payment. Good credit control procedures may not be the likely reason.

Any abnormal feature requires detailed investigation. It is advisable to inquire about the policy relating to credit period allowed for debtors. We have information about the industry alone but not about the firm's policies, which is also vital for commenting about the efficiency of working capital management.

Final conclusion: It shows the firm is grossly inadequate with the working capital, as finished goods holding is highly below the industry level. Another indicator is debtors' credit period, very low compared to the credit normally extended by industry. Firm has to find out the reasons for heavy raw materials' holding. If raw materials' holding is reduced, funds that are tied up would be available to improve the low stock level of finished stocks. If the firm makes necessary arrangements for improving its working capital, it is likely to improve sales and profitability further.

Working capital in terms of days/amount: Working capital is quantified in terms of days (operating cycle) or amount (requirement). Terms like stock/stock holding/stock conversion period/stock turnover are often used in numericals. If expressed in days, the concerned term is with reference to operating cycle. If shown in rupees, the same term is in terms of amount. Same is the treatment with debtors/debtors holding/debtors conversion period and creditors/creditors holding/creditors conversion period for solving the problems.

Illustration No. 9

Neelesh & Co. has obtained the following data concerning the average working capital cycle for the competing firm Dheeresh & Co. in the same industry:

Raw materials stock turnover	25 days
Work-in-progress turnover	10 days
Finished goods stock turnover	15 days
Debtors' collection period	30 days
	80 days
Creditors' payment period	30 days

Using the following data, calculate the current working capital cycle for Neelesh Ltd. and briefly comment on it, adding suggestions for improvement of working capital management. Analyse the data for exploring missing business opportunities, if any.

	(₹ In thousands)
Total sales	4,000
(includes cash sales 1,000)	
Cost of production	2,400
Cost of sales	3,000
Total purchases	800
(Credit purchases 700)	
Average raw material stock	90
Average work-in-progress	100
Average finished goods stock	200
Average creditors	100
Average debtors	450
Closing stock	—

Solution

Operating cycle of Neelesh & Co.

1. **Raw material**

$$\frac{\text{Average raw materials}}{\text{Total raw materials consumption}} \times 365 = \frac{90 \times 365}{800} = 41 \text{ days}$$

2. **Work-in-progress**

$$\frac{\text{Average work-in-process}}{\text{Total cost of production}} \times 365 = \frac{100 \times 365}{2,400} = 15 \text{ days}$$

3. **Finished goods**

$$\frac{\text{Average stock}}{\text{Total cost of sales}} \times 365 = \frac{200 \times 365}{3,000} = 24 \text{ days}$$

4. **Debtors**

$$\frac{\text{Average debtors}}{\text{Total credit sales}} \times 365 = \frac{450 \times 365}{3,000} = 55 \text{ days}$$

5. **Creditors**

$$\frac{\text{Average creditors}}{\text{Credit purchases}} \times 365 = \frac{100 \times 365}{700} = 52 \text{ days}$$

6. **Gross operating cycle** = 1 + 2 + 3 + 4
= 41 days + 15 days + 24 days + 55 days = 135 days

7. **Net operating cycle** = 6 – 5
= (41 days + 15 days + 24 days + 55 days) – 52 days
= 135 days – 52 days = 83 days

Comments and suggestions for improvement: For Neelesh & Co. the gross working capital cycle is 135 days, which is far above his competitor Dheeresh & Co. (80 days). Even the net operating cycle (83 days) is also more than his competitor (50 days).

Analysis shows the following reasons:

(A) Stock of raw materials is considerably higher. Holding of the firm is 41 days against that of competitor (25 days). This situation indicates that the stock control procedures are to be reviewed for reducing the inventory holding as funds are tied up, without adequate utilization. This may be the cause for delayed payment to its creditors.

(B) Work-in-progress cycle (15 days) is also more than the competitor, which is only 10 days. Sophisticated techniques adopted by the competitor in respect of manufacturing process needs inquiry.

(C) Finished stock is 24 days while it is only 15 days for the competitor. This may be due to lack of demand for the firm's goods or inefficient stock control procedures.

Inquiries are to be made whether the firm is holding any non-moving inventory. A comparison is to be made in respect of the range of materials maintained by both the firms and further analysis is to be made which product is more non-moving for initiating specific action.

(D) Debtor's collection period is 55 days while that of competitor is 30 days. This area requires improvement either by employing good credit control procedures or offering cash discount for early payment.

(E) Firm is taking 52 days to make payment to its creditors while its competitor is taking only 30 days. Reasons for this delay are to be inquired and whether this abnormal delay is affecting the firm in the form of increased prices and consequent profitability.

Firm has to concentrate to reduce its inventory holding of raw materials. Funds that are freed from better inventory control can be utilized for making payments to its creditors in time and take advantage of cash discounts, if any, to improve profitability of the firm. A thorough investigation is needed whether the firm is holding non-moving inventory.

Illustration No. 10

From the following information extracted from the books of Kalyan & Co., engaged in manufacturing activity, compute the operating cycle in terms of days and amount of working capital needed for the firm.

Period covered	365 days
Average period of credit allowed by suppliers	20 days
	(₹ In '000)
Average total debtors outstanding	480
Raw materials consumption	4,400
Total production cost	10,000
Total cost of sales	10,500
Sales for the year	16,000
Value of average stock maintained:	
Raw materials	320
Work-in-progress	350
Finished goods	260

Solution

Computation of Operating Cycle

(i) Raw materials held in stock

$$\frac{\text{Average stocks of raw materials held}}{\text{Total raw materials consumption}} \times 365 = \frac{320 \times 365}{4400} = 27 \text{ days}$$

(ii) Work-in-progress

$$\frac{\text{Average work-in-progress}}{\text{Total cost of production}} \times 365 = \frac{350 \times 365}{10{,}000} = 13 \text{ days}$$

(iii) Finished goods held in stock

$$\frac{\text{Average finished goods}}{\text{Total cost of sales}} \times 365 = \frac{260 \times 365}{10{,}500} = 9 \text{ days}$$

(iv) Credit period allowed to debtors

$$\frac{\text{Average debtors}}{\text{Total credit sales}} \times 365 = \frac{480 \times 365}{16{,}000} = 11 \text{ days}$$

Gross operating cycle period (i) + (ii) + (iii) + (iv)	60 days
Less: Average credit period allowed by suppliers	20 days
Net Operating Cycle Period	40 days

Number of operating cycles in a year = 365/40

= 9

$$\text{Amount of working capital required} = \frac{\text{Total cost of sales}}{\text{Number of operating cycles in a year}}$$

= 10,500/9

= 1,167

= ₹ 11,67,000

22.7 CLASSIFICATION OF WORKING CAPITAL—PERMANENT AND VARIABLE WORKING CAPITAL

The working capital is classified in two ways:

(A) On the basis of concept

(B) On the basis of time

On the basis of concept, working capital is classified as gross and net working capital, as discussed earlier.

On the basis of time, working capital is divided into two types:

(A) Permanent or fixed working capital

(B) Temporary or variable working capital

(A) Permanent or fixed working capital: Permanent or fixed working capital is that portion of working capital, which is necessarily required to carry on business operations. This amount is permanent in business as fixed assets are. For example, a certain amount of inventory or receivables is permanent in the business, irrespective of the volume of sales. This level would remain constant during the peak as well as non-peak season. In other words, this level does not fluctuate with the change in volume of business.

(B) Fluctuating or variable working capital: The extra working capital needed to support the changing production and sales is called the fluctuating or variable working capital. The classical example is Diwali period when sales are normally high. To manufacture the increased inventory, more raw materials are needed and equally work-in-process would also be more during the period of production. Once the season is over, increased inventory held for the season disappears. This picture appears in all seasonal business too. In seasonal industries, inventory would be the highest during the peak season. During the sugar cane crushing season, inventory level would be the highest when the season is in progress. Once season is over and inventory is sold, the working capital level would be the lowest.

Trends in Stable and Growing Firms: In case of stable firms permanent working capital is constant while the variable working capital increases and decreases, in other words fluctuates. This trend is seen in the following diagram.

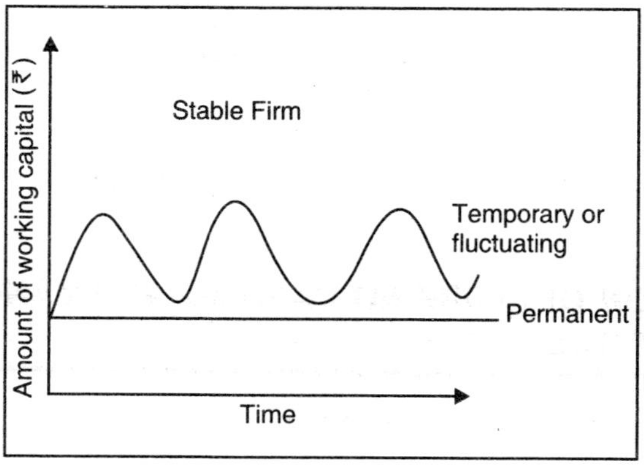

Stable Firm: Permanent and Temporary Working Capital

In progressive or growing firms, the permanent working capitals increases on a continuous basis to support the increasing trend of production and sales, unlike in stable firms. The temporary working capital increases or decreases similar to stable firms. So requirements of working capital would continuously increase in the growing firm as seen in the following diagram.

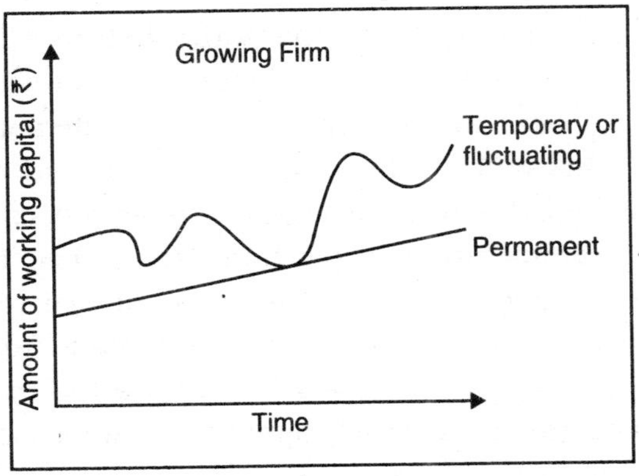

Growing Firm: Permanent and Temporary Working Capital

22.8 FACTORS OR DETERMINANTS OF WORKING CAPITAL

There are no set rules or formulae to determine the working capital requirements. The factors that influence the requirements vary from time to time. They cannot be ranked in the order of importance as the importance of each factor differs over time. However, the following is the description of the factors, which generally influence the requirement of working capital.

1. **Nature or character of business: Working capital requirement basically depends on the nature of business.** Public utility undertakings (like railways, water supply and electricity firms) deal in supply of services, not products, so they do not require any investment in inventory and receivables as their sales are total cash sales. So their working capital requirement is limited while they abundantly invest in fixed assets. However, trading and financial companies invest heavy amount in inventory and receivables so their working capital requirement is large. For example, a retail shop maintains heavy inventory to suit the varied tastes of clientele. For a housing construction firm, houses built for sale are the current assets as they are meant for sale, not to live in. So investment in working capital (houses built for sale) is more, with less investment in fixed assets. So it can be said that public utility undertakings stand on one extreme while trading and financial companies on the other extreme for working capital needs. In between these two extremes, manufacturing companies stand with a substantial amount of investment both in fixed assets as well as in working capital.

2. **Size of business/Scale of operations:** The working capital requirements are largely determined by the size of the unit or scale of operations. **If enterprise is big, the requirements are large and to a small firm, the requirements are low.** In some cases, even small units may require more working capital due to inefficient utilization of funds, high overhead charges and other economic disadvantages.
3. **Sales and demand conditions:** The working capital needs of a firm are directly related to sales. The firm has to build inventory before sales are expected. It is a normal feature to see heavy piles of stock before festival season. During the festive season, demand is large and to meet the anticipated demand, firms plan building up stock in advance. This type of demand is seasonal and during that period only additional working is needed. Once the season is over, stocks disappear and the need for additional working capital also goes off. Similarly, during the slack season demand falls and inventory level goes down and in consequence requirement for working capital decreases. In case, firm believes that the demand for the product has gone up steadily, it has to invest in fixed assets to increase the production facilities. Then additional current assets are also needed to match the increased volume of production and sales.

Firms need more working capital when sales are more and demand for the product is high.

4. **Technology and manufacturing policy: In manufacturing businesses, requirement of working capital is in direct proportion to the length of manufacturing process.** If the manufacturing process is long requirement of working capital is more. For example, BHEL, which produces boilers, takes one to two years to manufacture a boiler as the manufacture cycle is long. To reduce working capital needs, industries engaged in tailor-made products insist on advance payment. In case firm that placed the order cancels it, there would be no takers for that product. They insist on advance as the products are specific and do not meet the general demand in market. In contrast, requirement of working capital is low in firms, engaged in manufacturing chocolates, soaps and detergent powders, where the manufacturing cycle is short.

During manufacturing process, raw materials and other supplies have to be carried in the form of work-in-process. The investment is substantial and cannot be avoided in these forms as the manufacturing process demands. So, it is prudent to choose the shortest manufacturing process when there are alternative manufacturing processes to facilitate for lower working capital requirement. It is also necessary to ensure the manufacturing process is completed as per the schedule to avoid accumulation of larger work-in-process due to delays.

Non-manufacturing and service industries do not have manufacturing cycle and so their working capital requirement is uniform normally throughout the year, if they are not engaged in seasonal products.

5. **Credit Policy:** The credit policy influences the level of debtors. **Where a firm buys on cash and extends credit to its customers, requirement of working capital would be substantial.**

In certain industries, credit is a must. They buy on credit and sell on credit. Their need for working capital would not be too high as they enjoy and extend credit. In certain industries, credit terms depend upon the norms of the industry they belong to. In textiles, wholesalers normally extend three months credit to the retail shops and so the individual firms cannot influence credit policy. So, requirement of working capital of any firm normally would be in line with the pattern of industry. Whatever be the policy, every firm has to ensure collections from debtors in terms of the original credit period allowed to contain working capital requirements. Firms have to keep a close watch on prompt collections to ensure chance of bad debts to the absolute minimum level as bad debts erodes the profitability severely.

6. **Availability of credit:** When a firm is confident of raising additional finance from its banker, it manages with a lower amount of working capital in contrast to those firms not enjoying that type of facility or support. Similarly, firms enjoying liberal credit may not require much working capital. They can sell on cash, enjoying credit.

7. **Operating efficiency:** Firms may not able to control the prices of raw materials and wages of labour but are certainly capable of utilizing the resources efficiently without wastage of materials and idle labour.

Efficient firms can manage with lower working capital.

8. **Seasonal Business:** In certain industries, business is seasonal. The classical example is firecrackers. Even though firecrackers are used in marriages, now held through-out the year, the main demand for firecrackers is during Diwali season. To meet the huge demand during that period, production in those industries is carried out through- out the year. When there is no off take during non-peak season, inventories accumulate creating more need for working capital. The convenience is financial arrangements can be made well in advance for meeting seasonal requirements as they are known from beginning.

9. **Variable production competencies:** When an industry is able to develop alternative products, it can manufacture its main product during the period of increasing demand and other products during the non-peak season to use the production capacities evenly. This enables the firm to have uniform working capital requirement through-out the year.

10. **Business cycles:** Business cycles alternate to general expansion and contraction of business activity generally. During periods of boom, sales increase and the situation demands higher working capital. In depression, there is an all round dullness or declining trend in every activity and there would be a great fall in sales which reduces the working capital requirement.

11. **Price level changes:** When prices of raw materials increase, same level of assets need increased investment in current assets. The increasing shifts in price level result in increased requirement of working capital, if the firm is not able to revise selling prices immediately. This situation creates difficulty to the finance manager as he has to arrange additional working capital at short notice, which has not been foreseen. However, those firms do not get affected if they are able to pass on the increased prices of raw materials and inputs to their buyers.
12. **Working capital cycle:** The working capital cycle commences with purchase of raw materials and ends with realization of cash in a manufacturing enterprise. The raw materials move into work-in-process and finally to finished products. Later sales are made and often they are on credit. The credit period depends on the industry norms as well as the policy of firm. Once credit sales are realized firm ends with cash, which has been the starting point in the working capital cycle. The speed with which the entire cycle is completed determines the working capital requirement.

Longer the operating cycle, need for working capital is more.

Working Capital in terms of Amount

This method is popular with banks as they would like to know the working capital requirement in terms of amount.

Illustration No. 11

While preparing a project report on behalf of a client the following facts have been collected. Estimate the net working capital required for that project. Add 10% to computed figure to allow contingencies.

Estimated cost per unit of production	**Amount per unit (₹)**
Raw material	80
Direct labour	30
Overheads (exclusive of depreciation)	60
Total cost	170

Additional information:

Selling price	₹ 200 Per unit
Level of activity	1,04,000 units of production per annum
Raw materials in stock	average 4 weeks
Work in progress (assume 100% consumption of raw materials and 50% completion stage in respect of conversion costs)	average 2 weeks
Finished goods in stock	average 4 weeks

Credit allowed by suppliers	average 4 weeks
Credit allowed to debtors	average 8 weeks
Lag in payment of wages	average 1.5 weeks
Cash at bank is expected to be	₹ 25,000

Assume production is carried on evenly throughout the year (52 weeks) and wages and overheads accrue similarly. All sales are on credit basis only.

Solution

Net Working Capital = Current Assets – Current Liabilities

Current Assets:

Raw materials in stock	= 1,04,000 × 80 x 4/52		6,40,000
Work-in-progress:			
Raw Material (100% consumption)	= 1,04,000 × 80 × 2/52	= 3,20,000	
Wages	= 1,04,000 × 30 × 2/52 × 50%	= 60,000	
Overheads	= 1,04,000 × 60 × 2/52 × 50%	= 1,20,000	
			5,00,000
Debtors	= 1,04,000 × 170* × 8/ 52		27,20,000
Finished goods in stock	= 1,04,000 × 170 × 4/ 52		13,60,000
Cash			25,000
Total Current Assets			52,45,000
Current Liabilities:			
Creditors	= 1,04,000 × 80 × 4/ 52		6,40,000
Outstanding Wages	= 1,04,000 × 30 × 1.5/ 52		90,000
Total Current Liabilities			7,30,000
Net Working Capital	= Total current assets – Total current liabilities		
	= 52,45,000 – 7,30,000		45,15,000
10% Contingencies			4,51,500
Net Working Capital required			49,66,500

Assumption: * It is assumed that bank does not finance profit element while assessing working capital requirement.

Illustration No. 12

A newly formed company has applied for a loan to a commercial bank for financing its working capital requirements. You are requested by the bank to prepare an estimate of the requirements of working capital for the company. Add 10 per cent to your estimated figure to cover unforeseen contingencies.

The information about the projected profit and loss account of this company is as under:

(₹)

Sales	21,00,000
Cost of goods sold	15,30,000
Gross profit	5,70,000
Administrative expenses 1,40,000 Selling expenses 1,30,000	2,70,000
Profit before tax	3,00,000
Provision for tax	1,00,000
Profit after tax	2,00,000

Note: Cost of goods sold has been derived as follows:

(₹)

Materials used	8,40,000
Wages and manufacturing expenses	6,25,000
Depreciation	2,35,000
	17,00,000
Less Stock of finished goods (10 per cent not yet sold)	1,70,000
	15,30,000

The figures given above relate only to the goods that have been finished and not to work in progress; goods equal to 15 per cent of the year's production (in terms of physical units) are in progress on an average requiring full materials but only 40 per cent of other expenses. The company believes in keeping two months consumption of material in stock. Desired cash balance ₹ 40,000.

Average time lag in payment of all expenses is 1 month; suppliers of materials extend 1.5 months credit; sales are 20 per cent cash; rest is two months credit. 70 per cent of the income-tax has to be paid in advance in quarterly installments.

Bank does not finance depreciation component and profit element while assessing working capital requirements of the firm.

Other than above, you can make such other assumptions as you deem necessary for estimating working capital requirements.

(B.U. MBA- June, 2004)

Solution

Estimate of working capital requirement

Current Assets	₹
Cash	40,000
Inventories:	
Closing stock – Finished goods * $14,65,000 \times \frac{10}{100}$	1,46,500
Raw materials $8,40,000 \times \frac{2}{12}$	1,40,000
Work-in-progress:	
Raw materials $8,40,000 \times \frac{15}{100} = 1,26,000$ Wages and other mfg. exp $= 6,25,000 \times \frac{15}{100} \times \frac{40}{100}$ $= \underline{37,500}$	1,63,500
Debtors * *$12,95,000 \times \frac{80}{100} \times \frac{2}{12}$	1,72,667
Total current assets	6,62,667
Current liabilities	
Sundry creditors $8,40,000 \times \frac{1.5}{12}$	1,05,000
Outstanding Wages $6,25,000 \times \frac{1}{12}$	52,083
Outstanding administrative and Selling expenses $2,70,000 \times \frac{1}{12}$	22,500
Total Current Liabilities	1,79,583
Working Capital (Current Assets – Current Liabilities)	4,83,084
Unforeseen contingencies 10%	48,308
Total estimated working capital needed	5,31,392

Note: Bank does not finance depreciation component and profit element specifically also stated in the problem. So depreciation is excluded from closing stock and debtors.

* Closing stock:

Materials used	=	8,40,000
Wages & Mfg exp	=	6,25,000
		14,65,000

** Debtors:

Cost of sales – depreciation (15,30,000 – 2,35,000) = 12,95,000

Assumptions:

Taxes are not included in the estimate of total working capital as tax has to be paid only after the sale is made. Banks do not finance for payment of taxes as they are collected at the time of sale.

Illustration No. 13

The cost sheet of Kalyan & Kish Ltd. provides the following data:

	Cost per unit
Raw material	₹ 50
Direct labour	20
Overheads (including depreciation of ₹ 10)	40
Total cost	110
Profits	20
Selling price	130

Average raw material in stock is one month. Average material in the form of work-in-progress is for half month. Credit allowed by suppliers: one month; credit allowed to debtors: one month; Average time lag in payment of wages: 10 days; average time lag in payment of overhead is 30 days. 75% of the sales are on cash basis. Cash balance expected to be ₹ 1,00,000. Finished goods lie in the warehouse for one month.

You are required to prepare a statement of the working capital needed to finance a level of the activity of 54,000 units of output. Production is carried on evenly throughout the year and wages and overheads accrue similarly. State your assumptions, if any, clearly.

Solution

As the annual level of activity is given at 54,000 units, it means that the monthly turnover would be 54,000/12 = 4,500 units. The working capital requirement for this monthly turnover can now be estimated as follows:

Estimation of Working Capital Requirement

		Amount (₹)
I.	**Current Assets:**	
	Minimum Cash Balance	1,00,000
	Inventories:	
	Raw materials (4,500 × ₹ 50)	2,25,000
	Work-in-progress	
	Materials (4,500 × ₹ 50)/2	1,12,500
	Wages 50% of (4,500 × ₹ 20)/2	22,500
	Overheads 50% of (4,500 × ₹ 30)/2	33,750
	Finished Goods (4,500 × ₹100**)	4,50,000
	Debtors (4,500 × ₹ 100**) × 25%	1,12,500
	Total Current Assets	**10,56,250**
	Gross Working Capital	**10,56,250**
II.	**Current Liabilities:**	
	Creditors for Materials (4,500 × ₹ 50)	2,25,000
	Creditors for Wages (4,500 × ₹ 20)/3	30,000
	Creditors for Overhead (4,500 × ₹ 30)	1,35,000
	Total Current Liabilities	**3,90,000**
	Net Working Capital	**6,66,250**

Assumptions:

1. The Overheads of ₹ 40 per unit include a depreciation of ₹ 10 per unit, which is a non-cash item. This depreciation cost has been ignored for valuation of work-in-progress, finished goods and debtors. The overhead cost therefore has been taken at ₹ 30 per unit.
2. *In the valuation of work-in-progress, it is assumed that the materials have been used 100%, while wages and overheads are only 50%.
3. **It is assumed that the bank does not finance profits so profit element is also excluded from cost of sales for calculation of finished goods and debtors.
4. Since wages are paid with a time lag of 10 days, working capital provided by wages has been taken by dividing the monthly wages by 3 (assuming a month to consist of 30 days.)

Illustration No. 14

From the following cost sheet, prepare the working capital requirement of Nandi & Co.:

Estimated cost per unit of production	Amount per unit (₹)
Raw material	20
Direct labour	10
Overheads (inclusive of depreciation ₹ 10 per unit)	90
Total cost	120

Additional information:

Selling price	₹ 150 Per unit
Level of activity	60,000 units of production per annum
Raw materials in stock	average 2 weeks
Work in progress (assume 50% completion in respect of all costs)	average 1 week
Finished goods in stock	average 6 weeks
Credit allowed by suppliers	average 2 weeks
Credit allowed to debtors	average 4 weeks
Lag in payment of wages	average 2.5 weeks
Lag in payment of overheads	average 3 weeks
Overdraft at bank (average) is expected to be	₹ 12,000

You may assume that production is carried on evenly throughout the year (52 weeks) and wages and overheads accrue similarly. 50% of sales are on cash basis and the rest is on credit basis.

Solution

Estimated working capital requirement for a level of activity of 60,000 units of production (annual)

	₹
Current Assets:	
Raw materials 20 × 60,000 × 2/52 (two weeks stock)	46,153
Work-in-progress 110 × 60,000 × 50% × 1/52 (50% complete on average in all respects, one week)	63,462
Finished goods 110 × 60,000 × 6/52 (6 weeks in stock)	7,61,538
Debtors 110 × 60,000 × 4/52 × 50%	2,53,846

Contd...

(four weeks credit and 50% of sales only on credit)	
Total current assets (A)	**11,24,999**
Current Liabilities	
Creditors for raw materials 20 × 60,000 × 2/52	46,154
(two weeks credit)	
Wages 10 × 60,000 × 2.5/52	28,846
(Two and half a week credit)	
Overheads 80 × 60,000 × 3/52	2,76,923
(Three weeks credit)	
Overdraft at Bank (average)	12,000
Total Current Liabilities (B)	**3,63,923**
Working Capital (A – B)	**7,61,076**

Estimated working capital requirement of the firm for producing 60,000 units is 7,61,076.

Note: Depreciation is a non-cash item hence banks do not finance overheads. Profit on sales is also not financed by bank hence excluded in calculating debtors.

Illustration No. 15

From the following information of Kish & Co. Ltd., calculate the working capital requirement of firm.

Raw Materials holding period	4 weeks
Work-in-progress holding period	2 weeks
Finished goods holding period	3 weeks
Debtors holding period	6 weeks
Creditors holding period	8 weeks
Time lag in payment of salaries	1.5 weeks
Cost of production for the year	₹ 1,20,000
Cost of sales for the year	₹ 1,50,000
Total sales	₹ 1,80,000
(includes cash sales ₹ 20,000)	
Total purchases	₹ 1,60,000
(includes credit purchases ₹ 1,40,000)	
Salaries	₹ 20,000
Cash and bank balance	₹ 5,000

Contingencies are 10% on total current assets.

Make valid assumptions. Treat year is having 50 weeks.

Solution

Details of operating cycle have been given. Using the formulae of operating cycle, missing figures (current assets and current liabilities) have to be found out for calculation of working capital requirement.

Raw materials holding period = 4 weeks

Total consumption of raw materials* = 1,60,000

(Total purchases, no closing stock)

$$\text{Raw materials holding period} = \frac{\text{Raw materials holding}}{\text{Raw materials consumption}} \times 50$$

$$4 = \frac{\text{Raw materials holding}}{1{,}60{,}000} \times 50$$

$$\text{Raw materials holding} = \frac{1{,}60{,}000}{50} \times 4$$

$$= 12{,}800$$

Raw Materials = 12,800

Work-in-progress holding period = 2 weeks

Cost of production = 1,20,000

$$\text{Work-in-progress holding period} = \frac{\text{Work-in-progress holding}}{\text{Cost of production}} \times 50$$

$$2 = \frac{\text{Work-in-progress holding}}{1{,}20{,}000} \times 50$$

$$\text{Work-in-progress holding} = \frac{1{,}20{,}000 \times 2}{50}$$

$$= 4{,}800$$

Work-in-progress = 4,800

Finished goods holding period = 3 weeks

Total cost of sales = 1,50,000

$$\text{Finished goods holding period} = \frac{\text{Finished goods holding}}{\text{Cost of sales}} \times 50$$

$$3 = \frac{\text{Finished goods holding}}{1,50,000} \times 50$$

Finished goods holding $= \dfrac{1,50,000 \times 3}{50}$

$= 9,000$

Finished goods $= 9,000$

Debtors holding period $= 6$ weeks

Credit sales $= 1,60,000$

Debtors holding period $= \dfrac{\text{Debtors holding}}{\text{Credit sales}} \times 50$

$$6 = \frac{\text{Debtors holding}}{1,60,000} \times 50$$

Debtors holding $= \dfrac{1,60,000 \times 6}{50}$

$= 19,200$

Debtors $= 19,200$

Creditors holding period $= 8$ weeks

Credit purchases $= 1,40,000$

Creditors holding period $= \dfrac{\text{Creditors holding}}{\text{Credit purchases}} \times 50$

$$8 = \frac{\text{Creditors holding}}{1,40,000} \times 50$$

Creditors holding $= \dfrac{1,40,000 \times 8}{50}$

$= 22,400$

Creditors $= 22,400$

Time lag in payment of salaries $= 1.5$ weeks

Salaries $= 20,000$

Outstanding salaries period $= \dfrac{\text{Outstanding salaries}}{\text{Salaries}} \times 50$

$$1.5 = \frac{\text{Outstanding salaries}}{\text{Salaries}} \times 50$$

$$1.5 = \frac{\text{Outstanding salaries}}{20{,}000} \times 50$$

Outstanding salaries $= \dfrac{1.5 \times 20{,}000}{50}$

$= 600$

* **Assumption:** In the absence of opening and closing stock, total purchases are treated as consumption of raw materials.

Calculation of working capital

	(₹ in thousands)	
Current Assets:		
Raw materials	12,800	
Work-in-progress	4,800	
Finished goods	9,000	
Debtors	19,200	
Cash and Bank Balance	5,000	
Total Current Assets		50,800
Current Liabilities		
Creditors		22,400
Outstanding salaries		600
Total current liabilities		23,000
Working capital (Current assets – Current liabilities)		27,800
Add Contingencies 10% Current Assets		5,080
Total working capital requirement		32,880

Illustration No. 16

The following is the Profit and Loss Account and Balance Sheet of Suresha Ltd. for the year ended 31st March, 2008. You are required to calculate the working capital requirement under operating cycle method, showing gross operating cycle and net operating cycle.

Trading and Profit and Loss Account for the year ending 31st March, 2008

₹

Particulars	Amount	Particulars	Amount
To opening Stock		By Credit sales	1,90,000
Raw Materials	20,000	By Cash sales	1,10,000
Work-in-progress	10,000	By Closing stock	
Finished Goods	30,000	Raw materials	12,000
To Credit Purchases (Raw materials)	1,25,000	Work-in-progress	15,000
To Cash Purchases (Raw materials)	20,000	Finished goods	9,000
To Wages & Mfg expenses	5,000		
To Gross Profit c/d	1,26,000		
	3,36,000		3,36,000
To Administrative expenses	25,000	By Gross Profit b/d	1,26,000
To Selling & Distribution expenses	15,000		
To Net Profit	86,000		
	1,26,000		1,26,000

Balance Sheet of Suresha Ltd. as at 31st March, 2008

Liabilities	Amount	Assets	Amount
Share Capital			
(20,000 equity shares of ₹ 10 each)	2,00,000	Fixed assets	1,50,000
		Closing stock:	
Profit and Loss Account	40,000	Raw materials	12,000
Sundry creditors	70,000	Work-in-progress	15,000
Bills Payable	10,000	Finished goods	9,000
		Sundry debtors	70,000
		Bills receivable	15,000
		Bank	37,000
		Cash	12,000
	3,20,000		3,20,000

Solution

Calculation of operating cycle

Raw materials

Average raw materials = (Opening stock + Closing stock) /2

= (20,000 + 12,000)/2 = 16,000

Total consumption of Raw Materials = Opening stock + Credit purchases + Cash purchases – Closing stock

= 20,000 + 1,25,000 + 20,000 – 12,000

= 1,53,000

Raw materials holding period $= \dfrac{\text{***Average raw materials holding}}{\text{Raw materials consumption}} \times 365$

$= \dfrac{16,000}{1,53,000} \times 365$

= 38 days

Work-in-progress

Average WIP = (10,000 + 15,000)/2 = 12,500

Cost of production = Raw materials consumed + Wages & Mfg Exp + Opening balance of WIP – Closing balance of WIP

= 1,53,000 + 5,000 + 10,000 – 15,000

= 1,53,000

Work-in-progress holding period $= \dfrac{\text{Average work-in-progress holding}}{\text{Cost of production}} \times 365$

$= \dfrac{12,500}{1,53,000} \times 365$

= 30 days

Finished Goods

Average finished goods

(30,000 + 9,000)/2 = 19,500

Total cost of sales = Cost of production + Opening stock of finished goods – Closing stock of finished goods

$= 1,53,000 + 30,000 - 9,000$

$= 1,74,000$

Finished goods holding period $= \dfrac{\text{Average finished goods holding}}{\text{Cost of sales}} \times 365$

$= \dfrac{19,500}{1,74,000} \times 365$

$= 41$ days

Debtors

Debtors + Bills Receivable $= 70,000 + 15,000$

$= 85,000$

Debtors/Bills Receivable holding period $= \dfrac{\text{Debtors and bills receivable}}{\text{Credit sales}} \times 365$

$= \dfrac{85,000}{1,90,000} \times 365$

$= 163$ days

Creditors

Creditors + Bills Payable $= 70,000 + 10,000 = 80,000$

Creditors holding period $= \dfrac{\text{Creditors + Bills Payable **}}{\text{Credit purchases}} \times 365$

$= \dfrac{80,000}{1,25,000} \times 365$

$= 234$ days

Gross Operating cycle: 38 days + 30 days + 41 days + 163 days

= 272 days

Net Operating Cycle: 272 days – 234 days

= 38 days

* Bills receivable is another form of extending credit hence included.

** Bills payable is another form of getting credit hence included.

*** Where opening and closing balances are available, it is desirable to take their average to get a better picture rather than taking closing balance alone.

22.9 METHODS OF RAISING WORKING CAPITAL

Short-term funds are used to finance working capital. Two most significant sources of short-term sources of finance for working capital are: Trade credit and bank borrowings. Trade credit refers to the credit granted by the suppliers in supplying goods in the normal course of business. Accrued expenses and deferred income are the spontaneous sources of finance for meeting working capital needs.

Next is bank borrowing, which is the most important source of working capital finance. The different forms of bank finance are overdraft, cash credit, purchase or discounting of bills and working capital loan etc.

Cash Credit: Cash credit is the most popular form of financing for working capital requirements. Borrowers prefer this method of borrowing for the following reasons:

1. **Flexibility:** Borrower can deposit the sale proceeds into the cash credit account when funds are not needed. He can as withdraw when funds are needed from the cash credit account for purchase of stocks and other business expenses. Flexibility of deposit and withdrawal up to the drawing limit are the greatest attractions in a cash credit account. Deposit and withdrawal features are available only in a cash credit account while in a loan account only deposits are permitted but not withdrawals, even if installments are paid in advance.
2. **Economical form of borrowing:** Interest in cash credit is charged on daily basis, based on the outstanding balance in the account. Bank calculates daily product based on the outstanding balance and charges interest on quarterly basis. So, borrowers would like to deposit the sale proceeds immediately to reduce the outstanding balance for getting interest benefit. As and when funds are needed, borrower draws from the cash credit account. As no borrower would require funds to the extent of the sanctioned limit fully and throughout the year, actual interest cost works out very low on the total sanctioned limit. Borrower learns financial discipline too from this form of financing. Now-a-days, borrowers are highly cost conscious due to severe competition and cash credit form of borrowing is ideal to contain the costs to the minimum.
3. **Temporary Finance:** Additional drawings are normally permitted. Banks are always considerate to accommodate the good borrowers, even beyond the sanctioned limit, provided the drawing power is available. Unforeseen needs are always there in business despite the best planning. So, cash credit form of financing takes care of the additional requirements with the greatest ease. However, the temporary over drawings are to be cleared off, at the earliest, normally before the last friday of the concerned month.
4. **Extension of sanction (renewal of limit) is easy:** Banks normally sanction working capital facilities for a period of one year. Borrowers can request the bank for enhancement of the limits on submission of the required data. Now,

banks are flush with funds and they are also looking for good borrowers for better funds utilization and improving their own profitability. Good borrowers do not normally experience any difficulty in getting renewal of the limit at the same level.

5. **Increased working capital limits with increase in business:** Good borrowers do not experience any difficulty from banks for increasing limits for their genuine business needs. Though initial sanction is given for one year, banks often renew the sanction of the limit at the same or increased level depending on the past conduct of the account, business projected and assessment of their working capital needs. When the business firm is confident that there would be no problem to secure additional working capital for the increased volume of business, it can forget most of the financial worries and leave it to the bank to take care of its business needs.

Cash credit is the ideal form to raise working capital requirements of the firm, which is highly economical and flexible.

Letter of credit is another important source of indirect finance for meeting the working capital needs, in particular, to those firms engaged in import of goods.

All these areas are covered, in detail, in the chapter on short-term sources of finance.

Long-term source of funds: Another final and more important source of working capital is long-term funds. The long-term funds have to finance both the fixed assets as well the permanent component in the working capital. Long-term funds are equity share capital, preference share capital, reserves, debentures and long-term loans. There should be a judicial mix of funds both from short-term and long-term sources for meeting the working capital needs of organization.

22.10 APPROACHES FOR FINANCING CURRENT ASSETS

The modes of financing current assets can be divided into the following categories:

(A) Long-term financing
(B) Short-term financing
(C) Spontaneous financing

What should be the proportion of financing working capital? There are three approaches. The approach that is adopted by the firm depends upon its attitude towards risk and return. Risk assuming nature and return anticipating attitude differ from firm to firm. All firms do not behave alike. Depending on their attitude towards risk and return, the approaches are as under:

(A) Matching approach (Hedging Approach)
(B) Conservative approach
(C) Aggressive approach

(A) Matching Approach (Hedging Approach): A firm can adopt a financial plan in which the expected life of the assets is matched with the expected source of funds. If the life of the asset is 10 years, avail a 10 year loan so that revenue generated from the asset can meet the installment and interest over a period of 10 years. In other words, the life of the asset and repayment period of the loan should match so that the firm would not experience any difficulty in arranging the outgo of funds. Hence, it is known as matching approach.

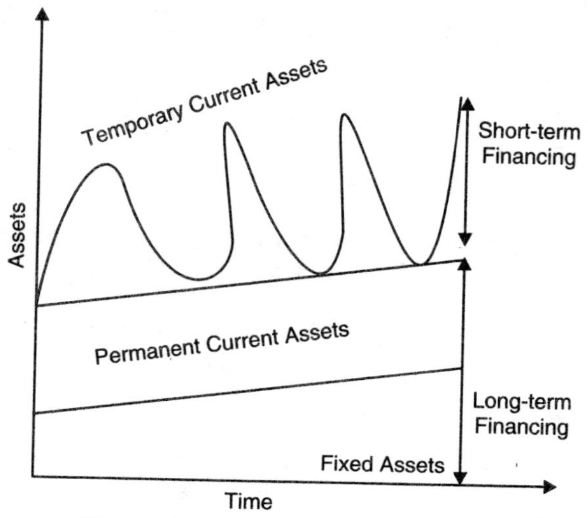

Financing under Matching Plan

From the above figure, it is clear that fixed assets are to be financed by long-term sources. Current assets consist of two components, permanent current assets and temporary current assets. Permanent current assets are constant in business as that portion does not change throughout the year. Temporary current assets change depending on the varying needs of business. As the level of temporary current assets increases, level of short-term funds also increases. Method of financing current assets depends on risk profile of company. The balanced approach is long-term sources of finance should finance fixed assets and permanent current assets portion totally. Short-term sources of finance should finance temporary current assets. In balanced approach, both risk and return are reconciled in a firm.

For example, a seasonal expansion in inventory should be financed with short-term loan or liabilities. The rationale of the hedging approach is straight forward. Once the season is over, cash flows are available to repay the short-term liabilities. If long-term sources are used to meet the seasonal needs, after expiry of season firm would have excess liquidity, which can be invested in marketable securities till the beginning of the next season. As marketable securities yield lesser return, profitability of the firm would be affected. The financing mix as suggested by the hedging approach is a desirable financing pattern. However, it is not possible to exact match the maturity period of current assets and sources of finance due to uncertainty of cash flows.

(B) Conservative Approach: According to this approach, firm depends more on long-term funds for financing needs. In this plan, firm finances its fixed assets, permanent current assets and a part of temporary current assets with long-term funds. Balance temporary current assets, part not financed by long-term assets, are financed with short-term funds. In the periods when the firm has no need for temporary current assets, the idle funds (long-term funds) can be invested in the marketable securities so that firm can conserve liquidity and also earn a small return. As the investment is made in marketable securities, even if there is an exigency to invest in temporary current assets, the funds are always available, at short notice, without any risk for reduction in their investment value.

The conservative policy heavily relies on long-term financing and therefore the firm has the least risk of facing the problem of shortage of funds. However, return would be less as the firm relies on long-term source of funds.

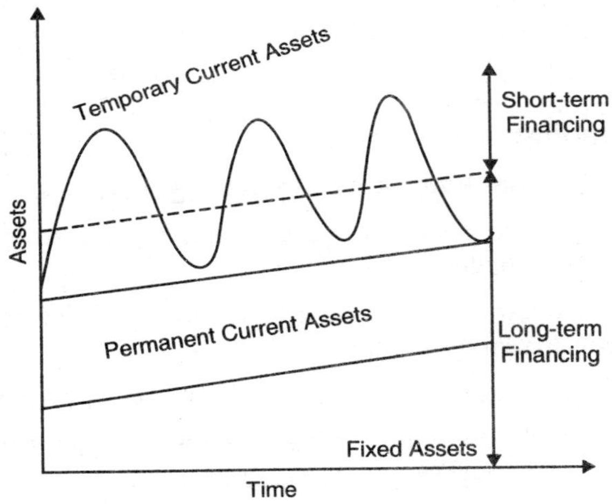

Conservative Financing

(C) Aggressive Approach: A firm may be aggressive in financing its current assets. Aggressive firm finances its total temporary current assets and a part of permanent current assets with short-term sources of financing. A firm is said to be aggressive as it uses more short-term funds in financing its current assets. This aggressive policy indicates higher risk and poor liquidity position as a part of permanent current assets are financed by short-term funds. But aggressive policy provides more returns.

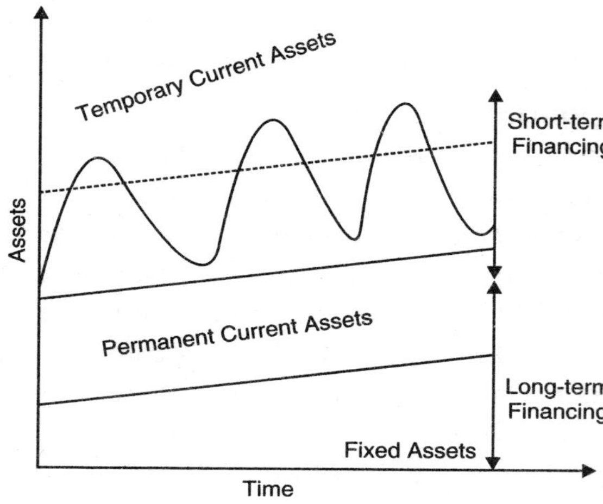

Aggressive Financing

Recommendation: Fixed assets are always to be financed by long-term sources only. Question of extent of financing temporary current assets and permanent current assets depends on the risk bearing nature of the firm. Attitude of the management decides the choice in type of financing. If risk is more, return would be more and vice versa. A balanced approach in financing current assets is desirable.

Check Your Understanding

(A) State whether the following statements are True or False

1. The gross working capital concept is a financial or going concern concept while net working capital is an accounting concept.
2. Permanent working capital is that portion of a firm's current assets, which is normally financed by long-term funds.
3. To meet the gap between the cash inflows and outflows, working capital is needed.
4. The working capital should be neither more nor less, but just adequate.
5. With the change in price levels, firms require more working capital even if they are able to pass on the increased prices of raw materials and inputs to their buyers totally.
6. The excess of current assets over the current liabilities can be expressed as gross working capital.
7. Every firm is interested in increasing the period of operating cycle.
8. Working capital is different from revolving or circulating capital.
9. Growing firms require more variable working capital on a continuous basis.
10. Permanent working capital is constant in a stable firm.
11. Net working capital refers to the capital invested in the total assets of a business.
12. Smaller the size of a business unit, higher will be the requirements of working capital.

13. Pattern of financing current assets depends on risk profile of the organization.
14. In conservative financing, risk and return are high to a firm.

Answers

1. True 2. True 3. True 4. True 5. False 6. False 7. False 8. False
9. False 10. True 11. False 12. False 13. True 14. False

(B) Detail brief reasons whether the following action would result in increase or decrease of total working capital requirements, presuming other factors being constant.

(A) Increase in the credit period allowed to customers from 15 days to 30 days.

(B) Realization of book debts by cash.

(C) Acquisition of additional fixed assets to increase production facilities.

(D) Change in the method of packing the product, involving no additional costs, but results in more sales, substantially.

(E) A credit sale.

(F) The decision to store in a larger quantity the new material whose price is expected to go up in future, needing more funds in a big way.

(G) Change in the method of depreciation.

(H) Bills receivable are received in place of sundry debtors.

(I) A policy decision to pay immediate cash to raw materials' suppliers for enjoying cash discounts.

(J) Receipt of sanction of cash credit limit communication from bank for working capital needs.

(K) Implementation of a scheme for reducing the production period.

(L) Debtors are accumulated due to slackness in collections but firm continues with the same amount of credit sales.

(M) A decision to increase the wages rates.

Answers

Tip: First, check the nature of transaction. Is it a temporary or permanent decision? Impact on working capital depends on the nature of decision. For example, examine the impact of one credit sale where business is conducted normally on cash and carry basis (cylinder gas business). Credit transaction is once and not occasional. So in place of stock, debtor has come into the firm. Only a change in the form of current assets–stock to debtor–does not affect working capital. Against this, consider a shift in nature of business from cash to credit–more credit sales instead of total cash sales. This decision results into more debtors in current assets. Cash is not available as earlier for purchase of raw materials as realization from debtors takes place only on the expiry of credit period. To purchase raw materials and run the business, more funds are needed in the form of additional working capital. You would observe an occasional transaction has not resulted in additional working capital, while the same type of transaction, if become permanent in nature results in more working capital.

(A) Increase—since the sundry debtors will increase. Nature of decision is long-term.

(B) No Change—one form of current asset is changed to another, increase of cash and decrease of debtors.

(C) Increase—since increased production requires increased investment in debtors, inventories and cash, etc.

(D) Increase—Improved packing has resulted in more sales and more stocks are needed to support the increased sales.

(E) No change—Inventory goes down and debtors increase. Only one credit sale does not result in additional working capital requirement.

(F) Increase—inventory increases and the increase in a big way is possible with more working capital.

(G) No change—neither the production time nor the inventory level is affected.

(H) No change—one form of current asset is changed to another.

(I) Increase—To avail cash discounts more cash is needed and so increased working capital is needed. Decision is a policy decision, which shows its long – term effects.

(J) No change—No change in the status of current assets and current liabilities.

(K) Decrease—investment in inventories decreases.

(L) Increase—debtors increase due to slackness in collections. More funds are needed to maintain same amount of credit sales.

(M) Increase—Cost of inventories goes up and work-in-process would be more.

(C) Objective Questions (Identify what is most appropriate)

1. Working capital is needed for financing
   (A) long-term assets (B) short-term assets
   (C) both (A) and (B) (D) none of the above

2. Working capital refers to those assets which are
   (A) converted into cash within one year.
   (B) converted into cash without any time limit.
   (C) permanent assets.
   (D) difference of assets and liabilities.

3. Gross working capital refers to
   (A) temporary liabilities (B) total current assets
   (C) total current liabilities (D) difference of current assets and current liabilities

4. When current liabilities exceed current assets, it is called
   (A) permanent capital (B) short-term funds
   (C) negative working capital (D) long-term funds

5. If sales increase while length of credit extended is same, normal requirements of working capital would be
   (A) less (B) more
   (C) same (D) unpredictable

6. This category treats adequate working capital position in the firm as a measure of safety and assurance for repayment on the due date.
   (A) Equity share holders (B) Preference share holders
   (C) Debenture holders (D) Creditors
7. When a firm does business on cash and carry basis, its requirements of working capital, compared to a firm that extends credit, would be
   (A) more (B) less
   (C) same (D) unpredictable
8. Difference between gross working capital cycle and payables deferred period is known as
   (A) net working capital (B) permanent capital
   (C) equity capital (D) temporary capital
9. Working capital requirement depends on
   (A) Width of operating cycle (B) Length of operating cycle
   (C) Both (A) and (B) (D) None of the above
10. For efficient working capital management, it is prudent to finance the portion of permanent working capital from
    (A) long-term sources (B) short-term sources
    (C) creditors (D) bills payable
11. Working capital is needed as the inflows and outflows are
    (A) predictable (B) certain
    (C) unpredictable and unforeseen (D) predictable and foreseen
12. A firm can exercise more control on
    (A) inflows (B) outflows
    (C) both inflows and outflows (D) none of the above
13. Net working capital refers to
    (A) temporary liabilities (B) total current assets
    (C) total current liabilities (D) diff. of current assets and current liabilities
14. Operating cycle is the length of period required to convert
    (A) cash into cash (B) cash into sales
    (C) purchases into cash (D) cash into purchases
15. Operating cycle would be short
    (A) if the manufacturing process time is long and realization period from debtors is more
    (B) if the manufacturing process time is short and realization period from debtors is low
    (C) no relationship with manufacturing process time and realization period from debtors
    (D) if stock holding is more
16. If the firm is holding finished goods more than its normal requirements, requirements of working capital would be
    (A) neutral (B) less
    (C) same (D) more

17. If more funds are locked in non-moving current assets, the firm would experience this problem
    (A) excess liquidity (B) liquidity crunch
    (C) excess profits (D) none of the above
18. If the firm experiences liquidity problem, the following is the consequence:
    (A) timely payments to suppliers and of wages
    (B) delayed payment to suppliers and labourers
    (C) profits would increase
    (D) no affect on the firm
19. The following investment mode is a proper and profitable use of excessive temporary liquid funds:
    (A) short-term deposit in a bank (B) long-term fixed deposit in a bank
    (C) purchase of a permanent fixed asset (D) speculative equity shares
20. For a manufacturing company, the gross working capital is =
    (A) Raw materials conversion period + Work-in-progress conversion period
    (B) Raw materials conversion period + Work-in-progress conversion period + Finished goods conversion period
    (C) Raw materials conversion period + Work-in-progress conversion period + Finished goods conversion period + Debtors conversion period
    (D) Raw materials conversion period + Finished goods conversion period + Debtors conversion period
21. For a trading company, the gross working capital is =
    (A) Finished goods conversion period + Work-in-progress conversion period
    (B) Work-in-progress conversion period + Finished goods conversion period
    (C) Raw materials conversion period + Work-in-progress conversion period + Finished goods conversion period + Debtors conversion period
    (D) Finished goods conversion period + Debtors conversion period
22. For a trading company, the net working capital is =
    (A) Finished goods conversion period + Work-in-progress conversion period–Payables deferred period
    (B) Finished goods conversion period + Debtors conversion period–Payables deferred period
    (C) Raw materials conversion period + Work-in-progress conversion period + Finished goods conversion period + Debtors conversion period–Payables deferred period
    (D) Gross working capital + Debtors conversion period–Payables deferred period
23. For an ongoing concern, this concept is relevant.
    (A) Gross working capital (B) Net working capital
    (C) Maximum working capital (D) Minimum working capital
24. This concept is relevant as an accounting concept:
    (A) Gross working capital (B) Net working capital
    (C) Maximum working capital (D) Minimum working capital

25. For calculation of debtors conversion period, this information is relevant:
    (A) Credit sales, debtors and bills receivable
    (B) Bills payable, creditors and cash sales
    (C) Bills receivable, creditors and cash sales
    (D) Credit sales, debtors and cash purchases

26. For calculating the period of credit allowed by suppliers, this information is relevant for calculating gross operating cycle:
    (A) Credit purchases, creditors and bills receivable
    (B) Credit purchases, creditors and bills payable
    (C) Credit sales, debtors and bills receivable
    (D) Cash purchases, creditors and bills receivable

27. Working capital efficiency of two comparable firms can be understood in terms of:
    (A) Net working capital cycle
    (B) Working capital in terms of amount
    (C) Both (A) and (B)
    (D) Neither (A) nor (B)

28. If the net operating cycle of firm A is longer than the firm B, when both the firms are comparable in their nature and working, it means
    (A) Working capital management of firm A is bad and B good, comparatively
    (B) Working capital management of firm A and B are equally good
    (C) Working capital management of firm A is good and B bad, comparatively
    (D) Working capital management of firm A and B is neither good nor bad

29. If net operating cycle increases, the consequence is
    (A) decrease in working capital requirement
    (B) increase in working capital requirement
    (C) no effect on working capital requirement
    (D) fluctuations in working capital requirement

30. Working capital requirements of borrowers are provided by this category at a cost on a regular basis.
    (A) Creditors
    (B) Term lending institutions
    (C) Commercial banks
    (D) Debenture holders

31. This factor does not influence the working capital requirements of a firm:
    (A) Business conditions
    (B) Length of operating cycle
    (C) Manufacturing time
    (D) Plant and Machinery cost

32. This is the greatest day to day challenge to a finance manager, if the firm experiences liquidity problems.
    (A) Term loan sanction
    (B) Working capital management
    (C) Managing production schedule
    (D) Sanction of letter of credit limit from bank

33. For temporary additional working capital requirements, this is the most economic form of financing for a firm.
    (A) Additional drawings in cash credit account of bank
    (B) Long-term loan from a bank
    (C) Creditors
    (D) Equity share capital

34. Working capital requirement can be expressed/measured in terms of
    (A) days (B) amount
    (C) both (A) and (B) (D) none of the above

35. Banks assess working capital requirements of borrowers in terms of
    (A) days (B) amount
    (C) both (A) and (B) (D) none of the above

36. Banks do not finance the following while assessing working capital requirements of a borrower.
    (A) cost of raw materials (B) depreciation
    (C) profit (D) both (B) and (C)

37. Depreciation is not financed by banks while assessing working capital requirements for the following reason.
    (A) Not an element of cost (B) No outgo of cash
    (C) No inflow of cash (D) Capital cost

38. Identify that asset which is not a current asset.
    (A) Cash (B) Bank
    (C) Bills receivable (D) Bills payable

39. For calculation of working capital, this information is not needed.
    (A) Goodwill (B) Fixed assets
    (C) Both (A) and (B) (D) Prepaid expenses

40. If working capital is inadequate, firm experiences this problem.
    (A) Lack of profitability (B) Liquidity
    (C) Surplus cash (D) Payments to creditors before due date

41. If working capital is excessive, firm experiences problem on this front.
    (A) Profitability (B) Liquidity
    (C) Surplus cash (D) Quick realization from debtors

42. It is necessary for every firm to have balanced working capital in this manner.
    (A) Adequacy of current assets (B) Individual proportion of current assets
    (C) Both (A) and (B) (D) None of the above

43. As a conventional rule, the current ratio is as below.
    (A) 2:1 (B) 1:2
    (C) 2:2 (D) 1:1

44. Lesser operating cycle, marginally, against the planned operating cycle is an indication of the following situation.
    (A) Inefficient working capital management
    (B) Efficient working capital management
    (C) Insufficiency of liquidity
    (D) Insufficiency of profitability

45. Working capital can be estimated by the following method.
    (A) Operating cycle (B) Working capital amount
    (C) Both (A) and (B) (D) None of the above

Answers

1. (B)	2. (A)	3. (B)	4. (C)	5. (B)	6. (D)	7. (B)	8. (A)
9. (B)	10. (A)	11. (C)	12. (B)	13. (D)	14. (A)	15. (B)	16. (D)
17. (B)	18. (B)	19. (A)	20. (C)	21. (D)	22. (B)	23. (A)	24. (B)
25. (A)	26. (B)	27. (C)	28. (A)	29. (B)	30 (C)	31. (D)	32. (B)
33. (A)	34. (C)	35. (B)	36. (D)	37. (B)	38. (D)	39. (C)	40. (B)
41. (A)	42. (C)	43. (A)	44. (B)	45. (C).			

Descriptive Questions

1. Explain the concept of working capital. Are gross and net working capital concepts exclusive. Discuss. **(22.2 and 22.3)**
2. To a finance manager, both gross working capital and net working capital are equally important. Justify. **(22.2 and 22.3)**
3. What is the importance and need of working capital in a business? Explain the impact of excess or paucity of working capital to a firm. **(22.4 and 22.4.2)**
4. Discuss the factors which influence the need for working capital management for a manufacturing concern. **(22.4 and 22.8)**
5. What is the impact of 'excess' or 'paucity' of working capital on the operations and profitability of the undertaking? **(22.4.2)**
6. Discuss the importance of operating cycle for estimating working capital requirement. **(22.6)**
7. Write a note on the classification of working capital and its role in a stable and growing firm with suitable pictorial presentation to explain the difference between the two categories. **(22.3 and 22.7)**
8. Explain the concept of 'Working Capital Flow'. Give examples of transactions that affect working capital, and that do not affect working capital. **(22.2 and check your understanding question & answer-B)**
9. Suggest the methods you consider most suitable for raising the required amount of working capital in the short and long run. **(22.9)**
10. "In bank finance, cash credit is the most economic form of working capital management" –Discuss. **(22.9)**
11. Describe the different approaches of financing current assets. Which method of financing is recommended? **(22.10)**

12. Whether working capital should be met from long-term or short-term sources? What impact this decision will have on risk and return of firm? **(22.10)**

Short Questions

Q.1. What is meant by 'operating cycle'?

Ans. The operating cycle may be defined as time duration starting from procurement of goods or raw materials and ending with sales realization in the form of cash. The length and nature of operating cycle may differ from one firm to another, depending upon the size and nature of firm. Basically, this is the length of period required to procure resources such as materials, power etc. and convert into cash. In other words, time taken to convert cash into cash is called operating cycle.

Q.2. How spontaneous sources of financing occur?

Ans. When goods are purchased on credit, credit is received from suppliers, which is a spontaneous source of financing. Period of credit depends on the market practice. Outstanding expenses like salaries, electricity charges and other payments for which services received, but not paid, are the other forms of spontaneous financing. Spontaneous financing occurs without any conscious effort by the company.

Q.3. What is the difference between gross operating cycle and cash conversion cycle?

Ans. Gross operating cycle refers to the length of time taken from the purchase of raw materials till the collection of sundry debtors in the sale of the final product. In other words, it is simply the number of days goods are tied up in inventory plus the number of days its sales are tied up in receivables. It is the average time period between buying inventory and receiving cash proceeds from its eventual sale. It is determined by adding the number of days inventory is held and the collection period for sundry debtors (accounts receivable).

Cash conversion cycle is calculated excluding depreciation from cost structure. Cash conversion cycle and gross operating cycle mean the same in the absence of depreciation in the cost structure of firm.

Q.4. What is the relationship between net operating cycle and working capital? In what manner does it affect profits of a company?

Ans. Net operating cycle it is the length of time (in terms of days) working capital is tied up. If net operating cycle is short (number of days low), working capital is tied up for less period in business. Shorter cash conversion period would better the company's bottom line (profits).

Q.5. Which type of financing is a balanced approach for financing assets of a business?

Ans. Fixed assets are to be financed by long-term sources. Current assets consist of two components, permanent current assets and temporary current assets. Permanent current assets are constant in business as that portion does not change throughout the year. Temporary current assets change depending on the varying needs of business. Method of financing current assets depends on risk profile of company. The balanced approach is long-term sources of finance should finance fixed assets and permanent current assets portion totally. Short-term sources of finance should finance temporary current assets. In balanced approach, both risk and return are reconciled in a firm.

Interview Questions

Q.1. What is spontaneous financing? Name the sources.

Ans. Spontaneous financing refers to the automatic sources of short-term funds that arise in the ordinary course of business. Trade credit and outstanding expenses for services are the common forms of spontaneous sources of financing.

Q.2. What is the need of working capital for a firm?

Ans. Funds are needed for purchase of raw materials, payment of wages and other day to day expenses. Adequate working capital is essential for every firm. To utilize fixed assets in an optimal manner, firm requires the support of working capital. Working capital is regarded as the life-blood of a business enterprise.

Q.3. What is the purpose of 'operating cycle'?

Ans. Operating cycle is the period that a firm takes from purchase of raw materials, completion of manufacturing process, sale of goods till collection of cash finally from debtors. In other words, it is starting from cash and ending with cash and the total time period for the entire process is known as 'operating cycle'. It is also known as 'Gross operating cycle'.

Q.4. A firm does not want to assume more risk in financing its current assets. Which method of financing the firm has to adopt and what are its implications?

Ans. When the firm does not want to assume more risk in financing its current assets, it has to adopt "Matching Approach' in financing its current assets. In matching approach, fixed assets and permanent current assets are totally financed from long-term sources. Temporary current assets are financed by short-term sources. As the firm adopts a balanced approach, its risk and return would be moderate.

Q.5. What is 'Treasury Management'?

Ans. Treasury means cash. Treasury Management means managing the funds of an organization. Basically, treasury management deals with planning, forecasting of cash flows and arranging them in an optimal manner with the least cost. It is concerned with rising of funds at a cheap interest rate, investing surplus funds for a return with the overall objective of minimizing cost of funds, achieving optimum utilization of funds. It involves ensuring funds when required and not letting the funds idle for a long period.

CHAPTER 23

Receivables Management

23.1 INTRODUCTION

Accounts receivables or debtors are created as and when goods are sold on credit. Debtors occupy a predominant place, next to inventories in current assets. In India, debtors constitute about 30% in the current assets. When it is the practice in industry to sell on credit, it is not possible for an individual firm to avoid credit sales.

23.2 IMPORTANCE OF RECEIVABLES

Meaning: Book debts arise with credit sales. Majority of trade is carried on credit. Very few firms are fortunate to carry trade on cash and carry basis like gas cylinder business. It is not possible even for such firms to make cash sales totally. Credit sales have serious implications in the form of investment and risk. Additional investment is necessary as funds get tied up in current assets. To contain the risk at an acceptable level, managerial control is essential for efficient management of debtors.

Characteristics: Book debts have three peculiar characteristics. The first and most important feature is 'risk' they carry. If payment is not received, sale turns into a bad debt, eroding the profitability of firm. Not only profit on that transaction but even the cost of goods is lost. In other words, profit made on other sales is at stake till realization of proceeds of sale. Second, the 'economic value' in the goods (ownership) is transferred immediately from the seller to buyer. After sale, seller stands at the convenience of the buyer to receive payment. The third characteristic is its 'uncertainty' feature. The seller receives payment at a later date. This future event—'receiving the payment'—is a contingent or uncertain event. Payment depends on the willingness and capacity of the buyer on the due date. Lot of changes can happen between selling date and due date for payment. This picture cannot be foreseen at the time of sale.

23.3 OBJECTIVES OF RECEIVABLES MANAGEMENT

The objectives of receivables management are

- **Improvement of sales,**
- **Elimination of bad debts,**
- **Reduction of transaction costs incidental to maintenance of accounts**
- **Collection of sale proceeds and**
- **Enhance profits of the firm.**

Trade credit: Credit provided by supplier to buyer as per terms of trade practice is known as 'Trade credit'. Funds are not free to any one. Funds carry economic cost. For this reason, firms charge a higher price when sold on credit compared to cash sale price, which is a known fact. At times, supplier may provide more credit to buyers to lure to buy higher quantum of goods. Credit sales help organizations to make extra profit.

> **Trade credit is not free to buyer. Seller includes the cost of funds in selling price, depending on credit period allowed.**

Marketing tool: Book debts are used as a marketing tool for improvement of business. If the firm wants to expand business, it has to sell necessarily on credit. Additional sales do not create additional production costs till a certain level due to the presence of fixed costs. The additional contribution totally goes towards profit, improving the profitability of firm.

Optimum Level of Investment in Receivables: To support sales, it is necessary for firms to make investment in receivables. Investment in receivables involves costs as funds are tied up in debtors. Further, there is additional risk in respect of bad debts too. On the other hand, receivables bring returns. If so, till what level investment is to be made in receivables? **Investment in receivables is to be made till the incremental costs are less than the incremental return.** Thus, the objective of receivables management is to make a sound investment in debtors. In the words of Bolton, S.E., the objective of receivables management is " to promote sales and profit until that point is reached where the return on investment in further funding of receivables is not less than the cost of funds raised to finance that additional credit".

In simple words, **the objective of receivables management is to make a sound investment in debtors till such a point where the cost of investment is less than the return on investment.** Risk perception of the firm also plays a key role in the decision-making process of deciding the level of investment in receivables.

23.4 DIMENSIONS OF RECEIVABLES MANAGEMENT

Receivables management involves consideration of the following two dimensions or facets:

(A) Credit Policy

(B) Monitoring Receivables

23.4.1 Credit Policy

For efficient management of receivables, each firm has to design its own credit policy. Credit policy relates to fixing credit period and credit terms. Credit policy involves decisions relating to

(a) Credit standards or selection of customers,

(b) Credit terms and

(c) Collection efforts

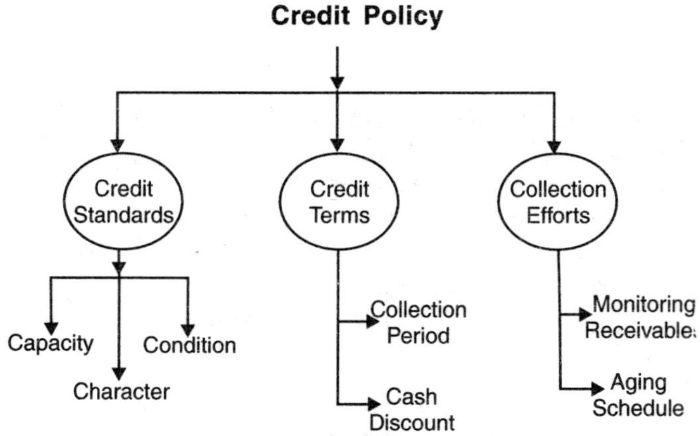

Managing Credit Policy

(a) **Credit standards or Selection of Customers: Credit standards are the criteria followed for selection customers for extending credit.** The volume of sales is influenced by the credit policy adopted by the firm. More sales can be created from more customers. But before credit is extended, investigation about creditworthiness of the potential customer is to be made to avoid bad debts and ensure repayment in the agreed time schedule. This process involves costs. In consequence, there is increased clerical work too to maintain more debtors' accounts in books of accounts and manage them. Additional staff is needed to make collections from them, in time. Above all, book debts may turn into bad debts. All this involves additional costs. On the other hand, more sales also result in more profits.

Firms have to strike a balance or bring a trade-off between incremental costs and incremental revenue that can be generated with additional sales.

The optimum sales would be that point where both additional costs and additional revenue are equal.

Selection of the customers should neither be too liberal nor too stringent. More liberal sales may add more revenue, but they also involve additional costs in the form of transaction costs for verifying the creditworthiness, clerical costs involved with maintenance of accounts and, finally, bad debts. With a liberal credit policy, firm sells to those whose creditworthiness is not known or not acceptable earlier. However, stringent policy also involves rejecting the customers who want to buy, but the firm is not willing to sell as it is not sure of their creditworthiness. In other words, the firm sells only to selective customers with a stringent policy. Both the policies of extreme stringent and lenient policies have shortcomings of their own. So, in practice, firms follow credit policies ranging between stringent and lenient policies.

The finance manager should consider three 'C's to form a reasonable judgment about the chances of default:

Character refers to customer's character, willingness to pay. Before sale is made, it is necessary for the seller to judge whether the customer would make adequate and reasonable efforts to honour the credit obligations. If customer does not have character, a basic requirement in business, chances of debt becoming bad are greater.

Capacity refers to the ability to pay. Ability is reflected in the financial position of the buyer. Financial position is found from ratio analysis.

Condition refers to the prevailing economic and other conditions which may affect customer's ability to pay on the due date. Condition on the sale date may be good but may deteriorate on the payment date. However, when goods are sold on short credit, chances of deterioration in such a short period are remote. Condition may be deteriorated on the sale date itself but may not to be known to the seller.

(b) Credit Terms: Credit terms refer to duration of credit and terms of payment by customers. Credit terms include

(i) Credit period and

(ii) Cash discount.

(i) Credit Period: Length of credit is influenced by the practice or custom prevalent in the industry. If a firm extends lower credit below the credit period allowed by the rest of the firms, its sales decline. So, by necessity, firms have to adopt similar practices followed by the industry. To attract new customers, some firms may give more credit than its competitors. It may extend more credit period, provided the existing customers agree to buy more quantity than their normal purchases. In other words, credit period is used as a marketing tool to improve the existing sales or arrest sales falling. But, more working capital is needed to extend more liberal period of credit. This also involves additional cost as there is cost of capital for the funds. The finance manager has to allow the firm so long as the incremental revenue is more than the additional costs that may be incurred by the firm by allowing liberal credit period, after analyzing the risk implications. Though credit period is allowed, firms allow cash discount to those firms, who pay earlier than the stipulated period of credit.

Cash Discount: Cash discount is not related to cash sales. There is some confusion amongst the students that cash discount is given by business firms when customers purchase on cash basis. This is not the case.

Cash discount has no connection with cash purchases. Cash discount is offered to lure customers, who purchase goods or services on credit to repay before the agreed period of credit.

A cash discount is a reduction offered, provided the payment is made, earlier, to the stipulated credit period allowed. So, the invoice should, clearly, state the rate of cash discount offered, period within which payment is to be made to avail the discount and also the normal credit period available, if discount is not availed. If the invoice states '2/20, net 30' it means discount of 2% is available, provided the payment is made within 20 days from the date of invoice. Otherwise, payment has to be made within the normal period of credit allowed, i.e. 30 days. The discount is, usually, expressed as a percentage of sales.

(c) **Collection efforts: Collection efforts influence the collection period.** If customers take longer period, higher amount would be blocked in receivables. The lower the collection period, the lower the investment and vice versa. If collection efforts become slack, investment in receivables becomes more unprofitable for the firms. Slackness in collections is the main cause for creation of bad debts. Debtors turn often bad because there is no follow up with them for payment in the form of reminders, personal as well as in writing. Bad debts happen on account of default on the part of delinquent customers. In case, results do not materialize in recovery, timely legal action is essential before the debts become time barred. Fixation of credit period itself is not sufficient, its execution in terms of follow up and recovery are important.

23.5 COST BENEFIT ANALYSIS

Firm may feel that it has been following liberal policy and incurring more bad debts and also more cost on the funds blocked by liberal credit. It may consider switching over to tight policy to overcome the bad debts as well reduce the cost involved in extending credit. Before the firm takes final decision, it has to weight the benefits and costs involved in the change of policy. If the benefits exceed the costs in the new policy—liberal to stringent or vice versa—it would be worthwhile for making a change. In case, costs exceed the benefits from the new policy, it is desirable to continue with the existing policy. Final bottom line, profitability is the deciding matter.

Whenever, firm changes existing credit policy—tight to liberal or vice versa—cost benefit analysis is essential.

Costs may be in the form of additional costs on funds blocked and additional selling and administrative costs. Interest burden is to be calculated, based on cost of goods sold. Benefits are generally in the form of additional contribution. A comprehensive and detailed calculation is needed before decision is taken for change of credit policy.

Illustration No. 1

Neha Kaushal & Co. is facing liquidity problem. To overcome liquidity problem, firm is planning to introduce cash discount to the customers who are enjoying credit sales. Presently, firm's credit policy is to extend a credit period of 60 days. It wants to change to '2/30, net 60'. Firm is paying an interest rate of 15% on the cash credit facility extended by the bank for meeting its working capital requirements. Make cost benefit analysis, if credit sales are ₹ 6,00,000 and it is estimated that 60% of customers are likely to avail the cash discount facility.

Jaya & Co. is making credit purchases of ₹ 1,00,000 from the above firm in a year. From the angle of Jaya & Co., do you consider it attractive to avail cash discount, if the firm is paying an interest rate of 15% to its bankers on its cash credit facility? Jaya & Co. does not experience any liquidity problem and bankers have no problem with them. Decide only on the basis of cost benefit analysis.

Consider year is of 360 days.

Solution

From the angle of Neha Kaushal & Co:

Cost:

Credit sales = ₹ 6,00,000

Customers who would avail cash discount facility (60%) = 3,60,000

Additional cost to the company in the form of cash discount = 2% on 3,60,000 = 7,200

Benefit:

Average period of credit saving = 60 – 30 = 30 days

Savings on interest paid to bank on cash credit account $= \frac{3,60,000}{360} \times 30 \times 15\% = 4,500$

Net cost to company on introduction of cash discount = Cost – Benefit

= 7,200 – 4,500 = 2,700

To ease liquidity problem, Neha Kaushal & Co. has to spend ₹ 2,700 additionally to introduce cash discount facility.

From the angle of Jaya & Co.

Cost:

Interest that is to be paid to avail cash discount

$$= \frac{1,00,000}{360} \times 30 \times 15\% = 1,250$$

Benefit:

Credit purchases in a year = 1,00,000

Cash discount would be availed = 1,00,000 × 2% = 2,000

Benefit to Jaya & Co. = Benefit – Cost = 2,000 – 1,250 = 750

Recommendation: It is desirable for Jaya & Co. to avail cash discount facility as it is beneficial by ₹ 750.

Illustration No. 2

To expand sales, Rupa & Co. plans to change their strategy of sales to overcome the liquidity problem it has been experiencing. It wants to introduce strict collection policies. At present, the firm sells 60,000 units per year with average collection period of 60 days. Collection charges amount of ₹ 20,000 and bad debts are 2% of sales. If collection procedures are tightened, it will reduce the collection period to 40 days. Bad debts losses reduce to 0.5% of sales. However, it involves additional collection charges of ₹ 3,000 and sales decline by 1,000 units.

Its present selling price is ₹ 40, which contains variable cost of ₹ 32. The average cost price is ₹ 35.

Advise firm on implementation of the proposed stringent selling policy. Assume 18% cost of funds.

Solution

Cost attached to proposal

(1) Loss of contribution

(1,000 units × ₹ 8) 8,000

Savings in variable costs.

(2) Additional collection expenses 3,000

(3) Savings on cost of funds –
decrease in investment
₹ 1,20,222 @ 18% 21,640
(Look to working notes)

32,640

Benefits attached to proposal

(1) Savings in bad debt losses
2% of old sales ₹ 24,00,000 48,000

36,200

0.5% of revised sales ₹ 23,60,000 (–) 11,800

Net benefit due to stringent policy (36,200 – 32,640) 3,560

As the benefits attached to the proposal to tighten the collection procedures exceed the costs attached to the same by ₹ 3,560 firm should implement the proposal.

Working Notes **Cost structure (Figure in ₹)**

	60,000 Units	59,000 Units
Sales (₹ 40/- per unit)	24,00,000	23,60,000
Variable cost (₹ 32/- per unit)	19,20,000	18,88,000
Fixed cost (35 – 32) x 6,000 units	1,80,000	1,80,000
Total cost	21,00,000	20,68,000
Average collection period	60 days	40 days
Daily outstanding investment (Assuming 360 days)	5833.33	5744.44
*Average investment, blocked throughout year	3,50,000	2,29,778
Savings in investment Savings in terms of cost on investment@ 18% **	1,20,222 21,640	

* Average investment is calculated by multiplying the daily outstanding with the number of days of credit allowed.

** Funds tied up in credit would remain outstanding throughout the year, so interest is calculated on the average investment for the year.

Illustration No. 3

A firm is proposing strict collection policies. At present, firm sells 36,000 units with average collection period of 60 days. Selling price of each unit is ₹ 32. Variable cost per unit is ₹ 25. Average cost of production per unit is ₹ 28. Collection charges:

₹ 10,000 and bad debts are 3% of sales. If collection procedures are tightened, it will reduce the collection period to 40 days and bad debts losses to 1% of sales. However, it involves additional collection charges of ₹ 20,000 and the sales decline by 2,000 units. Is it desirable to change the existing selling policy? Assume 15% cost of funds.

Solution

Cost attached to proposal

(1) Loss of contribution				
(2,000 units × ₹ 7)		14,000		
(2) Additional collection expenses		20,000		34,000

Benefits attached to proposal

(1) Savings in bad debts losses				
3% of old sales	₹ 11,52,000	34,560	23,680	
1% of revised sales	₹ 10,88,000	(–) 10,880		
(2) Savings in investment 15 % on 61,556 (Look to working notes)		9,233	9,233	32,913
Net cost due to proposed strict collection policy (34,000 – 32,913)				1,087

New policy, proposed stricter policy, would result in more costs (34,000) than the benefits (32,913). The new policy, if implemented, would reduce the existing profits by ₹ 1,087. So, the firm should continue to implement the existing policy and should not revise the proposed change.

Working Note	Cost structure	Figure in ₹
	36,000 Units	34,000 Units
Sales (₹ 32/- per unit)	11,52,000	10,88,000
Variable cost (₹ 25/- per unit)	9,00,000	8,50,000
Fixed cost (28 – 25) x 36,000	1,08,000	1,08,000
Total cost	10,08,000	9,58,000
Average collection period	60 days	40 days
Average outstanding investment	1,68,000	1,06,444
Savings in investment		61,556

23.6 CONFLICT BETWEEN LIQUIDITY AND PROFITABILITY

Both liquidity and profitability do not go together in receivables management. Let us see the situation when firm follows liberal credit policy. More credit sales require more working capital as more funds would be tied up in receivables. So when firm follows liberal credit policy, it experiences liquidity crunch. However, it would have higher profits. When the firm switches to follow stringent credit policy, it would discontinue sales to those customers who have been taking longer time for payments or their creditworthiness has become doubtful. Lesser sales ease the problem on liquidity front. As a result, firm would not have liquidity problems. However, less sales result in lesser profits and profitability problem commences. So profitability and liquidity are two conflicting issues.

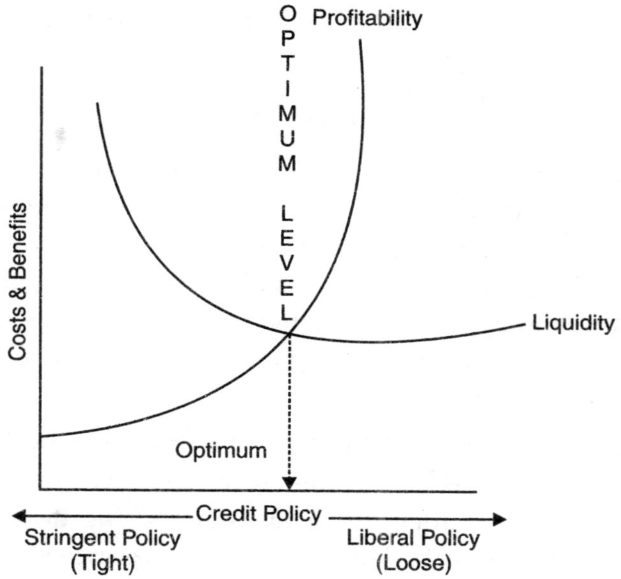

Optimum Size of Receivables

Optimum Credit Policy: As the firm moves towards liberal credit policy, sales would increase and as a result profitability would improve. However, liquidity would suffer as more funds would be tied up with more debtors. To correct the situation, when firm marches towards contraction of sales, adopting a stringent credit policy, sales would decrease. In consequence, liquidity would improve. But, in the process, profitability would be greatly affected due to reduction of sales.

> **Every firm tries to strike a balance between liquidity and profitability. This level is achieved when the incremental costs is equal to incremental revenue.**

Higher sales can be achieved by extending credit. It has two costs, interest on funds that are tied up from the date of sale till their realization and possibility of bad debts. Interest and bad debts increase costs while higher sales give more revenue. That level would be the optimum size of receivables where the incremental costs are equal to incremental revenue. So, optimum credit policy is the objective of management of receivables.

23.7 MONITORING RECEIVABLES

To monitor receivables, calculation of average period and comparing the actual period of credit with the credit period allowed is the first step for the purpose of monitoring the receivables in aggregate. The next step is preparation of aging schedule for identifying the group, where action is needed.

Average Collection Period: The average collection period is determined as follows:

$$ACP = \frac{\text{Debtors}}{\text{Credit sales}} \times 365$$

This collection period is to be compared with the credit terms fixed. This shows the efficiency of the collection department. For example, if credit period allowed is 30 days while the average collection period shows 60 days, it shows laxity of collection department. The average collection period is based on the aggregate data and it suffers from the limitation of showing specific picture where exact concentration or action is needed to tone up efficiency for improving the recoveries. This problem can be solved with the aging schedule.

Aging Schedule: The quality of debtors can be measured by looking at the age of debtors. Aging schedule breaks down debtors to the length of time for which they have been outstanding. This helps in identifying the slow-paying debtors' group. From the group, individual debtors have to be identified, who have exceeded the period of credit allowed. Concerted action has to be initiated in respect of those debtors. Legal action is the last step one has to resort when all other follow up measures have failed.

The following illustration is explained for understanding the picture better.

Illustration No. 4

Atul Ltd. has ₹ 7,50,000 in receivables on 31-12-2004. The amount contains sales of December ₹ 3,00,000; November ₹ 2,25,000; October ₹ 1,50,000 and remaining prior to October 2004. If the term of credit offered by the company is 'Net 30 days', prepare an aging schedule of receivables keeping in view the credit period and comment on the collection efforts of company. Do you offer any suggestion for improving collections?

Solution

Outstanding period (Months)	Outstanding amount of receivables (₹)	Percentage of total receivables
0 – 1	3,00,000	40 %
Above 1 –Below 2	2,25,000	30 %
Above 2 –Below 3	1,50,000	20 %
Above 3 Months	75,000	10 %
Total Debtors	7,50,000	100

Assessment of collection efforts: The first category is 40%, which is within the normal period of credit granted by the firm. This category does not cause any anxiety as the outstanding is within the normal period of credit allowed.

The rest 60% is overdue for payment. This is an abnormally high and anxiety causing.

This shows the collection department is inefficient and its follow up is not adequate. On account of the slow collections, firm must be experiencing liquidity problem. Delayed collections affect profitability of the firm too as funds carry cost.

Immediate action is needed for the last category, which is above 3 months. In fact, examination of individual debtors' accounts falling in this group is immediately required. If necessary, legal action may be initiated in respect of chronic cases before the cases are time barred by limitation.

Suggestion: It has to be examined whether the firm has made any assessment to introduce cash discount as an inducement to accelerate collections. The collection policy indicates the payment system as 30 days credit, which does not offer any inducement for earlier payments. It is advisable to adopt discount system after carefully examining the incremental costs as well as incremental revenue that may generate.

The risk the firm, already exposed too, also has also to be examined.

Illustration No. 5

Ajay Kumar Patel & Co. provides the following details and seeks your advice in respect of liberalizing credit policy of his company.

Sales	= ₹ 5,00,000
Selling price per unit	= ₹ 50
Variable cost per unit	= ₹ 30
Total cost per unit	= ₹ 45
Credit period allowed to customers	= one month

The firm is considering a proposal for a more liberal extension of credit which results in average collection period from one month to two months. This liberal credit policy is expected to increase the sales by 25% from its existing level.

Firm is borrowing at 20% in the market and additional sales shall result in payment of additional incentive of 8% on increased sales to total marketing personnel at the end of year.

Comment whether the new credit policy is beneficial or not? Calculate the return on additional investment in receivables.

Solution

Existing position:

Sales	= ₹ 5,00,000
Selling price per unit	= ₹ 50
No. of units sold	$= \frac{5,00,000}{50} = 10,000$ units

Total cost per unit = ₹ 45

Present total cost of sales = ₹ 45 × 10,000 units = ₹ 4,50,000

Existing investment (one month credit) $= \frac{4,50,000}{12}$ = ₹ 37,500

Proposed position:

Present sales = 10,000 units

Additional sales 25% = 2,500 units

Total sales = 12,500 units

Total sales value = 12,500 units x 50 = ₹ 6,25,000

Total cost of sales:

Existing = ₹ 4,50,000

Additional variable cost

@ ₹ 30 on 2,500 units = ₹ 75,000

₹ 5,25,000

Proposed investment (two months credit) $= \frac{5,25,000}{12} \times 2$ = ₹ 87,500

Additional investment = 87,500 – 37,500 = 50,000

Benefit:

Contribution = Selling price per unit – Variable cost per unit = 50 – 30 =20

Contribution on additional sales 2,500 × 20 = **₹ 50,000**

Cost:

Interest cost = Proposed investment (two months credit) – Existing investment (one month credit)

= 87,500 – 37,500 = 50,000

= 20 % on ₹ 50,000

= 10,000

Additional incentive 8% on 1,25,000 (6,25,000 – 5,00,000) = 10,000

Total cost **20,000**

Net benefit = 50,000 – 20,000 = 30,000

As there is net benefit, the new credit policy is beneficial.

Return on additional investment in receivables

$$= \frac{\text{Profitability of additional sales}}{\text{Additional investment in receivables}} \times 100$$

$$= \frac{30,000}{50,000} \times 100 = 60\%$$

Illustration No. 6

Zaliyappa & Co. wants to expand its sales. Its present sales are ₹ 4,00,000. Selling price per unit is ₹ 20. Variable cost is ₹ 10 and average cost is ₹ 14. Existing credit period is 30 days. Market survey reveals that the existing selling price is to be reduced by 10 % to make further sales. Presently, there are no bad debts. Liberal credit would result in bad debts by 1% on total sales. Credit involves cost and interest rate is 20% per annum. Assume 360 days in a year.

There are three following alternatives. Which alternative is recommended?

Credit policy	Increase in collection period	Increase in sales (₹)
A	15 days	1,00,000
B	30 days	2,00,000
C	45 days	2,50,000

Solution

Evaluation of different credit policies

Particulars	Present	A	B	C
Credit period	30 days	45 days	60 days	75 days
Sales (₹)	4,00,000	5,00,000	6,00,000	6,50,000
No. of units @ ₹ 20 per unit (present) and ₹ 18 per unit proposed	20,000	27,778	33,333	36,111
Variable cost ₹ 10 per unit	2,00,000	2,77,780	3,33,330	3,61,110
Fixed costs (Average cost ₹ 14 – Variable cost ₹ 10) x 20,000	80,000	80,000	80,000	80,000
Total costs	2,80,000	3,57,780	4,13,330	4,41,110
Profit (A)	1,20,000	1,42,220	1,86,670	2,08,890
Average debtors (at cost) Total costs / 360 days x Credit period	23,333	44,722	68,888	91,898
Cost of credit @ 20 % (B)	4,667	8,944	13,778	18,380
Bad debts (1% on total sales, if collection period is increased) (C)	Nil	5,000	6,000	6,500
Net Profit {A – (B + C)}	1,15,333	1,28,276	1,66,892	1,84,010

Recommendation: Credit Policy – C is giving the maximum amount of profit ₹ 1,84,010. It is recommended to adopt credit policy – C.

Test Your Analytical Skills

Explain the impact of receivables individually and other incidental implications in case of the following events, making the necessary valid assumptions?

(A) Boom

(B) Interest rate increases significantly.

(C) Production and selling costs increase due to inefficiency of the staff.

(D) Firm changes the credit terms from '3/10, net 30 to 4/10, net 30'.

(E) Depression

Answers

(A) Receivables increase. During boom, sales increase. More funds would be tied up in receivables and receivable increase. Profits also normally increase.

(B) Receivables normally increase. Increase in interest rate causes increase in cost of production. As a result, firm increases selling price to meet the increased cost of production to have the same profit margin. This is the likely situation as interest rate increase would affect the industry as a whole. A higher selling price results in increased receivables. However, if the firm absorbs the increase in cost from its profit margin and decides not to pass on the burden to its customers, there would be no impact on receivables.

(C) No impact on receivables. The increase in cost of production and selling costs is confined to this firm alone. The increase in costs is not applicable for all firms in the industry. If it increases the selling price to retain the profit margin, it is likely firm's sales would reduce. So, firm does not take any action on the front of increasing the selling price.

(D) Decrease in receivables. Firm is offering a higher discount rate of 4% instead of the existing discount rate of 3%. So, more buyers would be tempted to avail the benefit of cash discount. So, realizations would be fast and investment in receivables goes down improving liquidity of the firm. So, receivables go down. There may be impact on profitability due to higher discount rate unless the firm utilizes the improved liquidity in a better manner.

(E) Decrease in receivables. During depression, there would be lesser sales and the market would be dull. Lesser sales reduce the investment in receivables.

Check Your Understanding

(A) State whether the following statements are True or False

1. There would be no change in working capital to extend more liberal period of credit than presently allowed.
2. The lower the collection period, the lower the investment and vice versa.
3. Credit policy plays a vital role in determining the investment in receivables.
4. Bad debts happen on account of default on the part of delinquent customers.
5. It is desirable to follow stringent credit policy to avoid bad debts.
6. Aging schedule does not help in making assessment of the age of debtors' outstanding period.

7. Firm can extend more credit if the incremental revenue is higher than the incremental costs.
8. Credit standards indicate the selection criteria for the choice of customers to whom credit extension can be made.
9. The objectives of receivables management are to expand sales and increase profits.
10. Both extreme stringent and lenient policies of receivable management have shortcomings of their own.
11. The volume of sales is influenced by the credit policy adopted by the firm.
12. Firm's sales reduce when it follows a liberal credit policy.
13. Optimum credit policy is the objective of management of receivables.
14. Cash discount is usually expressed as a percentage of sales.
15. Slackness in collections is the not cause for creation of bad debts.

Answers

1. False 2. True 3. True 4. True 5. False 6. False 7. True 8. True
9. True 10. True 11. True 12. False 13. True 14. True 15. False.

(B) Objective Questions (Identify what is most appropriate)

1. When goods are sold on credit, this is created.
   (A) Accounts payable (B) Accounts receivable
   (C) Cash sales (D) Bills payable
2. As and when goods are sold on credit, this situation creates
   (A) additional investment and risk. (B) lower investment and safety.
   (C) same investment but more profits. (D) reduced investment with less profits.
3. Credit sales contain these important characteristics.
   (A) risk, safety and profits.
   (B) certainty of receipt in time and immediate change of ownership in goods.
   (C) risk and uncertainty in receipt of payment with immediate change of ownership in goods.
   (D) risk, certainty of receipt of payment and change of ownership in goods at a later date.
4. This is not the objective of receivables management.
   (A) Improvement of sales.
   (B) Elimination or reduction of bad debts.
   (C) Collection of sale proceeds in time.
   (D) Maintaining same level of profits.
5. Additional sales create this immediately, without an increase in fixed costs.
   (A) Contribution (B) Loss
   (C) More convenience in making sales
   (D) Lesser difficulties in managing marketing personnel

6. Investment in receivables is to be made till
   (A) incremental returns < incremental costs
   (B) incremental returns > incremental costs
   (C) incremental costs > incremental returns
   (D) None of the above

7. Credit policy does not involve this.
   (A) Credit standards or selection of customers
   (B) Fixing credit terms
   (C) Making collection efforts
   (D) Elimination of costs

8. While adopting a credit policy, firm can follow this policy depending on its approach.
   (A) liberal selection of customers to whom credit can be extended.
   (B) stringent credit policy .
   (C) Policy in between (A) and (B).
   (D) Any one of the above.

9. Stringent credit policy involves
   (A) Rejecting customers who want to buy but the firm is not willing to sell as their creditworthiness is not satisfactory or not known.
   (B) Accepting all customers who want to buy.
   (C) Rejecting all customers and not selling to any one.
   (D) Accepting those customers only who are willing to pay on cash.

10. Liberal credit policy means
   (A) Accepting those customers who are agreeable to pay cash immediately.
   (B) Rejecting those customers who do not agree to the existing credit terms.
   (C) Choosing those customers only whose creditworthiness is well known.
   (D) Extending credit to those who creditworthiness has not been accepted, earlier.

11. A balanced credit policy means
   (A) Liberal credit policy
   (B) Stringent credit policy
   (C) An approach in between total liberal and total stringent policy
   (D) None of the above

12. Liberal credit policy results in
   (A) more investment in debtors. (B) less investment in debtors.
   (C) more profits with less investment. (D) none of the above.

13. Credit terms does not involve
   (A) credit period. (B) cash discount.
   (C) credit period and cash discount.
   (D) selection of customers to whom credit is to be extended.

14. If the invoice states '2/20, net 30' it means
    (A) credit period of 30 days with no benefit for early payment.
    (B) credit period of 20 days with 2 % benefit for early payment.
    (C) benefit of 2% on cash sales.
    (D) credit period of 30 days with 2 % benefit for payment within 20 days.
15. In managing accounts receivables, when incremental costs are equal to incremental revenues, this level is known as
    (A) maximum sales.
    (B) minimum sales.
    (C) optimum level of investment in receivables.
    (D) break – even sales.
16. Credit policy covers
    (A) Selection of customers to whom credit sales are to be made.
    (B) Fixation of credit period.
    (C) Cash discount rate and its qualifying period.
    (D) All the above.
17. Optimum investment in receivables is the point where
    (A) incremental costs exceed incremental revenues.
    (B) incremental revenues exceed incremental costs.
    (C) incremental costs and incremental revenues are equal.
    (D) incremental costs and incremental revenues go together.
18. Purpose of aging schedule of accounts receivables is to find out
    (A) Age of each debtor.
    (B) Length of outstanding period for each group of debtors to monitor their realisation.
    (C) Both (A) and (B).
    (D) None of the above.
19. The average collection period of debtors is determined with the following formula.
    (A) $\frac{\text{Total debtors} \times 365}{\text{Cash sales}}$ (B) $\frac{\text{Total debtors} \times 365}{\text{Cash and credit sales}}$
    (C) $\frac{\text{Total creditors} \times 365}{\text{Cash sales}}$ (D) $\frac{\text{Total debtors} \times 365}{\text{Credit sales}}$
20. When the firm experiences liquidity problem, the following solution would improve collections of accounts receivables.
    (A) Introduction of cash discount with suitable qualifying period.
    (B) Slackening efforts of collection department.
    (C) Offering higher period of credit.
    (D) Removal of sales manager.

21. Before introduction of cash discount to improve liquidity of receivables, it is necessary for the firm to conduct
    (A) Credit benefit analysis.
    (B) Cost benefit analysis.
    (C) Cash benefit analysis.
    (D) Cost, credit and cash benefit analysis.

22. To determine the efficiency of collection department, this information is vital.
    (A) Period of credit allowed to debtors and actual period of their realization.
    (B) Average collection period of creditors with their realization.
    (C) Payment period of creditors.
    (D) Period of credit allowed to debtors for payment.

23. There is no relationship between the following terms.
    (A) Buyer and seller
    (B) Credit sale and risk
    (C) Investment and profit
    (D) Accounts receivable and accounts payable

Answers

1. (B)	2. (A)	3. (C)	4. (D)	5. (A)	6. (B)	7. (D)	8. (D)
9. (A)	10. (D)	11. (C)	12. (A)	13. (D)	14. (D)	15. (C)	16. (D)
17. (C)	18. (B)	19. (D)	20. (A)	21. (B)	22. (A)	23. (D)	

Descriptive Questions

1. What is 'Receivables Management'? How is it useful to business operations? **(23.1 and 23.2)**
2. Explain the meaning and objectives of receivables management. **(23.2 and 23.3)**
3. What should be the considerations in formulating a credit policy? **(23.4 and 23.4.1)**
4. Explain the objective of credit policy. What is an optimum credit policy and show it with pictorial presentation? **(23.4 and 23.4.1)**
5. Explain cost benefit analysis in the context of receivable management. **(23.5)**
6. 'Liquidity and Profitability are conflicting with each other while following credit policy'. How a firm can bring trade-off between the two? **(23.4 and 23.6)**
7. What are the different dimensions of 'Receivables Management'? **(23.4, 23.4.1 and 23.7)**
8. Explain significance of optimum credit policy. **(23.6)**

Short Questions

Q.1 What is 'Trade credit'? Is trade credit free to a buyer?

Ans. Majority of trade is carried on credit and period of credit depends on nature of business and practices followed in the industry to which the firm belongs to. Very few goods and services are sold on cash. Credit provided by supplier to buyer as per terms of trade practice is known as 'Trade credit'. At times, supplier may provide more credit to buyers to lure to buy higher quantum of goods.

Trade credit is not free to a buyer. Funds have economic cost and are not free to seller too. So, seller includes the cost of funds depending on credit period allowed in the selling price.

Q.2. Why supplier prefers to supply goods or services through a bill of exchange?

Ans. Bill of exchange facilitates documenting the trade transaction in a better way. This mode of trade is indeed better when buyer is new and his creditworthiness is also not known to seller. Bill of exchange is drawn by seller on buyer who accepts on it. Due date for payment is fixed in advance. When bill of exchange is presented on due date by seller or his banker, payment is made by buyer. In case, seller is in need of funds before due date, he can discount the bill of exchange with his banker and get payment, paying discount charges. Banker would feel confident too that credit is provided to facilitate genuine trading transaction. More so, bill of exchange has self-liquidating character as the advance is closed once bill is paid by buyer on the due date.

Interview Questions

Q.1. What is meant by credit policy?

Ans. Credit policy relates to fixing credit period and credit terms. Credit policy involves decisions relating to selection of customers, credit terms and collection efforts.

Q.2. What is the importance of credit policy?

Ans. Basically, credit policy is used to promote sales and in turn improve profitability. Credit policy is concerned with the selection of customers, determination of credit period and allowing cash discount. While determining credit policy, cost-benefit analysis is undertaken. If a change in credit policy results in more benefit compared to costs, new policy is welcome. Otherwise, there is no point in changing the existing credit policy.

Q.3. Why firms introduce cash discount?

Ans. Firms introduce cash discount to encourage its customers, availing credit, to repay before the stipulated credit period. Cash discount helps the firm to improve its liquidity position. Before extending cash discount, cost benefit analysis is always undertaken to decide the quantum of cash discount and period that would be eligible to get the benefit.

OO

CHAPTER

24

Inventory Management

24.1 INTRODUCTION

Inventories constitute a major component in current assets. It constitutes around 60% in the public limited companies in India. For the smooth running, every enterprise needs inventory. Inventories serve as a link between production and distribution processes. Due to its major composition in current assets, management of inventories occupies a key role in working capital management. Excessive investment affects the liquidity. Inadequate investment makes the firm to loose the business opportunities, otherwise available. Profitability would be affected with excessive or inadequate investment. So, **inventory management is essential to allow every firm to avail opportunities to improve profitability and at the same time does not impair its liquidity with excessive or unproductive investment.** A firm that neglects the inventory management jeopardizes its long-term profitability. So, it is absolutely imperative to control and manage inventory holding both efficiently and effectively to avoid unnecessary investment.

24.2 MEANING AND NATURE OF INVENTORY

Inventory means finished goods only in a retail business. However, it includes raw materials, work-in-process, finished goods and stores in a manufacturing organization.

> **A company's merchandise is raw materials, finished and unfinished products which have not yet been sold. These are considered liquid assets, since they can be converted into cash quite easily. There are various means of valuing these assets, but to be conservative the lowest value is usually used in financial statements.**

Raw Materials: Raw materials are the basic inputs, which are converted into finished products in the manufacturing process. They are needed to carry out the production, smoothly, uninterrupted. **Holding period of raw materials depends on the length of conversion cycle and time needed to replenish them.**

Work-in-progress: Work-in-progress is the semi-finished products. To become finished products still they are to undergo further process. They are in the intervening stage between raw materials and finished products. The quantum of work-in-progress depends upon time that is needed for completing the manufacturing process. **Longer the manufacturing process more amount would be blocked in the form of work-in-progress.**

Finished Goods: Finished goods are those, which are completely manufactured and ready for sale. When a firm manufactures, on receipt of order only, to suit the individual specific needs of the buyer, there will be minimum finished stock. Firms, which produce goods without waiting for any formal order have to maintain the finished goods.

Finished goods are a buffer between production and market.

Adequate stock with full range is necessary for marketing.

Stocks of raw materials and work-in-progress are necessary for the smooth production while finished stocks are important for marketing operations.

Nature of Business: The levels of the above inventories depend upon the nature of business. If the activity is manufacturing, large quantity is always blocked up in raw materials, finished goods and work-in-process. If the business is retail or wholesale, the inventory holding lies only in the form of finished goods only.

Supplies: Stores and spares are called as 'supplies', the last category of inventories. They do not enter into production but are very much necessary for production. Examples are brooms, soap, oil, fuel, light bulbs etc. The consumption pattern of spares is different from the normal consumption pattern of raw materials, work-in-progress and finished goods. They do not normally require any sophisticated system of inventory control technique for maintaining them unless the spares are highly expensive.

24.3 BENEFITS OF HOLDING INVENTORIES

Holding inventories is expensive in the form of storage costs, interest charges, deterioration of quality in holding stocks, theft and pilferage. Firms hold inventories basically for the following reasons:

Transaction Motive: Sufficient stocks of raw materials are to be maintained to facilitate uninterrupted production. There is always a time lag between the date of placing order and its actual receipt. There could be delays due to strikes, lock out and transport problems. Transaction motive takes care of these contingencies.

Precautionary Motive: Holding inventories is necessary to safeguard the unforeseen changes in demand and supply forces and other factors, which cannot be anticipated.

Production is dependent on demand of the finished product. If there is more demand for the product, more raw materials would be consumed. Consumption of raw materials cannot be forecast, with absolute accuracy. Sufficient stocks are to be maintained to suit the fluctuations in demand. Similarly, problems in supply may arise. Stocks are to be kept to guard against the changes in demand and supply, which are not foreseen.

> **Forces which could be foreseen are taken care by the transaction motive while forces that cannot be foreseen are guarded by precautionary motive.**

Speculative Motive: When firm anticipates increase in prices of raw materials in future, it stocks to take the advantage. Firm takes suitable decisions to change the stock holding pattern depending on increase or decrease in prices. Bulk order discounts may be offered to attract higher purchases. Reordering costs may be another factor in holding more quantity of inventories, than needed.

Example: A pan shop fellow purchases and stores cigarettes in bulk quantity before announcement of annual budget by the Finance Minister. It is a known fact that there would be some increase or other in excise duty on cigarettes every year. In consequence, prices of cigarettes invariably increase every year after budget. To take advantage of immediate price gain, almost every pan shop vendor and retail stores keeps more quantity than need before budget, in anticipation of price increase.

> **Even a pan shop vendor stocking cigarettes before annual budget is a classical example of speculative motive.**

24.4 RISK AND COST OF HOLDING INVENTORIES

The following are the risks and costs associated in holding inventories:

(A) Capital Costs: Holding inventories involves funds. Funds may be used from own sources or borrowings. If own sources are not blocked up in inventories, they can be used elsewhere profitably. This is the opportunity cost firm has incurred. If funds have been borrowed, interest is to be paid. So, in both the cases firm incurs cost. In case of own funds, it is opportunity cost and in case of borrowings, it is interest cost.

(B) Recurring Costs: Firm incurs recurring costs in the form of storage and insurance charges. Storage costs can be rent for godown or warehousing charges, if stored in outsiders' godowns.

(C) Risk of Deterioration: Stocks may deteriorate in quality due to long storage. Once goods loose their quality, they may not be even in saleable condition.

(D) Risk of Obsolescence: Goods may cease to be useful due to technological changes, changes in requirements and tastes etc. Now, we do not see floppy drive in the new computers coming into market as floppy drive has given place to CD drive.

24.5 OBJECTIVES OF INVENTORY MANAGEMENT

In inventory management, every firm is faced with two conflicting issues:

- Maximize investment by maintaining excessive quantity so that production is not affected and business opportunities are not lost for want of stocks.
- Minimize investment in inventories as they involve costs and affect profitability adversely.

Optimum stock: Excessive stocks and inadequate stocks, both are dangerous points. Excessive stocks result in additional costs due to storage charges, interest cost, and deterioration loss and obsolescence risk. Above all, funds are tied up in inventories and this creates liquidity problem. Inadequate stocks result in stock-out situations and cause loss in profits. In other words, excessive and inadequate stocks move in opposite directions. Both the extreme situations are unacceptable. Firm has to maintain that much stock, just enough to meet the production needs so that there is no interruption in production and no customer goes back disappointed for lack of stocks. This situation can be achieved by maintaining optimum stock level, which is in between the excessive stocks and inadequate stocks. So, every firm tries to achieve that optimum stock holding. The level of optimum stock holding is not static. The optimum level changes due to changes in demand and problems of supply. Demand for the product varies and supply constraints crop up, which are not anticipated. The finance manager has to ensure the optimum stock holding to achieve the conflicting objectives of profitability and liquidity at the same time.

The primary objective of inventory management is to maintain the right quantity of stocks in right location at right time to ensure uninterrupted production and at the same time minimize the investment in stock holding.

To sum up, the objectives of inventory management can be summarized:

- Maintain continuous supply of raw materials so that production is not affected,
- Minimize the carrying costs and lead-time in supplies,
- Maintain sufficient stocks of finished goods for smooth sales operations and business opportunities are not lost,
- Ensure perpetual inventory control so that physical stocks are always in agreement with stocks shown in records and
- Facilitate furnishing of data for short-term and long-term planning and inventory control.

24.6 TOOLS AND TECHNIQUES OF INVENTORY MANAGEMENT

Efficient inventory management requires effective control system. A proper inventory control system helps enterprises in solving problems of liquidity, eliminating excessive stocks and achieving increased profits with substantial reduction in working capital.

The following are the techniques of inventory management and control:

(A) Determination of stock levels

(B) Determination of Economic Order Quantity

(C) A.B.C Analysis

(D) V E D Analysis

(E) Perpetual Inventory System

(F) JIT Control System

(G) Inventory Turnover Ratios

24.7 DETERMINATION OF STOCK LEVELS

Carrying too much stock and too little stocks, both are detrimental to firms. If stock is too little, frequent stock-out situations firms face. Due to inadequacy of stocks, firms miss business opportunities. If it is too high, profitability will be affected due to increased cost of stock holding. In this context, it is relevant to discuss various types of stock levels.

(a) Minimum level: This is the minimum quantity that must be maintained, at all times. If the stock holding falls below this level, production stops due to shortage of materials. This level is fixed considering the following factors:

Lead-time: After placing the requisition for materials, some time is needed to process and place the order. If the material required is new, firm has to explore availability of options. Normally, every firm initiates tendering process to purchase at the most economic price. This involves time. Material does not come immediately as and when request for the material is made. After receipt of order, supplier too takes some time to execute the order. So, raw material holding is needed during the process time and execution time so that production does not suffer, which is called 'Lead Time".

Consumption rate: It is the average rate of consumption of raw materials in a factory. This rate of consumption can be calculated based on the earlier period's consumption rate, past experience and future plans. If factory enhances capacity to match increased production plans consumption rate also enhances.

Nature of materials: The nature of materials affects the minimum level. If firm produces soon after receipt of order only no minimum stock is needed.

The formula for computation of minimum stock is as under:

Minimum Stock Level = Re-ordering level – (Normal Consumption × Normal Re-order Period)

Normal re-order period means the period that is normally required to execute the order after placing order for supply of materials.

(b) Re-ordering Level: When the stock level reaches the re-ordering level, the order is placed for replenishment of stocks. This level is fixed in between the maximum stock and minimum stock. This level is decided after consideration of the following factors such as maximum consumption per day and maximum number of days required to supply the stocks. It is difficult to foresee the consumption pattern with full accuracy. Days that may be required to get supply of stocks may vary depending on unforeseen problems of transportation, bottlenecks and other factors. To be on safe side, maximum consideration is given for both the factors. Supply of materials would be received when the stock position reaches the minimum level; even when materials are consumed at the maximum requirement.

The formula for calculation is

Re-ordering Stock Level = Maximum Consumption per day × Maximum Re-order Period

Maximum Level: It is the level beyond which stock level should not exceed. If this level is exceeded, there would be blockage of working capital, loss due to wastages, risk of obsolescence and more rent for storage space etc.

The formula is as under:

Maximum Stock Level = Re-ordering Level + Re-ordering Quantity – (Minimum Consumption × Minimum Re-ordering Period)

Average Stock Level: The formula for calculating average stock is as under:

Average Stock Level = Minimum Stock Level + ½ of Re-order Quantity

Safety Stock: Consumption of raw materials depends upon production level. Production changes on the demand for finished products. The demand for the finished product is not always constant due to varying conditions. So, consumption of raw materials is not always constant. There should be safety stock to take care of fluctuations in consumption pattern of raw materials. The time taken for getting replenishment of stocks may also vary due to unforeseen problems of strikes or lockouts. So, every firm has to maintain certain amount of stock as safety stock to take care of unforeseen consumption pattern as well as extra unforeseen time for procurement of materials. Basically, safety stock is to meet unforeseen contingencies. Two costs are involved in determination of safety stocks i.e. opportunity cost of stock-outs and carrying costs. The stock-outs of raw materials cause disruption in production. Similarly, the stock-outs of finished goods provides an opportunity to competitors to capture firm's share, resulting in loss of profit on sales missed. This is a hidden cost. Customer service is also affected. On the other hand, larger quantity of safety stocks involves higher carrying costs.

Danger Level: This is the absolute minimum level below which stocks should not fall. When stock reaches this level, stock would be issued only to the emergency requirements and just to maintain the machinery working to avoid dry out situation.

The formula for calculating danger level is as under:

Danger Level = Average Consumption × Maximum re-order Period for Emergency Purchases

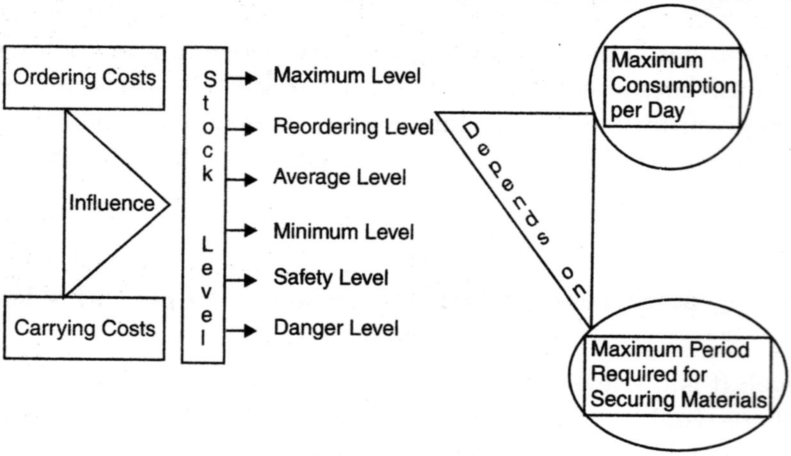

Inventory Levels

Illustration No. 1

In a firm, two types of materials 'A' and 'B' are used. Per week usage is as under:

	"A"	"B"
Normal usage	500 units	300 units
Maximum usage	750 units	400 units
Minimum usage	250 units	100 units
Re-order quantity	3000 units	5000 units
Re-order period	4 to 6 weeks	2 to 4 weeks

From the above information calculate:

(i) Re-order level (ii) Minimum stock level

(iii) Maximum stock level (iv) Average stock level

Solution

(i) Re-ordering Level: Maximum Consumption per week × Maximum Re-order Period

A = 750 × 6 = 4,500

B = 400 × 4 = 1,600

(ii) Minimum Stock Level = Re-ordering level – (Normal Consumption × Normal Re-order Period)

A = 4,500 – (500 × 4) = 4,500 – 2,000 = 2,500 units

B = 1,600 – (300 × 2) = 1,600 – 600 = 1,000 units

(iii) Maximum Stock Level = Re-ordering Level + Re-ordering Quantity – (Minimum Consumption × Minimum Re-ordering Period)

A = 4,500 + 3,000 – (250 × 4) = 4,500 + 3,000 – 1,000 = 6,500 units

B = 1,600 + 5,000 – (100 × 2) = 1,600 + 5,000 – 200 = 6,400 units

(iv) Average Stock Level = Minimum Stock Level + ½ of Re-order Quantity

A = 2,500 + ½ × 3,000 = 2,500 + 1,500 = 4,000 units

B = 1,000 + ½ × 5,000 = 1,000 + 2,500 = 3,500 units

Illustration No. 2

A TV manufacturing company purchases 1,600 units of a component. Its annual usage is 1,600 units. The order placing cost is ₹ 100 and the cost of carrying one unit per year is ₹ 8. Calculate the Economic Order Quantity. Prove that the total costs of ordering and storage are the least at EOQ quantity.

Solution

Formula for determining Economic Order Quantity = $EOQ = \sqrt{\frac{2AO}{C}}$

Where A = Annual consumption in terms of quantity

O = Cost of placing an order

C = Inventory carrying costs, per one unit

$$EOQ = \sqrt{\frac{2 \times 1,600 \times 100}{8}} = 200 \text{ units}$$

Table showing the Economic Order Quantity

Annual requirement	Orders per year	Units per order	Order placing costs @ 100 per unit	Average inventory in units (50% of order placed)	Carrying costs @ 8 per unit	Total Annual costs
1	2	3	4	5	6	(4+6)
1,600	1	1,600	100	800	6,400	6,500
	2	800	200	400	3,200	3,400
	3	533	300	267	2,136	2,436
	4	400	400	200	1,600	2,000
	5	320	500	160	1,280	1,780
	6	267	600	134	1,072	1,672
	7	229	700	115	920	1,620
	8	**200**	800	100	800	**1,600**
	9	178	900	89	712	1,612
	10	160	1,000	80	640	1,640

EOQ is 200 units. At this point, the total costs (ordering costs + storage costs) are the least. At all other levels, in excess and below 200 units, the total costs comprising and ordering costs are not the least. This proves that the total costs would be the least at EOQ quantity.

24.8 ECONOMIC ORDER QUANTITY

For effective inventory management, it is necessary to determine what should be the quantity of stock that has to be ordered for replenishment, periodically. The stock to be purchased should neither be small or big. To avoid accumulation of stocks, if frequent ordering of stock is made more ordering costs would be incurred. On the other hand, lesser number of stock orders results in accumulation of stocks, which result in higher carrying costs. Economic order quantity is that size lot which is economically viable.

Economic Order Quantity refers to that size of order which gives maximum economy in purchasing any item of raw materials and finished products.

Ordering Costs: These are the costs of placing an order and securing supplies. These are also known as buying costs as they are incurred at the time of purchase only.

Carrying Costs: Carrying costs are the costs for holding inventories. They are incurred for maintaining a given level of inventory. They are the costs for keeping items in stock. Carrying costs vary with the size of inventory. Higher the stock holding, larger would be carrying costs and they would be lower if the stocks are lower. Inventory may be high sometimes and low other times. For a proper calculation, carrying cost is calculated on the average inventory.

Ordering costs are referred as "costs of acquiring" while carrying costs are known as "costs of holding" inventory.

The components of costs for both the categories are as under:

Components of ordering costs and carrying costs

Ordering costs	Carrying costs
• Requisitioning costs (Indent for materials) • Processing & Placing order • Transportation of goods • Receiving and inspecting costs for incoming materials • Cost of stationery, typing, postage and telephone etc. • Clerical and staff costs for rendering the above services	• Interest on cost of capital, invested in inventories • Rent for storing • Handling costs • Clerical and staff costs for recording receipts and issues • Insurance • Deterioration and obsolescence loss • Cost of spoilage in handling materials

Both quanity and cost of goods in terms of value influence economic order quantity. Quantity influences ordering costs as well as storage costs. Value of goods influences the amount of capital invested, either own or borrowed funds, which in turn changes storage costs.

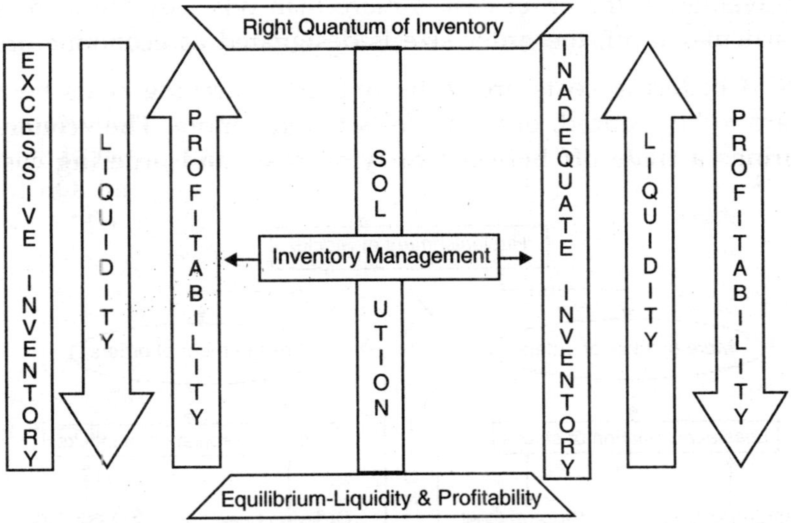

Efficient Inventory Management

24.8.1 Determination of Economic Order

Need for Determination of economic order: In inventory management, both stock-out and excessive stocks are unacceptable situations. If stock-outs are often in a firm, even loyal customers get frustrated. Customers' service gets affected. Competitors who look for opportunity to lure customers take advantage of the situation. Sales fall with frequent stock-outs affecting profitability adversely. To avoid such situation, if excessive stocks are maintained more funds get tied up in stocks and firm suffers liquidity problem. More stocks than necessary eats profitability too. The solution is fixing right economic order quantity.

Behaviour of Storage costs and Ordering costs: Ordering costs and storage costs are the aggregate costs for inventory holding. Ordering costs and carrying costs are inter-related and inverse in their relationship. In other words, they behave in an opposite direction. Let us explain their consequences. To avoid stock-outs, frequent re-orders have to be made. More orders result in more ordering costs. To reduce ordering costs, the other alternative is to fix a higher size while placing the order. With a higher size of stocks, more funds get tied up resulting in loss of liquidity. More so too much stocks result in more carrying costs. So, a higher level of stocks mean liquidity problem and also reduced profitability. To avoid accumulation of stocks, order size is to be reduced. This results in more number of orders with increased ordering costs. In other words, if ordering costs are to be reduced, carrying costs become more. If carrying costs are to be reduced, ordering costs become more.

Now, let us see the reaction of total cost in the entire process. The total cost declines initially due to reduction in the ordering cost on account of bigger size of order. But later the total cost (carrying cost + storage cost) starts increasing due to higher carrying cost as size of the order has gone up. The level when total cost starts increasing is when the decrease in average of the order cost is more than offset by the increase in carrying cost. At this particular level, the order size is designated as economic order quantity.

To sum up, if ordering costs are to be reduced, carrying costs become more. If carrying costs are to be reduced, ordering costs become more. **The economic order size of inventory brings a trade off between carrying costs and ordering costs.**

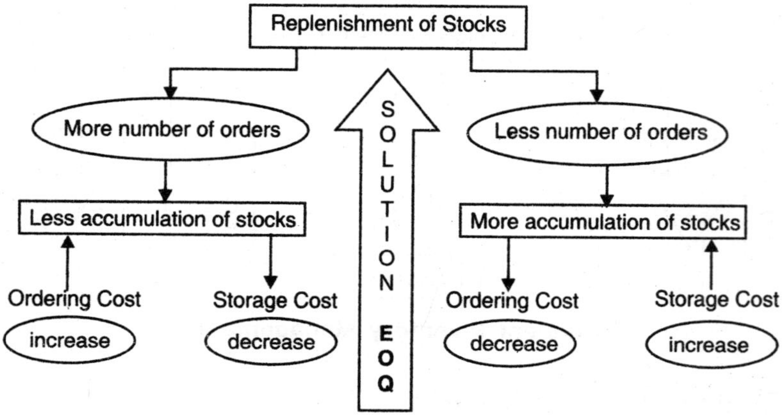

Behaviour of Storage costs & Ordering costs

The economic order size of inventory brings a trade off between carrying costs and ordering costs. If firm places the order for that item at that economic order quantity, then the annual cost of inventory of that item will be minimized.

The formula for determining Economic Order Quantity is:

$$EOQ = \sqrt{\frac{2AO}{C}}$$

where A = Annual consumption of unit in terms of quantity

O = Cost of placing an order

C = Inventory carrying costs per one unit

Assumptions: While calculating EOQ, the following assumptions are made:

(A) The total usage of a particular material is known and its usage is even throughout the year, Requirement of materials is certain.

(B) Material is readily available and there is no gap between placing an order and getting its supplies.

(C) Cost per order is constant.

(D) Cost of carrying inventory is also fixed and uniform throughout the period.

(E) There are no other costs other than carrying cost and ordering cost.

Graphical Presentation: The EOQ model can be presented graphically. The size of order is presented on the horizontal axis. The costs—carrying, ordering and total costs—are shown on the vertical axis. The picture shows that the order cost decreases with the increase in size of the order. To explain, let us take an example. If annual consumption of an item is 1,000 pieces and order is placed for 200 pieces each time, orders have to be placed five times in a year. If we increase size of the order from 200 to 500 pieces, number of orders gets reduced from 5 to 2. The ordering costs would be lower for two orders compared to five orders. In other words, with increase in size of order, total ordering costs would reduce.

As the size increases, the total number of orders for a particular item decreases as order costs are spread over a larger quantity. Due to increase in size of order, more stocks are purchased and more money is tied up in inventory, which results in increase of carrying cost. To reduce carrying cost firm starts cutting the size of the order. Then, the carrying cost starts falling. Carrying costs and ordering costs behave in opposite directions and reduction of one results in increase of other and vice versa.

> **In inventory Management, Economic Order Quantity is achieved when the total cost is at its minimum for the enterprise.**

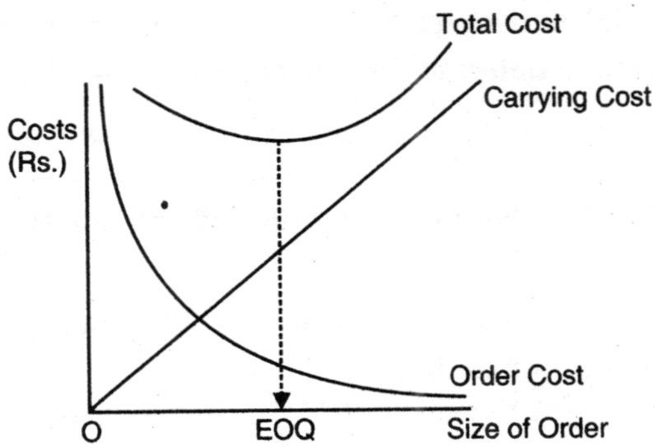

Graphical presentation of the EOQ model

EOQ is not the point, where ordering cost and carrying cost intersect. EOQ is that point, where total cost is at its minimum level.

Criticism:

1. **Not possible to predict consumption with accuracy:** It is not possible to predict the annual consumption with accuracy. The pattern of demand for finished products is likely to change. The actual demand for any item fluctuates. As and when demand for finished goods changes, production would also correspon-

dingly changes. It is not possible to predict demand of finished products correctly, which depends on consumer behaviour. In consequence, it is not possible to forecast the annual consumption of raw materials, correctly.

2. **Gap between date of placing order and receipt of materials:** Gap between date of placing order and receipt of materials is assumed nil. This assumption is totally unrealistic. It is unlikely that the supply of raw materials is available, without any delay.
3. **Ordering costs are fixed:** Another assumption with EOQ model is that the ordering costs are fixed and not a function of the size of the order. There are always economies of scale with larger order due to quantity discounts. So, the assumption is not realistic.
4. **Storage costs are fixed:** Storage costs are not always constant. With increase in quantity, storage efficiency develops resulting in lower storage costs.
5. **Exact quantity hypothetical:** Another shortcoming is that the exact quantity shown by EOQ model may be hypothetical. EOQ model may state the 567.2 units as the right quantity to place the order. It is not possible to pace the exact quantity due to fractions. Quite often, orders can be placed only in a particular multiple size i.e. multiples of dozens or 10's or 100's, which may be the normal practice with the wholesalers or industry. At best, EOQ can be a range, not a point.

EOQ is a basic model and extensions can be made to remove the shortcomings of EOQ model deleting its unrealistic presumptions.

Illustration No. 3

From the following particulars, calculate Economic Order Quantity and number of orders to be placed in each year:

Annual consumption of materials	= 5,000 kg.
Cost of placing per order	= ₹ 3
Cost per unit	= ₹ 2 per kg.
Storage and carrying cost	= 6% on average inventory

Solution

Formula for determining Economic Order Quantity =

$$EOQ = \sqrt{\frac{2AO}{C}}$$

A = Annual consumption in terms of quantity
O = Cost of Placing an order
C = Inventory Carrying costs, per one unit

$$EOQ = \sqrt{\frac{2 \times 5{,}000 \times 3}{2 \times 6\%}}$$

$$= 500 \text{ kg.}$$

$$\text{No. of orders to be placed per year} = \frac{\text{Total consumption per year}}{\text{Economic order quantity}}$$

$$= \frac{5{,}000}{500}$$

$$= 10 \text{ orders per year}$$

Economic Order Quantity is 500 kg and number of orders to be placed per year is 10.

Note: **While working out the problem annual consumption in number of units (quantity) is to be taken into account, not the cost of consumption in rupees. Most of the students take cost of consumption, which is incorrect. The economic order quantity is in units hence cost per unit has no significance.**

Illustration No. 4

Dheera & Co. is running a garment factory. Her factory makes 20,000 units of nighties annually. Cost per order is ₹ 75. Price per unit is ₹ 150. Storage cost is 12% per annum. Calculate economic order quantity.

Solution

$$EOQ = \sqrt{\frac{2AO}{C}}$$

A = Annual consumption in terms of quantity
O = Cost of placing an order
C = Inventory carrying costs per one unit

$$EOQ = \sqrt{\frac{2 \times 20{,}000 \times 75}{18}}$$

$$= 408 \text{ units}$$

Illustration No. 5

The following information is available in respect of an enterprise:

Annual consumption of a raw material	= 20,000 units
Ordering cost per order	= ₹ 1,875
Carrying cost	= ₹ 3 per unit/per annum

Find out the Economic Order Quantity of the raw material, number of orders to be placed in a year. Please verify the results, assuming any increased quantity and lower quantity.

Solution

The formula for determining Economic Order Quantity is:

$$EOQ = \sqrt{\frac{2AO}{C}}$$

where A = Annual consumption of unit in terms of quantity
O = Cost of placing an order
C = Inventory carrying costs per one unit

$$= \left[\frac{2 \times 20{,}000 \times 1{,}875}{3}\right]^{\frac{1}{2}}$$

$$= 5{,}000 \text{ units}$$

The total consumption in a year is 20,000 units and economic order quantity is 5,000. It means the number of orders in a year is 4 (20,000/5,000).

(A) If 5,000 units are the EOQ, let us check what the total cost is:

Total order cost = 1,875 × 4 = ₹ 7,500

Average inventory = 2,500 (5,000/2)

Total carrying cost = Average inventory × Carrying cost per unit
= 2,500 × 3 = 7,500

Total cost of inventory = Total order cost + Total carrying cost
= 7,500 + 7,500
= ₹ 15,000

(B) Let us check, what is the total cost for EOQ of 2,000 units

The total number of orders would be 10 (20,000/2,000)

Total order cost = 1,875 × 10 = ₹ 18,750

Average inventory = 1,000 (2,000/2)

Total carrying cost = Average inventory × Carrying cost per unit
= 1,000 × 3 = 3,000

Total cost of inventory = Total order cost + Total carrying cost
= 18,750 + 3,000
= ₹ 21,750

(C) Let us check, what is the total cost for EOQ of 10,000 units

The total number of orders would be 2 (20,000/10,000)

Total order cost = 1,875 × 2 = ₹ 3,750

Average inventory = 5,000 (10,000/2)

Total carrying cost = Average inventory × Carrying cost per unit

= 5,000 × 3 = 15,000

Total cost of inventory = Total order cost + Total carrying cost

= 3,750 + 15,000

= ₹ 18,750

Conclusion: It may be noted that total cost of holding inventory is the lowest at the economic order quantity. If the quantity per order is increased, the total cost increases. Similarly, if quantity per order is reduced even then the total cost increases. This only establishes that the total cost is the lowest, only at the economic order quantity.

> **EOQ is that quantity where the total costs associated with purchase (annual cost of consumption, storage costs and carrying costs) are the lowest.**

Control on purchase costs: Economic order quantity (EOQ) helps the firm to control purchase costs. When purchase costs are controlled, funds are not unnecessarily tied up in stocks and in consequence profitability of the firm greatly improves. When economic order quantity only is replenished, stocks do not lie in the firm, unnecessarily. At this level, the total costs associated with inventory, purchase costs, storage costs and ordering costs, in aggregate, would be the lowest.

> **Total inventory costs comprising purchase costs, ordering costs and storage costs are the least at economic order quantity level. Holding costs are minimum at this level.**

The following illustration explains the above.

Illustration No. 6

The following data is extracted from the books of Gopi Sailaja & Co.

Annual requirement = 10,000 units

Cost per order = ₹ 2

Cost per unit = ₹ 8

Carrying cost = 2%

Determine the economic order quantity. Establish that the total cost (cost of materials, ordering costs and storage costs) are the lowest at EOQ level only with any assumed figures. Your example has to prove that EOQ is in the best interests of the organization.

Solution

Economic order quantity = $EOQ = \sqrt{\frac{2AO}{C}}$

where A = Annual consumption of unit in terms of quantity
O = Cost of placing an order
C = Inventory carrying costs per one unit

Carrying cost per unit = 8 × 2%
= ₹ 0.16

$$EOQ = \sqrt{\frac{2 \times 10,000 \times 2}{0.16}}$$

= 500 units

Economic order quantity = 500 units

Number of orders per year (based on EOQ) $= \frac{10,000}{500} = 20$

The average quantity in stock (between fully replenished and empty) is EOQ/2.

Average quantity = Economic order quantity/2

Storage (Holding) cost = Average quantity in stock × carrying cost

Purchase costs = Cost per unit × Annual requirement

Total cost = Purchase costs + Ordering costs + Storage costs

Total cost = 8 × 10,000 + 2 (10,000/500) + 0.16 (500/2)

Total cost = 80,000 + 40 + 40

= ₹ 80,080

If we check the total cost for any order quantity other than 500 units (EOQ), we will see that the cost is higher.

For instance, suppose 600 units per order, then

Total cost = 8 × 10,000 + 2(10,000/600) + 0.16(600/2)

Total cost = 80,000 + 33 + 48

= ₹ 80,081

Suppose 400 units per order, then

Total cost = 8 × 10,000 + 2(10,000/400) + 0.16(400/2)

Total cost = 80,000 + 50 + 32

= ₹ 80,082

Similarly, if we choose 300 for the order quantity, then

Total cost = 8 × 10,000 + 2(10,000/300) + 0.16(300/2)

Total cost = 80,000 + 67 + 24

= ₹ 80,091

This proves that the economic order quantity is always in the best interests of the entity.

24.9 A.B.C ANALYSIS

'A.B.C' stands for 'always better control'. A.B.C analysis is concerned with selective control of inventory management. An analytical survey of the composition of inventory in most of the manufacturing organizations has revealed that 10% of the materials contribute for 70% of the cost of materials while 70% of the materials constitute 10% of the total cost. The first category, is classified as 'A' category while the later is 'C' category. In between falls the 'B' category, which contains 20% of costs as well as materials. If same importance is given in respect of control for all materials equally, result would not be effective.

> **The essence of selective control of inventory management is to allocate importance of control to goods based on their composition cost.**

It is desirable for organizations to give more concentration for 'A' category of items due to higher cost composition in the total inventory cost. As concentration is on the fewer items, result would be effective.

Under ABC analysis, item is allocated to the group depending on the amount of attention it deserves. "A" group requires the maximum concentration of the finance manager. This group constitutes a higher % in terms of value, while it occupies lesser significance in terms of number of units. "B" group requires lesser attention, compared to "A" group. The last group "C" has to be given the least attention as it constitutes less value in the total annual consumption.

In other words, the procedure is to divide the total inventory into three groups based on the total cost of each group. The first group should cover 70% of total cost of inventory where closer concentration has to be given to achieve better control on a selective basis. The second group should cover 20% while the last group falls into the category of 10% cost.

Method of Preparation: The method of preparation is as under:

(A) Calculate annual consumption of each item in a year.

(B) Arrange the annual consumption of different items of materials in descending order i.e. highest value first and then next like that.

(C) Calculate consumption of each item as a per cent of total consumption of all materials.

(D) Calculate the cumulative consumption in terms of per cent.

(E) When the total touches around 70%, the first group where concentration is needed is arrived at.

(F) The following groups are to be calculated for 20% and 10% accordingly.

An illustration explains the concept better.

Illustration No. 7

The following is the consumption of Dimpy & Co. for different items of inventory. Calculate the items as per ABC analysis and advise the group, where concentration is required most.

Item no.	Annual consumption (in terms of units)	Rate (per unit) (₹)	Total Value of consumption (₹)
1.	6,000	100	6,00,000
2.	10,000	65	6,50,000
3.	5,000	50	2,50,000
4.	25,000	2	50,000
5.	4,000	25	1,00,000
6.	15,000	10	1,50,000
7	25,000	6	1,50,000
8	10,000	5	50,000
Total	1,00,000		20,00,000

Solution

Priority order	Item no.	% each item in total no. of units	Total value of consumption (₹)	% of each item in total value	Cumulative %
1	2	10%	6,50,000	33%	33%
2	1	6%	6,00,000	30%	63%
3	3	5%	2,50,000	12%	75%
4	6	15%	1,50,000	8%	83%
5	7	25%	1,50,000	8%	91%
6	5	4%	1,00,000	5%	96%
7	4	25%	50,000	2%	98%
8	8	10%	50,000	2%	100%
Total		100%	20,00,000		

Group	Item No.	% Items (in units)	% Items (in value)
A	2, 1, 3	21%	75%
B	6, 7	40%	16%
C	5, 4, 8	39%	9%

Conclusion:

This exercise shows where concentration is needed.

Group 'A' = This group requires maximum monitoring by the finance manager. By concentrating on three items out of eight items, around 75% of materials, in terms of value, are monitored though the materials in number constitute only 21%. This proves how a lesser amount of concentration can yield better results.

Group 'B' = This is the next group where concentration is needed. Concentration of two products gives result for controlling 16% in terms of value while in number of materials the group constitutes 40%.

Group 'C' = Items 5, 4 and 8 requires the least concentration as their value is only 9%.

24.10 V E D ANALYSIS

The V E D Analysis is used for control of spare parts. A-B-C analysis is concerned with materials and is not totally and properly suitable for spares. Spares are divided into three categories, **Vital, Desirable and Essential.** Here, cost is not of importance but its necessity for smooth production assumes importance. If the spares are vital, a must for the smooth running, they are to be stored in adequate quantity. Highest importance is to be accorded for this category of spares. If the vital spares, required for uninterrupted production, are not available there would be havoc in production. **The classification has to be done by the technical staff depending on the necessity of spares for smooth running of production. It is important that no interference is to be made with the classification of technical department.** Vital items have to be kept in high quantity while essential items are to be kept in reasonable limits. If the desirable items are readily available on placing the order, no need to keep those items in large quantity, except a small quantity just to fill in the occasional need.

24.11 PERPETUAL INVENTORY SYSTEM

Normally, stock taking is done at the end of year. In perpetual inventory system, the stock taking may be done either regularly or continuously.

The procedure is as under:

(A) Stock taking team selects the storeroom where stock taking is to be done on a random basis.

(B) All bins in that storeroom are checked.

(C) The physical balance in the bin is counted or measured dependent on the type of material.

(D) The actual stock is recorded in the sheets provided for this purpose.

(E) There is no prior intimation to the stores department to maintain surprise element.

(F) All the stores are checked at least three or four times in a year on a rotation basis.

(G) There is a surprise element to the stores personnel so that shortages cannot be accommodated from other sources as intimation is given on the day of checking only.

(H) If there is discrepancy between stock ledgers and bin card with physical stocks, they are investigated immediately as there could be posting mistakes in stores ledger.

(I) Only after verification and obtaining proper approval, shortages and excesses, if any are recorded in the bin cards and stores ledger, as physical stocks rule the actual position.

Advantages: These are the following advantages:

1. **Stock records are always updated:** As the inventory taking programme is not known in advance, all the stores departments keep their bin records and stores ledgers updated always.
2. **Quick calculation of closing stock:** Stock taking need not be done separately at the end of the year. As a result, closing stock can be valued at the end of year without delay and financial statements like profit and loss account and balance sheet are prepared well in time.
3. **Check on stores personnel due to surprise element:** Due to surprise element, there is a regular check on the stores personnel. Stores personnel keep their records updated always. If advance intimation is given, there is a possibility for the stores personnel to accommodate the shortages from some other sources for a temporary period. Above all, there would be greater control on theft and pilferage.
4. **Errors and shortages easily detected:** Due to continuous verification, mistakes and irregularities come to light early for proper control. There would be fear that defalcations, if any, would be detected early. Laxity in control is avoided.
5. **Reconciliation between stores ledger and bin card with physical Stocks:** Reconciliation between stores ledger and bin card with physical stocks occurs periodically, which otherwise is not done in stock taking, except at the end of year.
6. **Helping in formulating purchase policies:** The system is helpful in formulating purchase policies. Stores personnel know when the materials are needed, which material is more needed by production department. They can provide the information relating to quantity, time and quality of materials, which helps

management in formulating suitable policies.

7. **Investment in inventory under check:** The system helps in fixing minimum and maximum quantity so that stock-out situation is avoided while controlling excessive maintenance of stocks. This helps in controlling investment in inventories.

8. **Increases the overall efficiency of organization:** The system tones up performance of the organization on all fronts which results in overall improvement in liquidity as well as profitability.

24.12 JUST IN TIME (JIT) INVENTORY CONTROL SYSTEM

The basic philosophy of JIT is to keep only enough quantity of stock on hand to meet the immediate production requirements.

> **JIT concept relies on the suppliers to furnish 'stock' 'just in time' as and when needed. It shows the level of confidence firm has on its suppliers for punctual delivery schedule.**

Just in time (JIT) inventory control system aims at eliminating wastages from every aspect of manufacturing. This was first introduced in Japan in 1950s. Toyota was the first company to practice this technique. Broadly, there are two aspects, (i) Just in time purchasing and (ii) Just in time production. JIT wants to avoid materials for storing and they should be available only when they are needed to meet its requirements.

Goal of JIT: The conventional inventory control system is totally in contrast to this concept. The traditional system is based on maintaining a healthy level of safety stock to protect against the uncertainties in production. The traditional system has worked well so long as interest costs and storage costs have been low. When the carrying cost has gone up due to high interest rate and other associated costs, the goal of JIT- maintain only essential stocks – is highly relevant in the current context of competitive environment.

> **The focus of JIT is to maintain relationship building with suppliers to enable them to purchase right quantities at right time. This underlines importance of meticulous planning both at buyers as well as suppliers end.**

The major thrust is to purchase or produce in response to need rather than as per plan and forecasts.

Objectives of JIT:

(A) Minimum/zero inventory and associated costs.

(B) Zero breakdown and continuous production.

(C) Manufacturing the right quantity at right time.

(D) Ensure timely delivery of inputs as well as outputs.

Major Advantages of JIT:

(A) Right quantities are purchased and produced in right time.

(B) Wastages are eliminated totally.

(C) Investment in inventory is controlled.

(D) Carrying cost is reduced.

24.13 INVENTORY TURNOVER RATIOS

Inventory turnover ratios indicate efficiency in using inventory. Inventory turnover ratio indicates the number of times the stock has turned over a period of one year. More the number of times, more efficient the organization is. The inventory conversion period shows number of days stock is blocked. A detailed coverage has already been made in the chapter dealing with Ratio Analysis.

Check Your Understanding

(A) State whether the following statements are True or False

1. Inventories serve as a link between production and distribution processes.
2. Stocks of raw materials and work-in-progress are necessary for marketing operations while finished stocks are important for the smooth production.
3. Holding period of raw materials depends on the length of conversion cycle and time needed to replenish them.
4. The primary objective of inventory management is to maintain the right quantity of stocks at right location and right time to ensure uninterrupted production and minimize the investment in stock holding.
5. The economic order size of inventory brings a trade off between carrying cost and ordering cost.
6. The costs that are associated with purchasing and placing an order is called carrying costs.
7. Higher the stock holding, larger would be carrying costs and they would be lower if the stocks are lower.
8. The time required to process and execute an order is called lead-time.
9. The total cost of inventory is not an aggregate of order cost and carrying cost.
10. ABC analysis is used to manage spare parts etc.
11. Ordering costs is also known as buying costs.
12. The total cost is the lowest at economic order quantity.
13. Raw materials' value is an important factor in determination of its economic order quantity.

Answers

1. True 2. False 3. True 4. True 5. True 6. False 7. True 8. True
9. False 10. False 11. True 12. True 13. False

(B) Objective Questions (Identify what is most appropriate)

1. This is the predominant component of current assets of any company
   (A) Cash and Bank (B) Debtors and Bills receivable
   (C) Inventory (D) Plant and Machinery
2. In a manufacturing organization, inventory means
   (A) Raw materials (B) Work-in-progress
   (C) Finished goods (D) Stores and spares
   (E) All the above
3. This component gives least value, if sold in its present form.
   (A) Raw materials (B) Work-in-progress
   (C) Finished goods (D) All the above
4. This current asset has to pass more stages to improve liquidity of the firm.
   (A) Bank balance (B) Bills receivable
   (C) Finished goods (D) Accounts receivable
5. This current assets disappears last, if the firm experiences liquidity problem.
   (A) Cash balance (B) Bank balance
   (C) Finished goods (D) Accounts receivable
6. When this asset is sold on credit, first it is to be sold and later has to be realized hence it is said that this asset is the least liquid.
   (A) Bank balance (B) Bills receivable
   (C) Accounts receivable (D) Finished goods
7. This current asset serves as a link between production and distribution process.
   (A) Inventories (B) Debtors
   (C) Bills payable (D) Creditors
8. For efficient working capital management, management of this asset plays a key role due to its major composition in current assets.
   (A) Bank balance (B) Inventories
   (C) Debtors (D) Bills receivable
   (E) Creditors
9. Excessive holding of inventories seriously affects
   (A) Liquidity of the firm (B) Profitability of the firm
   (C) Both (A) and (B) (D) Smooth production schedule of the firm
10. Inadequate investment in inventories affects
    (A) Business opportunities of the firm (B) Smooth production schedule of the firm
    (C) Both (A) and (B) (D) Neither (A) nor (B)
11. Efficient inventory management in the firm is essential to
    (A) improve profitability, without choking liquidity
    (B) decrease liquidity (C) decrease profitability
    (D) decrease liquidity and improve profitability

12. Determination of the quantity for which the order should be placed which gives maximum economy in purchasing raw materials depends upon
    (A) length of conversion cycle
    (B) Economic order quantity
    (C) Period needed to realize book debts
    (D) Period needed to make payment to suppliers of raw materials
13. This type of firms does not require finished stocks.
    (A) Firms engaged in tailor – made products.
    (B) Firms engaged in common products.
    (C) Firms engaged in those products, which are easily saleable.
    (D) Firms engaged in those products, which are difficult to be sold.
14. Finished goods serve this objective or purpose.
    (A) Transaction motive (B) Precautionary motive
    (C) Speculative motive (D) All the above
15. This takes care of those factors that cannot be foreseen.
    (A) Transaction motive (B) Precautionary motive
    (C) Speculative motive (D) All the above
16. Costs which are incurred for holding inventories are called
    (A) Carrying costs (B) Ordering costs
    (C) Both (A) and (B) (D) None of the above
17. If frequent orders are placed to control accumulation of stocks, these costs would increase.
    (A) Carrying costs (B) Ordering costs
    (C) Both (A) and (B) (D) None of the above
18. In inventory management, ordering costs and carrying costs behave in
    (A) opposite direction and maintain inverse relationship.
    (B) same direction and maintain opposite relationship
    (C) direction that cannot be predicted.
    (D) none of the above.
19. The time required to process and execute the order is called
    (A) short time (B) lead time
    (C) excess time (D) normal time
20. These are the costs which are associated with procurement (acquisition) of materials.
    (A) Carrying costs (B) Ordering costs
    (C) Both (A) and (B) (D) None of the above
21. At this level, the total inventory cost is minimum.
    (A) Minimum level (B) Maximum level
    (C) Normal level (D) EOQ level

22. This is the level at which an order should be placed for replenishment of stocks.
    (A) Re-order level (B) Maximum level
    (C) Normal level (D) EOQ level

23. Minimum stock level plus half of the re-order quantity is equal to
    (A) Minimum level (B) Average level
    (C) Normal level (D) EOQ level

24. Solution for purchasing the right quantum of stocks lies in determination of
    (A) Minimum level (B) Maximum level
    (C) Normal level (D) EOQ level

25. At this level, quantity purchased at one time is neither more nor less while achieving the objective of keeping the inventory costs at the lowest level.
    (A) EOQ level (B) Maximum level
    (C) Normal level (D) Minimum level

26. EOQ may sometimes give misleading results due to this assumption which does not happen in practical life.
    (A) Uniform consumption pattern of materials
    (B) No time lag between placing an order and receipt of materials
    (C) Carrying costs per unit are constant
    (D) Ordering costs per unit are fixed
    (E) All the above

27. Economic order quantity shows the
    (A) optimum level of order of stocks to be placed
    (B) optimum level of holding of stocks
    (C) Both (A) and (B)
    (D) None of the above

28. The following are the risks and costs associated in holding inventories.
    (A) Capital costs (B) Recurring costs
    (C) Risk of deterioration and obsolescence
    (D) (B) and (C) (E) None of the above

29. An efficient inventory management ensures
    (A) Maintaining minimum stocks (B) Maintaining maximum stocks
    (C) Maintaining normal stocks (D) Ensuring total costs of inventory lowest

30. Perpetual inventory control ensures
    (A) Agreement of physical stocks with book stocks
    (B) Ensuring early detection of errors and irregularities in stock records
    (C) Keeping stock records updated
    (D) All (A), (B) and (C)
    (E) None of the above

31. Inventory management decisions in a firm affect
    (A) liquidity
    (B) profitability
    (C) Both (A) and (B)
    (D) None of the above
32. EOQ of raw materials is based on
    (A) annual consumption of raw materials in quantity
    (B) raw materials in value influencing cost on borrowing
    (C) storage costs of raw materials
    (D) carrying costs of raw materials
    (E) All the above
33. EOQ helps in determining right quantum of
    (A) stock holding
    (B) stock ordering
    (C) both (A) and (B)
    (D) None of the above
34. Optimum stock holding is based on
    (A) maximum stocks
    (B) minimum stocks
    (C) neither excessive nor inadequate stocks
    (D) average stocks
35. Optimum stock holding is a
    (A) static situation
    (B) dynamic situation
    (C) passive situation
    (D) fixed situation
36. Optimum stock holding is based on
    (A) demand conditions for the goods at that particular time period.
    (B) supply conditions of the goods at that particular time period.
    (C) demand and supply conditions of the goods at that particular time period.
    (D) none of the above
37. If 'A' is annual consumption, 'C" is carrying costs and 'O' is ordering costs
    EOQ =
    (A) $-\sqrt{\frac{2AC}{O}}$
    (B) $\sqrt{\frac{2AC}{O}}$
    (C) $\sqrt{\frac{AO}{C}}$
    (D) $\sqrt{2AOC}$
38. The objective of inventory management is to ensure
    (A) control on ordering and storing costs.
    (B) uninterrupted production.
    (C) minimise investment in stock holding.
    (D) all the above.

39. If the firm follows the principle of economic order quantity, it's ordering and carrying costs would be
    (A) maximum (B) minimum
    (C) unpredictable (D) none of the above

40. Total costs comprising purchase costs, ordering costs and storage costs are the least at
    (A) above economic order quantity level (B) below economic order quantity level
    (C) economic order quantity level (D) none of the above

41. At economic order quantity level, holding and storage costs are
    (A) maximum (B) minimum
    (C) neutral (D) unpredictable

42. At economic order quantity, this cost is the least.
    (A) Aggregate of purchase cost, ordering costs and storage costs.
    (B) Ordering costs (C) Storage costs.
    (D) None of the above

43. This is not considered in the calculation of economic order quantity.
    (A) Carrying costs (B) Ordering costs
    (C) Value of materials (D) None of the above

44. The term 'inventory' refers to this.
    (A) Raw materials (B) Work-in-progress
    (C) Finished goods (D) All the above

45. Adequate quantity of this commodity is necessary for marketing operations of the firm.
    (A) Raw materials (B) Work-in-progress
    (C) Finished goods (D) None of the above

46. In a retail business, this is the major part of inventory in current assets.
    (A) Raw materials (B) Work-in-progress
    (C) Finished goods (D) Stores and spares

47. This commodity is very much necessary for production in a manufacturing business though does not enter into production.
    (A) Raw materials (B) Work-in-progress
    (C) Finished goods (D) Supplies

48. This is not a technique of inventory management.
    (A) A.B.C. Analysis (B) V E D Analysis
    (C) Determination of EOQ (D) Minimum level

49. To avoid stock out situation and stoppage of production, firm must maintain this level at all times.
    (A) Maximum level (B) Minimum level
    (C) Lead time (D) Consumption rate

50. '........ time' is the time taken for getting supplies after receipt of its requisition as supplier also needs time for its execution of order.

    (A) Normal time (B) Lead time
    (C) Sufficient time (D) Consumption time

51. In inventory management, normal re-order period means
    (A) Period required for placing the order
    (B) Period required for execution of the order
    (C) Quantity required for execution of the order
    (D) Period required for making payment for supplies made

ANSWERS

1. (C)	2. (E)	3. (B)	4. (C)	5. (C)	6. (D)	7. (A)	8. (B)
9. (C)	10. (C)	11. (A)	12. (B)	13. (A)	14. (D)	15. (B)	16. (A)
17. (B)	18. (A)	19. (B)	20. (B)	21. (D)	22. (A)	23. (B)	24. (D)
25. (A)	26. (E)	27. (C)	28. (D)	29. (D)	30. (D)	31. (C)	32. (E)
33. (C)	34. (C)	35. (B)	36. (C)	37. (B)	38. (D)	39. (B)	40. (C)
41. (B)	42. (A)	43. (C)	44. (D)	45. (C)	46. (C)	47. (D)	48. (D)
49. (B)	50. (B)	51. (B)					

Descriptive Questions

1. What is the importance of inventory management? Describe the objectives of inventory management? **(24.1, 24.2 and 24.5)**
2. "There are two dangerous situations that management should avoid in controlling the inventories". Elaborate? **(24.1 and 24.5)**
3. Explain the nature, meaning and benefits of holding inventory? **(24.1, 24.2 and 24.3)**
4. What type of risks and costs are involved in holding inventories? **(24.4)**
5. Define the economic order quantity? How it is computed? **(24.1, 24.8 and 24.8.1)**
6. "The management of inventories must meet two opposing needs". What are they? How a balance is brought between the opposing needs? **(24.1, 24.5 and 24.8)**
7. Define the term inventory control? What are the inventory control systems? **(24.6 to 24.13)**
8. Explain the various tools and techniques used for inventory management? **(24.6 to 24.13)**
9. What is meant by 'Economic order quantity'? What are the various costs which affect economic order quantity? **(24.8 and 24.8.1)**
10. What is a selective control of inventory? Why is it needed? **(24.9)**
11. "In inventory Management, Economic Order Quantity is achieved, when the total cost is at its minimum for the enterprise". Explain the concept, with suitable pictorial presentation? **(24.8 and 24.8.1)**
12. Write short notes on the following:

    (A) A.B.C. Analysis **(24.9)** (B) Perpetual inventory system **(24.11)**
    (C) V E D Analysis **(24.10)** (D) JIT **(24.12)**

Short Questions

Q.1. Explain the need of 'Economic order quantity'?

Ans. Determination of 'economic order quantity' is important to make the total cost of inventory the least. At this level, funds that are tied up in inventory would be low resulting in better management of liquidity. As costs of inventory are the least, profitability would also be more. For effective inventory management, it is necessary to determine what should be the quantity of stock that has to be ordered for replenishment, periodically. The stock to be purchased should neither be small nor big. Frequent orders of stock result in more ordering costs. On the other hand, lesser number of stock orders results in accumulation of stocks, which result in higher carrying costs. Economic order quantity is that size lot which is economically viable.

Q.2. What factors determine 'Economic order quantity'?

Ans. Three factors determine economic order quantity, which are annual consumption or requirement of materials in units (quantity), ordering costs and carrying costs. Cost of materials in rupees has no relevance in determination of economic order quantity. The total cost of inventory would be the least at this level.

Interview Questions

Q.1. What is the objective of 'Economic Order Quantity'?

Ans. The objective of 'Economic order quantity' is to determine the ordering size which is economically viable. The total annual cost of inventory (ordering cost and carrying costs) would be the least at economic order quantity.

Q.2. What is 'V E D Analysis'?

Ans. The V E D analysis is used for control of spare parts.

CHAPTER 25

Internal Financing

25.1 MEANING OF INTERNAL FINANCING

A new company can raise finances from external sources, public issue of shares, debentures, term loans and public deposits. It has no other alternative other than raising funds from external sources. However, an existing company can raise finances from internal sources additionally for future growth and expansion. Internal sources of financing are retained earnings in the form of balance in Profit and Loss account, general reserves, capital reserves and depreciation reserves. Internal sources of financing appear on the liabilities side of balance sheet.

25.2 RETAINED PROFITS OR PLOUGHING BACK OF PROFITS

A company can retain a portion of the profits it has earned without distributing to the shareholders. Portion of profits retained in the firm is known as "Retained Profits". It is strictly not a method of raising finance but refers to accumulation of profits. The process of retaining the profits year after year and their utilization in business is known as 'ploughing back profits'. Ploughing back of profits is called 'self-financing'.

According to the latest provisions of the Companies Act, a certain percentage, as prescribed by the Central Government (not exceeding 10%) of the net profits, after tax, has to be transferred every financial year to reserves, before declaring dividend for the year. These profits are transferred to General Reserves, Reserve Fund or Replacement Fund Account.

Need: The need for ploughing back the profits is to meet the following purposes:

1. Replacement of old assets, which have become obsolete.

2. Expansion and growth of business.
3. Purchase of fixed assets as well as meeting working capital requirements of business.
4. Making the company self-dependent and avoiding outside financing. Existing borrowing for working capital requirements may no longer be necessary.
5. Redemption of loans and debentures.

25.3 METHODS OF INTERNAL FINANCING

Retained earnings is a method of internal financing. They appear in the form of balance in profit and loss account, general reserves and depreciation reserves. All of them appear on the liabilities side of a balance sheet.

25.3.1 Depreciation as a source of finance

Meaning: Depreciation means decrease in the value of a fixed asset due to wear and tear, lapse of time, obsolescence, exhaustion and accident. Depreciation may be regarded as the capital cost of asset spread over its life. Even if a new fixed asset is not used still its value decreases. The typical example is a brand new vehicle. After purchase, if the new car is kept in a garage even though not used, its value goes down significantly. Here, the reason for providing for depreciation is for lapse of time.

Depreciation is an expense. However, depreciation is a simple book entry. While computing net profits, depreciation is provided. In fact, company cannot declare profits without providing for depreciation as per the provisions of Companies Act. Depreciation reduces value of the asset and profit of current year. Depreciation is an operating cost but there is no outflow of cash. By providing depreciation in books of accounts, there is no outflow of cash from the firm. While calculating funds from operations, depreciation is added back to the profits.

Source of Finance: Is depreciation a source of finance? **There cannot be definite 'yes' or 'no'. There is difference of opinion about depreciation as a source of finance.** Operating profits are a source of finance. If depreciation were really a source of finance by itself, any enterprise could have improved its position by simply increasing the provision for depreciation. Depreciation is a non-cash item of expense. Provision of depreciation does not affect the working capital. Working capital is neither increased nor decreased with depreciation. Working capital remains the same before and after providing for depreciation. So, it is argued that depreciation is not a source of finance.

Depreciation is a source of finance under the following circumstances:

Valuation of closing stock: Depreciation finds its way in the valuation of closing stock. Stock is valued at cost or market price, whichever is lower. As depreciation is an overhead, it is included as an element of cost. As closing stock is a part of current assets, working capital indirectly increases.

Saving of Funds: In the absence of fixed asset, it is hired and rent is paid which is a charge to profit and loss account. Once the asset is purchased for use, there is no rent. Depreciation does not generate funds but it definitely saves outflow of funds.

Reduces Tax Liability: Depreciation reduces taxable profits. As a result, tax liability is reduced with the provision of depreciation. To the extent of reduction of tax liability, depreciation saves out flow of funds. However, when the firm is in loss, there is no tax liability. In such a situation, the provision of depreciation does not result in saving of funds.

To sum it up, depreciation is not a direct source of funds, but it can be taken as a source of funds in a limited sense.

This will be clear through the following example.

Illustration No. 1

Income before depreciation is ₹ 1,00,000. Depreciation provided is ₹ 20,000. Tax rate is 50%. Establish depreciation creates internal source of financing.

Solution

	Case A	Case B
Income before depreciation	1,00,000	1,00,000
Depreciation provided (A)	------	20,000
Taxable income	1,00,000	80,000
Income tax @ 50%	50,000	40,000
Net income after tax (B)	50,000	40,000
Net flow of funds after tax (A + B)	50,000	60,000

In Case 'A', depreciation has not been provided while in Case 'B' depreciation has been provided to explain the impact of depreciation on flow of funds. In case 'B', the net flow of funds is more by ₹ 10,000. This is due to provision of depreciation which has been claimed as an expense while computing the taxable profits. On account of this, tax liability has been reduced by ₹ 10,000.

So, depreciation is a source of financing when the firm has made taxable profits.

25.4 FACTORS THAT INFLUENCE RETAINED EARNINGS

A number of factors influence the ploughing back of profits in an organization:

1. **Earning Capacity:** Earning capacity plays a key role in deciding the quantum of retained earnings. If the earning capacity of the firm is high, retained earnings also can be high. If a firm does not have adequate earning capacity, there is no possibility for retained earnings.
2. **Desire and Type of Shareholders:** The policy in respect of retained earnings is largely influenced by the desire and type of the shareholders the company has.

If majority of the shareholders are retired people, widows and who look for the dividend as a regular source of income then shareholders always prefer to have higher amount of dividend. A company having that category of shareholders cannot afford to retain more amounts in the form of retained earnings. A company that has wealthy shareholders may not mind if the company follows the policy of retained earnings.

3. **Future financial requirements:** The future financial requirements of the company affect the policy of retained profits. If the firm has more expansion plans, the requirement of funds is more. So, company prefers to retain profits rather than distribute higher dividends.
4. **Dividend Policy:** A company that wants to declare more dividends cannot afford to retain more profits. The dividend policy has a reciprocal relationship with the retention policy. **If more profits are retained, lesser amount of profit would be available for distribution and vice versa.**
5. **Taxation Policy:** A high taxation policy of the Government leaves lower amount in the hands of company towards retention of profits. On the other hand, a liberal policy of the Government allows more profits for retention in company as tax liability is less.

25.5 MERITS OF PLOUGHING BACK OF PROFITS

Ploughing back profits has several advantages to the company, shareholders and society.

(i) Advantages to company

(A) Cushion to absorb shocks: Ploughing Back of Profits acts as a cushion to the company. Trade cycles are not uncommon. During the period of depression-time when profits fall—the company with accumulated profits can withstand the shocks with more preparedness and comfort.

(B) Economical method of financing: Company need not depend upon outsiders for meeting the requirements of expansion and growth. Profits accumulated would be adequate to meet the requirements for expansion.

(C) Stable dividend policy: Stable dividend policy refers to the regularity in payment of dividends. A company can pay regular dividends even if the company has not made adequate profits in the lean years.

(D) Adds to creditworthiness: As the company would not have borrowing, it can declare itself as "No Borrowing Company". This adds to its public image in the minds of investors. When the company is not doing well, no financial institution comes forward to lend. Outsiders are just like fair weather friends. In case of need, they may not come to your rescue. A company with accumulated reserves does not require outsiders' assistance for the purpose of borrowing.

(E) **Increased needs of inflation:** The economy presently is passing through increase in prices. Machinery that has been purchased ten years back for ₹ 1,00,000 is not available for the same price, today. The amount provided towards depreciation is not adequate for the increased cost of the asset. The shortfall in the amount can be met out of the retained earnings.

(F) **Redemption of long-term liabilities:** With the creation of accumulated profits, firm can redeem its long-term liabilities such as debentures and can reduce the interest burden, which is a fixed commitment.

(ii) Advantages to shareholders

(A) **Enhances value of shares:** Ploughing back of profits enables the company to adopt stable dividend policy. With stable dividend policy, shareholders get dividend regularly. This increases the market price of equity share as investors gain confidence in the company to invest. Shareholders can sell their holding at an increased price in the market and enjoy higher earnings. Additionally, they can offer their higher valued holding as collateral security for any borrowing that is needed, in case of need.

(B) **Safety of investments:** Investors prefer to invest in those companies that can withstand any shocks the economy gives. Economy is never stable. Fluctuations are common. The shares of those companies are treated as safe investments.

(C) **Earning capacity enhanced:** With the increased investment opportunities, the company uses the retained earnings and, in consequence, the earnings of the company increase. In turn, the earning per share increases as there is no change in the number of shareholders.

(D) **No loss of control:** With retained profits, there would be no need for the company to issue new shares for meeting the additional financial requirements. If the company happens to issue new shares, the existing shareholders have to acquire the new shares to keep the same amount of control. In case, they do not have the funds to invest, there is a threat in respect of loss of control. With retained profits, this danger does not arise as there would be no need to issue new shares to meet the needs of expansion.

(iii) Advantages to society or economy

(A) **Capital formation:** Retained earnings help the economy as capital formation is made at a higher rate. It is beneficial to the society as well as economy.

(B) **Accelerated industrialization:** The capital formation stimulates accelerated industrialization of the economy and nation.

(C) **Higher standard of living:** As the economy progresses, productivity increases which results in reduced prices, better quality of goods and increased employment opportunities. The society, as a whole, would be benefited with higher standard of living.

25.6 LIMITATIONS OR DANGERS OF PLOUGHING BACK PROFITS

Financing through retained earnings is not free from evils or misuse. The demerits can be summarized as follows:

(A) **Manipulation in value of Shares:** Certain managements (directors), having vested interests, may use the concept of retained earnings to their personal advantage. They may skip the dividend in the name of plough back profits. Once the share price falls on account of skipping of dividend, they buy the shares of those companies at reduced price. They can use the retained earnings to cover their inefficiencies in managing the affairs of the company by declaring the same amount of dividend. Shareholders may remain under illusion about the continued satisfactory performance of the company as many do not go through the financial statements but observe the rate of dividend declared by the company. At times, the management can manipulate the value of the shares in the stock exchange with the retained earnings.

(B) **Creation of Monopolies:** Creation of retained earnings for a long period may create a possibility for the organization to grow into monopoly with all the evils. The company may expand to such levels that it may become uncontrollable.

(C) **Harmful to Society:** Retained earnings facilitate the organization to invest in the way it wishes. As retained earnings do not allow the shareholders to have dividends, the shareholders are not allowed to invest in those businesses which may be beneficial to the interests of the society.

(D) **Dissatisfaction to Small Shareholders:** Excessive retention of profits creates dissatisfaction amongst small shareholders. When the shareholders fall in low-income groups, they get dissatisfied with retained profits. They are prevented from having dividends to the extent of the retained earnings.

(E) **Misuse of retained earnings:** Management may develop the tendency to use retained earnings in unprofitable areas due to accumulation of profits in the company.

In nutshell, the quantum of retained profits is influenced by the dividend policy pursued by the firm. **The higher the dividend rate, lower is the amount of retained earnings and vice versa.**

Check Your Understanding

(A) State whether the following statements are True or False

1. Depreciation is a non-cash item of expense.
2. Whether the depreciation is a source of finance or not, there is difference of opinion on this important point.
3. Earning capacity plays a key role in deciding the quantum of retained earnings.

4. Ploughing back profits is used for self-financing.
5. Management of earnings has nothing to do with ploughing back of profits.
6. Capital reserves are built out of revenue profits.
7. As the retained earnings have a distinct merit to the company, the company should not distribute any dividend to its shareholders.
8. There is no gain to the shareholders if company adopts the policy of retained earnings.
9. Excessive retention of profits creates dissatisfaction amongst small shareholders.
10. Retention of profits may lead certain companies to become monopolistic.
11. Depreciation reduces taxable profits.

Answers

1. True 2. True 3. True 4. True 5. False 6. False 7. False 8. False
9. True 10. True 11. True

(B) Objective Questions (Identify what is most appropriate)

1. Retained profits mean
   (A) profits earned but not distributed. (B) profits distributed but not earned.
   (C) profits capitalized. (D) earnings capitalized.
2. If the firm retains more profits, it results in
   (A) more profits for distribution. (B) lesser profits for distribution.
   (C) no profits for distribution. (D) no impact.
3. A new company can raise external finance from the following source.
   (A) Public issue of shares (B) Debentures
   (C) Term loan (D) Public deposits
   (E) All the above
4. The internal sources of financing are
   (A) retained earnings. (B) depreciation.
   (C) both (A) and (B). (D) neither (A) nor (B).
5. The process of retaining profits, year after year, and utilizing in the business is called as
   (A) capitalization of profits. (B) ploughing back of profits.
   (C) redemption of debentures. (D) capitalization of bonus shares.
6. Retained profits are helpful to company for
   (A) expansion of business. (B) repayment of long-term loans.
   (C) replacement of fixed assets. (D) all the above.
7. Retained profits do not exist in a
   (A) New company (B) Existing company
   (C) Both (A) and (B) (D) None

8. Retained profits cannot be utilized for this purpose.
   (A) Redemption of preference shares (B) Repayment of debentures
   (C) Expansion of business (D) None

9. Retained profits is an indicator.
   (A) Strength of company (B) Weakness of company
   (C) Opportunity of company (D) Challenge to company

10. Retained profits are beneficial to
    (A) Company concerned. (B) Shareholders of company concerned.
    (C) Economy. (D) All of the above.

11. With retained profits, the following happens
    (A) No loss of control to existing shareholders.
    (B) Greater possibility for expansion of business.
    (C) Company can become free from borrowings with a sustained policy.
    (D) All the above.

12. Higher retained earnings in the past result in
    (A) Lower dividend rate in future. (B) Higher dividend rate in future.
    (C) No future plans. (D) None of the above.

13. The greatest disadvantage with higher retained earning is
    (A) Dissatisfaction to small shareholders.
    (B) Likely possibility for management to manipulate share value to suit their convenience.
    (C) Creation of monopolies.
    (D) All the above.

14. Companies belonging to this category follow a consistent policy to retain a part of their profits in the form of retained profits.
    (A) Prudent companies.
    (B) Companies which want to declare higher rate of dividends to satisfy shareholders.
    (C) Companies which do not have expansion plans.
    (D) Companies which wish to raise funds in market for future requirements.

15. Quantum of retained earnings in a company depends on
    (A) past earnings. (B) past savings policy.
    (C) expansion plans of company. (D) All (A), (B) and (C).

16. This is the purpose of 'ploughing back of profits'.
    (A) Self-financing (B) Self-borrowing
    (C) Private financing (D) External borrowing

17. A limited company can distribute all current year profits as dividend.
    (A) Yes.
    (B) No, a portion of profits are to be given in the next year.
    (C) No, a portion of profits is to be transferred to general reserves as per provisions of Companies Act.
    (D) Portion of profits to be transferred to general reserves is decided by board of directors.

18. This is the nature of depreciation.
    (A) Expense.
    (B) Only a book entry.
    (C) No outgo of funds.
    (D) All the above.
19. Company which follows the following policy can withstand well even in times of depression.
    (A) Policy of declaring all possible profits as dividend.
    (B) Policy to borrow when funds are needed.
    (C) Policy of plough back of profits.
    (D) Policy of raising funds from time to time in market to meet its needs.
20. Retained profits can be used for the following.
    (A) Replacement of fixed assets even with price escalation.
    (B) Redemption of long-term liabilities.
    (C) Expansion needs.
    (D) All the above.
21. Instead of distributing the entire earnings by way of dividend, companies normally follow this prudent step of keeping a certain percentage of it in the business which is known as
    (A) Self-financing.
    (B) Plough back of profits.
    (C) Internal financing.
    (D) All the above.

ANSWERS

1. (A)	2. (B)	3. (E)	4. (C)	5. (B)	6. (D)	7. (A)	8. (D)
9. (A)	10. (D)	11. (D)	12. (B)	13. (D)	14. (A)	15. (D)	16. (A)
17. (C)	18. (D)	19. (C)	20. (D)	21. (D).			

Descriptive Questions

1. What is meant by internal financing? Discuss the different methods of internal financing? **(25.1, 25.2 and 25.3)**
2. "Depreciation is not a direct source of funds, but can be taken as a source of funds in a limited sense". Explain? **(25.1 and 25.3)**
3. Discuss the factors that influence retained earnings? **(25.4)**
4. Discuss the role of retained earnings for the development of company, shareholders and society? **(25.2 and 25.5)**
5. What is meant by 'retained earnings'? Discuss the factors that influence retained earnings along with their merits and demerits? **(25.2, 25.4 and 25.5)**

Short Questions

Q.1. How external financing is different from internal financing?

Ans. A new company has only one option to raise finances through external financing such as equity shares, preference shares, debentures and long-term loans etc. However, an existing company can raise finances from internal sources additionally for future growth and expansion.

Q.2. What are internal sources of financing and where they appear in the financial statements?

Ans. Internal sources of financing are retained earnings in the form of balance in Profit and Loss account, general reserves, capital reserves and depreciation reserves. All of them appear on the liabilities side of a balance sheet.

Q.3. What is the need to plough back profits for a firm?

Ans. The process of retaining the profits year after year and their utilization in business is known as 'ploughing back profits'. Instead of raising finances externally for expansion, firm can utilize the ploughed back profits. Ploughed back profits can also supplement external sources of financing. Ploughed back profits can be re-introduced into the business for development. Such a phenomenon is called 'self-financing'.

Interview Questions

Q.1. What is meant by self-financing?

Ans. The process of retaining the profits year after year and their utilization in business is known as self-financing.

Q.2. What is meant by retained profits?

Ans. A company can retain a portion of the profits it has earned without distributing to the shareholders. Portion of profits retained in the firm is known as "Retained Profits".

❍ ❍

CHAPTER

26

Dividend Policy

26.1 INTRODUCTION

Dividend is a part of the profits earned by the company, distributed amongst its shareholders. The company distributes only a part of profits, while the balance is retained. The retained portion of profits is known as 'retained earnings'. Payment of dividend is necessary from the viewpoint of the shareholders as dividend constitutes the current earnings on the shares held by them. Dividend is to be paid to satisfy the expectations of the shareholders. Company cannot afford to ignore the expectations of shareholders totally as the aim of every company is to maximize the value of the shares held by equity shareholders and equally satisfy them.

26.2 DIVIDEND POLICY

The term 'Dividend policy' refers to the policy concerning quantum of profits to be distributed as dividend. A company's dividend policy influences the division of its net earnings into two parts: dividend and retained earnings. **What amount is to be retained and how much to be distributed is the essence of the dividend policy.**

Role of dividend in Wealth Maximization: The dividend policy is of crucial importance to the finance manager as it determines the amount to be distributed to the shareholders and the amount of profit to be retained as earnings for financing its long-term growth. There is a reciprocal relationship between dividends and retained earnings. If dividend distributed is more, lesser would be the amount of retained earnings. Less dividend payment results in larger retained earnings. **The finance manager takes into account the effect of the dividend decision on the maximization of the shareholders' wealth, the main objective of every company.** In case payment of dividend helps in achieving that objective, it is desirable to distribute dividend. In case dividend payment does not help in achieving the objective, it is desirable to retain the profits for financing investment programme. Thus, the dividend decision is largely concerned with the impact of dividend policy on the value of the firm. The value of the firm is reflected through the equity share price in the stock market.

Financing Decision: Dividend decision influences financing decision. External equity, raising funds by issue of shares or debentures, could be used for investment purposes. The alternative way is to use profits that have been earned by company for investment purposes. In such a case, company distributes the profit only when it does not have enough investment opportunities. In other words, company is retaining all the profits for the purpose of investment. **Instead of raising long-term funds, the company is totally using all its profits for the purpose of investment, without distributing any part in the form of dividend.** Reason may be that the external fund rising is more expensive. The idea behind in using retained profits is to avoid floatation costs, costs incurred at the time of raising capital. Approach of using retained funds for investment is adopted when companies anticipate their growth would be faster. With this approach, dividend decision is viewed as 'residual decision'.

Shareholders' Needs: Dividend on preference shares is fixed. Equity shareholders expect return when they invest in a company. Dividend received is their current earnings. When a firm opts not to distribute dividend and use the total profits for expansion, the equity shareholders do not get current dividend. They can expect capital gain when they subsequently sell the shares. Wealthy shareholders who are in a high tax bracket may be happy to receive the capital gain rather than the current dividend, if dividend is taxable. But, majority shareholders want current dividend. As and when company enhances the dividend rate its market price normally increases, if market does not expect more. When the company skips the payment of dividend for one reason or other, the market price would dip with the announcement of the company.

> **It is necessary to pay a certain portion of profits in the form of dividend to keep the majority of shareholders satisfied.**

Balanced Approach: The management of a company has to strike a balance between the above two conflicting approaches, dividend distribution and retention of profits for future growth. When the firm increases the retained portion, lesser amount is available for distribution. Firm can use the amount for expansion or other investment opportunities. The use of retained earnings increases the future earnings of the firm. On the other hand, when the dividend is declared, shareholders' current income increases. In consequence, the firm has to avoid some of the investment decisions immediately. The dividend policy is greatly influenced by the investment opportunities the firm has.

> **Every firm has to evolve an optimum way that increases the wealth of its equity shareholders which would satisfy their expectations as well as meeting its investment ideas.**

26.3 FACTORS OR DETERMINANTS OF DIVIDEND POLICY

The payment of dividend involves certain amount of legal and financial considerations. Some of the factors, which influence the dividend policy of the firm are:

(A) Legal Restrictions: A company can declare dividend out of the current profits or past profits only. **Before payment of dividend, provision of depreciation for the current year as well as arrears of depreciation, is necessary.** The other alternative way to pay dividend is out of the monies provided by the government when there is a government guarantee for dividend payment. Dividend can be paid in cash or by issuing fully paid bonus shares, capitalizing the profits. A company cannot pay dividend, which may result into the reduction of share capital. There are legal rules for compulsory transfer of profits to general reserves. Where the dividend proposed exceeds 20 per cent of the paid up capital, the amount to be transferred to reserves shall not be less than 10 per cent of the current profits.

(B) Shareholders' expectations: Board of directors recommends payment of dividend. Finally, equity shareholders of the company have to approve as they are the owners. Shareholders can reduce the rate of dividend, recommended by the board in the interests of the company. However, **shareholders do not have a right to increase the rate of dividend.** Shareholders' preference for dividend or capital gains depends on their economic status. If they are wealthy, tax considerations prevail. When the shareholders are people of small means or belong to retired category, they prefer current dividend as majority consider it as a supplementary source of earning.

(C) Financial Needs of the Company: The financial needs of a company may go in conflict with the desires of its shareholders. Firms want to retain while majority shareholders prefer to receive current dividends.

It is not wise to retain 100% of profits for investment or distribute whole profits as dividend.

A mature company can afford to distribute major amount of profits as dividend while retaining a small part for investment opportunities. A growing company prefers to retain a higher part of profits for the future expansion. When internal rate of return of the company is greater than the rate of return expected by the shareholders, it is to the advantage of its shareholders to allow the company to reinvest. However, when the rate of return required by the shareholders is more than the internal rate of return of the company, it is desirable to distribute. It is prudent to the company to retain a part of profits whether it has investment opportunities or not to maintain the company as a sound and solvent enterprise.

(D) Liquidity constraints: The payment of dividend involves cash outgo. Dividend is to be remitted to shareholders within 30 days of its declaration. Company might have made the profits, but its cash or liquidity position may not be comfortable to make the payment. It is, therefore, necessary for the company to take into consideration the cash and liquid position, both before and after payment of dividend. If the liquidity problem persists despite profits, it is desirable for the company to declare stock dividend i.e. issue of bonus shares to the existing shareholders. **The issue of bonus shares also satisfies the existing shareholders psychologically, without affecting company's liquid resources.**

(E) **Financial Condition:** If a company is already overburdened with debt and is having high degree of financial leverage, it prefers to retain a major part of earnings to strengthen its equity to reduce its financial leverage.

(F) **Access to Capital Market:** Easy accessibility provides the flexibility to company to raise the funds required for expansion or growth and distribute dividend from the profits. **If the ability of the firm is greater to raise funds in the market, greater would be the ability to distribute dividends.**

(G) **Restrictions in Loan Agreements: Lenders may put restrictions for payment of dividends at the time of lending.** At the time of sanction, lenders may impose restrictive conditions on payment of dividend. For example, condition can be that the company cannot declare dividend so long as the debt-equity ratio of company is more than 1.5 or the current ratio is less than 2. Once such conditions are incorporated in the contract, companies cannot declare dividend unless the stipulated conditions are complied with.

(H) **Control:** When additional equity shares are issued, the existing group may loose control if they do not have the necessary funds to acquire the new shares. They may be afraid that their control may .be diluted. To avoid rising of funds by issue of shares, the company may resort to accumulation of profits. In such an event, they may not distribute the dividend and use the profits for fresh investment opportunities, issuing bonus shares. **When bonus shares are issued, every shareholder gets additional shares so control is not lost.**

(I) **General State of Economy:** The general state of economy influences the firm to distribute dividend or retain profits more. **If the economy is passing through boom, investment opportunities would be more and so company wants to retain more funds for expansion, without distributing more dividends.** It is also easy for the company to raise funds during the boom period. During the period of depression, firms retain profits to absorb the future shocks, the economy may give. All depends on the dividend policy of the concerned company.

(J) **Nature of Earnings: A company having stable earnings can afford pay higher dividend with a higher dividend pay out ratio.** A company, which faces more competition with unstable earnings cannot declare higher dividend.

26.4 STABILITY OF DIVIDENDS

The term 'Stability' means consistency or lack of variability in the stream of dividend payments. Generally, shareholders prefer stable dividends to the fluctuating ones.

The stability of dividend can take any one of the following forms:

(i) **Constant dividend per share:** According to this policy, **shareholder is paid a fixed amount per share in the form of dividend.** For example, a company may declare ₹ 2 per equity share having a face value of ₹ 10. Whether the company makes more or less profits, the company declares ₹ 2 per share. In this case, there is no uncertainty about the payment of dividend. People who look for regular returns invest in such companies. As the company does not alter its pay out ratio irrespective of the level of earnings, investors look upon this dividend as their regular source of income and prefer such companies for investment.

(ii) **Constant percentage of Pay out: Companies pay regularly a fixed portion of their earnings as dividend.** If the earnings increase, the amount of dividend gets increased or vice versa. Suppose, a company fixes a proportion of 25% as dividend then the amount would be calculated accordingly and distributed amongst the number of equity shares outstanding. If there is no change in capital, the dividend payable per share is linked directly to the increase or decrease in earnings. In case, the share capital increases and the profits do not increase in the same proportion, the dividend payable to each share goes down.

(iii) **Stable dividend plus extra earning per share:** In this policy, the firm maintains stable dividend rate. So, shareholders are assured of the minimum amount of return on their investment. In case firm makes abnormal profits, it shares a part of the increased profits to its shareholders. The extra dividend is made available so long as the exceptional profits continue. Once the abnormal profits disappear, the regular dividend only continues.

Out of the above three policies, constant dividend per share is preferred by the shareholders. Some companies prefer the second method of making payment, constant percentage as the dividend is correlated to earnings they make. If their earnings increase, the shareholders would be benefited equally in the same proportion. In case the earnings fall, the return of shareholders also falls. But, the shareholders do not prefer this type of payment as there is uncertainty of dividend payment. In case the firm does not make any profits, there would be no dividend at all. In the case of stable dividend plus extra earning per share too, there is uncertainty about the amount of dividend receivable. One thing is clear, majority of shareholders expect regular dividend. So, firms try to adopt stable dividend policy to satisfy the shareholders, always.

26.5 SIGNIFICANCE OF STABILITY OF DIVIDENDS

A stable dividend policy is advantageous for the following reasons:

(A) Desire for Current Income: There are many investors such as retired persons or widows who look for regular income to meet their living expenses. To them, a constant or fixed amount of dividend would be supplementing their other resources to meet their expenses comfortably. Such persons invest in those companies who declare regular and fixed dividends rather than the companies that declare a fluctuating dividend.

(B) Perception of Stability: When the company declares regular dividend, investors consider the declaration as a continuation of normal operations. **When the company declares a reduced dividend rate, it looks as signal of dismal future.** Immediately, majority of investors sell their shares of that company in the market, without checking the reasons for reduction in dividend. A massive decision of majority selling creates ripples in the market and results in a drastic fall in market price. Such a situation can be avoided by following a consistent dividend payment.

(C) Requirements of Institutional Investors: Generally, public purchases shares of companies. Of late, even educational and social institutions and unit trusts have started investing heavily in private sector companies to improve their earnings. They find the investment as a good avenue to enlarge their earnings, more so when they are flush with funds. In India, institutional investors like IDBI, IFCI, UTI, LIC and other mutual trusts are the biggest investors. Every company wants to have the institutional investors as their shareholders as it indicates the image, reputation and strength of the company. More so, investment of the institutional investors is more or less committed. In other words, they look for the long-term growth, not to immediate short-term gains.

Institutional investors do not normally prefer a company that has an erratic track record of paying dividend.

So, a company prefers to follow a stable dividend policy to attract and retain the institutional investors.

(D) Raising additional finances: Stable dividend policy paves the easier way for raising the finances. Investors' prefer consistent dividend paying companies for investment. They recognize the share of such company as quality investment rather than a speculation. Their loyalty and goodwill will be sustained. As and when those companies issue new shares for raising finances, the existing shareholders would be more receptive to invest. Stable dividend policy serves as a way to spread ownership amongst many investors and in consequence chance of loss of control is reduced.

26.6 DANGER OF STABILITY OF DIVIDENDS

The greatest danger lies when a company, following stable dividend policy, skips to pay the dividend. Stable dividend paying companies create a 'clientele of shareholders' who depend on them for regular income for living and operating expenses. They consider a 'cut in dividend' as a 'cut in salary'. At times, directors of the company declare even when it is not prudent, not to depress the investors. Consequently, it is desirable to have a fixed rate of dividend on a lower side and declare additional dividend as and when the companies can afford with the increased earnings.

26.7 FORMS OF DIVIDENDS

Dividend can be classified into three categories depending upon the form in which they are paid. The various forms of dividend are as follows:

(A) Cash Dividend: Companies have to pay dividend in cash. This is a statutory requirement. In addition to cash dividend, some companies may issue bonus shares also. **As and when dividend is paid, there is outgo of cash.** So, companies should make advanced cash planning for dividend payment. Regular dividend paying companies should prepare cash budget to plan for such payment of dividends. This type of planning is possible with the companies, which have a consistent dividend declaring policy. However, this planning is not possible with companies which do not have stable dividend declaring policy as they may or may not declare dividend.

Effect on Market Price: After the payment of dividend, there would be reduction both in current assets and balance in profit and loss account or reserves. As a result, net worth of the company goes down. Due to reduction in net worth, there may be a fall in market price of the equity share. However, the fall in market price depends on several factors, in particular the perception of investors about the future of company. In share market, the likely future events relating to the company influence its share price in the market more than the past results. So, it is difficult to state with certainty that the fall in market price is due to reduction in net worth of the company. This could be one of the factors.

(B) Bonus shares (Stock Dividend): When the company does not have adequate cash resources, the other alternative to satisfy its equity shareholders is by way of issue of bonus shares. Issue of bonus shares, in lieu of dividend is not allowed. Issue of bonus shares represents distribution of shares to the existing equity shareholders freely. Bonus shares are issued, proportionately, to the shareholders. Bonus shares can be in lieu or addition to the cash dividend. Bonus shares are known as stock dividend, in U.S.A.

When a company issues shares to its existing equity shareholders freely, without their payment such shares are called as bonus shares. When a company has made profits but does not have enough cash to pay dividends, bonus shares are issued.

Bonus issue can be made out of the profits of the company, alone. Capital Reserves created by the revaluation of assets cannot be utilized for issue of bonus shares.

Sources of Bonus Issues

The bonus shares can be issued out of the following:

1. Balance in the profit and loss account.
2. General reserve.
3. Capital reserve. However, capital reserves created out of the revaluation of fixed assets cannot be utilized for issue of bonus shares.
4. Balance in sinking fund reserve for redemption of debentures after the debentures have been redeemed.
5. Capital redemption Reserve Account
6. Share premium account, if received in cash.

When share premium is available in share premium account, that balance is first utilized towards the issue of bonus shares. When there is no balance in the share premium account, then the balance in the profit and loss account or reserves is used for issue of bonus shares.

Impact on company: In what way, issue of bonus shares affects the earnings of the company? After issuance of bonus shares, earning per share gets diluted unless there is an increase in profits of the company.

Let us explain with a simple example. An individual has 1,000 shares in a company, while the total number of shares outstanding in the company is 10,000. The company has issued bonus shares in the ratio of 1 : 1. The individual would get 1,000 shares extra as present holding of one share entitles another share as bonus share. The earnings of the company are ₹ 50,000. Before issue of bonus shares, earnings per share are ₹ 5 (50,000/10,000). The individual would get ₹ 5,000 as dividend. If there is no change in the amount of earnings of the company, the same earnings of ₹ 50,000 have to be distributed by the increased number of shares i.e. 20,000. Now, the earning per share is ₹ 2.50 (50,000/20,000). Now, the individual continues to get ₹ 5,000 only as dividend (₹ 2.50 earning per share × 2,000 shares).

Accounting Treatment: When bonus shares are issued, profits are transferred from profit and Loss account/reserves to equity share capital account. In other words, there is a reduction in the aggregate profits and similar increase in equity share capital account. **Issue of bonus shares does not result in any change in the net worth of the company.** Due to increase in share capital, the number of equity share outstanding gets increased.

As there is no change in the investment opportunities to the company and if the same trend of profits continues, the same amount of profit or earnings has to be distributed by the increased number of equity shares. More so, the ownership in the company does not change. Earlier, the individual has 10% control in the company (1,000/10,000) and even after issue of bonus shares still he has only 10% control (2,000/20,000).

Capitalization of Profits: Issue of bonus shares does not affect the capital structure of the company. In other words, there would be no change in the net worth of the company. Issue of bonus shares results in the conversion of company's profits into equity share capital. This is known as capitalization of company's profits.

Illustration No. 1

The following is the capital structure of Dotty & Ltd.

	₹
Equity share capital (₹ 10 face value)	2,00,000
Share premium	2,50,000
Reserves and surplus	3,50,000
Total net worth	8,00, 000

The company issues bonus shares to the existing shareholders in the ratio of 1:10 at the market price of ₹ 15 per share. Company has decided to use reserves and surplus for ₹ 20,000 and balance from share premium account for issue of bonus shares.

You are required to show:

(i) the new capitalization of the company,

(ii) earning per share both before and after the bonus issue, presuming the net earnings as ₹ 80,000,

(iii) cherry is holding 100 shares in the above company. Calculate Cherry's earnings before and after issue of bonus shares and

(iv) what would be the market value of his total holding, before and after the issue of bonus shares? Make reasonable assumption about market price.

Solution

Dotty & Ltd. is issuing bonus shares in the ratio of 1:10. It means a shareholder who is having 10 shares presently would get one additional share, free of cost.

The share capital is ₹ 2,00,000 and its face value per share is ₹ 10. The number of shares in the company is 20,000 (2,00,000/10). As the allotment of bonus shares is 1:10, number of bonus shares issued are 2,000. Bonus shares are issued at the market rate of ₹ 15 (Face value ₹ 10 and premium ₹ 5).

Bonus issue = Number of existing shares 2,000 × 15 = ₹ 30,000

Composition of Bonus Issue:

Transfer from reserves to equity share capital 2,000 × 10 = 20,000

Transfer from share premium to share premium 2,000 × 5 = 10,000

(i) The new capitalization of the company will be as follows:

Equity share capital	2,20,000
(22,000 shares of ₹ 10 each)	
Share Premium (2,50,000 – 30,000 + 10,000)	2,30,000
Reserves & Surplus	3,50,000
Total Net Worth	8,00,000

For bonus issue, share premium is totally utilized. The above establishes that there would be no change in the net worth after the issuance of bonus shares as the net worth earlier too was ₹ 8,00,000.

(ii) Earning per share before bonus issue

Net Earnings	80,000
Number of Equity Shares	20,000
Earning per share	₹ 4

Earning per share after bonus issue

Net Earnings	80,000
Number of Equity Shares	22,000
Earning per share	3.64

(iii) Before bonus issue, Cherry's earnings are = ₹ 400 (100 × 4)

After bonus issue, Cherry's earnings are = ₹ 400 (110 × 3.64).

It will be seen that as a result of bonus issue the total earning of Cherry remains unchanged.

(iv) Market price normally falls after issue of bonus shares, if there is no increase in earnings. The market value of the equity share drops from ₹ 15 to ₹ 13.65.

(15 × 3.64/4) on account of the increase in number of shares with no corresponding increase in earnings. In other words, the same earnings are to be shared by the increased number of equity shares.

Reasonable assumption about market price: It is presumed that market price decreases in the same proportion of EPS, after issue of bonus shares.

Market Value of Cherry's holding (Before Bonus issue):

Market value of 100 shares = 100 × 15 = 1,500

Market Value of Cherry's holding (After Bonus issue):

Market value of 110 shares = 110 × 13.64 = 1,500

The issue of bonus shares will have no impact on the wealth of Cherry.

26.8 ADVANTAGES OF ISSUE OF BONUS SHARES

Issue of bonus shares is advantageous to the company as well as shareholders.

Advantages to the Company:

(A) **Conservation of cash:** Issue of bonus shares helps the company to retain the liquid or cash resources to finance profitable opportunities for investment purposes. The Board of Directors must consider the financial needs of the company and also satisfy the needs of the shareholders. These two objectives are often in conflict with payment of dividend. Dividend payment results in satisfaction to shareholders, but leaves reduced liquid resources for investment. Retained profit helps the company to go for investment but does not give dividend to the shareholders. Receipt of bonus shares satisfies the shareholders psychologically. So, **issue of bonus shares is a compromise to satisfy these conflicting objectives of the firm.** The company can retain the earnings as well as satisfy the expectations of the shareholders with the issue of bonus shares.

(B) **Keeps EPS at Reasonable Level:** The Company having a high EPS may have to face problems from its consumers as well as employees. Consumers may feel that the company is charging higher price on its products. They would advocate its higher EPS as a proof to support their thinking. The employees may feel that the company has been earning well by not passing on due salaries to them.

By issue of bonus shares, number of equity shares increases and EPS decreases. Reduced EPS level of the company would be more or less in line with the EPS of industry.

(C) **Only means to pay dividend under financial difficulties and contractual restrictions:** When a firm experiences liquidity crunch, the only option to replace cash dividend and satisfy the shareholders is by issuance of bonus shares.

Lenders may impose restrictions on the payment of dividend at the time of sanction of the loan. In such circumstances, company can issue bonus shares which satisfies the expectations of the shareholders without violating the terms of the covenant entered into with the lender.

(D) **Wider Marketability of Company' shares:** With an increase in business, established companies become highly profitable and so the market price of the shares of those companies would be high. The market price may not be within the range of the ordinary investors. Consequent on issue of bonus shares, the market price decreases and become within the reach of the ordinary investors to buy. The reasonable price of the share provides wider marketability to company's shares. However, wealth of the existing shareholders does not change. Bonus issue is used as a means to keep the market price of the share within a desired trading range.

Advantages to Investors

(A) High Psychological Value: News about the issue of bonus share normally is well received in the market, unless the market has been expecting more favourable bonus issue than the one declared. After the issue of bonus shares price normally falls as there would be no change in the earnings immediately and the number of shares that claim a share in the earnings increase. However, price of the share may not fall or even increase when market expects that the future earnings of the company increase. It is always to be remembered that the market price of a share is influenced by several factors, not one alone at any time.

(B) Increase in Future Dividends: Some companies may maintain a dividend policy of declaring a fixed amount of dividend, per share. When bonus shares are issued, the number of shares in a company increases. If the company continues the same policy of declaring a fixed amount of dividend per share, the shareholders would be benefited by larger dividend. If the company has issued 1:2 bonus shares, the shareholder holding 100 shares gets 50 bonus shares, increasing his total holding to 150. If the company has been declaring a dividend of ₹ 5 per share, the shareholder gets a dividend of ₹ 750 after issue of bonus shares in place of the earlier dividend of ₹ 500.

(C) Indication of higher Future Profits: Normally, companies issue bonus shares when they expect their future profits would increase and are hopeful to maintain the same dividend rate. If the future profit does not increase as expected, earning per share gets diluted. However, this gives the impression to the shareholders that the dividend rate has decreased after issue of bonus shares.

(D) Tax Benefits: If dividend is taxable, it is included in the income and tax is calculated. This tax rate normally is higher than the rate applicable to capital gains. The incidence of tax on capital gain, profit made on sale of share, is always lower than the normal tax rate. So, the shareholder can sell some of his shares, retaining the original holding to book profits and pay a reduced tax. Shareholder would have the benefit of capital gain while retaining the same number of shares held by him, before issue of bonus shares. This situation arises when the dividend is not tax-exempt.

Presently, dividend income is not taxable for the financial year 2010–11. It is not certain how long the exemption would continue.

(E) Booking Profit: Psychologically some investors do not want to sell their original shares considering them as their principal. However, they do not mind selling the bonus shares as they consider bonus shares as windfall gain and not a part of the principal.

Disadvantages of Bonus Issue

Bonus issue has the following limitations:

(A) **Shareholders' Wealth remains unaffected:** Bonus shares are considered valuable by a majority of shareholders. **But factually, there is no change in the wealth of the shareholders in real terms.** It is simply a division of the existing corporate pie into a larger number of pieces. Shareholders' proportional ownership and control does not change. But, it has a psychological impact on the shareholders.

(B) **Costly to Administer:** Company has to print more share certificates and post them to thousands of shareholders. With the increase in capital, more shareholders may come into existence as the existing shareholders may sell some of the shares. With the introduction of D mat concept, cost of administration has reduced. However by and large, cost of administration increases.

Bonus issue has following major effects:

1. Share capital gets increased according to the bonus issue ratio.
2. Liquidity of shares increases as more number of shares would be traded.
3. Effective earnings per share (EPS) and book value of share stand reduced.
4. Stock markets take the action usually as a favourable act.
5. Market price gets adjusted on issue of bonus shares.
6. Accumulated profits get reduced.

26.9 STOCK SPLIT

Stock split means splitting the existing equity shares. Stock split is normally done when the Net Asset Value (NAV) of the fund is at respectable levels. Corporate announces stock split when the share price goes to a respectable level and the management sees bright prospects for profitability and net worth.

Stock split

A stock split is a method to increase the number of shares outstanding, with proportional reduction in the par value of the shares. If the par value of share is ₹ 10 and outstanding shares are 10,000 in a company, it results in a capital structure of ₹ 1,00,000. When the par value share is divided into two, the par value becomes ₹ 5 and the number of outstanding shares increase to 20,000. There is no change in the share capital amount of ₹ 1,00,000.

Reasons for Stock Split

The following are the reasons for the split of shares:

(A) **To make shares Attractive:** When the price of the share is too high, only wealthy can afford to invest in a company. When the share is split, the market price is divided into the number the share is split into. If the par value of a share is ₹ 10 and its market value of a share is ₹ 10,000, when the share is split into ten parts, the par value becomes ₹ 1 and the market price becomes roughly ₹ 1,000. This price level would be within the range of many to buy.

(B) **Indication of Higher Future Profits:** The share splits are used by the management of the company to communicate to investors that the company is expected to earn higher profits in future.

Bonus Share vs Stock Split

The features of comparison between bonus share and stock split are as under:

1. Issue of bonus share increases the share capital amount while split share does not increase.
2. In case of bonus share, the balance in the profit and loss account, reserves decreases with a similar increase in the share capital account. Split share does not affect the balance in the profit and loss account, reserves and even share capital amount.

Check Your Understanding

(A) State whether the following statements are True or False

1. The term 'Dividend policy' refers to the policy concerning quantum of profits to be distributed as dividend.
2. Company can ignore the expectations of the shareholders while formulating dividend policy.
3. The essence of the dividend policy is what amount is to be retained and how much amount is to be distributed to the shareholders.
4. Issue of bonus shares results in the conversion of company's profits into equity share capital, which is known as capitalization of profits.
5. Once bonus shares are issued, there would be a change in net worth of the company.
6. A stock split is a method to increase the number of shares outstanding with proportionate reduction in the par value of the shares.
7. Once bonus issue is made at par, equivalent share capital amount is transferred from the accumulated profits and reserves to equity share capital account.

8. Payment of dividend does not involve any legal considerations.
9. It is desirable for a company to follow an ad-hoc dividend policy.
10. Bonus issue of 1 : 2 means two additional shares are issued to the shareholder who holds one share.
11. Issue of bonus shares is a compromise to satisfy the conflicting objectives of the firm as the company can retain the earnings as well as satisfy the expectations of the shareholders.
12. Balance in capital reserves created by revaluation of fixed assets can be utilized for issue of bonus shares.

Answers:

1. True 2. False 3. True 4. True 5. False 6. True 7. True 8. False
9. False 10. False 11. True 12. False.

(B) Objective Questions (Identify what is most appropriate)

1. Bonus shares are issued by
   (A) giving free shares to existing equity shareholders.
   (B) issuing new equity shares for cash.
   (C) both (A) and (B).
   (D) none of the above.
2. Bonus shares are issued to this category:
   (A) Preference shareholders. (B) Equity shareholders.
   (C) Debenture holders. (D) Redeemable preference shareholders.
3. Bonus shares can be issued by company to existing equity shareholders by
   (A) issuing partly paid shares. (B) issuing fully paid shares.
   (C) converting partly paid shares into fully paid shares.
   (D) Both (B) and (C).
4. Company prefers to utilize this category first for issue of bonus shares.
   (A) General reserves (B) Balance in profit and loss account
   (C) Share premium balance (D) All the above
5. Rights shares can be offered to
   (A) Preference shareholders (B) Equity shareholders
   (C) Debenture holders (D) Redeemable preference shareholders
6. When bonus shares are issued, this process happens in accounts.
   (A) Distribution of profits. (B) Capitalization of profits.
   (C) No payment of profits. (D) No capitalization of profits.
7. If the company wants to declare more than 20% of profits as dividend, it is necessary for the company to transfer a part of current year's profits to reserves, which is
   (A) 5% (B) 15%
   (C) 10% (D) Nil

8. When a company splits shares, par value of
   (A) existing shares which are already issued are split.
   (B) new shares that would be issued are also split.
   (C) Both (A) and (B).
   (D) Existing shares' face value is not disturbed.

9. Par value of a share means
   (A) issuing shares at its face value. (B) issuing shares at a discount.
   (C) issuing shares at a premium. (D) Both (B) and (C).

10. When total dividend distributed is less than current year's profits, this happens.
    (A) Retained earnings of current year decrease compared to last year.
    (B) Retained earnings of current year increase compared to last year.
    (C) Retained earnings of current year and last year are same.
    (D) No effect on retained earnings.

11. The relationship between dividend and retained earnings is
    (A) equal relationship. (B) reciprocal (inverse) relationship.
    (C) no relationship. (D) compromising relationship .

12. Dividend decision of a company
    (A) affects shareholders' satisfaction. (B) does not affect shareholders' satisfaction.
    (C) Both (A) and (B). (D) Neither (A) nor (B).

13. Floatation costs are those which are associated with the
    (A) issue of shares. (B) issue of debentures.
    (C) Both (A) and (B). (D) Neither (A) nor (B).

14. Dividend decision is interconnected with
    (A) financing decision. (B) Investment decision.
    (C) Liquidity decision. (D) All the above.

15. There is a legal restriction that a company cannot declare dividend
    (A) without providing for current year's depreciation.
    (B) without providing for arrear depreciation.
    (C) Both (A) and (B).
    (D) Neither (A) nor (B).

16. Final dividend is decided by this authority.
    (A) Board of directors.
    (B) Board of directors can only recommend which can be reduced by shareholders in the interests of company.
    (C) Government has full control on payment.
    (D) Board of directors can only recommend which can be increased by shareholders in the interests of company.

17. When the financial leverage of the company is very high and its financial position is vulnerable, prudent action on the part of the company is to
    (A) declare no dividend to improve the leverage.
    (B) declare same rate of dividend to reduce the leverage.
    (C) declare lesser dividend rate to improve the leverage.
    (D) take no steps to improve existing condition.

18. Dividend payment results in
    (A) inflow of cash.
    (B) outgo of cash.
    (C) no effect on cash.
    (D) increased borrowing even if the liquidity position is comfortable.

19. When the share capital of a company increases but profits do not increase in the same proportion and company declares all the profits in the form of dividend, this situation happens.
    (A) Dividend per share increases.
    (B) Dividend per share decreases.
    (C) No impact on dividend per share.
    (D) None of the above.

20. Stability of dividend means
    (A) constant rate of dividend per share.
    (B) constant percentage of profits earned.
    (C) Both (A) and (B).
    (D) Neither (A) nor (B).

21. Dividend on equity shares and preference shares respectively are
    (A) Fixed, Variable.
    (B) Variable, Fixed.
    (C) Both (A) and (B).
    (D) Neither (A) nor (B).

22. Interim dividend is decided by
    (A) board of directors in the board meeting.
    (B) general manager (Finance).
    (C) shareholders in annual general meeting.
    (D) CEO in consultation with all functional heads.

23. This security is called as variable income security as dividend is uncertain.
    (A) Preference shares.
    (B) Equity shares.
    (C) Debentures.
    (D) Redeemable preferences.

24. Stock dividend is another name of
    (A) preference shares.
    (B) equity shares.
    (C) debentures
    (D) bonus shares

25. Issue of bonus shares can be made from
    (A) general reserves.
    (B) profit and loss account.
    (C) capital reserves not created by revaluation of assets.
    (D) all the above.

26. Issue of bonus shares would not result in any change in
    (A) general reserves. (B) equity share capital.
    (C) net worth. (D) profit and loss account.

27. From the date of declaration of dividend, company has to remit it in cash within the following number of days to shareholders.
    (A) 15 days (B) 30 days
    (C) 40 days (D) 42 days

28. Company does not have enough liquid resources to increase the dividend rate despite abnormal increase in profits. Management has to satisfy the increased expectations of equity shareholders with the least economic cost. The compromise solution to meet the conflicting situation is to
    (A) issue preference shares to raise finances.
    (C) issue additional equity shares to raise finances.
    (C) issue debentures to raise finances.
    (D) issue bonus shares.

29. There would be no change in the following, before and after issue of bonus shares.
    (A) Net worth of company. (B) EPS of equity share.
    (C) Wealth of equity shareholders. (D) (A) and (C).

30. When a company declares a dividend rate of 10%, dividend amount is to be calculated on
    (A) face value of share.
    (B) market value of share.
    (C) cost price at which share was purchased.
    (D) decision of board of directors.

31. Before and after issue of bonus shares, change occurs in the following.
    (A) Net worth of company. (B) EPS of equity share.
    (C) Wealth of equity shareholders. (D) Equity share capital.
    (E) Both (B) and (D).

32. If the face value of an existing equity share is split into five, this situation happens.
    (A) Face value of existing equity share gets reduced.
    (B) Opportunity for more people to buy at an affordable rate.
    (C) New equity shares of that company are also to be issued at the split rate.
    (D) All the above.

33. After shares are split, availability of that company's shares in market
    (A) increases. (B) decreases.
    (C) unpredictable (D) remains same.

34. Dividend yield is calculated with the following formula.

(A) $\frac{\text{Dividend received} \times 100}{\text{Face value of share}}$ (B) $\frac{\text{Dividend received} \times 100}{\text{Market value of share}}$

(C) $\frac{\text{Face value of share} \times 100}{\text{Dividend received}}$ (D) $\frac{\text{Market value of share} \times 100}{\text{Dividend received}}$

35. When company follows stable dividend policy of constant dividend per equity share, in the event of increased earnings to company,
    (A) divided per equity share increases in proportion of earnings.
    (B) divided per equity share decreases in proportion of earnings.
    (C) divided per equity share remains constant.
    (D) divided per equity share is unpredictable.

36. Under the present Income Tax Act, dividend in the hands of investors is
    (A) taxable. (B) tax – free.
    (C) included in the total income of investor for calculation of applicable rate.
    (D) tax concessional.

37. The effect of a bonus issue is
    (A) reduction in the amount of cumulative profits.
    (B) increase in share capital to the corresponding extent of (A).
    (C) Both (A) and (B).
    (D) Neither (A) nor (B).

38. A limited company can issue bonus shares at this rate.
    (A) Face value (B) Market value
    (C) Any other value (D) Any one of the above

39. After issue of bonus shares, the normal impact on EPS and market price is as under.
    (A) Increase in market price and EPS.
    (B) Decrease in market price and EPS.
    (C) Same market price and EPS.
    (D) Can be increase or decrease both in market price and EPS.

40. This would be the situation after the issuance of bonus shares, if no significant improvement in the profits of the company is expected.
    (A) Decrease in number of equity shares and dividend per share.
    (B) Increase in number of equity shares and dividend per share.
    (C) Increase in number of equity shares and decrease in dividend per share.
    (D) Decrease in number of equity shares and increase in dividend per share.

ANSWERS

1. (A) 2. (B)

3. (B) Bonus issue cannot be made till existing partly paid shares are fully paid.

4. (C) 5. (B) 6. (B) 7. (C) 8. (C) 9. (A) 10. (B) 11. (B)

12. (A)	13. (C)	14. (D)	15. (C)	16. (B)	17. (C)	18. (B)	19 (B)
20. (C)	21. (B)	22. (A)	23. (B)	24. (D)	25. (D)	26. (C)	27. (B)
28. (D)	29. (D)	30. (A)	31. (E)	32. (D)	33. (A)	34. (B)	35. (C)
36. (B)	37. (C)	38. (D)	39. (B)	40. (C)			

Descriptive Questions

1. Explain the concept "Dividend Policy" and its role in the wealth maximization? **(26.1 and 26.2)**
2. If retained earnings and dividend are conflicting with each other in "Dividend Policy", what approach is to be adopted? **(26.1 and 26.2)**
3. What is meant by 'Dividend Policy' and indicate the factors that a company should consider while formulating the dividend policy? **(26.2 and 26.3)**
4. 'The primary purpose for which a firm exists is the payment of dividend. Therefore, irrespective of the firm's needs and the desires of the shareholders, a firm should follow of very high dividend payout'. Explain your reasoning? **(26.1 and 26.2)**
5. What are the factors which influence the management to pay a certain amount in the form of dividend every year? **(26.1 and 26.3)**
6. What is meant by stable dividends and explain its significance? What dangers are associated with stable dividends? **(26.4, 26.5 and 26.6)**
7. What are the different payout methods? How the shareholders react to these methods? **(26.7 and 26.8)**
8. What is a bonus issue or stock dividend? Evaluate its advantages with disadvantages? **(26.7 (Point B) and 26.8.**
9. What is a stock split? Why is it used? How does it differ from issue of bonus shares? **(26.9)**

Short Questions

Q.1. What is the importance of dividend policy?

Ans. The dividend policy is of crucial importance as it determines the amount to be distributed to the shareholders and the amount of profit to be retained for financing its long-term growth. Maximization of shareholders' wealth is the main objective of every company. In case payment of dividend helps in achieving that objective, it is desirable to distribute dividend. In case dividend payment does not help in achieving the objective, it is desirable to retain the profits in the company for financing investment programme. Thus, the dividend decision is largely based on the impact of dividend policy on the value of the firm.

Q.2. Why a company issues bonus shares?

Ans. It is legally necessary for a company to pay dividend in cash within 30 days of declaration of dividend. When a company is already experiencing liquidity worries or foresees them, dividend payment is to be avoided. If dividend is not paid, its equity shareholders get dissatisfied. In such circumstances, solution is declaration of bonus shares. Issue of bonus shares does not involve outgo of cash. The issue of bonus shares also satisfies the expectations of existing shareholders psychologically without affecting company's liquid resources.

Interview Questions

Q.1. What is meant by dividend?

Ans. Dividend is that part of profits which is distributed to the preference shareholders and equity shareholders. Dividend payment involves outgo of cash.

Q.2. What is the need to distribute dividends to equity shareholders?

Ans. Dividend is a common expectation of equity shareholders. Majority of shareholders in particular those belonging to retired community buy them for a supplementary income. Company cannot afford to ignore the expectations of shareholders totally as the aim of every company is to maximize the value of the shares held by equity shareholders and equally satisfy them.

Q.3. What is a bonus share? Why they are issued?

Ans. When a company issues shares to its existing equity shareholders without their payment, such shares are called as bonus shares. When a company has made profits but does not have enough cash to pay dividends, bonus shares are issued. If the company foresees liquidity problems after dividend payment, bonus shares are issued to avoid liquidity constraints while satisfying the expectations of equity shareholders.

Q.4. What is meant by capitalization of profits?

Ans. Conversion of company's profits into equity share capital is known as capitalization of profits. When bonus shares are issued, equivalent amount is transferred from general reserves or balance in profit and loss account to equity share capital account.

Q.5. Does issue of bonus shares change net worth of a company?

Ans. No. Issue of bonus shares does not change the net worth of a company. It results in reduction of reserves with a similar increase in equity share capital.

Q.6. What is meant by sweat equity shares?

Ans. Sweat equity shares mean equity shares issued by a company to its directors and/or employees at a discount or for consideration other than cash for providing know how or making available the rights in the nature of intellectual property rights or value additions.

❍ ❍

Glossary

ABC Analysis: ABC analysis is an inventory control technique that divides the total inventory items into three categories namely A, B and C category for greater control of inventory according to their usage value.

Accounts Receivables: The debts owed to the firm by customers arising from sale of goods or services on credit in the ordinary course of business.

Amortization: Amortization means gradual reduction of an amount at regular intervals over a certain time period. This term is used to refer to the reduction of debt by regular payment of loan installments during the life of a loan. It is also used for writing off an intangible asset such as goodwill.

Annuity: A stream (series) of equal or even cash flows.

Annuity Due: A stream of cash flows which occur at the beginning of the year.

Assets: The rights of owner whether it is tangible or intangible.

Average Cost: The average of various sources (specific) costs of the different components equity, preference shares, debentures, retained earnings of capital structure at a given time. This is used as the acceptance criteria for (capital budgeting) investment proposals.

Bond: A promissory note issued by a business firm or government unit for raising long-term debt.

Bond Dividend: Payment of dividend in the form of bond.

Bonus Shares: The issue of shares to the shareholders of a company, by capitalizing a part of the company's reserves. There is no inflow of cash to the company with issue of bonus shares as reserves are capitalized only.

Book Building: A process used to ascertain and record the indicative subscription bids of interested investors to a planned issue of securities.

Book Value: It is the amount of Net Assets that would be available per Equity Share, after a company pays off all Liabilities including Preference Shares from the sale proceeds of all its Assets liquidated at Balance Sheet values.

Business Risk: The risk that arises due to the variation in operating profit (PBIT).

Capital Budgeting: The firm's decision to invest its funds most efficiently in fixed assets with an expected flow of benefits over a series of years.

Capital rationing: Placing a limit on the amount of new investment undertaken by a firm is called capital rationing. This can be either by using a higher cost of capital, or by setting a maximum on the capital amount.

Capitalization: Capitalization refers to the **total** amount of securities issued by a company. The different securities are equity share capital, preference share capital and debentures etc.

Capital Structure: Capital structure refers to the **proportion** of securities issued. Capitalization refers to the total of long-term securities issued while capital structure refers to their proportion.

Cash Budget: A statement of expected cash (receipts) inflows and cash (payments) out flows and the net cash balance during a specified period (planning horizon).

Cash Conversion Cycle: The length of time between the date a firm pays its suppliers and the date it receives cash from its customers.

Cash Credit: An arrangement where a bank permits a borrower to withdraw money up to a sanctioned credit limit against tangible security. Deposits (inflow) and withdrawals (outflow) are permitted in this account.

Cash Discount: Cash discount is an incentive or reduction allowed by supplier to buyer for early payment than the normal credit period allowed.

Cash Dividend: Payment of dividend in the form of cash.

Collection Costs: The costs that are incurred in collecting the debts from the customers to whom the credit sales have been granted.

Combined Leverage: The percentage change in EPS due to the percentage change in sales.

Commercial Paper (CP): A short-term, unsecured Promissory Note issued by Blue Chip companies. Like other Money Market instruments, it is issued at a Discount on the Face Value and is freely marketable. Commercial Paper may be issued to any person including individuals, banks and companies.

Compound Interest: The interest that is paid both on the initial principle amount and the interest earned over previous period (s).

Consortium: A term generally used in banking. It refers to a group of banks associated for the purpose of meeting the financial requirements of a borrower, such as a term loan or working capital requirements.

Contingent Liabilities: The liabilities that may arise as a result of some future event which, though possible, is deemed unlikely, for example, a court judgment on a pending lawsuit that may result in a financial payment on a company.

Cost of Capital: It is the minimum rate of return required by investors. It is a price to be paid by the firm for obtaining capital. It is the minimum firm must earn on its investments in order to satisfy the expectations of investors who provide the required funds.

Cost of Debenture: It is the return expected by debenture holders to provide funds to the firm.

Cost of Equity: It is the minimum rate of return required by the equity shareholders.

Cost of Preference Share: It is the dividend payable to the preference shareholders.

Coupon Rate: It is the annual interest rate on the Par Value of Debentures or Bonds that an issuer promises to pay.

Credit Period: It is the period allowed by seller to customer to pay for goods sold on credit.

Credit Policy: Decisions relating to firm's credit period, credit standards and collection efforts.

Credit Standards: Relate to selection criteria for extending credit to customers.

Credit Terms: Statements of the credit period and any discount offered, for example 1/15, net 30 days discount of 1% is offered provided payment is received within 15 days instead of usual credit period of 30 days.

Current Asset: The assets that get converted into cash within a period of one year in the ordinary course of business, without reduction in value.

Current Liabilities: The claims against a company which are to be paid within a year.

Debenture: A debt security issued by company having a certain Maturity and bearing a stated Coupon Rate. Debentures may be unsecured or secured by Assets such as land and building of the issuing company. Debenture holders have a prior claim for interest on the earnings and repayment from Assets of the company in the event of liquidation as compared to Preference and equity shareholders.

Depreciation: Depreciation is an expense. Cost of a fixed asset such as a building or machinery is allocated as a periodic expense spread over the depreciable life of the Asset. Sometimes, it is called Amortization when the Asset is intangible. It is called as 'depletion' when the asset is a natural resource such as minerals.

Dividend: The portion of company's net profits that are distributed to the owners/equity shareholders of the firm. There is no decision making in respect of preference shareholders, since they are entitled to have a fixed rate of dividend).

Dividend Policy: The process of deciding the portion of earnings to be paid as dividends to equity shareholders and what portion is ploughed back (retained) in the firm for investment purpose.

Earnings per Share (EPS): Net income divided by the number of outstanding equity shares.

Economic Order Quantity (EOQ): The quantity of goods ordered at which the total inventory [ordering plus carrying less] cost is minimum.

Economic Value Added (EVA): EVA is return earned by the company in excess of the minimum expected return of the shareholders. It is a tool for evaluating managerial performance. An American consultancy firm, Stern Stewart is credited with the development of this tool in the late eighties. It is calculated by subtracting the total cost of capital from the after-tax operating profits of a company.

Escrow Account: It is a mechanism to ensure that the obligations under a contract are discharged. It is used typically in infrastructure projects such as power, roads or telecom. For example, an escrow account can be set up at a bank for depositing the payments of electricity bills. It is a technique of mitigating the risk to lenders.

Eurobond: Bond denominated in a currency other than that of the issuer's country. It is also denominated in a currency different from that of the country in which it is sold. They operate outside the jurisdiction of the central bank that issues that currency. Eurobonds are issued by multinational corporations; for example, a British company may issue a eurobond in Germany, denominating it in U.S. dollars. Bonds are not denominated in a pound though issued by a British company and also not in the currency of Germany(Euro).

Factoring: An arrangement for obtaining funds (working capital needs) by selling receivables to a specialized financing agency (factor). When factoring is contemplated, a firm's sales to different customers must have prior approval of the factor. Factor assumes the credit risk for collections.

Financial Leverage: The ability to magnify earnings available to equity shareholders, by the use of debt or fixed-charge securities. Generally, the higher the amount of debt in relation to total financing, the greater will be the impact on profits available to equity shareholders, other things being equal.

Financial Risk: The risk added by the use of debt financing in capital structure.

Float: The interval between the issuance of a cheque and its payment by the drawer's bank through the clearing system. The time involved in clearing cheques through the banking system allows greater flexibility in cash management. Funds need not be deposited in an account as soon as a cheque is issued.

Flotation Cost: The percentage cost of issuing new equity stock.

Gilt-edged Securities: A term often used to refer to Government Securities signifying that the securities have the highest degree of reliability. They are, however, vulnerable to Interest Rate Risk and Inflation Risk.

Gross Working Capital: The total current assets.

Hypothecation: It is a charge against property for funds borrowed. Bank lending for working capital involves a hypothecation of inventories and book debts. Under this arrangement, the current assets remain with the borrower, but in case of default, the bank may seek recovery of the loan by instituting a lawsuit to seize the hypothecated assets which can later be sold.

Indenture: A formal agreement between the issuer and the purchaser of the bond or debenture.

Inter-corporate Deposit: A short-term deposit made by one company with another. The period usually does not exceed six months, and it could be as short as one or a few days.

Internal Rate of Return: IRP is the discounting factor (rate of return) at which the present value of cash inflows equals to the present value of cash outflows.

Junk Bonds: The debt securities of companies bearing a considerable degree of risk that is reflected in their mediocre or poor credit ratings. They are 'Low-grade' or 'High-risk' bonds.

Lead-time: The total time required to receive the inventory from the date of placing the order till its receipt.

Letter of Credit: A financial instrument issued by a bank on behalf of a purchaser of goods, undertaking responsibility to pay a certain amount during a specified period for goods delivered.

Leverage: In the ordinary language, 'Leverage' means gaining strategic advantage. Using borrowed funds to magnify the earnings of equity shareholders is called leverage.

Limited Liability: A term which conveys that the responsibility of shareholders for debts and other Liabilities of their company, is limited to the extent of the amount remaining unpaid towards their shares in the company. In other words, each shareholder is liable to pay the full nominal value of shares held by him or her.

Liquid Asset: An asset that can be converted to cash quickly without having to reduce the asset's price very much.

Liquidity: Ability of an enterprise to make payments/obligations as and when they fall due for payment.

Lock-Box System: An arrangement where a firm rents a post office box and authorizes its bank to pick up cheques and drafts in the box for speedy collection of receivables.

Marginal Cost of Capital: The additional cost incurred to obtain additional funds required by a firm.

Market Capitalization: The value of equity shares outstanding at prevailing market prices.

Market capitalization = Number of shares × Market price of each share.

Maximum Level: The level of stock beyond which a firm should not maintain the stock.

Net Earnings: Earnings available to equity shareholders from where a firm actually declares dividends or retains profits for financing investment opportunities.

Net Present Value: A method of evaluating investment proposals. NPV is the difference between the present value of cash inflows associated with project and the present value of cash outflows.

Net Working Capital: The excess of current assets over current liabilities. It represents the portion of firm's current assets financed with long-term funds.

Net Worth: For a company, total assets minus total liabilities of a company is net worth. The funds belong to the shareholders of a company. Net worth includes equity share capital, general reserves, profit and loss account and preference shareholders.

Operating Cycle: The time that elapses between the purchase of raw materials and the collection of cash from debtors.

Operating profits: Earnings before interest and taxes.

Ordering Cost: The cost that is associated with the acquisition of raw materials. They include the cost incurred from placing an order till the receipt of inventory.

Payout Ratio: The proportion of earnings available to equity shareholders, which are paid out as dividends. Hence, if a company whose earnings per share is ₹ 10 pays a dividend of ₹ 2 per share, the payout ratio is 20 per cent. The payout ratio can be the basis for setting the long-term dividend policy.

Preference Share: The share, which is having preferential rights over the equity share in respect of dividend and repayment in the event of liquidation.

Present Value: The sum of all future values discounted by an appropriate capitalization rate.

Price-earnings Ratio: The market price of a share divided by earnings per share. PE ratio is useful whether a share is worth buying or selling.

Profit: Profit is the excess of sales revenues over operating costs. A company that earns more than it spends makes a profit.

Profitability: Profitability is the long-term ability of a company to make a profit. Profitability measures how well a company is making use of its capital by investing in assets that make goods and services that generate profits.

Ratio Analysis: The use of financial ratios for assessing the financial performance and financial position of a company by means of various ratios that relate to the liquidity, turnover, profitability, etc., of a company.

Reserves: Profits earned by company and saved for future needs, without distributing as dividend to shareholders. Reserves can be general (General reserves) or for a specific purpose (Capital reserves).

Retained Earnings: That portion of the firm's earnings that has been saved rather than paid out as dividends. Retained earnings can be in the form of reserves, profit and loss account etc.

Return on Investment (ROI): A profitability measure that evaluates the performance of a business by dividing net profit by net worth. It is usually expressed as an annual percentage return.

Safety Stock: The stock level that is needed to maintain to avoid stock out.

Scrip Dividend: An unusual type of dividend involving the distribution of promissory notes that calls for some type of payment at a future date. Scrip dividends generally signal that a firm is short of cash.

Sweat Equity: Equity shares allotted to certain employees of company either on discount or for consideration other than cash, as a reward for providing know-how or sharing intellectual rights or some other value addition to the company.

Systematic Risk: The portion of risk or variability that cannot be eliminated by diversification. These risks are a part of our system, hence called systematic risks. Risk is caused by factors, which affect the returns on all securities. Major political, economic and social phenomena, for instance, would affect all stocks, which imply systematic risk.

Temporary Working Capital: The amount required to maintain additional current assets temporarily over and over and above permanent working capital to satisfy cyclical demands.

Treasury bill (T-Bill): A short-term debt instrument of the Government of India. This security bears no Default Risk and has a high degree of Liquidity and low Interest Rate Risk in view of its short-term. The instrument is negotiable and is issued at a discount from the Face Value. At Maturity, the investor receives the face value. The increment amount constitutes the interest earned.

Unsystematic Risk: A risk that is unique to a firm or industry. The returns of company can be affected by occurrences such as a labour strike, changes in consumer preferences, or even wrong management decisions. The adverse impact of any such occurrence would be confined to one or a few firms. It means company-or industry-specific risk, as opposed to overall market risk, also known as specific risk, diversifiable risk and residual risk. Unsystematic risk can be reduced through diversification. As the saying goes. "Don't put all of your eggs in one basket."

Venture Capital: Funds made available for startup firms and small businesses with exceptional growth potential. Venture capital investments are generally made in cash in exchange for shares in the invested company. Purpose is to set up new products/inventions/innovations or to employ or commercialize new technologies. Thus, venture capital entails high risk but has the promise of attractive returns. It is, therefore, also known as 'Risk Capital'. Venture capital typically comes from institutional investors and high net worth individuals and is pooled together by dedicated investment firms.

Weighted Average Cost of Capital, WACC: A weighted average of the component costs of debt, preferred stock, and equity.

Working Capital: Short-term funds needed to meet operating expenses.

Zero-coupon Bond: A Bond that bears a zero Coupon Rate and hence is issued at a price substantially below its Face Value.

TABLES

Table A Compound Value of ₹ 1

Period	Interest Rate												
	1%	2%	3%	4%	5%	6%	7%	8%	9%	10%	12%	14%	16%
1	1.010	1.020	1.030	1.040	1.050	1.060	1.070	1.080	1.090	1.100	1.120	1.140	1.150
2	1.020	1.040	1.061	1.082	1.102	1.124	1.145	1.166	1.186	1.210	1.254	1.300	1.322
3	1.030	1.061	1.093	1.125	1.158	1.191	1.225	1.260	1.295	1.331	1.405	1.482	1.521
4	1.041	1.082	1.126	1.170	1.216	1.262	1.311	1.360	1.412	1.464	1.574	1.689	1.749
5	1.051	1.104	1.159	1.217	1.276	1.338	1.403	1.469	1.539	1.611	1.762	1.925	2.011
6	1.062	1.126	1.194	1.265	1.340	1.419	1.501	1.587	1.677	1.772	1.974	2.195	2.313
7	1.072	1.149	1.230	1.316	1.407	1.504	1.606	1.714	1.828	1.949	2.211	2.502	2.660
8	1.083	1.172	1.267	1.369	1.477	1.594	1.718	1.851	1.993	2.144	2.476	2.853	3.059
9	1.094	1.195	1.305	1.423	1.551	1.689	1.838	1.999	2.172	2.358	2.773	3.252	3.518
10	1.105	1.219	1.344	1.480	1.629	1.791	1.967	2.159	2.367	2.594	3.106	3.707	4.046
11	1.116	1.243	1.384	1.539	1.710	1.898	2.105	2.332	2.580	2.553	3.479	4.226	4.652
12	1.127	1.268	1.426	1.601	1.796	2.012	2.252	2.518	2.813	3.138	3.896	4.818	5.350
13	1.138	1.294	1.469	1.665	1.886	2.133	2.410	2.720	3.066	3.452	4.363	5.492	6.153
14	1.149	1.319	1.513	1.732	1.980	2.261	2.579	2.937	3.342	3.797	4.887	6.261	7.076
15	1.161	1.346	1.558	1.801	2.079	2.397	2.759	3.172	3.642	4.177	5.474	7.138	8.137
16	1.173	1.373	1.605	1.873	2.183	2.540	2.952	3.426	3.670	4.595	6.130	8.137	9.358
17	1.184	1.400	1.653	1.948	2.292	2.693	3.159	3.700	4.328	5.054	6.866	9.276	10.761
18	1.196	1.428	1.702	2.026	2.407	2.854	3.380	3.996	4.717	5.560	7.690	10.575	12.375
19	1.208	1.457	1.754	2.107	2.527	3.026	3.617	4.316	5.142	6.116	8.613	12.056	14.232
20	1.220	1.486	1.806	2.191	2.653	3.207	3.870	4.661	5.604	6.728	9.646	13.743	16.367
25	1.282	1.641	2.094	2.666	3.386	4.292	5.427	6.848	8.623	10.835	17.000	26.462	32.319
30	1.348	1.811	2.427	3.243	4.322	5.743	7.612	10.063	13.268	17.449	26.960	50.950	66.212

Table A Contd.

Period	Interest Rate											
	18%	20%	24%	28%	32%	36%	40%	50%	60%	70%	80%	90%
1	1.180	1.200	1.240	1.280	1.320	1.360	1.400	1.500	1.600	1.700	1.800	1.900
2	1.392	1.440	1.538	1.638	1.742	1.850	1.960	2.250	2.560	2.890	3.240	3.640
3	1.643	1.728	1.907	2.067	2.300	2.515	2.744	3.375	4.096	4.913	5.832	6.859
4	1.939	2.074	2.364	2.684	3.036	3.421	3.842	5.062	6.544	8.352	10.498	13.032
5	2.288	2.488	2.932	3.436	4.097	4.653	5.378	7.594	10.486	14.199	18.896	24.761
6	2.700	2.986	3.635	4.398	5.290	6.328	7.530	11.391	16.777	24.138	34.012	47.046
7	3.185	3.583	4.508	5.629	6.983	8.605	10.541	17.086	26.844	41.034	61.222	89.387
8	3.759	4.300	5.590	7.206	9.217	11.703	14.758	25.629	42.950	69.758	110.200	169.836
9	4.435	5.160	6.931	9.223	12.166	15.917	20.661	38.443	68.720	118.588	198.359	322.688
10	5.234	6.192	8.594	11.806	16.060	21.647	28.925	57.665	109.951	201.599	347.047	613.107
11	6.176	7.430	10.657	15.112	21.199	29.439	40.493	86.498	175.922	342.719	642.684	1164.902
12	7.288	8.916	13.215	19.343	27.983	40.037	56.694	129.746	281.475	582.622	1156.831	2213.314
13	8.599	10.699	16.386	24.759	36.937	54.451	79.372	194.619	450.360	990.457	2082.295	4205.297
14	10.147	12.839	20.319	31.961	48.757	74.053	111.120	291.929	720.576	1683.777	3748.131	7990.065
15	11.974	13.407	25.196	40.565	64.359	100.712	155.568	437.894	1152.921	2862.421	6746.636	15181.122
16	14.129	18.488	31.243	51.923	84.954	136.97	217.95	656.84	1844.7	4866.1	12144.000	28844.0
17	16.672	22.186	38.741	66.461	112.14	186.28	304.914	985.26	2951.5	8272.4	21859.0	54804.0
18	19.673	26.623	48.039	85.071	148.02	253.34	426.879	1477.9	4722.4	14063.0	39346.0	104130.0
19	23.214	31.948	59.568	108.89	195.39	344.54	597.630	2216.8	7555.8	23907.0	70824.0	197840.0
20	27.393	38.338	73.864	139.38	257.92	468.57	836.683	3325.3	12089.0	40642.0	12748.0	375900.0
25	62.669	95.396	216.542	478.90	1033.6	2180.1	4499.880	25251.0	126760.0	577060.0	2408900.0	9307600.0
30	143.371	237.376	634.820	1645.5	4142.1	10143.0	24201.432	191750.0	1329200.0	8193500.0	45517000.0	23047000.0

Table B Compound Value of an annuity of ₹ 1

Year	Interest Rate												
	1%	2%	3%	4%	5%	6%	7%	8%	9%	10%	12%	14%	16%
1	1.000	1.000	1.000	1.000	1.000	1.000	1.000	1.000	1.000	1.000	1.000	1.000	1.000
2	2.010	2.020	2.030	2.040	2.050	2.060	2.070	2.080	2.090	2.100	2.120	2.140	2.160
3	3.030	3.060	3.091	3.122	3.152	3.184	3.215	3.246	3.278	3.310	3.374	3.440	3.506
4	4.060	4.122	4.184	4.246	4.310	4.375	4.440	4.506	4.573	4.641	4.770	4.921	5.066
5	5.101	5.204	5.309	5.416	5.526	5.637	5.751	5.867	5.985	6.105	6.353	6.610	6.877
6	6.152	6.308	6.468	6.633	6.802	6.975	7.153	7.336	7.523	7.716	8.155	8.536	6.977
7	7.214	7.434	7.662	7.898	8.142	8.394	8.654	8.923	9.200	9.487	10.089	10.730	11.414
8	8.286	8.583	8.892	9.214	9.549	9.897	10.260	10.637	11.028	11.436	12.300	13.233	14.240
9	9.369	9.755	10.159	10.583	11.027	11.491	11.978	12.488	13.021	13.579	14.776	16.085	17.518
10	10.462	10.950	11.464	12.006	12.578	13.181	13.816	14.487	15.193	15.937	17.549	19.337	21.321
11	11.567	12.169	12.808	13.486	14.207	14.972	15.784	16.645	17.560	18.531	20.655	23.044	25.733
12	12.683	13.412	14.192	15.026	15.917	16.870	17.888	18.977	20.141	21.384	24.133	27.271	30.850
13	13.809	14.680	15.618	16.627	17.713	18.882	20.141	21.495	22.953	24.523	28.029	32.089	36.786
14	14.947	15.974	17.086	18.292	19.599	21.051	22.550	24.215	26.019	27.975	32.393	37.581	43.672
15	16.097	17.293	18.599	20.024	21.579	22.276	25.129	27.152	29.361	31.772	37.280	43.842	51.660
16	17.258	18.639	20.157	21.825	23.657	25.673	27.888	30.324	33.003	35.950	42.753	50.980	60.925
17	18.430	20.012	21.762	23.698	25.840	28.213	30.840	33.750	36.974	40.545	48.884	59.118	71.673
18	19.615	21.412	23.414	25.645	28.132	30.906	33.999	37.450	41.301	45.599	55.750	68.394	84.141
19	20.811	22.841	25.117	27.671	30.539	33.760	37.379	41.446	46.018	51.159	63.440	78.969	98.603
20	22.019	24.297	26.870	29.778	33.066	36.786	40.995	45.762	51.160	57.275	72.052	91.025	115.380
25	28.243	32.030	36.459	41.646	47.727	54.865	63.249	73.106	84.701	98.374	133.334	181.871	249.214
30	34.785	40.568	47.575	56.805	66.439	79.058	94.461	113.283	136.308	164.494	241.333	356.787	530.312

Table B Contd.

Period	Interest Rate										
	18%	20%	24%	28%	32%	36%	40%	50%	60%	70%	80%
1	1.000	1.000	1.000	1.000	1.000	1.000	1.000	1.000	1.000	1.000	1.000
2	2.180	2.200	2.240	2.280	2.320	2.360	2.400	2.500	2.600	2.700	2.800
3	3.572	3.640	3.778	3.918	4.062	4.210	4.360	4.750	5.160	5.590	6.040
4	5.215	5.368	5.684	6.016	6.362	6.725	7.104	8.125	9.256	10.503	11.872
5	7.154	7.442	8.048	8.700	9.398	10.146	10.846	13.188	15.810	18.855	22.370
6	9.442	9.930	10.980	12.136	13.406	14.799	16.324	20.781	26.295	33.054	41.265
7	12.142	12.916	14.615	16.534	18.696	21.126	23.853	32.172	43.073	57.191	75.278
8	15.327	16.499	19.123	22.163	25.678	29.732	34.395	49.258	69.916	98.225	136.500
9	19.086	20.799	24.712	29.369	34.895	41.435	49.153	74.887	112.866	167.983	246.699
10	23.521	25.959	31.643	38.592	47.062	57.352	69.814	113.330	181.585	286.570	445.058
11	28.755	32.150	40.238	50.399	63.122	48.998	98.739	170.995	291.536	488.170	802.105
12	34.931	39.580	50.985	65.510	84.320	108.437	139.235	257.493	467.458	830.388	1444.788
13	42.219	48.497	64.110	84.853	112.303	148.475	195.929	387.239	748.933	1413.510	2601.619
14	50.818	59.196	80.496	109.612	149.240	202.926	275.300	581.859	1199.293	2403.968	4683.914
15	60.965	72.035	100.815	141.303	197.997	276.979	386.420	873.788	1919.869	4087.745	8432.045
16	72.939	87.442	126.011	181.87	262.36	377.69	541.99	1311.7	3072.8	6950.2	15179.0
17	87.068	105.931	157.253	233.79	347.31	514.66	759.78	1968.5	4917.5	11816.0	27323.0
18	103.740	128.117	195.994	300.25	450.45	700.94	1064.7	2953.8	7868.9	20089.0	49182.0
19	123.414	154.740	244.033	385.32	607.47	954.28	1491.6	4331.7	12591.0	34152.0	88528.0
20	146.628	186.688	303.601	494.21	802.86	1298.8	2089.2	6648.5	20147.0	58059.0	159350.0
25	342.603	471.981	898.092	1706.8	3226.8	6053.0	11247.2	50500.0	211270.0	824370.0	3011100.4
30	790.948	1181.882	2640.916	5873.2	12941.0	28172.0	60501.0	383500.0	2215400.0	11705000.0	56896000.0

Table C Present Value of ₹ 1

Period	Interest Rate												
	1%	2%	3%	4%	5%	6%	7%	8%	9%	10%	12%	14%	15%
1	.990	.980	.971	.962	.952	.943	.935	.926	.917	.909	.893	.877	.870
2	.920	.961	.943	.925	.907	.890	.873	.857	.842	.826	.797	.769	.756
3	.971	.942	.915	.889	.864	.840	.816	.794	.772	.751	.712	.675	.658
4	.961	.924	.889	.855.	.823	.792	.763	.735	.708	.683	.636	.592	.572
5	.951	.906	.863	.822	.784	.747	.713	.681	.650	.621	.567	.519	.497
6	.942	.888	.838	.790	.746	.705	.666	.630	.596	.564	.507	.423.	.432
7	.933	.871	.813	.760	.711	.665	.623	.583	.547	.513	.452	.400	.376
8	.923	.853	.789	.731	.677	.627	.582	.540	.502	.467	.404	.351	.327
9	.914	.837	.766	.703	.645	.592	.544	.500	.460	.424	.361	.308	.284
10	.905	.820	.744	.676	.614	.558	.508	.463	.422	.386	.322	.270	.247
11	.896	.804	.722	.650	.585	.527	.475	.429	.388	.350	.287	.237	.215
12	.887	.788	.701	.625	.557	.497	.444	.397	.356	.319	.257	.208	.187
13	.879	.773	.681	.601	.530	.469	.415	.368	.326	.290	.229	.182	.163
14	.870	.758	.661	.577	.505	.442	.388	.340	.299	.263	.205	.160	.141
15	.861	.743	.642	.555	.481	.417	.362	.315	.275	.239	.183	.140	.123
16	.853	.728	.623	.534	.458	.394	.339	.292	.252	.218	.163	.123	.107
17	.844	.714	.605	.513.	436	.371	.317	.270	.231	.198	.146	.108	.093
18	.836	.700	.587	.494	.416	.350	.296	.250	.212	.180	.130	.095	.081
19	.828	.686	.570	.475	.396	.331	.276	.232	.194	.164	.116	.083	.070
20	.820	.673	.554	.456	.377	.312	.258	.215	.178	.149	.104	073	.061
25	.780	.610	.478	.375	.295	.233	.184	.146	.116	.092	.059	.039	.030
30	.742	.552	.412	.308	.231	.174	.131	.099	.075	.057	.033	.020	.015

Table C Contd.

Period	Interest Rate												
	16%	18%	20%	24%	28%	32%	36%	40%	50%	60%	70%	80%	90%
1	.862	.847	.833	.806	.781	.758	.735	.714	.667	.625	.588	.556	.526
2	.743	.718	.694	.650	.610	.574	.541	.510	.444	.391	.346	.309	.277
3	.641	.609	.579	.524	.477	.435	.398	.364	.296	.244	.204	.171	.146
4	.552	.516	.482	.423	.373	.329	.292	.260	.198	.153	.120	.095	.077
5	.476	.437	.402	.341	.291	.250	.215	.186	.132	.095	.070	.053	.040
6	.410	.370	.335	.275	.227	.189	.158	.133	.088	.060	.041	.029	.021
7	.354	.314	.279	.222	.178	.143	.116	.095	.059	.037	.024	.016	.011
8	.305	.266	.233	.179	.139	.108	.085	.068	.039	.023	.014	.009	.006
9	.263	.226	.194	.144	.108	.082	.063	.048	.026	.015	.008	.005	.003
10	.227	.191	.162	.116	.085	.062	.046	.035	.017	.009	.005	.003	.002
11	.195	.162	.135	.094	.066	.047	.034	.025	.012	.006	.003	.002	.001
12	.168	.137	.112	.076	.052	.036	.025	.018	.008	.004	.002	.001	.001
13	.145	.116	.093	.061	.040	.027	.018	.013	.005	.002	.001	.001	.001
14	.125	.099	.078	.049	.032	.021	.014	.009	.003	.001	.001	.000	.000
15	.108	.084	.065	.040	.025	.016	.010	.006	.002	.001	.000	.000	.000
16	.093	.071	.054	.032	.019	.012	.007	.005	.002	.001	.000	.000	.000
17	.080	.060	.045	.026	.015	.009	.005	.003	.001	.000	.000		
18	.069	.051	.038	.021	.012	.007	.004	.002	.000	.000	.000		
19	.060	.043	.031	.017	.009	.005	.003	.002	.000	.000			
20	.051	.037	.026	.014	.007	.004	.002	.001	.000	.000			
25	.024	.016	.010	.005	.002	.001	.000	.000					
30	.012	.007	.004	.002	.001	.000	.000						

Table D Present Value of an Annuity of ₹ 1

Period	Interest Rate									
	1%	2%	3%	4%	5%	6%	7%	8%	9%	10%
1	0.990	0.980	0.971	0.962	0.952	0.943	0.935	0.926	0.917	0.909
2	1.970	1.942	1.913	1.886	1.859	1.833	1.808	1.783	1.759	1.736
3	2.941	2.884	2.829	2.775	2.723	2.673	2.624	2.577	2.531	2.487
4	3.902	3.808	3.717	3.630	3.546	3.465	3.387	3.312	3.240	3.170
5	4.853	4.713	4.580	4.452	4.329	4.212	4.100	3.993	3.890	3.791
6	5.795	5.601	5.417	5.242	5.076	4.917	4.766	4.623	4.486	4.355
7	6.728	6.472	6.230	6.002	5.786	5.582	5.389	5.206	5.033	4.868
8	7.652	7.325	7.020	6.733	6.463	6.210	5.971	5.747	5.535	5.335
9	8.566	8.162	7.785	7.435	7.108	6.802	6.515	6.247	5.995	5.759
10	9.471	8.983	8.530	8.111	7.722	7.360	7.024	6.710	6.418	6.145
11	10.368	9.787	9.253	8.760	8.306	7.887	7.499	7.139	6.805	6.495
12	11.255	10.575	9.954	9.385	8.863	8.384	7.943	7.536	7.161	6.814
13	12.134	11.348	10.635	9.986	9.394	8.853	8.358	7.904	7.487	7.103
14	13.004	12.106	11.296	10.563	9.899	9.295	8.745	8.244	7.786	7.367
15	13.865	12.849	11.938	11.118	10.380	9.712	9.108	8.559	8.060	7.606
16	14.718	13.578	12.561	11.652	10.838	10.106	9.447	8.851	8.312	7.824
17	15.562	15.292	13.166	12.166	11.274	10.477	9.763	9.122	8.544	8.022
18	16.398	14.992	13.754	12.659	11.690	10.828	10.059	9.372	8.756	8.201
19	17.226	15.678	14.324	13.134	12.085	11.158	10.336	9.604	8.950	8.365
20	18.046	16.351	14.877	13.590	12.462	11.470	10.594	9.818	9.128	8.514
25	22.023	19.523	17.413	15.622	14.094	12.783	11.654	10.675	9.823	9.077
30	25.808	22.397	19.600	17.292	15.373	13.765	12.409	11.258	10.274	9.427

Table D Contd.

Period	Interest Rate								
	12%	14%	16%	18%	20%	24%	28%	32%	36%
1	0.893	0.877	0.862	0.847	0.833	0.806	0.781	0.758	0.735
2	1.690	1.647	1.605	1.566	1.528	1.457	1.392	1.332	1.276
3	2.402	2.322	2.246	2.174	2.106	1.981	1.868	1.766	1.674
4	3.037	2.914	2.798	2.690	2.589	2.404	2.241	2.096	1.966
5	3.605	3.433	3.274	3.127	2.991	2.745	2.532	2.345	2.181
6	4.111	3.889	3.685	3.498	3.326	3.020	2.759	2.534	2.339
7	4.564	4.288	4.039	3.812	3.605	3.242	2.937	2.678	2.455
8	4.968	4.639	4.344	4.078	3.837	3.421	3.076	2.786	2.540
9	5.328	4.946	4.607	4.303	4.031	3.566	3.184	2.868	2.603
10	5.650	5.216	4.833	4.494	4.193	3.682	3.269	2.930	2.650
11	5.938	5.453	5.029	4.656	4.327	3.776	3.335	2.978	2.683
12	6.194	5.660	5.197	4.793	4.439	3.851	3.387	3.013	2.708
13	6.424	6.842	5.342	4.910	4.533	3.912	3.427	3.040	2.727
14	6.628	6.002	5.468	5.008	4.611	3.962	3.459	3.061	2.740
15	6.811	6.142	5.575	5.092	4.675	4.001	3.483	3.076	2.750
16	6.974	6.265	5.669	5.162	4.730.	4.033	3.503	3.088	2.758
17	7.120	6.373	5.749	5.222	4.775	4.059	3.518	3.097	2.763
18	7.250	6.467	5.818	5.273	4.812	4.080	3.529	3.104	2.767
19	7.366	6.550	5.877	5.316	4.844	4.097	3.539	3.109	2.770
20	7.469	6.623	5.929	5.353	4.870	4.110	3.546	3.113	2.772
25	7.843	6.873	6.097	5.467	4.948	4.147	3.564	3.122	2.776
30	8.005	7.003	6.177	5.517	4.979	4.160	3.569	3.124	2.778